Canada since 1945:
Power, politics, and provincialism

UNIVERSITY OF TORONTO PRESS   Toronto   Buffalo   London

ROBERT BOTHWELL, IAN DRUMMOND, JOHN ENGLISH

Canada since 1945:
Power, Politics, and Provincialism

Revised edition

REVISED EDITION

© University of Toronto Press 1981, 1989
Published 1981. Revised edition 1989
Reprinted 1993, 1996, 2001
Toronto Buffalo London
Printed in Canada

ISBN 0-8020-2647-8 (cloth)
ISBN 0-8020-6672-0 (paper)

Canadian Cataloguing in Publication Data

Bothwell, Robert, 1944–
    Canada since 1945

    2nd ed.
    Bibliography: p.
    Includes index.
    ISBN 0-8020-2647-8 (bound) ISBN 0-8020-6672-0 (pbk.)

    1. Canada – History – 1945–   . 2. Canada –
    Politics and government – 1935–   .* 3. Canada –
    Economic conditions – 1945–   . I. Drummond,
    Ian M., 1933–   . II. English, John, 1945–   .
    III. Title.

    FC600.B68 1989   971.064   C89-093959-4
    F1034.2.B68 1989

The University of Toronto Press acknowledges the financial assistance to its publishing program of the Canada Council for the Arts and the Ontario Arts Council.

University of Toronto Press acknowledges the financial support for its publishing activities of the Government of Canada through the Book Publishing Industry Development Program (BPIDP).

To Charles Stacey,
scholar, colleague, and friend

Contents

Preface

A visitor seeing Canada for the first time since 1939 might well conclude that Canada, even more than nations devastated by war, has become another country. On the surface so much remains the same: the Liberals prevail in Ottawa; the provinces quarrel with Ottawa and among themselves; and we worry about Americans in our future. But most of the pieces have been rearranged, and the effect of the picture is quite different. In 1939 the prairie provinces were mostly dustbowls clouding over the nation's economic future. These one-time mendicants are now our new plutocrats, threatening long-established balances by the ferocity of their prosperity. Although nationalist sounds still emanate from Quebec City, their nuances would make them unrecognizable to the parochialists of 1939. To many Ontarians (and other English-speaking Canadians) in 1939, French Canada's problems lay primarily in its relationship with God: believing too much and breeding too often, French Canada was mired in the Middle Ages. Someday it would grow up, like its Anglo-Saxon brethren. But when it did grow up, the adult was wildly unexpected. So, for that matter, was the Ontario counterpart. By the 1970s over 40 per cent of Torontonians had been born outside Canada. Many more had come from the countryside and small towns, and had left much of their old lives behind. The sights, sounds, and smells of many city streets were new; only the street names remained to recall an older and very different time.

This is a book about our own times, and as such it expresses definite views. No reader will agree with everything we say. We have not tried to end debate; we have tried to clarify and broaden. We trust that our readers will be encouraged to seek for themselves a better understanding of where Canadians have been and what they have become.

If we were to thank all of those who have influenced this book, the list would be longer than the book. There are some who have worked on this manuscript who merit special thanks, especially Virgil Duff. Virgil gave early encouragement to this project and hastened its completion through frequent advice and generous advances. He is a model editor, a good friend, and as much a part of this book as the authors. Beverley Beetham, Margaret Woollard, and Jean Wilson were extremely competent editors who removed many stylistic abuses and corrected some egregious errors. It is often said that a picture is worth a thousand words and by this token the designer and our cover artist are responsible for a very significant and welcome addition to this volume, and we warmly acknowledge the splendid co-operation and imagination of Laurie Lewis and Don Evans. Others to whom we owe thanks for research assistance and timely help are Senator Carl Goldenberg, W.J. Bennett, Paul Evans, Catherine Barclay, Louise Driedger, and Dr Gerald Campbell. Much of the research on which the sections written by Bothwell and English are based was supported by the C.D. Howe Foundation, the Killam Foundation, and the Social Sciences and Humanities Research Council of Canada. We also want to thank Gail Heideman and Murielle Labrie for stalwart help with the typing.

Every reasonable precaution has been taken to trace the owners of copyright material and to make due acknowledgment. Any omission will be gladly rectified in future editions.

For the 1989 edition we wish to thank Bruce Uttley, Dave Batholemew, Carol Kieswetter, Jean Reilly, Irene Knell, Lorraine Ourom, John Parry, and, as always, our friendly editor, Virgil Duff.

RB, ID, JE

PART ONE

Patterns of Change

1

Beginnings

Canadian history is a success story – an account of coping with troubles and tri-umphing over adversities. Although the years since 1945 have contained their shares of disappointments, they have been more successful than most. From 1945 to 1975 the nation enjoyed thirty years of unprecedented economic advance. Living standards rose to heights undreamt of at the end of the war. Thanks to those economic achievements, Canadians could afford a social welfare system that few in 1945 had believed possible. It is true that, in the mid-1980s, the national government ran large budget deficits, and so did the provinces. Some blamed these on the 'expensive social services.' But the origins were more complex than that, and small increases in tax rates would have paid for the services. The problem was political will, not economic capacity. Between 1975 and 1988 the nation coped with inflation, the first post-war recession, and three major constitutional crises. All these troubles were surmounted, without damaging the social fabric or the institutions of representative democracy. Most states, not all of them poor and underdeveloped, could look with envy at that recent record. By 1975 the country had the apparatus of a humane and urbane society. That had not been present in 1945, and it was still present in the mid-1980s. Canadians had become a well-schooled and fairly thoughtful people, even though in education and learning – as opposed to schooling – a good deal may still remain to be desired. Canadians are certainly much less pious than in 1945, but perhaps they are a little more humane and a little less self-righteous. They give little to overseas missionaries, but much to economic development in poor countries. Their cities have grown and changed without turning into hell-holes of poverty, dirt, and insecurity. They worry about pollution, and actually do something to restrain it. They have grown more concerned about the preservation and conservation of national resources, both physical and intellectual.

These things are at once familiar and surprising. Once voiced, they are obvious, and yet in the atmosphere of shrillness and crisis that is created around every Canadian every day, they are very seldom said. If they sound banal, it is because the familiar is so seldom newsworthy. But a conscientious history of post-war Canada should stress them, as this book tries to do. If Canada suffers from a failure of nerve, it is partly because Canadians are so seldom told how much they have done, and how well.

We are sentimental enough to believe that one great nation – ocean to ocean, in the old phrase – is a better thing than an assemblage of squalling mini-states. There was a time when Canada was significant in world affairs, and perhaps it may be again. The authors must confess a preference for the relatively centralized but outward-looking Canada of the forties and fifties; later chapters detail with sadness the turns of events, some avoidable, some unavoidable, that have brought the country to its present pass. The developments of the past forty years may or may not have made Canadians nicer; they have certainly made them happier. Canadians have built the great cities, laid the pipelines, learned to be diligent and skilful. These habits and attitudes would remain, and the machines and equipment – the fabric of civilized life in the late twentieth century – would also survive. Even if Canadians were so unlucky as to slip a little way down the economic slope, barring an international catastrophe the halt would be a long way above the bottom, and far above the level of 1945. Even if the nation-state were to disintegrate Canadians would probably continue to live in much the same way as they do now. And it is the lives of persons, not nations, that really matter. However pessimistic one may sometimes feel about the latter, one should be optimistic about the former so far as Canada and Canadians are concerned.

Canada's history is not only a success story. Much of Canada's recent past is very funny indeed, and usually the humour is accidental, the humour of incident and situation. Harold Adams Innis once remarked that the principal danger in being a social scientist in Canada is that one might die of laughter. As usual Innis overstated his case, but as usual there was some truth in what he said. The history of post-war Canada is replete with pomposity, and therefore with absurdity. Naturally the 'pomposity coefficient' varies from year to year and, therefore, in the following pages, from chapter to chapter, as the reader who perseveres will discover. The country has its quota of fools and windbags; such people are most prominent in politics, where their inherent weaknesses seem less glaring and attract less ridicule than they would in other walks of life. Hence, in political history-writing they get more of the limelight than their importance really justifies. And so does the element of the absurd in Canadian life.

War, of course, is not funny at all, and no one in Canada has ever found it so, although much of the popular culture was once firmly rooted in war-based humour and in that legacy of war, the Canadian Legion hall. But Canada has been called the 'peaceful kingdom,' and since 1945 it has been just that. The nation managed rapid demobilization, reluctant rearmament to meet the Russian and Chinese threats in the early fifties, and then gradual and rather thoughtless re-disarmament for more than a quarter of a century. Intermittently, Canadians dreamed of middle-power status and fancied themselves as world peacekeepers. But when it became clear not only that soldiers could get killed but that no one loves a peacekeeper, the national temptation was to retire to gardens, cottages, and the endless elaboration of the social welfare state, a game that the provinces as well as Ottawa could play. Fortunately for Canada, the international balance of terror held, and no one actually asked Canadian troops to do anything much until, in 1970, they were used to pacify – some would say, subjugate – Quebec. Not for Canada an overseas empire of military power and influence both eco-nomic and political. Not for Canadians the complex careers, replete with risks and opportunities, that flowed to Americans from that nation's imperial role. Not for Canadians the dislike and detestation which that role so often produced; no one would accuse Canadians of cultural imperialism. They laughed about the 'American way of life' but rarely referred to their own, perhaps because it was so like the American. But whenever some American talked of exporting free-dom, democracy, capitalism, free enterprise, or that American way of life, some Canadian could be found in the background, quietly chuckling. And however much Canadians might dislike the 'other side' in the Cold War, on the whole they refused to preach at it.

However, when surveying non-democratic regimes that were on 'our side,' Canadians were far more critical, not to say moralistic, than Americans, for whom considerations of power politics reinforced worries about Communism. No doubt many Americans did not like the regimes in Spain, South Africa, Iran, or Vietnam. Nevertheless, except with respect to South Vietnam, Canadians were much more likely to stand up and complain and ask awkward questions about democracy and freedom of speech, and also to worry about racial discrim-ination.

At first, it may be thought, moralizing came easily to Canadians, who could all too readily believe that their own country was not merely democratic but also unprejudiced. As time passed, there was less assurance about the home base. Canadians gradually learned that their own society did impose some barriers to upward mobility, that ethnicity did sometimes matter, that some of their fellow citizens – Inuit, Amerindian, Métis, even Ukrainian, not to mention the relative-ly new but rapidly growing communities of East and West Indian origin – did face discrimination in some directions and believed they faced it in others. Also, in the sixties and especially in the seventies, anglophone Canadians heard much more about the unhappiness of the francophones, whose leaders, both in Quebec and elsewhere, spoke increasingly not just of misunderstanding but of grievance.

The response was interesting, and really quite encouraging. Canadians did not stop moralizing about racism and oppression abroad, but at home they began to take matters in hand, profiting, perhaps, from the American example. In this respect, the landmarks, although not the only measures, are John Diefenbaker's Bill of Rights, Pierre Trudeau's language legislation, and, in 1982, the national Charter of Rights. Whatever one may think of these measures in and of themselves, they were steps in a direction of which most Canadians approved, no matter how their viscera might respond to the sound of French and the sight of 'colour.' In some respects too little, perhaps too late, possibly misconceived in detail, the new laws nevertheless represented part of a humane adaptation not only to change but to a reality that had been present, although incompletely perceived, for a long time. Many other measures, both federal and provincial, tended in the same direction; it is hard to think of any retrograde steps, except for the Quebec language legislation of the late seventies. In these important respects the legal evolution of the sixties and seventies is part of Canada's success story, while unilingual language laws are blots on the national escutcheon, from whatever province they may have emanated.

This is not to say that all has been for the best in the best of all possible Canadas. There are many things to deplore besides linguistic bigotry. Compared with their fellow Canadians of the late seventies, Canadians in the nineteen-forties may appear boring and limited, but in many respects they were probably less confused and less uncertain. Many today deplore the tidal wave of self-seeking among artists, intellectuals, and other public subsidiaries and employees who must serve not only themselves but all Canadians. Some professions, both learned and semi- or pseudo-learned, show similar tendencies, to the obvious detriment not only of personal dignity but also of the standing of all professionals in the community.

But even here there are shreds of a silver lining inside the cloud of greed. When teachers strike, for instance, they are certainly behaving just like any other body of workers that wants more. The dedicated pedagogues have vanished, and in their stead stand suburbanites who want the same things their college buddies have. But is it altogether bad for teachers to make demands on the community? In the past, Canadians could all too readily congratulate themselves on the splendours of their educational system while shamelessly underpaying and exploiting the teachers who ran the schools and taught the kids. Those days will not come again. No one should be sorry to see them gone.

In the pages that follow, readers will find assessments and judgments about recent events – events through which the authors have lived. Many readers will have lived through these events as well, and their recollections may differ from the account of events that is put together here. This does not necessarily mean that the authors are wrong and the reader is right; memories can be faulty, as any reader of memoirs or writer of contemporary history must readily admit. Many things in the book may surprise the reader, therefore; some of them surprised the authors too. Time may have altered perceptions of events, and, especially for the events of the seventies and eighties, far more documentary material than any historian or journalist is now allowed to see will eventually be available. In particular, these years may come to look darker, or perhaps brighter, than the authors have found them. Still, it is important to assess the recent past, if only so that Canadians may better understand the present; whether history illumines the future only time will tell.

No part of Canada's history is as neglected or as misunderstood as that of the past forty years: people remember things selectively and often remember them wrong, and most people did not and could not know very much about what was really happening. The contemporary historian, therefore, checks recollections and fills in gaps by diligent research, or simply by careful exploitation of published but neglected materials. While checking and filling in, one often has cause to be critical of the mass media. In part this is just the snobbishness of university people. But it does appear that the media have deteriorated. They have become increasingly disinclined to give the Canadian people accurate and unbiased information in sufficient quantity. Also, one can detect a tendency to personalize, and therefore to trivialize, almost everything. Here is one of the darker sides to Canada's recent history. Was it inevitable? Did things have to go that way? It may be that television, compared with radio, is a trivializing medium. Perhaps Canada's media people learned too much from the great neighbour to the south, and learned the wrong things. Or perhaps, if better folk had been in charge at the top – whatever the reasons, it is partly because of the media that the readers of contemporary history, like the writer of it, are forced to reassess and relearn the past they have lived through.

Although this book concentrates on political developments, which have been so important for the shaping of post-war Canada, what follows is neither a straightforward narrative history nor a purely political history. The book tries to bring together political, economic, social, and cultural developments since the end of the Second World War. It has seemed useful to divide the material among chapters on the basis of the various governments – Mackenzie King, St Laurent, and so on. This does not mean that the authors believe political events have priority. In particular, political events *per se* have not much to do with the direction of social and economic change, where governments often respond but seldom lead or cause. Neither does it mean that politics can simply be considered a reflection of economic forces. Economic developments run right through the period with a continuity that is impressive or depressing, depending on one's point of view. Hence, the next chapter of this book offers a survey of economic and demographic change. It would be both arbitrary and misleading to divide up economic evolution into the political compartments with which the rest of this book is concerned.

In Canada political arguments have largely been about economic affairs, but most Canadians have only the vaguest ideas of what has really been happening in the economy, and a necessary part of the historian's job is to peel away the confusion, illusion, and misinformation that have clustered so thickly around it. Also, by beginning with these durable and deep-seated movements in economic life the reader may be able to put political disputations in a more appropriate perspective.

As for cultural and social developments, this material is distributed through the other parts. It also seemed convenient to follow common usage and speak of the culture of the forties, the fifties, and so on. Somewhat to the authors' surprise, on looking into the matter we found that in many important respects the decades really *are* different from one another. Why this should be so remains a mystery.

Much that some would find important has had to be omitted. It is to be hoped that nothing really crucial has been left out. Because the authors believe that the past is relevant to the present and the future, it is also to be hoped that this volume will enrich memory and stimulate thought.

2

Growth and Change

Demographic developments influenced society profoundly.[1] So did 'demographic echoes,' especially from the late 1920s and 1930s. It was births rather than deaths that mattered most. Admittedly there was a general tendency for people to live longer. In 1951, a male baby might expect to live sixty-six years and a female baby seventy-one years. By 1966 life expectancies had increased to sixty-nine years for males and seventy-five years for females. The death rate fell from 8.5 per thousand in the early fifties to 7.3 per thousand in the early seventies. These improvements were noticeable in all parts of the country. In the Yukon and Northwest Territories they were especially dramatic. In Saskatchewan and two Atlantic provinces death rates did not fall because young people tended to leave these provinces, but life expectancies increased.

In a general way we know why people were living longer. The body and its functions were better understood. The chemical industry had developed new and more effective medicines. The federal and provincial governments had introduced insurance schemes which reduced or removed the financial barriers to medical care. Relative to population there were more doctors and more dentists. As people became more prosperous they were more likely to be properly fed, clothed, and sheltered. These improvements offset the negative effects of prosperity on life expectancy because of drink, tobacco, food additives, pollution, and the risk of a car crash.

Although the elderly became more numerous, the population did not age very much. In 1951 7.7 per cent of the population was aged sixty-five or more; in 1981 the percentage was only 9.7. As the economy was becoming much more productive it could easily provide for the elderly. In this regard two things were

1 Data in this chapter are based on material in M.C. Urquhart and K.A.H. Buckley, eds., *Historical Statistics of Canada* (Toronto: Macmillan, 1965), the *Canada Year Book, Statistics Canada Daily,* the *National Income and Expenditure Accounts,* and the 1981 *Census* reports.

especially important. One was a contributory and relatively generous pension scheme, the Canada Pension Plan. Another was medical insurance, which is of special importance to the old. In addition, governments and private agencies did something to provide decent housing and other services for 'senior citizens.' Such things were needed because many urban families could not, and some families would not, care for their own elderly relatives. Detecting a 'crisis of the elderly,' social workers and publicists worked mightily to sway public opinion in the right direction; governments were impressed by the results, and they were not unaware that old people had votes.

Men were living longer chiefly because they were less likely to die in childhood or adolescence. From 1951 to 1981 the median life expectancy of a male increased by 4.2 years, and for a female the increase was seven years. In 1945-7, the one-year-old male could expect to live 68.3 years, and the one-year-old female, 72.4 years. In 1980-2 the figures were 71.6 and 78.7. In terms of life expectancy, therefore, women increased the lead that they had long enjoyed.

As infectious diseases were controlled by vaccination and drugs, and deficiency diseases by better nutrition and housing, some maladies dwindled in importance while others became much more important causes of death. By the early seventies almost no one died of syphilis, tuberculosis, cholera, typhoid, diphtheria, polio, or smallpox. The diseases of the young had been reduced almost to statistical insignificance. The principal killers were now heart disease, cancer, and accidents, including motor accidents. By 1987 a new disease – acquired immune deficiency syndrome, or AIDS – had surfaced. Its lethal potential, especially but not exclusively among homosexuals, was immense. Its full effect, however, was yet to be felt.

All these developments imposed strains on the medical services and on the ingenuity of governments and officials, who had to devise schemes first for financing health care and pensions and then for controlling the costs of the new programs. But the pressures and strains built up slowly. Because the changes were gradual, regular, and easy to predict, society digested them with relative ease. Unfortunately for Canada's governments, neither births. nor migrations behaved in so helpful a way.

In this century rates of national increase have fluctuated dramatically. They were high in the 1920s, but fell in the thirties, as fertility rates declined in a striking way. In 1946 they had risen to 1920s levels. Although among older women fertility rates were still lower than in the 1920s, among women in their twenties fertility rates were very much higher than they had been for many years, and for women in their early thirties fertility was almost as high as in the 1920s. The 'post-war baby boom' was under way.

In the forties and fifties young women became steadily more fertile, older women steadily less so. The peak was reached in 1959. The chances were better than one in five that if a woman was in her twenties, she would produce a baby in that year! Further, if the 1959 pattern had continued, the typical girl-baby of 1959 would in due course have produced 1.915 girl-babies. Population obviously would have grown very fast indeed, even if people lived no longer and even if Canada repelled all immigrants.

Fortunately the young women of Canada quickly came to their senses. Early in the 1960s they became much less fertile. Throughout the sixties and early seventies, age-specific fertility rates fell spectacularly. By 1971 the women of Canada were producing barely enough babies to reproduce the population. This pattern continued through the eighties.

In all provinces and territories the same general movements occurred. In the Northwest Territories fertility started higher, rose much higher, and stayed higher longer than elsewhere. In the Maritime provinces and Alberta, fertility rose so high as to pass the level of Quebec, which, with Newfoundland, had long possessed relatively high rates. But Quebec's collapse was extraordinarily speedy and complete. By 1987 Quebec's fertility was the third-lowest in the industrialized capitalist world.

Why does fertility change so much? No one really knows. Historians and demographers can provide some explanations for particular periods, but no one has a general theory that is worth much, especially because many countries seem to experience the same sorts of swing at the same times. Thus birth rates were low in the United States and western Europe during the 1930s, and the baby boom hit those countries just as much as Canada.

In popular culture the end of the baby boom is blamed on the 'pill,' which for the first time provided an almost foolproof, invisible, dignified contraceptive that women themselves could control. The first such pills became available late in the 1950s, and soon they were in common use. Perhaps if the country had been poorer they would not have been taken up so quickly. After all, in really poor countries they are not much used, even in the 1980s. Perhaps, too, if the churches had maintained their authority and their opposition to contraception, the pill would have had less effect. But in the 1960s the Roman Catholic Church was rapidly losing its authority in such matters, and Roman Catholics were increasingly willing to use the pill; other churches had long since abandoned their opposition. For Quebec, in particular, the attitude of the Church had once been of extreme importance in maintaining the birth rate. But the pill arrived just when the world-wide Church was trying to appear more flexible and up-to-date. At the same time, in Quebec, the role of the Church was changing, as ecclesiastical authorities turned over their institutions and programs to lay people and to the provincial government. By 1970, admittedly, Rome had thundered once more against birth control in general and the pill in particular. But by then the pope's words were falling on deaf ears.

Finally one must observe the effect of women's liberation and the women's movement. After all, it is very hard for a woman to have four or five babies and a career as well. Prosperous though Canada had become, few couples could afford the servants that would make such a life possible. As for day nurseries, these came only much later, in the sixties. Thus the educated housewife of the 1950s was often trapped in a world of green lawns, barbecues, and diapers which, many came to believe, offered little challenge and less diversion. It was not unusual by 1960 for newly married couples to think of limiting their family size so as to have a more pleasant and interesting style of life. By the mid-sixties the women's movement was on hand to provide an ideology and a justification that could move things only in the same direction.

These demographic developments created opportunities as well as problems. Before 1957, when the Canadian-born labour force was growing relatively slowly, it was fairly easy for the government to maintain full employment and also to admit large numbers of immigrants. For practical and humanitarian reasons immigration was a 'good thing': Canada could absorb displaced persons in the forties, refugee Hungarians in the mid-fifties, and disgruntled Britons throughout. Even after 1957, when the boom of the mid-fifties faded, for Canada's university graduates prospects remained relatively bright. For this there were two reasons. First, elementary and secondary schools were expanding rapidly and more and more often the schools insisted on hiring graduates. Second, business continued to hire new, qualified graduates. And because births had been few in the late 1930s, in the late 1950s such graduates were also few relative to demand.

In the 1960s the events of the late fifties produced an echo that might have been predicted. Observing that the better-educated had passed through the fifties unscathed, schools and parents tried to convince pupils to stay in secondary school and to seek higher education. Noticing that the economic expansion of the fifties had depended heavily on the importation of skills, the national government decided that Canada must have more technical and vocational education. These developments kept people in school longer, made secondary schools bigger, and thus delayed the movement from school to work while supporting an ever larger demand for teachers, especially in secondary schools and universities. Thus for graduates job prospects remained good, and once the economy began to grow faster the government felt justified in admitting more immigrants. In the forties and fifties Canada had digested them by the thousands; why not in the sixties and seventies?

The answer came with chilling directness. By 1970 elementary schools had begun to shrink, and it was already clear that, as the smaller classes of the sixties worked their way through the school system, secondary schools would shrink too. So would universities and community colleges, unless they could attract a larger fraction of each cohort. But now the market for graduates had softened: the economy was growing more slowly and irregularly, schoolteaching could no longer absorb many new graduates. Because such developments reduced the rewards from further study, they weakened the incentive to stay on in school, college, or university. The boom babies of the forties and fifties began to push their way onto the labour market. In any event they would not have stayed in school forever; sooner or later they would have emerged and looked for jobs. And on the labour market they met a tide of immigrant workers that the national government seemed unable or perhaps unwilling to control.

Canada has long been a country both of immigration and of emigration. Before 1914 the settlement of the prairies generated a wave of immigration that peaked in 1913, when 400,870 people were admitted. That figure has never since been approached. But in the late 1920s immigration again became substantial, only to fall away to almost nothing in the 1930s. Indeed, it is estimated that during that decade of depression Canada lost more by emigration than it gained by immigration. During the Second World War immigration dwindled still further, but it revived sharply after the end of hostilities, partly because Canada agreed to absorb refugees and displaced persons from continental Europe. Between the end of 1946 and the end of 1958 we absorbed 223,299 such people – chiefly Czechs, Germans, Jews, Hungarians, Poles, Ukrainians, Russians, and Yugoslavians. During those years refugee migration was only 13 per cent of the total; most migrants were of other sorts.

In the years since 1945 immigration has fluctuated, reflecting changes in government policy and variations in employment prospects here and abroad. The numbers rose from 12,000 in 1944 to 125,000 in 1948, then fell to 74,000 in 1950, only to rise to a post-war peak of 282,000 in 1957. In the slower growth of the late fifties and early sixties immigration fell to 72,000 in 1961. It then rose to 223,000 in 1967 and remained well over the 100,000 mark until 1978, when it fell to 70,000. In 1985-6 immigration averaged 92,000, of which less than one-quarter came from Britain and Europe, 42 per cent from Asia. Emigration has been important also, although one cannot be precise about the fluctuations because Canada does not keep any emigration statistics. Fortunately, by combining figures on natural increase, immigration, and population growth, one can estimate emigration and use the results to trace the movement of Canada's population and the sources of its change.

Throughout the post-war years natural increase accounted for most of the growth in Canada's population. Nevertheless, immigration has been sufficiently large and diverse to change Canada's ethnic mix. In the late forties, half of all Canadians were of British and Irish descent and 31 per cent of more distant French descent. By 1981 these proportions had fallen to 40 per cent and 27 per cent respectively. Those of other European extractions had become a little more numerous, rising from 18 per cent of the population to 19 per cent. Most prominent in this group were the German and Italian communities, but the Greek and Portuguese communities, although still not large in 1981, grew from virtually nothing in the late 1940s. The same thing happened to the West Indians, who entered Canada in some numbers for the first time in the 1960s. Relative to those of European origin, Canadians of Asiatic background were still not numerous in 1981, but their numbers increased quite rapidly, especially in the mid-1960s.

The new migrants affected the texture of Canadian life. Partly because they concentrated in the large cities, especially Toronto and Montreal, the impact was much greater than the raw numbers might lead one to suspect. Toronto in particular became a genuinely multiracial and multicultural society, while in Montreal the immigrants, who generally wanted to learn English and work in that language, appeared to threaten the demographic dominance of the francophones. In Vancouver the long-established communities of Chinese and East Indians were reinforced, and many other ethnic backgrounds were represented in some numbers for the first time. The result was a much more varied and interesting urban scene. The change was most noticeable in matters of shopping, eating, and drinking. Here, admittedly, it is hard to distinguish two causes: ethnic diversity and rising prosperity. Nevertheless it is clear that many of the new arrivals wanted to eat and drink the sorts of things they were used to. Other Canadians could, so to speak, go along for the ride.

Among native-born Canadians there was one development of such importance that it must be singled out for special attention. After many decades of decline, the Inuit and the native Indian peoples began to increase in numbers. In 1951 there were 9,733 Inuit and 155,874 native Indians – only 1.2 per cent of Canada's population. By 1981 there were 23,200 Inuit and 293,000 status and non-status Indians. In 1981 the two groups jointly accounted for 1.3 per cent of Canada's population. Of course there was little likelihood that the native peoples could achieve a 'revenge of the cradle.' However rapidly they might increase, they were simply too few to be other than a small minority group. Indeed, even in 1981 they were outnumbered within Canada by the Ukrainians, the Italians, the Scandinavians, and the Dutch. Similarly the West Indians and the other blacks outnumbered the Inuit, and so did such groups as Indians, Pakistanis, Lebanese, and Finns. Nevertheless, the demographic resurgence was both sign and cause of renewed self-confidence and assertiveness among the native peoples. Further, in the native economies this demographic pressure could often be serious, especially as the white man's economy pressed ever more closely on the areas where traditional hunting and gathering could be continued. In the 1930s it might have been expected that the 'Indian problem' would solve itself as the Indians gradually died out. In the 1980s no such expectation could be entertained, and Canada's whites were obliged to confront a series of questions and problems for which neither history nor attitude had prepared them.

Demography formed the background against which the economy developed. Some connections were obvious enough. Because Canada's population was growing quite quickly, and because in many industries labour productivity was rising, the economy would have to grow if all the new workers were to find jobs. Sometimes it did, and sometimes it did not. The history of unemployment, therefore, can be told as a sort of race between the growing supply of labour and the growing demand. But population growth might also affect the course of output-growth. For instance, the baby boom of the 1950s certainly stimulated demand for housing and for a host of consumer durables, and the same sort of stimulus may have been felt in the 1970s and 1980s because one-parent households were ever more common. Many other forces, however, were at work, helping to shape economic evolution.

Canadians can rarely bring themselves to praise their own economic performance. Yet if we compare that performance with the records of other countries, or with Canada's own record in earlier decades, Canada's economic story looks impressive. Only in 1945, 1946, 1954, and 1982 did output actually fall, and the first three declines were very small indeed, while in 1982 output fell 4.4 per cent – a distressing figure, but not large in comparison with the early 1930s. That 1982 recession was followed by a brisk recovery in output, one that was still continuing in the late eighties. Only in 1945, 1954, 1958, and 1982 did employment actually fall. The first of these declines reflects the aftermath of the Second World War, when the economy was converting to peacetime activities; the second, the slight recession after the Korean War of 1950-3; the third, the end of the fifties boom; the fourth, the world-wide recession of 1982. In 1945 4.4 million Canadians had civilian jobs; in mid-1987, almost 12 million.

Total consumption, meanwhile, has outgrown population, so that living standards have moved upward in the long run. The rise has not been unbroken, and it has been less rapid than in some European countries or in Japan, where labour productivity rose more rapidly than in Canada. In Canada, living standards rose regularly until the mid-seventies, fuelled by productivity-growth of 2.5 per cent per year on the average. From the mid-seventies to the mid-eighties there was little improvement, chiefly because productivity grew very slowly, or even, in 1980 and 1982, declined. In these circumstances living standards could not rise, and the recession of 1982 made things worse. Average family income fell from 1980 through 1984. With the revival of 1983 came a dramatic improvement in productivity-performance, which increased for the rest of the eighties at much the same respectable rate as in 1966-73. In 1984-7, average family income rose again. The slack of 1975-82 had to be made up, but the nation was laying the foundations for another period of improvement. In 1987 consumption per head was $9,284; in 1944, valuing goods and services at 1981 prices, it had been roughly $2,700.

The newspapers and parliamentary debates of the period give this remarkable progress and improvement relatively muted coverage, perhaps on the assumption that good news is not really news; instead they concerned themselves primarily with gloomier topics – inflation, unemployment, and regional disparities – and, in the seventies, energy problems. On all these scores national performance was less splendid than many observers and critics would have liked. In 1988, as in 1947, incomes and living standards were much lower in the Atlantic provinces and Quebec than in the rest of the country. Further, for much of the period there was a deterioration in Saskatchewan relative to Canada as a whole. As for inflation, by 1988 prices were much higher than in 1945, while unemployment had also tended to increase both absolutely and in relation to the labour force. Like the rate of inflation, the level and rate of unemployment changed in jerks and jolts. In seventeen of the years since 1945 the number of unemployed actually fell and, because the labour force was rising steadily, the percentage of unemployed naturally fell too. As an absolute magnitude, unemployment fell in 1947, 1948, 1951, 1955-6, 1959, 1962-6, 1973, and 1984-6; as a percentage of the labour force, unemployment fell in all these years and also in 1969 and 1974. But as an absolute magnitude unemployment rose in 1945-6, 1949-50, 1952-4, 1957-8, 1960-1, 1967-8, 1970-2, 1974-9, and 1982-3, and as a percentage of the labour force it rose in all those years except 1972 and 1974, when rising employment outran rising unemployment.

These developments are summarized in Figures 1 through 4. The first figure shows the movement in total output and consumption; the second shows total employment and total unemployment; the third shows the movement in the general price level, that is to say, the rate of inflation; the fourth shows unemployment as a percentage of the labour force. In the first two figures one can readily perceive the smooth progress described above, while in the last two one sees the irregular and painful developments on which political controversy concentrated. Figure 4 also shows a sort of broad wave-like pattern. Statistical analysis of this series reveals an upward trend, but the fit is not very good, and the picture may be distorted by high numbers at the end of the period, and low ones at the beginning.

Figure 1 Growth in national output and some of its components (1971 dollars)

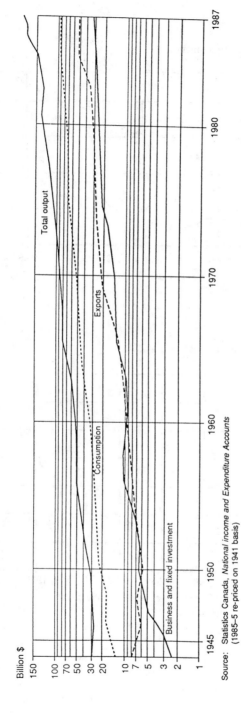

Billion $

Total output

Consumption

Exports

Business and fixed investment

150
100
70
50
30
20

10
7
5
3
2
1

1945   1950   1960   1970   1980   1987

Source: Statistics Canada, *National income and Expenditure Accounts*
          (1985–5 re-priced on 1941 basis)

Figure 2 Employment and unemployment

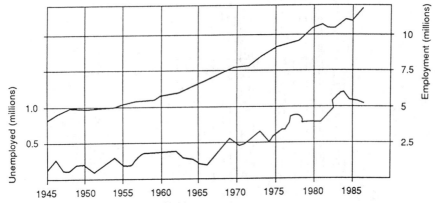

Source: Statistics Canada, *National Income and Expenditure Accounts; The Labour Force*
(recent years subject to revision)

Figure 3 Price index of national output (1971 = 100)

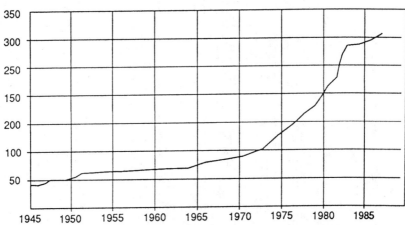

Source: Statistics Canada, *National Income and Expenditure Accounts;*
(recent years subject to revision)

Figure 4 Unemployment as a percentage of labour force

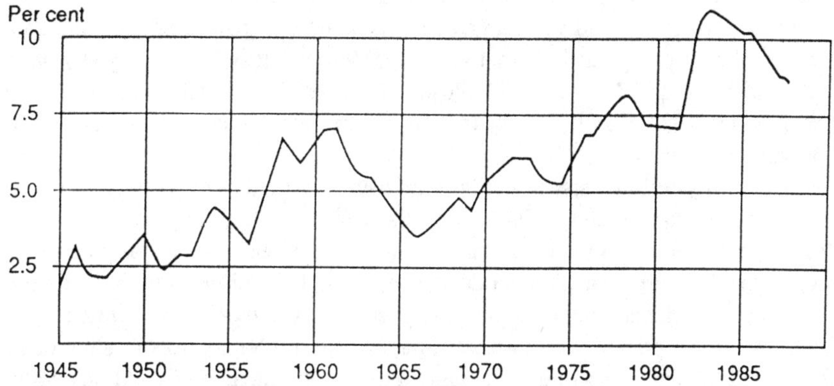

Source: Statistics Canada, *National Income and Expenditure Accounts; The Labour Force* (recent years subject to revision)

Our figures seem to show steady upward progress in output and employment until 1981; after a two-year recession, progress was resumed in 1983-8. From 1944 to the mid-seventies most Canadian families were improving their situations most of the time. The economy has grown almost fast enough to absorb the rapidly expanding labour force, which rose from 5.2 million in 1945 to over 13 million in 1988. Population rose from 11.9 million to more than 25 million, while output rose from $29.7 billion to $126.1 billion in 1978 (in both years outputs are valued at 1971 prices). It is not surprising, then, to find that the average income was much higher by the mid- to late seventies than in the mid-forties. In 1944 it was $2,486 per head; in 1978, $5,388. In forty-one years, hardly more than a generation, the average Canadian's living standard doubled. If we have lost ground with respect to pollution and congestion, we have certainly gained a great deal along more mundane and more measurable paths. This basic fact lies behind the cultural and social transformations of our time, no less than the economic.

Of course Canada's progress did not occur quite as smoothly as the figures' broad outlines suggest. The economy did not grow at the same rate year after year. Since the labour force was expanding remorselessly, and more rapidly in the sixties and seventies than in the forties and fifties, the economy sometimes failed to grow in step with its labour force, although sometimes it grew more rapidly. Hence the fluctuations in the number of jobless.

Why did the economy not grow more smoothly? In an economy like Canada's, citizens and businesses plan their own spending and over one-quarter of the nation's production is sold abroad. It is to be expected, economists agree, that these private spending plans, both domestic and foreign, will accumulate to produce periods of rapid growth and periods of slower growth, or even of slump. It is probably just good luck that Canadian output fell only in the post-war readjustment of 1945-6, in the readjustment of 1954 that followed the Korean War, and in 1982. It is also lucky that only in the last of these recessions did output fall perceptibly.

These 'mysterious' spurts and lags are usually linked to the behaviour of two big items – exports and investment outlays on new buildings, housing, plant, equipment, and inventories. Export volume and value depend on foreigners' willingness to buy Canada's goods and services. This will change from time to time, depending on many things: levels of economic activity in the United States and elsewhere; prices, exchange rates, tariffs, and import controls in other countries; and the discovery and development of new productive possibilities within Canada, especially in the resource-based industries such as oil and forest products. Investment outlays also vary. Some are made by governments, but in Canada most are made by businesses, and these businesses act with an eye to the chance of profit. These chances change from time to time, and so do both businessmen's perceptions of them and their assessments of the risks. Other changes, like those that occur from time to time in the cost of finance or its availability, can also affect businessmen's eagerness to build new things – new factories, perhaps, or new houses and apartment buildings. It is hardly surprising, then, that investment outlay, what economists often call 'capital formation,' does not simply rise every year, or that it sometimes falls. As for the other kinds of spending, the only major ones are household consumption outlays and government outlays on current operations. Although in principle each could change in such a way as to affect the growth rate, in practice both continue monotonously upward and, for the purposes of this discussion, can be safely ignored.

The following paragraphs trace the interactions among exports, new investment outlays, growth, and unemployment between 1944 and 1988. Data have been adjusted so as to eliminate the distorting effects of price increases. (Statistics Canada has produced series of output and expenditure data in which the prices of 1971 and 1981 are applied to the physical outputs of other years, and the results are then added up, year by year.) Naturally this calculation involves a good many estimates and some guesses; but the results are reliable enough for most purposes, including those of the present argument.

From 1944 until 1957, recovery and expansion were fuelled by business spending on new plant and equipment and by new house building. In the late forties, export volumes diminished sharply and almost continuously from the extremely high levels to which wartime demands had pushed them. Only in

1955 did export volumes pass the 1943-4 level: the increase from 1944 to 1957 was only 6 per cent. As national output rose 64 per cent over the same thirteen-year period, it was obviously not export volumes that were providing the engine for growth. On the other hand, export *prospects* were good, especially in the non-agricultural, resource-based industries; this fact was reflected in the high and rising level of new investment in plant and equipment. From 1952 to 1957 the level of new investment rose another 66 per cent, or 249 per cent since 1944. Meanwhile, governments were spending ever more on schools, roads, and other buildings and equipment; they were even spending a little on housing. Though still far smaller than the comparable sorts of private investment outlays, the volume of such government purchases was rising steadily and quickly.

Just as the expansion of 1946-57 was fuelled by investment outlays, so the deceleration of 1957-61 can be blamed on a falling away of investment. Admittedly national output did not fall. Neither did national consumption. Except in 1958, employment also increased with convenient speed in the late fifties and early sixties. National output grew 2.9 per cent per year, while consumption rose 3.4 per cent per year, comfortably outgrowing both population and labour force. Nevertheless, from 1946 to 1956 the record had been considerably better. Output had grown 5.3 per cent per year, and consumption 5.1 per cent; unemployment had been much lower.

What went wrong after 1956? The performance of exports was not to blame. Although export volumes fell in 1958, they revived thereafter, and in 1961 they were 16 per cent higher than in 1957, a better record than in the forties or the early fifties. As for other types of investment outlay, government spending on construction and equipment went up 35 per cent, and, in the private sector, house building went up 5 per cent. Unfortunately, the private sector was spending less on new non-residential structures, plant, and equipment. Such outlays declined in 1958, 1959, and 1960; in 1961 they were 9 per cent lower than they had been in 1957.

Since the Liberals gave up office to the Conservatives in 1957 and did not return to power until 1963, it might seem that the Conservatives were responsible for the slowdown of the late fifties and the Liberals for the revival in the sixties. But it would be inaccurate to distribute praise or blame in this way. Although the Liberals were still in office during the first half of 1957, the slowdown had already begun before the Conservatives took power: output in 1957 was only 2.3 per cent larger than in 1956, while unemployment was already rising. The Tories inherited a retardation, but they did not cause it. Whether their actions made it worse is a question that will be scrutinized in Part IV. Similarly, in the early sixties there were already signs of a change during 1961, although unemployment peaked in that year. Business was already spending a little more on plant and equipment, and there was a further increase in 1962, when total investment grew 4.5 per cent, exports 3.9 per cent, and total output 6.8 per cent. In 1962 unemployment was markedly lower than in 1961. The Liberals, then, inherited the beginnings of a boom; they did not create one, although perhaps their later actions may have prolonged it or increased its size. This question also is explored later, in Part v.

Once the boom of the sixties was under way, its progress was impressive. From 1961 until 1966, exports and business fixed investment rose together at rates of growth close to the rate at which investment had grown in the early fifties. The propulsive force was remarkably strong, and, thanks to this double impetus, output and employment rose steadily and rapidly, while unemployment fell. For a while, the growth of the economy once more outstripped the labour force. Between 1961 and 1966 unemployment fell from 7.2 per cent to 3.6 per cent of the labour force.

After 1966, while exports continued to rise steadily to 1973, fixed investment fell in 1967 and 1968, entirely because business was spending less on new non-residential plant and equipment. Because of this decline the unemployment rate began to rise once more, and although investment recovered in 1969 and thereafter, the expansion was not enough to absorb all the new workers. Thus employment, output, living standards, and unemployment all rose together. By 1971, 6.4 per cent of the labour force was out of work. Matters improved in 1972-4, when the economy grew 4.8 per cent per year and unemployment fell to 5.4 per cent, even though in 1974, for the first time since 1958, export volumes actually fell a little. Thereafter exports, investment, and output all faltered together. In 1975 export volumes fell still more, and the recovery in 1976 left the volume still below the 1974 level; but there were strong recoveries in 1977 and 1978, when export volumes rose 10 per cent per year. Investment outlays, unfortunately, were less accommodating. Total investment outlays rose strongly through 1973-5, rose a little more in 1976 and 1977, and then fell a little in 1978, when business did not raise its spending on new plant and equipment enough to offset the decline in spending on new housing. At the same time, physical output was rising, and the increase, though varying from year to year, was substantial, averaging 3.1 per cent per year from 1975 through 1978. Employment grew also – from 9.1 million in 1975 to 10 million in 1978 – but the labour force was growing still faster; and so the number of unemployed rose from half a million in 1974 to nine hundred thousand in 1978 and the unemployment rate rose from 5.3 to 8.4 per cent. In 1979 fixed investment and exports both rose strongly; in 1980 inventory investment fell, but fixed investment and exports rose again; in 1981 all three fell perceptibly, so that in 1980-1 the unemployment rate was 7.5 per cent – just what it had been in 1961. Sad to say, 1981 was the last 'good year': in 1982, everything seemed to turn downward.

As we noted above, the slump of 1982 was felt throughout the developed industrial world; it did not originate in Canada, nor did Canadian policies cause it. Thus it is not surprising that, in 1982, export volumes fell by 2 per cent. But domestic pressures certainly made the contraction much more painful. Both in 1982 and in 1983, Canada's non-agricultural businesses were depleting their inventories at an unprecedented rate. They were also cutting back on fixed investment, which fell by more than 11 per cent during 1982. All categories – housing, machinery, and non-residential building – were affected. Government investment spending went up a little, but this was a mere drop in the bucket. Even consumption fell, for the first time since 1948.

Recovery began in 1983, and the economy was still expanding in 1987. Much of the fuel came from exports, which rose 35 per cent from 1982 through 1986, and still more in 1987. Consumer expenditure resumed its advance, and inventories were again being built up, and at an increasing rate, adding further upward pressure. Fixed investment, however, was performing dismally. In 1983-4 business fixed investment was actually lower than in 1982, and although there was some increase in 1985-6, the levels of 1981 had yet to be reached again. The pattern was rather like that of the late 1950s. Exports and consumption were doing well, but investment was not.

The impressive economic growth of the period 1945-87 was paralleled by an equally dramatic change in the structure of the economy. Although few industries declined absolutely, some became less important relative to others. Not only did production patterns alter; there were far-reaching changes in the things Canadians worked at, and in the industries where they worked. Agriculture became far less important, both as producer and as absorber of labour. Indeed, the mining industry, though an insignificant employer, came to produce more than agriculture. The real Canadian 'growth industry' was 'public administration plus defence plus service activities' – that is, government offices, education, health, miscellaneous service industries, and, in principle, the armed forces, although these have actually declined since the war ended. In 1944-6 this sector was inflated in importance because of the war. By 1987, only 17 per cent of Canadian workers were employed in manufacturing, and only 4 per cent in agriculture, while 6.7 per cent laboured in public administration, where employment had risen from 479,000 in January 1970 to 914,000 in June 1987, and 32.5 per cent worked in 'community, business, and personal service.' Total employment in goods-producing industries was 30 per cent of the total, and the remaining 70 per cent worked in service-producing industries.

Compared with agriculture or manufacturing, the service industries employ disproportionately large numbers of white-collar workers, especially highly educated labour, because until the advent of the small cheap computer so few service tasks could be mechanized. Thus the transformation of employment was even more striking than the transformation of production. In 1945 non-agricultural blue-collar workers slightly outnumbered white-collar workers.[2] Thereafter, year by year, the proportions changed. Already by 1950 the white-collar workers were more numerous. By summer 1987, 66 per cent of all Canadian workers had white-collar jobs, 5.8 per cent were engaged in agricultural and other primary occupations, and only 28.2 per cent worked at non-agricultural blue-collar jobs.[3] Arguments about economic policy, and in particular about the subsidizing of industry and the freeing of international trade, continued to focus on the minority – barely a third – who did not do white-collar work. By 1988, nonetheless, some observers were asking whether the croaking of the dinosaurs would be heard forever.

Because of the expansion of white-collar jobs and the fact that so many white-collar workers had to be extensively educated and trained, until the late 1970s the well-educated usually had little trouble finding attractive jobs. Even then, it was the liberal-arts graduates, who, for so many 'baby boom' years in the fifties and sixties, could always find work in the schools, who had the most trouble in the new environment of the seventies and eighties. Regularly it was announced that 'top business executives' were trying to hire 'broadly educated liberal-arts types'; regularly the MBAs got the jobs and the philosophers and litterateurs did not. The occupational pattern was affected not only by the growth of service and administrative activities but by the increasing importance of wholesale and retail trade and finance, and by a change in the nature of production in manufacturing, transportation, and many other sectors, which demand ever more skilled workers, ever more white-collar workers, and ever fewer labourers. In Canada, as in other well-developed industrial countries, economic growth has gone hand in hand with a changing pattern of work and life.

These changes produced fewer stresses or strains than might have been expected. Because more and more young people were seeking more and more schooling, the expanding economy was generally able to get the sorts of worker it needed. Where gaps appeared, immigrants filled them. Cities grew because so many of the expanding activities were based in cities; and, although land and housing prices rose, this urbanization was noticeably trouble-free, especially in comparison with developments in some other countries. Agriculture had to shed labour, but in most parts of the country it could do so by attrition; the older

2   'White-collar' workers are those in managerial, professional, clerical, commercial, financial, and service occupations. 'Blue-collar' workers are all others, except for those in farming, forestry, fishing, trapping, or mining occupations.
3   The last figure includes 0.9 per cent 'unclassified.'

farmers retired, and their children, better schooled than their parents, moved off to city jobs. In some regions agricultural depression speeded the process because the new urban jobs paid much better than the old agricultural work. In other places, notably around the larger cities, the value of agricultural land rose dramatically, often because it was in demand for non-agricultural uses. This provided many farmers with an added incentive to retire – with very substantial nest-eggs. And even where farm prices and incomes were depressed, land prices often seemed tied to the general prosperity of the country, not to the troubled agricultural economy. Perhaps land-buyers hoped for better times. If so they were not disappointed; by the early 1970s agricultural prices were rising relative to other prices, and agricultural incomes had begun to rise dramatically relative to urban incomes. Sad to say, this development would be reversed in the eighties.

This is not to say that there were no problems. Some people, as always, were disappointed in their expectations and hopes for careers. For agriculture there were special troubles, chiefly in areas where land was not very good, where it had always been hard to make a decent living from the soil, and where alternative, non-agricultural uses did not appear. In such zones, largely in Quebec, the Atlantic provinces, and northern Ontario, the agricultural shrinkage was far from painless, and by the early sixties the national government had become concerned about the problem. In the eighties, the subsidized agricultural exports of other countries spelt trouble on Canada's prairies. Before 1957, some non-agricultural industries were hit by labour shortages: some businesses had trouble finding the skilled workers they wanted at the wages they were willing to pay, and it was hard for school boards to find enough teachers. These troubles reflected the slow growth of the Canadian labour force in the fifties and perhaps some deficiencies in the educational system, which has always had trouble producing skilled tradesmen.

As the domestic economy changed, so did the international economic environment. New trading colossi appeared – first the European Economic Community, and then, in the 1960s, Japan. Old trading patterns and partners became less important, as the British and Commonwealth markets faded away. There was new interest in the poverty-stricken Third World, first as a field for Canadian external aid, and then as a market for Canada's manufacturers and as a source of manufactured imports. Thanks in part to the Canadian-American Auto Pact of 1965, Canadian exports came to consist principally of complex manufactured goods. Uranium, the great growth-industry of the 1950s, did not remain a booming trade, while wheat exports flowed to new lands: once sold almost entirely in Britain and western Europe, by 1980 they went almost exclusively to the USSR, China, and the smaller socialist states of Eastern Europe.

Financial patterns changed too. In 1945 the industrialized capitalist world was one of fixed exchange rates and exchange controls. The Canadian dollar was not based on gold, or linked to it in any very simple way. Not since 1914 had there been any connection between the quantities of gold in the government vaults and the paper money in the hands of the public. In 1939 the Canadian government had pegged the Canadian dollar to the American, and by joining the International Monetary Fund (IMF) at the Bretton Woods Conference near the end of the war Canada pledged itself to maintain such a peg, and to keep its dollar within a narrow range in relation to the American. Many other states did the same thing, and like these other states, Canada retained the power to control transactions in foreign moneys. In 1950 Canada floated its dollar, but it needed the IMF's permission to do so, and in 1962 Canada repegged its dollar to the American. This arrangement lasted until 1970, but other developed countries maintained their dollar pegs until 1971-3, when the 'Bretton Woods system' broke down. In the fifties the Canadian dollar was unusual because it was one of the few floating currencies; in the seventies and eighties Canada was just one of the crowd. Even the US dollar, which had been convertible into gold at $35 per ounce from 1934 to 1971, was floated away from its golden mooring point. Meanwhile, throughout the industrial capitalist world there had been a gradual movement away from foreign-exchange controls. This development was halting, and there were many retrogressions. Further, it always affected non-residents more quickly and more completely than residents. For example, Britain and many western European countries abandoned exchange control for non-residents in the late 1950s, but it was 1979 before British residents could freely move money out of the United Kingdom. Here Canada was a leader: the Foreign Exchange Control Board, set up in 1939 to ration foreign moneys, was abolished in 1951.

Exchange control mattered because it interfered with the free international movement of funds. So long as a government permit was required before foreign money could be bought, and so long as any receipts of foreign money had to pass into government hands, each economy was to some extent cut off from all the others. For residents of the socialist states of eastern Europe this never ceased to be the case, and it was generally true of the Third World countries that gained their independence in the 1940s, 1950s, and 1960s. Conversely, the removal of exchange control in Canada was both a blessing and a curse: a blessing, because it meant that Canadians could travel, spend, borrow, and lend throughout the capitalist world; a curse, because without exchange control there could now be unbearable pressures on pegged exchange rates, or inconvenient swings in floating ones. Because Canada's exchange controls were always quite weak, it was one of the first nations to experience the former problem; because of the nation's early experiments with a floating rate, it gave lessons to the rest of the world with respect to the latter one.

Management of the exchange rate, whether fixed or floating, had been given in 1935 to the newly established Bank of Canada. The Bank could supply Canadian dollars or foreign money so as to maintain a pegged rate or to modulate the swings in a floating rate. The Bank also had important responsibilities with respect to the domestic monetary system. Although it never fixed the rates of interest at which ordinary banks borrow from the public or lend to it, it did fix the rate at which it itself will lend to the ordinary banks (in Canada, always called 'chartered banks'). In regard to its day-to-day operations, the Bank of Canada always operated quite independently, but, except for a brief period in the late fifties and early sixties, which we shall examine in Part IV, it always co-ordinated its monetary policy with the general direction of government economic policy. Before 1954 and after 1961 it was clear at all times that, if the government wanted one thing and the Bank wanted another, the government would eventually get its way, even if the governor of the Bank had to resign.

As time passed the Bank became more interesting. This was partly because people gradually came to understand that this strange government-owned institution did something more than circulate the paper currency. If an ordinary bank got into difficulties the Bank would have to help. Fortunately for everyone, that did not happen until 1985. Exchange rates and interest rates, however, were matters of burning public concern, and by the mid-1950s at the latest it was apparent that the Bank had something to do with these. Inflation, also, seemed to be the Bank's business, or its problem, at least in part.

From the end of the Second World War until the mid-eighties, prices generally rose with inconvenient speed. The pace was not a smooth one. The immediate post-war inflation was concentrated in the years 1946-8, and there was another, 'Korean-war inflation' in 1951-2. Thereafter prices rose little through 1957 and still more gradually until 1968, when inflation accelerated. Compared with the developments in 1972 and thereafter, however, the inflation of 1968-71 looks quite gentle – although it worried people at the time. The worst year of all was 1974, when prices rose 15.3 per cent. In 1968-71 the average annual increase was 3.9 per cent, and for the seventies as a whole, 8 per cent. Then came 1981 and 1982, when the general price level rose more than 10 per cent per year; the rest of the 1980s saw a deceleration to levels much the same as in 1968-71.

Although inflation has afflicted various countries at different rates, the inflationary experience was common throughout the Western world and throughout the Third World also. Canadian inflation, therefore, was part of a world-wide process, and the roots of the inflation were not to be found solely in Canada, which is a small part of the world economic system. Because the United States was Canada's major market and source of supply, Canadian prices were especially sensitive to developments south of the border. However, Canada was quite capable of adding its own fuel to the inflationary bonfire.

By the early seventies people had come to expect that prices would rise, and more and more people were adjusting their behaviour accordingly. In particular they were trying to allow for future inflation when negotiating wages, salaries, and professional fees; also they were seeking to buy assets, such as houses, land, and gold, whose value might be expected to keep pace with inflation. Further, on any kind of asset whose value was fixed in terms of money, such as a Canada Savings Bond, any other sort of bond, or a mortgage, lenders demanded much higher rates of interest to compensate them in whole or in part for the loss of purchasing power that would happen between the time of lending and the time of repayment, while borrowers were often happy to pay such interest charges because they expected their own earnings would rise in step with inflation. In the seventies, when prices rose much more rapidly than in the fifties or sixties, such adjustments and demands were especially noticeable, although by that time people had come to recognize that some plausible assets, such as common stocks, might very well not rise in step with the general price level.

Why did prices rise? Even if the specialists agreed, we could not provide a full answer here, except to note that several forces seemed to be at work – excess demand for goods and services, extravagant wage increases, higher costs for crucial materials such as oil, and the market-power of big firms, all interacting in complicated ways with the growth of the money supply. The general public tends to blame the 'big interests,' and perhaps government deficits; economists agreed at least that neither was chiefly to blame. Within Canada, certainly, the supply of money grew much more rapidly than the supply of goods and services. But as trade and finance became more tightly integrated throughout the Western world, Canadian developments mattered less in comparison with foreign ones. Politicians and officials, naturally, found it hard to accept this fact.

As the Canadian economy grew, so did the Bank of Canada. In the late thirties there had arisen a modest Art-Deco stone structure on Wellington Street in Ottawa – something Prime Minister King doubtless thought would add a new classic perspective to the capital. But this head-office building was soon far too small, and, at long last, late in the seventies, the old stone structure was surrounded by and embedded in an immense structure of reflecting glass that filled a city block. The net effect, one cynic remarked, resembled a Mack truck that had launched itself part way through a very large shop window. But by now Canada was a grown-up country, and its central bank presumably deserved the same sort of glass-walled sanctum that the chartered banks were pushing ever higher in Toronto.

What about the distribution of the gains from growth and change? Did all persons or groups share equally in the advance? Did anyone lose absolutely? Did the incomes of various groups come closer together, or move farther apart? Even if everyone gained, did some people – capitalists? city-dwellers? doctors? – gain by an unfair amount? Finally, what about the people of the various regions?

One may examine the 'distribution of income' from various angles. One can simply set up a list of categories – for instance, incomes below $1,000, between $1,000 and $10,000, over $10,000 – and then ask how many people or households fall into each category. Such results, drawn up for various dates and corrected for inflation, can then be analysed in various ways. Or one can take the average income of some group – farmers or Inuit or Newfoundlanders or coalminers – and compare it with the average income of some other group – mill workers or Indians or Ontarians or 'capitalists.' Canadians specialize in such comparisons, which can be trusted to breed resentment. Since different observers are interested in different groups this operation can go on forever. Further, since the comparison can be made in various ways there is no guarantee that any two observers will agree on the answer even if they are asking about the same groups.

Hypothetical questions often complicate the issue further. What would have happened to the distribution of income if the economy had not grown, and if consumption per head had not increased? Conditions in other, less well-off countries suggest that all Canadians have benefited from growth. The example of the aged is instructive here. With the passage of time, people move through an income cycle that parallels their life cycle. Usually the young adult earns less than he or she can expect to earn in middle life, while the elderly, whether employed or not, typically receive less than they did in their fifties. No one really expects that economic growth will somehow prevent this decline, although some reformers sometimes talk as if they think it ought to. In fact, by the seventies, Canada was making far better provision for the elderly than it had made in the forties or fifties, and the country could afford this, both economically and politically, because of economic growth.

The same is true of unemployment insurance and other forms of support for the able-bodied. Canada does far better under these headings than it did in the forties. Again, growth has provided the resources for an improvement in welfare and income-maintenance. Without such improvements, pensioners and the unemployed would be far worse off *than they are now,* whether or not they have become better off or worse off relative to the able-bodied employed or to capitalists or to some other reference group. It is widely thought that if a society does not use some of the fruits of growth to provide for the elderly and helpless in a more humane way there is something badly wrong with that society –

whatever the indices of growth or distribution may say. Judged by that criterion, Canada has not done badly in the past forty years.

In general, it seems clear that all the regions and most identifiable groups have shared in the economic advance of Canada since 1945. Living standards rose everywhere, and the vast majority of Canadians became far better off than their parents were forty years ago. They were also better off than they would have been or could have been if the income levels of 1945 had continued to 1965 or 1988. The fruits of growth were widely shared and widely enjoyed. Whether the sharing was fair, just, or equitable is of course another question.

It would be foolish, however, to claim that *everyone* became better off or that *nobody* lost, whether absolutely or relatively. The most obvious losers were the wheat farmers, whose earnings have not kept up with their costs. Here and there, too, workers and capitalists were unable to extract themselves and their funds from declining industries. Such people could not be called the victims of economic growth, since it was not the growth that caused their troubles. But certainly the growth did little for them, except in so far as government became more able and willing to pay subsidies, unemployment insurance, welfare benefits, and so forth.

Because the economic structure evolved in such a way as to create more openings in the white-collar and professional occupations, more and more Canadians found such jobs. In them, incomes were often relatively high and working conditions almost invariably better than in labouring or in routine factory work. It is true that for some of the lower-level white-collar skills, earnings fell relative to the earnings of factory workers. But hours of work generally were shorter and the working environment usually was more pleasant, while fringe benefits were often better. The professional and managerial groups, whose earnings were unequivocally higher than the average and whose working conditions were generally much more pleasant, increased in number relative to the total population, thus giving relatively high earnings to a comparatively large and fast-growing group. Indeed, for some components of this group (teachers and doctors, for example) earnings rose relative to the national average just when numbers were also growing unusually quickly. Thus, the period in question has seen a dramatic shift of population into higher-income occupations where working conditions are comparatively attractive. This shift has absorbed much of the increase in output per head because society was using so much more of these comparatively expensive kinds of labour. Most people would probably have approved of the result. It was one of the ways in which the fruits of economic growth were spread among larger numbers of Canadians. But whether this change could be said to have resulted in a more 'equal distribution of income' is questionable.

The best way to compare income-equality at different dates is to plot a cumulative percentage of spending units against a cumulative percentage of total income received. If incomes were perfectly equal, the poorest quarter of the families would receive 25 per cent of the income, and so would each succeeding quarter; if all the income went to one family, then the first three-quarters record no income, and the last quarter records it all. When comparing one year with another, it is important to make sure that definitions and coverage have not altered. Before 1971 there are problems with the Canadian data, so that it is necessary to 'make do,' but we have already argued[4] that between 1951 and 1977 there was no perceptible trend toward inequality. For the period 1971-84 there are perfectly comparable data, and these, further, have been adjusted to take account of inflation.[5] The results are clear: from 1971 to 1984, and in spite of the economic troubles of the early 1980s, the incomes of Canadians became slightly but perceptibly *more* equal. Thus, for instance, the poorest 45 per cent of the households received just over 23 per cent of the total income in 1971, and over 25 per cent in 1984. Not a large change, admittedly, but one that egalitarians ought to applaud.

The national statisticians regularly produce figures on average personal income in each province. By using these we can see whether the equalizing trend operated between regions also. The answer is simple: it certainly did. Whether one compares with the national average, or with Ontario, the highest-income province, the long-run picture is reasonably clear, although for some provinces there are big fluctuations from one year to another. For the Atlantic provinces the improvement was reasonably steady and consistent. In 1946 the average personal incomes in Prince Edward, Nova Scotia, and New Brunswick were respectively 50 per cent, 65 per cent, and 61 per cent of Ontario's; in 1984 the figures were 65, 74, and 68. When it entered Confederation in 1949, Newfoundland incomes were 43 per cent of Ontario's; in 1984 they were 67 per cent. Alberta and Quebec residents also improved their positions relative to Ontarians. For Manitoba and Saskatchewan, comparatively prosperous provinces in the mid-1940s, the picture is more mixed. Compared with Ontarians, Manitobans and Saskatchewanians lost ground during the 1950s and 1960s, only to regain most of their losses in the seventies and early eighties, so that they ended only slightly less worse off in comparative terms – and of course a great deal better off in absolute terms – than in 1946. In comparative terms British Columbians lost ground – but even in the mid-eighties their average incomes exceeded the national average and fell only slightly below those of Ontarians.

Why did Canada do well for more than forty years? In general it appears that

4 *Canada since 1945,* first edition, p. 22.
5 See Statistics Canada, *Income Distribution by Size in Canada, 1984* (catalogue 13-207), Table 1, for the raw data on which our calculation rests.

Canadians simply made good use of fundamentally favourable conditions. The nation's labour force was growing; new raw materials and new uses for old ones were discovered; much of the time world markets were favourable to Canada's exports; the country accumulated new, more productive, and more efficient plant and equipment; its workers grew more skilful and its managers more effective; and Canada eagerly imported new technical knowledge from the United States and elsewhere while developing more than a little for itself.

These are the normal processes by which an industrial economy raises its power to produce, and Canada, like the United States, western Europe, or Japan, has benefited from these processes, which have been at work here for a very long time. Nor has Canada's recent history been particularly unusual. It closely parallels the American experience, and although Britain has done less well and Japan very much better, the same sort of growth has been happening throughout the industrialized countries of the capitalist world. By using more 'inputs' – labour, machinery, natural resources – Canada raises its output; by using 'inputs' more efficiently it can raise its output per unit of input, thus getting a double return, so to speak. It is this double return that accounts for the rise in living standards. To achieve this all-important efficiency, up-to-date technology must be applied correctly in light of the supplies and costs of the various inputs and Canada's marketing opportunities; the ability to adapt despite the dislocation that a new machine or a new production process or a new arrangement may entail is also crucial. Where such changes have been resisted, as in the United Kingdom, the country has lost much of the benefit from technological progress and even from the accumulation of new plant. As a result, outputs and living standards have risen more slowly than they might have done. Where changes have been swallowed readily and eagerly, as in West Germany or Japan, outputs and living standards have risen very rapidly indeed. Relative to Britain, Canada and the United States have responded reasonably well to technological change and dislocation, at least during the period 1944-75.

After the mid-seventies, in Canada as elsewhere in the North Atlantic world, things went less well. Productivity grew more slowly than in the preceding thirty years. Specialists argued about the reasons, and they did not agree. Certainly every country had to absorb large numbers of comparatively unskilled new workers – women, immigrants, and the inexperienced young – who are probably less productive, on average, than workers in the prime of life. With time, doubtless, they learn on the job, so that productivity and living standards would drift upward once more. Indeed, by the mid-eighties, that was happening in Canada. There was also some sign that the pace of new investment, which is necessary to 'embody' new technology in plant and equipment, slackened off. This certainly occurred in Canada after 1981. Here, too, specialists hoped for a rebound, because old machinery was bound to wear out eventually – even in Sydney or on VIA Rail. A quite different problem resulted from the fact that, especially in North America, so many new jobs were in service industries and white-collar occupations where productivity is comparatively low, hard to raise, or both. Here again there was hope, by 1987, that with the spread of the computer and the microchip things might improve quite quickly. The coming of this new 'third industrial revolution' had already begun to affect white-collar workers just as much as blue-collar, or even more. In so far as featherbedding and other restrictive practices were part of the problem, wise government policy might eventually be deployed. Finally, even unemployment might eventually solve itself to some extent, simply because birth rates had been so low for so long.

In any event, the world of the eighties was so different from the world of the forties that to measure living standards by income per capita could now mislead. For one thing, in the eighties far more Canadians had come to belong to two-income households. For another, most of them possessed plenty of consumer durables, whose services were not counted as part of income. Equally important, 'do-it-yourself' had become a very large activity, partly because a household could so readily own or rent sophisticated tools. Finally, the tax system had created a large informal economy – the invisible 'black economy' whose activity largely escaped the statisticians' net. For all these reasons, in the late 1980s household living standards were certainly higher than they seemed, and since the mid-1970s they had risen considerably more than the statisticians thought.

Nevertheless, the recession of the early 1980s did create some problems, and these pressed on public consciousness in ways unknown since the 1930s. The most striking was 'homelessness.' Admittedly, this was to some extent the product of rent control, which made rental housing increasingly scarce, and to some extent the result of dementia, which made people unwilling or unable to seek the help that already existed. Rent control mattered because, having been installed in most provinces during the mid-1970s, by the mid-1980s it was having a cumulative effect. Dementia mattered because a high proportion of the homeless were disturbed. At an earlier time many might have been institutionalized. But for twenty years or more the mental-health authorities had been using drugs to empty their hospitals, just as completely and quickly as they could. Again the effect was cumulative. There was, finally, the problem of the broken marriage, an increasingly common circumstance. Family break-ups multiplied the physical demand for housing and often left one partner very hard up.

Almost equally noticeable was the reappearance of 'food banks,' which an earlier generation would have called soup kitchens or bread lines. Generally operated by churches and charitable organizations, these burgeoned in the early 1980s. In some places their main clientele was not destitute folk, but low-income people who used the free food to supplement the inadequate incomes they already received from work or from welfare. This was a pattern quite different from the destitution of the 1930s, which was, in addition, on a much larger scale. After all, in the worst of the 1982 slump the unemployment rate never rose as high as 13 per cent; in 1933, at the bottom of the Great Depression, 38 per cent of the non-farm labour force seems to have been without work. Nevertheless, the food banks did testify to urban misery – an inability fully to share in the 'good things' of city life.

The deprived, and their advocates in the anti-poverty lobby, could and did hope that salvation would come through 'redistribution.' By 1988 there was little sign, and not much hope, of such a thing. The Canadian heart might or might not have hardened since the 1960s, but government deficits, both federal and provincial, had certainly grown, so that no one could readily imagine a new program of public spending, except for Ottawa's day-care plan of 1988. In the budgets of the late 1980s, the hoped-for solvent seemed to be economic growth. An expanding economy would pay more taxes; deficits would fall; eventually governments would have more money to spend. But it would take time. Meanwhile, economic growth would create new jobs, as it had been doing for decades.

In the early 1970s it had been fashionable to say that economic growth was a bad thing – the cause of pollution, congestion, and the depletion of natural resources, the generator of pressure for change or for hard work, making people unhappy. Such criticisms were rare by 1988, although they could still be heard from pulpits and from the anti-nuclear lobby. They were not altogether empty. Growth implied change, which in turn meant risk. The latter has never been easy to bear, and the former is often painful. But for the great masses of Canadians economic growth provided an escape from a life of grinding poverty. That escape must be placed in the balance, along with the costs of congestion, stress, urbanization, and change. Also on the positive side of the balance must go many 'non-economic' benefits. Increased wealth had permitted Canada to subsidize the arts, run a decent social security system, look after the aged and most of the poor, deal with pollution if it chose to do so, and develop new technologies to offset, wholly or in part, the depletion of natural resources. The 'golden age' of the past had been at best a pretty tarnished piece of silver plate, with a large admixture of base metal.

PART TWO

The End of Mackenzie King 1945-8

3

Canada Adrift

'The sequence for sane Canadian thinking,' a foreign affairs commentator wrote in 1941, 'is, first, the British Commonwealth, second, the Anglo-Saxon union, and finally a world order, beyond the war, based on co-operation and justice.' Canadians reading these words nodded sagely. Thus it had always been; thus, once Hitler was disposed of, it would be again. The sentiment stands in poignant contrast to another observation, made about the same time, by Britain's ambassador in Washington. 'Boys,' he told a group of reporters, 'Britain's broke.'

A worried Mackenzie King reflected on what one of his dinner guests had just told him. 'Britain,' King was told, 'is a bankrupt country ... He had not conceived that England could ever be bankrupt ... but that was where she was now.' True in 1941, those words were truer in 1945. Some Canadians knew it. Speaking in August 1940, a University of Toronto professor of history, Frank Underhill, uttered these prescient words: 'We now have two loyalties – one to Britain and the other to North America. I venture to say it is the second, North America, that is going to be supreme now. The relative significance of Britain is going to sink, no matter what happens.' Underhill's candour was premature; he was almost fired for his pains and was saved only because his friends persuaded the premier of Ontario that his departure would be inexpedient. Britain, as far as public opinion was concerned, was still best.

The resultant gap between the ideal and the real in Canada's perception of the outside world bedevilled Mackenzie King's Liberal government. Ever since 1763 Canadian external relations had been dominated by one country – Britain. 'Foreign affairs' were in Canada styled 'external affairs' so that relations with the mother country could be included. Twice in the twentieth century Canadians had plunged into world wars at Britain's side, and between 1939 and 1945 over a million Canadian men and women disrupted their lives to serve in a cause whose symbol was, as always, Britain. In 1945 victory crowned British arms.

The empire still stood: why should things be any different?

But things were very different. Six years of war had disrupted the European economy and demoralized Europe's political society. At the war's end, the Soviet Union had advanced out of its Eurasian fastnesses and occupied the centre of Europe. The largest Soviet armies encircled Hitler's last bastion in Berlin, now to be governed jointly by the four major allies, Britain, France, the Soviet Union, and the United States.

Britain in 1945 disposed of large armies too, though never as large as the Soviet Union's. British troops occupied a vast swath of territory from Saigon to Hamburg, not to mention those parts of the empire recovered from enemy occupation. But the bright colours of the victory parades were soon forgotten. Soldiers returning to England after four or five years' absence found a very different country from the one they had left. Grey bread, tea served in jam jars, meagre rations of meat and butter, and dilapidated rolling stock on the railways, all testified to the sacrifices the civilian economy had made for victory.

Britain's new Labour government, contemplating the dismal scene, decided that it could not afford the luxury of empire very long. The Neilson's Chocolates map of the empire, for so long a feature of Canadian classrooms, began to shrink and change colour as the blotches of pink that represented the empire were replaced by unfamiliar greens and yellows. India was the Indian Empire no longer, but the Dominion of India – just like Canada – and then, in 1949, a republic. Beside it were new dominions, a largely Buddhist Ceylon and a Moslem Pakistan, the latter a testament to India's civil strife and religious disagreements. Burma left the empire entirely, and Palestine, with its warring Jewish and Arab factions, was abandoned in the spring of 1948. Only in Africa and the Caribbean did the empire hold on, but even there its days were numbered.

These developments were presented to Canadians in the cheery guise of liberal progress. Pakistan, India, and Ceylon remained in the Commonwealth; all had properly constituted parliamentary governments, like Canada's, free of the embarrassing encumbrances of British colonial rule. Canadians, who believed themselves to be a model for the Commonwealth's constitutional development, expected that the new nations would in time become exotic reproductions, modified for local colour, of Britain abroad. The Canadian government sat back approvingly, tendering much sympathy but little advice, as the British packed up and moved out.

The focus for the government's external perceptions was the Department of External Affairs, headed as was the custom by the Prime Minister himself. Its officers had matured in Mackenzie King's shadow. A highly intelligent group, they added tone to Canada's representation abroad, and lustre to the reports the government received. Inside Ottawa, foreign-service officers were admired as an élite corps in the civil service. But their influence did not match their prestige.

Mackenzie King took it to be axiomatic that external events, although they might affect Canada, were nevertheless beyond Canada's capacity to control, and usually beyond its ability to influence. King had, over the years, met most of the world's leading statesmen, from Theodore Roosevelt and Sir Edward Grey to Winston Churchill, Clement Attlee, and the new American president, Harry Truman. The Prime Minister prided himself on this accomplishment. He believed that it gave him a unique insight into the workings of the world and the preoccupations of its leaders. Liberal propagandists informed the electorate that King's influence, acquired over two generations, was irreplaceable.

It was an influence that King carefully conserved. Not for him the high-flying diplomatic exploits of his Conservative predecessor, Sir Robert Borden. Borden's turn as a world statesman in the First World War had done his party little good on the home front. Canada, Borden believed, had paid for its status in the world through the blood of its soldiers. Borden believed that sacrifice cemented national unity. King, however, suspected that blood was a pretty effective solvent. He dismissed the substance of influence abroad as a will-o'-the-wisp; far better, he concluded, to enjoy the appearance of influence, posing happily for the photographers at the Quebec Conference beside American President Franklin Roosevelt and British Prime Minister Churchill. Only King and his closest staff knew that the Canadians then left the scene.

In the election of 1945, King was presented as a beacon of stability and sense in a world that had to be set to rights. In fact, he was puzzled and disheartened by the chaos he perceived around him. In education and upbringing, Mackenzie King was a good Ontario Victorian, with family roots deep in British colonial soil. For King, London was the centre of the political and intellectual universe, the place outside Canada where he felt most at home and at ease. King's library was lined with British biographies and books on British politics and British thought – most of them unread, to be sure, but nevertheless a sure sign of their owner's tastes and affections. When King held his pre-war 'at homes' for the spirit world, it was British ghosts who came to call and proffer advice.

The ghosts could not tell the Prime Minister what to do, only reflect on what they, and he, had done. In 1945 there was a new addition to the pantheon, Franklin Roosevelt, the first American spectre to be admitted to the charmed circle. There, at least, was one American who could listen to and reassure King. King could reflect that Roosevelt was the only American president who took any time for Canada and who had even taken the trouble to advise King on the subjects that interested him most: national unity and Canadian politics. Roosevelt's advice, to assimilate the French Canadians to the English majority, was, of course, eccentric and politically unfeasible.

The new American president, Harry Truman, liked Canadians. He even knew one or two, and one of his first requests was that Canada appoint an old ex-Canadian crony of his a consul in Kansas City. From time to time Truman bestowed new marks of his esteem: Canadians were to be admitted to West Point, the military academy, just like Americans, Truman decided, and it took much bureaucratic shuffling by his embarrassed subordinates to bury the proposal. Relations between Truman and Mackenzie King, however, remained formal, polite, and minimal.

Fortunately other people in Washington liked Canadians, and some of them were in important posts. Professional diplomats admired the competence of Canada's fledgling foreign service and envied the compact tidiness of the Canadian government's ability to make decisions and then ratify and implement them, without messy reference to a fractious and ignorant legislature. In a war that was, on the American side, run largely by a powerful and increasingly arrogant military, American bureaucrats discovered fellow-feeling with Canadian diplomats in Washington: both were usually on the outside looking wistfully in. Common interests reinforced shared experience. During the war it had become increasingly common simply to pick up the phone and dial one's counterpart in the other capital. Almost always the Americans had something the Canadians wanted; less frequently, but still profitably, the Canadians could satisfy American demands.

Watching the United States go to war was an impressive experience. The Americans had, in 1945, over twelve million men and women in uniform. In 1947 the Americans produced over one-half of the manufactures of the whole world. In the same year they generated 43 per cent of the world's electricity and pumped 62 per cent of the world's oil. American productive capacity had determined the outcome of the Second World War, dethroning the Germans, the previous masters of the art of turning production into military predominance. With the American example so close and so obviously effective, it was natural and inevitable for Canadians to imitate the American model. Using American technology, American management skills, and largely American designs, Canadian industry surged ahead during the war, even surpassing, from time to time, American production records. Canadian achievements were, however, usually in terms of unit costs – making something quicker and cheaper than the Americans could, such as standardized merchant ships or artificial rubber. There was little question of making *more* of anything than the United States, which was still ten times bigger and fifteen times richer than its northern neighbour.

The Americans also had the atomic bomb. The bomb was the war's most closely guarded secret, known only to a handful of British and American statesmen, military officers, and scientists – and to Mackenzie King and a handful of

Canadians. Canada's participation in atomic research during the war derived from possession of a previously neglected metal, uranium, and from Britain's need for atomic research facilities. These Canada provided, first in Montreal and then in Chalk River, Ontario, and secured in return priceless training in the most advanced science and technology.

When the bomb was dropped on the Japanese cities of Hiroshima and Nagasaki in August 1945, and the war came to an abrupt end, the timing, but not the fact, was a surprise to the Canadian government. Although the existence of the bomb was no longer concealed, the United States embarked on an elaborate secrecy program, designed to preserve the atomic monopoly, with all its military and security advantages, for the United States alone. The American program was a fallacy, since the British too had the know-how, if not the facilities, to construct a similar device, and the Russians, not to be left behind, were hot on the trail.

So hot were the Russians that the Soviet government could not contain its eagerness to know as much as possible, as soon as possible, about the new wonder weapons. Fortunately for Moscow, some of the scientists engaged in atomic research were well disposed toward the Soviet cause, and some of these men worked in Canada. The revelation of this fact came all too quickly for Mackenzie King. On September 6, 1945, Norman Robertson, the Under Secretary of State for External Affairs, met the Prime Minister at his office. Something was terribly wrong, Robertson told King: 'A man had turned up, with his wife, at the office of the Minister of Justice. He asked to see the Minister. He said he was from the Russian Embassy.' It was not an official call, as could be seen from the Soviet official's observation that 'the Russian democracy was different from ours.'

How different Canadians were soon to learn. A shocked Prime Minister discovered that the Russian, Igor Gouzenko, had brought with him embassy documents proving the existence of a Soviet spy ring in Canada which had as its object the discovery of information on the making of the atomic bomb. It was a shattering awakening for a Victorian Canadian, even one as worldly and politically astute as King. King confided his shock and distress to his diary; Robertson, more practically, began to assemble one of Canada's finest collections of the literature of espionage. A royal commission was appointed to discover what it could about the spy ring. The findings were startling: a Member of Parliament, a prominent scientist, and minor members of the military and civil service were implicated. The suspects were rounded up in the early morning under the authority of the War Measures Act, Canada's emergency constitution, jailed, and interrogated. When brought to trial, about half of the accused, including Canada's only Communist MP, were convicted and sentenced to prison.

That was only the beginning. The Soviet Union professed to regard the publicity surrounding the spy scandal as malicious provocation by the Canadian government, part of an anti-Soviet strategy orchestrated by the Americans. As such, it was a nine-days' wonder internationally; for Canadians it was the end of innocence.

It was not difficult to connect what was happening domestically with what was going on internationally. Canadian diplomats stationed in Moscow had been sounding cautionary notes for some time. Even before the war was over, in April 1945, a Canadian dispatch from the Soviet capital called 'for a firm diplomatic line to be taken by the Western Powers in their dealings with the Soviet Union, and it is also desirable to consider building up those areas in Europe and elsewhere where Western influence is, or can be, dominant.'

Canada's advice on such an issue could not be decisive: that was left to the larger powers, the United States and Great Britain. What is noteworthy is the fact that most of the currents of the internal American debate over foreign policy were reproduced faithfully in a Canadian context. There were even some optimists who argued that it would still be possible for the great powers, including the Soviet Union, to agree among themselves, provided all parties kept their heads. But embedded in the optimism was a strain of bleak realism. Dana Wilgress, Canada's ambassador to Moscow, concluded that the chief interest of the Soviet Union was stability, domestically and internationally. That, he told Ottawa, was because Russia was the home of a 'new privileged class.' To preserve its dominance at home, the Soviet leadership required to be left alone, safe from interference from abroad. But would it be? Russia's new class was uncertain and fearful of Western intentions and influences, anxious to preserve its utopia from comparisons with Western freedom and affluence. When the Russians constructed a *cordon sanitaire* along their western frontier, establishing their own puppet governments under reliable personalities, the Western powers carped and balked. Russian diversions in the Far East and the Mediterranean, Wilgress explained, could be seen largely as a response to Western initiatives in Poland and the Balkans. They should not be taken seriously. 'On the whole,' he concluded, 'the interests of the Soviet privileged class are bound up with the maintenance of a long period of peace.'

If Wilgress was right, the world was in for a long period of division between two mutually exclusive economic and political systems. If there was little to fear, there was nothing to hope for. There would soon be a term for the situation, the Cold War, and a description of the boundary between West and East: the Iron Curtain. In the East there would be monolithic Communist regimes, firmly under the thumb of the spiritual grandfather of all Communists, Josef Stalin. In the West, there were the surviving traces of free economies and societies in western Europe and North America. In such a system, Canada's place was axiomatic: it belonged with its elder Anglo-Saxon partners.

The nub of the matter had been stated by Mackenzie King in 1938. 'We, too, as a good friendly neighbour, have our responsibilities. One of them is to see that our country is made as immune from possible invasion as we can reasonably be expected to make it, and, that should the occasion ever arise, enemy forces should not be able to make their way, either by land, sea or air, to the United States across Canadian territory.' That policy remained in effect in 1945; it would remain in effect for the next generation.

4

The End of the War

When General Alfred Jodl stepped out of a French schoolhouse on May 7, 1945, after signing the surrender of Nazi Germany, the Western world went wild with excitement. It hardly mattered to Canadians that their country was still at war with the Japanese and that the bloody battles of the Pacific might have another year to run. 'The war' was the war against Hitler, and Hitler was dead, his armies prisoners, his cities smashed, his people beaten, his country occupied.

Across Canada people celebrated according to their mood. Everyone left work, some heading for taverns to drink, others for the main streets to wave Union Jacks. In Ottawa, there was a solemn ceremony of thanksgiving. In Halifax, there was a riot.

It had been a long war. In five and a half years some 41 per cent of Canada's male population of military age (eighteen to forty-five) had passed through the armed forces – over a million men out of a total population of just over twelve million. The size of Canada's armed forces made Canada, temporarily, the fourth military power in the world in 1945, a significant factor in any equation of power.

The Canadian armed forces had a fine fighting record. Forty-two thousand had been killed during the war (fewer than during the First World War). Canadians had fought their way through Sicily and up the Italian peninsula, as well as across the lowlands of northern Europe. On May 7, 1945, Canada's own army, the First Canadian Army, on the allies' northern flank, was preparing to advance into the German fortress of Holland, to liberate the starving cities of Amsterdam, Rotterdam, and The Hague.

The Canadian government and the Canadian army had no intention of keeping Canada's military power in being. Canadian mobilization was an occasional thing, a temporary outing for a deeply civilian society. In 1944, with victory imminent, preparations for demobilization had been accelerated. The Canadian government informed the British that Canada would maintain a few formations in Europe to assist in the occupation of Germany – an offer the British gratefully accepted – but otherwise Canada's soldiers were to come home on the first available ships. And they did: 15,665 soldiers in June, and more thereafter. By the end of December, 184,000 had made the homeward voyage. Some brought new brides: in 1945 almost 7,000 adults and 3,700 children were admitted to Canada as 'soldiers' dependents.'

Some units were to be shipped to the Pacific theatre; otherwise priority was given to those who had served longest: first in, first out. Not everyone accepted the principle with equanimity. Riots broke out in overseas camps, with attendant publicity. A scandalized government decided to be quit of the whole matter as soon as possible. All troops would be brought home, previous pledges notwith-standing. In December 1945 the British were told that Canada's army would leave Europe no later than the summer of 1946. And by the autumn of that year it had.

On reaching Canadian soil, military units were disbanded as quickly as possi-ble. From a strength of 478,000 in May 1945, the army was reduced to 31,000 at the end of September 1946. The hopes of the generals, admirals, and air mar-shals that the government would show its gratitude for their military prowess by maintaining a military strength of 105,000 in peacetime were quickly dashed. Late in September 1946, the Cabinet Defence Committee decided that the army would have to live with a force level of between 20,000 and 25,000 soldiers, in-stead of the 55,000 it had requested. The air force received 15,000 to 20,000, and the navy 10,000. The military budget contracted, in spasms, until by fiscal 1947-8 (the Canadian fiscal year is measured from April 1 to March 31) it touched bottom at $240 million. This represented 12 per cent of the budget, a level dearly won against the opposition of more civilian-minded ministers by the Minister of National Defence, Brooke Claxton.

During the war, the civilian side of government had necessarily taken second place. Now the lid was off. Gross national product, in current dollars, had been $5.6 billion in 1939; it was $11.8 billion in 1945. Unemployment was negligi-ble: 163,000 in 1946, out of a civilian labour force of 4.8 million. Those who were unemployed benefited from the new unemployment insurance system.

Retrospectively, the picture looks rosy, but that was not the impression at the time. Canadians at the end of the war were deeply worried. 'What will we do if there's a slump after the war?' one young mother asked. 'I don't want my chil-dren to have the hardships I had.' Economists, businessmen, labour leaders, so-cial workers, and politicians all worried. 'Discontented youth formed the van-guard of revolutionary movements abroad after the last war,' the Canadian Youth Commission reported in 1945. 'They might well play a similar role here should prolonged unemployment destroy their faith in democratic institutions.'

With an eye to the future, businessmen and workers, free enterprisers and socialists alike, rushed to join what C.D. Howe, the Minister of Reconstruction, scornfully called 'the Security Brigade.' Fear of depression stimulated elaborate planning for the dreadful future. Typical was the proposal by Canada's tiny democratic socialist party, the Co-operative Commonwealth Federation (gratefully abridged by press and public to CCF), for a 'National Planning Commission, consisting of a small group of economists, engineers and statisticians assisted by an appropriate technical staff,' to advise the government what it could do with the economy and discover what would make a socialized Canada run. After all, the argument ran, it had been done in war; now it could be done in peace. Canadians, the CCF believed, would order 'Left Turn, Canada,' in the words of a party pamphlet.

The voters appeared to give their support to the CCF's analysis when they turned out two discredited provincial Liberal regimes, in Ontario (1943) and Saskatchewan (1944), installing the CCF as official opposition in Ontario and as the government in Saskatchewan. The voters had chosen the CCF, and the CCF stood for planning and socialization. Surely the signposts pointed left. Some of the signs, however, were deceptive. Part of the problem was that the public was undecided about which of its desires it wished to emphasize. The Canadian public wanted security; but it also craved material prosperity, consumer goods, cars, and a house in the suburbs. It had had a taste of prosperity during the war: personal expenditure on goods and services rose from $10.6 billion in 1938 to $14.1 billion in 1944 (in constant 1971 dollars). It wanted more of the same.

Alone of King's ministers C.D. Howe seized the mood of the public, and combined his perception with a grasp of the practicalities of planning. The real problem with the civilian economy after the war, he told King, would be shortages. Industry would be strained to the utmost to make up for fifteen years of depression and war. The facilities to exploit the potential boom were ready to hand, in capital investment in war industry. Indeed, in Howe's view, the true reconstruction of the Canadian economy had already taken place. All that was needed now was 'reconversion' to make the best new use of what existed.

King's preference did not go immediately to Howe or his program. There were alternatives, promoted by Ian Mackenzie and social planners under his patronage in the Department of Pensions and National Health. Mackenzie had sponsored the Committee on Reconstruction, chaired by Principal Cyril James of McGill University, to uncover the trouble spots in the Canadian economy and prescribe remedies that the government should adopt. From the James Committee's perspective, the chief post-war desideratum was employment; its chief premise, that there would be an economic slump. The government would, therefore, have to intervene in the economy to create employment, cushioning the shock with social welfare benefits such as unemployment insurance and health insurance. Meanwhile a committee of Mackenzie's own officials worked out a plan for a national health insurance scheme.

The problem with both the James Committee's plan and with the more modest health insurance scheme was that they were constitutionally unfeasible. 'I am inclined to think,' one of Mackenzie's French-Canadian colleagues warned in April 1942, 'that in considering the future policies of the Country we should not entirely forget the system which has been prevailing in our federal administration up to the present time.' Moreover, the minister added, 'I am somewhat doubtful as to the advisability of creating an entirely new organization of public activities which, among other things, would mean a rather complete condemnation of the present responsible system which we are defending and which young men of Canada are being asked to fight for.' In the opinion of some, the gospel of centralized social welfare was not all-powerful. In Quebec, at least, it might be politically dangerous.

The country wasn't ready, and neither was King. When the James Committee's research director, Leonard Marsh, issued a report on social planning early in 1943, it was firmly trodden on. The politicians found Marsh's proposals strange, and the civil servants found them actively offensive.

The civil servants knew, better than Marsh or James, how to make their opinions count. Their nerve centre was the Department of Finance. In pre-Depression days the finance department had been a sleepy accounting office, periodically spewing out new taxation and keeping the government's finances roughly in balance. All that had changed when, in 1932, King's Conservative predecessor, R.B. Bennett, had summoned W. Clifford Clark from Queen's University to become deputy minister of finance. Clark was a youngish man who had worked for the government at the end of the First World War and who had then left for the United States to make his fortune in private banking. That business had turned sour with the Depression, and Clark returned to academe to await better times.

But Dr Clark (as he became when Queen's awarded him an honorary degree) turned out to have talents, seldom found in an academic, that were more reminiscent of New York finance than of the university's dreaming spires. Clark combined his banker's flair with a talent for intrigue and a passion to arrive, and remain, at the centre of things. King, who shared many of the same qualities (besides a real PhD in economics), no doubt appreciated a kindred spirit and kept Clark on when he returned to power in 1935. Dr Clark and Dr King together made a formidable combination, as the cabinet discovered when King placed proposals for family allowances before them in January 1944. King summoned

Clark to the council table (in the absence of the Minister of Finance, who had pressing business elsewhere) to explain matters. 'I think,' King later wrote in his diary, 'most of the Ministers who have been opposing the idea did not feel equal to debating the matter with Clark.' Those who did were squelched.

Family allowances were just one of the opportunities the war brought to Clifford Clark. The budget expanded fivefold during the war (from $2.9 billion in 1939 to $19.4 billion in 1944, in constant 1971 dollars). Finance had to find how to raise it. To handle the problem, Clark assembled a strong team. First to come, just before the war, was R.B. Bryce, a product of John Maynard Keynes's seminar at Cambridge, who combined firm belief in the possibilities of government action with a clear and rational explanatory style. J.H. Perry and A.K. Eaton devised taxation policies, and for more specialized tasks Clark summoned an old colleague, W.A. Mackintosh, from Queen's.

Mackintosh was no stranger to Ottawa or governmental problems. His work for the pre-war Royal Commission on Dominion-Provincial Relations had helped to shape that group's perceptions of Canada's fundamental economic problems. Brilliant and persuasive on paper, Mackintosh was down-to-earth and blunt in person. Fertile in expedients and indefatigable in work, he became a much more powerful figure than his title, 'special assistant to the deputy minister,' indicated. 'Twin' or 'alter ego' would have been closer to the truth.

Mackintosh functioned most effectively on a special interdepartmental committee, created and chaired by Clark, called the Economic Advisory Committee. Its function was to purvey sound counsel to the cabinet on thorny economic problems on occasions when the Minister of Finance could not cope with them by himself. For the first three years of the war these problems were war-related. On topics such as taxation, wage control, and the balance of payments, the ministers were used to listening to and deferring to Clark's arguments. By 1942, however, the war was in principle won, and Clark could turn his attention to less immediate matters.

One such matter was the James Committee's report. When preliminary rumblings reached the cabinet in the autumn of 1942, they were referred to the Economic Advisory Committee. James recommended that a special department be established to guide reconstruction planning, or that at least a minister without portfolio be assigned the task of co-ordinating the government's reconstruction program. The Economic Advisory Committee poured cold water on James's proposals. It was then that James authorized Marsh to proceed with his famous report. It was ready on February 17, 1943.

Marsh failed to impress the civil servants. In an early comment, W.A. Mackintosh pointed out the defects, commenting that 'the full programme of social insurance here discussed is not at present within the powers of the Parliament of

Canada.' Marsh was not deterred. His report plumped for a 'comprehensive scheme' – health insurance, family allowances, unemployment insurance, children's allowances, and workmen's compensation – to be implemented by Ottawa alone. His sole concession to political reality was the observation that, 'There should be no danger if the whole situation were canvassed and agreed on in advance – possibly through the medium of a special conference of federal and provincial representatives.' Marsh prescribed, besides social welfare, a dominion 'works development programme' to combat unemployment in the inevitable economic downturn. The total cost of social security was estimated at $500 million, while public works might go as high as $1 billion. But even so, it would cost less than the war was costing in the fiscal year 1942-3.

Marsh was naturally proud of his creation, viewing it as an intellectual *tour de force*. It had not taken very long to complete, he told the press. Marsh's immodest observation provoked derision. Marsh's 'thinking was squeezed into a period of one week,' one of Mackintosh's friends, Walter Gordon, observed. 'Having in mind the "pie in the sky" era to which we are all looking forward,' Gordon added, 'I presume he means a working week of four or five days of perhaps six hours per day or a total of, say, thirty hours per one billion dollars.' Mackintosh reassured his friend. 'The so-called Marsh Report did not emanate from any of the Government departments,' he wrote, 'and I am afraid that it is likely to prove a boomerang.' Or a dead duck.

It was the sponsorship of the James Committee and the publicity that the Marsh Report received that helped to bury its proposals. But the spirit it represented had a profound effect on government thinking. James's and Marsh's views had a long and respectable ancestry in the writings of social workers and some economists. Britain's Beveridge Report, published the previous fall, had achieved bestseller status and was referred to by countless individuals, including Prime Minister King, who had never read it.

King moved slowly. Family allowances, recommended by the National War Labour Board as a means to circumvent wage control for the worst-paid in the work force, were brought before Parliament in 1944 and passed, though not before the Conservatives uttered some harsh thoughts about the French-Catholic families, with their unlimited breeding potential, for whom it was undoubtedly destined. A Department of Reconstruction was authorized, to serve as a coordinating agency for the government's reconstruction program. A cabinet committee was established to prepare for a dominion-provincial conference on reconstruction. A new Department of National Health and Welfare was established, and a special agency for veterans, the Department of Veterans Affairs, created. But the government's action was strictly circumscribed. No one questioned its ability to clean up after the war: war-making was a dominion responsibility. Family allowances arguably belonged within the dominion's sphere of action too. But the other schemes advocated by the enthusiasts for social welfare, planning, and government intervention in the economy did not.

While a cabinet committee wrestled with this problem (and while the committee's chairman, T.A. Crerar, a provincial rights' enthusiast, wrestled with his conscience and his colleagues), King was forced to come to a decision on reconstruction. The only possible appointee for the job was C.D. Howe, he decided, and in October 1944 Howe duly assumed the duties of Minister of Reconstruction. Reconstruction, he insisted, would follow the lines that he prescribed, and not those laid down by the woolly proponents of state planning. Reconstruction in fact would be reconversion.

Reconversion was in full swing, under the aegis of the wartime Department of Munitions and Supply. Under a 1944 budget provision, Howe was able to grant accelerated depreciation to companies converting their facilities to peacetime production. The accelerated depreciation would permit a quick write-off of extra expenses against current taxation; at the same time, if the economy turned downward, businesses would already have paid off their gamble on the future. If, as luck would have it, economic conditions were favourable after the war, they would be paying full taxes on their new but productive plant. Under Howe's program, funds for capital expansion were readily available.

Mackintosh, who had joined the Department of Reconstruction, was uneasy. A cautious and prudent man, he was opposed to putting all the reconstruction eggs into Howe's reconversion basket. Squeezing reluctant approval from his minister, Mackintosh set to work exploring a different line of country. From his labours emerged a general statement of the government's post-war economic policy, the White Paper on Employment and Income.

There had never before been a White Paper in Canada. Such a document committed the government to doctrine and policy, yet had no legislative effect. It could, however, attract attention and focus debate, both public and parliamentary. Mackintosh's first draft, when he laid it before Howe, took a spacious view of the government's capacities. There would be 'full employment' after the war, Mackintosh promised: the government would make it so. Howe bridled. 'Full employment was impossible,' he snorted, and any government that promised it would be a sitting duck collecting the pot shots of the press and the opposition. Far better, he thought, to take refuge in the circumlocution, 'high and stable level of employment.' That looked good, and yet promised nothing in particular. 'High and stable level' it was. Under that lumbering banner the Liberals marched out to the first post-war election, on June 11, 1945. Party orators had no hesitation in translating the 'high and stable level' into 'full employment' – after the election that would be forgotten. The Liberals, after all, had 'a plan.'

But the plan they had was not necessarily the one the electorate expected or, perhaps, voted for.

The real Liberal plan, whether by accident or design, was Howe's. It was based on optimism about the economy, and scepticism about the potentialities of planning. It would not be the economic abstractions of doctrinaire planners in Ottawa that would shape post-war Canada. The shaping would be left to business's self-interest, guided, prodded, and shaped by incentives that businessmen could understand. Post-war Canada would be a free enterprise society.

5

The Legacy of War

As Canadians struggled to regain their feet in civilian life and as their government endeavoured to inculcate the unfamiliar spirit of optimism in the electorate, certain phenomena remained constant. Among them was the Canadian constitution, the British North America (BNA) Act. That act divided Canadian government into pockets of authority and sovereignty labelled 'federal' (or dominion) and 'provincial.' Eighty years of interpretation by the courts had fixed clear limits to the ability of the central authority to exercise its powers.

Such limitation could be a political convenience. During the thirties, Mackenzie King's Liberal government was only too happy to slough off responsibility for the unemployed and the destitute on to the provinces and municipalities. It was only after the outbreak of war that the King government acted on the problem of unemployment, securing the provinces' consent to the transfer of authority over unemployment insurance to the central government, which alone possessed the necessary financial resources to grapple with the problem. As for the recommendations of the Royal Commission on Dominion-Provincial Relations, which in 1940 had suggested a much more fundamental restructuring of federal-provincial relationships, they were placed in a deep freeze for the duration of the war.

The staff of the Royal Commission dispersed to war work – more urgent and more necessary under the circumstances. The war took care of unemployment, and the emergency transferred ultimate authority to the central government (only in national emergencies did the central government's residual powers become active and effective).

The operative instrument of the dominion government's emergency powers was until 1988 the War Measures Act, passed in 1914 to cope with the First World War emergency. The act was a simple one. In a specified emergency the governor-in-council (the cabinet) may make 'orders and regulations [which] shall have the force of law' on any subject or for any purpose deemed 'necessary for the security, defence, peace, order and welfare of Canada.' During the Second World War the dominion government enacted 6,414 orders under the War Measures Act, orders that had the force of law and circumvented parliamentary debate. Using these orders, an army of civil servants, controllers, directors-general, and commissioners fanned out across the country, calculating, enforcing, regulating, and sometimes arresting persons or confiscating products.

The civil service expanded to match its growing powers. In 1939, the dominion bureaucracy totalled 46,000; in 1945 there were 116,000 civil servants. But that was not all. Unable to cram all of its administrators or functions into the tiny city of Ottawa, the central government set up specialized crown corporations to run essential aspects of the war effort. Crown corporations bought and stockpiled silk, mined uranium, built bombers, imported machine tools, refined fuel, ran telephone companies.

What the government did not ordain directly, it regulated through an army of controllers. That included transport, air, road and rail, petroleum products, hydroelectricity, and construction materials. Supplies for the war effort, scarce commodities for civilian life, all came under federal jurisdiction. Those who could demonstrate a valid need for one of the scarce commodities controlled by the Department of Munitions and Supply could apply for permission to use it. Those who could not, whether they wanted to put stainless steel railings in an office building or a new metal roof on a church, were told to wait until the end of the war.

Howe's controllers were concerned principally to supply raw materials to Canada's hungry factories. However, the government could not entirely ignore the needs of the rest of the economy, those parts that fed the war workers, clothed them, and kept public services in repair. Munitions and Supply symbolized what Minister of Finance James Ilsley called the 'real costs' of the war, 'the goods and services which have to be sacrificed out of our current production to meet the needs of war.' Those things that could not be sacrificed were doled out, and their prices controlled, by a parallel organization, the Wartime Prices and Trade Board, under its hard-driving chairman, Donald Gordon.

Gordon was by any standards a remarkable man. He had to be to face down the contending special interests that demanded his personal concentration and attention. Gordon enjoyed confronting his opponents, and he usually carried the day. The only exception to the rule was agriculture, where the Minister, Saskatchewan's Jimmy Gardiner, and the particular interests of farmers, reigned supreme. Gordon's attempts to integrate farmers into his system were seldom successful. But as Gardiner pointed out, farm production was booming ($570 million in 1939, it reached $1,320 million in 1944). Gordon wasted his profanity on

Gardiner.

In other spheres, the hard-drinking Gordon (he consumed a bottle of scotch a day, according to legend) was much more successful. His principal task, to keep the cost of living down, was achieved. The index of wholesale prices in December 1945 was a paltry 11.1 per cent over that of December 1941, while the cost of living reached only 120.1 (using 1935-9 as an average). Officials travelling out of their Ottawa fastnesses were pleasantly surprised at the relative absence of public complaint or resentment. The galloping inflation of the First World War had created an industrial crisis in Canada; there was hardly any repetition in the Second. Indeed, Canadians as a whole were better off than they had been before the war. For most, standards of living and disposable income had increased during the war. Only the business and professional classes and those on fixed incomes resented the large bites taken out of their salaries by stringent taxation. Gordon's organization pointed out proudly that food and clothing actually cost less in 1945 than they had in 1919, while fuel, home furnishings, and services cost just slightly more; only rents were substantially above 1919 levels.

Controls did not vanish with the end of Hitler's war. Servicemen released into the civilian economy created heavy demands on still-scarce supplies. Overseas, the liberation of Europe brought in its train millions of starving mouths to be fed. It was the same in the Far East. In July 1945 meat rationing had to be reintroduced (it had been abolished in 1944). Henceforth, Canadians could buy from one to three pounds of meat per person per week, depending on the type of meat. Butter, too, was rationed, and the allotment kept going down: in March 1946 it stood at four ounces per person per week. Sugar and preserves were also rationed, and so was clothing. There the object was to ensure that each newly discharged veteran got a new suit of clothes on leaving the service, and that meant hundreds of thousands of new suits. There was good news in one area, however: gasoline rationing was wound up in late 1945, and so was tire rationing. Canadians were released into the countryside for the first time in years. There were complications, of course. Since no new automobiles had been produced since 1942, Canada's highways looked like ambulatory motor museums. But shabby or not, motoring was one of the fruits of victory – liberation.

Other controls were lifted as soon as supplies became available. It was not always easy, however, to dispense with restrictions that had become customary and popular. The most important of these was rent control. This had been instituted early in the war to prevent landlords from gouging luckless tenants forced by war work to move into areas where housing was scarce. The end of the war naturally placed even greater strain on limited accommodation as soldiers returned to join their families and landlords struggled to escape from the web of wartime regulations in which their investments were enmeshed. The easiest device was to evict a tenant in order to occupy the premises oneself, although in some cases six months' notice would serve. There was, predictably, a flurry of eviction notices – 3,500 in Toronto, 1,100 in Vancouver, and 700 in Winnipeg in the summer of 1945 alone. Evicting an unwelcome tenant simply shifted the burden of accommodation to other shoulders, usually those of the government. In the first years after the war the dominion acted as landlord to thousands, using emergency shelters converted from barracks. More stringent controls on evictions naturally followed.

Housing was just one area where Canadians looked to Ottawa for solutions. Controls, for example, were good when it came to rent, bearable for meat and butter. Restraining private enterprise from gaudy excesses was justifiable in the public interest, whether or not that interest was enlightened. Socialists marvelled at the sight. Writing in 1945, the CCF intellectual Frank Scott observed that 'a central government which could not provide three square meals a day to the hundreds of thousands on relief ... now pours its billions annually among the astonished citizens and calls forth miracles of production from old and new enterprises.'

Wartime centralization did not stop with regulating business, large and small. Before the war Canadian labour had been governed under a crazy quilt of ten separate jurisdictions (one for the dominion and one for each of the nine provinces). Railways were under federal jurisdiction, so railway workers were regulated by the dominion's Industrial Disputes Investigation Act; but a Quebec streetcar conductor or a British Columbia hydro lineman came under the respective labour acts of those provinces. War's centralized economy could not tolerate jurisdictional particularities in labour law. Within a few months after the declaration of war, the federal government had brought war-related industries under its own jurisdiction, so that by the end of the war 85 per cent of the non-agricultural work force fell under federal sway. The dominion government prescribed union recognition, compulsory negotiation, and compulsory conciliation for employers and employees. It was a rational system, which was generally well administered. Most of the time it worked. It worked well enough to serve as a model for most provinces at the end of the war; their subsequent labour codes were based on the federal wartime regulations, rather than on pre-war experience.

Centralization had more indirect effects as well. All foreign-exchange transactions were placed under dominion control on the outbreak of war. Regulations were tightened drastically in 1940, and then supplemented by a series of special-priority arrangements between Canada and the United States governing the supply of goods essential to both countries' war effort. Spending on luxuries and tourism was strictly curtailed, although an inspection of import figures reveals that not all consumer cravings were prohibited. Oranges, for example, tipped the scale at twelve million cubic feet in 1945, while Scotch whisky reached Canada at the rate of 730,000 gallons in 1942. (Scotch, however, was a casualty of the battle of the Atlantic, dipping to 468,000 gallons in 1945.)

What interfered with provincial jurisdiction (for example, over liquor imports) also naturally affected provincial revenues and spending. The scope of provincial politics shrank, as their content was trivialized. Naturally the ferocity of provincial political contests grew in inverse relation to their actual importance, and federal issues played an ever larger part in provincial elections. Mackenzie King's temperance sentiments, normally strong, fierce, and sanctimonious, wobbled when confronted with the Ontario and Quebec provincial elections in 1943 and 1944. Could there not be, King mused, some means of easing controls? Provincial Liberals fervently agreed, out of hope before the elections (which they lost), and from despair afterward.

For most provinces the war provided a welcome respite from financial burdens. Capital projects now lay mostly within the federal sphere. Even if the provinces could procure the supplies necessary to carry out their own projects, it was by no means certain where they could find the money. As a consequence, provincial government departments quietly mouldered between 1939 and 1945. Comparisons between the levels of dominion and provincial spending are quite startling. Federal expenditure on goods and services, including capital formation, reached its wartime maximum in 1944 at $4,488 million. In the same year, provincial spending amounted to only $200 million ($539 million if local spending is added in).

For ordinary needs, the central government provided. The Wartime Tax Agreements of 1941 allowed the dominion government to 'occupy' the corporation and income-tax fields, which were 'vacated' by the provinces. In return, the dominion paid the provinces either the revenues they would have raised from the 'occupied' sources in the fiscal year 1940-1, or the service on the provincial debt, less certain amounts. In addition, the dominion paid the statutory subsidies under the BNA Act and 'fiscal-need subsidies' where a province could demonstrate urgent need for extra funds. These grants went to the poorest provinces: Saskatchewan, New Brunswick, Manitoba, and Prince Edward Island. In general, the provinces were able to pocket the federal compensation, run surpluses, and begin to retire their debts.

In the mean time Canadians got used to paying their taxes to the central government. A new fiscal device allowed the government to extract the money directly from the citizen's paycheque, eliminating, as far as possible, the direct pain of involuntary transfer from the subject to the chief magistrate. The effect in Ottawa was rather heady. From 1941 until 1945 Mackenzie King steered clear of any dominion-provincial gatherings, restricting his provincial contacts to occasional consultations with friendly Liberals. Most of his ministers came to view the provinces, not as rivals or antagonists, as they had been during the thirties, but as irrelevancies to be stroked or prodded according to whether they had a Liberal government or not. In an era of expansive action it was enough to contend with fellow ministers in the Treasury Board without worrying about parochial difficulties in one or another of the provinces.

Much of the central government's aggressive self-confidence derived from its collective belief that it monopolized the progressive ideas and the active intelligences of Canada's administrative system. You could look far in any single province, or in all the provinces put together, before spying the equals of Ottawa's mandarin team. With a successful record of wartime administration behind them, with all its invaluable and instructive experience, Clark and his colleagues were well placed to tell the King government what to do next. After devising national standards and policies that had been tested in war there could be no doubt that they could do it in peace as well. And what Clark and company could assemble would, or should, be superior to anything the provinces could imagine – or anyway, as with CCF Saskatchewan, afford.

Paradoxically, and despite Howe's strong confidence in the post-war economy, the central government's strongest card in its negotiations with the provinces was general uncertainty over what to expect. It would take strong medicine to banish the miseries of unemployment – strong centralized medicine. Masterful management of the economy by the dominion could not be achieved in the pre-war vacuum of power and initiative. Federal governments after the war would have to 'incur huge expenditures for housing and various construction projects' with or without help from the provinces, so as to fuel the economy and 'maintain a high level of national income.' It would therefore be, as the Minister of Finance explained to his colleagues in 1944, 'quite impossible for the Dominion Government to manage ... if we have to go back to our pre-war taxing system.'

If Canada's antiquated constitutional system could be cranked up to provide the necessary resources, then the Department of Finance had the answer. If the 'high and stable level of employment' promised by the White Paper were to be achieved, the government would have to promote the main sources of employment and income. These were four in number: export trade, private investment, consumption expenditure, and public investment. This was in conformity with the doctrines of the British economist Lord Keynes, whose ideas had so profoundly influenced Ottawa's own economic specialists.

Clark and Mackintosh undertook to translate Keynes for their political masters. It all, in the end, came down to one thing: Ottawa had to concentrate taxing and, to a large degree, spending authority in its own hands in order to provide a stable rudder for the economy. There must be a change in the rules by which peacetime Canada was run. As the White Paper said, 'when unemployment threatens,' the government would incur the necessary deficits to promote job creation, 'whether that policy in the circumstances is best applied through increased expenditures or reduced taxation.'

The war had accustomed many Canadians to thinking in national terms. Large problems, such as unemployment, must be solved on a large scale, and the largest Canadian dimension was the dominion government. Certain provinces whose finances were most threatened under a return to pre-war fiscal autonomy were anxious to assign some of their most onerous responsibilities to Ottawa. Liberal intellectuals, whose friends were in any case already in power in Ottawa, added their voices to the centralizing chorus. So did many businessmen, stirred by the memory of what had been done in the war. Canada, a business publicist pointed out in 1946, had enjoyed 'the most centralized – and perhaps the most efficient – war production organization in the world.' The experience had converted some reluctant businessmen to change their politics from reliable Tory blue to Liberal red, for, as long as C.D. Howe held the reins of economic power, business knew that it had a friend in Ottawa.

Next to King himself, and to St Laurent in Quebec, Howe was the best-known member of the cabinet. He had been the visible manifestation of the domestic war effort, criss-crossing the country to preside at the christening of the thousandth tank, the ten-thousandth plane, the millionth shell – jobs that Howe hated but tolerated for their considerable publicity value. Howe incarnated the business approach to administrative problems, contemptuous of theory, concentrating always on facts and specifics. Howe possessed manifest advantages. He had, in the first place, a quick mind and a decisive and impressive personality. 'When C.D. entered a room you knew it,' one of his business friends recalled. Howe caught people's attention with his pithy phrases (though he never uttered the one most often attributed to him, 'What's a million?') and his succinct summaries of problems too complicated, even insoluble, for everyone but himself. Howe sometimes horrified his colleagues, and his subordinates, by his willingness to speak off the cuff. Speaking one evening in the House of Commons, he unwittingly reversed the policy he was supposed to be defending. The next morning his assistant deputy minister came to tell him so. Howe was unperturbed. 'Fred,' he said, crossing his legs and lifting his feet to his desk, 'I've got news for you. Our policy changed at 9:57 last night.' Howe had the personal force to make his decisions, even the unconscious ones, stick. But he also had the information to formulate sensible policies. Using the statistics cranked out by his departmental economists, and combining them with the word-of-telephone by which he flourished, Howe knew in advance of most major investment decisions in Canada. He also knew, from the war, the men who would be making them, men like E.P. Taylor or Eric Phillips in Toronto, Frank Ross in Vancouver, or R.E. Powell in Montreal. Some though by no means all of Howe's business friends were Liberals: they became the backbone of the fund-raising system he perfected to fuel the Liberal party. But prominent Conservatives like Henry Borden, the president of Brazilian Traction, also supported Howe, if not his party.

Howe's closeness to business, his fishing trips and golf and bridge games with the Canadian rich, were part of his attraction to the economic élite. They were not designed to appeal to other segments of society. As Howe's colleague, Brooke Claxton, caustically observed, 'The mental climate of the businessman is ... unintellectual ... If a group of businessmen meet together for an afternoon or evening or for a week-end, the chances are that time will pass very enjoyably but that there will not be a moment's talk about politics, books or any serious subject.' Mackenzie King heartily agreed. When Howe lent his name to a book describing business leaders as 'Canadian strength,' King lamented that his minister showed a 'curious lack of proportion.' 'It is rather surprising,' the Prime Minister added, 'that any colleague should indicate that from his point of view Canadian strength was composed primarily of the heads of large corporations.' It was not the large corporations that voted, King knew, and the imposition of a corporate viewpoint on the Liberal party could bring in its train electoral dangers. Howe and the Minister of Finance (Douglas Abbott after 1946) were all too ready, in King's opinion, to 'impose their own will much too strongly through having a knowledge of certain matters respecting finance and trade and relations to the United States etc.' Howe scorned ignorant objections from colleagues too lazy or self-interested to see his point.

That was hurting the party, a delegation of Liberal Members of Parliament told the Prime Minister. The government 'was getting the reputation with the people of being icy cold; really not being in touch with the people at all.' The cabinet deferred too much to the wisdom of the finance department rather than to the sense of the caucus. But could the finance department garner votes?

It was not Howe, who despite his short temper was popular with backbenchers and the party rank and file, who epitomized the problem, but Douglas Abbott. Jaunty and cheerful, sensible and politically astute, Abbott had decided opinions on what was right and wrong in economic policy. Appearing before the Resolutions Committee at the national Liberal Convention in August 1948, Abbott lost no time in setting his audience straight. 'It doesn't matter,' Abbott told the party faithful, 'what resolutions you pass here. Pass any resolutions you like. But I am Minister of Finance and so long as I am, I will do what I think is right.'

It is normal for any party long in power to develop a hardening of the arteries in communications from bottom to top. The Canadian Liberal party was no exception. Through no particular fault of its own, it became a neutered cat, perfumed, brushed, belled, and fat (thanks to Howe's contribution system). As the cabinet's occasional pet, the party dragged its overweight carcass from election to election; in between, the cabinet's rigid propriety ensured that the party languished, without status or influence, on the sidelines. It was the civil servants, not the party, who had the ideas and the knowledge of how to run a country. In 1945, Mackintosh's White Paper was no mean banner to follow – a formula for national success that beat anything the grass roots could devise. The bush leagues would have to wait until after the election.

6

A Strategy for Economic Survival

In 1939 Canada ranked sixth among the world's trading nations. In terms of per capita trade, Canada was seventh, and in terms of per capita income also seventh. Canadians knew it well: their country was founded on trade and must trade to survive. 'It is only,' the Royal Commission on Dominion-Provincial Relations warned in 1940, 'by playing this role that Canada can maintain anything like her present standard of living and can support the great capital investment which has been made to equip her for this role.' That depended on international co-operation, for as the Commission observed, 'Canada is one of the least self-sufficient countries in the world.' It had paid the price during the thirties, along with other trading nations, suffering under the reign of 'Beggar my neighbour.'

There were no substantial alterations in Canada's official trade policy during the war. The policy was simply put in mothballs, superseded by innumerable practical arrangements between Canada and its principal trading partners, Britain and the United States. For five years, Canada had guaranteed exports, a market for all the war material the country could produce. The wartime bonanza had limited prospects, a fact that depressed the government's economic advisers. 'Adequate employment,' W.A. Mackintosh predicted, could not be achieved unless other countries co-operated to help 'maintain our external trade.'

The United States was Canada's biggest customer. In 1944 Canada bought $1,447,226,000 worth of imports from the United States and sold $1,334,554,000 in return. Britain was next, buying $1,238,078,000 worth of Canadian products, but selling Canada only $110,599,000 in return. The imbalance between British purchases and sales in Canada was a source of great concern. The Americans, when they bought from Canada, paid US dollars, which Canada needed to make up its purchases in the United States. The British, however, financed their Canadian imports with loans and credits from the Canadian government. Without governmental assistance, British purchases in Canada

would have been next to nothing. During the war the King government had become used to the British returning, time and again, to the Canadian treasury in
quest of more finance. It was provided, sometimes over the protest of parochial-
ly minded politicians who regarded Britain as the eternal incarnation of ill-
gotten imperialist wealth. For them, enlightenment would be late in dawning, if
it ever came. For the Liberals, dependent as they were on a suspicious Quebec
delegation, assistance to the descendants of Wolfe and Durham posed a particular problem.

But the government had to try. It was axiomatic, as Mackintosh told Mackenzie King, that 'only by promoting and participating in a collaboration between
the United States and the United Kingdom, with the threefold object of developing co-ordinated policies for maintaining employment, ensuring relative freedom of trade, and contributing to productive international investment, [could]
Canada ... find after the war the larger world economy necessary to her tolerable
existence.' Any such collaboration could scarcely be expected to develop out of
private initiative. Over the course of the war, the government had appropriated
most of Canada's private trading system. Most recently, in September 1943, the
government had suspended private trading in wheat in order to curb rising prices
and speculation on the Winnipeg Grain Exchange.

Wheat was a staple export whose markets were potentially extensive. The
same could not be said of Canada's manufactured exports. Shipping controls,
foreign exchange restrictions, and alternative war production had reduced civilian exports to a low ebb by the end of the war. It was partly the government's
(especially C.D. Howe's) anxiety to secure post-war markets for Canadian products that stimulated its stubborn insistence on membership in several allied
combined-supply boards toward the end of the war. What went to the military
today could go to refugees tomorrow and to reconstructed buyers the day after.
It was important, while Europe's industries lay prostrate, to encourage Europeans to think Canadian. It was pleasant to combine self-interest with altruism.

Canada would not define the terms, or secure the arena, for post-war trading
planning. That was the prerogative of the two senior allies, Britain and the United States. During the war the Americans had dispensed aid to virtually all com-
ers, as long as they were fighting the Germans. There would be no repayment. In
return for this startling generosity, the Americans asked only one small consideration: signature to a clause in the Lend-Lease (aid) agreements committing the
signatory to try to reduce its discriminatory trade practices and to join, after the
war, in a free multilateral trading system. Discussions (called Article VII talks,
after the numbered clause in the Lend-Lease master agreement) were to take
place before the end of the war, so as to be ready for a better trading world as
soon as hostilities ceased. Canada had remained aloof from Lend-Lease (though

it gladly cashed in some British benefits under the scheme) in order to emphasize its independence from American charity. But the dominion could hardly afford to be left outside the Article VII talks, so crucial to Canada's future. Canadian representatives gladly signed a separate note accepting the principles of Article VII, thereby qualifying Canada, it was hoped, for the great trading pow-wow.

Multilateral tariff reductions represented the best of all possible trading worlds from the Canadian point of view. A free flow of goods across one customs frontier was, of course, a distinct advantage to a trading nation, but a free flow across as many frontiers as possible was even more desirable. A diversified Canadian trading pattern would avoid undue reliance on a single customer, the United States, with all the dangerous political consequences that might entail.

Canadian officials during the war were not reluctant to urge their vision of multilateral trading on their American and British counterparts. They met a warm response among American officials, who also believed the goal of a multilateral, low-tariff or no-tariff world well worth pursuing. Unhappily, those Congressmen responsible for legislating American tariff policy were unlikely to take as broad or altruistic a perspective; discussions with the Americans therefore had a quality of fervent unreality all their own. The British also took the Canadian point. Their difficulty was not a divorce between an enlightened bureaucracy and a benighted Parliament, but the very real dangers of Britain's international economic position. Britain's standing in international trade had so far eroded by 1944 or 1945 that the British were forced to contemplate a variety of unpleasant alternatives, involving restricting trade with dollar countries, in order to stave off total collapse. Nevertheless, the British remained firmly committed, *in theory*, to multilateralism in trade. All they asked was that someone give them the means to put multilateralism into practical terms.

A distinct second best, from the Canadian perspective, was the possibility of some special bilateral trading arrangement with a powerful economic partner. Canada already participated in such an arrangement – known as Empire Preference – a system of reduced tariffs exchanged by the several parts of the British Empire. Until true multilateral trade was achieved, Empire Preference had its uses, not least as a bargaining counter with the suspicious and fearful Americans for whom the abolition of Empire Preference was a veritable grail of policy. Britain's economic weakness made it unrealistic to place too much reliance on the efficacy of imperial trading arrangements after the war. Dire necessity might make it imperative to contemplate another kind of special arrangement, this time with the United States. The concept was scouted in talks between Canadian and American diplomats toward the end of the war, but always as a highly theoretical possibility. Nevertheless, should the world slide into economic chaos, economic union with the United States might well become inevitable.

It was decidedly a time for bold initiatives. When Canadian ministers and their advisers considered the matter at a meeting in January 1945 their mood was gloomy. Clifford Clark as usual set the tone. 'The developing prospects ... [appear] to be so serious,' he argued, 'that they [justify] the Canadian Government doing what it could at the present time to improve matters.' Canada could not equably contemplate British withdrawal into economic isolation inside a 'soft currency' bloc made up of those states that could not afford to see their money converted into American (or Canadian) dollars. The British dilemma was real. To win the war, they had dissipated their foreign assets and piled up a mountain of debt, less with the Americans and Canadians than with the Indians, Egyptians, and South Africans. In the face of this terrible prospect, Canada should be prepared to loosen the national purse strings. One immediate measure was to write down most of the British debt accumulated during the war: it was traded off against costs incurred by Canadian soldiers and airmen abroad. Then, in the spring of 1945, the Canadians went further.

The British were offered a Canadian loan to tide them over their worst post-war troubles. The loan would allow the British to continue buying in Canada until their economy righted itself, even if that happy day were as much as two years away. The British were not unreceptive, as discussions in May 1945 indicated, but details were left until later. The continuation of the war against Japan ensured a continuing flow of American aid for the immediate future at least.

The unexpected conclusion of the war against Japan brought with it the immediate termination of American wartime aid. British missions swiftly sped across the Atlantic. They found the climate distinctly chilly. The Americans were not in a giving mood, and British hopes for a multi-billion-dollar aid program shrank under the icy impact of self-interested American parochialism. It took all of Keynes's persuasive powers to extract a grudging $3.75 billion from the Americans, to be repaid, with interest, over the next fifty years. In exchange, the British agreed to allow the pound sterling to be freely converted into the American dollar – except by British residents – no later than the middle of 1947, subject, as is usual in complicated financial agreements, to a number of limitations. They also agreed not to accept loans from other countries on terms more favourable than those received from the United States.

It would have been politically impossible for the Canadian government to offer better terms than those the British had received from the Americans. The American conditions were known: and the cabinet was not disposed to go one better than Uncle Sam. The British could expect essentially what they had got in Washington, a long-term loan, at low interest. What did cause comment was the size of the Canadian proposition. Canada would lend $1.25 billion, a third of the American subvention. It was as if the United States had proffered $12.5 billion (or more, considering the comparative magnitudes of the Canadian and American economies). The Canadians would have preferred a larger amount: both the Canadians and British negotiators regarded the American loan as dangerously small. Domestically, the Canadian loan was justified on the grounds of long-term trading benefits. Both government and business, the US embassy reported to Washington, hoped that the loan would help restore 'a normal volume of trade' with the United Kingdom, Canada's 'best market.'

By plumping for a vast loan to Britain, along with large credits to other European governments, Canada was trying to restore the pre-war pattern of trade, in which Britain and Europe served as a counterweight to the United States. The Canadian government was also trying to preserve export markets retained or acquired during the war. By 1946 it had become apparent that there would be no revolutionary changes in the world trading system. The United States, the chief supporter of liberalized trade, had surrendered its lead in 1945 when President Truman agreed to a simple continuation of the American reciprocal trading formula. Across-the-board cuts were ruled out: each tariff reduction would have to be bargained for individually. Ottawa was deeply disappointed.

Canadian negotiators thereafter had to make do with salvaging what they could from the wreck of the war's multilateral hopes. An attempt to found an International Trading Organization (ITO) foundered in futility on an American refusal to ratify its covenant. While the ITO millennium was still under discussion, the world's trading nations met in Geneva to explore ways of reducing tariffs on an interim basis. The American delegation, its hands partially tied by domestic legislation, worked closely with Canada's exceptionally competent delegates, led by Dana Wilgress. The chief American objective, loudly trumpeted, was to eliminate the British preference in imperial trade. That had been anticipated. What had not been was the skill with which the Canadian delegates talked round the thorny preferential issue, to emerge with both an agreement and, equally important, a method of reaching an agreement. The agreement was called the General Agreement on Tariffs and Trade, better known today as GATT. The method evolved in the course of the Geneva talks became known as the 'principal supplier rule,' whereby countries negotiate tariff concessions with the principal supplier of a given commodity. Canada, which was interested mainly in reducing American tariffs, thus assumed responsibility for certain primary products; European countries, more interested in supplying manufactured goods, took on the burden of those negotiations. The success of the Geneva talks hinged also on the willingness of the empire countries to make a gesture to the United States on imperial preference. Canada was not unwilling to do away with preference, and in an exchange of letters between the Canadian and the British governments, the bargain was struck: both countries undertook not to extend the preferential system to any new products and to reduce or abolish it if that were at all possible. (It was – but not until December 1979.)

The results of the Geneva conference were unexpectedly favourable for Canada. Tariffs on Canadian-American trade, the largest items in both countries' trade baskets, were reduced. In Canada's case, however, as one economic analyst has commented, there were 'only a limited number of reductions which have had a significant effect on the prices and competitive conditions' of Canada's protected industries. The British preferential system survived the Geneva negotiations virtually intact. An orderly forum for future negotiations, operating on the principle of non-discrimination, was established. The spectre of the tariff wars of the thirties was appeased, if not finally laid to rest. All this was measurable, valuable progress. But it was still a far cry from wartime visions of a great multilateral, low-tariff, trading system.

The key negotiations at Geneva were between the United States and the members of the British Commonwealth. (The terms Commonwealth and Empire were still used interchangeably, with Commonwealth gradually predominating.) The Commonwealth countries, especially Britain, were important parts of Canada's economic world. Britain's balance of payments difficulties were then important to Canada in a way that they would not be in a later generation, and the viability of Canada's external trade policy was measured in terms as much of its effect on trade with Britain as of its impact on trade with the United States.

The area most immediately affected by changing post-war trading policies was agriculture. Canadian agriculture had done well out of the war. Canadian farmers sold all they produced, and grew more. There was a startling recovery in farm prices, especially in wheat. As we have seen, the government responded by becoming more and more involved in the grain business, culminating in the establishment of the Canadian Wheat Board monopoly in September 1943.

Would the wheat boom be permanent? There had been such a boom in the First World War, and then a smash. Memories of hard times soured enjoyment of present prosperity for Canadian farmers, who communicated their anxiety to the federal Minister of Agriculture, Jimmy Gardiner.

Gardiner had represented Saskatchewan in the King cabinet since 1935. A former premier of the province, he was totally committed to serving what he perceived to be its interests, namely high farm prices and the supremacy of the Liberal party. Since for Gardiner there could be no contradiction between these principles, he was untroubled by qualms or political confusion. The same, the minister ruefully admitted, could not be said of Saskatchewan voters. In the 1945 general election only two Liberals were returned from the province to the dominion House of Commons; Gardiner was one. That September, welcoming the new CCF MPs from Saskatchewan to Ottawa, Gardiner observed that he should also congratulate himself on being there at all.

Gardiner knew that he would not be back after the next election unless the rural voters were reassured that the good times of war would not give way to the hard times of peace. Security and stability were the watchwords of farm interest groups, as they were of the rest of the population. Farmers appreciated the intervention of the central government during the war and concluded that more of the same might be beneficial. Ottawa might help in particular to guarantee better markets and higher prices and work to iron out the fluctuations of price so as to produce a stable and predictable income for risk-prone farmers, especially those dependent on export markets.

If Canadian farmers wanted security, Gardiner was ready to oblige. The options before him were much the same as those presented to Canada's other trade negotiators. In the case of wheat, the most attractive prospect was a multilateral agreement between the exporting countries (Canada, Australia, the United States, and Argentina) and the importers (Britain and the European continent). That would bring an end to cut-throat competition of the kind that had made the thirties so very unpleasant for primary producers. Unfortunately, the prospects in this area were dim. An international wheat agreement was stalled for the indefinite future, or so it seemed. And so Gardiner turned to the alternative. A bulk purchase agreement between Canada and Britain, its best customer, along the lines of wartime contracts, might prove useful for shoring up both the volumes of wheat exports and wheat prices. The British, now ruled by a socialist Labour government, were interested. In the spring of 1946 Gardiner accordingly rushed negotiations to a conclusion. So eager was the minister to reach a settlement that he swallowed the British terms virtually unaltered. After a feeble fluttering of multilateral pieties the Cabinet went along with the Minister of Agriculture. On July 25, 1946, the Anglo-Canadian wheat agreement was revealed to a delighted Parliament.

The terms were straightforward. In each of the 1946-7 and 1947-8 crop years, the British government would buy 160 million bushels of wheat, at $1.55 a bushel. In the next two crop years, the British would buy 140 million bushels: in 1948-9 at $1.25, and in 1949-50 at not less than $1.00 a bushel. These prices presumed that world wheat prices would fall over the term of the contract. In case they did not, the British offered, and Gardiner accepted, a clause that stipulated that at some later point the British government would 'have regard to' any price advantage it might secure in the first two years. In Gardiner's view, this meant that the prices paid by the British between 1948 and 1950 would balance off any difference between higher world prices and the contract in the first two. Soon the innocuous words 'have regard to' became an essential ingredient in any discussion of wheat marketing.

The trouble was that 'have regard to' was not specific. It seemed to promise much, but in fact delivered little or nothing. More careful drafting might have ironed out the problem, but in his haste Gardiner refused to take the trouble. And thereby hung a tale of political woe.

The announcement of the wheat sale was coupled with the government's decision to retain the Canadian Wheat Board as the sole agency for the distribution and sale of prairie wheat. That and the contract, the Canadian Federation of Agriculture proclaimed, were 'what organized agriculture ... had been urging upon the government for a long time.' In the seventies, when the Wheat Board was more than a little unpopular, farmers would have cause to remember their wartime demands and the government's response. From the beginning the private grain interests were naturally disgusted. Nobody worried about that; the Winnipeg Grain Exchange was sufficiently unpopular among farmers to make its denunciations a positive electoral blessing. The Grain Exchange did make one unpalatable and painful point, however: the bulk purchase price of $1.55 a bushel was considerably below world market values. Canadian farmers had gained security at a price.

Over the next four years this realization gnawed away at the satisfactions of the wheat agreement. When Gardiner belatedly tried to recoup for the farmers what he thought he had been promised, the British politely told him to read the contract. Gardiner's publicly expressed irritation and frequent admonitory visits to the United Kingdom did nothing to move the British government. Finally, in 1951, the Canadians and British agreed to bury the whole issue by applying the unspent residue of the Canadian loan – some $65 million – to the financial wounds of the wheat farmers.

In 1946, however, Gardiner had successfully sensed the public mood, and had exploited it. Nor was he alone in doing so. As the war contracts unwound and servicemen and women returned home, unemployment grew a little, and exports shrank. The autumn of 1945 looked bleak, and the future, if these trends continued, looked worse. But unemployment was cushioned by the Unemployment Insurance Act, now really useful for the first time, and many veterans were siphoned out of the labour market into retraining or education provided courtesy of the government. When, in the spring of 1946, the country paused to catch its breath, the shadow had passed. Employment was up, factories were reconverting smoothly to peacetime operations, and new investment was establishing new industry. Most important, consumer expenditure was beginning to rise. In 1944 the government had accounted for fully 40 per cent of national expenditures. In 1945 this fell abruptly to 29 per cent, and in 1946 to just under 16 per cent. Consumer expenditure rose from $14.1 billion in 1944 to $17.3 billion in 1946 and

$18.5 billion in 1947 (it had been $10.9 billion before the war).[1] It continued to rise for the rest of the decade.

Investment increased too. Expenditure on durable goods such as machinery rose steadily between 1945 and 1953, totalling $1.37 billion in 1945 and $2.5 billion in 1946. Besides buying and building anew, business was absorbing war surplus. It was C.D. Howe's policy, as Minister of Reconstruction, to sell the government's outmoded property to anyone who would guarantee to put it to productive use. Government telephone lines, aircraft plants, optical factories, and other facilities were knocked down to the best prospect and the highest bidder, although at a rate of return that exceeded the American government's on similar sales. Sometimes government plants were sold or leased to foreigners, the two best known being A.V. Roe of Great Britain, which took over the Victory Aircraft plant at Malton, Ontario, and the Electric Boat Company of Cleveland (despite its name, an aircraft company), which bought Canadair in Montreal. In both cases Howe was sure he had made a good deal: without a continuous infusion of foreign technology (and foreign technicians) the prospects for Canada's aircraft industry were dim. Howe had no wish to tie up government money in the hopeless pursuit of non-existent markets for costly Canadian planes. And, as Howe realized, factories for making bombers and fighters were no more than junk once the demand for their product ceased.

Having made the decision to continue the Canadian aircraft industry, Howe supported it to the utmost. Canadair married the American DC-4 airliner to the British Rolls-Royce engine. The result was a serviceable and reliable aircraft (dubbed the North Star), which Howe's Trans-Canada Airlines promptly bought. The North Star had only one slight defect: noise and vibration from the engines deafened its passengers and loosened the fillings in their teeth. As the North Stars lumbered across Canadian skies, perceptive observers must have reflected that Canada had not quite achieved technological maturity.

More generally, however, Canada had trouble attracting foreign capital between 1944 and 1949. There was little foreign direct investment, and little borrowing abroad by Canadians. On the securities markets of the United States Canada was a net lender, not the borrower it has usually been since. Perhaps Canadian exchange controls made Americans reluctant to move funds northward or to buy or build new plants here. It was true that the controls as they existed would not have prevented Americans from taking their money home whenever they liked. But who could be sure things would stay that way? After all, in other countries the trend seemed to be in the other direction – ever tighter controls and ever more stringent regulations on the movement of funds and the interest and

1 Measured in constant 1971 dollars.

dividends those funds had earned.

The lack of foreign investment was barely remarked in the late forties. The domestic economy was booming; but as it boomed, Canada's foreign exchange position started to slip. In 1946-9 the country was actually running a surplus on the current account of its balance of payments, a surplus of $1,040 million. There was, however, a very large deficit with the United States and a very large surplus with Britain and Europe. The deficit with the United States seemed inescapable. Canadians wanted to buy what had been denied them during the war. Businessmen, converting to new lines, turned to American suppliers. At first this was not thought to be a problem. Canada's export position was strong, and its reserves of convertible foreign exchange (gold or American dollars) were ample. In 1946, however, exports were off by almost a billion dollars, and the trade balance declined still more, by $1.3 billion. Exports would not again reach the levels of 1945 until 1951. The British began to draw on their huge loan, and simultaneously the Canadian government decided to revalue the dollar.

The problem with the dollar began with domestic decontrol. As price and wage controls were lifted, prices began to rise. Slowly at first, Canadians discovered that necessities were costing more. Inflation re-entered the political arena, and it did not take great perspicacity to predict the political problems it could cause. One contributing factor to Canadian inflation was price rises in the United States. With Canada dependent on a wide variety of American imports, any American inflation had drastic implications for Canada. To make matters worse, an American dollar cost $1.10 Canadian, so that prices of imports looked much higher than the original American price. In July 1946, therefore, the Canadian dollar was revalued to parity with the American.

Inflation continued to advance, however, and dollar reserves naturally continued to drop, since the cost of American goods was lower than before. And there was still the British loan to take into account. That had been intended to last for five years; by the spring of 1947, half had been drawn. Worst of all, it appeared that the loan was not enough. When the British fulfilled their part of the American loan bargain and made sterling convertible into American dollars, there was a run on the pound. After six weeks, the British suspended convertibility indefinitely. International trade was back where it had been in the summer of 1945.

The Canadian government was in a ticklish position. British needs were great, but Canada's own exchange position was precarious. The British were told to go more slowly in their drawings on the Canadian loan, but that was a palliative, not a cure. Finally, firm action could be avoided no longer. In November 1947, just after Mackenzie King announced the conclusion of the GATT agreements, Finance Minister Abbott went on the radio to proclaim economic measures of a different kind. The loss of exchange reserves had reached crisis proportions, Abbott told Canadians. To halt the drain the government had decided on a series of unpalatable, but essential, measures. Imports would be drastically reduced. Luxury items were banned altogether, and other imports would be subjected to quotas. Capital goods, machinery, and other imports essential to industrial reconversion would be admitted subject to special licences to be doled out by C.D. Howe, Minister of Reconstruction. To tide things over, the dollar would be supported by an emergency loan of $300 million from the American Import-Export Bank. In the understatement of the year, Abbott told his audience that he knew that his new policy would come as 'something of a shock,' but it would be temporary. Improvement was just around the corner.

Permanent improvement could come only if Washington willed it. The fundamental economic problem facing the Western world was a dollar shortage, a situation to which Congress had proved impervious the year before. But the American legislative logjam was shifting slightly. Britain's troubles and the fear of Soviet Communism had finally convinced the American government and, more important, Congress that something more imaginative would have to be tried if the United States were not to be isolated – rich and friendless in an impoverished world. Despite their ravished appearance, Britain and Europe still had immense reserves of skills, equipment, and technology; all that was needed was to get them started, with a substantial injection of American dollars to pay for imports of food, raw materials, and essential equipment for repair and modernization.

In the summer of 1947 the American government nerved itself to prescribe what was thought to be the magic elixir. Europe would, according to the Truman administration's plan, receive American aid on an unprecedented scale: money to buy capital goods and rebuild industry; money to buy supplies to feed and clothe the population; money to re-establish the European economy. Early in 1948 Congress approved the program, with the Canadian government watching anxiously from the sidelines. At the very least, the American proposals, called the Marshall Plan after their sponsor, Secretary of State George Marshall, would restore the self-respect of the democratic nations of western Europe and prevent them becoming a group of mendicants. Also, the money might save them from Communism.

While the Canadian government approved the American initiative, it worried about the implications for Canadian trade. Next only to solvency, diversification was the watchword of Canadian trade policy. It was easy to imagine what would become of Canada's exports if European purchases of goods under the Marshall Plan were restricted to the United States. Fortunately American officials took a broad view. Other nations were eligible to become 'off-shore' suppliers. Canada was, of course, an 'American' nation. There would be a place for Canada in the

Marshall Plan, allowing Europeans to buy Canadian goods with American dollars. It was, the Canadian ambassador in Washington reported, 'as generous an attitude towards Canada as I think we could possibly hope for.' The American attitude was not entirely altruistic: the United States wanted to preserve Canada as a strong ally, and its government hoped that Canada would keep it company in furnishing aid through the Marshall Plan (Canada escaped by pleading that the British loan and the wheat contract were enough foreign aid for a country of Canada's size).

Had the Marshall Plan not appeared, one stillborn proposal of the desperate autumn of 1947 might have come closer to realization. As Canada's dollar difficulties mounted, Canadian and American officials gave prolonged consideration to another approach to Canada's trade and balance of payment problems. One idea that struck both sides was a return to the wartime integration of the two economies. Then, American and Canadian agencies had freely purchased one another's supplies with little thought for the border. By removing tariffs along the frontier, perhaps the same end could be achieved. At least some officials thought it worth a try.

The proposal commended itself to high Canadian civil servants, especially John Deutsch of the Department of Finance and Lester Pearson, the recently appointed Under Secretary of State for External Affairs. Abbott and Howe were also interested, and King gave his officials the go-ahead to see what they could produce. But when, in March 1948, discussions did produce a tentative plan, the Prime Minister got cold feet. It reminded him too much of Sir Wilfrid Laurier's fatal reciprocity project of 1911, King confided to his diary, and it would be better to drop it. Drop it he did, to the incredulous dismay of his officials.

It would be comforting to believe that this was all there was to it. King had 'saved' Canada from economic annexation by the United States, which in 1948, as always, drooled over the prospect of inveigling its northern neighbour into economic servitude. Unfortunately American behaviour during the reciprocity negotiations, not to mention American self-interest, does not stand up to this analysis. Enthusiasm for free trade with Canada was confined to a small group of State Department officials, professional friends of Canada, who saw it as their professional duty to shore up the dominion as a bastion of democracy. The reciprocity project barely reached the political level in the American government; if it had surfaced, it would probably have been shelved for the duration of 1948, an election year, if not forever. It is difficult to imagine any situation in which the many special interests on the American side of the line could have been brought into harmony with their Canadian counterparts. Aborted on the Canadian side, continental free trade had few mourners on the American.

For better or worse, Canada was left to pursue an autonomous commercial policy in a fractious world. There was no permanent solution to Canada's economic dilemma, just the hope that the workings of the Marshall Plan would restore something of a balance in Canada's commercial relations with the outside world. That, as contemporary commentators pointed out, was an unstable and improbable contingency. More likely, Canada's attraction to the US market would continue and grow, as has actually happened.

Yet Canada's post-war economic adjustment can be rated a qualified success. The Canadian government, coping simultaneously with western Europe's economic troubles, inflation at home, reconversion of industry, and pent-up consumer demand, muddled through as best it could. Its reconstruction program was generally successful, maintaining high output and employment while effectively removing the government from the large sectors of the economy it had ruled so masterfully between 1939 and 1945. By underestimating the extent of Britain's needs and the imports Canada's reconstruction boom would suck in, the government had exposed Canada's foreign exchange weakness, exacerbated through the premature revaluation of the Canadian dollar in 1946. As a result, 1948 saw a return to some of the stringent economic controls of wartime and a perpetuation of the dominant role of the central government in the shaping of the Canadian economy.

7

Making a Better Country

When Prime Minister Mackenzie King rose in his place to open the Dominion-Provincial Conference on Reconstruction on August 6, 1945, he carried a heavy burden – a small green booklet, containing the proposals of the Government of Canada for the economic well-being of the country, a comprehensive plan to restructure Canadian federalism to give the central government the financial power and the legislative authority to guide the economy through the perils of depression, while insuring individual Canadians against disease, old age, and extended unemployment. It was an unusual moment. Never before had the King government laid such a comprehensive and audacious program before the public. Never before, King's advisers and colleagues believed, had there been such a heaven-sent opportunity to rescue Canada from constitutional stalemate and spare the country a repetition of the squabbling of the thirties. Finally Canada could shape a central government fit to cope with the uncertainties and dangers of the twentieth century.

King was alive to the potential of the moment. Never before, the Prime Minister told himself, had he placed so much at risk, and King hated risks and uncertainties. For over four years he had put off this moment, and its arrival left him fretful and perturbed. Perhaps this was neither the moment, nor the place, to attempt something of the magnitude of constitutional reform.

The sight that greeted King would scarcely have been encouraging. Around him sat the sleeping dogs of provincial power, yawning and stretching after five years in mothballs. Among the nine provincial premiers were some of King's bitterest political enemies. George Drew, the Conservative premier of Ontario, was a familiar foe. A passionate, self-assured, and strikingly handsome man, Drew could easily imagine himself in the place of the pudgy little fellow who occupied the prime minister's chair. And high time too, he liked to assure Ontario audiences. Drew's style had long since become frozen in bombast: attractive and interesting in small groups, he turned every gathering of over three people into a public meeting. On King's left sat another Tory, Maurice Duplessis, the Union Nationale premier of Quebec. Duplessis had started out as a Conservative but had discovered that a judicious mixture of nationalism with his *bleu* principles furnished just the right formula for winning elections. Duplessis stood foursquare for the stability of Quebec's traditional institutions and society; he was uninterested in new designs for Canada. But if Duplessis could not be counted on to promote a renewed Canada, he might not hinder it if events took their proper course. The same might have been said for Manning of Alberta, the youngest man at the conference table. Quiet, earnest, and efficient, Manning was an exponent of Social Credit evangelism. Could it be wedded to the central government's new economics? Tommy Douglas of Saskatchewan headed Canada's first (and last) CCF government. King liked Douglas, and philosophically there was no great gulf between them. But Douglas was also closer in spirit to the federal proposals than was the prime minister. Saskatchewan had suffered cruelly from drought and depression and well knew the value of a strong federal treasury.

The Liberal premiers were King's official allies. Stuart Garson of Manitoba was the best known. With a strong reputation for his work as provincial treasurer, Garson had a detailed understanding of the financial intricacies of dominion-provincial relations. His experience and his province's weak economic position made Garson a firm exponent of a strong central government. John Hart of British Columbia had been in office since 1941 as the chief of a Liberal-Conservative coalition. Tall, dry, dispassionate, Hart was not a dominating or disturbing element. The three Maritime premiers, all Liberals, were anything but colourless. John McNair of New Brunswick was an old political hand, raised in a political system that expected government to be the visible patron of the unfortunate, or at least of the unfortunate who voted for the right party. Five dollar bills were the welfare policy of New Brunswick. A.S. MacMillan of Nova Scotia was the oldest premier present, older even than King. He dozed gently next to Drew, waiting out the months until he retired to make way for Angus L. Macdonald, Nova Scotia Liberalism's legendary leader, who had recently returned to his native province from wartime service in Mackenzie King's cabinet. Macdonald was no friend of King's and held strong views on provincial rights, but for the moment he was unable to derail proceedings directly. Finally, there was Walter Jones, the farmer-premier of Prince Edward Island. Those who knew Jones suspected that farming came before politics in his personal order of priorities. 'There is not a worry on Prince Edward Island except tomorrow's hockey match and possibly the price of potatoes,' Jones told an interviewer.

In the final showdown, King knew the Liberal premiers would follow his lead

– if he looked like winning. But he could win only if he neutralized his two greatest opponents, Drew and Duplessis. That, King suspected, was a very doubtful proposition. Drew represented a tradition of assertive provincial rights – Ontario first, others last – that was deeply embedded in the province's political and administrative history. Even Drew's Liberal predecessor, Mitchell Hepburn, stood squarely in that tradition, although whether for reasons of state or personal spite remains a mystery. Drew, like Hepburn, strongly disliked King, and even King's masterful diplomatic skills usually failed on his marble exterior. Drew, however, depended on others, his treasury department, and its treasurer, Leslie Frost, for the details, if not the substance, of his policy.

So did King. The dominion government's proposals had their origins in the Department of Finance, with an assist from the Bank of Canada. Finance spoke for what had already been achieved. Thanks to the Wartime Tax Agreements Canada had for the first time a tidy, although temporary, tax system. Ottawa's decisions directed investment, shaped consumption, and secured resources for national goals, with no danger of competition from the provinces. In the King cabinet, Ilsley spoke up for Finance, and Ilsley was a powerful and effective advocate who had given his department's proposals his heart and soul. But Ilsley was not alone. Co-ordination of the dominion's proposals meant bringing to-gether a coalition of agencies and talents: that task King delegated in 1944 to his own parliamentary secretary, Brooke Claxton (later the Minister of National Health and Welfare) and to Alex Skelton of the Bank of Canada. Skelton had served as secretary to the Royal Commission on Dominion-Provincial Relations and had taken away from the experience a burning commitment to see the Cana-dian federal structure reformed and cleansed of petty provincialism and jurisdic-tional rivalries. Claxton, a consultant to the same royal commission, had come to believe that only a strong dominion government could provide the welfare poli-cies that the times demanded. A former Conservative, Claxton had become the most fervent, and one of the most politically astute, of Liberals. He combined his political passions with a strong administrative sense and indefatigable ener-gy; his only defect, though a large one, was an unappealing public personality.

Claxton and Skelton had first to convince the King cabinet that reform was essential, politically desirable, and safe. Some members of the cabinet proved most reluctant. T.A. Crerar, after King the most senior minister, was the most conservative and the most provincially minded of the group. Crerar had grown up in a world where the 'brains trust' of Finance and the Bank of Canada were unknown quantities; as W.A. Mackintosh once quipped to the minister, 'You don't think we have any brains, and you don't trust us.'

For Crerar, redistribution of federal and provincial powers and responsibili-ties would risk crippling the central government under a too vast weight of administration and expenditure. Crerar's views could be ascribed to an outdated and discredited view of the proper functioning of government, and they could be ignored as the prejudices of a minister whose political influence was in descent. The hesitations of the Minister of Justice, Louis St Laurent, were in a different category. St Laurent was no crank. His detailed knowledge of dominion-provincial problems derived from service as counsel to the Rowell-Sirois Commission in the late thirties, as well as from extensive experience in corporation law. He spoke, too, as the senior representative of Quebec, and, in King's government, views from such a source were listened to with respect.

St Laurent's orderly mind had an unusual capacity for assimilating facts and arguments quickly and then rendering judgment in a concise, pungent form. He had no use for timidity, and no patience for arguments that simply sought to avoid conflict. When, at a meeting of the cabinet committee on dominion-provincial relations in March 1945, Crerar advanced the familiar argument that an activist federal policy would 'precipitate acrimonious disputes with the provinces,' St Laurent readily agreed. But that was no reason not to go ahead, he told his colleagues: 'Acrimonious dispute was inevitable with Quebec in any case.' Crerar persisted. 'In a conflict,' he told the other ministers, 'the majority of the people would support the provincial governments against the Dominion.' 'Not at all,' St Laurent replied. The reason most Canadians turned to provincial governments first was because 'people were made constantly aware of the services which provincial governments render while they tended to think of the central government as the one imposing burdens such as taxation and conscription.' Family allowances would correct this situation, as would the other programs now contemplated by Ottawa.

By the time the dominion-provincial conference convened in August, St Laurent's side had prevailed. Crerar was gone from the cabinet, dismissed by King in April and promoted to the Senate. The needs of the finance department, newly rationalized in the White Paper on Employment and Income, and ably summarized by Alex Skelton and Brooke Claxton, shaped the conference's agenda. The dominion proposals were sweeping, logical, and uncompromising.

What the people wanted, Ottawa told the provinces, was security and stability. The central government knew how to provide these and had already outlined its strategy in the White Paper. There were four basic points: encouragement of export trade, private investment, consumer expenditure, and a program of public investment. There would also be encouragement of technological development and social security for the individual against 'large and uncertain risks' – those of old age, sickness, and unemployment. To finance the prospective expenditures, Ottawa must secure an adequate base in taxation. Ilsley's officials proposed that in return for federal participation in and contribution to social security expenditures (many of which were located in provincial jurisdiction) the provinces should surrender to Ottawa the right to levy income, corporate, and succession taxes. In return, the provinces would receive an annual per capita grant indexed to the fluctuating value of the gross national product. Because the latter had grown substantially since the last adjustment in 1941, there would be an immediate and large increase in provincial revenues.

As King stressed to the premiers, Ottawa's proposals relied on co-operation, not coercion. No constitutional amendment was contemplated; instead, there would be joint agreements enforced by little more than the power of public opinion. But that public opinion, in the minds of King's officials, was now firmly on the side of the dominion government.

August had seemed a likely time for a conference, at the beginning of the breathing space provided by the end of the war against Germany and before the end of the war against Japan. That event might be as much as a year away, and during that year Ottawa's ideas could be circulated and popularized. But within a month the war was over, Japan surrendered, and the emergency powers of the central government were soon due to expire. Within a measurable and very short period Ottawa would have to hand back to the provinces what it had appropriated in 1939.

Some of the provinces were determined to turn the clock right back to the thirties. Ontario's Drew took the lead. First, he secured a delay in the conference's proceedings. The federal proposals were so sweeping and so sudden, he maintained, that he would have to take them home to Toronto for study. Even on brief acquaintance they looked unpromising. They were little more than a scheme to replace the provinces with a unitary government, contrary to the expressed federalist wishes of the hallowed Fathers of Confederation. The dominion's jurisdiction did not need rounding out; rather, the provinces should be on their guard against centralizing encroachments. In Drew's view, the provinces would bear the primary responsibility for post-war social policy, and for that purpose they would need more, not less, revenue. Certainly Ontario would not agree to surrender its right to income and other direct taxes. After Drew's salvo, it was Duplessis's turn: the Quebec premier happily followed where his Ontario ally had led.

Immediate agreement being impossible, the dominion delegation had no option but to send its proposals to a Dominion-Provincial Co-ordinating Committee for study and elaboration. There followed a winter of hope and uncertainty. Drew was actually encouraging, so federal officials believed, and for a time it seemed that he might be persuaded to go along with a redistribution of taxation and, subsequently, the dominion's social security package. Duplessis, according to Alex Skelton, who served as Ottawa's roving ambassador, did not appear even to have read the federal proposals. But maybe that was encouraging: if he hadn't read them, presumably he had not finally made up his mind on the subject. Hart of British Columbia provided an unexpected snag. Ottawa's financial proposals worried him, even after plentiful reassurances were provided. Naturally, Nova Scotia's attitude took a distinct turn for the worse after Angus L. Macdonald's return as premier. Macdonald sympathized with provincial rights and nursed a healthy distrust of any propositions that bore the imprint of Mackenzie King's cloven hoof.

The uncertainties of the autumn surfaced in January 1946. King and the premiers met in Ottawa to examine the provinces' reactions to the dominion proposals. Drew's counter-proposal grudgingly accepted the utility of the central government as the collection agent for income tax (it would reap thereby the unpopularity that derives from visible taxation), but he insisted on the right of the individual provinces to charge their own rates. In exchange for this dubious concession, Drew insisted that the dominion promise never to return to or to invade any new fields of direct taxation. As for the federal proposal that the central government serve as the economic balance-wheel of the federation, Drew could concede only that 10 per cent of the proceeds of provincial income taxes be placed in a fund to be administered jointly by the dominion and the provinces. The poorer provinces could petition the fund for relief according to their needs. Drew's proposals stimulated a further need for contemplation; the conference adjourned until April.

The last session of the Dominion-Provincial Conference on Reconstruction met on April 25, 1946. It was a depressing day. Drew denounced centralization and its socialistic spawn, health insurance. Duplessis chimed in, beating the drum for provincial autonomy and comparing the dominion proposals to the works of Hitler and Mussolini. Angus L. Macdonald hymned the virtues of autonomy and locality. Stuart Garson's protests were swept away in a rhapsody of provincial rights.

For Minister of Finance James Ilsley it was a sad moment. He had hoped that his six years as finance minister would end triumphantly in the recasting of Canadian fiscal federalism, only to be balked by parochial obstruction that he considered ridiculous and unworthy. King adjourned the conference *sine die*. W.C. Clark scornfully characterized Drew's final proposals as 'full of misstatements and half-truths' and with his External Affairs counterpart Norman Robertson mournfully told an American diplomat: 'If the selfish interests of the two principal Provinces are going to hamstring the Federal Government in its efforts to provide machinery which will permit it to fulfill the functions of a central government in this modern age, then Confederation is a failure and Canada cannot be a nation.' Clark's words were prophetic. Yet his handling of the delicate and

LaPalme, 1948   *Le Canada*

The Pimp: 'Mais, mon frère, en sommes-nous rendus là?'
Premier Duplessis, seated at table, rents Quebec to American investors, thereby affirming
provincial control over resources (LaPalme, 1948). Reproduced with the permission of
Robert LaPalme

complicated dominion proposals had not been without fault. As Mackenzie King commented, as the conference was collapsing around him, 'you cannot get Clark, whose mind is wholly academic, to realize that no matter how theoretically accurate you may be or in accord with strict financial rules that [sic] what you are doing is no good unless you can get the public to understand and support it.'

Canada, in any case, survived Clark's disappointment. King steadfastly refused Drew's demands to reconvene the conference. To regularize the fiscal relations between the dominion and the provinces, emergency powers were gradually wound up and returned to the provinces, while instead of the comprehensive taxation and social security scheme of 1945, the national government offered 'tax rental' to the provinces. Under this scheme, the federal government would occupy completely the fields of income, corporation, and succession taxes. In return for their abstention from taxing these fields, the provinces received payments based on complicated formulas designed to provide both a per capita grant and their statutory subsidies under the BNA Act. The per capita grants varied, with Nova Scotia and Saskatchewan receiving higher amounts than the other provinces. Quebec and Ontario predictably rejected the federal terms and in 1947 re-established their own autonomous taxation systems. The remaining provinces did accept, and in 1949 they were joined by the newest province of Newfoundland. Through tax rental, Ilsley hoped, the poorer provinces would escape the worst consequences of their unequal tax bases and unequal resources.

The dominion's case might have had more force, and more point, had Canada been facing a genuine economic crisis in 1945 or 1946. If a real crisis of unemployment had developed, then popular support might have been mobilized behind national control of government taxing and spending. In the event, without a centralized fiscal system, the nation's income recovered and then began to grow. The real problem, as C.D. Howe informed his colleagues in September 1945, was not going to be labour surplus but labour shortage. The popular mood changed, and with it Canada's political imperatives.

Nor was the dominion government, despite the gloom of some of its officials, prepared to wither away. St Laurent was right when he observed that a government with a tangible presence and a real function attracted attention and focused loyalty. Many federal programs did not depend on provincial co-operation for their implementation, and these proceeded. Where provincial co-operation was constitutionally inescapable, the lesson of 1945 was thoughtfully applied. Sensible co-operation being impossible, it was best to present the provinces with financial inducements to go along with predetermined national initiatives. If a province was prepared to do without a dominion program and the attached subsidy, then it could justify the lack to its own electors.

The most prominent programs of the post-war era did not infringe on provincial rights, nor did they excite much controversy. Veterans were the government's first concern. Legislation in 1944 and 1945 established a framework of demobilization grants based on time served in the armed forces and time served overseas. Incapacitated veterans received full medical care, and invalids were pensioned to the full extent of their individual disability. Those veterans who wished to go on to university or technical schools received free tuition and a living allowance that corresponded, month for month, with the time they had spent in the armed services. Veterans wishing to take up farming or to buy land for small businesses were assisted under the Veterans' Land Act. Those who wished to return to their pre-war jobs were handed their old jobs back, with seniority as if they had never been away to war. Unemployed veterans received out-of-work allowances. At first it seemed as if this last category would be alarmingly large: in January 1947 over 50,000 veterans of the Second World War were registered as seeking work. By September of the same year, however, only 15,000 were still jobless, and even the seasonal rise in unemployment failed to reproduce the previous winter's large figures. In any case the Department of Labour preferred to look on the bright side, emphasizing that almost a million people had been discharged from the armed forces by September 1947, and that 810,000 placements had been made.

If the education and employment of veterans produced few serious complaints, the same was not true of the homes they proposed to occupy. The problem was of long standing. In 1930, the Dominion Bureau of Statistics later concluded, Canadians had been under-housed: there were not enough dwelling units to accommodate the number of families available to occupy them. During the 1930s this condition was masked because large numbers of families doubled up in single units to make ends meet; thus, vacancy rates did not reflect real needs. The war, which placed large amounts of money for the first time in the hands of many families, resulted in an explosion of housing demand and, until rent control was imposed, in skyrocketing rents. Rent control proved popular and was difficult to get rid of after the war. The central government eventually offered to vacate the field in favour of any province willing to take up the burden, and slowly some provinces responded, first Saskatchewan and then, in 1951, Quebec. Not surprisingly, rent controls directed capital into houses for sale rather than into new apartment buildings. Housing construction was, nevertheless, extraordinary. Measured in constant (1971) dollars, private residential construction totalled $713 million in 1944, $1,033 million in 1945, and $1,342 million in 1948 (the government accounted for about $3 million worth in each year). In 1947, for the first time, new dwelling units exceeded the rate of family formation, no small boast, since the number of marriages in that boom year was 130,000 (1938: 90,709). Between 1945 and 1949, no less than 367,900 new dwelling units were completed.

To help people pay for their new homes, the national government made mortgages available under the National Housing Act of 1944. Between 1945 and 1947 over 19,000 loans were approved under the new legislation. Most interesting of all, of the 76,738 dwelling units built during 1947, no less than 76 per cent were for single-family dwellings. Whatever else post-war Canada might be, one thing was clear: it would be a country of individual owner-occupied homes.

The first consequences of this became immediately apparent. Cities and suburbs began to spread. Some subdivisions were built especially for veterans according to government specifications. Profiting from wartime experience, the government's Central Mortgage and Housing Corporation[1] promoted a National Building Code to simplify its financial tasks in evaluating new housing. And so across Canada distinctively 'Canadian' suburbs began to appear: solid, well-built, and generally unimaginative houses of wood or brick, conforming to the 'Canadian federal' style of architecture. Canadian cities sprawled, and municipalities spread outward to follow their inhabitants.

Had visiting sociologists wished to examine the beliefs of the average Canadian, or the typical Canadian family, they might have done worse than to study the largely unregarded growth of the central government's housing policy. Possibly because there was so little conflict between that policy and what the electorate thought was natural, it passed without much in the way of general comment. 'Today,' an English visitor wrote in 1961, 'about three-quarters of all Canadians own their own houses.'[2] Canadians, he added, also tended to move out of rented accommodation as soon as they could. With such aspirations, and such a lifestyle, it was not surprising that few Canadians seemed to blaze with resentment of social injustice or revolutionary ferment.

Canada remained a country of homeowners scattered across miles of suburbs and preoccupied with the arrival of the next sewer line in the vicinity, or with the paving of the streets, where diaper services helped cope with another post-war phenomenon: the baby boom. In 1948, Canada's total population was estimated at 12,850,000. Of that total, over two and a half million were aged nine and under, born since the outbreak of the Second World War. The birth rate had risen during the war; it rose still further when the war was over (23.5 births per thousand between 1941 and 1945; 27.4 per thousand between 1946 and 1950). 'To-day,' a caustic critic lamented, '... the five-room bungalow [is] the object of life and every woman in sight [is] pregnant.'[3]

Housing can be accounted a success. There was a reasonable national consen-

---

1 Now called Canada Mortgage and Housing Corporation, but still CMHC.
2 Alistair Horne, *Canada and the Canadians* (London and Toronto: Macmillan, 1961), p. 235.
3 A.R.M. Lower, *Canadians in the Making* (Toronto: Longmans, 1958), p. 417.

sus on goals and agreement on guidelines. But other forms of social programs did not fare so well. Health insurance, one of the centrepieces of social security, would not come for years. The central government made health grants for certain diseases, as well as hospital grants, available to the provinces for the improvement of their health-care facilities. The Department of National Health and Welfare acquired a new minister when, in December 1946, its founder, Brooke Claxton, moved to National Defence. Paul Martin, the new minister, strongly believed in the appropriateness and the inevitability of national health insurance. But the obstacles – stubborn and conservative provincial governments and a preference in Ottawa for other forms of economic action – hobbled him. Martin discovered that the cardinal virtues of a Minister of National Health and Welfare in an increasingly conservative society were patience and tolerance. Martin settled down to wait.

8

Making a Better World

Word of Germany's surrender reached Mackenzie King at a hotel in San Francisco. The California city had been chosen to host the founding conference of the new international organization that would replace the failed League of Nations. This time, nothing was left to the imagination: the new world body would be called the United Nations.

As King heard the news, he uttered 'a prayer of thanksgiving.' Then he added, 'and of rededication to the service of my fellow-men.' Most international bodies had need of rededication and renewal that spring. Few had managed to survive the war, and those that had were safely peripheral to great events. A start had already been made on restoration, however. Attention had turned first to economic reconstruction.

It is difficult to imagine any world economic order on which the Grand Alliance that won the war against Hitler could have agreed. Britain, the Soviet Union, and the United States were deeply divided in their notions of what the ideal world economy would be. When the representatives of the allied nations met in Bretton Woods, a New Hampshire resort, in the summer of 1944, the British and Americans had enough trouble agreeing among themselves about the reform of the international monetary system. The Russians, who arrived late, sat dourly on the sidelines and waited for the results. What capitalists did among themselves did not greatly concern the Soviet Union, which knew, as an article of faith, that the West was doomed to economic stagnation and depression as soon as the war was over.

Although the main action at Bretton Woods involved the British and the Americans, Canada was there too, represented by an exceptionally capable delegation headed by Louis Rasminsky of the Bank of Canada. The Canadians were well informed about the respective states of mind of the Americans and the British; they arrived in Bretton Woods determined to bridge any gaps that might open between Canada's two principal allies. It was one occasion in which Canada's self-designated role of 'helpful fixer' or 'linchpin' actually worked. The competence and diligence of Canada's representatives won them the confidence of both sides and helped bring about a solution that both sides perceived as respectable and viable. Canadian suggestions, a British observer wrote, 'were intelligent and constructive, and the British and Americans were always anxious to have them.'

The Bretton Woods agreements established an International Monetary Fund (IMF) and an International Bank for Reconstruction and Development (later called the World Bank). The agreements had various purposes: one was to establish a means for regulating the currencies of the world. To this end the governments subscribing to the IMF agreed to give their currencies 'par values,' pegging them to the US dollar, allowing these currencies to deviate no more than 1 per cent from 'par,' and consulting about changes in these 'par values.' To help its members manage their currencies, the IMF provided short-term credits.

The American government conceived of the Bretton Woods agreements as the best response available to the monetary wars of the thirties. Accepting the arrangements would benefit all nations by removing one of the causes of economic instability. Canadian officials agreed, in general, with this point of view. There was, Louis Rasminsky later pointed out, a 'great increase in international consultation and collaboration' as a result of establishment of the Fund. The mere existence of an agreed international forum for the discussion of economic policies was a great advantage. Relief and guarded optimism notwithstanding, there were still some forebodings. The IMF and the Bank would not be enough to help finance countries through their reconstruction difficulties; but the United States had been unwilling to pledge more, and the Americans had their way. W.A. Mackintosh was worried by the manner in which the United States had achieved its goals and perturbed at the American assumption that the United States could now benevolently prescribe what rules the rest of the trading world should follow. This was familiar stuff to a Canadian raised in the British Empire, and it amounted, in Mackintosh's view, to 'imperialism.' Mackintosh did not, of course, regard imperialism as the ultimate political sin that the term now implies, but he did question the practicality and desirability of its American variant. 'The United States,' the economist wrote, 'with its inevitable minorities, is incapable of following any consistent imperialistic policy. It would also be defeated by the Fifth Column within its own country. What it could, and may, do is to defeat any adequate programme by abortive imperialism.'

Mackintosh's views found an echo mainly among Canadians with direct experience of the American government. Canadian diplomats in Washington smarted when Canada was left out of discussions preparing for the future world security organization. Although Canada would have to accept the consequences of great-power decision-making, the dominion was seldom consulted. External Affairs officials dug into the theory of international relations and came up with a concept that fitted, or appeared to fit, the Canadian case: 'functionalism' or functional representation. Broadly speaking, functionalism was interpreted to mean that Canada had a right and a capacity to be consulted about decisions for which this country would later have to take responsibility. This, as John Holmes has noted, was linked to a belief in the efficacy of international action in reducing the level of international conflict.[1]

Functionalism found a home in some Canadian international negotiations (for example, in aviation conferences), but never in high-level political discussions. On that lofty plane, King knew, the smaller powers were expected to show their appreciation and not indulge their own peculiar ideas. Canada's contribution to the drafting of the charter of the new world security organization was a minor one.

The United Nations was born for all that. Like the old League of Nations, it had a Security Council, housing the great powers, with permanent seats, and elected representatives chosen from among the other members of the organization. Some votes in the Security Council were more equal than others, for the great powers could veto any substantive (as opposed to procedural) motion. Without the insurance of a veto it is doubtful if either the Soviet Union or the United States would have consented to join. In the General Assembly, which included all members, things were theoretically more equal. The same was true of the various specialized agencies belonging to the UN. To reflect the new realities of power, the United Nations would have its seat not in Geneva, but in New York. A site was donated by the Rockefellers, and a new ultramodern building was soon under construction. Canada's contribution was a set of metal doors.

As the new UN building rose above the East River, high diplomacy made a last perambulation around Europe. The early sessions of the UN were held in London and Paris, and in Paris, too, was convened the first post-war peace conference. The conference was meant to restore the formalities of peace between the allies and Germany's former satellites. In the end it did so, but that was not its lasting achievement. What the Paris Peace Conference did do was to make people think of a new war. Soviet, British, French, and American diplomats and ministers growled and spat and snarled for the benefit of the world's press. It was the first time the world (or that part of it with a free press) had been furnished such an instructive vista of the gulf between the wartime allies, but it would not be the last.

1 See the discussion in John Holmes, *The Shaping of Peace* (Toronto: University of Toronto Press, 1979), p. 72.

Canadian sympathies lay with the United States and Great Britain. The revelation of a Russian spy ring in March 1946 helped. So did a speech by Winston Churchill at a small college in Fulton, Missouri. On a continent-wide radio hook-up, Canadians heard Churchill intone: 'From Stettin in the Baltic to Trieste in the Adriatic, an iron curtain has descended across the continent.' On all sides, Churchill told his audience, the Russians and their Communist sympathizers constituted 'a growing challenge and peril to Christian civilization.' The Russians had no intention of going to war while they could get what they wanted by bluff: 'What they desire is the fruits of war and the indefinite expansion of their power and doctrines.' Only by strength could the Russians be stopped, and the only powers in a position to show strength were the British Commonwealth and the United States. Mackenzie King, whom Churchill consulted about the speech, was deeply moved. 'I confess,' he wrote in his diary, 'I personally believe that as regards Russia the rest of the world is not in a very different position than other countries in Europe were when Hitler had made up his mind to aim at the conquest of Europe.'

King soon got a taste of Soviet diplomacy at first hand. Travelling to Paris for the peace conference, King had a front-row seat as the great powers quarrelled among themselves. A Canadian reporter watched the Prime Minister sit fascinated through a diatribe by the Soviet delegate, Vishinsky. 'Oh Smith,' King later lamented to the reporter, 'I'm aghast. Isn't this ghastly.' 'And in his eyes,' Smith commented, 'were sadness, fear and disillusion.'[2]

King's reaction might have been duplicated across Canada as citizens followed in their papers or on the radio the progress of the Sovietization of eastern Europe. It all sounded very familiar: rigged elections, arrests, show trials, and the steady growth in power of the local Communist parties. The news made a profound impression in Ottawa as well.

In Ottawa there had been a cabinet shuffle. Mackenzie King, who had been both Minister of External Affairs and Prime Minister, handed over the former to the Minister of Justice, Louis St Laurent. King chose as St Laurent's deputy Lester Pearson, Canada's ambassador to the United States, and sent Hume Wrong, one of the country's ablest diplomats, to replace Pearson in Washington. St Laurent, Pearson, and Wrong were only the most visible level of an exceptionally competent team. The team's first and most important task was to confront the problem of Soviet expansion in Europe and to assess its implications for Canada. The problem seemed obvious: very recent history had shown what could happen if aggression were not resisted and if totalitarian states were allowed to run roughshod over their weaker neighbours. By tolerating or counte-

2   I.N. Smith, *A Reporter Reports* (Toronto: Ryerson, 1954), p. 28.

nancing Soviet expansion in Europe, Canada would only be weakening its own position in a showdown with the Soviet Union. Canada's liberal democratic institutions, its economic welfare, and its hope for political survival were all bound up in the fate of Europe.

St Laurent expounded the External Affairs viewpoint in a speech at the University of Toronto in January 1947. Canadian policy in external relations, he told his audience, was founded on five basic principles: national unity, political liberty, the rule of law, the values of Christian civilization, and a 'willingness to accept international responsibilities.' All these principles were at stake in western Europe, and that, St Laurent added, was a matter of the gravest concern to Canada. 'We have realized,' St Laurent told his listeners, 'that a threat to the liberty of western Europe, where our own political ideas were nurtured, was a threat to our own way of life.'

If that was the threat, what should be the response? New manifestations of the Soviet threat arose daily. In February 1948, there was a coup in Czechoslovakia, placing a Communist regime in firm control. Within months, Czechoslovakia's democratic parties and institutions were suppressed, and its most prominent non-Communist politician, the foreign minister Jan Masaryk, was mysteriously dead on the pavement outside his apartment. 'Suicide,' the Czech government claimed. Further north, around Berlin, the Soviet grip tightened. Berlin was occupied by the four principal allies, deep inside the Russian zone. Access depended on land, water, and air corridors across East Germany. When the Western allies implemented a currency reform, in June 1948, these routes were blocked – all except the air corridor. There followed the Berlin airlift, a symbol of Western determination and initiative in the face of Soviet pressure. Britain, France, the United States, even Australia and South Africa sent planes and pilots. Canada, virtually disarmed, could send only sympathy.

The government in Ottawa, especially Mackenzie King, pondered what to do. In December 1947, after a trip to England, where British reports on the European situation thoroughly alarmed him, King disclosed the secret to his cabinet, telling it 'perhaps more than I should have about inside of situation in Europe as I knew it and believe is about to break.' The cabinet was 'stunned,' King wrote. 'It is just too terrible to contemplate, but it does look increasingly to me as if the men at the head of affairs in Russia have got it into their minds that they can conquer the world.' Typically, however, King hesitated to take any final or irrevocable action.

The first reaction to the Communist coup in Prague came from western Europe. There, the British, French, Dutch, Belgian, and Luxembourg governments signed the Treaty of Brussels on March 17, 1948, pledging mutual aid in case of aggression. A week before, British Prime Minister Attlee had sent King an important message noting the dangers posed by Soviet pressures on Norway and proposing, as a counter-measure, establishment of 'a regional Atlantic pact of mutual assistance in which all the countries threatened by a Russian move on the Atlantic could participate.' King promptly convened an urgent meeting of his foreign policy advisers – St Laurent, Claxton, and Pearson – in his office on the afternoon of March 11, 1948. A prompt and affirmative reply was dispatched at once to Attlee. 'Collective measures seem to me to be essential to establish some sense of security and to preserve the peace. Such collective measures will, of course, require the active leadership of the United Kingdom and of the United States.' To assist in Anglo-American deliberations King arranged for immediate Canadian participation in secret talks in Washington. Though no commitments had as yet been made, they were now clearly envisaged.

As discussions proceeded in Washington, Louis St Laurent and his officials undertook the delicate task of selling an Atlantic alliance to Canadian public opinion. Most Canadians were by this time anti-Communist and deeply mistrustful of the Soviet Union. The Canadian Communist party (then travelling under the name of Labour Progressive party) collected a negligible handful of votes in national elections. Its influence, and that of allied 'peace' groups, could be discounted. But there were others besides Communists who found the prospect of a peacetime military alliance with the United States less than alluring. A few intellectuals, among them a trio from the University of Toronto – Harold Adams Innis, Donald Creighton, and Frank Underhill – poured scorn on the idea of an alliance from a variety of perspectives. Innis disgustedly wrote that 'Pearson seems to be as active as possible in selling us down the river to the United States.'[3]

The Toronto trio spoke for few besides themselves. But there were other, and more significant, sources of opposition. French Canada, with its history of isolationism, was a likely source of dissent. Even there, however, disagreement with Ottawa's alliance policy was scattered, confined to a few fractious politicians and the Montreal newspaper *Le Devoir*. St Laurent, it appeared, spoke for Quebec as well as Canada when he preached his alliance crusade. As for the non-Communist left, it had little choice but to follow the leadership of the national CCF in support of an Atlantic alliance. With battles against domestic Communists in the labour movement just behind it, the CCF found it natural to extend the fight to the realm of external affairs.

With these minor exceptions, Canadian opinion on foreign policy was remarkably coherent: a consensus had gradually been established that would last, without serious opposition, for the best part of the next decade. When St Laurent

3   Public reaction is ably discussed in James Eayrs, *In Defence of Canada*, IV (Toronto: University of Toronto Press, 1980), pp. 51-8.

spoke to the House of Commons of a 'dynamic counter-attraction of a free, prosperous and progressive society ... opposed to the totalitarian and reactionary society of the communist world,' he was addressing the converted.

In his wake, the vigorous and firmly committed Minister of External Affairs dragged a reluctant Mackenzie King. It was not that King was unimpressed by the Soviet threat, or that he regarded a Western grouping as unnecessary. But he was getting old, tired, and depressed at the awful prospect of an indefinite Cold War (as the new bi-polar international system was beginning to be called). Increasingly, King's leadership in cabinet seemed directed to demonstrating that he was, indeed, still leader and Prime Minister: 'the last bellows of the leader of the herd before he cashed in his cheques,' as Brooke Claxton unkindly put it. At the end of 1947 King announced his impending retirement and summoned a Liberal convention, the first since 1919, to meet in Ottawa and choose his successor. The choice was purely formal. King knew, and most Liberals knew too, who the choice must be. The convention ratified the choice, making St Laurent the new Liberal leader and, on November 15, 1948, prime minister of Canada.

Mackenzie King shuffled off into retirement. He had good reason to be content with his legacy. He had handed on a prosperous country with a sound government. The Liberal party was flourishing. Its successful leadership during the war had stimulated a wave of national pride and self-confidence which the Liberals were not slow to exploit. The central government and its policies were in the forefront of the nation's consciousness; it was to Ottawa that Canadians looked for direction and, given the unhappy world situation, protection. It was, after all, better to be united against an uncertain future than to resume domestic quarrelling on the model of the 1930s.

Under firm and strong leadership, Canadians could turn their attention to domestic concerns.

9

Popular Culture

In 1948 Canada was still a relatively pious country compared with Britain, France, or other European states. In this respect, as in so many others, its residents resembled the Americans with whom they had such close connections. Whether Roman Catholic, Protestant, or Anglican, Canadians went to church on Sunday. Unless they were Catholic, they met a sermon-dominated liturgy that had much to say about piety and obligations, and not much to say about anything else. For Catholics, whose liturgical tradition centred on the mass and on Mariological devotional exercises, the experience was rather different. But this difference was less important than the fact that almost all Canadians professed some religion. Both for believers and for non-believers religion was a serious matter. Faith was a spur to action, although it did not necessarily point unequivocally in any one direction. Among Catholics there were plentiful recruits for the religious orders, whose members staffed hospitals and schools throughout the dominion. In other denominations there was a perpetual war between the 'social gospellers,' who wanted to enlist Christianity in the service of socioeconomic reform, and the devotionally and sacramentally inclined, who were more interested in individual purification and sanctity. All denominations, however, believed in 'mission.' Hence the Canadian churches supported Indian and Eskimo work at home and medical missions abroad. The Canadian churches, like the American, were deeply involved in China. Unlike the American, they had also committed themselves to India, while the Catholics had many projects in Latin America also.

Regardless of denomination, people looked to their priest, minister, or pastor for spiritual guidance. They might think the minister odd, they often told themselves that they paid his salary, but they did not ignore him. Often, of course, the clergyman was the only educated person with whom ordinary people had contact. However irrelevant that education to the mid-century situation, or to the perplexities of the parishioners, it helped to strengthen the clergyman's ex-officio authority. Conscious of their followings and of their influence, clergymen of all denominations were inclined to say that Canada was a Christian country. The state schools reflected this influence. There were Bible readings, prayers, and, in some provinces, formal religious instruction. Indeed, during the period 1944-8 such exercises became more numerous, and in many places they were enforced more rigorously than before. The churches, in effect, were enlisting the power of the state, hoping that governments could do what the churches themselves had not managed to achieve.

Christianity is meant chiefly to turn man toward God. There are various aspects of this turning – worship, prayer, alms-giving, good works, respect for one's fellows, and love of them. Canada's churches were reasonably good at worship. Some had a good record of alms-giving and other good works. As for respect and love, the record was mixed, and certainly it was much less satisfactory. All the churches tended to convert love into law. Thus, for instance, the Roman Catholic Church tried to ban birth control and divorce, while the United Church tried to ban 'beverage alcohol.' In such matters the flocks may or may not have heeded their pastors. But governments certainly did.

Broadcasting, too, was permeated by a rather simple sort of morality, the doctrine of uplift. In the 1930s the Canadian Radio League had propagated this doctrine, and the Canadian Broadcasting Corporation (CBC) had been founded largely to embody it. Canadian broadcasting was supposed to unify the country, displace American programming, and improve the cultural and moral condition of the people.

During the war, CBC radio had come of age. Admittedly, both in production and in transmission the arrangements were often primitive. For the English network the main programming centre was a derelict girls' secondary school in one of the less savoury parts of Toronto. The French network was no better served. The ambitious framework of 50,000-watt transmitters adumbrated in 1936 had barely been commenced when war began, and it could not be further expanded until after 1945. Many CBC stations, therefore, had rather limited ranges. The AM band was then much less crowded than it later became, and, especially at night, a relatively weak AM signal could often be heard for considerable distances. The CBC also had the power to affiliate privately owned stations to itself, and this power was used with vigour, especially for the networking of news, public affairs, drama, and music. In Toronto, Watrous, Saskatchewan, Montreal, and Sackville, New Brunswick, the CBC did own four high-power transmitters. As yet there were no television transmitters, no cable systems, and no FM; but through landline linkages between its owned and affiliated stations, CBC AM radio reached a large proportion of Canada's population.

Broadcasting was regulated by the legislation of 1936. This stated that there was a single national system, in which privately owned elements co-operated with the state-owned element and were regulated by it. Private stations depended on advertising revenues, but if affiliated to the national network they got CBC programming free, or very cheaply indeed. The CBC also got some revenue from advertising, but it depended chiefly on the licence fees that radio listeners paid. That licence system was cumbersome and costly to enforce, but it had been designed to ensure that government could not influence programming: since Parliament did not vote any money to the CBC, in theory the state-owned system was independent of government control. In fact, of course, things could never have been quite so simple; Parliament did determine the size of the licence fee and, especially in wartime, there must have been many occasions when government ministers made suggestions to broadcasters. On the whole, however, CBC broadcasters evinced a sturdy independence, not just of government but also of public opinion. Like the British broadcasters on whom so many of them had modelled themselves, they were concerned to purify and improve the public taste, not slavishly to follow it.

The CBC aimed at 'balanced programming' – a mixture of information, entertainment, and uplift, with something for everyone in the course of a week. In the big cities, unaffiliated private stations provided alternatives. But these stations were not allowed to form networks, or to link themselves with the American chains: Columbia Broadcasting, Mutual, or the Red and Blue Networks of NBC. Nor could they be foreign-owned. However, most Canadian cities were within range of American AM transmitters, and so American programming was widely available in the dominion. The CBC itself transmitted a certain amount of American material and it drew a good deal of news from the British Broadcasting Corporation. But although there were no 'Canadian content' regulations, the CBC concentrated on Canadian programming, almost all of which went out 'live.'

For much CBC programming the audience was massive. All over the dominion people huddled around their loudspeakers on Saturday nights to hear Foster Hewitt narrate 'Hockey Night in Canada.' For news and public affairs there was also a mass audience, especially while the war continued. In these spheres, CBC programming showed seriousness together with thoroughness and attention to the large and important issues. Commentators treated the issues as if they thought the public wanted to understand important questions and think about them.

Here, one supposes, the war itself was a considerable help. Most Canadian families – at least the English-speaking ones – had relatives on the battlefields; everyone cared about the conduct of the war and the shaping of the post-war scene. But other forces were at work too, traditions of popular education and uplift that were partly borrowed from the BBC and the Fabian tradition and partly generated from the native soil of populism, puritanism, Protestantism, the Grange, and the labour movement. Hence the intense seriousness of such programs as Citizens' Forum and National Farm Radio Forum; hence, too, the considerable audiences for such things.

The privately owned broadcasters cared little about the arts and letters, or about public affairs. The CBC, however, cared passionately, and it compelled many private radio stations to carry some of the programs that it produced or purchased. From the United States the CBC acquired the Metropolitan Opera and New York Philharmonic programs, which it 'networked' throughout the dominion. From Canadian sources it picked up the Toronto, Montreal, and Vancouver symphony orchestras, the only substantial symphony orchestras that the country possessed. It aired immense amounts of music for small orchestras and for soloists. It developed a remarkable offering of drama, including morning soap opera – *Laura Limited* and her friends and relations, modelled closely on American prototypes. Some was aimed at particular audiences, the regional family dramas modelled on BBC programming and aimed solely at farm families. But a great deal was meant to be culture and high art, and many remember it with admiration and gratitude. Every Sunday night in Toronto, on CBC *Stage,* Andrew Allan produced a major play. Some were new plays, the words of such Canadian authors as Lister Sinclair and Len Petersen. Some were adaptations, borrowings from the great plays and novels of world literature, past and present. From other centres came similar though less ambitious series. Such programming provided invaluable opportunities for Canadian authors and actors. On Wednesday nights, from 1947 until 1963, the CBC transmitted a full evening of serious music, talks, and drama. Modelled on the BBC Third Programme, CBC Wednesday Night never achieved a mass following, but it did not aspire to one. Its producers were confident that they were doing good and useful work, no matter how small the audience ratings might be. In a sense, such programming was 'broadcasting for the sake of the broadcaster.' But it treated the radio audience with respect. And although American commercial radio then broadcast somewhat more serious matter than American commercial television would later transmit, CBC radio had no competitors, and no parallels, south of the border. At that time, there was no 'public broadcasting' in the United States.

In its more relaxed and less serious moments, the CBC joined with Canadian private broadcasters and American stations in the transmission and diffusion of North American popular culture. In such matters there was some effort at Canadian programming, but it is hard to find much that was distinctive. From Charlottetown every afternoon for fifteen minutes came Don Messer and his Islanders; from the West came Wilf Carter and his cowboy friends and relations.

Here and there, too, one detected the beginnings of a perhaps slightly self-conscious cult of the folk-song. Nevertheless, Canadian popular music prospered in so far as it assimilated itself to American models: in Canada there was a mass audience for the staples of American network programming: *The Hit Parade,* Bob Hope and Francis Langford, Fred Allen, Jack Benny, *Fibber McGee and Molly.* Thanks to the CBC there was Canadian content, and Canadian competition, from such worthies as Juliette, or the Happy Gang, or Wayne and Schuster. On New Year's Eve, as the American networks followed the old year across the continent from New York to San Francisco, the CBC moved, time zone after time zone, from Halifax to Vancouver. On both sides of the border, the big band sound was much the same, but the Americans were better at it; on both sides of the border enthusiasts followed the evolution of jazz, but few Canadians tried to play it.

Like present-day television programming, radio programming was based on the assumption that audiences would actually settle down and pay attention. There were identifiable separate programs, typically lasting fifteen minutes or half an hour. Advertising breaks, where they occurred, intervened every ten or fifteen minutes. Many CBC programs, especially the cultural ones, carried no advertising at all, and many ran for an hour or more.

By 1944 the North American radio and record industries had established the symbiotic relationship that has characterized them ever since. In the 1920s and early 1930s the new phenomenon of radio had almost destroyed the much older recording industry. But in the late thirties record sales gradually revived. The Depression was passing; the quality of the records had dramatically improved; people were beginning to buy recordings they heard on the radio. As RCA Victor explained in its advertising, records gave you 'the music you want, when you want it.'

Although the electronically recorded discs of the forties were spectacularly better than the acoustically processed discs of the twenties, by the standards of the 1980s they were nasty, brutish, and short. Because records revolved at 78 rpm, the standard ten-inch disc played for only three minutes per side, and the standard twelve-inch for five. Records were pressed out of highly breakable wax or slightly less breakable laminates and were played with fibre or steel needles. Reproduction systems were unable to reproduce a wide range of sound, and recording technique was adjusted to this fact. High fidelity, therefore, was unknown, and stereophonic sound was inconceivable. Records, too, were expensive relative to current earnings. In 1945 an RCA Victor Red Seal disc cost $1.35 and yielded only ten minutes of music; lower-quality ten-inch discs might cost as little as 85 cents. Popular music was tailored to the three-minute format that the ten-inch disc imposed and to the sound the discs were capable of reproducing.

By present-day standards the recording companies were few and catalogues were thin. While some discs were pressed in Canada, almost no masters were produced here; the masters came from Britain and the United States. In Canada, Columbia and RCA Victor – both subsidiaries of American record and radio conglomerates – dominated the industry.

As classical albums were heavy, bulky, and extremely expensive relative to earnings, few people could attempt to build a large collection of serious music, and in most parts of the country classical discs were almost unavailable, except on special order. Popular discs, especially dance records, were more widely sold, but even here the range was limited and was dominated by the radio programming of the *Hit Parade* and its imitators. Disc jockeys existed, but their influence was relatively slight, because nationally networked live programming absorbed so much of the broadcast week.

As for the printed media, the war had given them an unexpected fillip. As Canada tightened its exchange controls, Canadians were unable to spend American dollars on the more frivolous American publications – specifically, comic books – and the result was the short-lived flowering of the Canadian comic-book industry. For a few years Adrian Dingle could make a living out of *Johnny Canuck*. The war itself provided the basic scenario: upright and clean-cut Canadian youths confronted the slimy and corrupt 'Fascist beast.' But such efflorescences did not long survive the arrival of peace and the easing of exchange controls.

As for the more serious periodicals, the war provided a new relevance for such newsmagazines as *Maclean's* and *Saturday Night*. The specialized trade publications, as always, did well. So did the women's magazines. The *Canadian Forum* soldiered on, as it had done since 1922, bringing uplift and a vague socialism to its 2,000 subscribers. In Toronto, Kingston, and Halifax the universities produced literary quarterlies that aspired unsuccessfully to interest the literate public. However, *Time* and *Life* had already penetrated deep into the Canadian scene, and *Reader's Digest* was not far behind. Such periodicals were too 'serious' to be excluded under the exchange control.

More durable publishing was modest in quantity and uncertain in quality. In the forties, as for many years previously, the Canadian publishing industry rested on two pedestals. The typical company made most of its living from the distributing of American or British books. Some did well, instead or in addition, by producing school texts. The more earnest firms used the proceeds to subsidize the publication of Canadian material: poetry, fiction, and works of scholarship. Many such firms were owned abroad: Macmillan of Canada and J.M. Dent were British-owned, although both firms published and distributed – often at a loss – many Canadian scholarly books.

Radio mattered, partly because the population was still so dispersed, and partly because even in cities there was so little else. As a French diplomat said of wartime Ottawa, 'Le cinéma! Toujours le cinéma!' But for the Canadians who lived on farms and in small towns, even the cinema was a rare and exotic treat, and the only recreation was likely to be found in the Canadian Legion bar or the Orange Lodge. As for the city-dweller, by present-day standards the fare was remarkably sparse.

The discothèque had not yet been invented. In the larger cities there were a few 'supper clubs,' where cabaret could be seen. But outside Quebec these led a dim and sequestered life because they could not serve alcoholic drinks. They could and would sell 'mixers'; their tables were all equipped with floor-length tablecloths; and when patrons came bearing anonymous brown paper bags, the managements were understanding. Here and there the Canadian Legion clubs offered entertainment of a sordid and derivative kind.

Many cities had theatres, often built for vaudeville and once used by touring players and repertory companies. But in the 1930s most of these buildings had been converted into cinemas, and some were derelict. Not much theatre or vaudeville had survived the onslaught of the talkies; because the war made touring impossible it administered the *coup de grâce,* and live professional theatre did not revive promptly with the coming of peace.

In music the situation was better, but only slightly. Vancouver and Toronto had professional symphony orchestras, and Montreal had a semi-professional one. But Toronto was the only Canadian city to have a proper concert hall. In Vancouver the symphony performed sometimes in a cinema and sometimes in a hockey rink; Les Concerts symphoniques de Montréal used a high school auditorium. Canadian musical audiences were timid in the extreme. In 1946, for example, a rendition of Jan Sibelius's Fourth Symphony by the Toronto Symphony Orchestra was prefaced by a plea from the podium for tolerance for this new and strange work.

Nor were museums and art galleries numerous or impressive. In Ottawa the National Gallery had lived since 1907 in the National Science Museum, where the lighting was bad and the ambiance depressing. In Montreal and Toronto there were substantial galleries, but private donors had provided the buildings and the contents. Toronto had the Royal Ontario Museum, where a distinguished collection had been accumulated. Vancouver had a small municipal art gallery. Other cities had little or nothing.

In big cities and towns the movies were everywhere, and they were available in profusion. Every suburb had its local cinema, where films were shown cheaply within weeks after they had opened in the big downtown palaces. These palaces, in turn, were numerous and immense. Dating from the 1920s or before, some had begun as proper theatres or as vaudeville houses; but many possessing small stages or no stages at all had been built and designed as picture palaces.

In a downtown theatre, a film would often run for several weeks. In the suburbs, the typical run was two or three days, so that in a single week a suburban theatre would show two or three complete programs, each including a main feature film, a supporting full-length production, a newsreel, a cartoon, and sometimes a travelogue or other short subject. Most suburban theatres also had a Saturday 'kiddy matinee' – one or two features, lots of cartoons, and an exciting serial such as *Batman* or *Captain Marvel*.

People went to the movies a great deal, sometimes two or three times a week. Movies were not only exciting and undemanding; they were cheap, too. In Vancouver, in 1947-8, for example, the suburban kiddy matinee cost twelve cents – about the price of two bottles of Coca Cola or two rides on the streetcar. The sociologist may suspect that the age of the movie was based on escapism; the economist is fairly sure that it was based on cheapness. Hence its vulnerability to the competition of television, which *appears* to be even cheaper – indeed, free. By 1948 there was still no television in Canada, but its arrival was foreshadowed.

Regular television broadcasting began in 1936, when the BBC commenced transmission in London. These broadcasts ceased in 1939 when war broke out. By then, the National Broadcasting Company had begun experimental broadcasting near New York. When the United States entered the war in 1941 its transmission ended. In North America, therefore, commercial television began only in 1946, when the US Federal Communications Commission defined and allocated twelve VHF channels.

Television is different from AM radio in that the TV signal does not follow the curvature of the earth. Hence the height of the transmission tower really determines the range of the signal. American radio could penetrate Canada readily; American TV could do so only with difficulty. Montreal could receive Plattsburgh, Toronto could get Buffalo, and Vancouver could receive Bellingham, but only with expensive equipment and tall antennas. By 1948, Canadians were beginning to watch the 'box in the corner' (by 1949, there were at least 3,600 sets in the dominion), but the sets were inconvenient to tune and their pictures were small: the ten-inch picture tube was the standard. They were still extremely expensive, too, so that the TV set was a luxury and a status symbol. So long as TV sets were few there was little economic justification for cable connection, even though all programming came from relatively remote transmitters in the United States. Cable systems came later, when the sets were more common and when the signals were more numerous.

When they went to the movies, Canadians saw British and American films.

The war had cut off the supply of films from continental Europe, but even before 1939 such films were rarely seen. After 1945 the Soviet Union sent one or two art films, which achieved critical acclaim and very limited exposure. Canada's National Film Board laboured worthily, producing a torrent of short subjects, but there was no Canadian feature film industry, and no sign of one.

Most of the cinemas were grouped in a few great chains. The largest, Odeon, was British-owned. Famous Players and Twentieth Century belonged to American interests. The British and American owners, in turn, had close links with the great film studios of Hollywood and London. Some observers have deduced from this that the chains conspired to show foreign films, suppressing Canadian talent and corrupting the Canadian consciousness, but the claim has only dubious plausibility. Naturally each chain tried to release the products of its parent studio, but there were many more studios than chains, and no chain showed only the products of its parent. Moreover, no studio produced enough feature films to satisfy the demand from its own chain. The suburban cinemas, it should be remembered, showed from four to six feature films every week and almost never showed re-runs or revivals. Each chain offered the products of several large American studios – Twentieth Century Fox, Warner Brothers, Universal-International, and the rest. Although British films might appear first in Odeon cinemas, they were shown in other movie houses too. It is reasonable to suppose, therefore, that if there had been a Canadian feature film industry, and if theatre managers had thought its products saleable, the films would have been shown.

In recent years, Canada has developed a feature film industry, just when the feature film, as a form of mass entertainment, is declining. As so often in our history, the timing is wrong. It might well be argued that if the government had provided some subsidies in the 1940s, as seed money, Canada might have developed a film industry at a time when there was a genuine mass market – at a time, that is, when film-making was really part of popular culture. But the government of the day did not see things in that light. It did not subsidize the arts, music, drama, or sport; it subsidized higher education only with extreme reluctance. How could it have been expected to subsidize film-making? Symphony orchestras and operas, at least, were recognized money-losers the world over, but the movies were an enormously remunerative business, not just for the studios but for the distributors. A less plausible field for subsidy would have been hard to imagine.

In the film era, especially during the war and immediately after it, the newsreel had an importance that the TV newscast would later assume. Like feature films, newsreels came from British and American companies. Most of the footage came from abroad, but for Canadian distribution the producers usually added a good deal of 'Canadian content.' The newsreels also gave some attention to sport, both professional and amateur; although the coverage of sport, as of other matters, was far more sketchy than that which TV would later provide. The newsreel was short and was assembled with considerable trouble. Typically it covered all the events of a week in twenty minutes or less. It assembled its raw materials by train, ship, and airplane, but not by satellite or by landline; it distributed its finished product in the same pre-electronic way. It could hardly aim at immediacy, depth, or thoroughness, but at least it gave ordinary people the feeling that they had seen what was going on in the great world.

Vying with the movies for popular attention were the sports arena and the beer parlour. In Canada, sports-madness grew with television, which exposed Canadians to an intensive dose of sport both commonplace and exotic and converted national sports and many foreign sports into nation-wide events. In the era of radio and film, however, such things could not occur. The range of sports, too, was more limited than it has later become; few schools had the facilities for such things as gymnastics or swimming, for example, and skiing was both exotic and expensive. Although some cities provided parks, no one did anything to subsidize the amateur. In each age group, only a small number completed secondary school or attended university, so that participation was limited largely to sandlot baseball and local hockey. Few people persevered in either sport after the end of formal schooling. As for professional sport, the range was less complete and the atmosphere less intense than it became in the 1950s and 1960s. Of course, Torontonians and Montrealers flocked to football and hockey. The National Hockey League comprised six teams, of which two were Canadian; many people could remember the time when there were no American teams at all. But the season for professional football was short and the teams were few. Neither hockey nor football reached the west coast until later.

However, there was a great deal of baseball. In this, as in so many other respects, Canadians showed their identification with the North American culture. Canadian cities fielded teams in various American leagues, not the National or the American, but various second- or third-level gatherings such as the International and Western International leagues. In Canada, as in the United States, baseball stadiums were often rickety and primitive; nevertheless, Canadians found baseball a suitable diversion for the hot Saturday afternoons of midsummer. And if they kept away from Maple Leaf Stadium or Capilano Stadium, they followed the American major-league broadcasts on the Liberty Broadcasting System. Admittedly, Liberty had no outlets in Canada, but its American affiliates were nearby.

To the observer of the 1980s the spectator sports of the 1940s, like the movies, look cheap relative to incomes. Drink, however, was neither cheap nor plentiful. By 1944, everywhere in Canada except in Prince Edward Island, where until 1948 drink was available only on prescription, the days of prohibition were long past. Even so, everywhere the buying of drink was inconvenient, and, except in Quebec, the buyer was made to feel slightly daring. No one could drink, or buy drink, before the age of twenty-one. Through the outlets of the provincial liquor control boards one bought spirits, wine, and, in most provinces, beer. During the war spirits were rationed and watered. After the war rationing ended, but watering has continued to this day. Only in Quebec were there cocktail bars; only there could one get a drink with a meal. Elsewhere there was nothing but the 'licensed premises,' or 'beverage room,' or 'beer parlour.' These remarkable places were always attached to hotels. In them one could buy a glass of beer, and usually nothing else – not even food. Normally an unattached man was not allowed to drink beer in the same room as a woman, attached or not; in some cities it was impossible for a man and a woman to drink beer in the same room at all. About many other things, too, there were regulations. One of the more notorious related to the number of draught glasses that could rest on a table at any one time. Outside Quebec, no one was allowed to sell wine or spirits by the glass, and bottles could be bought only in provincial outlets or, in some provinces, in the wineries' own stores as well. Hence it was impossible to have wine with one's meal, except at home. On Sundays, nothing was sold and nothing was open. No wonder the average Canadian consumed only a few litres of wine in a year. One province even employed a teetotaller to handle its wine buying.

To Americans and Europeans these arrangements were incredible. Canadians, however, were inclined to accept them as inevitable, if not altogether natural. And, as the country was still relatively poor, they did have certain advantages. Simply because drink was so hard to come by, drunkenness must have been less common than it would have been if beer, wine, and spirits had been widely available.

In the 1970s many observers were inclined to be nostalgic about the popular culture of the 1940s. Many things *were* a good deal simpler, often extremely cheap, and often, too, less commercialized than they had since become. But fundamentally things were pretty bleak. Even in 1944 the Toronto Maple Leafs were a money-making proposition. The Vancouver Capilanos were run for profit, not for fun. Commercial radio was as blatantly commercial as commercial television was later to become. In popular music, in cinema, and in all sports but hockey, Americanization was all but complete. The CBC had not yet abandoned the battle for standards and sense, but its impact was probably small, except when it was participating in the diffusion of North American mass culture. In the forties, broadcasting was certainly more imaginative than in the seventies; it aired a great deal of Canadian material, much of it was very good indeed. But of this programming most Canadians knew little and cared less. As for high culture and the arts, Canada had precious little of either.

Among those who lived through the war and its aftermath, 'the sounds of the forties,' and the sights of that depressing decade, can often produce a *frisson* of excitement. But the 'big band sound' could grow monotonous when little else was available. Frank Sinatra was embarrassingly sentimental, while 'Shep Fields and his Rippling Rhythm' was simply embarrassing. Jitterbugging or jiving was fun but formless, while the 'slow fox trots' of the era were soporific – though at a time when sexual continence was still the norm, cheek-to-cheek dancing had an obvious place in the scheme of things. It is as well to remember that, in the last years of the Mackenzie King era, most Canadians were rather poor, extremely busy, and more than a little timid. There was little time and less income to give to frivolities. Also, the young were relatively few. In the late twenties and throughout the thirties Canadian birth rates had been low, while in the thirties immigration had been slight; thus by 1945 there were remarkably few teenagers or young adults. Compared with the late sixties or the seventies, the population was middle-aged. The dominion looked grey partly because so many of its people were greying.

What, then, has changed in the forty years since 1948? First and most important, we are all a great deal better off. We spend casually on things that our parents and grandparents would have thought unattainable luxuries. There are many more of us, too, and the age distribution has changed a great deal. In 1945 there were about eleven million Canadians; in 1988 there were over twenty-six million. In popular and high culture, as in many other things, opportunities expand with the growth of the market. Relative to the total population there are far more adolescents and young adults who, in turn, are far more prosperous than their predecessors. In the eighties, furthermore, there are 'yuppies' – a breed unknown in the forties. Governments are more willing to subsidize and control, and the public is more willing to bear the costs of the former and the irritations of the latter. Relative to incomes some things have become very much cheaper. Television bathes us in 'free' entertainment. Thanks to technical change and progress, records and televisions are no longer the luxuries that they were in the late forties, and the quality of sound-reproduction and transmission has improved dramatically. In 1988 it was simply impossible to find anything as ghastly as the standard five-tube superheterodyne table radio of 1948. But such a radio could cost fifty dollars or more in 1948, at a time when few families made five thousand dollars per year. Travel, too, is now cheaper: air travel and bus transport have perfected themselves, and car travel became steadily cheaper relative to incomes throughout the fifties and sixties. Conversely, many older pleasures, such as streetcar rides and sermons, have become relatively costly, either in money or in time and effort. Popular consumption responds accordingly, and popular culture is transformed.

10

Education

For many years, enrolments in elementary and secondary schools had been growing very slowly or declining in most provinces. In Ontario, between 1934 and 1946 enrolments fell by nearly 30,000, or 4 per cent. In the prairie provinces the declines were more dramatic – 18 per cent in Manitoba, 22 per cent in Saskatchewan, and 9.5 per cent in Alberta. In British Columbia, enrolments rose by 13 per cent in twelve years, and in Newfoundland and the Maritimes by 7.2 per cent; but Quebec enrolments, having risen in the 1930s, then declined by 11.6 per cent from a 1938 peak. These patterns reflected the demographic developments of the late twenties and thirties, when birth rates had been relatively low in most parts of the country. High-school attendance was little more fashionable in 1946 than it had been in 1939. It was no less expensive, whether the measure is sacrificed income or out-of-pocket costs relative to family earnings.

Where enrolments had been rising, as in the Atlantic provinces and British Columbia, expansion had been so slow that the provincial and local authorities could provide extra teachers and facilities with very little extra strain: new buildings were rarely necessary, instructional media were simple and cheap, and teachers could readily be found, although a remote and unattractive area might have to settle for an 'unqualified' person. Where enrolments had been falling, as in Ontario, the decline was so gentle that it posed few problems for the educational authorities. Rather, it provided opportunities: by lowering the pupil-teacher ratio, and by lengthening the period of teacher-training, the authorities could perhaps raise the quality of education. In all provinces such developments can be traced during the years before 1944 or 1946.

Even where enrolments were falling, teachers became more numerous. Everywhere, on average, they became better qualified. In Quebec, for example, in 1930 only 14 per cent of all teachers had any training beyond junior matriculation, the end of high school, and 64 per cent had not completed high school; in

1950 only 23 per cent had not completed high school and 44 per cent had progressed beyond junior matriculation. Although in other provinces teachers had been better qualified than in Quebec, in all provinces there was a movement in the same general direction. In Ontario, in 1930, 63 per cent of teachers had studied for only one year past junior matriculation, and only 10.6 per cent had university degrees; in 1950 the former figure had fallen to 16 and the latter was 17.

In eight of the nine provinces, Canadian schools operated under provincial regimes that generally gave relatively little power to local schools and teachers and relatively great power to provincial education departments. The provincial authorities, not the schools, set the curricula and chose the textbooks. They also arranged for exit examinations – junior matriculation after eleven or twelve years of schooling, and senior matriculation after twelve or thirteen years. In Quebec, where there was no department of education, the Protestant schools operated in the same way as the public schools elsewhere in Canada. That is, they prepared pupils for matriculation examinations which admitted graduates directly into university. Matriculation examinations were set and marked by provincial authorities, not by schools. High-school teaching often centred on these external examinations because teachers were often judged by their success in getting pupils through them.

In some of the western provinces, the matriculation examinations were no longer compulsory by 1946. A promising candidate could be 'recommended' for university entrance on the basis of his or her high-school work. Nevertheless, even in such provinces the provincial examinations remained in existence. They had to be sat by any pupils who had not earned 'recommendation,' and no one could receive a provincial university scholarship without competing in them. Such scholarships were few, and neither the dominion nor the provinces ran any general scheme of student aid.

Each provincial system bred up its own officialdom and produced most of the instructors for its own teacher-training institutions. Teachers of teachers might go away for higher studies, but would generally return to the province of origin. Thus each school system had a career ladder – teacher to principal to inspector to government official, with a branching path into teacher-training. This self-containment helped to make each system rather stable and tradition-minded, and public attitudes tended in the same direction. In 1946, most people appear to have demanded much the same things from the school system as their parents and grandparents had demanded in the 1920s or even before 1914.

These centrally regulated systems made a great deal of sense when teachers were badly schooled and when parents and children were badly informed, or timid, or both. The arrangements had developed at a time when the typical teacher could not have been trusted to devise a program of study, choose textbooks, or maintain standards, and when pupils and parents were ignorant and knew it. The arrangements also rested on an implicit assumption that most pupils would leave school before matriculation. In some provinces, and in some cities, efforts had been made to provide various sorts of secondary school, not only academic, but also vocational, technical, and commercial. These non-academic schools and streams did not lead to matriculation and university entrance; they were meant to give more practical training that would lead directly into work. But such schools could not be established everywhere, and, when obliged to choose, the educational authorities would set up an academic high school – in some provinces, a 'collegiate institute.' Few citizens expected that the typical adolescent would stay in school, any kind of school, until he or she had completed some sort of course. It was expected that the vast majority would leave school as soon as the law allowed. Thus the external apparatus of academic curriculum and external examination was never meant to process more than a small fraction of each age group. It was implicitly assumed, too, that numbers would rise slowly, or not at all. Although elementary schooling was compulsory everywhere by 1945, no one was compelled to complete a secondary education of any sort. Teachers and parents might worry about 'drop-outs' and hope that the more promising adolescents would stay in school, but the authorities, as yet, were not really concerned.

In time, all these circumstances changed. With more education and more self-confidence, teachers became more assertive. With more training and more mobility came more knowledge of other arrangements, systems, and assumptions, especially American ones. Parents and pupils grew less docile and the schools were asked to do more sorts of things: to develop personality, treat neuroses, instruct in the right use of the automobile and the right attitudes toward alcohol and the opposite sex. Schools and politicians now began to share teachers' worries about 'drop-outs,' and their worryings affected curricula. Most important of all, perhaps, was the rising tide of high-school students. In later decades, and especially in the 1960s, these and other pressures transformed both the English- and the French-speaking school systems, but in the forties they were not much in evidence.

Admittedly, numbers were increasing, and compared with the thirties or earlier forties these increases were considerable. But compared with the 1950s they were small. The 'baby boom' of the forties had started to affect enrolments, but the pressure had only begun. From 1945 to 1950 elementary enrolments rose 12 per cent and secondary enrolments 13 per cent; in the next quinquennium the increases were 27 per cent and 29 per cent. In the forties it was possible to go on much as before. One hired more teachers; one worried about their qualifications; one put more pupils into the same school buildings, many of which had been under-used since their construction two or more decades before.

The Catholic schools of Quebec provided almost all of the province's French-language teaching and a very little of its English. They were not at all like Quebec's Protestant system, or like the public-school systems in the other provinces.

In the first place, Quebec's local primary schools were generally staffed by members of religious orders, and normally the parish priest took a special interest in the school and its work. Such staffing could and did occur in other provinces, either in independent Roman Catholic parochial schools or in tax-supported 'separate schools.' But although monks and nuns might staff such schools, and although public-school supporters might fulminate against them, the provincial educational authorities controlled both the separate and also the parochial schools, where enrolments relative to public schools were small. Not so in Quebec.

In the second place, Quebec really had no general integrated system of secondary schooling. The provincial authorities had established various special schools for technical and agricultural training. And there were public 'post-primary' schools that did not lead to university entrances. But for French Catholic pupils with academic aspiration there was only the 'classical college.' There they might remain for one to five years. Having completed the course they would receive the baccalaureate degree and could proceed to university, having got somewhat beyond senior matriculation on the English-Canadian scale. Although aided by government grants, the classical colleges were independent institutions. Almost all of them were owned and staffed by members of religious orders. Their curricula were severely academic, and somewhat more specialized than those of the English-speaking systems. Typically they concentrated on theology, philosophy, and languages; few made any effort to teach science.

Outside Quebec there were some classical colleges. Usually these were based in a French-speaking area, and generally they were affiliated for purposes of credit and transfer to a francophone university, often the University of Ottawa. English-speaking Canadians found the classical colleges puzzling. The more virulent Protestants saw them as yet another agency of Catholic thought-control. Such criticisms were understandable but rather unfair. Admittedly, the colleges taught theology and usually ignored science. Admittedly, too, although they attempted some university-level work they probably did not always attain that level in fact. But in Quebec the public authorities were not yet concerned to suggest an alternative, much less to devise and introduce one. It would be better to praise the monks and nuns whose efforts filled a gap in the state system.

Beyond the secondary schools and the classical colleges Canada had universities and almost nothing else. There were military colleges at Kingston and Victoria. Some provinces had created higher schools in such things as agriculture and forestry that did not grant degrees. Most provinces had teacher-training colleges that took and processed both high-school and university graduates. Here and there, too, one found colleges that were affiliated to some university and that did some university-level teaching. In the Maritimes there were specialized professional colleges that granted degrees. In Ontario and elsewhere there were Bible colleges that did not. Everywhere there were theological colleges, most affiliated to universities. But there were no full-blown community colleges or institutes of technology and only a few junior colleges. As for the universities, because so few Canadians sought university degrees in 1944, they were few and small. They had always been that way, and little had changed for a long, long time.

In 1920 Canada contained 21,869 full-time undergraduates and an insignificant number of postgraduate and professional students. By 1930 the total had risen to 30,209, and by 1944 to 35,132, of which one-quarter were women. Full-time faculty numbered 4,503. Through the twenties and thirties enrolments had grown steadily, but slowly – 61 per cent in twenty-four years, or less than 2 per cent a year on average. Universities, like schools, were thus adjusted to an extremely gradual pattern of growth. Further, the Depression had hurt them severely because provincial grants and private benefactions had fallen together.

The universities of Canada originated in different ways. Some were provincial foundations; others came from the efforts of religious groups – Roman Catholic and Anglican bishops, Protestant churches, various sorts of pious conventicles; a few had been founded by private benefactions on a non-sectarian basis; and many had severed their church ties wholly or in large part. But in Ontario, Quebec, Manitoba, and the Maritime provinces the religious dimension was still very much in evidence, and it was not altogether absent elsewhere. Universities received no federal funds, and provincial governments financed them in various ways. However, some universities received nothing from the government. A few, such as McGill, had large endowments. A few received subventions from churches, and the Roman Catholic colleges and universities gained from their ability to employ a clerical and monastic staff whose pay was small. But many universities depended to a quite remarkable extent on tuition fees, and for all universities this fee revenue was important.

This tranquil scene was transformed when the dominion government announced late in the war that it would send veterans to universities. Tuition fees would be paid; there would be a subsistence allowance; each university would get a federal government grant, the size dependent on the number of veterans who had enrolled. This grant was meant to help the universities hire extra staff, buy books, and provide for other current expenses.

No one expected, or hoped, that there would be time to construct new buildings. Indeed, because the 'veteran bulge' was bound to leave the universities before many years had passed, the new program did little to justify such building. Nor could it justify expansion of the permanent staff. The universities, therefore, were forced into a series of heroic improvisations. Temporary lecturers joined the somewhat frail and elderly permanent staffs, most of whom had been appointed in the 1920s or before. Branch campuses were set up in old army camps. Prefabricated army hutments were moved from camps to campuses, where some are still to be found. Lecturers spoke in theatres, churches, and halls of all sorts. Classes became enormous – or so it seemed at the time.

In the academic year 1945-6, Canadian universities had enrolled 38,776 full-time undergraduates. In 1946-7 the figure was 61,861, and at the peak in 1948, there were 79,346 full-time undergraduates. In three years, enrolments had almost doubled.

Fortunately veterans tended to prefer arts and commerce courses, where equipment was of little importance and where lecturers could to some extent be substituted for the books that the university libraries did not have. There was pressure in science and engineering also, but it was less severe. This was just as well, since the heroic improvisations would have been much less practicable, and much less successful, in laboratory-based subjects.

The university staffs found the veterans stimulating and refreshing. One wonders whether the veterans thought the same of the professors. Most Canadian universities were then rather dim and limited places. For generations the provincial authorities had been pinching pennies, and private benefactions had not made up the deficiency. Of the churches' contributions the less said the better. Libraries, therefore, were often very incomplete, and the array of courses was limited in quantity, while quality was at best variable. Although some professors tried to keep up with current scholarship in the humanities and social sciences there were no funds for research or travel. As university staffs were miserably paid, few professors were able to attend learned gatherings or to finance their own investigations. Many were unable to purchase current learned journals or to follow current developments in other ways. In terms of purchasing power, from 1938 until 1955 the average professorial stipend *fell*, before taxes, even though from 1939 until 1944 the tax burden increased substantially, and even though after 1945 most Canadians became steadily better off. Although there were a few private scholarships for postgraduate study, in the arts and social sciences there were no government scholarships and no loan funds. The aspiring scholar could hope only to capture an American university award or one of the few private grants that might take him to Britain. Canadian governments contributed nothing to any of these grants or awards. As for the results of scholarly investigations, in 1948 there were still no government grants to aid scholarly publication in the arts and social sciences. The dominion contained one anglophone university press, whose operations were subsidized only by the profits of the printing plant with which that press was affiliated.

In medicine and the natural sciences matters were somewhat better. Since 1917 the National Research Council had provided some funds for university research and helped to finance graduate fellowships; it also operated several learned journals. There were similar arrangements for medicine. In agriculture and in some other specialized subjects the dominion and the provinces did something to finance and aid research. But on most Canadian campuses such subjects were not predominant, and on some they were absent entirely.

However dim the universities may have seemed, and however dedicated solely to teaching their staffs may have appeared, some interesting work was under way. University physicists had been deeply involved in the wartime atomic-energy program. After the war this involvement continued. In literature, universities provided the bases from which writers like Birney, Klein, Pratt, and Child produced works of imagination and power. Although in history the dominant tendency was a sort of curricular boredom, here and there scholars were at work, forming and reshaping the several national myths. In economics the eccentric genius of Harold Innis was already attracting attention in Britain and the United States. Here and there, scholars brooded on the significance of the prairie wheat economy, on dominion status, on democracy in the British dominions. However great their physical isolation, and however deep their poverty, Canadian university people felt they belonged to an international community of learning. So far as they could, they contributed to that corpus of knowledge.

In universities, as in schools, the staffs of the forties had formal qualifications that were relatively low and extremely various. Outside the sciences, few professors had doctorates, and many had the sort of British MA that is earned not by formal work but by the effluxion of time. However, typically they took their teaching responsibilities very seriously, and many took a great interest in the later careers of their students. Perhaps they were serious about teaching because they could not hope for recognition as researchers. Perhaps they simply manifested and transmitted a seriousness of purpose that then manifested itself in many aspects of Canadian life. We shall see more of this seriousness in Part III.

PART THREE

The St Laurent Years 1948-57

11

A New Cabinet and Its Foreign Policy

The new Prime Minister, Louis St Laurent, was a late-comer to politics, but no stranger to public life. Sixty-six when he took office in November 1948, he had been a practising politician for not quite seven years. In his cabinet he was dwarfed in seniority by C.D. Howe and James G. (Jimmy) Gardiner, the Ministers of Trade and Commerce and of Agriculture, respectively, and by James MacKinnon, Alberta's representative in the government. MacKinnon, an amiable and respectable lightweight, would soon shuffle out of active politics into the Senate. Howe and Gardiner, however, were the St Laurent government's heavy artillery, as they had been in the King ministry. Fortunately, St Laurent and Howe were fast friends and firm allies, for Howe had no ambition to become leader or prime minister, tasks for which he felt unsuitable and unsuited. Gardiner was a different matter. A former premier of Saskatchewan, Gardiner was raised in the heavily partisan politics of a bygone age. He was a professional politician and proud of it. 'I don't think Mr St Laurent was a politician at all,' Gardiner once commented. 'He was a lawyer's lawyer ... but that isn't politics.'[1]

Many of St Laurent's colleagues, then and later, would have agreed. St Laurent was a good and faithful Liberal, to be sure (his *Who's Who* entries noted the fact long before he entered partisan politics), but he had no experience in political organization and little interest in learning about it. That he left to the more overtly political members of his cabinet, C.D. Howe, the party's chief fundraiser, and Brooke Claxton, its chief electoral strategist. St Laurent's strong points were administrative and personal. Endowed with a clear and quick understanding, St Laurent had an uncanny ability to grasp and epitomize the essence of an argument, an invaluable attribute in a period when cabinet agendas were becoming longer and more complicated, and when the questions placed before

1 Quoted in R. Bothwell and W. Kilbourn, *C.D. Howe: A Biography* (Toronto: McClelland and Stewart, 1979), p. 226.

cabinet were becoming increasingly technical. Although others might shine more brightly in the House of Commons and on the hustings, St Laurent was master of his cabinet and of the civil servants who appeared before it.

The links between cabinet and civil service were strong, and becoming stronger. The Liberals had grown grey in office during their thirteen years in the East Block. Howe and Gardiner had been around longer than the 'permanent' heads of their departments. It was small wonder that the civil servants relied on their ministers for tradition and guidance, or, where they did not, freely exchanged advice on policy for advice on political impact. St Laurent's ministers had their politics – and their administration – well under control. A case in point may be found in the finance department, the citadel of economic power in St Laurent's Ottawa. There the deputy minister, Clifford Clark, still reigned supreme. Journalists specializing in financial or economic questions regarded Clark with unstinting admiration: 'brilliant,' one wrote; 'gentle and civilized to his fingertips,' another recorded, 'perhaps the most lovable of Ottawa's top-flight officials, utterly free of "side" or pomposity and incapable of pettiness.' Equally formidable, however, was the minister: Douglas Abbott. Abbott, a Montreal lawyer, had scant knowledge of economics; but he was a skilled politician, with abundant confidence in his own abilities and common sense. Abbott acted as a valuable brake on his economists' enthusiasms. On one occasion, shortly after the end of the war, Abbott's officials informed the minister that the government should run a large surplus in the next budget to combat inflation. 'You fellows tell me we should have surpluses, in inflationary conditions,' Abbott is said to have replied. That, he told the officials, was out of the question. If he predicted surplus, his backbenchers would expect it to be shared out in the form of tax relief. The thing to do, Abbott explained, was to forecast a small surplus, rather than the large one actually anticipated. Then, when the large surplus occurred, it could be put down to good fortune and good management. And so it was.

For the first six months of the St Laurent government's life it seemed that Abbott's surpluses would make little difference to the Liberals' political fate. They would not, pundits decided, be around much longer. The Conservatives had a bright new leader, George Drew, newly translated from his Ontario fastness. What Drew had done for the Ontario Tories, his supporters reasoned, he could repeat on the national level. He looked like a leader: tall, handsome, authoritative, and experienced; and the leader had an issue – Communists in government. Ottawa was full of them, Drew told a startled House of Commons. The country's first priority should be to fire the Reds and outlaw their party. Secure at home, Canada could then turn to face the enemy abroad. The only trouble, Drew explained, was that the government refused to take the situation as seriously as he did.

It looked like a winning issue. 'Communists in government' was playing to packed political houses south of the border; soon it would become even more popular. When Drew unlimbered his parliamentary big gun in the session of January 1949, he was firing the first salvo of a campaign that might shortly blow the Liberals out of office altogether. St Laurent, caught off guard, was initially hesitant and uncertain. Suddenly, just as his troops were losing heart, he rallied. No, St Laurent affirmed, Canada would not outlaw the Communist party, however repugnant its beliefs might be. There was no real threat and no excuse for such drastic measures. As for the Communists in government, they hardly existed. St Laurent's reasoned reply to Drew's charges probably had less impact than another exchange that occurred at about the same time. When Drew tried to pin the spectre of Karl Marx on the Liberal cabinet, Abbott easily replied that Drew reminded him of Marx, too: 'Groucho, not Karl.'

Drew's charges were dissolved in ridicule. The minor chord of Communism disposed of, the Liberals introduced the main theme of their electoral hymn: prosperity. When Parliament was dissolved on April 30, 1949, the Liberal symphony was in full blast under Brooke Claxton's skilful direction. Drew, thumping the stale Communist issue, was overwhelmed. The Liberals attracted 49 per cent of the popular vote in the June election (not counting Liberals who won their seats by acclamation), and 193 of the 262 seats in the House of Commons. Only in Alberta, where they elected five members, did the Liberals receive less than half the total number of MPs. Louis St Laurent, who had shed his lawyerly shyness to become everybody's favourite 'Uncle Louis,' proved to be an unbeatable electoral asset. Canadians liked him, they liked his cabinet, and they approved of his party. They decidedly did not like George Drew, who earned a meagre forty-one seats, or the CCF, which fell from twenty-eight members in 1945 to thirteen in 1949. The CCF would be in the future a minor electoral sect, distinguished mostly for its earnestness and its parliamentary skills.

For the next eight years Canadian politics followed the line set down in 1949: a powerful government, sustained by an overwhelming majority in the House of Commons, dominated the political world. The proposition that it could not, if it wished, push any legislation it desired through Parliament was unthinkable, even laughable; and since the Liberals consistently led in the public opinion polls there was no prospect of change. At the time of the next election, in 1953, a Toronto philosopher, Marcus Long, explained to a television audience why this should be so: 'I pointed out,' he wrote to a prominent Liberal, 'that change is of no value unless it represents improvement ... I then suggested that there was no point in changing a government that had done so much for Canada, nationally and internationally ... Finally I expressed the opinion that I could not see Mr

Drew and his Conservative Party as an improvement.' Most Canadians agreed. Eighteen years into office, the Liberals won another resounding victory in August 1953: Liberals 172; Conservatives 51; CCF 23; Social Credit 15; others 4.

The cabinet took the electorate's endorsement as a well-deserved compliment. Some of the cabinet's stars began to believe that their term in office was limited only by mortality. Canada had never had a finance minister as smooth and cheerful as Douglas Abbott, a trade minister as capable and commanding as C.D. Howe, or an external affairs minister as charming and plausible as Lester Pearson. St Laurent gave his colleagues their head, subject to his overall supervision. In St Laurent's systematic and orderly government there were few surprises. The circulation of cabinet papers warned ministers of their colleagues' plans and saved tedious exposition. It had another, unexpected effect. The power of the finance minister, already great, was increased. Forewarned, Abbott or his successor, Walter Harris, could come to cabinet and deliver instant opinions on the financial soundness of any ministerial proposal. The system guaranteed that the St Laurent government would pay a great deal of attention to the voice of responsible finance, and it confirmed the already great power of the Department of Finance.

That institution shared some of its authority with other agencies and departments. Clifford Clark, together with the 'cool, detached, objective' Graham Towers, governor of the Bank of Canada, with an assist from Mitchell Sharp at Trade and Commerce, shaped and implemented Canada's fiscal and monetary policies. These men, assisted by a corps of senior officials, were the top rung of what came to be called the Ottawa 'mandarinate.' The civil service mandarinate is a mysterious concept, evoking visions of languid, broad-browed intellectuals formulating government policy in between sips of tea. This picture is naturally overdrawn, but there are some elements of truth in it.

Most of the mandarins were not the scions of Canada's privileged urban élite. Of the government's top officials, the Clerk of the Privy Council, J.W. Pickersgill, was raised in rural Manitoba; Mitchell Sharp, Winnipeg-born, was anything but privileged in background; Clifford Clark, the dean of the mandarinate, hailed from a tiny Ontario hamlet just outside Cornwall. Though predominantly Anglo-Saxon and Protestant, the mandarins were not exclusively so: the prominence in their ranks of John Deutsch (Catholic), Louis Rasminsky (Jewish), or Jules Léger would indicate that government, more than business, furnished a road open to all talents.

The most obvious common characteristic of the higher civil servants was that they were educated far above the average. At a minimum, the senior public servants had earned an undergraduate degree, most frequently at the University of Toronto, Queen's University, the University of British Columbia, or, less frequently, one of the western provincial universities. There were few French Canadians. Of the 201 foreign service officers employed in the Department of External Affairs in December 1949, only 43 were of French origin. And External Affairs fared better than most Ottawa departments in its French-Canadian recruiting.

What was true of External Affairs was generally true of other government departments. They were officered by men (very few women reached senior levels) recruited usually direct from university into the civil service. Even at the highest level, the average age was comparatively low. At the most senior level, only Clifford Clark himself and the president of the National Research Council, C.J. Mackenzie, exceeded sixty in 1949; most of their peers ('the juniors') had not reached even fifty. There was, as a result, surprising stability and continuity in the senior civil service. To a large extent, the history of the central government between 1945 and 1970 is the story of a single and coherent group.

In 1945, it had been expected that the central government's preoccupation would be social security and domestic improvement. Instead, it turned out to be defence. In 1948 Canada was practically disarmed. The defence budget in fiscal 1947-8 touched a post-war low of $240 million; in mid-1948 all the armed services were below authorized strength. Spending on defence had dropped to 12 per cent of the government's total budget, and although some increase was contemplated, it would not be swift in coming. There were other priorities for the moment: winding up reconstruction, expanding national services (the St Lawrence Seaway and the Trans-Canada Highway were in the offing), and, above all, reestablishing Canada's shaky foreign exchange balance. Social services, a gleam in the eye of the health and welfare minister, Paul Martin, were deferred, and defence would have to take its turn.

It was a safe projection, however, that defence spending would be in the offing. In October 1948, shortly before the change of government, External Affairs Minister Lester Pearson placed before his cabinet colleagues the recommendation that Canada join an Atlantic alliance. Such an alliance, Pearson stated, 'would provide the basis for the organization of an overwhelming preponderance of force – military, economic and moral – over the Soviet Union and a sufficient degree of unity to ensure that this preponderance of force may be so used as to guarantee that the free nations will not be defeated one by one.'[2] The security of Europe was vital to Canada's defence, in Pearson's view; and it was vital in other ways as well. A world without a democratic and friendly Europe would throw Canada into the arms of the United States. Reviewing Canada's established policy, Maurice Lamontagne wrote in 1948 that 'the only long-run solu-

2   Cited in James Eayrs, *In Defence of Canada*, IV:97.

tion compatible with our national independence' was to help Europe to reconstruct itself so that it might once more become a viable trading partner for Canada.[3] If a true Canadian national identity were ever to emerge, it had to balance itself on something other than unilateral dependence on the friendly southern neighbour.

In talks in Washington late in 1948, Canadian negotiators tried to define what they meant by an Atlantic alliance. It would be restricted to the democracies of northwestern Europe: Britain, France, Benelux, and Scandinavia. It would exclude dictatorships, and it would not extend to areas outside the North Atlantic sphere. And it should, if possible, be more than a military alliance.

Canada's strictures on membership did not survive intact. Portugal, a functioning dictatorship, was included because of its highly strategic location. Italy, a democracy far from the Atlantic, was included because its omission would have disheartened democratic forces in that country. The Algerian departments of France were included at French insistence. Ireland, a genuine North Atlantic democracy, had to be excluded because it insisted on an immediate settlement of the problem of Northern Ireland (and settlement, in Dublin's eyes, could only mean the inclusion of the North in the South, whether the majority of northerners wanted it or not).

The proposition that the Atlantic pact should be more than a military alliance was vigorously pursued. A North Atlantic treaty, the Canadians proposed, should include 'some general provision which would encourage economic and social collaboration between the members ... The Treaty should be something more than a defence treaty or a defensive military alliance.' It could be an instrument for the pursuit of broad multilateral objectives: trade, economic development and investment, and cultural exchanges. Perhaps, ultimately, it could become the framework for a new transatlantic superstate, in which the overwhelmingly dominant power, the Americans, would be more equal than they were at present. This conception, which later travelled under the name 'Atlanticism,' drew much of its strength from wartime idealism. Its proponents laboured under the strain of knowing that what might just be possible in critical times would be forgotten in more normal ones. The winter of 1948-9 was such a critical time.

Some Americans shared the vision, but many did not. Those who did not were more important. Their leadership was located in Congress, fearful as always of turning over the keys of the American treasure chest to a horde of untrustworthy foreigners, themselves one short step removed from Communism. Congressional complaints perturbed officials in the executive branch, accus-

3 M. Lamontagne, 'Some Political Aspects of Canada's Trade Problem,' in J.D. Gibson, ed., *Canada's Economy in a Changing World* (Toronto: Macmillan, 1948), p. 37.

tomed to the dangerous consequences of ignoring legislative whims. The Secretary of State, Dean Acheson, classified the Canadians' Atlantic dream as a time-wasting delusion. Even the Canadian ambassador in Washington, Hume Wrong, had his doubts. But under pressure from his own government Wrong persevered, and eventually Acheson gave in. The North Atlantic Treaty would have a Canadian clause, Article 2, which promised economic co-operation (and cultural too). It would come to nothing, Acheson predicted, and he was right.

When the North Atlantic Treaty was signed, on April 4, 1949, by Canada, the United States, the United Kingdom, France, Italy, Portugal, Norway, Denmark, The Netherlands, Belgium, and Luxembourg, Canada committed itself to the defence of western Europe against Russian attack. The western Europeans, less plausibly, were pledged to come to the aid of Canada and the United States should those countries be attacked separately; in any case it was assumed that the defence of one would be the defence of all.

But how to organize the defence? That was the concern of the generals, in particular of the Chief of the General Staff, General Charles Foulkes. A competent officer and a canny negotiator, Foulkes had his plans ready before the ink on the treaty was dry. 'It is interesting to note,' he later wrote, 'that the organization of the military aspects of NATO suggested in our proposal of 7 March 1949, is very similar to the present organization.'[4] There would be a supreme military commander, an American, and a series of staff committees, some strategic, some regional in character. Eventually a Standing Group was decided upon, consisting of the principal military powers in the Alliance, the United States, Britain, and France. The other members, including Canada, had a right to be consulted before the Standing Group disposed of their forces or resources.

For the moment, Canadian forces were a notional concept. Canadian resources, however, were not. Article 3 of the treaty provided for mutual aid among the allies on Second World War lines – equipment for the allies to help them, as the treaty put it, to 'maintain and develop their individual and collective capacity to resist armed attack.' In Ottawa it was decided that Canada should contribute in kind, obsolescent British-type equipment now being discarded in favour of up-to-date American lines. In fiscal 1950-1 this Canadian mutual aid amounted to almost $200 million; as stocks were drawn down, and as Canada's balance-of-payments position eased, other types of aid would become possible.

The Americans and the Europeans were anxious for more. Canada, cautiously balancing its budgets, was reluctant to pledge more for the immediate future. Armament and rearmament proposals were calculated to furnish a rational and long-lived re-equipment of the armed forces; those forces would total less than

4   Quoted in Eayrs, *In Defence of Canada*, IV:133.

50,000. That calculation was thrown overboard in the wake of a most unexpected event in June 1950.

On June 25, the army of North Korea invaded South Korea. North Korea was a state on the Soviet model, complete with local dictator, an omnipotent Communist party organization, and an insatiable desire to fulfil its destiny by absorbing the southern half of the divided country. South Korea, established by the Americans under UN auspices, was an overpopulated and impoverished piece of rocky real estate ruled by a less efficient (and therefore more benign) autocrat named Syngman Rhee. In January 1950 the American government had indicated to those who wanted to listen that it considered South Korea outside its strategic perimeter – not, presumably, to be defended at all costs. It is at least possible that this news was taken very seriously in North Korea, and in Moscow, which was handling the equipment of the North's oversized army. Whether with Moscow's collusion or not – the absence of contemporary documentary research in the Soviet Union is an obstacle to those who wish to understand its policies with any certainty, although, as this volume goes to press, there are signs of real progress the North Koreans decided that the time was opportune for an excursion.

Initially, their attack delivered all that could have been hoped. The South Korean army, poorly equipped and badly led, crumbled. American reaction was initially uncertain. Soon, however, that reaction took shape. President Truman and his advisers decided that North Korea's aggression was intolerable and must be stopped. To Truman, it was the 1930s all over again: then, dictators had been permitted to escape with their loot in order to avoid a wide and destructive war. That reasoning had proved fallacious, and it was high time that the proper deductions were drawn from the experience. North Korea had to be stopped; Truman appealed to the United Nations to stop it.

Because the Soviet Union was boycotting the Security Council in order to secure Nationalist China's replacement by Communist China in the international body, the Americans were able to get speedy agreement from the international organization. No other Communist state, besides the Soviet Union, had a veto over UN action; soon, North Korea was branded an aggressor and a UN force was being organized to put it in its place.

Most of the UN force was American. No other country had the army, air force, sea transport, or money that action in a far-off Asian country required. Other nations sending troops and equipment found their contributions integrated into a larger, American command. Although a coalition in form, the UN side in the Korean conflict inevitably leaned heavily in the direction of what the United States desired and expected.

The Canadian government, like the American, was taken by surprise at the outbreak of hostilities in Korea. Parliament was about to adjourn for the summer; the nation's attention was riveted on domestic matters. Even after the American response became clear, the Canadian government temporized; it would send some aid, but no ground forces. It would, naturally, support the United Nations in attempting to end aggression. For July 1950, the principal deployment for Canadian troops was the state funeral of Mackenzie King, who was given a magnificent send-off that must have gratified his hovering spirit.

On the train back to Ottawa from King's burial in Toronto, the cabinet discussed the Korean situation. Newspapers were demanding that Canada contribute something more tangible than a few ships and transport planes, and public opinion was not opposed to firmer action. Action there would have to be, the cabinet decided: on August 7, Prime Minister St Laurent and the Minister of National Defence, Brooke Claxton, went on the radio to announce that Canada would raise a special army brigade to go to Korea, or anywhere else that necessity might dictate. For, as St Laurent warned his listeners, 'No one can guarantee that, through the action we are now taking, the free nations will succeed in preventing a general war.'

What perturbed the cabinet was the possibility that the conflict in Korea was the first stage in a general Communist assault on Western defences. Korea, after all, was at best of marginal importance to Western strength, but if crucial resources were diverted there and bottled up, it would be all the more difficult to respond to a real offensive by the Red Army in Europe. It was obvious that Canada would have to do more than send troops to Korea; through the winter of 1950-1 defence planners, economists, and politicians laboured to decide just how much more was required.

When the planners got through, Canada's armed forces had doubled in size, to 100,000, and the massive sum of $5 billion was earmarked for rearmament, over three years. As Claxton explained to the House of Commons, 'It is the view of this and the other allied governments that the vital centre of our global defence is in Western Europe.' Accordingly, Canada agreed to send a brigade group (some 6,670 strong) and an air division (eleven, later twelve, squadrons of fighter aircraft). A NATO command structure was established, with an American general on top. Canadian troops in Europe, however, would serve not with the Americans but with the British, a sign of Canada's traditional associations, as well as of Claxton's mistrust of the US army.

As Canadian troops set sail for Europe, their fellows in Korea were bogged down in a hopeless, seemingly endless war. There was no longer any possibility of a Communist victory: the North Koreans had been stopped and their army virtually destroyed in the autumn of 1950. The victorious UN troops, spurred on by the Americans, unwisely pressed their advantage too far and were defeated in their turn by a Chinese offensive over the Manchurian border. The US government hesitated to take the war into China; the United Kingdom and Canada begged the American government not to use its nuclear weapons to rescue its hard-pressed ground forces. President Truman had had no serious intention of doing so, and in any case a front was soon stabilized across the waist of the Korean peninsula. There it rested from late 1951 until mid-1953, when a ceasefire was finally declared. When the war ended, on July 27, 1953, 1,577 Canadians were casualties and of these 312 had died.

Much of the last stage of the war was taken up by diplomatic wrangling among the Western allies as to how best to make peace. Pearson, who was also president of the UN General Assembly in 1952-3, played a key role in the discussions. His object was to bring a quick end to the conflict, which he saw as an increasingly unnecessary diversion of attention and resources from the central, European front. He had his doubts on the wisdom of American policy, which he found too belligerent and unyielding. The Americans, in turn, were furious at the ingratitude and obstruction of an ally whose contribution to the Korean War was minuscule. Pearson's relations with some of his American diplomatic counterparts would never be the same again.

Relations with the British were more cordial. The British economy had made a remarkable recovery after the catastrophes of 1940-9, and soon it would be possible to contemplate normal relations with the mother country again. And, after the truncating of the British Empire in 1947 and 1948, when India, Pakistan, Ceylon, Burma, and Israel had become independent, the rest of the colonial empire seemed momentarily contented and healthy. In October 1951, St Laurent and the cabinet were the proud hosts to Princess Elizabeth, the heiress to the throne, and her consort, the Duke of Edinburgh. Canada wallowed in royalist ecstasy as the handsome young couple proceeded from coast to coast. Editors loosed their fashion writers, starving for prey, in the direction of the royal party; the CBC, not to be outdone, tried to make up in purple prose and breathless enthusiasm for Canada's continuing lack of television. When the royal couple went to a football game at the University of British Columbia, the home team was so excited that it posted its first win for many years.

Elizabeth and Philip were received, like previous visiting royalty, by a British peer serving a term as Canadian Governor General. But a change was in the offing. The next Governor General would not be from Britain at all, St Laurent decided; he would be a Canadian. The Prime Minister toyed with the idea of making C.D. Howe Governor General, a selection that would surely have provoked howls of Conservative outrage from Halifax, Westmount, Toronto, and Victoria – and some points in between. Circumstances came to St Laurent's rescue. Howe was unavailable; he liked politics, and power, too much. The next

Governor General, therefore, would be Vincent Massey, Canada's long-serving High Commissioner in London, a man who, in habits and attitudes, was more British than the British themselves. Massey succeeded to his new dignity in February 1952.

Massey's appointment was overshadowed by yet another royal event. George VI died that month, and his daughter succeeded him as Elizabeth II. Her coronation was scheduled for June 1953. That year, the Canadian Parliament was wound up early and a general election postponed so that platoons of politicians and other dignitaries could sail to London – few people, even then, preferred to fly – for the social event of the decade. Among their numbers were a select few who had been allowed to purchase their admission through generous donations to one or another of Canada's impoverished universities – the useful inspiration of a former university lecturer, now the secretary to the cabinet, J.W. Pickersgill.

The festivities surrounding Elizabeth II's coronation reflected more than simple loyalty to the Crown, although there was plenty of that. They represented a hope, almost a faith, on the part of millions of Canadians that Britain had recovered from the war and was now back near the top of the international heap. The Commonwealth Conference that coincided with the coronation showed that Canada was still an important member of a functioning international organization, the most important after Britain itself. The Commonwealth, representing Britain and the 'old dominions,' Canada, Australia, New Zealand, and South Africa, as well as the new members, India, Pakistan, and Ceylon, held out the promise that it would be a genuine bridge between the underdeveloped world and the Western powers.

Canadians prided themselves on the fact that the Commonwealth had made the transition from a 'pure white' body to a multi-racial association, where there could be no risk of centralized control and where the rule would be decentralized co-operation. But that change implied another: old Commonwealth arrangements lost their significance. Defence co-operation, for example, gradually unravelled. It was generally admitted that the Commonwealth could not go to war as a single entity, because its members could hardly be expected to agree on what would be important enough to fight about. This had happened already, when Ireland chose neutrality in the Second World War; it would happen again, in Korea. Indeed, the time would come when Commonwealth members would war against each other.

The Commonwealth's internal contradictions remained on a family basis in the mid-fifties. It was possible to dream that Canada and India had formed a Commonwealth axis; in support of that dream, and in recognition of India's unceasing preaching of peace, Canada furnished the Indians with a nuclear reactor. It was a celebration simultaneously of Canadian technology, of Canadian good intentions, and of Canadian faith in the permanence of India's pacific internationalism.

Some of Canada's good intentions were discharged on the Americans. American politics in the early fifties were a discouraging sight. Prominent politicians fought Communism and won popularity with the weapons of bombast and defamation. The Democrats lost the presidency and control of Congress in the 1952 elections. The new American president, Dwight D. Eisenhower, had been a genuine war leader, uncertain of his directions in domestic politics. The politicians in his Republican party, including his Secretary of State, John Foster Dulles, were only too willing to guide his steps. Dulles, who came from northern New York state, even knew where Canada was, and where it should be. Treating a congressional committee to a *tour d'horizon* of American foreign policy, Dulles started with Canada. 'He takes a few slams at Canada,' one State Department official remembered, '– their inferiority complex, their ambivalent attitude to the U.S. – but points out that it's a very important piece of real estate that should be humored along.'[5] Dulles's testimony had to be sanitized by his horrified aides before it could be released to an unsuspecting public.

Sure of itself and conscious of its rectitude, the Eisenhower administration treated Canada with friendly unconcern. Sometimes the unconcern turned into uncomprehending annoyance, as in disputes over membership in the United Nations or discussions of the West's obligations to Nationalist China's refugee regime on Taiwan. On economic matters Eisenhower did not bring back old-fashioned high-tariff Republicanism, but he did enforce a blind devotion to domestic economic interests to the exclusion of those of America's allies. Giveaways of American surplus wheat gratified American farmers, disrupted world wheat markets, and brought pain to the heart of C.D. Howe, who as minister responsible for selling Canadian wheat abroad now faced horrendous political problems at home.

Surface tranquillity was preserved, however. It was with the British rather than the Americans that obvious trouble first surfaced. The likelihood of a serious difference increased after the replacement of the Labour party by the Conservatives in the 1951 British general election. The returning Conservatives, under the wartime hero Winston Churchill, still tended to believe in the great power status of Great Britain. Churchill's successor, Anthony Eden (who became Prime Minister in 1955), was more conscious than his elder colleague of Britain's precarious economic position and its weakened defence forces, but he hoped through skilful negotiation to make the illusion of power last a little longer. And for a while he did. The most painful pressure on Britain's strained re-

5   Quoted in Leonard Mosley, *Dulles* (New York: Dell, 1979), p. 358.

sources was at the Suez Canal in Egypt, where 70,000 British troops were tied down defending a line of navigable water and its connecting ports and water supplies. It was a terrible drain on the British army, which had problems elsewhere, and on the British Treasury. It seemed sensible to seek a negotiated solution with Egypt, which wanted the canal and was encouraging terrorist attacks to make trouble for the British.

In 1954, while serving as British Foreign Secretary, Eden found what he was looking for – an agreement with the Egyptian leader, Gamal Abd-al Nasser, providing for the withdrawal of British troops but the preservation of the Suez Canal as the property of a private foreign company. In case of war, Nasser promised to let British troops back in to protect the canal. The last of the British garrison left Egypt in June 1956.

Barely a month later, Anglo-Egyptian relations were inflamed anew when the British and American governments announced that they could not agree to furnish Egypt with a loan to build a new dam across the Nile at Aswan. In response, Nasser nationalized the Suez Canal. Eden, now British prime minister, decided that Nasser had been allowed to go too far. If the Egyptian dictator could not be persuaded to disgorge the canal, he would have to be compelled to do so. The effort of returning to Egypt so soon after leaving it was almost beyond Britain's resources, but the French were happy to help, and so were the Israelis. Gradually an allied plan of attack was worked out, and combined forces moved into position.

Canada had no direct role in these events. The Commonwealth prime ministers met in London at the end of June 1956, too early to have anything to say about Egypt or the Suez Canal. When the crisis emerged later in the summer, it was obvious that the Commonwealth could not hope to meet it as a united body. India, bastion of ostentatious neutrality, was consolidating its position as the leader of a third force in world politics, the 'non-aligned nations.' Its partner in this enterprise was none other than Gamal Abd-al Nasser. Clearly India would oppose any move that could result in the humiliation or deposition of its Egyptian friends. The Canadian government required no great perspicacity to see that the future of the Commonwealth was at risk. British intervention in Egypt, Pearson wrote to Norman Robertson, would 'split the Commonwealth.' Worse still, it might fracture Britain's alliance with the United States, which had absolutely no intention of going along with Eden's scheme. It seemed impossible that Eden did not realize what he had to lose, in comparison with the doubtful and expensive gains his troops could secure; nevertheless, he persisted.

Eden's irresponsibility became even more galling when, in October 1956, serious rifts appeared in Russia's eastern European sphere of influence. In Poland, the government was toppled, to be replaced by a more secure (but ostensibly more liberal) nationalist Communist regime. In Hungary, a similar process started, and then began to go farther than the Soviets could tolerate. Hungary actually wanted to throw off Russian control and assert its national independence. Western correspondents, including a CBC team, scented a story and rushed to Budapest. They sent back dramatic reports of the mass rejection of ten years of Communist indoctrination, symbolized best by the free-standing bronze legs that had until recently supported a statue of Stalin. ('He stooped to pick up a stolen wristwatch,' the Hungarians helpfully explained.)

It was infuriating that just as the Soviet Union faced international embarrassment and imperial disruption, the British were fumbling back into their discarded colonial costumes, picking up the imperial elephant gun, and going hunting for an 'emerging nation.' Third World countries were not impressed. Egypt was much closer to them in fact and spirit than Hungary, and it was about Egypt that they proposed to excite themselves. As the British and French landed in Egypt, at the beginning of November, international attention swung away from Hungary – just as the Russians completed their preparations to reinvade their erstwhile satellite. The United Nations demanded immediate action in Egypt to throw the imperialists out. The Americans ostentatiously stood aside. In Ottawa there was consternation and incredulity.

Commonwealth consultation, such as it was, had completely broken down. The British hoped that the Canadians would endorse their action but, fearing that they would not, had not bothered to inform them of its details. Despite this lack of consultation, the Commonwealth connection was still strong at the level of public opinion, where old memories and older sentiments compensated for the lack of substantial common interest. A Gallup Poll showed that 43 per cent of Canadians thought that the Anglo-French invasion was a good idea, while 40 per cent opposed it. St Laurent and Pearson would not be able to count on the support of united public opinion if they openly differed with the British.

Pearson knew that Canada's international standing would suffer if his country associated itself with the British action. He knew, too, that the Anglo-French invasion had little chance of long-term success, regardless of what might be achieved in the short run. Worst of all, permanent Western occupation of the Suez Canal zone could drive wavering non-aligned countries to conclude that the West, not the Soviet Union, threatened their essential interests. Pearson was not alone on the issue; many, even in Britain, agreed that there was no point in the British seizing something that events had shown they neither wanted nor controlled.

Fortunately Pearson had several assets (besides a clear understanding of the circumstances) at his disposal. His own standing was high, both at the United Nations and in Great Britain. So was Canada's, thanks largely to the superior diplomatic skills of Canadian representatives abroad. Pearson therefore put all his considerable negotiating skills to work in the cause of covering an Anglo-French withdrawal from Suez. There should be a United Nations force sent to Suez to keep the peace and incidentally provide a face-saving cover for the withdrawal of British, French, and Israeli troops. After several tense days and sleepless nights, Pearson's emergency diplomacy paid off. The British and French invasion was floundering, economic pressure was mounting, and American displeasure was increasing. The Anglo-French invasion was halted. Shortly thereafter, a United Nations Emergency Force (UNEF) was organized and dispatched to Egypt. It later took up positions along the Egyptian-Israeli border, hoping to separate the two perennial combatants. Canadian troops participated; indeed, for the sake of the St Laurent government's internal prestige it was essential that they should.

Pearson later won the Nobel Peace Prize for his efforts, but many at home failed to applaud his performance. St Laurent, who completely supported his external affairs minister throughout, made matters worse by letting slip a damaging phrase, 'the supermen of Europe,' to describe the British and French. Their day was over, St Laurent told the House of Commons, whether people recognized it or not. Many Canadians refused to. The Conservatives introduced a motion deploring the government's policy; although defeated by the Liberals with CCF support, it evoked ancestral memories inside and outside Parliament – some of them acutely dangerous to the government's political health.

The classic expression of English Canada's folk memories was given by Howard Green in a speech in the House of Commons. Canada, the Conservative MP for Vancouver-Quadra proclaimed, had turned its back on Britain and France. This was no surprise; in fact it was the logical conclusion of the whole external policy of the Liberals, from Mackenzie King on. Now Canada was nothing more than 'a chore boy' for the United States. 'In the last ten years,' Green declaimed, 'this government has been currying favour with the United States. Ever since the Second World War, that has been the policy of the Canadian government.' Many Canadians agreed. The Americans were the wrong people to work with.

That feeling became well-nigh irresistible the next spring when the Canadian ambassador to Egypt, Herbert Norman, jumped to his death. Norman had been accused, not for the first time, of Communist sympathies because of his pre-war communist activities. Although Pearson knew that some of the allegations were true – though Norman denied them – he kept Norman on as a diplomat. It could not be proved that Norman was a Soviet spy, and Pearson refused to punish him for what he must have considered a youthful indiscretion. But security officials are trained to consider risks as well as acts; in their view Norman remained a risk. Pearson's decision to stand by his friend had, therefore, elements of tragedy. Doubtless it contributed to further suspicion that included not only Norman but his minister. At the root of the tragedy was the juxtaposition of security and individual rights, a conundrum that has still not been resolved.

Pearson's statement to the House of Commons on Norman's death signalled a twenty-year low in Canadian-American relations. The statement was far too moderate for many. Americans were everywhere, circling around the world, dominating NATO, humiliating Britain, affronting Canadian intellectuals with their loud Hawaiian shirts and breezy Bermuda shorts. As one Calgary matron exclaimed, there were now so many Americans in Alberta that 'I feel like staying away from the club; there are so many Americans here ... *They're forever trying to make me feel at home in my own club!'* [6] Once an American, always an American, a Conservative MP reminded the House of Commons in the summer of 1956. He was referring to the Minister of Trade and Commerce, C.D. Howe, an American by birth. The listener was left to infer that Howe's American origins had determined his choice of an American-financed consortium to build the new Trans-Canada Pipeline. The fact that the pipeline would run entirely in Canada and prevent Canada from becoming dependent on American gas supply was not stressed. The Americans were everywhere!

And if the Americans were not, their dupes were. When Pearson spoke in Florida, the Conservative Toronto *Telegram* interpreted his words for its readers. Pearson's speech was 'a public renunciation of Canadian sovereignty' that ranged Canada 'among the banana republics, a satellite state proclaimed by Pearson.' [7]

But while the Canadian élite knew what it didn't like, it could hardly agree on what it wanted. American investment, American culture, and American alliances were condemned by some intellectuals, and even a few politicians. Yet the alternatives were most unclear: the fuzzy Commonwealth, even less significant or united since the Suez fiasco, the forlorn hope of a closer relationship with Europe, perhaps a retreat into a monarchist bastion in the northern half of North America. *Freedom Wears a Crown* was the title of a book widely read and discussed in Conservative and intellectual circles in the fifties. But while freedom and royalty were hobnobbing in the common rooms of Canadian universities, ordinary Canadians were watching *I Love Lucy* from the United States. Would freedom survive the removal of the United States's protecting armed umbrella? Most Canadians thought not.

A later commentator observed that Canada's foreign and defence policies

6 Quoted in Joseph Barber, *Good Fences Make Good Neighbors* (Toronto: McClelland & Stewart, 1958), p. 67.
7 Judith Robinson, *This Is on the House* (Toronto: McClelland and Stewart, 1957), pp. 59-61.

enjoyed unusual support – 'consensus' – in the decade from 1948 to 1957. That support was remarkably uniform geographically and racially, both coast to coast and among French and English. From the CCF on the left to the Social Credit on the right, the political parties agreed that NATO was a good thing, and Communism a bad thing, that a close association with Europe was desirable, and that the Commonwealth embodied a glorious past. It could not be denied that Canada's international standing was high, and would remain high until war-devastated Europe recovered completely. There were differences over techniques, but none over objectives. It was not until 1956, when the controversy about American leadership and American investment merged into the pipeline debate and then into recriminations over Suez, that public support for Canada's foreign policy came unstuck. Foreign policy, from being a winning issue for the Liberals, was fast becoming a losing one.

12

Liberal Centralization

External relations are only a part of the diplomatic life of a Canadian government. Canada, as a country, is fully equipped with a collection of jealous provincial jurisdictions: four in 1867, nine in 1905, and ten in 1949.

The tenth was the island of Newfoundland, Britain's oldest colony, which had stood out against the Confederation tide in 1867 and ever since had viewed the possibility of union with Canada with the deepest suspicion. Newfoundland's fish- and forest-based economy had collapsed completely during the depression of the 1930s, so completely that its government had to be bailed out by the British, who underwrote most of the colony's budget in return for suspension of the island's responsible government. The truce on political activity lasted through the Second World War, as Newfoundland's economy gradually righted itself under the stimulus of high prices and demand. Newfoundland was the gateway to North America and a strategic link on the air and sea routes connecting Canada and the United States to Great Britain; to defend the island, the Canadian and American governments poured in thousands of troops whose spending power also helped to restore the local economy. The Canadian government made sure that a Canadian officer was the senior commander on Newfoundland.

Canada's plans for Newfoundland were indefinite. Clearly the dominion did not want to see its large eastern neighbour pass under the control of the United States. But it was not sure that it wanted Newfoundland to become part of Canada either. That had been tried three times before, in the 1860s, in the 1890s, and in the 1910s, and each time the proposition was wrecked on the shoals of Newfoundland particularism and demands for money, which provoked a reciprocal Canadian meanness. It could happen again. Generations of Newfoundlanders had proudly sung, 'Draw near at your peril, Canadian wolf.' Some Canadians did not see things quite that way; Canada was in their eyes a sheep in wolf's clothing; union would entail shearing the sheep.

The initiative for union came not from Canada, but from Newfoundland. It came from one man, Joseph R. ('Joey') Smallwood, a frustrated ex-politician and failed pig farmer who had honed his remarkable oratorical talents as a radio announcer during the war. Smallwood was a born orator, a master of vivid, earthy imagery, and he proved to be no mean political strategist. When a convention was called in St John's to consider the colony's future government, Smallwood became a delegate. The convention's proceedings were broadcast, and Smallwood took advantage of his familiarity with the medium to drum into his listeners' ears his own preferred solution: confederation with Canada. Most of the convention was hostile to the idea, but Smallwood knew that it was not his real audience. That audience was sitting every night in the parlours and kitchens of Newfoundland waiting for the latest news from St John's.

Smallwood contrived to have a delegation sent to Ottawa to explore terms of union with the Canadian government. With the help of Mackenzie King's secretary, J.W. Pickersgill, a cabinet committee drafted proposals. These were a combination of Canadian social security and special financial compensation for the loss of Newfoundland's existing tariff revenues. In addition, Canada would pick up most of Newfoundland's debt, and Labrador, the subject of covetous glances from Quebec, would remain an indisputable part of the new province.

Initially, these proposals were badly received in Newfoundland. Two plebiscites were held to test public opinion. In the first, confederation with Canada ran second (41.13 per cent) among three possible options. Because there was no clear majority, a run-off was held, and on July 22, 1948, the cause of confederation prevailed, 78,323 to 71,334. Starting from virtually nothing, Smallwood had created a winning coalition that had reversed Newfoundland's history, overturned its traditional political leadership, and reoriented the province's economy to the west and away from the Atlantic.

At the time it seemed that Newfoundland had hardly any choice. The province's historic export industries – fish, timber, pulp and paper, and iron ore – were often precarious. It was the decline in world market prices for fish and forest products that had undermined Newfoundland's autonomy in the 1930s. Even with the return of prosperity Newfoundland could not afford a Canadian level of government expenditures, and the British, beset with their own economic troubles, were unwilling to foot the bills of a distant, dollar-consuming economy. Confederation indeed performed what it promised: there were family allowance cheques, pensions, unemployment insurance, and federal grants-in-aid for various provincial projects, including, until 1988, the province's infamous, rickety, narrow-gauge railway. With the help of federal subsidies, Smallwood dragged the province out of the isolation of centuries. It became a commonplace, in the 1950s and 1960s, as Smallwood's roads reached previously roadless fishing villages, for the inhabitants to take to those same roads, heading for St John's or points west, away from the way of life of their ancestors.

Everyone was affected. Some of the province's traditional élite, beaten at their own game of politics, adapted to the times. One of the leaders of the anti-confederation movement was pensioned off with the federal position of director of civil defence for Newfoundland; another, Don Jamieson, joined the national Liberal party and eventually became Canada's Minister of External Affairs. Not everything worked well, however. Ottawa's fisheries' policy was unsatisfactory: help for the fishing industry came too late to help it modernize or to preserve its fishing grounds and markets abroad. But it was difficult to see what fundamental changes in Canadian policy would have kept Newfoundland's economy in its traditional orbit. In any case, it was not enough to sustain all the Newfoundland-ers that a high birth rate (consistently the highest in the country) turned out. In 1971, out of 594,000 persons born in Newfoundland and still residing in Cana-da, no less than 98,000 had moved outside the province.[1]

Newfoundland's entry into Canada on March 31, 1949, was generally wel-comed. The St Laurent government easily secured approval from Parliament for the financial terms and brushed aside protests from the provincially minded Conservatives (their leader was, after all, a very recent provincial premier) that the other provinces should be consulted and allowed to give their consent. The same point was repeated, more strongly, by Quebec's Premier Maurice Duples-sis, who had claims of his own – the ownership of most of Labrador – to enter against the new province. But St Laurent refuted their arguments. The Ottawa government represented all of Canada, and it had no reason to go running to the provinces for ratification of a national act. It was in the national interest that Newfoundland be admitted to Canada, and the national government would not shirk its responsibilities.

St Laurent's government was among the most nationally minded that Canada had ever seen. Its national direction reflected Ottawa's strong position *vis-à-vis* the provinces. In 1948, Ottawa spent $1.767 billion – compared with the $810 million spent by all the provinces taken together and the $715 million spent by Canada's municipalities – over 50 per cent of all government expenditures in Canada. By 1952, with the Korean War and rearmament in full swing, the differ-ence was even greater: $4 billion as against a combined provincial and munici-pal total of $2.3 billion. Of the federal total, defence and mutual aid accounted for $1.9 billion – almost half.

Few questioned the necessity of heavy defence spending in the face of a pow-erful Red Army in Europe and war in Asia. Such heavy national spending

---

1   It should be pointed out, in fairness, that Saskatchewan had the largest out-migration: in 1971 some 371,000 Saskatchewanians lived outside their native province, inside Canada.

seemed the natural order of things, although as recently as 1939 spending by the provinces alone had far surpassed that of the central government.

St Laurent, with his confident belief in Ottawa's ability to act, and in its right to act, was hardly the man to dismantle the national government's administrative apparatus. As far as he could, he strengthened it. In 1949-50 he turned his attention to the question of the Canadian constitution. The British North America (BNA) Act, Canada's fundamental constitutional document, still required to be amended in Britain. True, the British freely amended the act on request, but it was embarrassing and inconsistent with Canada's national stature to have to beg favours from another country, however friendly and closely related, in order to have the country's internal affairs set to rights. St Laurent's solution was simple. For matters that lay inside the national sphere, as defined by the BNA Act, the federal government would act alone: Canada's Parliament would in future handle its own amendments. Where it was a question of provincial jurisdiction, the additional consent of all the provinces would be required. At the last moment, however, St Laurent drew back. On the advice of J.W. Pickersgill, who had been passed on by King to his successor, he decided to let sleeping dogs lie; only the federal government's power to amend its part of the constitution was enacted. It was a missed opportunity. St Laurent had the power and the prestige to override opposition both in Ottawa and in the provinces. Most Canadians were probably in favour, even though they might not have assigned constitutional amendment a very high place on their list of governmental priorities. But once abandoned, the idea of patriating Canada's constitution was dormant for a decade. When it was revived, ten years later, the circumstances were very different.

Canada's bifurcated constitution was still a manageable and generally comfortable framework for government. Duplessis periodically ranted about the waste of Quebec dollars on aid to unbelievers and Communists abroad ('Duplessis donne à sa province, St-Laurent donne aux autres,' read one slogan), but for the moment he undertook no serious moves to challenge federal dominance. Between St Laurent and Leslie Frost, George Drew's successor as premier of Ontario, there was positive warmth. Frost did not care much for Drew, his methods, or his policies. A warm, practical, and friendly man, Frost had no ambition to promote Ontario's local concerns into full-dress constitutional battles. Instead, Frost let the federal Liberals know that he, for one, was willing to live and let live politically. If that meant abandoning George Drew and his federal party, Frost could live with that. Frost kept Ontario's taxes down and its expenditures low, and he ended the tax feud with Ottawa. In 1952 Ontario officially entered Ottawa's tax rental scheme. Henceforth only Quebec remained outside the single, national, income tax system.

Quebec levied no income tax, so that Quebec taxpayers were not penalized for remaining outside the tax rental system. Duplessis made it clear that this was a matter of convenience, not of principle. In his reading of the constitution, the provinces had priority in direct taxation, including income tax, and by occupying the field the federal government was usurping provincial prerogatives. When, in 1954, Duplessis did impose a Quebec income tax, to be collected separately by the provincial government, he embodied his constitutional argument in the preamble to the legislation.

Although St Laurent remained a strong Canadian nationalist, he was no longer sure that the voters of Quebec would share his view that all provinces should enter Ottawa's existing tax rental agreement, or, as he put it, that 'Quebec can be a province like any other.' He preferred to manoeuvre to avoid a head-on collision over taxation. Duplessis remained obdurate, refusing to grasp any of the olive branches tendered by Ottawa in the spring and summer of 1954. Annoyed, St Laurent put aside his misgivings and told his audience: 'In certain parts of the province of Quebec, the idea that there should be a Canadian nation, united and strong, holding an important place in the family of nations, does not please everybody.' St Laurent repeated his assertion in an even stronger speech before the Reform Club in Quebec City on September 18. He stressed his belief that Ottawa's policies did not constitute centralization, as his opponent claimed, but added that his government also believed that the provinces were not more important, singly or collectively, than the whole country. St Laurent again offered a compromise, if Duplessis would take it.

Duplessis, sensing that he now had a lively and possibly advantageous political issue, sent off a counter-blast instead. At the same time, he asked St Laurent for a personal meeting, which took place in Montreal's elegant Windsor Hotel early in October. At the meeting, Duplessis made some concessions. His provincial income tax act would be amended to remove his claim to provincial priority in direct taxation. He assured St Laurent that Quebec's income tax would not amount to more than 10 per cent of its federal counterpart. In return, once Duplessis's figures were in, St Laurent agreed to amend the federal income tax act to allow inhabitants of a province outside the tax rental system (i.e., Quebec) to reduce their federal tax by 10 per cent.

This defused the confrontation. The two contending governments had chosen the path of co-operation and had found a workable solution. But there were some disquieting elements, nevertheless, in St Laurent's ready agreement with Duplessis. There was no disguising the fact that Duplessis had secured terms that made Quebec, in fact if not in law, a province different from the others. He claimed that this was because of Quebec's special need to safeguard its language and particular institutions. St Laurent, of course, admitted no such thing, but his dry defence of equity and reasonableness had less impact than Duplessis' intonations on the theme of provincial sovereignty and Quebec's special situation. Some of St Laurent's followers in Quebec believed that he should have pursued his fight with Duplessis to the end. By pitting his own considerable prestige against that of the Quebec premier, the federal champion must prevail. By pandering to Duplessis, St Laurent was bowing before precisely those nationalist elements he had so caustically denounced in September. In a serious political confrontation, Ottawa had shied away from defending its predominance as the national government over the demands and interests of a provincial government. This did not augur particularly well.

The breach in the tax rental agreements opened by Quebec's decision to impose its own income tax system raised the possibility that other provinces, for their own reasons, would do the same. If that happened, the federal grants to the poorer provinces under the tax rental system would be jeopardized. In any case, some of the provinces were complaining that their burdens were growing and that the tax rental payments designed to meet their needs were simply inadequate. The national government had already promised to help with provincial social assistance to the long-term unemployed; now it was forced to contemplate further measures to supplement and stabilize the revenues of the 'have-not' provinces. The brainchild of John Deutsch, a lively and imaginative economist serving in the finance department, the new proposals were summed up under the title 'equalization.' What equalization meant was comparatively simple. In the first place, the old tax rental system would be abandoned. In its place there would be a system of tax points, equivalent to a percentage system. A province would be allowed to collect 10 per cent of the federal personal income tax, 10 per cent of the taxable income of corporations, and 50 per cent of federal succession duties. Then an average would be taken of the amounts that could be collected by the two wealthiest provinces, Ontario and British Columbia, and grants to the remaining provinces would be 'equalized' or brought up to that standard.

With the substantial advantages promised by the equalization grants, it was unlikely that the 'have-not' provinces, even Quebec, would stand out against them; and they did not. When the last tax rental agreement expired, on March 31, 1957, the new arrangement came into effect. It was not, it is true, without its detractors, principally Premier Frost of Ontario, who wanted the federal government to raise its basic tax rate so that Ontario could garner more from its 10 per cent of federal corporate and personal income taxes. St Laurent, facing a federal election within the year and mindful of larger fiscal considerations, refused, arguing that the tax level was already high enough. Frost would have to seek his extra revenue elsewhere – if not from his taxpayers, then from his political friends in Ottawa, the Conservatives.

The end of tax rental has been severely criticized as a sellout of federal power and the beginning of an auction of federal tax points for momentary political advantage to the government of the day. Worse, it has been portrayed as a political ransom to buy off the insatiable provinces for a year or two at a time. But in context it looks very different. Its proponents arguably took a more realistic view of taxation and expenditures than did their opponents. The absolute federal dominance of Canada's finances that characterized the post-war period was an exceptional phenomenon. It existed because of a war emergency that began almost twenty years before. It was sustained because of the critical problems – economic, military, and political – that Canada faced in its dealings with the outside world. Under these circumstances, it would have been difficult for any province to decry the federal government's large budgets and its strategy of economic management. But, as the years passed, it was becoming easier to discover provincial priorities that were either distorted or suppressed by the dominant position of Ottawa in the country's tax fields. The provinces saw the lush green grass of revenue and yearned to graze in the federal field; like any good political husbandman, St Laurent opened the gate before the beasts kicked down the fence. Equalization, for some, was a bonus – a sort of extra feeding.

13

Roads and Resources

The St Laurent years were a time of high employment, a high birth rate, and high immigration. From an estimated 12,823,000 in 1948, the population grew to an estimated 16,610,000 in 1957. Some of the increase derived from more than 1.5 million immigrants; the rest from more than 4.1 million births. Few Canadians left; of those who did, most went to the United States. These tended to come from the better-educated technical and professional classes. There were 46,000 emigrants from Canada to the United States in 1957; of these, some 32,000 were Canadian-born.

But there were plenty of Canadians to go around. The birth rate soared, hovering above twenty-seven per thousand for the whole nine-year period. Within Canada, the largest number of births was in the province of Quebec, some of whose publicists hoped by this means to overcome English Canada's numerical advantage, founded as it was merely on immigration and a lower (though not much lower) birth rate. The census of 1941, taken after a decade of minimal immigration, had pointed in the right direction, but the hopes aroused were doomed to disappointment in the 1951 census. The flow of immigration after the Second World War landed hundreds of thousands whose sole desire was to adapt as quickly as possible to English-speaking society, whether by residence in an English-speaking province or within the English minority inside Quebec. The census of 1951 also disclosed another trend: Canadians migrating within Canada were congregating in just two provinces, Ontario and British Columbia. Between 1941 and 1951 every other province lost some of its natural increase from the trickle of 5,000 departing Prince Edward Island to the 150,000 leaving Saskatchewan.

Moving from Saskatchewan meant, in most cases, leaving the farm. Canada's rural blood was perceptibly thinning, in proportionate if not absolute terms. While, in 1941, 4.9 million Canadians lived in rural areas and 6.5 million in ur-

Bell, 1948

Sask. Leader Post

'Doesn't seem to scare them any more …'
Premier T.C. Douglas of Saskatchewan discussing his campaign strategy (Bell, 1948).
Reproduced with the permission of Charles E. Bell

ban centres, by 1956 urban dwellers totalled 10.7 million, and rural inhabitants 5.3 million (of whom only 2.6 million actually lived on farms). The cities offered manifold advantages. To begin with, there were modern conveniences such as electricity, no small matter as late as 1951 when 44 per cent of all homes in Saskatchewan were heated by gas or kerosene. Even where electricity lines reached, it is difficult to know what appliances existed. In 1951, of 3,409,295 Canadian homes (or 'dwelling units' as the census put it: a dwelling unit, to adapt a phrase of the time, need not be a home), 1,485,055 relied on wood stoves for cooking, and 1,136,585 had no refrigerators whatsoever, not even the time-honoured icebox still employed in over 621,000 others.

The absence of modern appliances was not an exclusively rural or farm phenomenon, but the quality of rural life as a whole suffered by comparison with its urban cousin. To take another revealing statistic, in 1951 some 885,690 'occupied dwellings' in Canada had neither hot nor cold running water (583,835 had only cold): of these, 758,950 were rural. Similarly, 998,660 dwellings had 'other' than a flush or chemical toilet, and of these 845,810 were in rural areas. There was, it was true, much evidence of progress, as the statisticians pointed out. In 1941 only 61 per cent of Canadian homes had running water; in 1951, 75 per cent; and by 1961, 89 per cent. It was hard not to see 'Canada's century' – the boom of the industrial age and the improvements that it brought in its train – as an urban phenomenon. In the 1950s many thousands, indeed several millions, of Canadians still lived in many respects as their ancestors had: not surprisingly, they did not want to live that way any more.

The number of Canadian farms steadily declined during this period. Between 1951 and 1961 the number of farms sank from 623,000 to 570,000. Perhaps as a consequence, the normal trend to home ownership among Canadians in general was not as pronounced between 1951 and 1961 as it had been between 1941 and 1951. Yet in all provinces except Quebec the majority of homes were owner-occupied. Many were brand-new: almost a million new dwellings were constructed between 1948 and 1957. Most were single-family dwellings: Canadians liked the feeling of space and independence that owning their houses gave them.

As a result, Canadian cities sprawled, overflowing their pre-Second World War municipal boundaries and invading the surrounding rural townships. The townships were hard-put to keep abreast of the invasion, even where their own hunger for revenue had encouraged it. One early consequence was the development of metropolitan government. Toronto's population grew from 667,500 in 1941 to a scant 675,800 in 1951, while its suburban satellites positively blossomed in the same period from 242,500 to 441,700. By 1961 they would grow further, to 946,000, and thereby outnumber the city itself. The suburban municipalities proved unable to handle the strain separately. Chaos in sewage facilities, road building and maintenance, and water-supply finally forced the province to intervene. As a result, in 1953, Metropolitan Toronto was established, a federation of the city and twelve suburbs (later reduced to the city and five boroughs), enjoying centralized services for important regional matters (such as water-supply) while preserving local autonomy on other matters.

The drift to the suburbs helped to accentuate another development: the growing use of the automobile. Between 1941 and 1951 automobile ownership increased only marginally: 36.7 per cent of Canadian households reported owning one in 1941 as compared to 43 per cent in 1951. But by 1961 the automobile boom was on in earnest: 68.4 per cent of Canadian homes boasted at least one car, although ownership varied from a low of 37.8 per cent in Newfoundland to a high of 76 per cent in Ontario. Cars soon came to occupy a central place in Canadian life: the convenience absolutely essential to recreation, travel – and commuting. So central, so obvious, had automobile traffic become that when a social historian analysed recent trends in Canadian life in the late 1950s he could find none so representative as 'the god CAR.' CARS, according to A.R.M. Lower, 'invaded every urban open space and threatened to destroy every blade of urban grass. They knocked down houses. They called imperiously for straight, wide roads to be carved out of our diminishing fertile fields.' They were also, as Lower could not fail to note, ostentatious and vulgar to a degree.[1]

But they were inescapably, ineluctably popular, as more and more Canadians took up the challenge to 'tour the broad highway in a Chev-ro-let' or selected the Chrysler Corporation's hideous fin-tailed 'forward look'; vast chrome-encrusted vehicles belched their way over the landscape or more often than not treated their owners to traffic jams on overcrowded highways and arterial roads. And so the several provincial governments girded themselves for a renewed highway-building program. They had a long way to go. In 1949, Canada boasted some 10,000 miles of paved roads and 540,000 miles of unpaved roads (improved or unimproved). The total cost of improving and maintaining such a highway system was vast, and it fell almost entirely on the budgets of the provinces (and, to a much lesser extent, on those of their subordinate municipalities). It was, therefore, something of a godsend when, in 1948, the central government decided to contribute some $150 million to the construction of the Trans-Canada Highway according to an agreed national standard. If the provinces agreed to co-operate in such a project, the federal government would meet 50 per cent of the construction costs, and indeed 50 per cent of the cost since 1928 of any existing part of the route that the provinces chose to donate. The St Laurent government optimistically set the date for completion as 1956. It took nine years

---

1   A.R.M. Lower, *Canadians in the Making* (Toronto: Longmans, 1958), p. 424.

longer. When the final segment of the Trans-Canada Highway was officially opened in November 1965, it had cost $924 million, of which the federal government had contributed $587 million. All the provinces eventually joined in the program, even Quebec, which held out until the early 1960s and joined in only when it discovered that the fiscal lures were great enough to overcome the most rigid constitutional scruples.

A joint project of a different kind was the St Lawrence Seaway, a deep-water system to link the Great Lakes with tide-water. Long the subject of negotiations between Canada and the United States, the Seaway was finally given top priority by the St Laurent government in 1951. Unless the United States stopped dragging its feet in this matter, the government announced, Canada would proceed by itself in digging the deep-water ditch; ancillary power benefits would be shared by Ontario and New York State, which was only too happy to co-operate. Even the province of Quebec, loud and fierce in its opposition in the 1930s, agreed to stay mum. Canada's case was reinforced from the American side by the report of a presidential commission on raw materials, which urged that it was in the American national interest to proceed as soon as possible to bring Labrador iron ore to the steel furnaces of the Midwest. With the lukewarm support of American President Eisenhower, the pro-Seaway forces finally prevailed in Congress, and a treaty was signed in 1954 providing for joint construction and ownership of the Seaway works.

This news was greeted with relief in Ottawa, where the Minister of Trade and Commerce, C.D. Howe, was looking about for a 'big project' to fuel the Canadian economy. As for the stricter meaning of fuel, the Seaway's hydro development would come in handy as well, because southern Canada, especially Ontario, was running out of sites for large hydroelectric plants. The St Lawrence would be the last; thereafter southern Ontario would have to rely on steam generators, burning coal or oil, for new electricity – or possibly using a newer energy source, uranium.

Canadian uranium development went back to the beginnings of the atomic age, to the development of the atomic bomb during the Second World War. At that time, Canada's allies, Britain and the United States, had approached Mackenzie King with two requests: first, that the Canadian government secure control of an obscure and inactive uranium and radium mine on the shores of Great Bear Lake in the Northwest Territories and, second, that the Canadian government welcome to its shores a British atomic research team. The mine was a relatively simple proposition. Eldorado Mining and Refining Limited became a Crown corporation, and eventually the exclusive agent for uranium sales within Canada, sending its product south to the American nuclear laboratories to be fashioned into atomic weaponry. Uranium sales began modestly, only

$4,050,000 in 1948, but as American demand expanded the Canadian and American governments jointly raised the incentives they were prepared to offer for uranium development. A uranium boom followed, first in northern Saskatchewan and then in northern Ontario. At one time, uranium contracts with the United States totalled over $1.5 billion, and annual deliveries reached the very large sum of $331 million in 1959.

The other side of atomic development was equally intriguing, though less immediately profitable. During the war Canada had co-operated closely with British atomic scientists, thereby acquiring basic information and technology that made the dominion, in 1945, one of the three 'atomic powers.' Canadian atomic research was centred at a new laboratory and reactor complex up the Ottawa River at Chalk River, Ontario. The potential use of atomic energy for electrical generation had always been regarded as possible, but by the 1950s it was on the threshold of economic feasibility. Putting together a consortium of Canadian utilities with his own Atomic Energy of Canada Limited, C.D. Howe instructed his officials to begin active development of atomic power. By 1955, Atomic Energy of Canada Limited was ready to start work on a prototype commercial reactor, later known as the CANDU (Canadian Deuterium-Uranium).

Although the government now knew that atomic power was feasible, it was obvious that large-scale nuclear power plants were little more than a gleam in an engineer's eye. More fuel would be needed before atomic energy became widespread, and the most obvious source was natural gas, found in large quantities in Alberta. It seemed to make sense to bring Alberta's gas straight to the major Canadian market – southern Ontario – and C.D. Howe began in the early 1950s to encourage gas promoters to think in terms of a trans-Canada pipeline, running exclusively in Canada. Rival groupings soon formed, some to compete for the pipeline on Howe's terms, others to argue that to be economically viable such a pipeline would have to pass through the United States. Still others argued that it made more sense to pipe Alberta gas directly south and west, to the United States, and to supply Ontario with American gas from the south and southwest. Though Howe solved most of the organizational problems of the projected gas line by merging two rival groups (one of them American) into a single company, Trans-Canada Pipelines Limited, he was unable to solve its difficult financial problems. As a result the Liberal government confronted the thorny problem of furnishing the company with emergency financial aid to allow it to buy pipe and start construction. But only Parliament could provide the money.

What had seemed to Howe and his cabinet colleagues a straightforward economic proposition was for the opposition in Parliament the opportunity of a political lifetime. By filibustering the pipeline bill it would force the powerful Liberals either to back down and hand the pipeline over to a purely Canadian company (which meant for the CCF a national Crown corporation, for the Conservatives a private company with different principals) or to push the bill through Parliament using closure, the parliamentary device that limits debate and forces a vote on issues before the House of Commons. As a royal commission later observed, the government had few alternatives. If Howe wanted the pipeline built he had to choose closure. The pipeline company needed its money in early June. By the time the government nerved itself to apply the device, in mid-May 1956, it had only sixteen days left for debate: ample time, under ordinary circumstances, for ventilating the most controversial legislation. But the legislation, as such, was hardly discussed. Instead the Commons chamber rang with points of order, accusations that the Liberals, slavishly pro-American as they were, were selling Canada out to a bunch of Texas oil buccaneers, and arguments that the whole thing could have been done differently, in some unexplained way. It was a pyrotechnic parliamentary circus for the opposition, whose sole object was to perform death-defying feats of oratory to talk out the government bill. The press was impressed, and when the Liberals brought in closure, the nation's newspapers reported that democracy was in danger at the hands of the Liberal majority in Parliament. Although Howe's pipeline bill finally passed, under closure, the debate proved a public relations disaster for the government.

Construction of the pipeline started immediately. Trans-Canada Pipelines surmounted its financial problems and in February 1957 repaid the government its loan. Far from ending up as the fief of Texas oil buccaneers, Trans-Canada Pipelines became a majority Canadian-owned company. And in October 1958 natural gas reached Toronto and Montreal. That was cold comfort for the Liberals: by then they – and Howe – were out of office.

14

Building the Welfare State

While C.D. Howe was preoccupying himself with industrial stratagems, worrying over fuel supplies, and weighing the reports his economists gave him for signs of boom or bust, other Liberals worried about a very different problem.

Abandoned in the wreckage of the dominion-provincial disputation in 1946 were the government's plans for an expanded and comprehensive welfare system to ensure Canadians against want. As far as most members of the Liberal cabinet were concerned, those plans were now museum pieces, relics of bygone hopes that were now, because of the economic boom, fortunately outdated. But not everyone took that view. The flame of welfare burnt bright inside the Department of National Health and Welfare in Ottawa, in the hearts of its minister, Paul Martin, and its deputy minister, George Davidson, and in regional chapels on the prairies and the west coast.

For while Ottawa paused, dallied, and then dozed, the first stages of health insurance went ahead in Saskatchewan and British Columbia. In Saskatchewan, the CCF government of T.C. Douglas determined that, despite the collapse of the federal proposals for a national scheme, Saskatchewan ought to enjoy hospital insurance as soon as possible, at any rate before the next provincial election. Accordingly a Hospital Insurance Act was introduced and passed in the legislature in 1946, to take effect on January 1, 1947. On that day the first universal, compulsory system of medical insurance in Canada with a uniform rate of contribution began. It was not the last such program; indeed, it became the model. Saskatchewan's plan proved successful, though costly – far costlier than its proponents had imagined. In this too Saskatchewan set a precedent.

Barely a year after Saskatchewan, the coalition Liberal-Conservative government of British Columbia also took the plunge into hospital insurance. The BC plan proved an administrative nightmare: those who paid their insurance might nevertheless be left without coverage; those who did not pay might receive an entitlement card anyway. For delinquents, the government reserved powers to garnishee wages and prosecute offenders. None of these features was popular: they helped to bring about the resignation of the responsible minister, and then the chaos of the program as a whole served as a principal factor in the defeat of the coalition by the maverick Social Credit party in 1952.

Hospital insurance in British Columbia survived the change of government. Understandably, the new Social Credit regime of W.A.C. Bennett became an enthusiastic supporter of a national program of hospital insurance, if only to relieve some of the political and financial burden of the BC plan. But the Ottawa Liberals remained obdurate, taking refuge in the formula that they would, and could, agree to a national plan only when they had enough money and when a majority of the provinces agreed to join. That, they were confident, would never be.

The stronghold of conservatism in Canada was the 'blue' province of Ontario, governed for most of the period since 1905 by the Conservative party. Ontario had been in the forefront of the opposition to the federal proposals in 1945 under the leadership of its blustering Premier, George Drew. But while the Premier was thundering his anathemas at Liberal centralization, his provincial treasurer, Leslie Frost, was taking a longer and quieter look at the whole situation (one story even holds that Frost sought advice from the Liberal Premier of Manitoba, Stuart Garson).

When Frost succeeded to the premiership in 1949, a new day dawned, politically and administratively, for Canada's largest province. Frost got on well with St Laurent, ideologically, politically, and personally. Tax rental held no terrors for 'old man Ontario,' and he negotiated reasonable terms for joining the national program in 1952. Projects like the Trans-Canada Pipeline likewise appealed to the Ontario premier: he and C.D. Howe saw eye to eye on that, although Frost's influence was not enough to prevent his Conservative brethren in Ottawa from running amok. He and St Laurent agreed about something else too. After a conversation with Frost in January 1956, St Laurent turned wonderingly to a companion and remarked: 'You know, Mr Frost doesn't like health insurance either.'

But it was Frost who made national hospital insurance in Canada politically inevitable. Although personally uninvolved in the health insurance advocates' enthusiasm, Frost seems to have perceived that hospital insurance, at least, was a sign of the times, an idea whose hour had very nearly struck. He had no particular commitment or attachment to the private insurance companies (on his sixtieth birthday, in September 1955, two of his personal health insurance policies were thoughtfully cancelled) and was unmoved by their claim that the government should confine itself to insuring the uninsurables, while the private companies skimmed off the cream of the crop.

Accordingly, in 1955, Frost opened a public campaign to push the federal government into a national hospital insurance scheme. Except for Maurice Duplessis of Quebec, Frost's fellow premiers supported him with varying degrees of warmth, urging that Ottawa make an immediate commitment to hospital insurance and back up its pledge with federal funds. Frost's *démarche* struck an answering chord in the federal cabinet, where Paul Martin bluntly informed St Laurent that he could not remain in the government if it failed to take up Frost's challenge. St Laurent's response to Frost was a careful and qualified 'maybe' instead of the flat 'no' he would doubtless have preferred.

Martin had been briefing himself for seven years in readiness for this moment. He had already implemented a health grants program and had prepared an authoritative survey of the health needs of Canadians. His officials were willing and able to move on hospital insurance as soon as he gave the word. After prolonged and frustrating negotiations, agreement was reached between the national government and the provinces in the late winter of 1957. In April Martin introduced a national hospital insurance scheme, the Hospital Insurance and Diagnostic Services Act, to the House of Commons. It was unanimously passed.

One other major welfare proposal reached fruition during this period. Since 1927, Canada had had an old age pension, a joint federal-provincial affair which, since Quebec's accession in 1936, was national in scope. But the pension, which was low, was dependent on a means test, and it was limited to the over-seventy age group. The test was inadequate and humiliating, and there was considerable agitation during the 1940s for its abolition. St Laurent and the finance department would have preferred a contributory scheme (one paid for directly by individuals), but the agitation inside and outside the Liberal party was too much to withstand. In the 1949 general election all parties promised to do something about the means test. A joint committee of the Senate and House of Commons examined the issue and eventually recommended a universal pension for Canadians over seventy and the introduction of a means-test pension for those between sixty-five and sixty-nine. The St Laurent government was surprised, but acquiesced. The consent of the provinces to a limited constitutional amendment (necessary because welfare was basically a provincial field) was secured, and a new old age pension regime came into operation in 1951. Special Old Age Security taxes were enacted to pay for it.

Throughout the St Laurent government's tenure of office, it could rely on a ginger group to the left to push it further than it might have been willing to go. The CCF party, largely confined to its prairie base in Saskatchewan, was generally admitted to have no hope of securing power. Its members, most of them sedate and responsible, recalled St Laurent's phrase that the CCFers were really only 'Liberals in a hurry.' But if the CCF was hurrying anywhere, it was not toward the seats of power.

This fact perturbed both the professional CCF politicians and their allies in the Canadian Congress of Labour, one of the country's three umbrella labour organizations (the others were the Trades and Labour Congress and the Confédération des travailleurs catholiques du Canada). Both the CCF and the CCL stood for a democratic-socialist-labour party in Canada; to that end, both had weeded Communist sympathizers out of their ranks or expelled unions that remained obdurately Communist-dominated. In a futile attempt to attract the attention of voters whose sympathies were wedded to the political centre and the existing economic system, the CCF even undertook to modify the socialist rhetoric that had enveloped its platform since the 1930s. All in vain: by the 1957 election the CCF was sinking in the public opinion polls and was moving further from the prospect of power than ever before.

If the CCF was floundering, its union affiliates were flourishing. Union membership was going up and passed the million mark for the first time in 1949. Expanding membership was reflected in strike action, which was, however, firmly directed toward amelioration of wages and working conditions and conspicuously lacked the revolutionary verbiage that had accompanied the strikes of the post-First World War period. The issue of compulsory union membership for all employees in a unionized company was met by the system of compulsory check-offs of dues (a formula devised by Mr Justice Ivan Rand and consequently known as the Rand formula), whether or not the individual concerned belonged to a union.

Although the fifties were not lacking in bitter and sometimes violent strikes, observers noted a decline in basic conflict between unions and most management, and between unions and government. There was also a reduction in interunion hostility, as the Trades and Labour Congress (affiliated with the American Federation of Labor) and the Canadian Congress of Labour (affiliated with the Congress of Industrial Organizations, or CIO, in the United States) grew closer together. In 1953 both organizations appointed a Unity Committee which in 1954 produced a No-raiding Agreement and then in 1955 a Merger Agreement. The latter was implemented in April 1956 when the Trades and Labour Congress and the Canadian Congress of Labour officially merged into the Canadian Labour Congress (CLC), under the leadership of the veteran labour leader Claude Jodoin.

Jodoin's physique, large and solid, and amiable appearance reassured a public still skittish of 'radical' innovations. Harmony among the unions prefigures harmony in society in general. The economic order no longer demanded fundamental reform, and virtually no one was asking for it any more. Progress and prosperity seemed to have obliterated discontent almost everywhere, leaving only a few isolated pockets of misery and malcontents. In the fullness of time these too would join the past where, so it seemed, they already belonged.

15

Stratford, Elvis, and the Happy Gang

The effects of prosperity were most evident in a sector where Canada had little past to live down – culture. Culture was a matter of bookstores, a couple of theatres (some professional, but many more amateur), and literary salons. The state, whether federal or provincial, had little business there.

Indirectly, the Canadian government had slowly and almost accidentally acquired a galaxy of cultural institutions. Out of the Department of Agriculture, for example, there had sprung the National Gallery – housed, it is true, behind the dinosaur collection in the National Museum. There was the National Film Board (NFB) and, above all, the Canadian Broadcasting Corporation (CBC). Overall, support for these institutions was meagre, for there was no Canadian tradition of state support for the arts as in Europe. Worse, the private foundations that so generously contributed to artistic endeavours in the United States were also lacking. Canadian philanthropists and American foundations had built some concert halls and libraries and endowed some scholarships. But there was still little to boast of, and the cultural facilities of Canadian cities compared badly with those of their American counterparts and even with those in the bombed-out European cities. Symphony concerts in hockey rinks, movie theatres, or high-school auditoriums were common, as we have seen, and great performers all too often shunned Canada on North American tours. George Bernard Shaw refused to visit Canada lest he die of intellectual starvation in a land of primitive ruffians.

Shaw's comments were an exaggerated reflection of a common view of Canadian development. Canada was a coarse-grained adolescent still clearing the land, lacking the leisure and taste for refinement. After the war, many Canadians were embarrassed by this image, and prominent among these were two internationalists (and Liberal ministers), Brooke Claxton and Lester Pearson. Claxton was irritated when the National Liberal Convention in August 1948 failed to support a resolution for a commission on the arts. Once Mackenzie King was out of the way, however, Claxton believed that such a commission was both possible and workable. He spoke to Pearson and Jack Pickersgill about the idea, and both enthusiastically supported it. Louis St Laurent had his doubts – he told Pickersgill that he was sceptical about 'subsidizing "ballet dancing" ' – but eventually he came round. For chairman of the Royal Commission on National Development in the Arts, Letters and Sciences, Claxton suggested Vincent Massey, the most apparently cultured Canadian of his day. It would give Massey something to do, Claxton argued; without his job, the former diplomat might leave for England for good. Massey's appointment was announced on April 8, 1949; the other commission members were Laval social scientist Father Georges-Henri Lévesque, Montreal engineer Arthur Surveyer, Saskatchewan historian Hilda Neatby, and the president of the University of British Columbia, Norman MacKenzie.

The Massey Commission, as it soon became known, examined the work of numerous federal agencies, including the CBC, the NFB, the National Research Council (NRC), and the National Gallery. It also confronted a difficult constitutional problem on federal aid to universities, and even the old question of what kind of honours Canadians should receive. Massey, characteristically, approached these tasks with broader, grander aims in view. The report would be an official statement on Canadian 'culture' – what it lacked, what it could and should be. The report, submitted to St Laurent on June 1, 1951, took an appropriately large view of its subject. Canadian culture, the commissioners reported, existed on the margin of society. It was time to end the isolation and irrelevance of the Canadian writer and the Canadian artist and make them 'an integral part' of the Canadian environment. Only then could 'the spiritual foundations' of our national life be secured.

To that end, the report recommended that a 'Canada Council for the Encouragement of the Arts, Letters, Humanities and Social Sciences' be established. In general, traditional institutions such as the CBC and the National Gallery should also be more generously supported lest American cultural influence become, for Canada, 'permanent dependence.' Federal grants must strengthen Canadian universities in order to increase their role in the life of the nation. Otherwise the nation would not long endure. In fact, as Norman MacKenzie later explained, 'I was the only member of the Commission who felt that this should be done and that it was possible under the general terms of our constitution despite the importance of education to the provinces.' Understandably, however, MacKenzie's views were popular with his fellow university presidents, many of whom viewed the possibility of federal aid to their institutions with an anxiety born of years of budgetary starvation.[1]

The tone of the Massey Report sounds archaic today. The state now promotes Canadian culture to a degree that the Massey commissioners could never have imagined and probably would not have fully approved. Their criticisms, then, are no longer valid. Neither, it seems, is the particular notion of 'culture' that Massey so carefully defined and employed. The Massey Commission reflected not only post-war nationalistic optimism, but also a conservative view of the Western cultural tradition, a view that had appeared in the wake of, and in response to, the holocaust. Massey's fear of 'mass culture,' his identification of culture and art, his confidence in the continuity and the excellence of the Western intellectual tradition were Canadian counterparts of T.S. Eliot's post-war inquiry into the meaning of our cultural tradition and Friedrich Meinecke's call for a return to the traditional values of 'civilization,' which he claimed were the strongest barricades against the return of the barbarians of the 1930s. The Massey Report was as much an echo of the past as it was a forecast of the future. Most of its institutional recommendations have been followed, but the institutions created have not shaped Canadian cultural life into the forms that the commissioners expected. The report's nationalism is as different from the English-Canadian radical variant of the 1960s as is traditional French-Canadian nationalism from (René) Lévesque-style separatism. They are related, but not fraternally.

The Massey Report was greeted with acclaim by most of the Canadian artistic and intellectual community. There were dissenters: Frank Underhill complained of the identification of mass culture with the United States, claiming that mass culture was an inevitable concomitant of modern democracy and not some peculiar 'American' evil. More troubling to the government was the attitude of the Quebec government, which attacked the commission as an infringement of the province's rights in the field of culture. The conception of federal grants to the universities was repugnant not only to Premier Duplessis (although he accepted them for a year) but also to some of his strongest opponents, such as the Montreal editor and publisher Pierre Trudeau. Nevertheless, St Laurent decided to make the grants; as he told a University of Toronto audience in 1950, 'Some means must be found to ensure to our universities the financial capacity to perform the many services which are required in the interest of the nation.' The government established the National Library in 1953 as called for in the report,

---

1 One minor indication of the state of the universities may be found in the real income of faculty. A senior economist at the University of Toronto, Vincent Bladen, calculated that his disposable income in 1971 dollars was less in 1951 ($11,000) than it had been in 1941 ($11,900) or indeed in 1933 ($11,100). *Bladen on Bladen: The Memoirs of a Political Economist* (Toronto: privately printed, 1978), p. 218.

but it delayed action on Massey's most important recommendation, the Canada Council. Members of the government, including Claxton, were nervous about the impact such a purely cultural policy would have on the electorate. When a windfall from succession duties did make the Canada Council possible in 1957, a Social Credit MP predicted that it would subvert religion and the family. Claxton blamed a popular backlash against the new body for some of the Liberals' unpopularity and defeat in the 1957 election.

The Canada Council survived to become the major federal government commitment to the support of Canadian culture and a forerunner of many other agencies and programs created to make the Canadian artist and intellectual 'an integral part' of the Canadian environment.

Whether the Council has played a major role in the appearance of a sophisticated Canadian cultural life is debatable, as are all historic relationships between patrons and scholars and artists. *The Literary History of Canada,* for example, stresses the continuity between the 1940s and the 1950s in the development of Canadian literature since the war. One might also point to many Canadian writers who spurn the Council's largesse but who produce many of our finest works. It does seem, then, that the rise of a distinctive Canadian literary world and consciousness owes less to official patronage than to general improvement in the level of education and what George Woodcock calls 'the shift in national tone from the bucolic to the urbane.'[2]

The most dramatic indication of the shift occurred in the small city of Stratford, Ontario. Tom Patterson, a Stratford resident, thought that Stratford, whose best days seemed to have passed with the decline of the railway, might find in culture what it lacked in industry and trade. He persuaded the practical burghers on the city council to pay Tyrone Guthrie, a distinguished English director, five hundred dollars to come to Stratford to consider founding a Shakespearean theatre. At first glance Stratford offered only its name and that of its river – the Avon – but Guthrie soon caught Patterson's enthusiasm. In 1953 the Stratford Shakespearean Festival opened in a circus tent with Alec Guinness starring in *Richard III.* The performance was good; Stratford became a pleasant summer diversion for thousands of North Americans and the source of employment and income for a few actors and actresses, as well as for the city.

In a sense Stratford was premature because Canadians had not yet acquired the training demanded by distinguished theatre. The casts of early plays were sprinkled with Canadians among more eminent imports. No one complained much. Theatre in the 1950s, after Stratford, was consumer-oriented. The audience got what it wanted; after all, who would have travelled to an Ontario coun-

2   George Woodcock, *Canada and the Canadians* (Toronto: Macmillan, 1970), p. 253.

try town for a Robertson Davies or Merrill Denison festival?

For the time, it was enough that new facilities were being built. Other theatre companies appeared, not only at Stratford. Gratien Gélinas and Jean Gascon's Théâtre du Nouveau Monde in Montreal did much to reinvigorate French-language theatre, and Gascon was soon making links with Stratford. The small number of people involved in Canadian theatre in the 1950s made such links important and possible. While this could lead to an 'in-group' atmosphere – and in the 1960s all too often it did – it endowed Canadian theatre with the excitement that derives from new discovery and growth. Moreover, there were some critics, most notably Nathan Cohen of the *Toronto Daily Star,* who would not tolerate the second-rate even when produced by friends. Inexperience was no excuse.

Stratford did not eclipse other equally notable cultural developments. The Canadian Ballet Festival, beginning in 1948, led to increasing interest in and support for the dance in Canada. In ballet Winnipeg took the lead with a professional company established in 1950. Gweneth Lloyd's efforts in Winnipeg were soon followed by British-born Celia Franca's work in building the National Ballet Company, centred in Toronto. These professional companies, which toured widely, soon overshadowed the amateur Ballet Festival, which died out in mid-decade. Canadians were less willing to accept amateur performances when professional ones were readily accessible on radio or television. Television was to become an additional means of support for the arts, but not so strong as many had hoped. Television as a medium is best discussed under the heading of popular culture.

A more enduring prop for the arts in Canada was the university. An extremely high proportion of Canada's functioning writers and critics were associated with the universities. The most prominent example was Northrop Frye, who evaluated the efforts of Canadian writers year by year in the *University of Toronto Quarterly.* There was, nevertheless, much scepticism when George Woodcock and the University of British Columbia established *Canadian Literature* in 1959. This quarterly presented serious criticism of Canadian writing, past and present, and from its first issue it strove to avoid a narrow nationalism that might impair critical standards. Its endurance testifies to its success.

The universities contributed to a general atmosphere where the arts were tolerated if not encouraged. All too often there was an intellectual barrenness to the fervour civic leaders brought to the promotion of the arts. The 'edifice complex' – buildings being constructed without much thought for their eventual function – affected too many Canadian cities and the institutions within them. The origins of this complex may be discerned in the perception of the future held by Canadians of middle age in the fifties. For them the task was to accommodate wealth and progress; for their children there would be a different and richer life, one in which leisure and refinement would be possible as the hard edges of Canadian life wore off. The post-war generation would not only be better housed and fed; it would also be university-trained (if not better educated). University administrators sensed this mood early in the fifties, and when they scanned the post-war birth-rate figures they realized that their classrooms might soon be overwhelmed. Their enthusiasm for the federal grants advocated by the Massey Commission may be gauged accordingly. University presidents sounded dire warnings about the future, predicting that enrolments would and must double between 1955 and 1965. Where would these students find their professors, much less their residences? This time Cassandra was believed, but only late in the day and after much incidental help from the Russians.

On October 4, 1957, the Soviet Union launched the first global satellite, and the heavens seemed to confirm the worst fear of all: 'The Russians are ahead of us.' Suddenly penny-wise politicians began to orate about millions and even billions for engineers, for scientists, and for the universities that would train them. Beer, football, and fraternity frolics now began to seem slightly seditious, certainly irrelevant. Educators began to stress how serious education must be. Hilda Neatby who, in 1953, had published *So Little for the Mind,* an indictment of Canadian pre-university training, now became a prophet whose all-too-accurate warnings about child-oriented progressive education had been unwisely ignored. Now serious purpose must return to the classroom, from kindergarten through to university; otherwise, in the continuing struggle of freedom against darkness, freedom would perish. One indication of the shock inspired by the Soviet menace was the statement by University of Toronto political scientist James Eayrs that Canada should consider merging with the United States if that proved necessary for the defence of the 'free world.' University administrators began to envisage themselves as the leaders of a national mission. No argument for funds was so effective as national security, and it was widely and loosely used. New universities sprang up on muddy Waterloo cow pastures, the barren plains of Downsview, and even on a small mountaintop in Burnaby. Bulldozers became a normal feature of the campus scene in the late fifties and early sixties, as the 'edifice complex' spread to the universities.

The baby boom had other effects as well. There were acute teacher shortages, first at the elementary and secondary levels, and then at the universities as well. To stock the universities there was an inflow of American and European academics. Canadian graduate schools, comparatively underdeveloped, could not meet the demand. Canadians who went abroad to finish their education often did not return. In the pure sciences, many aspiring PhDs found the research facilities inadequate – and moved; in the social sciences, many liked where they studied –

and stayed. Canadian universities responded by raising their incentives in the form of salaries and research grants.[3] Besides money, there was deference, an intangible but enjoyable 'perk' for the professoriate. Still, as universities expanded, many found that their staffs were less than 50 per cent Canadian. Given that expansion must occur, and no one seemed to disagree, there was simply no alternative.

There seems to have been a curious hiatus of scholarship in Canada as the universities prepared for the deluge. Several distinguished individual works appeared during the fifties, but, as in literature, scholarship seemed to take few new departures from the patterns of the previous decade. Historians were probably the most productive scholars. Donald Creighton's two-volume biography of Sir John A. Macdonald attracted much public attention, a reflection of reawakened interest in Canada's past as well as of the popular taste for biography. At a time when history as an academic discipline was adopting more frequently a neopositivist approach, Creighton's study emphasized the traditional linkage of history with narrative and imaginative literature.

Creighton's work attracted few disciplines and even fewer successful imitators. Harold Innis, Creighton's friend and colleague at the University of Toronto, produced some stimulating works (*Empire and Communications,* 1950, *The Bias of Communication,* 1951, and *Changing Concepts of Time,* 1952) just before his untimely death in 1952, but, as Carl Berger has observed, Innis's abrupt departure from his earlier field of economic history was met with 'a mixture of admiration for his intellectual daring and courage and bewilderment over what he was driving at.'[4] One who seemed to sense where Innis might lead was the literary scholar Marshall McLuhan who, along with other academics, was studying the problem of technology, communications, and culture in his book *The Mechanical Bride* and the journal *Explorations.* McLuhan's impact, however, was minimal in the fifties, when his work was viewed mainly as a manifestation of quixotic curiosity.

The curiosity of English-Canadian social scientists seemed to focus upon deviant cases in the Canadian consensus. Social Credit in Alberta received more attention than any other topic as the Social Science Research Council endowed an excellent series on that subject. Social Credit lay outside the mainstream of Canadian political thought and tradition, and the reasons for its appearance and survival seemed important to an understanding of what the mainstream might be. Even Canadian socialism was being assimilated to the Canadian liberal consensus, as we have seen above. The thirties, seen from the prosperous fifties,

3 Using Vincent Bladen's figures (cited in note 1 above), we find his salary in 1971 dollars rising from $11,000 in 1951 to $23,000 in 1960.
4 *The Writing of Canadian History* (Toronto: Oxford University Press, 1976), p. 194.

seemed an aberration, and the CCF's Regina Manifesto of 1933 appeared to some little more than an outdated collection of anti-capitalist ravings. Such sentiments were often expressed in the *Canadian Forum* in the fifties, when that traditionally left-wing periodical generally supported American leadership in the world struggle against Communism and, in domestic affairs, an 'end of ideology' approach to Canadian politics which emphasized the absence of sharp class division and class conflict in Canadian politics. Not all agreed. When Seymour Martin Lipset, an American who had studied the 'anomaly' of agrarian socialism in Saskatchewan, contended that ideology was irrelevant to North American politics and that the Canadian and American political cultures were fundamentally similar, a young prairie socialist and *Forum* contributor, Ramsay Cook, strongly dissented, expressing his belief in the separate historical identity of Canadian socialism and the autonomy of the Canadian political tradition. And yet Canadian social science and social philosophy did not clearly identify what that unique tradition might be. Attempts to uncover the tradition in the British connection (as in John Farthing's book, *Freedom Wears a Crown*) or in a new conservatism were unconvincing when not simply hackneyed.

French Canada's intellectual life was considerably livelier. There was little tendency to minimize political and social antagonism as Quebec's young intellectuals expressed their hostility to Maurice Duplessis and actively sought to break up the foundations of the old premier's conservative sway. Among French-Canadian social scientists and historians there was a distinct decision to break with the past, a recognition that their tasks were new, and, in the context of the 1950s, perhaps even revolutionary. Scholarly detachment and reserve had little appeal for scholars like Guy Frégault, Fernand Dumont, Maurice Séguin, or Jean-Charles Falardeau. Epitomizing the view of the past held by so many Quebec scholars during the fifties, Pierre Trudeau declared that 'in Quebec, during the first half of the twentieth century, our social thinking was so idealistic, so *a priori,* so far removed from reality and to be blunt, so ineffectual, that it practically never became a real part of the community's living and evolving institutions.'[5] This, of course, naturally exaggerated the sins of the past and ignored the consequences for scholarship of the commitment to change that such remarks seemed to demand. But it is undeniable that in the debates about church and society, man and politics, the meaning of modernization and nationalism, French-Canadian intellectuals outshone their English-Canadian counterparts in originality, depth, and, most of all, vitality.

In Quebec, too, academic discourse and popular debate were not widely separated. After all, change required popular support and that demanded public edu-

5   From 'Quebec on the Eve of the Asbestos Strike,' in Ramsay Cook, ed., *French-Canadian Nationalism* (Toronto: Macmillan, 1979; 1st ed. 1970), p. 32.

cation. Thus academics took up their pens and wrote political pamphlets, and on the French-language CBC (a federal institution where Duplessis's long arm could not reach) Pierre Trudeau was a commonplace figure, along with other intellectuals and critics of the Quebec regime, exhorting the people to awaken and accept responsibility for their political fate. Other CBC programs were less obviously political but equally didactic. René Lévesque, for example, became familiar as a lecturer on international affairs on the television program *Point de Mire*. From this time the relationship between the media and public life took a different form than in English Canada. Journalists who saw themselves primarily as educators often became politicians, and the distinction between the crafts was often blurred. The 'new journalism' and the reporter engagé were seen in Quebec long before the term became popular in the United States in the mid-sixties. (Duplessis recognized the phenomenon when he barred a reporter from *Le Devoir* from his office.)

Quebec led in other ways as well. The painters Alfred Pellan and Paul Emile Borduas had brought to Canada from Paris a post-impressionist experimental mood that rejected representational art. In English Canada, the influence of the Group of Seven and landscape art remained strong, but in 1953 a group of Toronto abstract expressionists formed Painters Eleven. Influenced by American art theory and practice, but possessing strong individual traits, these painters (among them Harold Town and Jock Macdonald) attracted much attention and, naturally, criticism. The National Gallery under the directorship of Alan Jarvis became a patron to the abstract artists and gave them a respectability which a cautious Canadian art market might not otherwise have afforded.

Respectability, however, was less definable by the end of the fifties than at the beginning. The Massey Report had followed the traditional distinctions between high culture and popular culture, and, for the commissioners, high culture was associated with refinement, with education, with taste. These provided critical standards against which artistic effort could be clearly measured. Yet what happened when artistic effort was directed against these same standards, as was the case with some modern artists? How, too, did one judge films now that they had passed beyond slapstick and melodrama and had 'serious' intentions? And finally, what was one to make of the challenge to traditional restraints and to the puritan ethic which could be found in what most agreed was 'good' literature?

These questions were not answered directly, but their declining relevance was to be discerned in the crumbling support for censorship. The most spectacular censorship case of the decade, Quebec's banning of the film *Martin Luther*, gave critics of censorship a 'respectable' point of departure. As the decade advanced, the rules of censorship became perceptibly more liberal. Grace Metalious's *Peyton Place*, a steamy novel of life and lust in rural New England, was doubtless junk, but what could one say of Vladimir Nabokov's *Lolita* or James Joyce's *Ulysses,* both modern classics but both affronts to the censorship laws? The good burghers of Fort William and Port Arthur publicly burned D.H. Lawrence's *Lady Chatterley's Lover,* but thousands of others simply bought and read it. By 1960 the majority seemed clearly on the side of liberalization and the courts and politicians were quick to respond.

Their response, unfortunately, did not arise from a mature consideration of the relationship between what people read and saw and what it made them do. Traditional controls on public information broke down with mass education, affluence, and the appearance of new means of communication, especially television. In the United States, television programming had been from the beginning a medium for entertainment. Dependent on advertisers, the American networks needed consumers. The Massey commissioners had feared that Canada would follow such a pattern and had urged strict control over the growth of Canadian television. The experience of Canadian radio should have been enlightening, but it was not. Instead of the strictly regulated and edifying fare envisaged by the Massey Commission, Canadian television, when it took to the airwaves in 1952, proved to have much more in common with raucous American television than with any abstract educational model. With antennae facing south, Canadians indicated their preference for *I Love Lucy* (considerately carried by the CBC as well as the American networks), *Jackie Gleason,* and, after Gleason on Saturday nights, *Hockey Night in Canada.* Where the CBC did not directly buy American programs, it imitated them. Thus the Canadian program *Space Command,* complete with cardboard sets, challenged American space operas, and a Canadian *Howdy Doody* disputed conclusions and audiences with the celebrated American puppet. Perhaps the most successful original Canadian programming came from the CBC's French network. It was noticed that one French program was attracting an unusual amount of attention in English Canada: *La Famille Plouffe,* a creation of the novelist Roger Lemelin. Duly translated and rebaptized *The Plouffe Family,* it proved capable of attracting English-language audiences to its own homely version of French-Canadian family life.

Although the CBC directed some of its attention to the provision of high-quality cultural fare to its audiences (Nathan Cohen's *Fighting Words* and the CBC's drama flagship *Folio* are examples), its pandering to Americanized Canadian audiences distressed academics and potential performers. Would it not be better to take a stand on principle, rejecting American mass culture for the next generation? The answers to these questions must have been unpleasant for those who asked. From every juke-box playing popular music, for every watcher of *American Bandstand* or *Trans-Canada Hit Parade* (playing American songs, though with Canadian performers), the sound of a common North American experience burst forth. Popular music sounded the same in Chicago, Vancouver, Moose Jaw, or Toronto, and Canadians rushed to buy the latest records and the latest styles that American pop stars produced. The most shocking to the sedate tastes of the fifties was the Tennessee singer Elvis Presley, whose visits on tour to Canada stimulated the same crowds of shrieking teenagers that an earlier idol, Frank Sinatra, had enjoyed. Canadian parents worried, and Canadian pundits pondered: was rock 'n' roll uniquely bad, or was it just the most recent example of a deplorable and inevitable drift of the young into American mass culture? Some Canadians were appeased when Canadian singers appeared to show that they could do it too. A young Ottawa resident, Paul Anka, was the first, with his gold record 'Diana.' There would be many more for Anka, but few other Canadians had such success in these years. Many radio stations turned to continuous music programming, usually 'rock,' but, on the 'Top 40,' only one or two at most were Canadian efforts.

No one cared very much. Radio survived the shock of television by becoming specialized. The CBC gradually brought its popular Dominion Network to an end (the flag station, CJBC in Toronto, turned French in the early sixties). *The Happy Gang,* an afternoon diversion since the thirties, finally broke up. CBC radio began to concentrate on reaching specialized audiences (the 'highbrows' through CBC 'Wednesday Night') or catering to regional or special interest groups. The CBC at least had solid financing behind it. For radio stations that didn't, the way was clear: maximum audiences, with maximum advertising impact, could be achieved only by catering to youth. Without the 'Top 40' many stations simply could not have existed. They survived, and their frenzied, sometimes raucous, voices became the inescapable background music for Canadian beaches and drive-in restaurants.

As younger Canadians adopted the tastes of young Americans in music, food, and dress, they became less doubtful of American behaviour than their parents had been. Divorce, for example, seemed less an indication of a decadent American society than an effective, though drastic, solution to marital incompatibility. The number of divorces went up at the end of the Second World War, and it stayed up, between 6,000 and 7,000 a year compared to 1,000 to 2,000 in the thirties. Canada's divorce laws were increasingly condemned as archaic; so were Sunday closing laws and drinking restrictions outside Quebec. The opponents of change hung on, fighting every plebiscite, hoping that the temper of the times would change. But despite ostentatious displays of public and official piety, it never did. The reward of the moral conservatives was cruel caricature, and for none more than the United Church's James Mutchmor. Mutchmor, a serious and intelligent critic of contemporary society, was depicted as a foe of human happiness, a relic of the age of Carrie Nation and her axe-carrying disciples. 'Much less of Mutchmor,' one critic remarked.

The real trend was up: up for alcoholic beverages and Sunday movies and other forms of public indulgence. Cocktail lounges opened and spread. More restaurants listed wine on their menus. Yet, by international standards, Canada remained an abstemious society. In 1953 Canadians drank 13.72 gallons of beer, 0.74 gallons of spirits, and 0.36 gallons of wine per capita. By 1960 beer consumption had dropped to 13.41, although spirit consumption rose to 0.82 and wine to 0.44 gallons. It was still a mild trend. In large cities, except Montreal, it was exceedingly difficult, if not impossible, to get a drink on Sunday. Canadians could still not read a Sunday paper, unless they bought the *New York Times* or another American paper. It would be in the next decade that the real changes would be felt.

16

Crosscurrents in
Economic Affairs and Policy

The heart of the St Laurent government's policy structure lay far from the rhythms of 'ballet dancing' and closer to cycles of a different sort. Down Parliament Hill from the House of Commons, in a Gothic office tower, dwelt the Department of Finance, the focus of the capital's mandarinate, the conduit through which all other departments' spending projects must travel. Many of Finance's proceedings were classed as secret and jealously guarded: the making of the budget was the most secret process of all, revealed only to the Prime Minister himself, and that at a late date. If some of Finance's workings were not secret, they were judged so arcane as to be beyond the understanding of the average citizen or bureaucrat. Into the language of its officers were creeping terms like 'macroeconomic policy,' puzzling to a cabinet consisting largely of lawyers, and more puzzling still to the press outside, which began to interpret the doings of the government's economists as a kind of benign wizardry.[1]

Today the wizardry would be interpreted rather more easily. 'Macroeconomic policy,' the conundrum of the fifties, is quite simply that area of government policy that tries to manage the level of unemployment, inflation, and the balance of payments. In restraining inflation and combating unemployment, the St Laurent government could use standard textbook weapons: engineering changes in tax rates and outlays, increasing or decreasing the flow of credit from the Bank of Canada, cutting or raising tariff rates, lowering or raising the exchange rate, imposing or removing exchange controls, or other sorts of direct regulation. Economists studying the matter have usually argued that although the St Laurent government's actual actions were not always correct, at least the administration was fully committed to this kind of macroeconomic management, and tried hard to do the right thing. The pattern was different in the United States, where the

1 The untimely death of Kenneth R. Wilson, the *Financial Post*'s economic correspondent, appreciably lowered the level of economic reporting in Canada.

Truman administration (1945-53) understood such matters only dimly, and the Eisenhower administration (1953-61) did not understand them at all. Of course these things were more easily managed in a parliamentary system like Canada's or Britain's than in a congressional one, especially when the government enjoyed a secure majority in the House of Commons. However, because 'junior governments' – provinces and municipalities – bulk so large on the Canadian scene, macroeconomic policy-making has always been more difficult in Canada's federal system than in unitary countries like Great Britain. Indeed, during the St Laurent years the 'federal problem' became much more awkward as the junior governments waxed larger and more importunate. Further, with the dismantling of wartime controls in Canada and elsewhere the Canadian economy became more closely integrated with the others, especially with the American economy, whose share in Canada's import and export trade rose steadily. Trade with Britain grew absolutely but diminished relatively; as yet continental Europe and Japan mattered little, and neither mainland China nor the Soviet Union was yet buying Canadian wheat. By 1957 Canada's trading pattern made it plain that this was a North American country whose trade and financial connections would be with the United States. Not all Canadians rejoiced at the prospect. Imperial longings were not extinct, as the Diefenbaker years were to show. Ignoring the repeated attempts of the Canadian government to encourage Anglo-Canadian trade, some commentators and mythmakers began to chatter about the American dominance of the Canadian economy. In the prosperous and complacent fifties, their warnings had little impact. Canadians enjoying the rising, American-style standard of living were not inclined to listen to prophets of economic and political doom; if anything, they were inclined to overestimate the contribution of American money and American markets to the new national prosperity.

The economy was functioning well: trade and investment figures proved it. If anything could reinforce belief in the effortless superiority of the Ottawa mandarins, this was it. All that a perceptive observer had to do was witness a dominion-provincial conference to mark the difference in competence between the Ottawa civil servants and their provincial counterparts. Saskatchewan had a competent group of administrators, but their horizons were limited. In the Atlantic provinces, as always, politicians ran things, and they did no better and no worse than ever. In Newfoundland and British Columbia, where they followed the wizard principle, governments had some disastrous experiences with 'special advisers' whose advice cost millions and who occasionally vanished without trace or landed in jail. Although the provinces were spending more than ever before, they had yet to develop the expert bureaucrats who could meet their Ottawa opposite numbers as equals. Thus, although provincial revenues and expenditures were rising, and Ottawa's were falling relatively, the central government's dominant expertise allowed it to retain the financial leadership of the Canadian federation for a little while longer.

Yet the grasp of Ottawa was far less all-embracing than it would later become. Compared with the Pearson or Trudeau government, St Laurent's appears almost 'minimalist' in its approach to the role of government in the national economy. There was no regional development program, and there were few shared-cost programs (in which the national and provincial governments jointly finance projects). Major initiatives were comparatively few, the St Lawrence Seaway and the Trans-Canada Highway being the biggest and the most important. Nothing was done to stimulate competition, except in so far as tariff reductions and the ending of exchange control had this incidental effect. The feeble Combines Investigation Act, inherited from the King era, was amended in 1952, but it was not strengthened. Ottawa did support a few agricultural prices under 1944 legislation, and it ran the Canadian Wheat Board for the marketing of prairie grain, but the wheat crop was sold without government guarantee and the provinces ran all the other marketing boards. Pressure from wheat farmers to get Ottawa to pay more attention to their economic plight was either resolutely ignored, or responded to grudgingly.

By 1957 federal price and rent controls had long been things of the past, and no one yet talked of an 'incomes policy' that would regulate wages. With the return of peace the provinces had regained their authority in this area, and in other aspects of social policy as well. Only 5 per cent of the labour force was subject to federal regulation (although that 5 per cent was in key areas, as the railway strike of 1950 demonstrated); in labour as in agriculture Ottawa did not try to encroach on the provincial sphere. No one doubted that the provinces were entitled to collect revenue from the natural resources they owned and to control resource development if they wished. Off-shore oil was another matter, because no one was sure who owned it, but before 1957 no one very much cared. Ottawa had assumed control over uranium, it was true, but in the atomic age that power was not yet seriously questioned. The central government did regulate energy exports and was still reluctant to allow the sale of electricity abroad; on one notable occasion, C.D. Howe used his power over energy exports to block an American aluminum plant in Alaska that would have competed with a Canadian facility, Kitimat, just across the line. But when it came to oil and gas, Ottawa was more eager to find US markets than to limit development. As for subsidies to universities, the central government justified its action as an aspect of the spending power. The provinces were not obliged to accept federal grants (and after a year Quebec refused them); Ottawa was merely topping up inadequate provincial funding. When the government set up the Canada Council in 1957 the constitutional logic was the same, and to this federal initiative no one objected.

The provinces, it might be observed, had problems of their own. Expenditures were surging upward as governments built more things, schooled more children, spent more on old age security, and, in British Columbia and Saskatchewan, began to spend on hospital insurance. Fortunately, by 1950 it was possible to borrow, not only at home but in the United States. The rigid limits on provincial spending and revenues during the Second World War had had their beneficial side: provinces and municipalities, relieved from spending, improved their financial standing. Better credit ratings and the abolition of Canadian exchange control reopened American money markets to Canadian borrowers, and after 1950 the Bank of Canada pursued a financial policy that encouraged them to go there. Everyone believed that to maintain a decent pace of development and modernization Canada would have to draw money from abroad. Nevertheless, in spite of their borrowings, the junior governments needed more current revenues – from taxes, natural resources, and their increasingly profitable liquor monopolies.

Naturally the provinces criticized the dominion, which, they claimed, took too much in taxation and gave back too little. The tax agreements of 1947 (see above), though acceptable, did limit provincial taxing powers. Tax rental payments steadily grew, as did other forms of federal transfers to the provinces. Unconditional grants to the provinces totalled $103.9 million in 1949, $338.7 million in 1952, and $382.6 million in 1957.[2] During the same period conditional transfers fluctuated between $115.9 million in 1949 and $144.8 million in 1957. To give the provinces some leeway, the central government repealed its own taxes on gasoline and amusements, and the provinces soon occupied these fields wholly or in part. In 1950 the St Laurent government offered an amendment to the BNA Act that would have permitted the provinces to levy 'indirect' sales taxes at the retail level. Ontario, however, refused, and the proposal lapsed. The provinces could and did impose 'direct' retail sales taxes. Saskatchewan had been doing so since 1937, and in Quebec there had been municipal sales taxes since 1935. Ontario held out against the trend until 1961, and Alberta, oil-rich since the late 1940s, has never needed a retail sales tax at all. But in most provinces the fiscal stresses and strains of the St Laurent years forced governments to tap this one remaining source of funds.

In some provinces resource revenues could help float the ship of state. After

2 Here and elsewhere in this book data on government receipts and expenditures are presented on a calendar-year basis, using the definitions that Statistics Canada employs in its *National Income and Expenditure Accounts*. Although the numerical results can be reconciled with the *Public Accounts* they are almost never the same. Increasingly, when discussing budgets, taxes, and estimates, finance ministers have used both the National Accounts basis and the Public Accounts basis, thus recognizing that the former is more meaningful than the latter.

the Leduc discoveries, Alberta's oil production rapidly increased, and so did the province's output of natural gas. The same thing happened, although to a lesser extent, in British Columbia and Saskatchewan. Pipelines opened new markets in Ontario and the United States. Economic growth stimulated buoyant markets. By the mid-fifties Alberta was debt-free, an achievement that some attributed to the exotic effects of the Social Credit doctrine; others, more realistically, ascribed it to frugal financial management and the oil bonanza. In British Columbia and in some other provinces the North American construction boom produced active demand for forest products, and mining developments provided royalties from provincially owned minerals. But some provinces liked to tax the resource industries relatively lightly so as to encourage development, and perhaps to pay off political obligations. Thus only in Alberta were the resource revenues really large enough to meet the public demand for government services – roads, schools, public buildings, sewers, water mains, hospitals, welfare services, and pensions – areas where nothing much had been done since the 1920s.

There was talk of other initiatives. In 1950 Ontario dallied with a provincial income tax before joining the tax rental system, and, as we have seen, Quebec actually did impose one in 1954.

All these developments created problems for Ottawa's mandarin macroeconomic managers. In 1947 the dominion collected 70 per cent of all government revenue and spent 60 per cent of all government outlay. By 1957, in spite of the defence build-up and the new old age pensions, the percentages were 62 and 55. Worse, the provincial and local share in government capital outlays, always high relative to the federal share, was now 83 per cent. Worse still, the ten provinces and the thousands of municipalities made their own spending plans, without any kind of central co-ordination. Thus if Ottawa were to raise taxes or cut spending so as to restrain inflation, the junior governments could and did offset the impact. In principle Ottawa might press harder, offsetting the offsetting, as it were. But there were limits to this. By 1957, 73 per cent of the outlays of the national government consisted of wages, salaries, interest on debt, and other payments to persons and junior governments. In the remaining 27 per cent only 4 percentage points came from capital outlay – the easiest sort to turn on and off – while the rest was spent on the raw materials of government, everything from electricity and paper to the fuel for Canada's mighty air force and the red tape with which to bundle reports on government spending. On the revenue side of the account, tax hikes were unpopular with everyone except the provinces, since the central government did the collecting everywhere except Quebec. Whenever Ottawa ran a surplus, the provinces could be relied on to ask for a larger handout. By 1957 the optimistic statements of the 1945 White Paper and the reconstruction conference seemed remote and unreal. If any ministers ever thought about them, they must have been thankful that C.D. Howe had forced his officials to speak not of 'full employment' but of 'high and stable levels of employment.' Nor is it surprising that Ottawa was increasingly inclined to rely on old-style monetary management, not only on new-style Keynesian fiscal management, to control the inflationary pressures of the 1954-7 boom.

Throughout the St Laurent period the central government sought to combat the menace of inflation. Hence the government deliberately ran surpluses and managed expenditures so as to reduce the inflationary pressure. Only in 1953-4, when there was a brief recession, was the fiscal engine used to create extra jobs. In 1948-53 and in 1955-7, the national government's surpluses were very substantial – 15 per cent of total revenues in the first period and 7 per cent in the second. The funds were used mostly to finance Crown agencies, such as the Central Mortgage and Housing Corporation (CMHC), and to reduce the national debt. In and of themselves the surpluses certainly reduced inflationary pressure, although it has sometimes been argued that they could have been used in ways that would have reduced that pressure still more. In particular, it was probably a pity that so much of the retired debt belonged to ordinary citizens instead of to chartered banks and the Bank of Canada. It was also a pity that Ottawa was still pumping funds into the housing market through CMHC.

When the National Housing Act was modified in 1954, Ottawa had hoped to end the direct mortgage loans that it had been providing, under one guise or another, since 1935. But the authorities were reluctant to face the possibility that fewer houses would be built. During the minor recession of 1954 these worries were especially understandable. And of course the housing shortage was still a very live political issue. Thus CMHC drifted back into the business of direct lending. By the end of 1957 it had been authorized to draw up to $400 million from the public purse for this purpose. The impact was considerable: $400 million was 40 per cent of the federal surplus in 1955-7. In principle, of course, CMHC activity was subject to government control. In practice, it was rapidly becoming another means of offsetting the tax-changing and expenditure-planning with which Keynesian fiscal policy is chiefly concerned.

By 1948-9 it appeared that the major taxes had been reduced far enough from their wartime peaks. Although personal income tax was further reduced in 1949, and although various commodity taxes were reduced in both years, the government seems to have been concerned chiefly to encourage new investment not just in the resource industries but throughout the economy. Thus there were various tax changes to that end, but no changes of macroeconomic direction. To fight inflation the government continued to run surpluses, as it had done in 1947. In terms of the goods and services it actually used up, government expenditure fell noticeably in 1948 and rose only a little in 1949. A measure of government expenditures may be found in the force levels of the armed services – 35,000 in 1948. The Korean War would reverse the trend.

In February 1951 the government unveiled its plans for rearmament. The strength of the armed forces would rise from 90,000 full-time employees (service and civilian) to 148,000. The government would modernize and upgrade military equipment, and the changes would cost $5 billion. Defence as a percentage of federal budgetary outlays rose from 16 per cent in 1950 to 45 per cent in 1953.

The rearmament program coincided with the new old age pension scheme (above), which added another $250 million a year to federal outlays. Although these were apparently vast sums, they could have been absorbed without much difficulty. There had been a budgetary surplus of $484 million in 1949. But war had rekindled the fires of inflation around the world; in order to combat that menace the government decided to raise its tax rate. In the fall of 1950 Parliament approved rises in corporation taxes and various commodity taxes. In April 1951 the government raised them again, and added a 20 per cent surcharge on personal income taxes. When, in the autumn of 1951, the government made fiscal provision for old age pensions, costs went up, but revenues went up still more. As a result, in 1951 the federal surplus was almost $1 billion. This vigorous Keynesian fiscal policy nevertheless failed to halt inflation. From 1949 to 1952 consumer prices rose 17 per cent, and from 1951 to 1952, the period of greatest pressure, they rose 10 per cent. Modest though these increases now appear, by the standards of their time they were shocking. But if the government had not deliberately counteracted inflation by running large surpluses, they would have been larger still.

By 1952 prices were rising very little, and, in 1953, for the first time since the early 1930s, the price index actually fell a little. Hence in 1952 Ottawa could reduce some commodity taxes, and in 1953 it reduced income taxes to the 1949 level while also lowering commodity and corporation taxation. The provinces were handed a little more room for income taxation. In 1952 and 1953 the national government still ran surpluses, but these were smaller than those in 1950 and 1951, and relative to federal outlays or national production they were too small to be interesting – less than 1 per cent of gross national product in 1952, and still less in 1953.

In 1954 there was actually a federal deficit – a small one, less than 1 per cent of total federal outlays. The deficit helped, in a minor way, to offset the recession of that year, when gross national product actually declined a little. Since the risk of recession had been foreseen, the Minister of Finance had already cut personal and corporate income taxes and reduced or removed various sales and excise taxes. Because the rearmament effort was winding down, government outlays actually fell somewhat, but the tax cuts and the recession itself reduced government revenues still more.

The last years of the St Laurent government, 1954-7, saw an inflationary expansion, but Ottawa's expenditures provided none of the fuel. Although the national government was spending more on goods and services, thanks to inflation it was actually buying less: in 1957 the national government bought less, in physical terms, than in 1954. Revenues, in contrast, rose sharply both in terms of current dollars and in dollars of constant purchasing power; hence the rising surpluses, which peaked in 1956 and then shrank in 1957 as the economy decelerated. Ottawa fought inflation by controlling its own outlays, while growth and inflation were automatically pushing its revenue up. Tax cuts would have been perverse in an inflationary environment, and nobody pressed for them. But tax increases would have been unpopular, especially as the 1957 election drew near, and they were not imposed.

Ottawa's restraint was a contrast to, not a model for, the activities of the provinces and municipalities, whose capital and current outlays rose sharply. And so Canadians were presented with a paradox that – outside the cloistered inner circles of government – was only dimly understood. Ottawa was helping to restrain inflation, while the provinces were helping to create it.

Of course, taxes were not the government's only weapon in a war on inflation. The St Laurent government had the option of choosing a relatively high exchange rate and enforcing a policy of monetary restraint – high interest and tight credit. But high interest rates were unpopular with borrowers, and a high exchange rate did not hold much appeal for hard-pressed exporters. Accordingly, after 1954 the government increasingly relied on a novel interpretation of the Bank of Canada Act. By following the letter of the act, it appeared that the governor of the Bank, rather than the government of the day, determined monetary policy.

Under the first governor, Graham Towers, it was always understood that in any ultimate confrontation over monetary policy the Bank would have to take direction from the cabinet. But James Coyne, who succeeded Towers in 1954, was as inclined to demand his statutory independence as the government was to emphasize it. Yet one may reasonably suppose that if the Bank's 'tight money' policy had actually annoyed the responsible ministers in 1955-7 they would have taken steps to dispose of the governor, just as the Diefenbaker government eventually had to do in 1961. On the one hand, Coyne really believed that Canadians should tighten their belts, borrow less, pay more for their borrowings, and live within their collective means. On the other hand, the government found it politically convenient to have a governor who would carry the can for a monetary policy that the government would in any event have wanted to follow.

In the early 1950s, Governor Towers had provided extra reserves so that the banking system could expand credit in step with higher prices. But in 1952 Towers applied the brakes. Thereafter, banks' reserves rose very little indeed, and in 1953 and 1954 actually fell. It would seem that Towers was determined to pump out the extra dose of reserves that he had injected, and in a sense he may be said to have succeeded. Between 1945 and 1954, reserves rose at an annual average rate of 1.9 per cent, while output rose 1.96 per cent a year: monetary policy was modestly contractionary throughout, although these averages mask the year-to-year changes in growth rates that were such a marked feature of the Towers regime, as of those of his successors. Thus there were years in which the reserves and the money supply outgrew output and years in which they lagged behind, deflating output and employment as well as inflation.

When James Coyne took office in 1954 he changed central bank policy in two obvious respects. First, he began to change the bank rate – the Bank's charge for credit to the chartered banks – far more frequently. In the central bank's first twenty years, Towers had only once altered the rate. Since the banks did not need to borrow and preferred not to do so, this stability was perhaps understandable. But the bank rate was changed three times in Coyne's first year as governor, and he was just as active during 1956. Indeed, he arranged in November 1956 that the bank rate would move up and down weekly, in a fixed relation to the cost at which the government could borrow. Indirectly, the Bank could affect that cost, because it entered the government bond market regularly as a buyer or seller of government bonds. But to the uninformed, bank rate now looked like a piece of automatism, as divorced from the Bank's control as from the government's.

Second, the new governor began to use his annual reports as a means of self-justification. He was anxious to explain his policies, much more so than his predecessor. For reasons that never became explicit, he wanted to influence inflationary pressure by controlling the money supply itself, not just interest rates or other aspects of credit conditions. The idea, which became familiar and fashionable once more in the late seventies, was really quite simple and sensible. By first fixing the supply of credit through its decisions about the growth of the money supply, the Bank would affect the financial markets, where, given the demands for credit, interest rates would be fixed in an automatic way by the interaction of supply and demand. Coyne, unlike his successors in the late seventies, never stated what rate of growth he thought appropriate, but if we are to judge by his performance we must conclude that he thought the money supply should rise less rapidly than output, thus applying upward pressure on interest rates and downward pressure on prices. That was the pattern from 1954 until 1957, and indeed for most of Coyne's remaining years as governor.

The Bank's tight-money policy encouraged Canadians to borrow abroad, chiefly in the United States. Thus it tended to raise Canada's foreign indebtedness, which would in any event have been rising because of the attractions Canada held as a place for Americans to build new factories and develop new industries, especially in the resource field. But the Bank's policy was deflationary in three respects.

It provided the foreign money with which to pay for imports, thus reducing the pressure on Canada's own productive capacities. It caused the floating Canadian dollar to float higher, thus reducing the Canadian-dollar price of imports. Because it made exporting less profitable this high Canadian dollar tended to discourage exports, thus releasing labour and machinery to produce more for the domestic market. For the government there were obvious political advantages: it helped to have the exchange rate of the dollar determined by unseen market forces, not by government policy.

This had not always been so. During the war, the external value of the Canadian dollar had been strictly controlled at 90.9 cents (US). In July 1946 the government changed the peg, making one Canadian dollar equal to one American. As we have seen above, Canada's foreign exchange reserves dribbled away in the next two years, leading directly to the emergency program of November 1947, which imposed heavy taxation and import control. The Marshall Plan helped: in 1948-9 Marshall Plan procurements in Canada totalled $1,027 million when net direct American investment amounted to only $145 million. From the end of 1947 until early 1950 Canada's gold and exchange reserves rose by nearly $500 million. The emergency restrictions by themselves do not account for this improvement; at best, they prevented some erosion that would otherwise have occurred during 1948. Their loosening during 1949 reflected the new exchange position.

In 1949 various things changed. Net direct American investment jumped from $84 million in 1949 to $200 million in 1950, and although American investment in bonds and stocks was now negative Canada attracted an enormous flow of short-term capital, largely from the United States. It seems that people expected the Canadian dollar to rise relative to other currencies, especially the American. Presumably the speculators believed that the 1949 devaluation of the Canadian dollar (back to 90.9 cents, US) had fixed too low a value. So they were buying Canadian money as fast as they could. Thus in the first nine months of 1950 Canada's reserves rose from $1 billion to about $1.7 billion, even though for the first time in twenty years Canadians imported more than they exported.

For the government the situation was a difficult one. Having joined the International Monetary Fund (IMF), Canada was supposed to keep its exchange rate fixed relative to the American dollar. Only the narrowest fluctuations were permissible: beyond the limits set by the IMF the Canadian government was supposed to consult the Fund, whose arrangements did not provide for floating exchange rates at all. But the inflow of foreign money was an embarrassment. It was producing extra inflationary pressure just when Korean War inflation was beginning. Because it was not embedding itself in new plant and equipment it might leave just as quickly as it had come. The obvious solution was to give in to the speculators and peg the Canadian dollar higher. But then the speculators would have won their gamble. They might then remove their funds from Canada, producing downward pressure on Canadian reserves and creating renewed demands for a change in the exchange rate, this time in the opposite direction. Thus the government might face an absurd oscillation whereby it would first raise the value of the dollar only to be forced to reduce it shortly afterward.

It is surely not surprising that the government decided to avoid the whole problem by floating the rate, returning in effect to the regime of the 1930s. The decision, taken in October 1950, was meant to be temporary. The IMF acquiesced on the understanding that Canada would fix its rate as soon as it could. But the floating rate became a habit, and it was not until 1962 that it was pegged to the American dollar once more.

For more than eleven years the Canadian authorities entered the foreign exchange market only to prevent large day-to-day fluctuations. As a result Canadian foreign exchange reserves changed very little: the government was neither piling up heaps of US dollars nor spending its hoard. But the price of the Canadian dollar changed a great deal. It rose from 90.9 US cents in September 1950 to 95 US cents in November. Thus, after fluctuating, it rose again to $1.04 US in the third quarter of 1952. After falling to par with the American dollar in 1956, it rose again, touching $1.05 US in the third quarter of 1957. Under the Diefenbaker government these oscillations continued, but, as we shall see below, the dollar remained well above par until after 1960.

After 1950 the Canadian dollar danced to the tune of supply and demand. But who had written the score? The answer to that question lies buried in Canada's export and import figures, interpreted in the light of Canadian commercial commitments and American trade policies. We must also explore the reasons why the Canadian economy was booming in 1950-3 and 1954-7. Finally we must examine the policy of the Bank of Canada, increasingly independent under Coyne's governorship.

From the beginning of 1950 Canada was exporting less than it was importing. In 1952, there was a small surplus, but that was swamped by the deficits of other years. In 1951 and 1953-7 Canada ran a deficit even on merchandise trade – purchases and sales of goods and services not counting interest and dividends. In 1950 there was a merchandise surplus, but the weight of interest and dividend obligations converted this surplus into a current account deficit.

Canada ran a deficit fundamentally because the great boom of the fifties was based on domestic spending – consumption, domestic accumulation of plant and equipment, new building, and, especially in the later stages, the spending programs of junior governments. As noted in Part I (above), the boom was not export-led. That is to say, it was not a growth in Canadian export receipts that was responsible for the country's increasing prosperity; instead it was based on domestic spending. Indeed, some export industries were in serious trouble. This was most obviously true of the prairie wheat economy, where the revival of European production combined with the advent of subsidized American competition to produce a collapse of prices and farm incomes. Admittedly, much domestic spending, especially in the resource industries, was made with an eye to *future* export prospects. In this regard the American Paley Report, which had underlined American needs for resources from abroad, certainly played a part. But these investment programs did nothing for *current* export earnings, while directly they demanded large imports of machinery and equipment; indirectly they also stimulated the importation of consumer goods and services. It was in the later St Laurent years that Canadians first became really noticeable at tropical resorts in Florida, Hawaii, and the Caribbean.

Meanwhile, developments in commercial policy, both Canadian and foreign, may have hindered rather than helped Canada's current account position. The Marshall Plan ended in 1953. European production was reviving, and, although the dollar shortage was disappearing, this revival implied further competition for Canadian exports. In the United States, thanks to a system of domestic price supports, there was now an ever-growing heap of produce that the world would not accept on ordinary commercial terms. In response Congress passed Public Law 480, a measure that provided for the subsidized export of agricultural products, especially grain. Many of the buyers were poor countries that might not have bought Canadian grain in any event. But Public Law 480 certainly did not help Canada's export trade, and at least at the margin it harmed us more than a little.

In the area of tariffs the St Laurent years also saw some changes. In 1948 the Canadian tariff was lowered so as to implement the General Agreement on Tariffs and Trade (GATT) signed the previous year (above). The reduction of Canada's emergency exchange controls also served to encourage trade, as did the end of the rationing of foreign exchange in 1950. In 1950-1 there were new GATT negotiations at the English resort town of Torquay, and in 1953-4 at Geneva again. Thanks to these negotiations the Canadian tariff fell further. So far as imports were concerned, these changes opened the Canadian market more widely to foreign competition, even though for many goods the Canadian tariff was still prohibitive. Although other countries also reduced their duties, so many Canadian products already enjoyed duty-free entry, especially to Britain and the United States, that on balance the GATT agreements probably raised imports rather than exports for Canada. Meanwhile, although the United States welcomed ever more Canadian goods, on certain agricultural products there were exceptions, and on fish sticks American duties were actually raised. Continental Europe, now recovered, was also returning with a rush to its immemorial habits of agricultural protectionism.

Given this pattern, imports could be expected to rise relative to exports, pushing the Canadian current account into deficit, just as the actual experience of the fifties indicates. But why, then, did the floating dollar not fall? What kept it up was the inflow of capital funds. Some of the inflow was directed at raising Canada's export capacity, but most was not. Much direct investment was aimed at the domestic market, while little of the junior governments' borrowings was aimed at helping Canada to produce more.

The Bank of Canada is relevant to this story because its policies made external finance more attractive. If the Bank had allowed credit to expand more rapidly within Canada, domestic credit would have been cheaper and more plentiful, relative to American credit, than in fact it was. In the immediate post-war years the Bank had not worried much about these matters. Whenever extra money was needed to support the prices of Canadian bonds, the Bank had created credit with gay abandon. In effect, whenever the public wanted to sell inconvenient quantities of the bonds it had bought during the war the Bank simply printed extra dollars with which to buy the bonds. Gradually, however, the Bank awoke to the fact that by controlling the supply of credit it could restrain inflationary pressure. Thus in 1948 it allowed the prices of dominion war bonds to sag a bit, and in 1950 it declared its monetary independence by raising its own lending rate to 2 per cent – the first increase since the rate was fixed at 1.5 per cent in 1934. The increase was a signal that the Bank would try to control money and credit so as to reduce inflationary pressure. The Bank also convened the chartered banks and insurance companies, both of which agreed to restrain their lending. Meanwhile the government imposed a ceiling on bank credit and acted to prevent an undue expansion of consumer credit. By autumn 1953 the authorities were worried more about unemployment than about inflation, and so in 1954 the Bank Act was modified in an expansionary direction. But in 1955, when inflationary pressures were visible once more, the Bank asked the chartered banks and other lenders to restrain credit. Although the Bank did let the chartered banks lend a good deal more, interest rates rose, to the embarrassment of the government and the delight of the opposition.

With the election of 1957 the end of the inflationary boom was already in sight. In 1956 prices rose 4 per cent, and in 1957 only 2 per cent. But of course the government was blamed not just for the inflation, which its actions had helped to moderate, but for the 'high rates' (translated for the electorate into the slogan 'tight money') that had helped to control the inflation. Ministers responded by blaming the Bank for the credit squeeze, and the world situation for the inflation. The electorate, it seemed, was not convinced.

It was a salutary lesson for economists. In the textbooks of macroeconomics, governments are imagined to make policy – manipulate taxes, spending programs, and the monetary system and exchanges – without regard to elections. It is assumed either that a government does not have to worry about re-election or that the electorate understands the game the government is playing and rewards the government that plays it properly. Clearly neither assumption is true, as finance minister Abbott understood, and few governments have behaved as if they believed them. In Britain it has been shown that since the war there has been a 'political cycle' in macroeconomic policy. Governments often have cut taxes and developed new spending programs just before elections, regardless of the economic climate. Of course all democratic governments must be tempted to behave this way; the problem about modern macroeconomic policy is that governments now think they can more readily get away with it. Fortunately for the St Laurent government, in Canada the political and economic imperatives often pointed in the same direction. In 1949 and 1953 it made economic sense to cut tax rates, but because elections were on the way it also made political sense. The results produced such massive Liberal majorities that the government might well have concluded that it was as safe to heed its technocrats as it was to consult its ward heelers. In 1955-6, especially in 1956, the situation was altogether different. In an inflationary boom with elections in the offing the political and economic imperatives pointed in opposite directions, and the government's attack on inflation was accordingly less than wholehearted. Nevertheless, as we have seen, it did move in the right direction, and on the whole the Bank of Canada was helpful. In the 1957 elections, did sensible policy win votes or cost votes? Or did the pipeline battle plus prairie populist rhetoric add up to a winning combination that would have swept the Liberals from office regardless? We shall never know.

17

The Twilight of the Grits

It is an axiom of politics that oppositions do not win elections; governments lose them. Most observers did not expect the Liberals to lose the general election of June 10, 1957; when they did, by a margin of seven seats (112 Conservatives, 105 Liberals, and 48 MPs from the minor parties), it seemed as if the foundations of the earth had shifted.

For three decades since 1957 commentators and political scientists have laboured to explain the inexplicable. Why did a government that had ruled for so long, and generally so well, with such a minimum of fuss and bother, suddenly collapse? What did it portend for the Canadian political system, and what did it demonstrate about the nature of Canada?

The simplest explanation for the defeat may be the one offered by a former member of the St Laurent cabinet: 'The electorate got bored,' he said. 'St Laurent made it seem so easy to govern Canada that the electorate decided that anybody could do it. And so the people elected anybody.' Equally simple is the reverse proposition: the Liberals were afflicted with incurable arrogance, *hubris,* the quality of blind conceit that invites divine retribution which was administered, in this case, by the votes of an aroused populace. There is some truth in both arguments.

The art of government seemed easy under St Laurent. St Laurent's own qualities had something to do with the phenomenon – his grandfatherly appearance, his mastery of his cabinet, the grace and apparent effortlessness of his administrative style. So did the political balance within Canada. The federal government was still politically predominant, as reflected in the overall sizes of federal and provincial budgets. But, as we have noted, the figures of expenditure on capital account tell a different story, particularly if defence expenditures are excluded. The tale of Canada's capital expenditures prefigured a different kind of politics, although what kind could as yet hardly be guessed at. The age of masterful management of a disparate federal system was clearly coming to an end. Its approaching conclusion was masked only by the mystique of power that wafted along the grey corridors of Ottawa: hence, in some sense, the *hubris* that commentators have depicted.

A more complicated explanation would point out that in twenty-two years in power any democratic government will necessarily offend a large variety of interest groups across the country, especially in a country as large (spatially) and diverse as Canada. It was the Liberals' fate, during their last ten years in office, to offend many. The party's heaviest losses occurred in the western wheatfields where farmers cherished an acute sense of grievance at the government's inability to sell their wheat on glutted international markets, or to offer them compensation for their efforts comparable to what their American cousins were getting. In social policy, despite Paul Martin's best efforts, the Liberals had patently lost the initiative to the provinces, even to Conservative Ontario, where the ideological commitment to social reform was even less, if possible, than that of the majority of the St Laurent cabinet. And, as we have seen, when the government tried to follow the prescriptions of Keynesian finance, it eventually reaped a whirlwind of popular abuse and hostility. 'The Liberal dynasty had simply run out of ideas,' C.D. Howe heavily concluded, after the fall.

Yet it is still possible to view the St Laurent government's legislative program and administrative style, right up to the end, as relatively successful and efficient, certainly by comparison with what came after. St Laurent and his colleagues perceived what most of his critics then and since did not, that the bases for the federal government's predominance were shifting and that, short of attempting a formal constitutional revolution, some accommodation had become inevitable. The flexible attitude to Duplessis's Quebec income tax, the new fiscal arrangements, the willingness to reach an agreement over medicare with Leslie Frost, all betokened the government's conviction that it should be possible to reach a *modus vivendi* with its several opposite numbers in the provinces. They were all partners in administration, after all.

And so they were, over the short term. Because the Liberal government negotiated from a position of strength, it was still able to offer its planning and co-ordinating services to the provinces, to integrate its bureaucrats with their bureaucrats, and to rely on the stronger federal team to prevail. If there was no longer an overt colonial dominance between the national government and its provincial satellites, there might be an administrative colonial bond, sustained by a subterranean administrative politics in which the true actors did all the real bargaining offstage, behind closed doors, in joint co-ordinating committees whose existence the electorate, and most of the politicians, only dimly suspected.

Such a system of accommodation, rather than confrontation, suited St Laurent's personal style – that of the corporation lawyer. It did not appeal to his more politically minded colleagues. 'Mr St Laurent was a lawyer's lawyer,' as Jimmy Gardiner commented. 'He wasn't a politician at all.' St Laurent as prime minister and party leader was indifferent to the needs and well-being of the Liberal party's local organization; though a partisan when he had to be, he interpreted his partisan responsibilities strictly, and in a limited fashion. They did not include close cohabitation with the Liberals' provincial branches, and it is remarkable that during the nine years of St Laurent's term of office the Liberal governments of British Columbia, New Brunswick, and Nova Scotia went down to defeat, while the Liberal parties of Ontario, Quebec, Saskatchewan, and Alberta regularly suffered drubbings at the polls. In a peculiar way the dismal records of the provincial parties brought them closer to the national organization: they became its pensioners, demoralized but docile.

The real dangers of the erosion of the Liberals' provincial bases were concealed by the phenomenal federal election victories of 1949 and 1953. It seemed self-evident that voters could maintain one allegiance provincially and vote, without self-contradiction, for another party in Ottawa. If that were true, then the fate of the provincial parties was indeed a matter of little moment for the Liberal chieftains in the national capital. But it was not so. The cases of Ontario and Quebec are particularly instructive. Leslie Frost, premier of Ontario, was a natural complement to St Laurent. As we have seen, Old Man Ontario took the path of co-operation rather than confrontation with the national government. His cool relations with the national leader of the Conservatives, George Drew, fostered the view that Ontario had, late in the day, discovered the path of true statesmanship that would mute partisan loyalties and provincial entanglements. That proved true in the late forties and early fifties, but only until some other conflict arose between the government of Ontario and the government of Canada. That conflict did arise in the mid-fifties over the proportion of the tax dollar that should go to the provinces, to Ontario in particular. In the 1957 federal election Premier Frost's Conservative partisanship reasserted itself, and, while the subsequent loss of thirty Liberal seats in Ontario cannot be blamed entirely on the weight of the provincial Conservative organization, there were many Liberals who wished that they had more viable provincial allies in the struggle against a revived Conservative party.

The situation in Quebec was even more serious, although its consequences were delayed until the 1958 federal election. There, the provincial Liberal party had been left to perish by the national leadership. And perish it did, annihilated in the 1948 provincial election by Maurice Duplessis's Union Nationale. The Liberals' provincial remnant was itself infiltrated by the Union Nationale (the party caucus in the mid-fifties had to take the unusual step of expelling some disguised Unionistes from its legislative ranks), while federal Liberal MPs often took refuge in electoral pacts with their provincial Union Nationale counterparts: neither, it was agreed, would campaign against the other. And neither did, until Duplessis's organization undertook a pre-emptive strike in 1958, reducing the Liberals in Quebec to a corporal's guard of twenty-five.

The Liberals' provincial weakness was compounded by another oddity. Although the Liberal government enjoyed closer relations with Canadian business than any other twentieth-century Canadian administration, it had not secured business's electoral support. Indeed, one of the keys to C.D. Howe's success as the government's link to the financial and industrial community was his utter indifference to partisan considerations where economic affairs were concerned. The businessmen with whom he dealt admired him, sought his advice, and fed him information; some even followed him into the Liberal party. But not all, and, indeed, not most. Howe continued to enjoy the company of his business friends after the 1957 Liberal débâcle, never more than when his lunch table of bank presidents and mining directors began grumbling about the new Conservative prime minister they had helped to elect. 'Well,' Howe would say, smiling sweetly, 'I didn't vote for him.'

It is tempting to conclude that the Liberal party marched into its electoral Armageddon imbued with the primitive belief that partisan bullets could not touch it. Secure in its administrative non-partisanship, its co-operative competence, and its credo that most problems could be resolved administratively, it met an enemy for which it was totally unprepared. Psychologically disarmed, bereft of their provincial militia, the Liberals were easy prey. With their defeat the post-war period came to an end; a new era of doubtful, contentious politics had arrived.

PART FOUR

The Diefenbaker Years 1957-63

18

The Shape of Things

On June 21, 1957, John Diefenbaker became Prime Minister of Canada. He was the first Conservative to have led the country since 1935, when R.B. Bennett's five-year rule had ended. Canada had grown accustomed to Liberal rule. So had Ottawa. Eventually there were fourteen members in the new cabinet, including the Prime Minister himself. In forming a cabinet there were special problems about Quebec because the Tories had won so few seats there. An anglophone prime minister is expected to have a francophone lieutenant, but Quebec had supplied only nine Tory MPs, of whom few were distinguished and some were anti-Diefenbaker. In the end there were just three ministers from Quebec: only two were francophone, and neither of these received an important portfolio. The significant ministers were Donald Fleming (Finance), George Hees (Transport), George Pearkes (Defence), Gordon Churchill (Trade and Commerce), Davie Fulton (Justice), Douglas Harkness (Agriculture), Michael Starr (Labour), and Alvin Hamilton (Northern Affairs and Natural Resources). When the cabinet membership was announced the press became especially excited about Starr: the Oshawa MP was the first Canadian of Ukrainian origin to sit in cabinet. Later Sidney Smith left the presidency of the University of Toronto to take up External Affairs, which at first Diefenbaker had retained for himself. All the ministers were inexperienced: none had held cabinet office, either federally or provincially, although some had run other things. George Hees, the new transport minister, for instance, had operated the family business before entering politics; George Pearkes, the new Minister of National Defence, had been a senior army commander.

The new ministers were suspicious of the senior civil service; the officials were nervous about the new ministry. The Conservatives knew that most officials were Liberal-appointed and Liberal-trained; the officials suspected that some ministers were madmen and that others were incompetent. In the event, things went better than might have been expected. Some mandarins and some ministers came to respect one another. In some cases, indeed, the ministers relied utterly on their senior officials; the relationships were as varied as the departments. There were troubles, none the less. Some ministers wanted officials who could tell them how to do things and were not happy when officials told them why something could *not* be done. During the long Liberal regime, civil servants had learned to propose and dispose. It was not easy for them to convert themselves into mere executors of cabinet desires. But they tried and, on the whole, succeeded.

Among the most suspicious was the prime minister himself. In his memoirs Diefenbaker reveals just how deeply he distrusted the officials, especially in External Affairs. While in office, he behaved in ways that clogged the diplomatic machine while confusing his associates. Presumably these things happened because he did not trust the officials. George Drew, Canada's new High Commissioner in London, communicated directly with the prime minister, instead of through External Affairs. And, as one adviser later reported, when President Kennedy sent confidential messages from Washington they went directly to Diefenbaker, who would open them, 'look mysterious,' and then lose them. The same thing happened when Harold Macmillan, the British prime minister, sent confidential messages. Nor were such letters answered, by Diefenbaker or by anyone else. After a few awkward encounters between the American embassy and the Department of External Affairs, the adviser trained the maids in the Diefenbaker home to trace down the missing papers – 'between his mattress, or ... in one of those deep drawers, or ... in a pocket in a clothes cupboard somewhere, or under the blotter.'[1]

Thanks to Liberal co-operation, during the session of 1957-8 things in Parliament went well. The new government was able to legislate, and it shoved masses of paper through the House machine. In this first year the prime minister appeared dynamic and decisive. In 1958, thanks to a maladroit Liberal manoeuvre, Diefenbaker was able to call a snap election; and, partly because of Union Nationale support in Quebec, the Conservatives swept the country, winning 208 seats out of 265. Henceforth Diefenbaker was much less decisive. It was almost as if he were afraid that his immense majority might become a steamroller. After all, he had long defended the rights of Parliament and in 1957 the Conservatives had campaigned largely on that issue. From 1958 until 1963 there would be plenty of time for debate; the opposition would be given enough rope; everything would be referred to the House of Commons. In other words, although the parliamentary machine continued to grind out new matter at an

1 Peter Stursberg, *Diefenbaker: Leadership Gained 1956-62* (Toronto: University of Toronto Press, 1975), pp. 172-3.

impressive rate it seemed to have slowed down. Media people, anxious to denigrate Diefenbaker, made the most of the chance with which he had presented them.

Relations between Diefenbaker and his ministers were seldom easy. 'The Chief' had his ways, and often enough the ministers were expected to furnish the means. In his memoirs Donald Fleming described the process of preparing the 1959 budget, and getting it past Diefenbaker and the cabinet, as 'almost degrading' – 'close to humiliation.' No fewer than six futile cabinet meetings were devoted to the subject, to Fleming's intense irritation. Fleming consoled himself with the prospect of balancing the budget the next year, only to have his hopes blasted by increasing expenditures. 'This will prevent us from balancing the budget,' the finance minister protested. 'There is no chance of balancing the budget,' Diefenbaker grinned. 'There never was.'[2]

In 1962 the Conservative government went to the country once more, but its popularity had melted away. In much of the country the leader no longer exerted the magnetism he had displayed in 1957 and 1958. Only on the prairies did the folk hold to the true Tory vision. Perhaps in the cities people had lost their taste for populist oratory; perhaps people were dismayed by the evidence of economic mismanagement, and, in defence policy, by signs of confusion or worse. In Quebec, the Liberals were in power and the Union Nationale machine had crumbled in disarray. Thus, in the election of 1962, the Tories garnered only 116 seats – 17 short of a majority. For a few months more, propped up by the Social Credit members, Diefenbaker clung to office. Then in 1963 another election was forced upon him, and this time, although no party won a majority, the Tories were defeated as definitely as the Liberals had been in 1957.

---

2 Donald Fleming, *So Very Near: The Political Memoirs of the Honourable Donald M. Fleming* (Toronto: McClelland & Stewart, 1985), pp. 39-40, 220.

19

Delusions Complete or Partial

In the 1957 election campaign, and much more forcefully in 1958, Diefenbaker and the Conservatives spoke of a national 'vision.' Some of this related to social welfare measures and to the equalization of opportunity and development throughout the dominion. But most related to the North, and it was Diefenbaker's northern vision that captured the national imagination. Reminding us that he had already thought of this in 1956, Diefenbaker has written, 'In emphasizing the question of northern development and northern vision, I advocated a twentieth-century equivalent of Sir John Macdonald's national policy, a uniquely Canadian economic dream.'[1] Thanks to the intervention of Dr Merril Menzies, the northern dream acquired new substance. Menzies was a Saskatchewan-born economist who had written a doctoral dissertation on Canada's grain trade. Early in 1957 he had sent Diefenbaker a long brief on the development of the North. This, Diefenbaker tells us, captured his interest, inspiring 'the dream of opening Canada to its polar reaches.'[2] For the 1957 campaign he made Menzies a speechwriter, and later Menzies was assistant and economic adviser. In office, Diefenbaker discussed Menzies's ideas with Alvin Hamilton, a devoted Saskatchewan supporter who first entered Parliament in 1957. Hamilton became the Conservatives' Minister of Northern Affairs and Natural Resources and held this portfolio until he moved to agriculture in 1960. He devoted himself to the 'vision' with vigour.

There is every reason to believe that the Prime Minister and Alvin Hamilton took the vision seriously. Certainly Merril Menzies did; once the campaign was over, he worked as an adviser who could help make it come about – whenever he was not advising Diefenbaker directly. As for the Conservative party, it is

1 John G. Diefenbaker, *One Canada: The Crusading Years 1895 to 1956* (Toronto: Macmillan, 1975), p. 11.
2 Ibid., p. 12.

hard to believe that it did not detect the wonderful opportunities for regional patronage that the vision could present. Linking 'regional development' with a 'drive to the North' made everything possible – the South Saskatchewan Dam, a bridge at Prince Albert, a railway to Pine Point where Cominco had discovered a new mine, not to mention a host of branch railway lines and 'roads to resources.' Menzies thought that Canada needed national goals and priorities together with some definite developmental projects, such as a national energy policy with a grid that would cover both power and pipelines. He and Diefenbaker also wanted to build an inventory of all Canadian resources, so as to plan their development. Out of these ideas came the Royal Commission on Energy, the National Energy Board, the roads to resources program, and a conference called 'Resources for Tomorrow.' The government also became interested in the prospects of finding Arctic oil and gas. From Ottawa's perspective, of course, Arctic resources had one great advantage: because they were not in any province they were wholly under dominion control. To Diefenbaker in particular, a vision of national development was especially appealing because of the tradition of Sir John A. Macdonald, on whom the Prime Minister was increasingly inclined to model himself.

But what actually happened? Unable to bring Diefenbaker to the point, in 1959 Menzies became an ordinary civil servant, working hard on the marketing of grain. An energy policy did come, but chiefly because it was politically essential to secure a protected vent for Alberta's overpriced oil. A power grid was discussed, and in the Columbia and Peace River conversations with British Columbia it played some part, but by 1962 the scheme had vanished without trace. Of course some dams, railways, and roads were built, often in co-operation with the provinces. At Frobisher and Inuvik work continued on the planning of modern townsites. During the Diefenbaker years there was plenty of oil exploration in the Arctic, thanks to the incentives with which the government had tried to encourage this, but there was no new production. A good deal was done for ice-breaking, harbours, and airports in the North, and for Eskimo (Inuit today) education. Thanks to the new railway, the Pine Point lead-zinc mine began to produce. In the Northwest Territories explorers found one great tungsten deposit and an immense mass of iron ore. But in all the Diefenbaker years there were only two new northern mines – one gold and one tungsten – while in the North the two uranium mines and the one copper-nickel mine all shut down. In short, although by 1963 the vision had given Canada some useful and expensive new facilities, it had not transformed the economy or even significantly changed it. Moreover a serious national development strategy was still undefined.

In 1958 the Liberals made fun of the vision. They spoke of roads from igloo to igloo – good politics perhaps, but sketchy analysis. They did not ask the questions that now arise: what of the fragile ecology? What of the native peoples and their land claims? What of the markets for Arctic products and the prudence of early development? Indeed none of the parties, including the CCF, worried about these things or mentioned them. As for foreign ownership, the government had considered this matter and tried to exclude foreign control in the northern lands. But as there was little more than exploration in the Arctic during the Diefenbaker years, these devices could not affect the balance between domestic and foreign control. In fact, the vision was the last gasp of Canadian developmentomania. In the eighties Canadians can still get excited about great projects, like a Hibernia oil field or a gas pipeline from Alaska, but nowadays they ask hard questions about need, impact, cost, and pay-off. In Diefenbaker's North the costs would have been immense, the need debatable, the impact destructive, and the pay-off negligible. The North is full of blackflies and mosquitoes. Its winter climate is appalling. It has little soil and not much by way of timber. In present-day terms, it is good only for oil drilling and mining. But mines and oil wells do not support a large or closely settled population, so it is not surprising that so few white Canadians want to live in the North.

For the masses who would linger in the south, cuddled up for warmth close to the American border, Mr Diefenbaker offered something else – a bill of rights. He had demanded this since the mid-thirties; he placed it in campaign platforms in 1957 and again in 1958; at length, in 1960, his Bill for the Recognition and Protection of Human Rights and Fundamental Freedoms received royal assent. In no time Conservative MPs assisted by a patriotic toothpaste manufacturer were scattering the act broadcast.

A simple statute of Parliament, the Bill of Rights could apply only in the federal sphere, and in principle it could be amended, repealed, or overruled by any later Parliament at any time. It also contained escape clauses to protect the security of the state. However, as Diefenbaker himself loved to explain, in Britain such parliamentary enactments had stood for centuries without anyone's trying to repeal them or supersede them; besides which the bill was so drafted as to give it a certain primacy over other laws. Unless some other dominion statute stated that it was to 'operate notwithstanding the Canadian Bill of Rights,' then that other statute was to be 'construed and applied' on the basis of the new bill.

In 1960 Professor Edward McWhinney wrote that the bill might or might not be effective; if it were, it would work by strengthening the tendencies toward libertarianism that had been present in the courts since 1949. Ten years passed before a 'Bill of Rights case' reached the Supreme Court. Writing in 1976 Diefenbaker himself was still proud of his bill, although he observed that the courts had been shying away from it and he noted that in their recent judgments the courts had shown a 'desire to chisel away at some of the freedoms Parliament intended to protect.'[3] It has since been superseded by Pierre Trudeau's Charter of Rights and Freedoms.

Paralleling virtue at home there was virtue abroad. From 1959 until the fall of the Conservative government, Howard Green and Diefenbaker laboured long and hard, although not particularly helpfully, to produce world disarmament and the liberation of captive peoples. The United Nations provided them with a forum, but little was accomplished. When the United Nations tried to stabilize the newly independent Congo (now Zaire), Canada sent a signals unit and helped to finance the UN airlift. Much further north, Canadian troops lingered in the sands of the Middle East hoping to keep the Egyptians and the Israelis apart. Through the Commonwealth Scholarship Plan (1960), the Colombo Plan (1950), and various bilateral and multilateral arrangements Canada gave modest sums to educate the poor countries and to help them grow. The totals were small – by 1961-2, $69.32 million per year in grant aid, or 0.19 per cent of GNP – far, far below the 1 per cent figure that had already begun to circulate as an aid target. But the Canadian public, Diefenbaker believed, would not willingly shell out more. As yet Canada had no 'aid community' that could lobby for larger subventions and sway public opinion. That would come in the sixties – first CUSO, then CIDA, then a steadily rising aid budget.

Diefenbaker was honestly attached to the British connection and genuinely distressed about the ever-closer integration between the Canadian and American economies. He worried about the extent of American direct investment and about the increasing importance of the United States as market and supplier. In the 1957 election campaign he announced that he would try to increase Canada's trading links with the United Kingdom, so as to reduce its dependence on the United States. He must also have been meditating about ways by which to control the inflow of American capital.

With respect to Anglo-Canadian trade, the Conservatives faced a difficult task. In 1872, Britain had supplied 60 per cent of Canada's imports, and the United States, 32 per cent; in 1938 the percentages had been 18 and 63, and in 1957, 9 and 71. As for exports, over the same period Britain's share had shrunk from 47 per cent to 41 per cent and then to 15 per cent, while the American share had changed from 44 per cent to 32 per cent and 59 per cent. These developments occurred in spite of the system of preferential tariffs, whose elaboration Canada had begun in 1897. During the period 1919-32, both Britain and Canada expanded their mutual tariff concessions. Canada acquired a protected British market for certain goods, especially automobiles and foodstuffs, in exchange for tariff cuts on some British manufactures. The Ottawa Agreements of 1932 did

3   John Diefenbaker, *One Canada* (Toronto: Macmillan, 1976), 2:263-4.

something for some Canadian farmers and processors, but little for Britain, as the British share of Canadian import trade continued to fall. After the Second World War Britain mounted an export drive that increased its total sales on the Canadian market. This drive was helped by the preferential tariffs, which accorded duty-free entry to some British products, such as cars and parts. Even so, Britain's share still drifted downward. In addition, for many British manufactures there were serious problems about quality control, spare parts, delivery dates, design, and after-sales service.

The American market was close and familiar; many Canadian producers depended on parts and components from American suppliers, often their own parent firms; Canadian consumers were more accustomed to American designs; Canadian businesses tended to buy American machinery because they could expect speedy and convenient after-sales service, and spare parts, from nearby American sources. These considerations militated against any easy switch from American to British suppliers. Further, nothing could be done by way of new preferential tariffs. The General Agreement on Tariffs and Trade (GATT), which both Canada and Britain had signed, prohibited any extension of preferential tariffs. During the war and the post-war years, Britain made further unilateral commitments to the United States, in which it promised not to invent any new preferences. In the brave new world of multilateral non-discrimination, free trade zones could be created, but new preferential concessions could not be granted or preferential margins widened. Thus Canada could not extend the privileges that Britain already enjoyed. Nor was it obvious how Canada could divert its own exports from American markets to other places, either in Britain or elsewhere. Because the British economy was the slowest growing in the industrialized world, and was in any event relatively small, Britain could not absorb much more of the traditional Canadian exports – wheat, minerals, and forest products. Nor could it buy large quantities of Canadian manufactures, many of which were not price competitive even after preferential concessions had been made. Moreover, from 1940 to 1958 Britain, Europe, and Japan had been obliged by their shortages of dollars to discriminate against goods from the dollar zone. As for the Communist economies in Europe and Asia, they practised rigorous exchange control, buying only what they absolutely required to feed their people and to industrialize. Neither salesmanship nor competitive pricing could make much difference when trying to sell to the Soviet Union, China, or Albania. In Britain, western Europe, and Japan, dollar discrimination was already fading, but there was little Canada could do to speed its departure.

In July 1957, responding to reporters' questions, Diefenbaker proposed to divert 15 per cent of Canada's import trade from the United States to Britain. It seems that the figure occurred to him in the course of the interview. The United

Kingdom responded by offering to form an Anglo-Canadian free trade area, the only sort of thing that the GATT rules would have permitted: over fifteen years duties would be gradually reduced to zero. Neither Diefenbaker nor Fleming was prepared to consider the idea, which by late 1957 had sunk without trace. In his memoirs, Diefenbaker implies that the proposal was never intended seriously. For the rest of his years in office, nothing more was heard about trade diversion; indeed, in its later years his government took certain measures that discouraged Canadian purchases in the United Kingdom.

Export trade was another matter. Coming from the prairies and believing himself to be at one with the small merchants and farmers of Canada, Diefenbaker was especially sensitive to the proposals for a European common market that had already begun to circulate when he became prime minister. What would happen in Europe was still obscure. The United Kingdom was pressing for a free trade area that would cover only manufactures and that would not have a common external tariff. Such a scheme would have let Britain retain its own system of external duties, imperial preferences on Canadian goods, and free entry for wheat and other agricultural products. Britain could also have kept its own system of agricultural assistance, a system that could readily coexist with large-scale imports of grain, meat, dairy products, apples, and other fruits. France and West Germany, however, wanted genuine economic integration, with a common external tariff and internal free trade not just in manufactures but also in agricultural goods. No one knew just how agriculture would be protected in such a common market, but as France and West Germany already had high tariffs and quotas it was clear that Canadian foodstuffs would have hard sledding if Europe should integrate on a non-British model.

When the Conservatives came to power in 1957 the Treaty of Rome had just been signed, establishing the European Economic Community (EEC) on the Franco-German model, with Britain outside. The United Kingdom proceeded to form a Free Trade Area with the Scandinavian countries and some of the other European states that had not joined the Community. However, the British authorities quickly decided that their future lay inside the Community, not outside it, and in 1961 the United Kingdom applied for entrance. Many years afterward, Diefenbaker maintained that French President General de Gaulle had told him that France would never allow Britain to join. If so, it is difficult to understand the barrage of hostility with which the Conservative government of Canada greeted Britain's request. Canada, it seemed, could accept Britain's membership only if all Canada's preferential trading privileges remained intact. When the Commonwealth's prime ministers met in London in September 1962, Diefenbaker criticized not only Britain's application but the 'common market' itself. Fortunately for the Canadian government but unhappily for Britain, France did indeed veto Britain's membership; only in 1973 did the United Kingdom finally win entry, taking Denmark and Ireland in with it.

Regrettably, although Ottawa officials had expected some sort of European economic union since the early 1950s, there is no sign that Diefenbaker or his ministers understood or tried to understand the forces that were impelling Britain into Europe. The rapidly growing markets were on the continent, where the post-war economic miracle had already been under way for more than a decade. Even if the Commonwealth markets had been fully open to Britain's goods, such markets as Canada and Australia could never be as receptive to Britain's manufactures as France, West Germany, or Italy might prove to be. In any event, the Commonwealth countries wanted to industrialize too, and all of them pursued protectionist policies that limited Britain's ability to supply their markets. Admittedly the common market would raise the price of food in Britain. But the British standard of living had risen so high that the typical British family did not spend much of its income on food – at least, not on the raw imported component thereof. When food prices rose, living standards would drop, but only a little and only temporarily; however, when British manufactures enjoyed duty-free access to the immense European market there might well be a boom in British industry whose effects would soon swamp the effect of the more expensive food. In any event, ever since 1931 Britain had wanted to protect its own farmers against competition, and Commonwealth foodstuffs were not exempted from this desire. Even if the British were to stay out of the Community there was no guarantee that Britain would continue to allow relatively free access to Canada's foodstuffs. For Canadian grain growers the dynamic markets would be in the Communist countries and in the Third World, not in Britain or in western Europe. In defending the Commonwealth preferences Diefenbaker was simply defending the past.[4]

Soon after the Conservatives took office the Gordon Commission issued its final report. In this report Walter Gordon expressed his concern about the size of American direct investment in Canada and made a few mild and tentative suggestions for ensuring that Canadians could have access to jobs, research opportunities, and shareholdings in foreign-owned businesses. In his memoirs, written nearly twenty years later, Diefenbaker echoed Gordon's concerns: too much American capital, too few export orders, too little Canadian control. Whatever one may think about Diefenbaker's own feelings while actually in office, there is no doubt that some members of his government did worry about these things. In September 1957, Diefenbaker himself told an American audience that American firms should offer stock to Canadians and should not regard Canada as an

4   See John G. Diefenbaker, *One Canada: The Years of Achievement 1957-1962* (Toronto: Macmillan, 1976), p. 264.

extension of the American market. In framing new regulations for resource development in the Northwest Territories, the Diefenbaker government insisted that firms should be controlled in Canada and that the majority of shares be owned in the dominion also. The regulations of 1960 required that oil and gas leases be granted only to Canadian citizens and residents, or to Canadian incorporated companies with shares either listed on a Canadian exchange or at least 50 per cent owned by Canadian residents and citizens. Of course these rules did not apply to the provinces, where provincial authorities determined policy with respect to resources. Nor was anything similar done with respect to manufacturing, finance, or real estate. In other words, the Diefenbaker government took some steps down the path recommended by the Gordon Commission, but tentatively and timidly. Nor did the government recognize, until after 1960, that the monetary policies of the Bank of Canada were encouraging exactly the sort of capital inflow that Gordon and Diefenbaker seemed to deplore. This topic is explored more fully in Chapter 20.

The prime minister believed in personal diplomacy and in world travel. Regrettably, the public became increasingly sceptical about the value of these adventures, and Diefenbaker himself eventually lost interest in them. It was all very well while President Eisenhower was installed in the White House, because the two old men understood and liked one another. It was different when the young and energetic John Kennedy came to power. Nor was the Prime Minister altogether happy in his Commonwealth relationships, seriously though he took them.

Diefenbaker also made many trips to the United States, where he conferred with both Eisenhower and Kennedy. He found the former congenial, but soon fell out with the latter, whose brashness offended him. Perhaps he was surprised to discover that Kennedy was as concerned to defend and advance American interests as he himself was anxious to advance Canadian. The Canadian position was admittedly difficult. Anxious to assert an independent national direction, in contra-distinction to the 'Pearson pattern' which they saw as unduly acquiescent, the Conservatives none the less had no particular goals that they wished to attain in international affairs. They were, in fact, consistently negative. Canada would not join the Organization of American States (OAS); it would not recognize Communist China; it would not approve the American response – or the Soviet initiative – in the Cuban missile crisis of 1962, when the Soviet Union installed ballistic missiles in Cuba and President Kennedy used a naval blockade to get them removed. As for its own defences, Canada would neither withdraw from NATO nor increase its contributions to the alliance; Canada would cancel the production of its own interceptor-fighter and buy American Bomarc missiles, but it would not purchase the atomic warheads for which these missiles were designed. It would not force South Africa out of the Commonwealth but would devise a form of words that would induce the South Africans to withdraw and not apply for readmission.

Apart from the problem of the EEC, the main item on the Commonwealth agenda was the South African perplex. At the end of the Second World War the Commonwealth consisted of Britain, Ireland, Canada, Australia, New Zealand, and South Africa. Ireland quickly departed, but India, Pakistan, and Ceylon were soon admitted, and in 1957 Ghana and Malaya became members also. It had been established that if a Commonwealth country became a republic it could remain a member so long as it acknowledged the British sovereign as head of the Commonwealth; Ireland withdrew before that fact had become clear. Formally, on becoming a republic a country had to reapply for Commonwealth membership. In 1961 South Africa became a republic. At that time its racial policies had long been a world scandal; the question was whether it should, or could, be readmitted, given these policies. The Commonwealth tradition was one of non-interference in the internal affairs of members; it was different, however, if a country was applying or reapplying to join the club. Also, it was possible to argue that if South Africa were inside the Commonwealth it might be more amenable to suggestion. Perhaps in time it might be led to adopt less dreadful policies. At the Commonwealth Prime Ministers' Conference of May 1960, Diefenbaker did his best to convince the South African delegates that their nation's racial policies were repugnant to civilized opinion everywhere. Soon thereafter, South Africa asked to be assured that if it became a republic it would be welcomed back into the Commonwealth. Diefenbaker argued that no such assurance could be given in advance, but that an application could certainly be considered.

Later in 1960, South Africa held a referendum on the question of republican status, toward which it moved early in 1961. The South African authorities told their electorate that they would apply for readmission to the Commonwealth and suggested that other countries would welcome South Africa back. However, Diefenbaker later wrote that he did not see how he could support South Africa's readmission if the Union government would not even pay lip service to the concept of racial equality. He was not anxious to drive South Africa out of the club, but when the Commonwealth leaders reassembled in March 1961 he supported a passage in the draft communiqué that labelled apartheid as inconsistent with Commonwealth ideals and that committed Commonwealth countries to work for equality of opportunity, 'irrespective of race, colour, or creed.' Unable to accept such a declaration, the South Africans withdrew their proposal to rejoin the club. At the time, Diefenbaker regretted their decision, but he later wrote, 'in retrospect I consider it fortunate that the South Africans withdrew their application.'[5]

American wheat policy was a worry to the Conservative government. For some time, the United States had been producing surplus wheat, because it supported wheat prices at a level that consistently produced an excess of supply over demand. The US government bought the excess and stored it. This accumulation was worrying in and of itself; more worrying still, the United States had begun to give food aid and to sell wheat in exchange for 'soft currencies.' Such sales were, in effect, gifts. Although Canada did not support the price of wheat, the Canadian Wheat Board controlled the marketing of the crop, and as it was not willing to sell wheat at very low prices it piled up surpluses first in the elevators and then, once the elevators were full, on the farms. In Britain and Europe, governments were ever more inclined to protect their own farmers; in Asia and the rest of the Third World, Canadian grain met competition from subsidized American grain and from American food aid. In December 1957 Diefenbaker proposed to the NATO council a World Food Bank to hold stocks and supply them to countries in need. Unfortunately, in 1957 the United States was not interested in a food bank, although by 1960 there was a new secretary of state in Washington, and a new Food for Peace program. In 1958, the United States believed that to store all the food would cost too much. In 1960, when Diefenbaker and Eisenhower met once more, Eisenhower was more forthcoming, and later that year Canada and the United States jointly sponsored a UN resolution for a food bank. The resolution was adopted unanimously but, like most UN resolutions, came to nothing.

In May 1961, four months after his inauguration as president, John F. Kennedy came to Ottawa. Having explained his worries about Cuba, he pressed Canada to join the OAS. The Canadian elder statesman was not impressed by the young American leader, nor did Kennedy enjoy Diefenbaker. In Ottawa, the President mislaid a memorandum that fell into Diefenbaker's hands. Rather than return it, Diefenbaker used it to charge Kennedy with interference. Kennedy, we are told, vowed never to meet Diefenbaker again. It has also been suggested that he smoothed the path that led an eminent American public relations firm onto the Liberal payroll.

Such manoeuvres were not the best way to create confidence between the two great countries of North America. No doubt there was guilt on both sides, or perhaps one should say errors of judgment. But there were also substantive problems, and these really were not affected by the histrionics with which Diefenbaker loved to decorate the sober fabric of Canadian-American diplomacy.

Like other Canadian governments, Diefenbaker's loved royal commissions.

5   Ibid., pp. 209-21.

Among those it established were the Glassco Commission, which looked into the organization of the public service, the Borden Commission, on energy, the Hall Commission, on health care, the Macpherson Commission, on transportation, the Porter Commission, on banking, the Carter Commission, on taxation, and the O'Leary Commission, on the problems of Canadian magazines. The Glassco Commission's report led to some rearrangements in the federal administration. The Hall and Carter commissions, which reported long after Pearson's Liberals had taken office, embarked on enormous research programs and produced voluminous reports that have not markedly affected events. The Porter Commission, which also reported after Diefenbaker's fall, did affect banking arrangements. The Borden Commission developed a plan to reserve the Ontario market for Alberta oil. As for the O'Leary Commission's report, when it appeared in June 1961 it embarrassed the government greatly.

The 'magazine problem' had arisen because some American publications, especially *Time* and *Reader's Digest,* were producing special runs for Canadian distribution for which they solicited Canadian advertising. At that time there was already a Canadian edition of *Reader's Digest,* and *Time* was planning to print in Canada and to bring out a distinctive Canadian edition. Canadian mass magazines complained that such editions, plus the overflow of American magazines into Canada, amounted to unfair competition. Canadian magazines had to bear editorial costs but could not attract much advertising revenue; American magazines did not have very heavy editorial costs relating to Canada, but because they had large Canadian circulations they could and did draw advertising revenue away from the Canadian magazines.

No doubt the Americans were doing well out of selling magazines in Canada. But there was no reason to believe that Canadian advertisers would stick to the Canadian media, so long as the American media were so widely read in Canada. The O'Leary Commission suggested that Canada should prohibit the importation of any magazine that contained advertising for the Canadian market. Thus if Imperial Oil advertised in *Newsweek,* Canadian Customs would bar *Newsweek* at the frontier. It also suggested that if a Canadian taxpayer advertised in any 'foreign' periodical, whether printed abroad or in Canada, his advertising outlays should not count as a business outlay for tax purposes. Canadians would still be able to buy foreign magazines so long as these did not have any advertising that was specifically directed at the Canadian market. As for the change in tax treatment, it was reasonable to suppose that Canadian advertisers would swallow the extra outlay for the sake of the circulation and that to counter the tax change American publishers might lower their advertising rates in their 'Canadian editions.' If, as was alleged, they were doing so well out of their Canadian operations, presumably they could have afforded to do so, although of course they did not want to tell the government so. In his memoirs Diefenbaker explains that he received strong representations from *Reader's Digest* and *Time*. He mentions no pressure from the US government, and it is reasonable to suppose that if there had been any pressure he would not have concealed the fact.

The government adopted the O'Leary recommendations, but before it could do anything about its decision, it fell from office. Like so many other matters, the 'magazine question' remained to perplex future governments.

The St Laurent government had set up a royal commission on broadcasting, under the chairmanship of Robert Fowler. In October 1958 it reported, and the government based much of the new Broadcasting Act on that report. No longer would the CBC license and regulate the private stations. Henceforth this would be done by the Board of Broadcast Governors, or BBG, the ancestor of the present CRTC. Now there could be private television networking, and private TV stations in the big cities as well as in the small towns. New licences were eagerly sought and quickly awarded. No one was surprised that some new licences, such as the Toronto one, went to ardent Conservatives.

There was also the Bladen Commission on the automobile industry. Formed because the Canadian car industry had lost its export markets and much of its domestic market too, the commission recommended various inducements that might produce a more extended integration of the North American car industry. Although the Auto Pact of 1965 did not resemble the Bladen Plan, it originated with the Bladen Commission's report. Professor Bladen also wanted the government to put an import duty on British cars and remove the excise tax from Canadian-made cars. He got the latter but not the former. Not that it mattered much; already the British competitive position was eroding, and soon that erosion would have gone far enough to do the work for which Bladen suggested an import duty. On December 11, 1979, another Conservative government announced that it was ending the preferential tariff concessions to Britain, not just on cars and parts but across the board. By then, however, almost no one noticed, and certainly no one cared. Like Britain's imperial power, imperial preferences had faded into the woodwork, and as foci for debate they now mattered not at all. Other and more pressing economic issues perplexed the Conservative cabinet; to these issues we now turn our attention.

20

Managing the Economy:
Budgets, the Bank, and the Diefenbuck

Like most Canadian prime ministers, Diefenbaker was not particularly interested in economic affairs except in so far as they might affect his fate at the polling stations. But like most of his Liberal predecessors he was genuinely anxious to apply the power of the state to help the downtrodden and the disadvantaged. He was, in other words, a populist or a Red Tory, not a neo-conservative of the sort that surfaced in the late seventies. Coming as he did from Saskatchewan, the Prime Minister was especially interested in the fate of the farmers, the one group that seemed to have gained nothing and lost something in the great post-war boom. At first, it appeared, Diefenbaker was content to leave the problems of macroeconomic management – monetary policy, taxing, and spending – to the officials and to his competent and respected Minister of Finance, Donald Fleming. Unfortunately for Diefenbaker, the economy would not be left alone. Unemployment was inconveniently high. The management at the Bank of Canada soon revealed itself to be both inflexible and intractable. Finally, in 1961-2, the government itself provoked a flight from the Canadian dollar, after which it was obliged to pick up the pieces in an embarrassingly public way. In this chapter we present the story of these misadventures: the Conservative budgets; the crisis at the Bank of Canada; the dollar crisis; and Tory agricultural policy.

In 1957 there were already signs of economic trouble. After taking office Diefenbaker was able to make parliamentary play with the evidence that the Liberals had known what was afoot. But there was little point in blaming the Liberals for their failure to prevent unemployment if the Conservative government could not manage to dispel it. Thereafter, although the unemployment rate fluctuated from time to time it remained embarrassingly high throughout the Diefenbaker years.

Things were further complicated for the Tories by the fact that James Coyne was governor of the Bank of Canada. A Liberal appointee and a friend of Liberal ministers, Coyne was a man the Tories would instinctively distrust. Worse, he had his own views on economic policy, and these proved not to be the same as the new cabinet's, although within the cabinet Coyne certainly had some supporters. Worst of all, although Coyne would manage the Bank's affairs to accommodate the government's needs he would not co-operate in any program of fiscal and monetary expansion – the medicine that some ministers and most economists would have prescribed at the time, given the slow growth and rising unemployment of the late fifties.

At least as serious were the troubles of the resource industries, whose development had helped to fuel the expansion of the early and middle fifties. The market for uranium did not develop as rapidly as governments and companies had hoped. By 1960 mines were closing, and in the new mining towns life had become alarmingly insecure. The Americans were still subsidizing the export of wheat. As a consequence grain piled up on Canada's farms and prices fell disconcertingly. Thanks to competition and the ever-growing tanker fleet the oil of Venezuela and the Middle East was becoming cheaper, and it penetrated ever more deeply into the American and Canadian markets, with painful effects on Alberta's oil industry. The emerging European trade blocs would do further damage to Canada's metals industries, lumbering, and wheat; although Britain and Europe were dismantling the discriminations against dollar goods that had survived the years of post-war reconstruction, there was no reason to be optimistic about future demand for Canada's staple exports.

As these storm clouds gathered on the horizon the government was much more preoccupied with a tempest in a teapot – what to do about the unemployment insurance system. At March 31, 1957, the unemployment insurance fund held a surplus of $871 million. The surplus had accumulated because in planning the contributions in the early forties the actuaries had assumed that unemployment would be higher than it had proved to be from 1940 to 1957. Although the St Laurent government had revised the scheme so as to make the payouts larger, nevertheless the fund had continued to grow. Since the end of 1952 unemployment benefits had been larger than current contributions, but until the end of 1956 the fund had been earning enough interest to maintain itself and even to increase. Then, with rising unemployment, the fund began to shrink; and thereafter it declined inexorably throughout the Diefenbaker years. Although the government raised the rates of contribution it also made the payout easier and more generous, while at the same time unemployment stayed high. Hence annual outlays rose from $210 million in 1956 to $494 million in 1962, while the fund shrank away to nothing.

It was easy for opponents and journalists to claim that there was something wrong about all this. Was not the government dissipating the unemployment insurance fund? Economists saw the matter rather differently. When people received unemployment benefits they spent the money, creating extra demand and extra jobs at a time when there were not enough jobs to go around. If government had tried to 'protect the fund,' it would have had to cut benefits or raise contribution rates – thereby reducing the after-tax income that people could spend. Certainly, if jobs and output are seen as being of paramount importance, then the government was right to spend the fund, and it would have been wrong to find the money for additional benefits by raising taxes.

The same general argument applies to the old age security payments, which also fell outside the ordinary budget. Here, too, the special tax collections did not cover the outlays, and this had been the case since 1952, when the special old age security fund was set up. Unlike the unemployment insurance fund, however, this 'fund' had never contained anything and had always required subsidy from the ordinary budget. The Diefenbaker government raised the old age pension without raising old age security taxes. When unemployment was relatively high, both decisions were certainly wise.

So much for the largest extra-budgetary items. What of the budgets themselves?

During the Diefenbaker years there was constant conflict both within the cabinet and among the government's advisers with respect to taxing and spending policy. Donald Fleming, the Minister of Finance, preferred to balance his budgets, although he was never able to do so. Many advisers, especially those in the Department of Finance, argued in the same way. Afraid of inflation, they disliked new spending and they hoped that the government would cut taxes. However, Dr Merril Menzies thought that the government should try to eliminate unemployment by cutting tax rates and by new spending, especially on national and northern development. The Prime Minister and many members of the cabinet thought the same. Thus before the end of 1957 the Conservatives had asked Parliament to cut the income tax and to authorize various new kinds of spending programs. In later years the government did more of the same, although it was more and more inclined to concentrate on extra spending, not tax cuts.[1]

It was easy to make fun of the results. On the one hand, the finance minister was known to want balanced budgets; on the other hand, the accounts were never balanced, and only twice did Fleming dare even to forecast a surplus. As time passed, Fleming himself became even less attached to the idea of a balanced budget, and from December 1960 through spring 1962 he wanted to cut taxes and raise spending so as to create new jobs. Although the budgetary expenditures were consistently higher than budgetary revenues, in only one of his seven

1   See Fleming's memoir, *So Very Near: The Summit Years* (Toronto: McClelland and Stewart, 1985), vol. 2, especially chap. 52, 55, 59, 66, and 71.

Tory cakewalk.
Prime Minister Diefenbaker, Minister of Finance Donald Fleming, and Minister of
Trade and Commerce George Hees (Macpherson, 1961). Reproduced with the
permission of the *Toronto Star*

budgets did Fleming actually raise tax rates; in all the other budgets, rates were reduced. Fun was also made of the fact that things never came out the way Fleming said they would. But there was nothing really discreditable about all this. Fleming's forecasts went wrong partly because the economy grew rather slowly, and partly because his colleagues kept inventing new ways to spend money. Thanks to the latter, spending ran ahead of the estimates; thanks to the former, revenue rose less rapidly than one might have hoped. What would have been really discreditable would have been to make reality march with the forecast by cutting expenditure or raising tax rates. Given the high unemployment and the slow growth, neither medicine would have been a good prescription.

Because unemployment was higher than desired, while prices were barely rising and the economy was growing rather slowly, it was sensible for the Conservative government to cut tax rates and to devise new spending schemes. Relative to government spending or national output the results were far from bad. In the event, of course, these measures were not enough to get rid of all the unemployment, although they were certainly large enough to reduce it. But should the deficits have been larger? Or could they have been?

It is always easy for Parliament to cut tax rates and to give citizens more grants and larger subsidies. The same goes for intergovernmental payments – transfers from the dominion to the provinces and municipalities. And it is always easy to prescribe such medicine when unemployment rises. But history has taught us that after unemployment has risen it generally falls. At such times a prudent government may want to *raise* the tax rates and *reduce* the subsidies to citizens and junior governments, although politically that is a much harder thing to do. And, of course, the grants and subsidies and benefits and welfare payments get built into the economic and social system so that people come to depend on them. Thus a prudent government, hoping to fight unemployment by cutting tax rates and by pumping out grants and subsidies, might do well to restrain itself. Indeed, some observers think that the Conservative government was not sufficiently restrained. Then there are new kinds of government spending on goods and services, especially on such installations as roads, canals, public buildings, and the like. The Conservatives were very interested in such things. Diefenbaker, prompted by Merril Menzies, had seen a 'northern vision,' and he did not just dream dreams about it; he set out to build railways and roads in northern Canada, and he meditated on a second Trans-Canada Highway. Under his leadership the government began to spend much more on technical surveys, so as to map Canada's natural wealth. In the 1962 election campaign he came near to enunciating a still more grandiose developmental vision.

As anti-unemployment weapons such schemes have one important advantage: they need not go on forever. One can build a few 'roads to resources' without committing oneself to build a thousand miles or so, every year, indefinitely. As regional and personal patronage they are ideal, too. But the projects take time to work out, and at any given time there may be only a limited number of projects that a government can sensibly undertake. It is easy to talk of extra spending, but sometimes it is hard to find anything useful to spend on. And compared with the St Laurent government, Diefenbaker's was certainly an ingenious and imaginative spender!

It is also important to remember that in the late fifties there was a good deal of confusion about the *source* or *origin* of the unemployment. When unemployment is too high because demand is too low, it makes sense to cut tax rates, devise new spending programs, and pay larger subsidies to citizens and junior governments. When output and employment have fallen from a previous peak, it is reasonable to suppose that the trouble is deficient demand. But as shown in Part I, output and employment *rose* during the Diefenbaker years. It was certainly not a depression, or even a recession, but rather a deceleration. This fact worried politicians and officials who thought the standard Keynesian medicine too crude. Moreover, many observers thought there was something odd about the unemployed themselves. Inside and outside government it was noticed that the unemployed were chiefly those who had few skills and little or no education. The better educated, it seemed, had no trouble finding or holding a job, so perhaps the real trouble was lack of education. The Department of Labour had discovered that in the post-war expansion, Canada had drawn many skilled workers from Britain and Europe, but relatively few from its own native-born population. Perhaps the real trouble was a mismatch between labour supply and labour demand, it reasoned. Or perhaps the real trouble was 'automation,' the replacement of men by machines. In the late fifties, automation was a vogue word in the media and among the literati; its function was much the same as 'energy crisis' in the seventies, or 'informatics' in the eighties.

These conflicting counsels inspired the Diefenbaker government to try various things. Grants to universities were doubled, and arrangements were made by which the Quebec universities, for the first time, might receive dominion funds. In 1960, legislation was passed to allow the dominion to help bear the costs of technical and vocational education. Co-operating with the provinces and sharing the costs, the dominion financed many new technical and vocational schools and gave large grants for school staff and equipment. A propaganda campaign, aimed at keeping pupils in school, was also instituted. About automation nothing could be done, although by increasing the period of entitlement to unemployment benefits from sixteen to fifty-two weeks the government may have helped to cushion its impact.

The problem of winter unemployment had always been a serious matter in

Canada, but now it, too, attracted still more attention. Strictly speaking, it cannot have affected the average level of unemployment, which was adjusted for seasonal variation; there was no reason to believe that winter unemployment was more severe under Diefenbaker than under St Laurent or King. But it was a distressing social problem, and one that the public was less and less willing to accept as a fact of life. The St Laurent government had introduced a system of 'seasonal unemployment benefits,' which allowed workers to receive special assistance even if they had not contributed enough to qualify for the ordinary unemployment benefit. The Diefenbaker government made the terms more generous and extended seasonal benefits to farm labourers and fishermen, but by subsidizing municipalities and the construction trades it tried to encourage winter *work* as well. These subsidies were withdrawn under Pearson, but they seem to have changed the behaviour of the Canadian construction industry, which learned a good deal about year-round working.

Of course these educational and climatic schemes had their impact on the budget, and therefore on the level of spending in the economy. But they were not introduced for that reason. Rather, they were meant to improve the economic *structure,* making the economy perform better in the longer run. Indeed, years would pass before the university funding and the vocational education plan could affect the labour market in any important way. The Conservatives must have realized this fact, but it did not deter them.

Nor should one forget George Hees, the Minister of Trade and Commerce, who mobilized our trade commissioners and businessmen in the interest of the export trade. No one knows just how effective Hees's razzle-dazzle methods may have been, but certainly they were pushing in the right direction. It is a pity that until 1961 they were impeded by the exchange rate: when the Canadian dollar stood relatively high while productivity was relatively low and wage rates were not low enough to offset these two facts, Canadian manufacturers had difficulty keeping their domestic markets, to say nothing of finding new foreign ones.

Fleming himself later explained that he knew unemployment was growing 'into '59.' He argues, however, that the government's approach was 'realistic ... We did take measures to increase direct employment by government programs.' Michael Starr, then Minister of Labour, has said that the winter works and the school programs were meant 'to relieve unemployment.' Fleming has also explained that although he was proud of the balanced budget that he introduced in 1960, three weeks later things were looking much worse. 'It was necessary then, as we thought, to resort to more fiscal measures to accompany any measures in the monetary field that the Bank of Canada might see fit to take.' Alvin Hamilton has asserted that the 'tight money budget' of 1959 actually stopped a recovery.[2] It was only when devaluation began in mid-1961, he argues, that Canada really began to absorb this unemployment. But Hamilton exaggerates the effect of Fleming's tax increases – foolish though these doubtless were, given the levels of unemployment and prices. There is no doubt that by June 1961 the government was consciously planning to force the dollar down so as to make jobs, a sensible step that might well have been taken sooner.

As Fleming explained to Diefenbaker shortly after making his first budget speech on June 17, 1958, the government would have trouble borrowing the sums that would be needed both to pay its current bills and also to retire or roll over $19 billion in old loans. Matters would quickly get even worse, since, between the beginning of 1959 and mid-1966, Ottawa would also have to repay some $10 billion in old Victory Loans. For the time being the government would not be able to borrow on a long-term basis; instead, it would have to raise $400 million from the Bank of Canada. Fleming also suggested that the government might convert $6.4 billion of the old 3 per cent Victory Loans into new bonds. These would pay higher interest and would have various terms; there would be cash bonuses for those who agreed to convert their holdings of the old bonds into new ones. As Diefenbaker later explained: 'This proposal ... would lift from the market the burden of the substantial amount of early maturities. For years afterward, debt management would be simpler. Above all, this would restore confidence and give us the opportunity to carry on with our development plans.'[3]

The conversion involved an immense selling effort: by September 15, 1958, some 90 per cent of the old Victory Loans had been converted into the new government bonds. Unfortunately, the new terms were not attractive enough to make people hold the bonds, once converted. Thus at once the public began to sell the new paper. For a time the Bank of Canada supported the market by buying goverment bonds. But early in October 1958 it decided that it could not go on doing so: to buy up the bonds the Bank had to create new money, and this it was unwilling to do on the necessary scale. Thus, as interest rates went up, the bonds depreciated. The people who had converted their Victory Bonds were annoyed and criticized the government for 'mismanaging the conversion.' For those who had held relatively short-dated Victory Bonds the complaint had some merit: they could have held their old bonds to maturity, cashed in each $100 bond for its full face value, and started again; now if they wanted to get the face value they would have to hold the new bonds for some time, often for a

2 Peter Stursberg, *Diefenbaker: Leadership Gained 1956-62* (Toronto: University of Toronto Press, 1975), pp. 210-11, 213, 214.
3 John G. Diefenbaker, *One Canada: The Years of Achievement 1957 to 1962* (Toronto: Macmillan, 1976), p. 276.

good many years, as the new issues ranged in term from three and a quarter to twenty-five years.

More serious was the economists' complaint that because the conversion had replaced short-term bonds with longer-term ones it lengthened the average term of the national debt. Because short-term bonds feel more like money, if the average term rises the public is likely to spend and buy less – hardly what one should prescribe for the late 1950s. However, to facilitate the conversion and to support the new bonds for a couple of weeks the Bank of Canada had had to create $1 billion of new money. By expanding the money supply, the Bank may well have offset the contractionary effect that would normally have followed from the conversion itself. If the Bank had allowed the money supply to rise further there would be no reason to criticize the conversion operation, or even to mention it. As things were, however, the operation is interesting not only for its effects but also for what it revealed about the relations between the Conservative government and the governor of the Bank of Canada.

During Coyne's term as governor, the Bank allowed chartered bank reserves to rise by 4 per cent per year, while output grew 3.1 per cent per year on the average. Thus it would seem at first sight that money was outgrowing output, contributing to inflationary pressure rather than restraining it. However, the extra reserves were concentrated in the single year 1958, when the central bank was financing both a massive bond issue and the conversion plan that has just been described. Coyne regretted the resultant increase in the reserves and in the money supply. Although he thought it 'justified and unavoidable' that the Bank should help to finance the government's deficit and its conversion plan, he believed that the increase was 'substantially greater than would have been necessary for monetary and economic reasons alone.'[4] This statement appears to mean that he would have preferred to see the money supply grow more slowly, in spite of the rising unemployment rate, which he knew was becoming a social and economic problem in 1958, and in spite of the fact that the general price level was no longer rising.

The following year, having explained once more that 'the primary function of the central bank is to regulate the total quantity of money,' Coyne went on to say that he had kept chartered bank reserves 'on a broadly stable basis.'[5] In fact, although prices were still stable and unemployment was still high, bank reserves *fell* by 4.7 per cent while output *rose* nearly 4 per cent! The Bank was applying a genuine squeeze. It is hardly surprising that in Canada the cost of credit rose, both absolutely and in comparison with American interest rates. With respect to the cost and availability of credit, government and governor were already on a

4   Bank of Canada, *Annual Report of the Governor*, 1959.
5   Bank of Canada, *Annual Report of the Governor*, 1960.

collision course.

Coyne knew that too many Canadians were out of work. He knew that many Canadians, inside and outside government, blamed him. But he refused to accept any blame. Since unemployment rates had been rising for a decade, he argued that the cause must be some long-standing underlying structural deficiency, not Bank of Canada policies. There was no shortage of money, he said, and no deficiency of demand. The problem, he wrote in 1961, was an excessive deficit on the balance of payments. What was needed was tighter control over imports so that Canada could live within its means.[6]

Unfortunately, by tightening credit relative to the situation in the United States Coyne had indirectly and probably unintentionally helped to create the problem of which he complained. In 1959 short-term loans earned 4.81 per cent in Canada and 3.42 per cent in the United States, while long-term government bonds paid 4.93 per cent in the former country and 4.06 per cent in the latter. It was hardly surprising that, whenever possible, Canadian businesses and junior governments were raising funds abroad. When they brought their borrowings home they had to exchange American dollars for Canadian, thus forcing up the exchange rate – the price of Canadian dollars – and encouraging Canada to import more goods and to export less. Since the exchange rate was floating, any extra inflow of money tended to force up the rate, generating an extra current account deficit. For an underemployed economy a more unwise policy would have been hard to devise. It would have been more sensible to use monetary policy in the reverse direction, making credit cheaper in Canada relative to the United States so as to discourage foreign borrowing and encouraging the exchange rate to float down. But this sensible policy Coyne would not countenance.

During 1958-61, Canadian productive capacity rose much more rapidly than production. Hence the level of unemployment went up, hovering between 6 and 7 per cent for four years. Yet during those years Canada imported $4.9 billion in foreign capital. Believing that the unemployment problem was deeply rooted in Canada's economic structure, Coyne asserted that it was 'unsound and dangerous' to increase the money supply fast, or at all. Thus he continued to fight inflation because he thought it was right to do so, even though prices had been almost stable since mid-1957.

Among Canadian economists the policies of Governor Coyne created rage and dismay so strong that, in 1961, many of them signed an open letter that requested his dismissal on grounds of incompetence. In Ottawa, government mandarins closed ranks, defending one of their own against outside criticism. To

6 Bank of Canada, *Annual Report of the Governor*, 1961.

ensure that none of the offending economists would ever receive government employment, a black list was prepared and extensively circulated. However, the government itself was becoming alarmed. Coyne's monetary policies were creating difficulties that were as much political as economic. We do not know when Diefenbaker first perceived Coyne as a political problem. It may have been in 1960, when Coyne began to make speeches urging Canadians to tighten their belts and live within their means, though Diefenbaker himself later protested that he had always seen the governor as 'an unregenerate Grit.'[7] Coyne proposed reducing living standards, discouraging capital inflows, raising taxes, and decreasing public expenditures. His message was by any standard sensational; coming from a high public official its effect on the political scene was disquieting.

Some observers deduced that Donald Fleming was not all that far from Coyne's position. He was willing to act against capital inflows; he seemed to distrust the idea of deficit financing. While Fleming was inclined to defend the governor as a public servant, Coyne's speeches, and indications that his views lacked support among economists in and out of government as well as among Canadian banks, undermined the minister's confidence. In March 1961 Fleming began to cast about for ways to secure Coyne's departure.[8]

In the process he discovered that the previous year the Bank's board of directors (most of them Tory appointees) had fixed Coyne's annual pension at the very high sum of $25,000. The government had been routinely notified, but had not noticed. Fleming would have been well advised to let this sleeping dog lie; instead he passed on his startling information to the cabinet.

The effect on the cabinet and on Diefenbaker was electric. They made a fatal choice to confuse the essentially private pension issue with larger questions of public policy. Fleming was authorized to ask for Coyne's immediate resignation, though in the ordinary course of events his term had only seven months to run. This Fleming did on May 30, 1961.

In the subsequent discussion Fleming stressed the disagreement over policy but also brought up the pension. Coyne took umbrage, as well he might: the government had the means to know, and he assumed the government had known. He could not know that those whose duty it was to report the matter had not done so. Again, it would have been better to let the issue die; instead, it was now not merely allowed, but encouraged, to take the shape of a battle over Coyne's personal integrity.[9]

To the government's surprise, public opinion swung round to support Coyne,

7   Ibid.
8   Fleming, *So Very Near*, II:302-14.
9   Ibid., pp. 315-20.

who refused to resign in the face of the slur cast upon his honour. The cabinet now placed a bill calling for his dismissal before Parliament. It was passed by the House of Commons after a bitter debate, notable for evidently unfounded allegations that Coyne was being advised by the Liberal opposition. To add insult to injury, Coyne was not allowed to testify before a committee of the House.

But if the Conservatives controlled the House, the Liberals controlled the Senate by virtue of the tremendous backlog of King and St Laurent appointees who enjoyed tenure for as long as they drew breath. A Senate committee listened sympathetically as Coyne defined the issue as one not of policy but of character assassination. The Senate rejected the government's bill. Claiming vindication, Coyne finally resigned, and was replaced by Louis Rasminsky, who issued a statement affirming that the ultimate responsibility for monetary policy lay with the government of the day.[10]

Responsible observers, including some of Diefenbaker's cabinet, have laid most of the blame at the Chief's feet, and Diefenbaker's subsequent attempt at self-exculpation is not convincing. In the history of the decline of the Diefenbaker government's reputation and authority, the Coyne affair therefore takes pride of place, the more so because it was so needless and pointless. In that, Canadians were beginning to conclude, it was typical of Diefenbaker.

What difference had Coyne really made? Even now it is hard to tell. No doubt his 'tight money' policies raised Canadian interest rates, both absolutely and relative to American rates. Hence the policies encouraged Canadians to borrow abroad. As the exchange rate was floating, these foreign borrowings raised the exchange rate when the borrowers exchanged their US dollars for Canadian dollars in the foreign exchange markets. Imports of goods were encouraged, and exports discouraged, at least to some extent. On the domestic scene, Coyne's influence may have strengthened the forces within the government that wanted to control borrowing and outlays, so as to prevent inflation, while working toward a more nearly balanced budget. But some ministers, such as Donald Fleming, had similar desires, and so did some of the senior Finance officials. Scanning Diefenbaker's spending programs, one sees little sight of fiscal rectitude on the 'Coynesian' model. As for the crusade against foreign investment and the reduction in the exchange rate, by 1960 the Prime Minister himself was talking of the former, while important ministers, such as Alvin Hamilton, were arguing for the latter. In 1960-1, commentators often examined the entrails of government and ministerial statements in an effort to discover whether Coynesianism or Keynesianism was in the ascendant. But Coyne probably had little effect on the course of government fiscal policy. Indeed, it may have been because he

10 See J.W. Pickersgill's version of events in his *The Road Back* (Toronto: University of Toronto Press, 1986), pp. 102-31.

himself realized this fact that he began his ill-starred program of public pronouncements.

In the 1962 campaign, and thereafter, Liberal publicists such as Walter Gordon made much of the Coyne affair. Few observers thought that the government had been wrong to ditch a recalcitrant governor; although some thought it would have been more tactful to let the man serve out the remaining six months of his term, many thought he should have been eased out long before. Some held that the government had mismanaged the ejection by concentrating excessively on the pension question instead of on the more general and important questions of economic policy that Coyne's line had raised. These charges were certainly justified. Others believed that the Coyne affair had sapped business confidence, thus depressing investment and helping to cause the outflow of funds in 1961 and the exchange crisis of 1962. As to investment, it is hard to believe that any businessman forgoes a chance of profit just because he thinks that the government is inept. With regard to capital flight, however, only Diefenbaker doubted that the Coyne affair made financiers very nervous indeed.

In June 1961, having disposed of Coyne, the government began to contrive a depreciation of the floating Canadian dollar. In principle such a thing is easy to manage: the government can buy foreign money in the market and supply Canadian dollars to the market, thus changing the supply-demand balance. The Canadian dollar would decline because there were more Canadian dollars on offer relative to the demand for them. In the June budget of 1961 Donald Fleming announced that the government would do exactly this. But he did not say how far the dollar would go. Therefore he set up a one-way option for speculators. Everyone knew that the dollar would fall. Hence everyone wanted to sell dollars now, not later. For some time the government's Exchange Fund was absorbing foreign money so as to depreciate the Canadian dollar. But as summer 1961 passed into winter the market got the message, and private operators moved rapidly out of Canadian currency. Where it had once *absorbed* foreign money so as to force our dollar down, now the Exchange Fund was *supplying* foreign money so as to slow its descent. Further, the International Monetary Fund had become worried. A signatory to the IMF agreement, Canada was supposed to maintain a fixed exchange rate and was definitely not supposed to manipulate the rate so as to gain a competitive advantage. In 1950 the IMF had allowed Canada to float the rate, but only on the understanding that it would not manipulate it. Since June 1961 Canada had been doing exactly that. Clearly in this respect, as in others, Canada was ignoring its international commitments.

In June 1961, an American dollar cost $1.0055 Canadian. The 'exchange premium' had gone. From July through October the price of a US dollar was around $1.03, but in November and December it slid upward, so that from January through May 95 cents US would buy one Canadian dollar. In June 1961, when Fleming had announced the new policy, our exchange reserves were $1,985 million (US). By December they had risen to $2,056 million. In spring 1962 the reserves fell month by month, from $1,922 million in January to $1,495 million in May. When the exchange rate and the reserves are falling together, it is a sure sign that the Exchange Fund is spending reserves to slow the descent of the currency. Although by mid-March it seemed that the government was trying to stabilize the Canadian dollar at 95 cents US, no one could be sure about the future. As Professor Donald Forster wrote at the time, 'Many speculated that the massive reductions in reserves might destroy market confidence that the authorities could control the rate.'[11]

On April 10, Fleming explained that although the government would not hesitate to spend its reserves so as to 'prevent sudden or erratic movements in our exchange rate,' it was not willing to fix any particular rate. It would seem that the Prime Minister did not notice what his Minister of Finance was saying; in any event, he later denied any knowledge of the problem. Three weeks later, on May 2, 1962, the exchange rate was pegged at 92.5 American cents. it would remain there until mid-1970.

The government did its best to convince the electorate that the devaluation would do no harm. The external value was one thing; the domestic purchasing power was another. Devaluation, in other words, did not mean inflation. Of course this was absurd. Canada imports almost 25 per cent of what it uses. When our dollar falls relative to other currencies, prices naturally rise. Indeed, this happened almost at once after the devaluation of May 2.

Donald Fleming has since argued that no one in government foresaw the crisis. This statement is hard to accept: anyone could see that to keep the rate at 95 cents the government had been spending its exchange reserves. When the problem came to his attention late in April, Fleming conferred with his officials and with Louis Rasminsky, the new governor of the Bank of Canada. Fleming decided that the rate must be pegged. But the officials could not agree on a rate. So Fleming himself chose 92.5 cents. Having dispatched officials to the IMF in Washington, he reported his decision to the Prime Minister. Diefenbaker reluctantly agreed with the action. Already he feared that the Diefendollar would cost his party the election. He was probably right.

Thanks to the election campaign, the cabinet was scattered across the country. The Prime Minister was in Quebec. Alvin Hamilton, the agriculture minister, who had wanted devaluation for more than a year, was in Vancouver, where he knew nothing and cared less about the means by which Fleming had chosen

11 *Canadian Annual Review, 1962*, p. 178.

the rate. Nevertheless, on June 8 he announced that it was a compromise between two groups of cabinet members, one group favouring 90 cents and the other 95 cents. The speech made Fleming and Diefenbaker very angry. It also sparked a further speculative run because it suggested that the government might not defend the new rate. On June 10 Fleming did his best to repair the damage. His efforts were without effect. The election of June 18, returning as it did a House of minorities, may have made matters worse. Perhaps the financial community assumed that there would be confusion, runaway budget deficits, and inflation; perhaps it was simply nervous. Whatever the cause, in the second quarter of 1962 Canada had to cope with an outflow of capital funds that reached $245 million. And it was mainly Canadian residents who were speculating against their own money by moving funds out of the dominion.

Diefenbaker still maintained in his memoirs that he did not know of the problem until April 29. It was wrong of the officials, he implies, not to have told him earlier. As for the decision to peg at 92.5 cents, he argued that this cost him the 1962 election, and that it was unnecessary. Better, he maintained, to have used the national exchange reserves to hold the rate at some target figure until after the election; at that more propitious time the government could have chosen an exchange rate and announced it.

In the Conservative leader's account the whole incident is given an overtone or undertone of conspiracy. The officials, he suggested, might have been influenced by 'partisan considerations.' As for the crisis itself, that too received a conspiratorial explanation from a leader whom journalists were already calling the Father of Lies. Diefenbaker wrote in his memoirs: 'The only explanation of the 1962 crisis that makes any sense is that it was orchestrated for political reasons ... The crisis began with a "spooking" of the New York money market. I believe that it is more than possible, indeed highly probable, that the administration of President Kennedy used its influence to bring this about.'[12]

Diefenbaker admitted that he had no proof. Others have suggested, with no better evidence, that the trouble began with Liberal financiers in Toronto. Presumably we are to imagine that Walter Gordon, who was running the Liberal campaign, instructed all the corporations whose accounts his firms audited to speculate against the Canadian dollar.

Until we have much more documentation no historian can refute such allegations or even discuss them seriously. In any case they are not very plausible. First, they assume that financiers and industrialists readily respond when politicians issue commands for political reasons. All our experience suggests that this assumption is not correct. Second, they ignore the possibility that there were

12 John G. Diefenbaker, *One Canada: The Tumultuous Years 1962 to 1967* (Toronto: Macmillan, 1977), p. 124.

good economic reasons for speculating against the Canadian dollar. Such reasons certainly did exist. The government had said that it wanted the dollar to fall. Noticing that fact, financiers would naturally sell Canadian dollars and buy other moneys so long as the fall had not yet occurred. In so doing they would make the Canadian dollar fall, and this fall would bring further nervous men into the market as sellers of Canadian dollars. Third, these and other conspiracy theories ignore the possibility that, apart from speculation on a fall, there were good reasons for a weakening of Canada's balance of payments. Since the departure of Coyne the Bank of Canada had become much more expansionist. In 1961, for instance, it increased chartered bank reserves by 14.4 per cent, an increase that far outstripped the growth in Canada's GNP. Compared with American interest rates, Canadian interest rates had fallen. Canadian borrowers were therefore far less inclined to seek funds in the United States. Given the fact that Canada's export earnings did not pay for all its imports, to support any particular exchange rate the country needed an inflow of foreign capital funds. If that flow should flag the Canadian dollar would fall. That is exactly what happened before the crisis of April and May 1962.

On June 21 the government was forced to seek foreign assistance – temporary credits from Britain and the United States, and $400 million from the International Monetary Fund. All in all there were lines of credit for $1,050 million. To restore confidence in the dollar the government thought it should also announce an 'austerity program,' although such a scheme ran against the prime ministerial grain. There would be tariff surcharges on almost all of Canada's imports; government outlays would be cut by $250 million; there were cuts in the duty-free exemptions for tourists; if the government's Exchange Fund had to sell foreign money and buy Canadian dollars it would not lend the results to the government.

The crisis was soon over. So as to protect the newly pegged rate the Bank had to become restrictive once again. In 1962 the national output rose 6.8 per cent but the Bank provided only 6 per cent more in chartered bank reserves, thereby applying downward pressure on prices and upward pressure on the cost and availability of credit. This fact, plus the government's demonstration that it was serious about the new exchange rate, brought capital funds flowing back to Canada. Thanks to devaluation and higher tariffs, the current account improved. As Canadian interest rates were still higher than American, Canadian firms and junior governments were still borrowing in the United States. In a matter of months the dominion could repay its emergency foreign borrowing. By the end of 1962 the Exchange Fund held $1 billion more than it had contained a year before. The tariff surcharges were removed in stages, the last being abolished on April Fool's Day 1963. The dominion civil service, frozen since June 1962, began to grow once more.

In the 1962 election campaign the Liberals made great play with the 'Diefen-dollar' or 'Diefenbuck.' Doubtless many citizens did believe that the devaluation of May 2 was proof of government incompetence: either the Prime Minister should have told the electorate what was up, or he should not have let the dollar down. As we have seen, Diefenbaker himself maintained that until April 29 he himself had not known what was going on. As Fleming has indicated, that statement is quite plausible. Diefenbaker had no particular interest in financial or economic matters; lacking such interest, he could not expect that officials would keep him posted on exchange developments, and it is perfectly possible that they did not.

As for the fall itself, at the time economists argued that devaluation would be a Good Thing because it would encourage exports and discourage imports. Because the economy was far from full employment in 1962, Canada could readily replace imports with domestic output, and it could quickly expand exports. Indeed, many people thought that for years the Canadian dollar had been worth too much on the foreign exchange markets. As we have seen, that was one of the main elements in the economists' attack on Coyne. Although it was good politics to attack the 'Diefendevaluation' it was bad economics to do so. No doubt the Liberals realized this, for until 1970 they kept the exchange rate where Diefenbaker had put it.

If one is to believe the picture that Diefenbaker later painted in his memoirs, one has to conclude that until his dying day the Chief never understood the larger issues of economic policy and management that lay behind the Coyne crisis and the dollar débâcle. But he understood the west – the old west of the prairie wheat economy and the new west of oil and gas and potash. And he cared about farmers wherever they lived. From the moment he took office he was anxious to find ways to help them.

There is more than one route to aid farmers. One way is simply to give them money. The Diefenbaker government was quite willing to do so. Another is to try to raise the prices of the things they sell. In 1958, through the Agricultural Stabilization Act, the government provided new price supports for some twenty-four products. Still another is to provide subsidies for credit and insurance. The Conservatives did both. A government might allow farmers to form marketing monopolies, or force them to do so; monopolies, with luck and skill, mean better prices for crops. The Conservatives preserved the Wheat Board's monopoly in the selling of prairie wheat and coarse grains, but they did not set up any new monopolies. This task they left to the provincial marketing boards, whose skills and energies were already apparent. Finally, the government can help the farmer to farm better, or to leave the land. For many decades, through agricultural extension and research, the dominion had been busy with the former; in 1961, under the Agricultural Rehabilitation and Development Act (ARDA), it undertook to help with the latter.

All such devices have obvious political pay-offs. Less obviously, they have economic disadvantages. Doubtless the civil servants explained these to the cabinet. Certainly there was argument within the cabinet. But as usual in agricultural matters, politics and expediency won. Price supports often produce surpluses, because support prices are typically high relative to demand. A selling monopoly has only limited power if its crop is exported or if imports are allowed. No amount of price-raising can really help the small farmer, because he has so little to sell; all price-raising measures tend to help the richer farmer who is marketing a great deal. No matter; farmers have votes.

Until the 1950s Canada could not have afforded the agricultural programs that the Diefenbaker government introduced. The country had not been rich enough, and its farmers had been too numerous. But with the rising prosperity of the forties and fifties went a sharp fall in the absolute number of farm families, and an even sharper fall in their numbers as a proportion of the population. A government can much more easily find a subsidy or build a safety net when the subsidees are few relative to the subsidizers, and when the latter are quickly becoming richer and more numerous. Also, as Canada's city-dwellers became richer, they spent a smaller proportion of their incomes on food. Thus farm prices could be raised to help farmers without disrupting city budgets.

In 1957-60 the government could rely on American example and on farm pressure groups for suggestions in plenty. In quick succession Parliament authorized loans for farm-stored grain, other agricultural price supports, acreage subsidies, and fodder subsidies. Many prairie farmers wanted a two-price system by which their wheat would sell for a higher price at home than it would abroad. This they were not given. Diefenbaker later argued that the 'acreage payments' of 1960, by which the dominion simply paid $142 million to the wheat growers, were meant as a substitute. But prairie farmers wanted even more.

Wheat prices were still depressed and prospects were bad; no one had yet envisaged the Chinese wheat sales and it was feared that Europe would buy less wheat in future. Hence the pressure for a compensatory grant and a price floor. At the same time there were signs that with respect to tariffs the Conservative government was becoming more protectionist. Certain rates were raised in 1959 and early 1960, while the bases of valuation were changed in ways that raised also tariffs and prices within Canada. It seemed that the Tories were returning to their old protectionist ways, and in the west protective tariffs had never been popular. However, in 1958 the prairies had voted heavily for the Conservatives, and the Prime Minister and other members of cabinet were deeply rooted in the western soil. There is no doubt that they were sincerely interested in agricultural rehabilitation and welfare. But politics pushed them in the same direction, and a mixture of economic and political pressure probably explains the ARDA legislation of late 1960.

The ARDA legislation was actually passed in May 1961, having been introduced in the autumn session of 1960. In spring 1960 Alvin Hamilton, since 1957 the Minister of Northern Affairs and Natural Resources, took the agricultural portfolio. Although he later said that he spent 60 per cent of his time worrying about wheat sales, he was responsible for the devising of the ARDA legislation. The measure was an odd one. Even when introducing it to the House, Hamilton was unable to give a definite account of what it would actually *do*. The provinces, if willing, would co-operate in a program whose aims were clear enough. Small farmers would be helped to improve the use of their land, to consolidate small farms into more economically viable units, to modernize their houses, and to learn how to farm better. There would be help for those who wished to leave the land; there would be trees and pastures where worn-out or infertile land was still under crops. Other things might be possible; doubtless, the minister explained, they would be. If the provinces agreed, large sums of money would be spent in agricultural areas throughout the dominion. (Later in the 1960s, long after the Conservatives had left office, ARDA blossomed into DREE, the Department of Regional Economic Expansion. Hamilton originally thought ARDA might spend $15 million a year – $6 million in the west and $9 million in the east. DREE was soon spending over half a billion.)

No one knows what ARDA actually accomplished. For one thing, progress of the type that ARDA was meant to encourage was already beginning to be made. Small farmers were leaving the land; arable land was turning to forest and pasture; farmers were finding other things that they could combine with small-scale agriculture to produce a better living. In the sixties such things became more common, but one cannot give ARDA the credit.

Meanwhile there were glimmers of hope with respect to wheat marketing, and the glimmers soon burst into a blaze of light in whose reflection the Tories have been basking ever since. The new light came from an unexpected corner of the world – from Communist China and from the USSR. The Soviet Union began in 1957 to buy Canadian grain. But until 1963 Soviet purchases were small and irregular. It was the Chinese market that captured the national imagination.

Before 1957 Canadian officials had already begun to explore the possibilities of entering the Chinese wheat market. In 1958 the Canadian trade commissioner in Hong Kong asked for permission to go to mainland China and sell wheat. The commissioner, C.M. Forsyth-Smith, visited the country and managed to obtain orders for eight shiploads of grain. The grain was sent, but nothing further happened until November 1960, when two Chinese officials arrived unannounced in Montreal, carrying $63 million in letters of credit. Alvin Hamilton, the Minister of Agriculture, at once sent them to visit the Wheat Board in Winnipeg, where a sale was quickly arranged. Canadian officials then went to Peking. This visit, plus a guarantee of credit by the Canadian cabinet, produced an enormous export order. In April 1961 the Wheat Board was able to announce that by December 1963 it would sell at least three million tons of wheat and at least 600,000 tons of barley. In the end, sales totalled 240 million bushels, and Canada earned about $425 million. In those years China was Canada's second-best customer for wheat, and, as Diefenbaker later explained, 'These sales helped to restore our prairie economy to its rightful place in the Canadian scheme of things.' It was he who had made the crucial decision over considerable opposition in cabinet; Canada could safely provide the necessary credit, because the word of a Chinese 'was as good as his bond.'[13]

Although the American government would not let its own citizens trade with China, Washington does not appear to have opposed the grain sales themselves. However, there were troubles about bunker oil and grain-handling equipment – 'vacuators.' Diefenbaker was not pleased to find that the Americans' Trading with the Enemy Act might prevent Imperial Oil from supplying oil fuel for the grain steamers. At length, after angry discussion, Washington agreed to exempt Canadian subsidiaries from the relevant regulations. The vacuators, however, were actually produced in the United States. The shipowners, not the Chinese government, had ordered them, and they had already been delivered to Canadian ports. When the US authorities tried to get the local representatives of the manufacturers to ship the equipment back to the United States, Diefenbaker went directly to President Kennedy, explaining that this was no business of the Americans. Kennedy agreed to release the equipment, but Diefenbaker believed that this incident ended 'any friendly personal relationship between President Kennedy and myself.'[14]

For prairie farmers the Chinese purchases were a bonanza. The Wheat Board sold all its surplus stocks; wheat prices rose from $1.60 to $2.19 a bushel; the Minister of Agriculture told the farmers to grow all they could; net farm income tripled in three years. It is no wonder that the prairies have voted Conservative ever since. Admittedly the Diefenbaker government deserves little credit for the sales. Neither Diefenbaker nor the Wheat Board caused the two years of crop failures that drove the Chinese onto the world market. Nor were Canadians responsible for the American embargo that gave Canada such an opportunity. At worst, the cabinet might have refused the necessary credits, or refused to deal

13 Diefenbaker, *One Canada ... 1957-1962*, pp. 178-80.
14 Ibid., pp. 180-1.

with Communist officials. There was a political risk, as the cabinet recognized; ethnic votes might be lost because the Conservatives were helping to prop up world Communism. But it was reasonable to hope that Diefenbaker's performances in the United Nations would keep new Canadians in the Tory camp. Anyway, as Alvin Hamilton argued in cabinet, the economic risks were small relative to the pay-offs. In effect the chance was too good to miss.

Although the United States did not really object to Canada's new trans-Pacific grain trade, Washington was very far from happy to find that its northern neighbour wanted to go on trading with Cuba, where, in 1959, Fidel Castro's regime replaced the unpleasant oligarchy of Fulgencio Batista. Canada at once recognized the new regime, but as Cuba moved fairly rapidly into the Soviet orbit the United States eventually severed diplomatic relations and imposed a trade embargo. Although the volume of Canadian-Cuban trade was not large, for some Canadian firms the Cuban market was welcome.

Equally welcome was the American market for natural gas, where shipments were authorized for the first time in April 1960. Although the Alberta authorities were always nervously anxious to give local consumers a sure supply of cheap gas, by this time there seemed to be plenty of gas in Alberta and British Columbia, and the American market was willing although not eager to buy it. It might now be said that the export was ill advised or that prices were too low. But at the time the prices seemed fair, and there was no sign of an 'energy crisis.' The sales were welcomed not only in Alberta but throughout the country. It was thought that Canada would soon be earning $75 million a year by selling natural gas. In light of our chronic current account deficit, those millions seemed a welcome windfall.

Much the same applied to oil. In the late 1950s the United States was worrying about oil imports, which threatened the profits of domestic oilwell owners and might imperil national security. The great oil companies, by and large, were eager to import, because South American and Middle East crude oil was cheaper than American; the owners of oil lands, especially in the Gulf States and California, naturally wanted to keep out foreign crude so as to keep their prices up; the Pentagon worried lest too much of American needs were supplied from overseas. Until March 1959 the United States had limited oil imports only through 'voluntary controls,' which the oil companies operated. But on March 10, 1959, the US government imposed mandatory controls, and until April 30 these applied to Canada. The Canadian government was extremely anxious to win re-entry to the American market, and it argued that in time of war Canada's wells and pipelines would be as secure as America's own. In the background, of course, was the current account deficit, and the government's need to placate Alberta and the other western provinces. As yet it had done little for the wheat farmer, and already it was under attack from the west. Fortunately for the Diefenbaker government, Washington saw reason, and removed the controls. Hence, for more than a decade, Canadian oil flowed freely south.

21

Bad Luck and Bad Management: Dominion-Provincial Perplexities

Like every Canadian government, John Diefenbaker's had troubles with the provinces. Unlike its immediate predecessors it also had trouble with defence policy, and therefore its relations with the United States became very disturbed. This chapter treats first the internal perplexities and then the international ones, where bad luck and bad judgment are inextricably intertwined.

Compared with what it became during the Pearson and Trudeau years, the dominion-provincial scene was still relatively tranquil. The oil-pumpers of Alberta had little leverage. Indeed, the dominion had to protect them by giving them a guaranteed Ontario market for their expensive crude and by holding open the taps on the pipelines to the United States. Honouring its promises, in 1958 the dominion began to build the South Saskatchewan Dam, a project that would irrigate immense areas in the arid belt. The Atlantic provinces got special adjustment grants. In the northern parts of the western provinces the dominion's 'Roads to Resources' scheme opened up large areas by road and rail. For Maritime coal production and transport there were new subsidies. But of course the provinces were not satisfied. No junior government ever is.

At Queen's Park the Tories ruled; in Quebec City the Union Nationale was in firm control until 1960. These facts made life no easier for the Tory cabinet in Ottawa, or for its leader. All the provinces wanted more money. More than one was sensitive about autonomy and federal intrusion. Most were unhappy about the tax-sharing arrangements that the St Laurent government had imposed in 1957. Only after 1959 would Quebec allow its universities to accept the federal grants that other universities had received since 1951. Planning to develop the hydro power on the Columbia River, Ottawa found Victoria as obstreperous as Washington, and a good deal less trustworthy.

The dominion's shared-cost programs made matters worse. In 1953-4 the dominion had provided $75 million through conditional grant programs; by

Le chant du signe.
An obituary cartoon for Premier Maurice Duplessis, who is saying, 'Shut up!'
(Hudon, 1959). Reproduced with the permission of Norman Hudon

1964-5 it distributed $935,500,000. The Diefenbaker government had expanded some old programs and introduced at least fifteen minor shared-cost programs and five major ones, of which the most expensive was the hospital insurance plan. By 1963-4 this plan, enacted by the St Laurent government but accelerated and actually implemented by Diefenbaker, was costing Ottawa $391,297,000 per year. Other large programs were the technical education scheme, assistance for the needy unemployed, old age assistance, and the Trans-Canada Highway – all initiated before Diefenbaker took office. Costs were shared on a variety of bases. Commonly the provinces were asked to pay 50 per cent of the costs, but their shares might be as low as 10 per cent or as high as 75 per cent.

It is far from clear that the dominion authorities actually worked out what such things as hospital insurance, the technical education program, or the Trans-Canada Highway would cost the provinces. There was no obvious reason why costs should be split in any particular way. By bearing a larger share, the dominion authorities could have spared themselves the agonized screams of provincial authorities who on the one hand could not say no to federal largesse but on the other had to raise some of the cost. At the same time all the provinces faced heavy outlays for such things as road-building and universities, while some wanted to help municipalities with the costs of schools and public utilities. Naturally the provincial governments did not want to impose new taxes, although by 1963 almost all were collecting a new sort of tax, the retail sales tax, at rates ranging from 3 to 6 per cent. As for the 'shared tax fields' – income tax, corporation tax, and succession duties – no province liked to impose more tax than the 'abatement from federal tax' that the dominion was prepared to give. Hence all the provinces pressed Ottawa for a bigger share of these jointly occupied taxes. In addition, the poorer provinces pressed for 'equalization grants' that would let them provide the same level of public service as the richer provinces could provide. Differences between federal and provincial priorities further complicated things. Saskatchewan and British Columbia introduced hospital insurance before Ottawa; both were anxious to get federal funds for the schemes they had already set up. But in Ontario and Quebec neither government wanted hospital insurance at all; neither was anxious for Ottawa to set up a shared-cost program that for political reasons it would have to join. There was also a metaphysical-constitutional problem that worried some theorists and politicians, especially in Quebec. By using its spending power to finance a shared-cost program, the dominion seemed to encroach on the provincial sphere. In theory a province might refuse to take part, but in practice it would have to participate. Thereby, it was argued, provincial priorities were distorted, and the writ of the dominion was made to run within the provinces. Much better, some argued, to give the provinces the money and let them do what they liked with it.

As we saw in earlier chapters, after the Second World War the Liberal government had proposed a system of 'tax rental agreements,' and most provinces had agreed to levy no personal income tax and to limit their taxation of corporation profits. They could tax estates as they wished, and the dominion would treat provincial succession duties as credits against the federal impost. In exchange for their taxing powers, the provinces got subsidies. The agreements were renewed in 1957, just before Diefenbaker took office. The Conservatives had promised to give the provinces a better deal, and they did give a special adjustment grant to the Atlantic provinces – $25 million annually for four years. Also, in 1958-9 they increased the income tax rebate from 10 to 13 per cent. Further, the government was attached to the principle of equalization payments, which were meant to supplement the tax powers of the poorer provinces. By 1960 Ontario publicists were loud in their denunciation of equalization payments, although the governments of Saskatchewan, Manitoba, and the Atlantic provinces were understandably extremely attached to them.

In July 1960 there was a dominion-provincial conference. Meant to work out a new plan for sharing tax fields, it ended in deadlock. All the provinces wanted more; no two wanted the same things. In October, when the conference reconvened, Diefenbaker proposed that when the tax rental agreements expired in March 1962 they should not be renewed. Still no agreement was possible. In February 1962, at another session of the conference, Diefenbaker simply told the provinces what would happen with the expiry of the agreements on March 31. Equalization grants would continue, but would be calculated differently. The dominion would guarantee that under the new regime no province's revenue could fall by more than 5 per cent. This was the 'stabilization' provision. Adjustment grants would be continued and increased. There would be a special grant for Newfoundland. As for the three shared tax fields, Ottawa would abate half of its succession duties, 9 per cent of its corporation income taxes, and a rising share of its income taxation: starting at 16 per cent of federal tax in 1962, the abatement would rise to 20 per cent in 1967. Then all provinces could impose their own taxes at their own rates. So long as a province calculated its income tax as a percentage of the federal tax, Ottawa would collect income taxation on behalf of that province.

The Prime Minister announced that he liked this scheme because it would give back to the provinces their constitutional right to impose what taxes they wished. On the whole, the provinces did not like the new regime. Some were disappointed because they had not gained more; others were annoyed because they would get less. Some economists and social theorists were annoyed because in the new regime the dominion alone would not determine the weight of personal direct taxation. Hence Ottawa could no longer be sure that it could manage the level of spending and the pace of economic activity by cutting income taxes or raising them. If Ottawa were to change its tax rates, the provinces might change theirs in the opposite direction, offsetting the effect.

In the event, however, the new regime has proved to be much like the old. The provinces have continued to demand that the federal government should vacate more of the shared fields. With the passage of time they have got their way. The abatements became larger in 1963, once the Liberals returned to office, and they have been increased many times since. For provinces that opted out of various shared-cost programs there have been special abatements. This arrangement began in 1960, so that the Quebec government could subsidize its own universities. In the mid- and late sixties, as we show in Part V, the practice became general. Although the provinces do tax incomes at different rates, and although Quebec has imposed and collected its own income tax, there has not been a return to the 'tax jungle' of the 1930s. No province wants to tax incomes much more heavily than other provinces; every province prefers to demand more of the jointly occupied fields – by 1978, overwhelmingly the income tax, as the dominion no longer taxes estates and as few provinces can raise much money by taxing corporations. As for economic management, although federal taxing and spending have lost ground relative to provincial, relative to the whole economy federal activity has grown a great deal, and nobody would now complain that Ottawa has lost the power to manage the economy. It may not have the *will,* but that is another question. In addition, through federal-provincial conferences and through informal contacts Ottawa often attempts to co-ordinate provincial tax and spending plans with federal and is sometimes able to do so.

Although the disputes about taxing and spending were intertwined with disagreements about constitutional propriety, during the Diefenbaker years there was no great pressure for constitutional reform. Doubtless Diefenbaker would have been happier about his bill of rights if it had applied to provincial activities as well as federal. Although the Prime Minister would have liked to 'patriate' the British North America Act so that it could be amended in Canada, as late as June 1960 he did not expect that Canada would quickly devise a formula. At the July dominion-provincial conference, Premier Lesage urged that something be done at once; Diefenbaker then announced that E. Davie Fulton, the federal Minister of Justice, would meet with provincial attorneys general early in October to consider the question of 'patriation.'

The provinces quickly realized that there was no point in patriating the constitution unless they and the dominion could agree on an amendment formula. Ever since 1867 the Parliament at Westminster had amended the BNA Act on request; what would replace this procedure? In November, it was quickly agreed that the language and education provisions, and one or two others, should be 'entrenched.' That is, only if all the provinces agreed could the dominion amend such provisions. With respect to the rest, there were various proposals aimed at providing greater or less flexibility. Some provinces hoped that if more of the provincial sphere were 'entrenched' there should also be some arrangement by which a province could delegate some of its powers to the dominion. In January 1961 this was agreed to, although Quebec was nervous lest others might delegate too much, leaving it as the only province to cling to the full panoply of provincial pomp and power. Saskatchewan, its CCF government anxious for national marketing boards and comprehensive national planning, was most reluctant to entrench 'property and civil rights.' Quebec, meanwhile, wanted to transfer unemployment insurance back from federal to provincial control. On December 1 Fulton revealed his draft bill. All provincial powers and rights, language, and education were to be entrenched, except that Newfoundland could not veto educational changes. There was some provision for the provinces to delegate functions to the national government. If four provinces wanted to legislate in a federal field, the dominion could consent. Beyond the entrenched clauses, the dominion Parliament could amend the constitution if supported by two-thirds of the provinces containing 50 per cent of the people. The amending formula itself was also to be entrenched.

On December 7, 1961, Quebec rejected the 'Fulton formula' because it did not give the provinces unemployment insurance. And, for the time being, that was that.

Meanwhile there were puzzlements about off-shore oil. In the Yukon, the Northwest Territories, and Hudson Bay, the dominion controlled natural resources, although on provincial dry land control lay with the provinces. But 'Canada' extended three miles out to sea, and already by 1960 it was obvious that in due course it would advance its seaward frontier. In 1958 and 1960 Canadian representatives had told the Americans that Canada would not always allow American fishing inside a *twelve*-mile limit. Under the waves there might be minerals, especially oil and gas. Who controlled *them*?

The answer was unclear. Ottawa argued that its oil and gas regulations, drafted in 1960 to cover the Arctic, applied to all off-shore waters, and in July 1961 it gave Shell an off-shore exploration permit in the Pacific Ocean. British Columbia was annoyed, claiming that Victoria, not Ottawa, should give the permits and garner the royalties. Premier Bennett proceeded to offer exploration rights for fifteen million acres of the blue Pacific, including the eleven million that Ottawa had assigned to Shell. Although Richfield had protected itself by taking out both federal and provincial permits, Shell did not do so. When the rights auction occurred on September 1, other bidders bought the province's permission to drill in Shell's area. Late in 1962 British Columbia took the question to the courts, where it lingered until 1979, when the Clark government decided to give off-shore minerals to the provinces. With the Liberal victory of 1980, the issue was unsettled once more, and the issue remains uncertain.

The same might be said for amending and patriating the constitution. In October 1964 the Liberal government got the provinces to swallow the scheme of 1961-2, now known as the 'Fulton-Favreau formula.' Premier Lesage thought the formula a great achievement; Diefenbaker thought it would make Quebec an associate state, not a province like the others; the NDP thought it too rigid. In many minds the question became entangled with the 'special status' issue: was Quebec a province like the others? One by one the provinces gave their approval. Only Quebec remained uncommitted. In that province the Union Nationale mounted a strong campaign against the formula, while other groups also opposed it. In the end, on October 22, Lesage told the legislature that he would neither approve the formula nor reject it. Once more, it seemed, the question was dead, or perhaps dormant.

Meanwhile the provinces had taken courage from Diefenbaker's attitude toward disallowance. Theoretically the dominion could disallow any provincial measure; in practice the power had not been used since 1943. In the winter of 1958-9 there was trouble in the woods of Newfoundland. The Smallwood government passed a law that decertified the union of the International Woodworkers of America, which happened to be on strike. When the provincial authorities asked for RCMP reinforcements to help keep order, Fulton and Diefenbaker refused to send them, at least partly because they did not want the RCMP to appear to be strike-breakers. L.H. Nicholson, head of the RCMP, resigned over the incident, because he thought that the government's decision was a breach of the contract by which the RCMP provided police in the province. Diefenbaker later wrote, 'I was not prepared to sacrifice the reputation of the RCMP to save either Mr. Smallwood or the reactionary corporations which owned the Newfoundland forest industry.'[1] After waiting until 1960, however, the dominion would not disallow the decertification measure; indeed, Diefenbaker said that he did not think Ottawa should ever disallow anything. The federal government, he explained, should not be judge and jury over the provincial legislatures that the people had elected. His logic is hard to follow: apparently it is wrong to use the RCMP for strike-breaking when a legitimately elected provincial government asks for its help, and equally wrong to use the pre-eminent power of the dominion to prevent a provincial government from breaking strikes. Although the question of disallowance would surface once more in the late 1960s, in effect the Conservative government's decision had banished it from the constitutional

1   John G. Diefenbaker, *One Canada: The Years of Achievement 1957 to 1962* (Toronto: Macmillan, 1976), p. 317.

scene. In their own spheres the provinces were now pre-eminent. As John Saywell wrote in 1960, 'It was a far cry from the view of Sir John A. Macdonald.'[2]

Not the least of the dominion-provincial perplexities was the plan for a Columbia River dam, which one journalist thought might better be called the dam' Columbia River plan. This had an international dimension because it required Canada and the United States to co-operate; it also had a dominion-provincial dimension, partly because the BC government had its own plans for power development in the Rocky Mountains. Although Ottawa emerged from the fracas with much credit and British Columbia came out with little or none, it was the dominion that failed to get its way.

Both Diefenbaker and President Eisenhower were anxious to conclude an agreement for the development of the Columbia River, which meandered through British Columbia for hundreds of miles before finally crossing the forty-ninth parallel. As the generating plants were to be in the United States and the water storage in Canada, neither government could proceed without the co-operation of the other. After discussion with British Columbia and with the International Joint Commission, the parties completed a treaty. It was signed in January 1961, three days before Eisenhower left office.

The scheme had been gestating for more than fifteen years. In the early 1940s studies had begun, and the International Joint Commission had been asked to report on the proposal. If the Americans had been allowed to build the dam they first wanted to build, the full hydraulic potential would not have been developed, then or ever. Only when the United States agreed to pay Canada for downstream benefits could Ottawa agree to a draft treaty. The treaty was to last sixty years. Canada would build three storage dams, receiving in return half of the power that the United States would generate downstream. Canada could divert some Kootenay water into the Columbia so as to generate some power within Canada; it would also get $64.4 million for the flood-control benefits in the United States.

Because the Bennett government in British Columbia had already proposed private development of Peace River power, it did not like the new plan. It also quibbled about the sharing of costs between federal and provincial treasuries. What it really wanted was to develop the Peace and Columbia projects, selling the downstream benefits to the Americans instead of importing them in the form of cheap electric power. There was also a chance that the dominion would declare the Columbia project to be for the general interest of Canada; it could then control the project, importing the power and selling it to the BC Electric Company, the private corporation that then supplied Vancouver and Victoria. To fore-

---

2 *Canadian Annual Review, 1960* (Toronto: University of Toronto Press, 1961), p. 51.

stall this, in August 1961 Bennett took over BC Electric and also the Peace River Development Company. The United States was prepared to buy the power from the Columbia and was probably eager to do so, but it did not take sides in the dispute; Bennett hoped that by selling twenty years' worth of the downstream benefits he would garner enough to develop the Peace. Meanwhile the dominion argued that Columbia power would be cheaper power for British Columbia and that if sales were allowed for a term of years Canada might have trouble reclaiming its power when it was needed. As we have seen, the government also hoped to set up a national power grid within Canada, and it feared that by exporting power from the western end of the country it might have trouble supplying power to the prairies.

Early in 1962 the Americans announced that if the Canadians could not settle their row, the United States might have to look elsewhere for power. Bennett, Ottawa learned, would supply Peace River power to a national grid if he could sell Columbia power in the United States. On May 11 the dominion announced that it would soon call for dam tenders, and on May 27 Diefenbaker spoke warmly of the Peace project. On September 27 the throne speech forecast that the treaty would be ratified and power exports permitted. However, there was no legislation before the Conservatives fell from power. It was left to the Liberals, in July 1963, to patch up an agreement with British Columbia. It was decided that the province would get the benefits, sell them back to the United States, and use the proceeds to finance the Peace River project. The verdict was not popular. Many journalists and politicians disliked the new arrangements even more than the old proposal, which General McNaughton, the former chairman of the International Joint Commission, had thought a sell-out. To Ottawa the new arrangement was a humiliation; to W.A.C. Bennett it was a political triumph; to the citizens of British Columbia it meant expensive hydro power from the Peace, not cheap power from the Columbia; to Washington it was a swap of money for energy, a trade that the US government was only too eager to make.

Much more serious and far more alarming were the arguments about defence. In Ottawa no one doubted that Canada should stick with NATO and with an integrated air defence system for North America. In July 1957, with little thought and without cabinet scrutiny, Diefenbaker had committed Canada to NORAD – the North American air defence plan by which Canadian and American officers would jointly administer an integrated air defence force under supreme American command. The St Laurent government had known about NORAD but had deferred action until after the 1957 election. How was Canada to contribute to NORAD, and what sort of weapons would it use?

The Conservatives had also inherited an embarrassing item. At Malton, Ontario, with government funding, A.V. Roe Canada (AVRO) was building an all-Canadian supersonic fighter plane, the AVRO Arrow, and Orenda Engines was developing the Iroquois engine that would make the plane fly. The two companies had assembled a formidable technical team but had a depressing record of profligacy and budget overruns. Other companies were at work on Arrow weaponry and electronics. The Arrow had been specially designed for Canadian conditions. No doubt the plane and the engine were superb. AVRO said so; the engineers said so; the RCAF said so. But they were expensive, and no other government seemed to want any. The Liberals had intended to cancel the project after the 1957 election. After an embarrassed pause, in 1959 the Tory cabinet decided to abandon both the Iroquois and the Arrow. AVRO promptly laid off 14,000 workers. Torontonians fulminated. Either on Diefenbaker's orders or on AVRO's, the existing aircraft – all five of them – were destroyed. And for air defence Canada would have to find some other weapon.

Before scrapping the Arrow, the cabinet found the Bomarc anti-aircraft missile. This was an American ballistic device that was meant to intercept Soviet planes, but not rockets. It would be controlled by NORAD's joint Canadian-American headquarters in Colorado Springs. Canada would build two Bomarc sites, and the Americans would supply missiles. The total cost to Canada would be $14 million, far less than the cost of 100 Arrows. The RCAF had originally expected to order 500 Arrows, but, on learning that reservists would be unable to fly so complex an aircraft, it had decided that 100 would have to do.

Meanwhile, the military knew full well that Canada would sooner or later have to buy some new interceptor aircraft for northern defence. The old ones were already obsolete. Every day there were numbers of unidentified aircraft on the radar screens. One could not fire Bomarcs at all of them. At length, in 1961, the government bought sixty-six F-101 Voodoo aircraft from the United States. The government had had to wait until it could make a satisfactory deal with the United States by which American procurements in Canada could provide work for Canada's aircraft industry and offset the cost of the Voodoos. It had also wanted to wait until the hubbub about the Arrow had died down.

These decisions did not kill Canada's aircraft industry. De Havilland and Canadair continued to do original design work; Orenda continued to build engines under licence; most of AVRO was eventually sold to Douglas Aircraft. To assist the aircraft industry the government made various special deals. This industry also gained from the Development and Production Sharing Program, which Diefenbaker and Eisenhower devised in July 1958. Under this new program, which resembled the wartime Hyde Park Agreement, Canadian firms were able to share in orders from American military procurement. The agreement produced a sharp increase in American purchases of Canadian arms, which quickly came to exceed Canadian purchases of American. It was in this way that the

Diefenbaker government defended Canada against the horrors of continentalism.

The Arrow was a very good aircraft, and many Canadians have wondered why the United States would not buy it. The answer seems to be threefold. First, it did not precisely fit American needs. Second, it was not built in the United States. Third, it was very expensive relative to the alternatives. Indeed, for Canadian defence production the demise of the Arrow and the purchase of the Bomarc represented a sort of handwriting on the wall. For a decade or so, it had seemed reasonable to believe that Canada could design the most sophisticated military hardware and equip itself therewith. Canada might even expect to sell such things abroad. But by 1958 development costs were rising to insupportable levels, especially if spread over the small outputs that Canada could possibly afford or need. All over the capitalist world the smaller airframe makers and the 'national' airframe industries were in trouble. The economies of large-scale production were very significant, and research, too, had become immensely costly. Closure, merger, and government subsidy – these were the orders of the day, even in Britain and France. In 1946 C.D. Howe had hoped that by selling Canada's wartime airframe plants to American and British firms Canada would get some of the international action. To some extent it has done so, chiefly by using other people's airframe designs and by building components, such as wings. But even later the production-sharing arrangements have also made a big difference.

By spring 1960 Canada had begun to build its first Bomarc base at North Bay, Ontario. Unfortunately, the system was still untried, and no one was sure it would work, much less do the job of interception for which it was intended. Also, in the United States the US Army was lobbying in favour of an alternative system, the Nike-Hercules short-range missile. The US Air Force had to defend the Bomarc, its brainchild, against Army sniping. In 1960 there were congressional inquisitions. To Canada these were intensely embarrassing, as they suggested that Canada might have bought a pig in a poke. More embarrassing was the fact that Canada's Bomarcs would have to carry nuclear warheads. They had not been designed to handle high explosives. Diefenbaker later maintained that he had thought that they could be armed either way. If so, he cannot have read the specifications for Bomarc B. He also suggested that by 1959 the Bomarc was already junk, because by this time the threat was intercontinental ballistic missiles (ICBMs), not the manned bombers that Bomarc was meant to repel. If he thought this in 1960, it seems curious that he went on with the Bomarc program. In any event, neither he nor his military advisers can have believed that the day of the manned bomber was really over. If North America had dismantled all its bomber defences, there would have been nothing to stop the Soviet Union from building bombers and sending them over the North Pole. As the threat was dual, the country would need defences against both sorts of weapon. Indeed, the government recognized this in 1961 when it bought the Voodoos.

But the government had still not decided what to do about the nuclear warheads. In 1960 General Pearkes, the Minister of National Defence, reported that he was discussing the matter with the Americans. Thus he revealed that Canada had chosen the Bomarc without deciding to arm it. And as Bomarcs were gradually installed in the two Canadian sites, they were 'armed' with sandbags. The United States was naturally concerned. Although Canada itself had asked to locate the two sites in Canada, both were part of the North American defence system; unarmed, they left holes that made the United States more vulnerable. If the government had decided at once, perhaps no one would have noticed. But by 1960 there was a large and vocal lobby arguing for nuclear disarmament. In Britain, continental Europe, and Canada there was an active 'ban the bomb' campaign. Thousands of people marched to and from Aldermaston, where Britain's atomic research was concentrated. Swimmers defied American nuclear submarines in Scotland's Loch. Although there was no indication that the Soviet Union would disarm, in western Europe and in Canada the optimistic and the naïve believed that through a great act of self-abnegation they would bring Russia round – or at least, if they did not, their own lands would remain ritually pure until the moment when the Third World War actually began. The Americans and the Russians, it was argued, had plenty of atomic weaponry. Why proliferate the weapons, especially since the United States was prepared to shoulder the risk and the responsibility?

In Canada the Liberals and the CCF did not want nuclear weapons. Many Conservatives and some cabinet members felt the same way. After accepting the External Affairs portfolio in 1959 Howard Green laboured mightily, at the United Nations and elsewhere, for the cause of disarmament. How could he do so, if Canada were to accept the new weapons? Rereading the arguments nearly twenty years later, one detects the last gasps of the Protestant conscience in an incompletely secularized disguise. Canada should be pure; by an act of will it *can* be pure; it has no larger responsibilities that might compel it to share in the impurities of the world, the flesh, or its allies. Diefenbaker maintained that the government had not promised anything about warheads, but he never explained why it was spending several million dollars to erect a series of empty metal towers at North Bay.

In 1961 it became clear that Douglas Harkness, the new Minister of National Defence, wanted to accept nuclear arms, both for air and for ground use. That year the first Bomarcs were installed, and in 1962 Canada's NATO ground forces began to deploy the Honest John missiles that were meant for atomic arming. The basic decision had been taken in 1958. Moreover, in 1959 the government had agreed that in Europe the RCAF should play a 'strike reconnaissance' role, one that assumed that Canada's planes would carry tactical nuclear weapons. For this purpose it arranged to produce an American-designed aircraft, the CF-104 Starfighter. In February 1962 Boeing turned over the North Bay base to the RCAF. Still there were no warheads for its twenty-eight Bomarcs. Still the government havered.

Diefenbaker later argued that the real problem was one of control. Under US law, Canada could not acquire title to atomic weapons because these would have to be bought from the Americans. Indeed, they would have to remain in American custody, being released to the Canadians only in time of need. By September 1961, Diefenbaker has written, he believed that President Kennedy would not allow joint control of such weapons on Canadian soil,[3] although he and everyone else knew that the American government did want to see nuclear arming of Canada's Bomarcs and Voodoos. It is certain that Diefenbaker was wrong about control. In March 1962 the American Secretary of State remarked: 'The United States is willing to work out arrangements for joint control consistent with national sovereignty.' With other countries such as Britain the Americans had already devised 'two-key' systems which amounted to a mutual veto. In Canada, however, there was really no will to solve the problem. The Prime Minister seems to have believed that if war should break out there would be time to bring in the nuclear arms and install them for use. He liked the plan for a 'missing piece,' by which part of a warhead would be stored in Canada and part would be flown from the United States in case of need. This might work for the Bomarc, an anti-aircraft missile. But it was already known that a Soviet ICBM could reach North America in seventeen minutes. If war did break out there would be no time for such foolishness. Also, to keep such a transfer system in constant readiness would be immensely expensive.

By mid-1962, when the election occurred, nothing had been done. In the campaign the NDP said that it wanted Canada to leave NORAD, abandon NATO if pressed to take nuclear arms, and form a non-nuclear club. Lester Pearson, the Liberal leader, did not want to take nuclear weapons, and his party sat on the fence, while his wife joined the anti-nuclear Voice of Women.

As *La Presse* observed, 'O shades of Mackenzie King! ... Not necessarily nuclear arms but nuclear arms if necessary.' Diefenbaker explained that Canada would not acquire nuclear warheads for the present, although 'we are in a position to defend ourselves if war breaks out.'[4] By what means he did not explain. Nor could he do so after the election. The second Bomarc base was almost ready. The new aircraft was leaving for Germany. These facts did not sway him.

---

3 John G. Diefenbaker, *One Canada: The Tumultuous Years 1962 to 1967* (Toronto: Macmillan, 1977), p. 74.
4 *Canadian Annual Review, 1962*, p. 4.

In October 1962 the Americans detected Soviet missiles in Cuba and risked world war to force withdrawal. The cabinet refused to place Canada's NORAD force on alert; it refused to let the United States fly nuclear-armed fighters to arctic bases; it did not arm the Bomarcs or the Voodoos. As Professor Spencer explains, 'Fear of adding to the tension and of sharpening the crisis appears to have held the government back; and Canada emerged from it with its defence policies in disarray, its reputation a little tarnished, but its nuclear virginity intact.'[5]

By this time some cabinet members rated survival – military and political – ahead of virginity or ritual purity. Thanks to Green's meditations and Diefenbaker's indecisions the country was defended only by the Americans, and the Tory party was in peril. The Prime Minister must decide, or leave office. As Peter C. Newman later observed, 'In acquiring the CF-101B, the Bomarc, the Honest John and the CF-104 and then refusing to arm them, Canada under John Diefenbaker's management had spent $685 millions for the most impressive collection of blank cartridges in the history of military science.'[6] Something would have to be done. Meanwhile, the Prime Minister was ever more moody and erratic, while the business of Parliament remained undone.

In November 1962 a group of ten cabinet ministers began to consider the future of Diefenbaker and the Tory party. George Hees was their leader. Nothing came of their discussions, but Douglas Harkness, since 1960 the defence minister, was increasingly disinclined to follow Diefenbaker on his trek through Wonderland. In February 1963, following a dramatic cabinet session, Harkness resigned. Canadian-American relations broke down; Canada recalled its ambassador following an American revelation that Canada had 'not yet proposed any arrangement sufficiently practical to contribute effectively to North American defence.' In the Parliament Buildings the conspirators were active once more. They would bid for Social Credit support, replace Diefenbaker with George Nowlan, and hold a leadership convention.

But Dief the Chief refused to co-operate or to give any assurances. Instead, he mobilized his supporters in cabinet and on the back-benches. But the Social Crediters, NDPers, and Liberals could combine and defeat him. On February 5 they did so. For the second time in this century, a vote in the House had brought down a government.

The Prime Minister tried to unite his cabinet behind him for the coming election battle. But first he had to digest the resignation not only of Hees but also of Pierre Sévigny, the Acting Minister of National Defence. Both were unhappy about Diefenbaker's anti-American posturing; neither could stand his

5 Ibid., p. 136.
6 Peter C. Newman, *Renegade in Power* (Toronto: McClelland & Stewart, 1973), p. 354.

The nuclear weapons crisis of 1963: Minister of Defence Douglas Harkness quits (Macpherson, 1963). Reproduced with the permission of the *Toronto Star*

shilly-shallying on defence.

In the 1962 election campaign Lester Pearson and the Liberals had tried to evade the nuclear question. But on January 12, 1963, distressed both by the Cuban crisis and by private as well as public information that had revealed the full weakness and dishonesty of the Canadian position, Pearson had promised that if elected he would honour the Diefenbaker commitments: he would accept nuclear arms.

As public opinion polls quickly showed, Pearson had caught the public mood. Canadians wanted their government to live up to its commitments even if, as Pearson also proposed, it would then renegotiate them out of existence. Diefenbaker, many if not most Canadians thought, had not kept Canada's word, and when the American government publicly rebuked Canada in a statement at the end of January it was John Kennedy and not John Diefenbaker whom most Canadians believed.

In the campaign that followed, many prominent Canadians transferred their trust to Pearson and the Liberals. To Pierre Berton, the campaign meant that 'national sovereignty is on the wane. If this election proves anything it proves that anti-Americanism is finished as a political issue. We have cast our lot with this continent for better or worse and the people know it. The world is reassembling itself into larger units and I doubt we could escape the tide even if we wished to.'[7] Reading these words reminds one how much Pierre Berton and Canada changed during the Pearson years.

On polling day, April 8, the Conservatives won only 95 seats and the Liberals, 129. Thanks to the NDP and Social Credit members, neither major party had a majority. But John Diefenbaker had lost power forever, and the nuclear question was to be settled. Pearson and Kennedy quickly agreed on a system of joint control, and Canada began to acquire the nuclear weapons for which its delivery systems had been designed.

There had been other election issues. There were other examples of Conservative indecisiveness and confusion, with which the opposition parties had made great play. But the historian must find the weapons question the most important, and the most alarming, of all the matters that the Diefenbaker government bungled. First Diefenbaker had made commitments without understanding their import. Then he had refused either to honour the commitments or to withdraw from them. In the end he had succeeded only in dividing his party, infuriating Canada's allies, weakening its defences, and disrupting its alliances. He cannot even have won many votes: Canada's 'ban-the-bombers' presumably voted NDP or Communist, and the opinion polls showed that most Canadians wanted nuclear arms.

In his memoirs Diefenbaker explained that he was the victim of a plot. According to him, Washington set out to manipulate Canadian politics. It suborned Pearson, who changed his tune at Kennedy's behest; the Pentagon had a 'supragovernmental relationship' with the RCAF, which had suborned Harkness and Sévigny; and, in the basement of his embassy, the American ambassador was giving secret lectures to Canadian newsmen, so that they could best 'undermine my government's policy on nuclear weapons.'[8] All was orchestrated from the American Department of State. Diefenbaker believed this in 1963; he still believed it in 1977, fighting once more in his memoirs for the causes that served

7 Pierre Berton, untitled article, *Maclean's,* 7 (April 6, 1963), p. 62.
8 Diefenbaker, *One Canada ... 1962 to 1967,* p. 3.

him so ill in that election campaign. The Conservatives were defending Canada's sovereignty against the big bad wolf to the south; the Liberals, we are told, were Kennedy's running-dogs.

Of course the Americans wanted Canada to decide, and, if possible, to arm the weapons it had willingly acquired; and of course they tried to change Canada's behaviour. However, they did not compel Canada, or try to compel it, to do anything in particular, and therefore did not infringe its sovereignty. Nor was Diefenbaker consistent when he criticized the American government, or American soldiers, for making public statements or granting interviews that embarrassed his government. With respect to South Africa and the Commonwealth, or Britain and the EEC, Diefenbaker himself had done exactly the same thing. Indeed, he and his ministers had threatened the British, adopting a tactic to which Washington did not stoop. In any event it was the Canadian voters, not the Toronto media, the old Bay Street gang, or the Washington establishment, that decided to turn the rascals out. Diefenbaker believed that he spoke to and for the ordinary people. In April 1963 they told him that they no longer trusted him to do so.

Diefenbaker was right when he claimed that in Canada the press did not treat him fairly. Indeed, it handled his foibles in a way that was both insulting and cruel. While he was in office the media developed a habit that is probably now unalterable. Having constituted themselves a sort of popular tribune, they attempt to destroy the reputations of political leaders. This is not to be confused with old-style political partisanship. It is applied with malice but without discrimination to the leading figures of both major parties, no matter which is in power; it serves to conceal matters of substance not only from the public but from the journalists themselves. Minor parties get the same treatment from time to time, although for some reason the CCF and NDP leaders have always been exempted, perhaps because in the federal House they are so powerless that it is no fun to make them look ridiculous. Reporters wrote of Diefenbudgets, Diefendollars, Diefenbubbles, and Diefenbabble, as later they were to write about Peter Elliott Waterhole; no one converts Broadbent into Narrowtwist, or Coldwell into Warmspring. Of course the glossy young people of Toronto and Montreal did not understand the elderly populist orator from Prince Albert. His style was not theirs; to them his interests and his worries were more foreign than those of Ho Chi Minh. By 1963 it was they, not the Bay Street plotters within the Conservative party, who were Diefenbaker's most dangerous enemies.

Certainly Diefenbaker had little reason to fear that the New Democratic Party (NDP), the retreaded version of the old CCF, could replace him in office. With money from the unions and with a broader organizational base, in the federal sphere it might hope for great things. Nevertheless, it did not do as well as its promoters had hoped. In the 1962 election, it raised its share of the popular vote from 9.4 per cent to 13.4 per cent, and it took nineteen seats, compared with twenty-five for the CCF in 1957 and eight in 1958. In 1963 and thereafter, the NDP vote would be one of the awkward things that could deny a majority to either major party. But most observers think that it was erstwhile Liberal voters who moved into the NDP. For the Tory vote, especially in 1962 and 1963, a much more serious threat came from the Social Credit party.

In 1957, Social Credit won nineteen seats, all in Alberta and British Columbia. In 1958, it won none. In 1962, it rebounded to a new and much higher level, winning thirty seats, largely because in rural Quebec voters turned from the Tories to the colourful leadership of Réal Caouette. Unlike the Albertans and British Columbians who ran the federal party, Caouette actually believed in the 'funny money' ideas of Major Douglas, the inventor of Social Credit doctrine. Among small businessmen and on impoverished farmlands these doctrines had a natural appeal. If Caouette and Social Credit had not existed, presumably some Quebec voters would have stayed with the Tories, in spite of the Diefenbaker disarray, while more would have gone back to their former Liberal affiliation. Certainly the Liberals expected this outcome, only to receive a painful surprise. In Alberta and British Columbia, Social Credit's traditional happy hunting grounds, in the absence of Social Credit the Tories would have attracted the Socred voters, who were emphatically anti-socialist and generally anti-Liberal as well. Some Albertans and British Columbians must also have voted Socred simply because the party, based and led in the west, was 'theirs.' Such voters must have worried about the sudden appearance of francophone Socred members, and of a French-Canadian deputy leader. Through the 1960s the Social Credit party would be a source of distress to the two major parties, especially to the Tories, for, though responsibly led, it did help to prevent any party from getting a clear majority. But with the passage of time it became less important. In Quebec it was unable to make much progress in cities, and with the dwindling of the rural population its support dribbled away. In the far west, as provincial Socred governments lost first credibility and then office, so in federal elections voters drifted back to their natural homes in the Conservative party. It was unfortunate for Diefenbaker that before this drift was well under way he had lost the Tory leadership.

Perhaps it did not really matter very much. The last few Diefenbaker years saw a profound change in style, a change that made the Chief's ideas less and less compelling, his own style more and more repellent. The country was turning from old ways to new, and we must now proceed to chronicle that turning.

22

From the Old Ways to the New:
The Changing Atmosphere of the
Early Sixties

In 1960, as John Kennedy hailed the passing of the torch to a new generation in the United States, the sixty-three-year-old John Diefenbaker still held a torch lit three years before, a torch whose flame now flickered weakly. Canadians were thus diverted by the brilliance of the American blaze, of that new Camelot in Washington that had finally lifted the Republican pall from the American capital. There was something symbolic when Beverly Baxter wrote his last London Letter for *Maclean's* on July 30, 1960, declaring that he hoped he had made Britain more understandable for Canadians 'far across the sea.' This British *ave atque vale* was followed soon by a special issue: 'America 1960' – a '100-page report on the people all the shouting is about.' The issue celebrated American variety; the incredible women of Madison Avenue, a 'vision of energy, neuroses and high income'; Wall Street, 'the damned and exalted canyon'; and Flora, Illinois, or Middletown, 'where the bull sessions were at Honest John Throgmorton's drugstore instead of the barbershop these days, but the bull sounds the same, the white paint on the veranda rails looks as clean, and the piano lessons last as long as they always did.' Small wonder the Americans shouted; no wonder Canadians listened. From Britain the noises were already feeble and plaintive.

Naturally there were Canadians who did not like what they heard. Hugh Mac-Lennan lamented the 'Americanization' of Canada, the 'swamping of our national purpose by that of the United States and of our habits by a state of mind totally American.' There had been no conquest; it had been 'more like a seduction in which the lady keeps murmuring that she can't help herself.' Canadian intellectuals were as always more wary of the American pandemonium than businessmen, bureaucrats, and, above all, the young. In the past Canada's intellectuals had accepted the criticism of American mass culture and politics which American intellectuals themselves had so eloquently delivered. But the new style and the new intellectuals troubled Canadians. There was the popular, Canadian-born economist John Kenneth Galbraith ensconced in Washington; there were the poets Archibald MacLeish and Robert Frost too; the historian Arthur Schlesinger was settled in the White House and sometimes swam in the presidential pool. Where was academic distance, much less alienation, in all this?

The picture was certainly confused. Scepticism was difficult when Kennedy talked to Americans in language almost Periclean in its balance, simplicity, and purpose, while Diefenbaker hectored Canadians in the fashion of a tiresome fire-and-brimstone evangelist. Frankly, Dief the Chief was embarrassing for Canadian intellectuals. Could one imagine Diefenbaker discussing the fashionable Protestant theologian Reinhold Niebuhr with Schlesinger? Or with anyone else? The image quickly became comic. Diefenbaker himself knew that a teetotalling Baptist could not live on the new frontier. Wisely he did not try; less wisely, he let his resentment of the new way turn into a bitterness that affected Canada's relations with the United States and that ultimately speeded his own decline.

The United States, then, was a land to shout about. *Maclean's* had seen the future, and it seemed to work. And not only for Americans. The stream of technology ran broadly, easily crossing over the undefended border; so too could American wealth and life. *Maclean's* recognized that Canadians would share the icons and legends of Camelot, and to prepare them it listed on its first page 'ninety things and people to watch for from the US.' The list lacks neither amusement nor irony. Mack Jones, the new 'slugger' for the Milwaukee Braves, soon could be watched again in the minor leagues. The Desert Rat (gin and lemon bitters) never quite made it as a cocktail, although Quincy Jones and Buddy Rich certainly did as musicians. Lighted wallpaper intended to replace light bulbs remains a seductive idea but nothing more, yet frozen orange juice in paper cartons is now a part of daily life. The irony in the list would not be understood for over a decade, but it was there. Among people to watch for was Sam (Mooney) Giancana, 'a Chicago hood who is taking over from gangster czar Tony Arcado.' No one watched Sam until it was learned, a decade and a half later, that he and the new president had shared the same mistress. But by that time Camelot was only a memory tinged with sadness and ambivalence. The dynamic young president was soon dead; the American scene soon turned sour.

The immediate impact of Camelot was on politics and especially on the relations between politics and the media. In a sense, however, the Quebec election of June 1960 had anticipated the American election of November. Quebec intellectuals had become closely involved with political life, and effective use was made of the media, especially television. Underlying the appeal of the Liberals was a sense that change was inevitable and, more important, that it was good. As

John Saywell pointed out, 'The Liberal leaders – Jean Lesage, Georges La-palme, Paul Gérin-Lajoie, René Lévesque, and others – gave the impression of intellectual ability, progressive view, youth and vigour, and lent strength to the plea that it was "time for a change." ' This, of course, was the stuff of Camelot. The early successes in Quebec suggest that Canadians were ready to sympathize with the New Frontiersmen even before they had ridden into battle.

Lester Pearson and Walter Gordon realized this fact as they began to recon-struct the federal Liberal party from the rubble of 1958. Two important events occurred in 1960. Richard O'Hagan, a Toronto advertising executive and Gor-don's friend, became Pearson's special assistant. O'Hagan saw what Kennedy's media people had done, and in similar fashion he began to shape Pearson's rath-er ragged and soft image into something smoother, harder, and more progres-sive. Pearson soon stopped wearing bow-ties and began speaking simpler and shorter sentences. But Pearson could never have the Kennedy style, and his re-fashioners wisely refrained from any attempt to recast him in that image. Much was made of his interest in hockey; little or nothing was said of his university background.

Meanwhile, another event also sought to attach the progressive label to the Liberal party. In early September the party held a thinkers' conference in Kings-ton to which it invited numerous 'liberal' Canadians. This was the first such conference since the early thirties – apparently 'thinking' was not required in the mean time, while the Liberals ruled – and the tone, as in the thirties, was dis-tinctly to the left of the party's when it had been in power. Tom Kent attracted most attention when this new Pearson adviser called for a state medical system, sickness insurance, more unemployment benefits, retraining programs, subsidi-zation of industries in depressed areas, and an urban renewal plan. This was a forecast of a future that Kent would help shape. Less accurate as a prophet was non-Liberal James Eayrs, who reminded the audience that the Soviet danger remained and that we should contribute to its containment by increasing our contribution to NATO and NORAD. Eayrs would change his mind, but in 1960 most thought with him that his remarks were progressive, a Canadian reflection of what one heard in Boston or Berkeley or Foggy Bottom. Power was still an opportunity, not a threat.

The thinkers' conference was followed by a giant Liberal policy rally in Jan-uary 1961. The Conservatives too held larger and more enthusiastic conventions. Both parties' conventions had a similar theme: political participation was no longer for only a few. The 'process,' as it came to be called, must be open to all. This view was endorsed even more heartily by the New Party, then being brought to birth from the marriage of the labour movement and the CCF. During 1960, seminars proliferated, spawning New Party organizations throughout

Canada, all in preparation for the party's founding convention on July 31, 1961. The enthusiasm was immense, although the new infant was not quite so much unlike the other parties as the CCF had claimed to be. Over 2,000 delegates assembled in Ottawa's Coliseum and debated vigorously and long, passing resolutions as regularly as they wiped their brows in the sweltering August evenings. The party decided to call itself the New Democratic Party, and delegate Ramsay Cook termed it 'symbolic because [the convention] represented a victory of the rank and file over the officials and what better word than "democratic" to describe such a victory.' Living with 'democracy' in the sixties proved harder than the 'moderate majority' of the NDP realized at the time. Some of them, including leadership candidate Hazen Argue and Ramsay Cook himself, later left the party when the majority lost its moderation.

But the convention was not a prayer meeting worshipping the saints of the socialist past as had happened so often before, and as would occur again. There was still ritual, but, as Cook reported, the platform was 'Galbraithian in terms,' the 'music folksy and the liturgy strongly American in flavour.'[1] Because the United States seemed to be pioneering in the adaptation of social democracy to Galbraith's affluent society, the American flavour appealed to the NDP in 1961. Nor was it yet time for the socialists to come in from the Cold War, with the Russians flaunting their abuse of basic human rights in the new concrete and barbed-wire barrier dividing Berlin. NATO was endorsed by the NDP, and, although NORAD charmed neither the new party nor the Liberals, the attack was directed mainly toward nuclear weapons, not the American alliance.

The Bomb was an easy, albeit genuine, target for leftist fear and rage. In July 1960 the spirit of public action exemplified by the broader party conventions led to the creation of the Voice of Women, a peace movement dedicated to the abolition of nuclear weapons. The Voice created little controversy at first; when it called on Howard Green in January 1961, the External Affairs minister warmly greeted the delegates, congratulating them on the service they were rendering mankind. The women left with little comment. In the autumn of 1961, however, the women dispensed with the friendly social call on the minister. Together with the Combined Universities Campaign for Nuclear Disarmament they organized a large, seventy-two-hour anti-nuclear demonstration on Parliament Hill and presented a 142,000-signature petition to government officials. The nuclear question is discussed elsewhere in Part IV; what is of interest here is the shift in the emphasis of this political pressure group from direct contact with policymakers to 'media events' designed to influence public opinion. This technique, honed to perfection by the civil rights marchers in the United States, became

1 Ramsay Cook, 'The Labor-Socialist Wedding: Moderation Wins Down the Line in NDP,' *Saturday Night* 77, no. 18 (September 2, 1961), pp. 9-12.

characteristic of public action during the sixties. 'Participatory democracy,' it came to be termed, although the participation was decidedly selective and the democracy questionable at best. But as the American leftist Tom Hayden, who originated the term, later said, 'It was a call to action when students wanted to take action.' The action, then, was rebellious, whatever the role might be. Form was as important as content. In the end, for many North American movements only the husk of form counted; the core of content was dead.

In the early sixties, however, the 'citizens movements' were invariably earnest, and their cause was generally well defined. There was perhaps a too simple belief in the efficacy of such movements, a belief that led to later frustration and, in a few cases, violence. The belief in the possibility of change through direct action enlivened and complicated the political process, and it was a reflection of a new willingness to test limits, a thirst to taste what was new.

Among things new in 1963 was 'pop art,' which appeared in three Toronto shows late in the year. Pop art puzzled Toronto's critics and attracted few buyers, yet it presaged an important debate among artists, writers, and critics about the nature of culture and the meaning of the avant-garde. But this debate came late to Canada, and in the early sixties Canadian critics continued mainly to lament Canada's isolation and consequent conservatism. As Robert Fulford, surveying the literary landscape in 1962, said of those times, there was a sense in which Canadian literature reflected the fact that Canadians were not living in the twentieth century. We had, Fulford observed, a habit of learning about cultural events a decade after they occurred. Elizabeth Kilbourn discussed art in terms that echoed Fulford when she spoke of the 'spell which for so many years ... locked Canadian painting into perpetual isolation from the rest of the world.'[2] The recognition accorded the Canadian painter Jean-Paul Riopelle at the 1962 Venice Biennale was a happy exception, but the embarrassing failure of the National Gallery to detect the fakes when it exhibited a large collection of purported old masters in the same year afforded further testimony in support of the general rule.

The Canadian artistic community was nevertheless in a generally optimistic mood. These years were marked by a confidence, surprising in retrospect, that the solution to Canada's cultural deprivation was a more educated public and a more beneficent government. The solution seemed near, for never had universities expanded so fast and never had the government's and the public's support for the arts been so strong. In 1963 alone, the Molson Foundation established several $15,000 awards for outstanding Canadian achievement in the fields of arts and letters; the province of Ontario established its own Arts Council; the

2 Elizabeth Kilbourn in John Saywell, ed., *Canadian Annual Review for 1962* (Toronto: University of Toronto Press, 1963), p. 416.

federal government announced plans for a $9-million arts centre in Ottawa that eventually cost over $40 million; a new Place des Arts opened in Montreal; Brian Doherty founded the Shaw Festival at Niagara-on-the-Lake; and on Dominion Day in Halifax the Neptune Theatre welcomed its first visitors. Extraordinary beginnings that lasted.

The Neptune found its home in an old movie theatre, but other efforts required new structures to house them. Sometimes these simply mimicked the uninteresting buildings about them, but occasionally the architect was more adventurous and the building became an ornament to the downtown area and a happy contrast to the dross of 1960s development and redevelopment. While sections of cities disappeared, the Victorian touches that so marked Canada's downtowns until the fifties were destroyed forever. In the early sixties there was still little objection to this kind of destruction except from a few specialists, and it must be admitted that many of the old buildings were pretty undistinguished. Toronto, for instance, would have little cause to regret the vanishing of Shea's Theatre and the clutter of tumble-down shops and doss houses that lay around it. Architects on the whole were too busy drafting new plans to concern themselves about the old, and the obligations to their predecessors seemed less important than the legacy that would be left by their own generation, not only in city centres but also on university campuses, which became laboratories for architectural experimentation. Unfortunately the results of the experiments were mixed at best. Simon Fraser University was placed in a group of elegant pavilions on a mountaintop near Vancouver. The University of Toronto devised a suburban campus (Scarborough) that attracted international attention, while on its downtown site it erected a row of tasteless and uncomfortable monoliths that did not even have the virtues of homogeneity. At Massey College, in Toronto, and at Trent, in Peterborough, Ron Thom experimented with modern adaptations of Oxbridge collegiality. And in London, the University of Western Ontario, eschewing innovation, continued to build in 'collegiate gothic.'

Perhaps the results were so mixed because architects had to draft hastily and contractors had to work as fast as they could. The universities faced extraordinary pressure to expand after 1960. By 1961 the number of university students had reached 113,000. This was 50 per cent higher than in 1956, and 200,000 were expected by 1966. (In fact, the number was closer to 300,000.) Surveys consistently showed that Canadians thought this expansion a remarkably good thing, but of course they expected that their children would be part of that good thing. The federal government responded by increasing its grants in support of higher education. In their campaign platform of 1963, Liberals offered a system of national scholarships that would open higher education to able but needy students. The willingness of the federal government to become involved with this traditionally provincial area met with few objections, even in Quebec. Indeed, one 1963 poll indicated that 72.5 per cent of Canadians thought that education should be a federal responsibility.

The most important federal initiative in education during the Diefenbaker years may well have been the Technical and Vocational Assistance Act, mentioned above in connection with economic policy. This provided for a type of conditional grant whereby the federal government paid 75 per cent of the total a province spent on the building and equipping of vocational training schools. By late 1963 Ottawa had approved new construction, additions, or alterations to 538 technical schools. Of this total, 265 were totally new institutions. To serve national needs the new technology demanded its own servants. The Technical and Vocational Assistance Act was a partial attempt to provide them. Although it stressed the classroom rather than the work experience, the act deserves little criticism on that score. Canadian schoolchildren and their parents were no longer prepared to accept the dependent relationships and the low wages of the apprenticeship system, which in any event had never worked very well anywhere in North America. Government policy did not destroy apprenticeship; Canadian middle-class values were effective enough in erasing this ancient avenue to technical and vocational skill.

The pervasiveness of middle-class values was clear in all the studies that examined Canadian society in the early sixties. Raymond Breton and John C. McDonald found that in 1961 the majority of Canadian male and female students with four or more years of secondary schooling wanted and indeed expected a high-status occupation. There were regional differences, to be sure, but the trend held true in all regions. A 1963 study of adolescent high-school culture concluded that 'Canadian high school youth act in a conventional manner and are bearers of a conventional culture.' Yet another 1963 survey indicated that Canadian high-school students shared the values of their parents, esteeming heterosexuality, sports, and 'having fun.' There was scarcely a sign of a generation gap in 1963 high schools – and precious little indication of a flowering of interest in high culture.

University students, too, exhibited much less anti-establishment emotion than anti-Diefenbakerism. The fundamental goals of Canadian society were scarcely questioned by the student body. To Canadians who went abroad to graduate schools in the mid-fifties and returned to university appointments in the early sixties the scene was much the same as the one they had known as first-year students – bigger and more challenging in terms of intellectual demands, but not fundamentally different. There was some concern that the students came too much from the upper middle classes. Evidence seemed to support this belief. In 1961 the Dominion Bureau of Statistics showed that although 31 per cent of all families had incomes over \$5,000, 70 per cent of students reported parental incomes in that range. What this meant was hard to say: students often did not know what their parents' incomes really were, and the parents of students naturally belong to an age group whose incomes are very much higher on average than the incomes of families as a whole. Nevertheless, the numbers were disturbing, because they seemed to suggest that the benefits of higher education flowed chiefly to the children of the prosperous.

The answer urged by university administrators and governments was, naturally, enlargement of the universities, combined with more generous student aid. If fees were kept low and bursaries were generous, there could be a spot for everyone no matter how poor his or her original state. The solution seemed easy; its pedagogical consequences were too obscure to consider. There were some objections, to be sure. Frank Underhill and Peter Dale Scott lamented the loss of 'community' in the new large university, but Robin Mathews in reply praised the American university in which he had begun but not completed his doctoral studies. In that institution of 25,000 students, he wrote, he had not been 'one whit less in touch with faculty' than 'as one of twelve honours students in a Department with half a dozen graduate students in Canada.' A larger university meant more diversity and thus more stimulating minds. According to Mathews, Canada need not fear the 'Ohio States' in its future.[3] Nor had Mathews yet begun to fear the Americans who would come in such numbers to staff them.

Although Claude Bissell has suggested that there was 'a widespread popular radicalism in the early sixties,' this radicalism was apparent only in scattered traces within English-Canadian writing of the pre-1963 period. Most of these traces were no more than notices of the Beat poetry of Allen Ginsberg, of the philosophical anarchism of Paul Goodman, or of the founding of the Students for a Democratic Society in 1962, at Port Huron, just across the bridge from Sarnia. Seemingly more important for Canadians was Frank Underhill's *In Search of Canadian Liberalism,* a record of Underhill's intellectual migration and an investigation of the authenticity of the Canadian liberal tradition. For Underhill the rounding of the Canadian circle came in the joining together of the radical and liberal traditions. Where did this leave Underhill and other Canadians? Certainly far from the radicalism of the mid-sixties, which eschewed both the historical approach and the liberal tradition.

Another work derived from the same tradition was *Social Purpose for Canada* (1961), an anthology of essays on the need for continuing social change in Canada. The tone was pragmatic, optimistic, 'responsible,' and managerial, rather than radical. Michael Oliver's preface rather unconvincingly disavowed any

3 Robin Mathews, 'The New University: An Old Role,' *Canadian Forum* 77 (May 1963), pp. 35-6.

direct connection between the appearance of the book and the founding of the NDP: 'The ideas contained in this book will, we hope, influence not only the New Party but all political parties in Canada.' They did so more directly than Oliver imagined: seven years later one of the authors became Canada's prime minister and Liberal leader.

Pierre Trudeau was like many French-Canadian intellectuals and literary figures in being more directly involved with political life and political publicity than his English-Canadian counterparts. The Quiet Revolution did, perhaps, accompany a widespread popular 'radicalism' in Quebec. Books such as Jean-Paul Desbiens's *Les impertinences du Frère Untel* and Abbés Gérard Dion and Louis O'Neill's *Les Chrétiens et les élections* influenced action in a fashion unknown in the rest of Canada. There was often a scatological, ribald tone to French-Canadian satire in this period, one that carried over easily to the new radicalism later and to the unique political/cultural nationalism of Quebec. Among new writers, Marie-Claire Blais captured most attention with her remarkable *La belle bête* (1959), an experimental and lurid tale of rural Quebec. Her style, too, passed easily into the bold and surreal attack upon limits in art and life so characteristic of the new left. Still, these works seem more like early shoots rather than solid growths; only watering and nurturing would assure survival of the plants. In 1963 no one yet knew what form that nurture would take.

There were too many early shoots to know what the future would bring. The early sixties were mainly a period of transition in which optimism mingled with uncertainty and social liberalism accompanied middle-class conformity. By 1963 Canadians seemed to be embarrassed about their conservative reputation, and one heard much less of the gleeful comparisons of Canadian and American divorce rates. Even the churches, especially the mainline Protestant churches, sought to cloak themselves in new, more colourful raiments. For some there was a return to the social gospel with a call for an 'activist' Christianity, one that lived in the streets and the slums. The Student Christian Movement, which had branches at almost every college campus in English Canada, was most receptive to such notions, and endless nights were spent discussing how Christians should live in this particular world. Most concluded that they should not live as they had. Even the moderator of the United Church could describe his organization as 'too pietistic and irrelevant in the face of the real stuff of life and great issues of our day.' The church, the Very Reverend Angus MacQueen continued, was merely 'the feeble guardian of personal decency and the fount of tranquillity and optimism.' These virtues counted far less than commitment and change. To spur their complacent parishioners, the head offices of the United and Anglican churches sponsored popular publications that excoriated 'the comfortable pew.' One of these publications, by agnostic Pierre Berton, got much wider distribution than the Bible in some churches, and certainly it was read with more attention. A more lasting and important document than Berton's was Pope John XXIII's 1961 encyclical, *Mater et Magistra.* Yet this historic document also reflected the demand that the church must be less comfortable and more 'involved.' The pope's message was well received by Canadian Catholics, some of whom interpreted it as a call 'to plunge ... into the forefront of the reforms needed in society.' Catholic trade unionists and reformers were particularly pleased at the encyclical's cautious approval of state action and its implied disavowal of the Catholic Church's traditional anti-socialist stand.

Even the Christmas and Easter church-goer could not fail to notice the change in the faith. The distance between priest and parishioner shortened; familiarity crept into the ritual and liturgy. Folk masses echoed through sanctuaries, and Pete Seeger added his name to the roster as a composer of sacred music. There were study groups where doctrine was to be discussed, not just received. Even the existence of God was debated, and an occasional theological radical could be found to take the negative side. The Anglican, Presbyterian, and United churches seemed to have taken a road that would lead eventually to union, and other churches heeded similar calls for brotherhood. In his 1960 presidential address to the Canadian Council of Churches, the Very Reverend George Dorey proclaimed that 'the fearsome monsters of denominational prejudice and animosity, like the prehistoric monsters whose skeletons we see in the museums, have died.'

But of course the fearsome monsters were still alive. They lingered in the hearts of many church-goers who resented the liberalizing and ecumenicizing trends in their faiths. Some left old allegiances to join the fundamentalist sects which grew and proliferated throughout the period. Others became dissenters within their churches, modern Jeremiahs warning of new enemies bearing the seeds of moral and spiritual degradation both of the society and of the faith. They could find signs everywhere – in the moral vacuity of Canada's schools, in the disintegration of family life, in the permissive attitude toward sex, in the collapse of censorship. The railings at modern society quickly became tiresome, and the press virtually ignored them, choosing to emphasize the progressive trends in modern religion. The People's Church and the Pentecostals were there, but they were not to be noticed by polite society except when their behaviour found a place in a newspaper's morning or afternoon 'smile.' This reaction was understandable, but it led to distortion. Too often the press and even the clergy failed to notice the reservations that accompanied church leaders' professions of reform. *Mater et Magistra,* for example, warned of the serious dangers in the process of modernization at the same time as it revised some of the Roman Catholic Church's traditional attitudes. The latter was usually hailed; the former was generally ignored. Thus many were greatly surprised when the fabric of their faith later did not give way to permit any and every new form of personal and social behaviour.

No topic symbolized this liberal expectation and conservative result so much as birth control, especially 'the Pill.' The US Food and Drug Administration approved the use of Enovid, an oral contraceptive, in May 1960. Tests showed it to be 100 per cent effective – history's first full guarantee against pregnancy, apart from abstention. No one expected a sudden sexual revolution, and at the time none came, even though birth rates began to fall almost at once. Studies in the early sixties indicated that pre-marital and extra-marital sexual activity had increased very little over that reported by Alfred Kinsey in the late forties. And yet the possibility was there. Earlier, contraception tended to be a male responsibility, and one that was often not accepted. Contraception usually meant condoms, which were normally hidden beneath the drugstore shelf and, with revealing evasiveness, sold 'for the prevention of diease only.' When needed, they were often not to hand.

The new freedom for women and the gradual awareness of this freedom are described by Nora Ephron. After her 1962 graduation Ephron moved to New York and immediately decided she must do something about birth control. She was naturally frightened: she told the nurse she was engaged, although she knew she did not have to say any such thing. But within a few minutes, in the 16th Street brownstone that housed the Margaret Sanger clinic, 'a long and happy relationship' began between Ephron and the pill:

When I first started with the pill I would stop taking them every time I broke up with someone. I had a problem making a commitment to sex; I guess it was a hangover from the whole Fifties virgin thing. The first man I went to bed with, I was in love with and wanted to marry. The second one I was in love with, but didn't have to marry him. With the third one, I thought I *might* fall in love. It was impossible for me to think that I might be a person who 'had sex,' so whenever I had no boyfriend it was always a terrible emotional mess. I couldn't start sleeping with someone until I could begin the pill's cycle again. It was awful. Finally, my new gynecologist explained it all to me. 'Dahlink, who knows what's coming around the corner?'[4]

In those days, in so many ways, no one did.

Meanwhile, in Ottawa, the political game was played much as before, but social change had begun to affect the process, the assumptions, and the results. On February 5, 1963, Canada's Prime Minister walked into the House of Com-

4 Nora Ephron, 'The Pill and I,' in Lynda Rosen Obst, ed., *The Sixties* (New York: Rolling Stone, 1977), pp. 71-2.

mons with his hands behind his back, his fingers crossed. The old-fashioned gesture was futile, and John Diefenbaker's minority government fell. The crossed fingers seemed to symbolize a superstitious man locked in a prison of his own past and his own narrow beliefs. That, at least, was the way most Canadian journalists saw things. Diefenbaker's political obituaries were written before the campaign began. Only four newspapers remained loyal to the Tory cause, and their defence of the Chief often faltered. The electricity that had startled the nation five years before now seemed mere hocus-pocus. The conjuror's hands had become too slow to fool anyone but the gullible and the senile. To those many Canadians who admired the cybernetic aura of the New Frontier, Diefenbaker had become a national embarrassment.

On the cover of *Newsweek* for February 18, 1963, Diefenbaker's wrinkled, contorted face glowered. The cover story was no more flattering in its description: 'The india-rubber features twist and contort in grotesque and gargoyle-like grimaces; beneath the electric gray of the hairline, the eyebrows beat up and down like bats' wings, the agate-blue eyes blaze forth cold fire.' Some people claimed that older, female Tories found Diefenbaker's face rugged, kind, pleasant, even soothing. His enemies need not have been concerned, for in 1963 one saw few young people at Tory rallies, especially in the cities. To younger Canadians Diefenbaker seemed sadly out of tune with their times.

It is all too easy to be sarcastic about Dief the Chief and his merry band of individualists, not least because Diefenbaker's Conservative-populist government could so easily be made to look foolish and uncoordinated – no happy posture for any government, especially for so actively interventionist a one. In economic affairs, the government's record was at best mixed, and with respect to defence and foreign affairs its performance was dismal. No wonder journalists and university people, now as then, have inclined to make fun of the old man from Prince Albert. By 1963 it had become hard to take the Conservatives seriously as an alternative governing party, and the Pearson Liberals were not slow to learn how to compare Conservative incompetence with Liberal wit and dispatch. Nor did they fail to exploit the Kennedy comparison, misleading and inaccurate though that comparison was. Looking back on 1963 from the eighties, the authors are inclined to think that so far as confusion and incompetence are concerned, it is really hard to distinguish between Liberal Tweedledee and Conservative Tweedledum in the years after 1957. What is really sad about the Diefenbaker years is that for the time being the Conservatives lost their chance to become a properly national party, strong in Quebec as well as elsewhere. If the Québécois had a federalist choice in which they could believe, surely Canada's national politics would have been healthier in the sixties and seventies. But was the choice lost? stolen? mislaid? or did it ever exist at all? Was the 1958 election a fluke from which nothing may be inferred? However real the missed opportunities, two things are clear. Diefenbaker was not interested in party organization. And he did not care about Quebec. In both respects, the Mulroney years would be different.

What happened on election day, April 8, 1963, was more complicated than Diefenbaker, *Newsweek,* or the young Canadians who shunned the Tory rallies realized. The Liberals won 129 seats with 41.7 per cent of the popular vote, and the Conservatives took 95 seats with 32.8 per cent. As for the minor parties, the NDP garnered 17 seats with 13.2 per cent of the vote, and Social Credit collected 24 seats with 11.9 per cent of the vote.

Canada had another minority government. This much is clear; its significance is not. Soon after the election, political commentators presented interpretations that suggested the election of 1963 had been decisive, at least symbolically. In 1965 the political philosopher George Grant lamented Diefenbaker's defeat, seeing it as definitive proof that there could no longer be 'an alternative to the American republic being built on the northern half of this continent.' Grant admitted Diefenbaker's weaknesses but honoured his 'telling historical sense' that harked back to earlier days when for 'young Ontarians ... the character of the country was self-evident.' The passion of Grant's argument and its intellectual sophistication and subtlety apotheosized the Diefenbaker government, shielding its contradictions behind a historical dialectic. While Grant's lament told us much about Canadian myths and the discontinuities of Canadian history, it did not succeed in fitting Diefenbaker convincingly into its interpretive framework. A decade later Diefenbaker's memoirs showed Canadians how much the Chief, with his curiously ambivalent attitude toward the Americans and with his banal understanding of political ideas, stood outside the historical pattern that Grant had so cleverly constructed.

Grant's interpretation of Canadian history rightly commands attention, but a more useful analysis of what happened in April 1963 is found in Peter Regenstreif's study of voting patterns between 1957 and 1963. Regenstreif pointed out that the political affiliations had become 'remarkably unstable.' Canadians were casting off their old political raiments as they moved from their parents' homes, from their familiar communities, and from traditional to new forms of behaviour. There was no Canadian consensus in 1963; but, Regenstreif added, Canada did possess an élite population that was reasonably small and localized. By 1963 Diefenbaker had offended most segments of this élite. The 'crucial lesson' of the Diefenbaker period, he argued, was that 'if any party coming to office nationally does not do so with the support of élite opinion, it must gain that support immediately and then hold it if it wishes to remain in office.' This Diefenbaker had not done; relying on rural and traditional support was not enough; his defeat inevitably followed.

If Diefenbaker failed, Pearson scarcely did better. The controversy over nuclear weapons brought credit neither to government nor to opposition. But the Liberals were to have sixteen years in office, and then another four. During this time they could disentangle the confusion they had inherited, while making mistakes of their own. They would also observe and have to cope with the further evolution of Quebec's Quiet Revolution, which became steadily less tranquil as year followed year through the sixties. If Canada's relationship with the United States was one of the two foci of political change during the early sixties, the other was the place of French Canada and Quebec in Canadian Confederation.

Apart from Peter Gzowski's sensitive articles in *Maclean's,* there was little but superficial comment on Quebec in the English-Canadian media prior to 1963. There was much sympathy but little understanding of what the so-called Quiet Revolution might mean. Most important, there was little recognition of the demands that Quebec's changes would make on the rest of Canada. Most English Canadians appeared to think that their country could remain the one they knew. Among Protestant and post-Protestant opinion there was a widespread feeling of relief that Quebec was at last casting off the 'fetters of Catholicism.' No longer 'priest-ridden,' the province would at long last be a fit partner for the progressive and secular forces that had long run English Canada while looking down on their francophone fellow citizens.

But Quebec was not yet a 'province like the others.' The nuclear question underlined the differences. Pierre Berton, in his comments urging Canada to take nuclear weapons, castigated his country for its weakness during the Korean War. Why had Canada been so spineless as to send a 'token' force? Why had conscription not been decreed? To ask the question was to forget the past and misunderstand the future. In fact, nuclear weapons were most unpopular in Quebec. Pearson's announcement led almost all important Quebec newspapers to oppose him. Social Credit received an immense boost, and Pearson lost some valuable potential candidates who became vociferous opponents. In a sarcastic *Cité libre* editorial, Pierre Trudeau charged that 'les Hipsters' of Camelot had decided to destroy Diefenbaker: 'You think that I dramatize? ... You believe that it is by inadvertence that the State Department had sent to the newspapers on January 30 a communiqué reinforcing Mr. Pearson's positions and where Mr. Diefenbaker was called a liar?'[5] Trudeau's caustic questions remain unanswered. They are most important for what they reveal about the questioner – cynical, emotional, and thoroughly distrustful of the Ottawa that Trudeau observed from a distance.

5 *Canadian Annual Review 1963* (Toronto: University of Toronto Press, 1964), p. 32.

Pearson's nuclear weapons policy cost him élite support in Quebec which earlier statements had attracted. In December 1962 Pearson had shown, in a speech drafted by Maurice Lamontagne, that he was prepared to move to meet the new Quebec. This was probably the most important speech of Pearson's life; it was scarcely noticed outside Quebec. Pearson called for an inquiry to investigate 'the means of developing the bicultural character of Canada.' He admitted that English Canadians and the federal government had held a narrow vision of the rights of French-speaking Canadians. 'This meant that, for all practical purposes, there would be an English-speaking Canada with a bilingual Quebec. What is called the "French fact" was to be provincial only.' As a description of the past the statement was fair, but the assumption that the vision of Canada's anglophones could be easily broadened was too facile. The Pearson government and its successor would try to reshape Canada's mentality; the task would prove far more difficult than Pearson himself had imagined possible.

PART FIVE

The Pearson Years 1963-8

23

Coming Apart and Changing Together

'Even citizens of a South American republic might have envied Canadians in 1963.' The usually dour *Canadian Annual Review* thus began its 1963 issue with this unfamiliar comparison of Canada to a banana republic. The new prime minister, Lester Pearson, might, the *Review*'s editor declared, respond as Franklin Roosevelt had when told he would be the greatest American president: 'Either the greatest or the last.' He was neither; but perhaps he was closer to both than we have realized.

In the eighties, we forget how serious the strains upon Confederation seemed in the mid-sixties. Canada had outgrown its old political garments, and it had to try out new ones or refashion the old. Internal growth had strained the fabric of Confederation, and, by the mid-sixties, few thought simple readjustments would ease the strain. There were external influences, too, that forced Canada to change. The grey threads now seemed merely dull, not stolidly respectable, and in any case that respectability that had marked Canada's earlier style was no longer a value Canadians or others cherished. Throughout the country we cleaned out our closets, but we were uncertain whether we would refill them with the new fashions we saw.

Nowhere was this uncertainty more obvious than in the English-Canadian reaction to events in Quebec. The English-Canadian media showed a generosity toward the Quiet Revolution that rested upon too superficial an appreciation of the nature of the social, economic, and political changes occurring in Quebec. The first stirrings of separatism in the form of the Rassemblement pour l'indépendance nationale troubled English Canadians: the bombs in Montreal mailboxes outraged them. Too often, all dissent was lumped into a general mass called separatism. How could one interpret Liberal cabinet minister René Lévesque's warning that 'there must be a new Canada within five years or Quebec will quit Confederation'? Lévesque admitted being 'first and foremost ... a Québécois and second – with a rather growing doubt – a Canadian.' Graduates from the University of Toronto's University College in 1963 applauded Lévesque enthusiastically, but the enthusiasm may have simply masked confusion. The parts of Confederation were no longer fitting into the familiar mental images they had learned in the classroom.

What they had learned created many of the problems, not least Lester Pearson's. Pearson's background made it easier for him to accept the demands for change emanating from within Canada. Conversely, he was ill prepared for the changes that occurred beyond his nation's boundaries. To understand Pearson's idea of Canada requires consideration of his idea of internationalism. Pearson had spent his formative years outside Canada. His memoirs reveal how important to him were the First World War, Oxford, and, above all, the international anarchy of the 1930s that he observed as a bystander in London and Geneva. He sensed both the fragility of international order and his nation's unwillingness to face the impact on it of the world beyond its borders. This always distressed him; in the 1930s it frustrated him and formed in his mind strong ideas about the need for internationalism. In the 1950s and 1960s, he determined that he must break down those crustaceous formations that limited the growth of Canadians. Pearson's internationalism and his domestic politics thus were obverse sides of the same coin. By leading Canada into the bracing winds of international activity, Pearson hoped to open his countrymen to fuller awareness of the possibilities of, and threats to, humanity. There could be light in this world, but the dark was always nearby. 'The dark,' he once wrote, 'comes from our fears and our hates, our wrong priorities and our rooted prejudices, the destructive use to which we put so much of our technology, and poisoning and polluting of our environment, weariness, and a declining public commitment to new international responsibilities.' Of these fears and hates, his nation had too many.

Like the turn-of-the-century imperialists, Pearson looked beyond Canada because he did not like the limits he saw within. Yet unlike his critic George Grant, Pearson was not a part of that conservative tradition. Pearson might have admitted that in earlier days the British connection had been an essential ingredient of a distinctive Canadian identity for English Canadians. For Pearson, however, an identity was not an end in itself. His diplomatic career had led him toward a cosmopolitanism that accepted progress, relativism, and liberalism. His direct experience with Europe in the 1930s had made him distrust the irrational in politics and also the values of the past. Thus, the only historian who became prime minister was, in some ways, the most eager to break with the past. In his view, Canada could not remain a nation if it continued to dwell upon its past. This was the intellectual foundation of Pearson's determination to give Canada a distinct flag, to promote bilingualism and biculturalism, and to heighten the activity of the Canadian state in cultural and social realms. Education, mobility, and affluence would clear the path toward modernism. In 1963, Pearson could not foresee how many Canadians of his own background would hesitate to take the path that he himself had followed so easily.

It would be wrong to regard Pearson as an outsider to Canadian intellectual traditions. Like Frank Underhill, J.W. Dafoe, and, in 1963, Peter C. Newman and Pierre Berton, Pearson shared an acceptance of Canada as a North American nation. Like Berton, he believed that Canada had 'cast [its] lot with this continent for better or worse.' Since 1945, that lot had been mostly good. The Americans had made many mistakes; they had shown too little regard for Canadian sensitivities and too much alarm toward the Communist threat. Yet their aims seemed fundamentally decent and beneficent; certainly the benefits of American economic and military leadership in the free world were great for Canada. Like most of his generation, Pearson recalled American isolationism and attributed to it many of the catastrophes of the pre-1939 period. He and his fellow Canadian diplomats took some credit for weaning the Americans away from isolationism and toward responsible leadership. What Peter C. Newman expressed in a pre-election (March 7, 1963) *Maclean's* article summarized Pearson's attitude well: 'The future prosperity and even the existence of Canada depend directly on the goodwill of the USA. This doesn't mean we should toady to Washington. But it does mean that we can hardly expect our point of view to carry much weight, if our chief emissary in future bargaining with the US president is a politician elected on the basis of blatant anti-Americanism.' Canada was part of the American team; quarrels over strategy were for the privacy of the clubhouse, not for the playing field.

Although cordiality characterized Mike Pearson's first official meeting with Jack Kennedy at Hyannis Port in May 1963, the rapport between the two leaders did not automatically eliminate all differences between their countries. This became clear in the reaction to Walter Gordon's first budget, which alarmed American businessmen and officials who regarded the proposed tax on takeovers of Canadian firms as discriminatory and 'protectionist.' Still, ultimately, it was the Canadian reaction not the American protest that led Gordon to withdraw the tax. The embarrassment of Gordon continued when in late July Kennedy proposed to Congress an interest equalization tax to be applied to foreign borrowings in the United States. The Liberals, having ridiculed the ninety-two-and-a-half-cent Diefenbuck, could not accept without protest a policy that might cause further dollar devaluation. Thus Canada's most nationalistic finance minister had to beseech the Americans to make Canada an exception to the new tax. The special relationship still held; Canada got its exemption. Ironically, the exemption that Gordon did so much to obtain contributed to greater American involvement in the Canadian economy. To the nationalist finance minister, the incident was 'another sharp reminder of Canada's dependency on the United States.' Further contact with Americans convinced Gordon that 'at least the more junior people in the State and Treasury Departments held decidedly imperialistic views about Canada.' Further contact with Gordon convinced Americans that Canada's finance minister possessed limited competence but abundant paranoia. On the Liberals' second time around, things would not be the same.

Despite Canada's strong links with the United States, Pearson and Secretary of State for External Affairs Paul Martin were troubled by the zeal with which American Defense Secretary Robert McNamara and Secretary of State Dean Rusk sought deeper involvement in Vietnam. They believed that such impetuosity prevented careful evaluation of the effects of Asian involvement on allies, on public opinion, and on the United States itself.

Kennedy's foreign policy troubled Canadian officials, but his domestic policy commanded respect and imitation. The Liberal party's domestic program drew its spirit, if not its form, from the reinvigorated liberalism of the Kennedy administration. In the early 1960s political liberalism enjoyed its post-war heyday. The unattractiveness of authoritarian alternatives seemed indubitably proven by the wall at Berlin, by Solzhenitsyn's *One Day in the Life of Ivan Denisovich,* and by the affluence and confidence of Western society. The case for civil rights and for the abolition of irrational and archaic restraints on individual behaviour had never been so strong as in the summer of 1963. Canadians applauded and admired the massive, peaceful, and eloquent demonstrations with which American blacks sought to redress ancient wrongs. They watched attentively and with sympathy for they could see the future working and knew that it might be Canada's as well as America's, even if it came second hand.

The strength of the bond with the United States was revealed on November 22, 1963, when suddenly the light seemed much further away and blackness so near. On that late fall day, the death of John F. Kennedy in Dallas stunned Canadians. Like Americans, they stopped to watch what they could not believe. That one day is imprinted on the memories of an entire generation. For Peter Gzowski, twenty-nine on November 22, 1963, 'no other event in public history – not V-E Day, not the beginnings of the October crisis in Quebec, not the first landing of mankind on the moon ... stands so clearly in my private memory.' He could never again see the world as it was before. It was not public history but our private selves that changed most. Ten years later, Gzowski remembered: 'I guess there are two things that I hope for the son who saw me weep that day. The first is that he will understand why. And the second is that, if something should happen to him, the way it happened to all of us, that he will weep too, and survive.'[1] There was, though, much that did not survive that day.

Kennedy's articulate administration concealed how much it reflected the past, not the future. His beliefs in American possibilities were Whitmanesque, redolent of the last century's most lavish visions. His confidence in the capacity of Americans to 'bear any burden' derived from those heady post-war days when, with a devastated Europe, American leadership was craved and its economic muscles barely tested. Europe had rebuilt and was flexing its own muscles. And the rapidly appearing Third World was showing a hostility to the American liberal-capitalist model that surprised Americans. Like the new Johnson administration, the Pearson government's legislative enthusiasm derived in part from the contemporary American belief that good government could be measured by programs, agencies, and activity. Doubts about Johnson's international activism rarely surfaced in Canada in 1964, not least because he seemed so much more pacific than his right-wing opponent, Barry Goldwater. In February 1965, for example, James Eayrs could argue that Johnson's approach represented a retreat from American activism internationally. Domestic policy was being placed ahead of foreign policy. Nevertheless, in the next few years the definition of objectives would remain elusive. America's burdens had become too much to bear.

A decade earlier Canada would probably have lent its strength to share these burdens. Now there was growing reluctance. By late 1964, one could find increasing criticism of American foreign policy, especially in Quebec. Canadian officials also saw that there was some advantage in creating distance between American and Canadian objectives. In that year of the first Chinese atomic test, Canada considered a break with the Americans over the question of Chinese admission to the United Nations. Paul Martin and his officials soon learned, however, that the domestic gains from such action (polls showed Canadians favoured recognition of China) could not offset the difficulties with the Americans that such an action would create. Canada still had serious balance of payments problems, and American forbearance was essential. Moreover, the chronic problems of the automobile industry seemed finally close to a lasting solution through the Canada-United States Automotive Agreement, the Auto Pact, which was announced on December 11, 1964. This agreement meant more Canadian jobs and industry; the alternative was a protectionism that even Walter Gordon rejected.

Banking emerged as a second economic area where Canadian policy created difficulties. In 1963, despite a warning from Gordon that the Canadian government opposed foreign control of any chartered bank, James Rockefeller, presi-

1 Peter Gzowski, *Peter Gzowski's Book about This Country in the Morning* (Edmonton: Hurtig, 1974), p. 155.

dent of Citibank, attempted a takeover of the small Dutch-controlled Mercantile Bank of Canada. The result was a government decision to revise the Bank Act and thereby prevent Mercantile from expanding under foreign ownership. American observers wondered at the retroactivity of this action. If applied to other American interests the impact of the legislation could be immense. The government stood firm, and by the end of 1965 the substance of the case lay submerged beneath the nationalism it had aroused.

Another catalyst to nationalism in Canada was the government's failure to expel American magazines from the Canadian scene. In his 1965 budget Gordon, in an attempt to divert Canadian advertising to Canadian media, disallowed income tax deductions for advertising in non-Canadian newspapers or magazines, with the notable exceptions of *Time* and *Reader's Digest*. The *Globe and Mail* felt that this was akin to locking in 'the two biggest wolves with the sheep.' Most in the Liberal caucus agreed, and it was left to Gordon to explain that despite his personal objections 'this was the price we had to pay to get approval of the automotive agreement' and to assume that *La Presse* would not be sold to 'European interests sympathetic to the Separatist cause' and The *Globe and Mail* to Americans. Whether the *Globe* and *La Presse* rumours had any substance is unknown. The argument nevertheless convinced the caucus, and the legislation was passed. The controversy illustrated the difficulties inherent in reducing Canada's cultural involvement with the United States. The *Winnipeg Free Press* denounced Gordon's bill as undemocratic. To clarify its point it printed Gordon's picture beside those of Hitler, Stalin, and Mussolini. The *Toronto Star,* published by Gordon's friend and fellow nationalist Beland Honderich, was kinder, defending the finance minister as a Canadian patriot. In the end, however, no one was fully happy with the bill.

The change in Canadian attitudes toward the United States was revealed in the reaction to a report entitled *Canada and the United States: Principles for Partnership*. The authors, Canadian Arnold Heeney and American Livingston Merchant, had been asked by Pearson and Johnson to study how the two countries could 'make it easier to avoid divergencies in economic and other policies.' Their report came in July 1965 when the value of avoiding divergence was no longer so widely assumed. The controversies about magazines, banks, and the balance of payments were only a part of the broader interaction that had created new bruises and reservations. In February 1965 the United States began to bomb North Vietnam, and, in the following month, American combat troops began to fight there. During this time and before, Canada, primarily through Blair Seaborn, a member of the Canadian delegation to the International Control Commission, had tried to find the key to peace. Seaborn had warned Hanoi of the violence that would follow if it did not desist, while simultaneously offering, on behalf of the Americans, negotiating points. Seaborn got nowhere.

Pearson and Martin fumbled as they saw the United States lurch toward full war in the early spring of 1965. When they met Americans they trusted, such as Mike Mansfield, Bill Fulbright, and Scotty Reston, they heard dire warnings about the unreliability of Johnson's judgments. In April 1965, Pearson decided he must raise his voice to express his doubts. The occasion he selected was a convocation address at Temple University in Philadelphia. He called for a halt to American bombing of North Vietnam, not forever, perhaps, but simply as a test of the possibility of negotiation. It seemed cautious, but the Americans were inordinately sensitive. In fact, Johnson exploded. At Camp David, he grabbed Pearson by the lapels, stopping barely short of physical violence in an angry rebuke. Publicly, Pearson pretended nothing had happened. Privately, he had learned that this American president was unlike others, a bully who threatened, a vulgar manipulator who tested one's mettle.

After the Temple University speech, Pearson and Johnson never repaired their relationship. Pearson, knowing that his nation still craved the benefits of a close association, apologized to Johnson for his remarks, but the situation improved little. In August Johnson refused to permit Pearson to publish their correspondence on Vietnam, embarrassing the Canadian, who had promised he would do so. If the politicians lost trust in the United States, so did the population, but more slowly. The August 1965 Gallup Poll revealed that 58 per cent of Canadians regarded the United States as Canada's best friend. In the following spring both Young Liberals and Young Conservatives debated whether Canada should contribute directly to the American effort in Vietnam. They decided that Canada should not, but the rejection of the motion was neither overwhelming nor immediate. Where the change was most noticeable was among the literary and intellectual élite, groups that before Vietnam had been most critical of American influence on Canadian life. Vietnam provided substance for their case. Canadians, taken together, were confused.

The kaleidoscope of confusing images created in Canada a fear that the nation might fall prey to the virus sweeping the United States. After all, the smoke from Detroit's race riots drifted very quickly over the river. This time the defenders of Canadian independence came, not, as in the past, from the right, but from the left. The change was sudden. In 1964 the new leftist periodical *Canadian Dimension,* edited by former American Cy Gonick, still looked instinctively south for leadership in social matters. The United States has discovered poverty, Gonick wrote in May 1964; 'it is curious that this subject is being ignored by Canadian counterparts.' The defeat of the Saskatchewan CCF government in the spring of 1964 was attributed to the fact that after the introduction of medicare there was nothing remaining for a socialist government to do. Two years later the left had a program: the protection of Canada from the malignant wave sweeping the United States. A *Canadian Dimension* poll of 'leading Canadian thinkers' in the early part of 1967 revealed that most expected that Canada would soon be ruled by a nationalist-socialist government, one that would derive its force from its success in insulating Canada from the American sickness. Two books of essays by Canadian intellectuals revealed the new mood: *Close the 49th Parallel* and *The New Romans*. The Canadian consensus, these books declared, could be found only in opposing the liberal capitalism of Canada's neighbour. Canadians could finally be free only when they rejected the economic system that had created the American virus. So strong was the current that even those who, like Mordecai Richler, had looked forward 'to the day when [Canada] might disappear and we would join fully in the American adventure' resisted no longer: 'Vietnam and Ronald Reagan, among other things, have tempered my enthusiasm. Looked at another way, yes we *are* nicer. And suddenly that's important.'

But the United States still absorbed Canadian thoughts. Perceptive observers of the first 'teach-in' at the University of Toronto against the Vietnam War in 1965 commented on the striking absence of Canadian material. Others remarked upon the derivative quality of anti-American criticism in Canada: were Canadians saying anything different than Herbert Marcuse and Robert Wolff, or, for that matter, J.K. Galbraith and Walter Lippmann? No, there was little originality in the Canadian critique; there was mainly the satisfaction for Canadians that the airing somehow made us feel 'nicer.' This new self-confidence, this sense that Canada was a better nation and Canadians a better people, struck us suddenly. Since the Second World War Canadians had not thought this way. Now Americans told us, and because they did, Canadians believed.

Polls clearly showed that public opinion had shifted toward a nationalistic stance by 1967. In 1965, a *Maclean's* poll had shown a strong disposition toward free trade with the United States and a relatively benign attitude toward foreign investment. In 1967, nationalistic responses dominated a *Toronto Daily Star* poll: 67 per cent thought that 'the Canadian government [should] take steps to reduce foreign control of Canadian industry'; 47 per cent believed that 'foreign control of Canadian industry' was an issue of major importance; and 63 per cent believed that Canada did not show enough independence in its dealings with the United States.

For Pearson and Martin, this nationalism presented major policy difficulties. Pearson had been literally shaken by Johnson's treatment of his dissent on the question of bombing. He feared the consequences of further and broader dissents not only on Canadian-American relations but on the Atlantic alliance, which he continued to believe was the best guarantee of world peace. To dissent openly and vigorously would be to lose influence on the United States in its most irrational international moment. Was this not, in a nuclear age, an irresponsible act? Pearson never decided how to answer this question. He was faced with asserting Canadian independence while at the same time trying to tame the American war machine now out of control.

To the government's critics, independence meant cutting most of the links Canada had built up with the United States. NORAD was a prime target; so too was NATO, which the critics charged was a European extension of American imperialism. For Canada NATO meant, Kenneth McNaught declaimed, 'acquiescence in Washington's ideological anti-communism.' The Cold War was over; its symbols must end. Written before Russian tanks rolled over Prague in 1968, and soon after the test-ban treaty, at a moment when apparent Soviet restraint in Asia contrasted with apparent American zeal, and when de Gaulle's short-lived European vision challenged the bi-polarity of the post-war world, McNaught's analysis seemed to carry more weight than it actually did. Those who followed McNaught's fashion included Walter Gordon, Dalton Camp, the New Democratic Party (the CCF's successor), and some influential Liberal MPs, notably Pierre Trudeau, Donald Macdonald, Jean Marchand, and Gérard Pelletier.

Even policies that had little to do directly with the United States became involved in the debate. Defence minister Paul Hellyer had assumed office in 1963 as a staunch supporter of the American and NATO alliances, of nuclear weapons for Canada, and of modernization of the Canadian armed forces. In March 1964 the White Paper on Defence had called for integration of the armed forces and a single chief of defence staff. Naturally some members of the military saw this as an attack on the traditions of the Canadian armed forces. The admirals and generals rallied the opponents of unification, arguing that Hellyer was reducing Canada's armed forces to 'a special peacetime force to undertake small police actions in foreign countries.' This was not Hellyer's intention, but some were delighted to think it was. The NATO-NORAD commitments were made in another day, in different circumstances: they could now lead us down mine-strewn paths where Canadians need not tread. Thus, armed forces integration became a means that could attain the greater end of an independent foreign policy. There were other examples. In the Mercantile Bank case the government refused to back down when, in April 1966, the Americans officially protested against 'discrimination against American-owned banks.' In November the message was tougher, threatening retaliation against the Canadian banks' lucrative American activities. Over the next six months the Liberals fought among themselves about the appropriate response, with Mitchell Sharp, the finance minister, pitted against his predecessor, Walter Gordon. The result was a compromise that irritated the Americans (but they did not retaliate) and that emphasized the divisions within the Liberal party and the cabinet on the nationalist question.

On Vietnam, Martin tried desperately to obtain peace and to establish an independent Canadian position. He sought to do this by sending the retired Canadian diplomat Chester Ronning to Hanoi in early 1966. The United States reluctantly approved, because, as the Pentagon papers put it, 'there seemed no proper response other than encouragement.' Pearson was unenthusiastic, and by the end of 1966 Canada has lost face not only in Washington but also in Hanoi.

In that same year Canada also tried to develop a separate policy toward China. In fact the Ronning trip was part of this plan. He was to go to Peking, where it was thought that his well-known sympathy for the People's Republic would guarantee him a warm reception. It did not get him past the border guards at Canton. Although Ronning brought no new information, Martin and Pearson decided to take some initiative and were surprised when they received American encouragement. This support was short-lived. When the Canadians decided to go ahead and change their vote on Chinese admission at the United Nations, Dean Rusk warned Martin that such an action would greatly offend the United States and many of its allies. In the end, the Canadian 'One China-One Taiwan' resolution failed.

By early 1967 Canadian-American relations had, in Rusk's diplomatic euphemism, 'deteriorated.' Pearson and Johnson bore mutual suspicion and avoided meetings. In fact, Johnson initially refused to visit Canada during the 1967 Centennial and only relented hours before visiting Expo '67 in Montreal on the US national day. It was the last time that Pearson and Johnson met. Neither had regrets.

In the fall of 1967 Martin publicly called for a bombing halt. In the din of American and other international protest, hardly anyone noticed. Johnson by this time had hardened to criticism, and there was no retaliation. To critics of earlier Canadian policy, this American silence proved that Canada need not restrain itself in criticizing the war or in moving out of the American orbit generally. In that maelstrom of international politics of the mid-sixties, 'independence' seemed to many Canadians a life preserver that would save them from drowning or at least prevent them from whirling mindlessly in the patterns of the past. Alas, they did not know exactly what was sought. Independence remained an amorphous substance whose definition eluded common agreement. To the Marxist-nationalists, independence meant closing the forty-ninth parallel, severing forever the ties that had bound Canada to the United States and creating in Canada s socialist society where state ownership predominated. Others regarded independence as a kind of old-fashioned isolationism, and in this respect Stephen Clarkson's concept of independence meaning equality – the right to say no – was not much different from O.D. Skelton's in the 1930s, with the Third

World now offering the 'freedom' that the United States seemed to offer in the 1930s before the Second World War broke out. But, as in the 1930s, so too in the 1960s: independence for what?[2]

An independent foreign policy, Clarkson argued, is 'ethically just.' Perhaps, but as Peyton Lyon pointed out at the time, it does not mean that 'a policy of non-alignment and tub-thumping diplomacy would augment Canada's influence in world affairs.' We would be most foolish, Lyon wrote, 'to abandon a foreign policy that has been generally helpful, and admired by foreign experts, for a new policy that might prove to be counter-productive, even in helping Canadian intellectuals to overcome their inferiority complex.'

In retrospect, it is clear that the debate had meaning only for the moment – for the Vietnam years and after the first misleading glimpses of détente and arms control. When a critic of Pearsonian diplomacy, Pierre Trudeau, succeeded Pearson as prime minister, he discovered how much the changing circumstances of the world beyond Canada's borders made the premises of the tub-thumpers and their opponents irrelevant. Foreign policy once again went beyond the interest and understanding of most Canadians, and the many tubs thumping now seemed a single hand clapping.

'Il faut que ça change.' 'Things have got to change,' the Quebec Liberals declared in the 1960 provincial election. And things did, not only in Quebec but in Canada as a whole. They did so in a way few had imagined in 1960 when the former Minister of Northern Affairs and Natural Resources in the St Laurent government, Jean Lesage, became premier of Quebec. An elegant, imposing man who combined administrative efficiency with strong business and political attachments, Lesage contrasted sharply with Maurice Duplessis, whose vulgarity had been so calculated and whose administrative and political style derived mostly from the pork-barrelling, parish-pump politics of the past. That at least was the first impression. English-Canadian journalists welcomed Lesage as the modernizer that the 'backward' Quebec had so long required. Now, finally, the oldest province might come of age.

In the first few years of the Lesage government, this sympathy persisted. It was an English-Canadian journalist who referred approvingly to post-1960 events in Quebec as the Quiet Revolution. The change that must come would come quietly and conservatively, through the mediation of the modern manager so fashionable then in Ottawa, Toronto, and, of course, Washington. Thus when Liberal senator Tom Crerar, cantankerous and sceptical in his old age, com-

2 Stephen Clarkson, ed., *An Independent Foreign Policy for Canada?* (Toronto: McClelland & Stewart, 1968). This book contains numerous essays reflecting nationalist criticism of Canadian-American relations.

plained that Quebec was changing too rapidly, that its new self-confidence would threaten the Canadian consensus, historian Blair Neatby told him that Quebec would have difficulties in passing through these changes but that, in the end, it would become more North American.

As Dale Posgate and Kenneth McRoberts noted later, for English Canadians the Union Nationale's traditional nationalism and the 'lag' in political modernization meant that the Quebec 'problem' had 'a deceptive air of manageability.' Indeed, there was a dream that finally a common nationality might come from the 'modernization' of Quebec and the breakdown of the barrier of traditional Quebec nationalism. This was, of course, a dream unfulfilled. Change came to Quebec less quietly than was first thought and, when it came, proved far more resistant to management and government control than political scientists suggested. When Lesage, now the 'prime minister of the state of Quebec,' was asked by his former colleague Mike Pearson where his government and his province were going, Lesage replied, 'I don't know.' The reply was honest; no one else knew either.

Today historians tend to emphasize the continuity of the Quiet Revolution with the past, yet none denies the rapidity of change in Quebec in the 1950s and 1960s. The physical signs were everywhere, from Gaspé villages to Montreal graffiti, in the churches now become coffeehouses or union halls, in the argot of the street and the jargon of the academy. Some of this change can be measured, and what the available statistics reveal is a society undergoing rapid transformation socially, economically, and culturally.

The image of Quebec as a rural province has not been valid in the twentieth century, but agriculture was for Quebeckers a main occupation as well as a symbol of a way of life until long after the war. Nevertheless, between 1951 and 1971 the number of farms fell from 134,366 to 61,257. At the same time the number of farm inhabitants fell from 19.5 per cent of the total population to 5.6 per cent. This decline in agricultural importance was not matched by a concomitant increase in manufacturing, which saw employment decline from 36 per cent to 31.9 per cent of the labour force between 1946 and 1966. Where growth occurred most rapidly in Quebec, as in Canada as a whole, was in the service sector, where employment during the same period rose from 37.2 per cent to 59.7 per cent of the labour force. These changes in employment brought (especially for French Canada) changes in the way people lived. The city was an irresistible siren to young French Canadians wanting employment. In 1941, 55 per cent of the French-origin population of Quebec lived in urban areas; by 1951, 63 per cent did; and in 1971, 78 per cent did. City air brought some new freedoms perhaps, but it also created a propinquity that identified inequities. The French Canadians found themselves facing barriers that seemingly prevented them from

Table 1
Agriculture 1951–71

	1951	1961	1971
Number of farms	134,366	95,777	61,257
Per cent of population on farms	19.5	11.1	5.6

Table 2
Distribution of Male Labour Force, Quebec 1951–71

1951

Ethnic group	Total (%)	Proprietary & managerial (%)	Professional (%)	Clerical (%)	Industrial (%)	Agriculture (%)
French	79.9	65.4	63.9	67.2	79.1	91.7
British	13.3	19.0	27.2	26.5	12.3	7.0
Other	6.8	15.6	8.9	6.3	8.6	1.3

1961

Ethnic group	Total (%)	Managerial (%)	Professional & technical (%)	Clerical & sales (%)	Industrial (%)	Agriculture (%)
French	77.5	63.8	72.9	72.3	80.2	91.1
British	11.8	19.0	22.5	17.1	8.8	6.1
Other	10.7	17.2	14.6	10.6	11.0	2.8

1971

Ethnic group	Total (%)	Managerial/ administrative (%)	Professional & technical (%)	Clerical & sales (%)	Industrial (%)	Agriculture (%)
French	75.8	61.9	69.2	72.7	79.5	87.9
British	11.7	22.8	15.9	14.5	8.6	7.9
Other	12.5	15.3	14.9	12.8	11.9	4.2

SOURCE: 1951 *Census of Canada* Volume IV, Table 13 (p 13.9), and Dale Posgate and Kenneth McRoberts, *Quebec: Social Change and Political Crisis* (Toronto: McClelland and Stewart 1976), 38 reaching the heights in those occupations that a liberal capitalist society most esteems. Although statistics indicate that most Quebec francophones lived better lives, their frustrations are eloquently felt in Gabrielle Roy's *Bonheur d'occasion,* Roger Lemelin's *Au pied de la pente douce,* and Pierre Vallières's *Nègres blancs d'Amérique.* Worse, acquiring the appropriate raiments – education, language, and experience – did not seem to guarantee francophone entry to the boardrooms where economic power lay. Wallace Clement found in 1972 that only 8.4 per cent of the Canadian economic élite was francophone, only 1.7 per cent higher than in 1951 (according to and using John Porter's analysis of the economic élite). Another study by economists argued that, in 1961, 60 per cent of the difference in income between francophones and anglophones in Quebec derived from discrimination in favour of anglophones for high-level positions. Some institutions altered little, but others changed very much and in a fashion that created new tensions within the society.

The Lesage victory in 1960 was the triumph of the city over the country, the articulate over the mute. It had been easy to believe that Quebec was 'backward' and rural under Duplessis because the style of so many of the Union Nationale members was redolent of the barnyard. Lesage's ministers struck one immediately as 'street smart,' men for the city season. Indeed, journalists in the 1960s often remarked that the Quebec government was much closer in style to Kennedy's Camelot than to Ottawa. René Lévesque strode easily from the television screen into politics, leaving the impression that every policy could and should be explained in a thirty-minute spot. Some policies had as much substance as the puffs of smoke that surrounded him, but with Lévesque the medium was the message, the image of vitality and commitment. The Minister of Youth, Paul Gérin-Lajoie, had the habits of Oxford common rooms, and the new bureaucrats who began to move into offices where party jobs were previously the major concern brought with them very sharply honed technical skills. They were the equals, if not the betters, of those in Ottawa in talent, suavity, and commitment.

Lesage drew electoral support as well as talent from the anglophone and francophone middle class. Workers and farmers did not take so quickly to the Lesage program and style. But as we have seen, the farmers were dwindling, and their doubts about change were drowned out by the very articulate spokesmen who were urging fundamental transformation of society. By 1962 the momentum was clear, and the Lesage government knew it had to move beyond where it had stood. What this implied was a more overt commitment to the use of the state than Quebec had ever known. 'Anti-étatisme' (anti-statism) was a Quebec tradition, though often honoured in the breach, and the tradition itself did not pass to the younger, more secular generation that influenced the Liberal party in Quebec at the time. The central debate occurred over the issue of nationalization of hydro in the province. Without the consent of the cabinet or the premier, Lévesque called for such nationalization on February 12, 1962. St James Street trembled only slightly at the news; the presence of George Marler, a financial conservative, in the cabinet, as well as Lesage's own corporate law experience, seemed to guarantee that this was one more whiff of smoke that would pass. Nationalization was not popular; it reeked of the musty socialism of the 1930s about which even socialists (including the newly formed New Democratic Party) seemed embarrassed.

On Labour Day weekend in 1962, the Quebec cabinet met to consider Lévesque's disregard of cabinet solidarity in promoting nationalization. The importance of nationalization to its proponents transcended the action itself, and Lesage called an election on the issue. Of course those who denied the need for nationalization attracted the sting of nationalist rhetoric. When Daniel Johnson, the Union Nationale leader, suggested partial nationalization, Lesage accused him of 'refusing to collaborate in the most important task of economic liberation.' Political freedom was not enough; now the state, which alone of all major institutions the Québécois could control, must grasp the levers that could bring 'economic liberation.'

The campaign obscured the question of what came next, and it proved to Canadians generally that nationalism in Quebec was not a casualty of the Quiet Revolution but rather a beneficiary. Yet this nationalism possessed a different flavour, one that English Canadians could not so easily identify. When the results of the election came in on November 14, 1962, the Liberals had won sixty-three of the ninety-five seats in the legislature. Workers and farmers remained resistant to the Liberal appeal, but the anglophone and francophone middle class had combined to give Lesage his victory.

In an analysis of what it all meant, Albert Breton argued that nationalization of hydro and, by implication, most of the projects of the Lesage years were patronage or 'public works' for the francophone middle class. Nationalism in Quebec, Breton wrote, 'is a tool used by the new middle class to accede to wealth and power.' The francophone engineers, managers, and technicians reaped the rewards of nationalization as they secured positions anglophones had previously held or would have held.[3] Whether the francophone middle class perceived its economic gain so rationally is perhaps questionable, but Breton's analysis has considerable validity. The activist state became the focus of francophone middle class expectations and for very many the provider of economic livelihood. The rapid expansion and secularization of the educational system, almost inevitable following the 1962 election, worked the same way. Educational expansion

3 Albert Breton, 'The Economics of Nationalism,' *Journal of Political Economy* LXXII (August 1964).

swelled the ranks of the foot soldiers of the Quiet Revolution over the next decades. For these people, the government's slogan to promote education had a special meaning: 'Qui s'instruit, s'enrichit.'

Sometime in 1962 or 1963, the Quiet Revolution became the Quebec problem. To English Canadians and to federal politicians generally, what had been expected in Quebec had not occurred. The federal Liberals had expected to benefit from Quebec's disillusionment with Diefenbaker, but in the election of 1962 the twenty-six seats won by Réal Caouette's Social Credit confused and disappointed them. As in the Quebec election, voting patterns revealed fear and resistance to change, as well as serious divisions within Quebec society. Fortunately for the Liberals, Prime Minister Diefenbaker, who had lost most of his Quebec members, seemed neither to know what to do nor to care to do it.

For federal politicians, trouble was there, but also opportunity. Pearson made an attempt to seize it, even though by background he seemed almost as unsuited for the task as Diefenbaker. In the forties, when he was first discussed as a possible Liberal leader, an American diplomat had reported to Washington that Pearson's greatest liability was his lack of knowledge of French Canada and his centralist disposition. In 1962 his French still sounded as if it had been learned – badly – in a Methodist manse, but his sympathies for Quebec's demands were real. There were other advantages: Jean Lesage was his former parliamentary secretary; Maurice Sauvé advised both federal and provincial Liberal parties; and Maurice Lamontagne, another Pearson friend and adviser, realized how serious the Quebec problem was. It was Lamontagne who drafted Pearson's December 1962 speech in which he called for an inquiry and said: 'It is now clear to all of us, I think, that French-speaking Canadians are determined to become directors of their economic and cultural destiny in their own changed and changing society ... they also ask for equal and full opportunity to participate in all federal government services, in which their own language will be fully recognized.' This meant, in Pearson's view, 'the greatest possible constitutional decentralization and ... special recognition of the French fact and the rights of French-speaking Canadians in Confederation.' Pearson's 'doctrine of federalism' was 'to decentralize up to a certain point as the way to strengthen, indeed to establish and maintain, unity.'

This speech and the policy it foretold won widespread support, even though many of Pearson's caucus, including Walter Gordon, opposed its delivery at that time. Bilingualism became an election plank for the Liberals in Quebec, but what it gained there for the Liberals, Pearson's nuclear weapons policy probably lost. The French press in Quebec quickly turned against Pearson generally, choosing to support no one in the campaign, though *Le Devoir* backed the NDP and others noted with approval that the Créditistes opposed nuclear weapons.

More important probably was the disaffection of some intellectuals who, because of the weakness of Quebec representation in Ottawa, were considering running for the Liberals. Jean Marchand, Pierre Trudeau, and Gérard Pelletier decided that they could not run, and in Trudeau's case the decision was accompanied by an angry denunciation of Pearson as immoral. Instead of presenting scrub-faced reformers, the Liberals fought the Créditistes with a brawling bush fighter, Yvon Dupuis, who confronted the Créditiste reaction with the methods of the past. The Liberals scarcely seemed the party to deal with Quebec's future. During the campaign, Lesage, although friendly toward the Pearson Liberals, made it clear that his increasingly hard stance against 'Ottawa' would not change. No longer would all Quebec Liberals believe in 'Rouge à Quebec, et rouge à Ottawa.'

Both parties had separate identities, and both capitals, Quebec City and Ottawa, had to have their separate attraction for the Québécois. After his victory of April 8, 1963, Pearson, with forty-seven Quebec members, moved to make French a language of caucus and of cabinet discussion. In the civil service, bilingualism and the hiring of francophones were to be encouraged. Finally on July 22, 1963, Pearson announced the membership of the Royal Commission on Bilingualism and Biculturalism that he had promised as opposition leader.

That biculturalism remains an elusive concept, that the commission knew from the beginning what it would report, and that its formation aroused passions are not items meriting condemnation. Moreover, the implementation of bilingualism in the federal civil service had only an indirect relationship with the commission: the Pearson government made that commitment prior to and independently of the appointment of the commission. The 'B&B Commission' in fact did what it was intended to do: alert Canadians to the gravity of their national crisis. Its February 1965 preliminary report put the point bluntly and accurately: 'Canada, without being fully conscious of the fact, is passing through the greatest crisis in its history.' The commission contributed little directly to solving the crisis, but one may certainly ask what kind of direct contribution it could have made. Events moved too quickly. The commission began with a bang, punctuated by the explosions in Montreal mailboxes; it ended in a rallentando of whimpers – about its cost, about its purpose, and, most of all, about the future of the country.

Jean Lesage believed that the fundamental grievance of Quebec in 1963 was its inability to have 'full exercise of its powers under the Constitution.' In his first federal-provincial conference in July 1960 Lesage had called for an end to shared-cost programs and for appropriate compensation to the provinces. At each succeeding conference he repeated his demand, and in the 1963 campaign the federal Liberals had vaguely supported his 'opting out' of some established programs. Lesage wanted a more specific commitment. Three days before the April 8 federal election Lesage strengthened his ultimatum: 'Twelve months will go by before the next budget speech. Either the federal government, whatever party is elected on April 8, and I repeat, whatever the party elected on April 8, the central government will have made use of the 12 months to make allowance for Quebec's needs or else we in Quebec will have taken steps on our own side to make the required decisions in fiscal policy. And the decisions will be those imposed on us by the aims of economic, social, and cultural affirmation we have set ourselves at the request of the people of Quebec.' In Pearson, Lesage found a sympathetic listener and a skilled mediator, but one whose knowledge of international law and practice far exceeded that of domestic constitutional law and practice. He was, as he later said, 'prepared to make substantial concessions to Quebec (and to the provinces) in the interests of national unity.'

The provinces, especially Quebec, did not need any extra powers merely because they were taking a more active part in the domestic, social, and economic life of their people. They already had powers aplenty. But they did need more money, and some, including Quebec, aspired to an international role also. Adding to the problem was the minority Pearson government's need to show that it too was progressive. In the 1963 campaign a Liberal slogan declared 'Better Pensions for All.' Once elected, the Liberals moved quickly – too quickly – to put the pension resolution on the order paper of the House of Commons. The minister responsible for the plan, Judy LaMarsh, dubbed it an 'instant plan.' Little resistance was expected, but it came none the less, first from Ontario, where Premier John Robarts became irritated when provincial Liberals drew the issue into a provincial campaign, and then from Quebec, where the objections struck more strongly at Canadian constitutional practice. At the September and November 1963 federal-provincial conferences, the federal government was in a weak position because of the clumsiness of Pearson's first 'sixty days of decision' and because the provincial responses had not been anticipated. Quebec had passed a unanimous resolution of the legislature declaring that the province would not accept the federal plan. It had its own plan and would support a constitutional amendment only if it could 'opt out' of the federal plan.

The deadlock continued and the deadline on Lesage's taxation ultimatum loomed nearer. Lesage seemed to take the initiative when he invited the premiers and Pearson to Quebec for a federal-provincial conference from March 31 to April 3, 1964. The welcome was not as warm as expected. The Château Frontenac had a bomb threat; federal ministers had guards with them everywhere. Lesage was more confident, and, to the astonishment of the conference, he presented his own pension plan in lavish and full detail. Its benefits were better, and, for provincial governments, its funding most lucrative, because they could borrow from the fund for their social programs in the future. The response, Pearson aide Tom Kent recalled, was electric and 'the federal government position was destroyed ... The most extraordinary thing about the whole situation was that the federal government had been so completely unprepared for it, for the whole aggressive, powerful stance of the provinces in relation to the federal government.' On the plane returning to Ottawa, some passengers reportedly predicted Confederation's death.

Within a few days, both sides decided to heal the wounds opened at Quebec. Maurice Sauvé and Tom Kent for the federal government and Claude Morin and Claude Castonguay for Quebec worked out a compromise that essentially adopted Quebec's plan and accepted the right of any province to have its own plan. Although Morin later claimed that Quebec gained no more than was its due, that was not the reaction at the time, nor was it the case. Jean Lesage dramatically told the legislature: 'I have lived for the past month a terrifying life. I have worked for my province as no man has ever worked for it. I have made use of all the means which Providence granted me ... so that Quebec, finally, could be recognized as a province which has a *statut spécial* in Confederation, and I have succeeded.' Not only did Quebec secure its pension plan but it also obtained Ottawa's commitment to negotiate, first, Quebec's 'opting out' of many shared-cost programs, and, second, a larger share of the personal income tax for all provinces. By the end of 1964 the federal government knew that it was seen as the loser. The events of 1964 were and still are a triumph for Lesage.

Aware of the weakness of his government's position, Pearson decided that he had to strengthen the influence of Quebec in Ottawa. The pension controversy had revealed how talented the Quebec public servants were and how Quebec was attracting the loyalties of the brightest French Canadians. Lionel Chevrier, the senior Quebec minister, left the cabinet early in 1964. Pearson then promoted two younger Quebec members, Guy Favreau to Justice and Sauvé to Forestry, but he knew that this was not enough. In January 1965, he met Lesage in Florida and asked him to come to Ottawa. It was his duty as a Canadian. The answer was no. Pearson and Lesage parted, with Pearson more uncertain of the future than ever before but more aware of the difficulties facing him and his government.

Pearson carried his search for new men further, but at the moment when the need became clearer, recruitment had become more difficult. Even before the conversation with Lesage, a series of scandals had profoundly damaged Quebec Liberalism. Favreau stumbled badly when confronted with evidence that a narcotics-peddling thug named Lucien Rivard had prominent Liberals act on his behalf to prevent extradition. Pearson's own parliamentary secretary, Guy

Rouleau, had unwisely, if not illegally, interceded on behalf of Rivard. Pearson fired him. Raymond Denis, an executive assistant, had tried to bribe a Montreal lawyer. Two other Quebec ministers, Maurice Lamontagne and Réne Tremblay, were accused of receiving free furniture from a Montreal furniture company. At the same time, December 1964, Pearson learned that the recently appointed Minister without Portfolio, Yvon Dupuis, faced charges of corruption. Pearson asked for his resignation, and although Dupuis initially refused, he resigned several embarrassing days later.

Favreau also resigned when the inquiry he had demanded questioned his judgment in its report. Although the French-Canadian ministers wanted Favreau to stay, Pearson encouraged the resignation. Favreau had become a ghostly figure whose sallow skin and hollow eyes eerily and accurately foretold his death in 1967. At a moment when Quebec's attitude toward Confederation was becoming more and more ambiguous, the collapse and isolation of French-Canadian cabinet members were ominous.

What can one say of Pearson's performance? Perhaps the opinion of Tom Kent, his aide, is fairest and most revealing: 'Mr. Pearson was a diplomat. His skill was in settling differences and sometimes that perhaps meant evading the expression of differences. There was an element of escapism, and no question, Mr. Pearson could be an escapist. He found it very difficult to say anything unpleasant to anybody face to face, and most people who talked to Mr. Pearson tended to leave him thinking that he'd agreed with them. That was true even if the views of A and B in succession were rather diverse, and that sometimes left lots of problems to sort out afterward.'

Consequently, the Pearson government in its first years never possessed a coherent image, never managed to let Canadians know what it intended to do. For this, it suffered.

The decision to call a federal election in 1965 had little to do with Quebec. The advocates of an election came from Ontario, and they tended to blame the government's malaise upon its minority status. Walter Gordon, fearful that a more popular leader might replace Diefenbaker, had begun to urge an election in the spring and summer of 1965. By early September he had convinced Pearson, if not all his colleagues. The election would be held on November 8.

The Liberal party entered this election with John Diefenbaker as its major issue. Diefenbaker in turn dwelt upon the scandals. The result was a bitter campaign, and the electors came to believe that there could be no escape from the miasma that surrounded Ottawa. The Liberals entered the election knowing they would carry Quebec. To many Quebec Liberals that was simply not enough. This popular support would be for ministers whom Quebec thought were wronged but whom Quebec knew could no longer have much influence in

Crossing the Styx.
Prime Minister Pearson, Minister of Transport Jack Pickersgill, and Minister of Justice
Guy Favreau confront a sea of Diefenbakers (Macpherson, 1964). Reproduced with the
permission of the *Toronto Star*

Ottawa. One of these ministers, Maurice Lamontagne, thought it essential that
Quebec's influence in Ottawa be strengthened lest Quebec City become even
more the focus of francophone attention and loyalties. He and Sauvé agreed that
Jean Marchand, who had not run in 1963 because of Pearson's acceptance of
nuclear weapons, must run in 1965. Sauvé, and Marchand himself, believed that
Gérard Pelletier and Pierre Trudeau must run with Marchand. This was not so
easily accomplished: Pelletier's and Trudeau's acid pens – Pelletier had recently
compared the Liberal party to a garbage can – were not forgotten or forgiven by
Liberal MPs. Nevertheless, Marchand insisted, and on September 10 the three
announced that they would run for the Liberals. Their commitment to Liberalism
was weak, but to Quebec and Canada strong. Marchand recalled what they said
to each other then: 'Well, there is a vacuum [in Ottawa], and if we believe in this
country and we want to do something for the country, we have to do it in Ottawa
– and we have to do it in the party which has a chance to be in power.'

'Now for my next act–'
Prime Minister Pearson displays the art of government (Macpherson, 1965). Reproduced with the permission of the *Toronto Star*

Although the presence of the so-called three wise men probably won few votes, their entry into federal politics was the most significant event of the election. Ironically, as the left wing of the party was strengthened in Quebec, the right wing gained in English Canada. In the campaign Diefenbaker drew upon the final drops of Conservative loyalty while Pearson's expected appeal to the young middle class proved less enticing than originally expected. Thus on November 8 little had changed; the Liberals had two more seats (131) than in 1963, but the Conservatives also had two more (97). There was no majority, and, for Pearson, no relief.

Gordon accepted responsibility for the failure to achieve a majority. He re-

Table 3
Results of 1965 General Election

Seats	Liberal	PC	NDP	Créditiste	Socred	Ind.
Newfoundland	7 (7)	–	–			
PEI	0 (2)	4 (2)	–			
NS	2 (5)	10 (7)	–			
NB	6 (6)	4 (4)	–			
Quebec	56 (47)	8 (8)	–	9 (0)	0 (20)	2 (0)
Ontario	51 (52)	25 (27)	9 (6)			
Manitoba	1 (2)	10 (10)	3 (2)			
Saskatchewan	–	17 (17)				
Alberta	0 (1)	15 (14)	–		2 (2)	
BC	7 (7)	3 (4)	9 (9)		3 (2)	
Yukon	–	1 (1)	–			
NWT	1 (0)	0 (1)	–			
Popular vote	40	32	18	5	4	1

signed, and so did national organizer Keith Davey. Others drifted away, Tom Kent to the bureaucracy, Dick O'Hagan to the Washington embassy. Most troubling, though, were the departures of Lamontagne and Tremblay. After the furniture revelations, they had remained in the cabinet. There were no alternatives, but, in the case of Tremblay especially, the charges were unfair. Yet after the election, without proper consultation, Pearson fired them. They were, Pearson said, honourable men; unfortunately his actions did not lead others to see this. What they saw was Marchand, a new member, becoming immediately the most important Quebec minister. However clumsy Pearson's actions were, they made one thing certain: there would be a new look to French Canada in Ottawa.

That at least was Pearson's hope. In late winter 1966, however, the new look seemed old indeed. Once again there was scandal; once again a French Canadian was at the centre – the new Minister of Justice, Lucien Cardin. On March 10, while defending his revelation on national television that Vancouver postal clerk George Victor Spencer, a Soviet spy fired but not prosecuted by the government, would be watched for the rest of his life, Cardin was asked by the press to explain what he had meant the previous Friday (March 4) when he spoke of Diefenbaker's participation in the 'Monseigneur case.' The Press Club was already alive with rumour: 'Monseigneur,' a stunning German who was spying for the Russians, had slept with a former Tory minister who sported a moustache. Most guessed the wrong minister. Diefenbaker had known this, but had done nothing. Cardin claimed that since Munsinger was dead only Diefenbaker and his colleagues could take the blame. The Liberals, Cardin declared, had a 'working ar-rangement' to make sure that Diefenbaker did not escape punishment. 'We are going to fight and fight hard and, if we have to, use the same methods that are being used and have been used against us for the past three years.'

It was an unfortunate statement laced with inaccuracies. Gerda Munsinger was soon discovered, very much alive, and working as a hostess in a Munich bar. When *Toronto Daily Star* reporter Robert Reguly found her she said simply, 'I suppose you want to ask me about Sévigny.' The man with the moustache was now known. Reporters thronged before his door before he had a chance to shave. An emotional Sévigny appeared with his wife and children beside him, admitted seeing Gerda 'socially,' and then cited his fine war record as proof of his loyalty to Canada. The defence was a bit embarrassing and hardly to the point, but Sévigny did win much sympathy when Larry Zolf, with a cameraman behind him, beat upon the Sévignys' door. Sévigny opened it and then answered with his cane, which came down in the vicinity of Zolf's imposing nose.

Soon Gerda became familiar to all Canadian viewers over the age of sixteen (the networks discreetly saved her for the later hours). *Maclean's* sponsored a limerick contest. This one won.[4]

There was a young lady from Munich
Whose bosom distended her tunic.
Her main undertaking
Was cabinet making
In fashions bilingue et unique.

Gerda proved garrulous. She identified George Hees as the other minister she knew. Reporters, Christian or not, took this to mean the biblical 'to know.' Hees protested, accurately, that he had simply had lunch with her. But the press con-tinued to hint, in defiance of most human experience, that men and women who eat together must inevitably sleep together.

Cardin declared in the House of Commons that Munsinger's involvement with the Associate Minister of National Defence was a serious security breach. Diefenbaker charged that Munsinger was being used by the Liberals to blot out their own scandals. The whole business smelled. Gerda said it best: 'I knew Pierre as a man. He knew me as a woman. That's all there was to it.' And that's all there should have been.

Pearson had taken little part in the Munsinger debates. He talked of resigna-tion; he did not resign, but most knew his time was short. With Diefenbaker, too,

4 Quoted in Peter Newman, *The Distemper of Our Times* (Toronto: McClelland & Stewart, 1968), p. 403.

Two solitudes.
John Diefenbaker has problems with his 'Quebec lieutenant,' Léon Balcer
(Berthio, 1965). Reproduced with the permission of Roland Berthiaume

it was clear that the end was approaching. Indeed some Conservatives had approached Pearson during the Munsinger debate asking for help in removing their leader. After the spring, what remained of Pearson's and Diefenbaker's time was really an interregnum. It was for this reason, perhaps, that the expected damage to Quebec from the Cardin difficulties never materialized. Marchand stayed, as did all the other Quebec ministers. It was, in fact, a show of strength.

Journalists later would divide the Pearson government's relationship with Quebec into the pre-1965 years, when the emphasis was on 'co-operative federalism' and accommodation, and the later period, when a 'harder' line was followed. The influence of Marchand, Trudeau, and Pelletier, who strongly opposed 'special status' for Quebec, is usually deemed to be paramount in the post-1965 period. This interpretation misleads in the sharp distinction it draws between Pearson's supposed 'soft' attitude and the new Quebec ministers' intransigency. One might better describe 1963-5 as the years in which the federal government, unprepared for what it faced, simply reacted to events in Quebec. Compromise was thus an instinctive, natural response. By 1966, however, Pearson knew better what he faced, feared it more, and was much less inclined to appease the Quebec government, although he had become even more willing to commit the federal government itself to bilingualism and biculturalism. In April 1966 he announced that all future university graduates joining the federal public service would have to be bilingual or willing to become so. Every Canadian, he declared, must have the right to service by federal officials in the citizen's official language. The Prime Minister's Office itself took on a Gallic air as Pierre Trudeau became parliamentary secretary and Marc Lalonde and Jean Beetz moved into important positions in that office.

No longer reactive, the federal government in 1966 seized the initiative in federal-provincial financial negotiations. The new finance minister, Mitchell Sharp, announced in September 1966 that the federal government would no longer 'make room' for the provinces by turning over tax 'points' as it had done earlier. Shared-cost programs would also be reduced in scope. This was mainly a device intended to reduce Quebec's special status. For the first time since the Quiet Revolution, the federal government began a federal-provincial conference with the best-prepared case on its side. The conference in October 1966 was, in the words of a participant, a disaster, yet it revealed that Ottawa had finally found the limits of its generosity.

There was yet another area where the limits of Ottawa's patience and constitutional capacity were most severely tested. This was, of course, the extraordinary liaison between Quebec and France.

Quebec's Quiet Revolution almost immediately captured attention beyond Canada. In 1960, Charles de Gaulle, restored to the leadership of France by the generals two years before, visited Canada; on his return he told his culture minister, André Malraux, to watch for 'interesting events' in French Canada. Malraux's sharp eye soon spotted what he termed 'un climat nouveau' in Quebec and in relations between Quebec and France. From October 1961, when Malraux made this observation at the opening of Quebec's délégation générale in Paris, Gaullist France wooed an increasingly receptive Quebec, and the seductiveness was not merely one-sided. De Gaulle saw in French Canada a French people infused with the spirit which, twenty years after the liberation, France so obviously lacked. Quebec, too, was a modern nation, part of the North American technical miracle and yet French: the lure was irresistible. As the transatlantic romance warmed, the Canadian mixed marriage seemed more strained than ever before. The Gallic flirtation was, to Ottawa, the most serious threat to Confederation of the middle and later 1960s.

That Mike Pearson's government should be so disturbed about Quebec's interest in international ties is not surprising. Pearson himself had seen in the 1920s and 1930s how Canada's step-by-step road to autonomy had led Canada away from Britain and toward independence in all aspects of foreign as well as domestic affairs. The Pearson government thus moved to ensure a federal presence in the France-Quebec relationship. Ottawa had to represent French Canada abroad, and Canada's international personality had to be a fusion of Canada's bicultural character. If it were not, many Ottawa officials believed, independence for Quebec was both inevitable and logical. As one official later remarked, one day we would awaken and suddenly realize Quebec had left not through a declaration of independence but quietly through the back door. Then it would all be too late.   '

During the 1963 campaign Pearson announced that he would add Paris to the traditional London and Washington visits that began a new prime minister's tenure. He kept this promise on January 15, 1964, and early suspicions about the warmth of de Gaulle's welcome soon disappeared as the French president spoke eloquently of the special and natural solidarity between France and 'votre Etat fédéral.' Officials worked out new arrangements for technical, cultural, and educational exchanges. The mood, however, was deceptive: de Gaulle, increasingly isolated from his allies, needed Canada's voice and help in 1964. He wanted to buy Canadian uranium and to sell French Caravelle jets to Canada. In NATO, Canada was taking a more understanding attitude than most to France's criticisms of the alliance. Thus, despite the growing differences between Canada and France in 1965, which grew out of de Gaulle's new audacity in international policies, the French showed little interest in offending Canada: Quebec was not yet worth a mess.

But propinquity bred affection, especially for Quebec. Jean Lesage and several of his ministers luxuriated in the banquets, the champagne toasts, and the affection that accompanied their Parisian visits. For provincial politicians, these whiffs of the glamour of international diplomacy were intoxicating. By 1964 the Quebec government had begun negotiations for an educational accord. As Ottawa watched Quebec warily, the French displayed proper hesitation. It took ten months before final agreement occurred. On February 27, 1965, Quebec and France signed an 'entente' and Canada and France exchanged 'notes' to give the curious specimen diplomatic authenticity. The Quebec signatory, Paul Gérin-Lajoie, sought to give it much broader meaning. He declared in Paris that the agreement was the first step toward a francophone cultural commonwealth in which Quebec would represent French Canada. Later in Montreal, Gérin-Lajoie advanced this argument further, claiming that the Quebec state was 'the political instrument of a distinct cultural group' with the right to sign international agreements in realms of provincial jurisdiction and to participate in international organizations that dealt with provincial matters.

Martin and Pearson moved to protect the federal position through the creation of 'umbrella agreements' with foreign powers whereby provinces could reach agreements with foreign governments under the protection and signature of a covering federal umbrella. This, it was hoped, legitimized Quebec's dealings while simultaneously treating Quebec as a province like the others. What was not clear was the part Ottawa would play in what went on under the umbrella. In Quebec's view, federal officials would form the audience; in Ottawa's view they were part of the team.

This difference in perception caused acrimony when France and Canada signed their umbrella agreement ('accord cadre') in November 1965, which was followed by a second, broader, Quebec-France entente. Quebec would not accept a federal role in Quebec-France dealings. Claude Morin, the Quebec senior civil servant most closely connected with this stance, later wrote: 'Ottawa only realized later that, in its direct relations with France, Quebec was now poised not only to hatch new exchange programs or even simply discuss political problems with French representatives, but also to consult with Paris as if it were a virtually sovereign state and, thanks to French support, be bidden to international gatherings on the same basis as the other nations of the world.'[5]

Morin, who by 1965 was considered a separatist by Ottawa officials, is only partly correct. Ottawa was not so ignorant as he suggests, but it is true that French support of Quebec's attitude had become much stronger. In Paris, Canadians were being treated differently. Even Canadian ambassador Jules Léger faced continuous snubs from the Elysée Palace.

Other Canadians felt the Gaullist cold shoulder as well. Governor General Georges Vanier, distressed by the Franco-Canadian difficulties, thought a personal visit to his wartime colleague and friend might help. He was mistaken, as de Gaulle's refusal to offer him head-of-state status can attest. Vanier never saw Paris again, and his beloved France sent only a low-ranking representative to his state funeral when he died in office in 1967.

Other French actions seemed also deliberate attempts to repudiate past ties. On February 21, 1966, de Gaulle demanded that Canadian forces leave French soil. Infuriated, Pearson asked 'a high-ranking French public servant' whether Canada would have to take its hundred thousand dead in French graves to Germany along with its planes and soldiers. In a similar vein, de Gaulle refused to attend April 1967 ceremonies at Vimy Ridge because the Canadians had invited Prince Philip. On that spring day at Vimy only a few French local officials honoured Canada's greatest military triumph. Despite enormous irritation, Pearson remained mum. Events had made protest too dangerous.

On June 5, 1966, the Lesage government was defeated at the polls, and the Union Nationale under Daniel Johnson took power with a platform of 'Québec d'abord.' Quebec, the platform declared, should possess extended powers and sovereignty internationally. By the fall, a ministry of intergovernmental affairs

5   Claude Morin, *Quebec versus Ottawa: The Struggle for Self-Government 1960-72* (Toronto: University of Toronto Press, 1976), p. 37.

President de Gaulle receives a state visitor in style: Quebec's Minister of Education Jean-Guy Cardinal (Macpherson, 1969). Reproduced with the permission of the *Toronto Star*

was created to 'co-ordinate' Quebec's dealings with 'foreign governments.' Johnson was raising the stakes.

The bluff came over General de Gaulle's 1967 visit. Canada's centennial celebrations meant that all heads of state must be invited to Canada. De Gaulle received his invitation in spring 1966. On August 4, Pearson learned that Johnson had extended two personal invitations to de Gaulle and the pope. He was immediately suspicious and became more so as some Union Nationale ministers spoke publicly of France's willingness to treat Quebec as a 'sovereign' state. As for de Gaulle, his foreign policy in late 1966 was ever more theatrical and infused with symbolic gesture. He was, in short, unpredictable and, for Ottawa, an unwelcome guest who could not be provoked.

Naturally, both Quebec and Ottawa wanted to establish primacy in preparing for the visit. Ottawa insisted that it had a role in all aspects of the tour. Quebec denied that Ottawa should have a pre-eminent role in the Quebec portion of the visit. In mid-1966, André Patry, a constitutional law specialist, was placed in charge of official visits in the Quebec government's Department of Intergovernmental Affairs. In fall 1966 Patry refused to heed federal demands that he not deal directly with foreign states. By the spring of 1967 Patry was speaking publicly and privately to baffled foreign diplomats about reciprocal rights and privileges for Quebec 'diplomats.' France already appeared to be offering special privileges. In March 1967 Ottawa learned through a rumour of a plan worked out between Quebec and French officials whereby de Gaulle would come in a warship to visit Quebec first and alone. Pearson angrily told his officials that there could be no visit unless de Gaulle came to Ottawa. Moreover, the federal government should control the entire visit, which, barring exceptional circumstances, must begin in Ottawa.

A few days later, the rumour was confirmed to Paul Martin, who decided to see de Gaulle, Pearson, and Johnson. The Pearson-Johnson conversation was friendly, and Pearson recorded in his diary that Johnson was 'prone to excuse his own lapses from common sense and moderation by the necessity of handling carefully his "wilder men".' But the fundamental disagreement was not discussed. This amiable meeting clarified little and settled nothing. The same was true of the Martin-de Gaulle visit, although the French did then agree that de Gaulle should visit Ottawa first.[6]

Within two weeks this agreement disappeared, as did the amicability. The French, clearly after consultation with Quebec, presented a new itinerary in which de Gaulle visited Montreal first. At the same time, in early May, Ottawa and Quebec had a bitter argument over the signing of a Belgian-Canadian cultural accord. In May Johnson went to Paris and the lights of the city had rarely shone so brightly. The welcome, Johnson declared, was 'glittering.' In this atmosphere, the Quebec premier persuaded de Gaulle to begin his historical visit in Quebec and then to travel the *chemin du roi* to Montreal. Ottawa could only agree; dissent would court disaster. In the remaining two months, Quebec and Ottawa quarrelled continually over the length of receptions, seating plans, and the height of flagpoles. Such trivia suddenly bore much meaning. The game was played secretly; the public knew nothing.

De Gaulle arrived on board the *Colbert* the morning of July 23, 1967. The welcome, *La Presse* assured the visitor, would be 'royal.' For the Québécois the

6 See the excellent account of the Canadian-French relationship in Paul Martin, *A Very Double Life* (Toronto, Deneau, 1986).

world would now learn what they had not forgotten. 'Le monde,' Johnson announced on July 21, 'saura que nous existons.'

As de Gaulle left the *Colbert* at Quebec, he heard a thunderous roar; for newly installed Governor General Roland Michener, there were scattered boos. Soon, Johnson took away the general. They passed through the streets of old Quebec, to the shrine at Ste Anne de Beaupré, and then back to the old city, all in an open car, through seas of waving flags and ceaseless chants – 'De Gaulle, de Gaulle. Vive la France.' That night at a banquet de Gaulle talked eloquently of the return of France to North America. The next day along the historic north shore trail, rechristened the *chemin du roi,* de Gaulle responded in kingly fashion to the regal welcome. The long caravan snaked its way to Montreal, where half a million thronged the streets and squares before the Hôtel de Ville.

Finally he was on the balcony, arms outstretched to embrace the crowd's warmth. He hesitated, then spoke: 'C'est une immense émotion qui remplit mon coeur en voyant devant moi la ville française de Montréal. Au nom du vieux pays, au nom de la France, je vous sabre de tout mon coeur. Je vais vous confier un sécret que vous ne répéterez pas. Ce soir, ici, et tout le long de ma route, je me suis trouvé dans une atmosphère du même genre que celle de la Libération.'

The liberation, his most cherished memory, was alive again. France, he dramatically concluded, would know, watch, and listen to all that passed in its oldest offspring: 'Vive Montréal! Vive le Québec! Vive le Québec libre!'

The cries reverberated; but they struck different keys. By the next day Pearson was declaring the remarks intolerable: 'The people of Canada are free. Every province of Canada is free. Canadians do not need to be liberated.' The anglophone press agreed, questioning de Gaulle's mental stability. So did Pearson's French-speaking colleagues. The francophone press and the Quebec government saw it differently. Claude Ryan in *Le Devoir* denounced the anglophone and federal government reaction as excessive, hysterical, betraying fear and animosity. Daniel Johnson confessed that he found Pearson's reaction inexplicable: De Gaulle's purpose was blameless. He had simply evoked 'le problème de l'identité distincte du Québec et son immense effort d'affirmation. Le Québec n'a jamais été une province comme les autres.' Polls indicated that Quebec agreed: 69.3 per cent thought the voyage worthwhile; 58.7 per cent disagreed with Pearson's statement. Only 20 per cent thought that de Gaulle wanted to encourage separation.

Frenchmen, however, had a different view; even the Communist *L'Humanité* thought de Gaulle had interfered, and the conservative *Le Figaro* deemed the intrusion in Canadian affairs disgraceful. That de Gaulle's French interpreters were correct he soon made clear. On his return he expanded upon his encounter with a people possessing 'a unanimous and indescribable will for emancipation.'

In a historic and histrionic November 26 press conference the general relived his passage along the *chemin du roi,* claiming once more that the spirit of liberation still dwelt in these people, Frenchmen thousands of miles away. They would inevitably attain the rank of sovereign state and become masters of their own destiny.

The echo did not have the force of the original. In another year de Gaulle was gone; so were Pearson and Johnson. So much had changed. The spectacle at the Hôtel de Ville had merely ended the prologue to the drama. In September 1967 René Lévesque issued 'Option Québec,' a disjointed but direct appeal for Quebec sovereignty. The Quebec Liberals fumbled, uncertain how to handle the renegade. This time there could be neither compromise nor excuse, and at the Quebec Liberals' October 1967 convention Option Quebec was defeated. On November 18, 1967, the Mouvement Souveraineté-Association was formed in a Montreal monastery, its leader René Lévesque. The debate about Quebec was now on different ground; the debaters, too, were different.

That de Gaulle contributed to the spirit of Québécois nationalism and separatism cannot be doubted. That he created a French popular consciousness of Quebec is also true. He and Lévesque also alerted other Canadians to the crisis of Confederation. As Centennial year came to an end, the century to come seemed as uncertain as the first had been at its beginning.

24

The Economy and the Flowering
of the Social Service State

The tension between Quebec and Ottawa derived in part from the claims that both capitals were staking in the area of social reform. The sixties finally brought to Canada that social service state whose first glimmerings had been seen during the First World War but whose form had remained inchoate so long. During the decade many streams merged to create a torrent of legislation that surprised even the optimistic reformers of the 1950s. Prosperity, the sense of security arising from the stability of post-war society, and the general reformist orientation of the media made this full measure of reform possible. So did the need of politicians to win elections. In Ottawa it became fashionable to throw money at problems. Thanks to inflation and economic growth the government discovered that its take was increasing. Because employment was growing and unemployment was falling, unemployment insurance became self-financing once more, and the government did not concern itself about 'bankruptcy' of the fund. Governments could turn to other needs.

In the election campaign of 1963, Mike Pearson caught this new mood. He promised 'sixty days of decision' and talked about a health plan, a two-price system for wheat, a $1.25 minimum wage, a forty-hour week, portable old age pensions, a municipal loan fund, a department of industry, and a national development corporation, later known as the Canada Development Corporation (CDC). He also promised to help the Atlantic provinces. One by one, in his difficult years in office, the pieces of this ambitious program took on legislative substance.

In 1963 the Municipal Development and Loan Act provided $400 million for municipalities to be lent at 5.25 per cent interest. There was a new measure to subsidize housebuilding in winter; the provinces were creating planning bodies of their own, with co-ordination or urging from Ottawa. To make medium-term forecasts and to advise the government, the dominion invented the Economic

Council of Canada (ECC), which replaced the National Productivity Council (NPC) that the Tories had formed in 1961. The NPC had been notable chiefly for the elaborate rejoicings that marked its regional conferences; the ECC was to be notable chiefly for the self-conscious earnestness of its *Annual Review* and for the quantity of its research work. Nevertheless, it was the council that helped to launch Canada's own version of the American War on Poverty. By 1963 it was already clear that the wind was blowing in that direction. Inside the new Liberal cabinet Walter Gordon and July LaMarsh led the 'progressive' forces. In 1962 Saskatchewan had forced its doctors to operate a medicare plan; in 1963 Alberta introduced voluntary medicare, and Ontario proposed to do the same. And, most important of all, both Quebec and Ottawa were planning to introduce new pension plans.

In Quebec it was hoped that the pension scheme would provide finance for provincial development. Hence the rates of contribution would be large enough to build up a sizeable fund in the first decade. Ottawa wanted a pay-as-you-go plan, whereby current contributions would pay for current pensions. As the real cost of a pension plan is the consumption of the pensioners, the real economic burden would be the same in either case, whether or not a pension plan was 'funded.' But the Quebec plan had an obvious attraction to a capital-poor government, and other provinces were quick to notice this fact. As we saw earlier in this part, after a lengthy wrangle with the provinces, federal legislation was introduced early in November 1964 and passed in March 1965. Quebec and the other provinces got their way. The pensions were partially indexed against inflation, and they would also rise along with average real incomes. They would coexist with the old flat-rate pension.[1]

After the pensions came medicare. In 1963 Pearson had promised to introduce it within four years. To do so he needed the provinces' co-operation. Already some provinces had universal medicare, while others had voluntary programs. But some did not want medicare at all. At last, in July 1965, Pearson announced that the federal government would contribute funds to any provincial scheme that was 'universal and portable,' so long as it covered all general and specialist services without using private firms or groups. The final rule was important. In some provinces, such as Ontario and British Columbia, the doctors operated large and successful medicare plans; in some provinces private insurance firms had been active. Almost everywhere there was Blue Cross. In the provinces with more conservative governments the natural tendency was to provide medical insurance through these 'private carriers.' But Ottawa wanted the provinces themselves to administer medicare. One by one, often after much

---

1 For more detail on the pension, monetary, and budget topics discussed in this chapter see our first edition, chapter 27.

grumbling, the provinces accepted the federal scheme. It would have been political suicide to refuse. Anyway, as several provinces were already running their own medicare schemes while others proposed to do so, the federal money would come in handy. In 1968 nation-wide medicare began.

Medicare was welcomed as a triumph of 'progressive' politics and thought. During the sixties 'progressive' thinking was increasingly critical of the status quo. It was not enough that real per capita output was rising; now more and more Canadian publicists and politicians worried about *inequality* of incomes, about the relations between Canada's affluent whites and much poorer native peoples, and about the nation's responsibilities in world economic and social development. Although Canada escaped the serious disturbances of American and German universities, there was much academic activism and dissent which helped to create a widespread mood of unease and a questioning of social and economic institutions which, before 1962, nearly everyone had accepted.

During the 1940s and 1950s, the national authorities had put their faith largely in macroeconomic monetary and fiscal policies. They appeared to need little more. But such policies had disadvantages. They were too complicated for many politicians and most citizens to understand, and only a strong and self-confident government could enforce them; nor could they be used for political patronage as social reform measures sometimes could. Further, after 1958 certain intellectual currents were pulling strongly in a contrary direction. As we saw in Part IV, by the late fifties some officials had noticed that Canada was depending strongly on skilled migrants at a time when unemployment was concentrated almost wholly among the unskilled. These officials, the educational establishments, and the more 'structurally' inclined economists were convinced that unemployment was chiefly or wholly a mismatching of supply and demand: raise the level of education and skills and everyone would find a job. Here was an area where academic dissenters and the politicians could find common ground. Governments had also begun to notice that in the agricultural regions where population was falling, many individuals were stranded, unable to move, yet unable to make decent livings under changed price-cost conditions.

Diefenbaker had provided massive national funding for provincial efforts in secondary technical education and money for the retraining and educational upgrading of adults, especially the unemployed. The Pearson government continued the program, and added to it. In 1967 it took full responsibility for the training and retraining of adults, while it agreed to continue construction grants until every province had received at least $800 per capita. It also offered allowances to any adult who enrolled in a retraining course. By 1971 the national government had spent $1,100 million on the construction of technical schools, and the provinces had spent many millions more.

In 1965, intergovernmental ARDA agreements were revised so as to concentrate on the relief of rural poverty. In 1966 the federal government created a $50-million Fund for Rural Economic Development (FRED), which would make grants in rural areas, especially for schools, adult education, land purchase, and re-establishment. This fund began to offer guaranteed minimum incomes to elderly farmers who would agree to leave the land. The spending ceiling was quickly raised. In 1968, it was used to underwrite far-ranging provincial plans for eastern Quebec and Prince Edward Island.

These agricultural and educational plans were not meant to help the poorer regions as such. But since the agricultural problems were concentrated in the low-income districts, and since education was especially bad in the eastern low-income provinces, they inevitably had this effect. Paralleling these plans were new government subsidies for depressed areas. First applied in 1960, these subsidies rapidly proliferated.

Further, there were grants to persons. In 1965 the Manpower Mobility Program appeared. It offered loans and, in certain circumstances, grants to would-be movers. At first the scheme did not amount to much. But in 1967 it was made more liberal; grants replaced loans, and the government said that it would finance more kinds of movement. Hence, in 1968, 10,000 people received assistance.

All these schemes raised government spending substantially. In 1950 Canada's governments spent just over $1 billion on health and social welfare. In 1971 they spent some $9 billion. They consistently spent some 24 per cent of their total outlays in this way, thus accounting for some 9 per cent of national product in the late 1960s.

These developments should be seen as extensions of the welfare state and of the paternalistic, interventionist state with which we have become so familiar in the 1980s. They should not be seen as socialism, either creeping or revolutionary. In most respects the private sector grew and flourished as never before, although of course businessfolk disliked taxation and complained about it. As for the protection of the consumer and the protection of competition, the Pearson government was less active than its successor, although somewhat more vigilant than its predecessor. It did not amend the Combines Investigation Act, and it rarely invoked it. Hence mergers and the construction of conglomerates proceeded with little check from Ottawa. Nor did the government appear to worry about the power of the trade unions. Indeed, it seemed to welcome the extension and expansion of unions and their rights. Strong unions, it seemed, were a palliative to capitalist guilt.

After the end of the Second World War, Canada had returned to the divided jurisdiction in labour matters that it has maintained ever since. The national government has power to legislate with respect to workers only in certain industries, while the residual power, covering almost 95 per cent of the labour force, rests with the ten provinces. Hence one cannot give any compact and accurate account of the eleven codes of labour law, or of their evolution. Only a few points can safely be made. First of all, because the several provinces began the post-war period with the general national regulation of the war years, they started with similar codes. Employers were obliged to recognize and bargain with unions that had been certified as bargaining agents by the relevant government board. The authorities provided compulsory mediation and conciliation, but not arbitration, except when the national government might impose such arbitration ad hoc, as was done several times, especially in railway disputes. Strikes could occur legally only after both union and management had passed through the several steps of negotiation that the law prescribed. Contracts were legally binding for a stated term. Hence, compared with some other countries, in Canada strikes were relatively few but relatively lengthy, and were usually 'official.'

This legal code protected labour unions and encouraged their growth, which had continued – from 711,000 members in 1945 to 1,459,200 in 1960, and 2.2 million in 1971. Throughout the period, nearly 70 per cent of all unionists belonged to 'international' unions. Between 1946 and 1971 there was only a slight change in union membership relative to non-agricultural employees. The unionized proportion rose only from 28 per cent to 33 per cent. But since agriculture became much less significant during these years, unionism became much more important for the labour force as a whole. In 1946 only 17 per cent of Canada's labour force belonged to unions, while in 1971 the percentage was 27.2.

By the late sixties, the Canadian Labour Congress (CLC) contained three-quarters of all Canadian unionists. The Canadian and Catholic Confederation of Labour changed its name and orientation, becoming the Confederation of National Trades Unions (CNTU). By the late sixties it had 10 per cent of the unionists. The unions also changed their relationship with the political parties and movements. In the early 1960s the CLC had become closely connected with the New Democratic Party, which depended heavily on union financing. In the mid-sixties the CNTU became very deeply involved with political and linguistic agitation in Quebec, where its membership was concentrated. While unions might deliver the money, they still could not deliver the vote.

In 1963 the unions began to ask themselves how they might advance from the blue-collar trades into the white-collar occupations where most new jobs were appearing. In that year two unions merged to form the Canadian Union of Public Employees (CUPE). As yet, most government employees were forbidden to join unions or to bargain collectively; however, both in Ottawa and in many provincial legislatures the laws would soon change. CUPE would soon be joined by a horde of what one might call 'white-collar craft unions,' most of whose members worked for government. Many of these unions were very small, mainly because so many based themselves on occupational affinity, not on industry. Thus, for example, every airport had an air traffic controllers' union and a host of other specialized unions, not a union for the airport industry. Because the Canadian system of labour relations is good at defining and certifying a network of 'bargaining units,' outside Quebec there were not many of those jurisdictional disputes in which two or more unions fight for the right to organize the workers or represent them. But by the late sixties there were plenty of simple old-fashioned strikes over wages, working conditions, fringe benefits, and the like. And because the bargaining units were often so small and specialized, a tiny group of public employees could cause a good deal of trouble, bringing large industries or government departments to a halt.

The worries of 1960-2, when the unions had wondered if they would even penetrate the expanding industries – chiefly service trades and the various public services – proved premature. In the Pearson years the unions penetrated ever more pervasively. In 1963 Ontario gave civil servants bargaining rights, although it withheld the right to strike, providing instead binding arbitration. The federal government agreed to the same thing in principle, and Ottawa set up a committee to draft proposals. Already, however, the postal workers were pressing for the right to strike. Provincial employees, too, were pressing for the right to strike. Usually though not always they got their way. For hospital employees there was discussion of compulsory arbitration, largely because some hospital strikes were already occurring. In Quebec the government proposed compulsory binding arbitration for civil servants. Submitting to pressure from public employees, the Quebec government gave most civil servants and all teachers the right to strike over wages, thereby setting the stage for some protracted and bitter disputes in the late sixties and the seventies. Already the teachers had formed the Quebec Teachers' Corporation; teachers and other public employees were co-operating ever more closely with the CNTU, which, in turn, was growing ever more nationalistic and which competed ever more fiercely with the Quebec Federation of Labour, the provincial arm of the CLC.

In 1965 Ontario also set up an arbitration system for civil servants, while banning hospital strikes. For federal civil servants the Heeney Committee recommended bargaining with binding arbitration, not strikes. But by that time customs workers, like postal workers, wanted to be allowed to strike. In 1966 the federal government introduced legislation along the Heeney lines. But for the leaders of the public services and their cabinet supporters, this was not enough. The cabinet debated the issue at length. The 'liberals,' like former labour leader Jean Marchand, and others anxious to woo the urban worker from the NDP, decided that civil servants should be allowed to strike like everyone else. The former civil servants – Bud Drury, Mitchell Sharp, Jack Pickersgill, and Pearson himself – did not much like the idea. But in February 1967 they gave way, and Parliament quickly gave its assent.

The extension of the right to strike did not quell labour unrest, and it seemed that strikes were everywhere – in municipal services in Vancouver and Toronto, in hospitals in Quebec, in the post office, in 1968, and, of course, in the traditional areas. Many blamed a seaway workers' strike in 1966 for these troubles. In that strike, a majority conciliation board recommended a 14 per cent wage increase over two years. The union rejected this, but, before the strike could begin, the government-appointed mediator announced that a settlement had been reached which granted a 20 per cent increase retroactive to January 1 and 10 per cent more on January 1, 1967. Certainly this encouraged others to push negotiations to the final stages and to seek higher settlements, but it would be wrong to attribute too much influence to it. Bystanders had already begun to suspect that there might be something wrong with the Canadian system of labour relations. These new developments were not generally popular. In a sense, admittedly, they were not really new. There had always been railway strikes from time to time, and in several provinces such vital services as city transit, telephones, and even electricity had potentially been at risk. But in the past governments had usually acted quickly to prevent such strikes or stop them. Indeed, it had long been argued that on the railways collective bargaining was a fraud, because in case of any real dispute the federal government would impose a solution sooner rather than later.

But in the 1960s such disputes became more common and more disruptive; also, because a small group could now cause so much trouble the strikes looked less sensible, while because there were often no alternatives they also looked more irresponsible. When glue workers or car assemblers strike, it is clear that they are striking against their employer; the public does not really suffer. But what of those who work in government monopolies? The public loses all the service, but the employer does not suffer any financial loss because governments do not make profits, and in the end the public pays through higher taxes. And what of strikes in such 'essential services' as hospital, police, and fire services? The public pays for the settlement not only through higher taxes but also through unnecessary deaths, illnesses, crimes, and fire losses. Hence it was easy to argue that such strikes were really 'strikes against the public.' But workers suspected that if they were refused the right to strike they would lose leverage, whether or not governments offered to accept arbitration instead. These fears were hardly surprising, since in several provinces the authorities were already trying to limit the powers and effectiveness of unions. At least, union leaders thought that this was so. The debate continues, with neither resolution nor winners.

Looking through the newspapers of the middle and late sixties, one might quickly conclude that those were years of economic turmoil. Alarms sounded regularly, but the crises they foretold passed surprisingly quickly. The crises normally arose from our investment and trading patterns and characteristics.

The Pearson government inherited a dollar that its predecessors had pegged at 92.5 American cents in 1962. That exchange rate outlasted Lester Pearson. Indeed, it was maintained by his successors until May 1970. At no time in these years would any minister or any official admit that the rate might be changed – Ottawa had learned a lesson from the Tory mishaps of 1961-2. But the rate was maintained only with difficulty. Year after year Canada imported more than it exported, covering the difference by importation of capital, chiefly from the United States. In the boom atmosphere of the 1960s such foreign money was not hard to attract. Foreigners were anxious to invest in Canada, and Canadians were anxious to borrow abroad. Nevertheless, the waters that had been so tranquil in the 1950s were now scattered with reefs and shoals, around which Canada's monetary authorities had to navigate with care. For the first time in more than sixty years the American government was worried about its own payments position. Although the US economy regularly produced a current account surplus, American firms were so eager to invest abroad that the gold in Fort Knox, once so massively impregnable, was melting away, while foreigners were heaping up ever-larger holdings of US dollars, all of which were convertible into gold, on demand, at the fixed price of $35 per ounce. Thus the US government began to discourage the export of capital funds just when Canadians had become very dependent on capital import.

The first crisis occurred in July 1963, when the US government announced that it would ask Congress to levy an 'interest equalization tax.' This tax was based on the cost of credit in the United States, where loans were cheaper than in most countries. Its purpose was to discourage foreigners from borrowing so much in the United States by equalizing the cost of domestic and foreign funds. The US government wanted it because Americans were lending more than the American current account surplus would cover. Although Canada was not a special target, the original idea was to cover *all* foreign borrowing, and Canadians believed that the tax would have the effect of adding a full percentage point to the cost of any new loans they might raise in the United States. Canada could offset the tax by raising its cost of credit, but the result would be a painful monetary contraction. The Canadian government and central bank therefore asked for an exemption, and the US government agreed. Three days after Washington had proposed the tax to Congress, it announced that so long as Canada would not try to increase its reserves of foreign money, it would ask Congress to exempt new Canadian borrowings. That is, so long as Canada borrowed just enough to cover its own current account deficit the United States would not subject it to the tax.

Because Canadian-US trade accounted for all of the Canadian deficit, it was obvious, even in Washington, that by borrowing just to cover its deficit Canada could not possibly hurt the American balance of payments. But if Canada borrowed to increase its reserves it would pull gold from American vaults, or add to its holdings of US dollars, the two things the US government wanted to prevent.

Until Congress had legislated there was great uncertainty about the impact of the tax. Although in the end Canadian borrowings were exempted, for the rest of 1963 and for much of 1964 the American bond market was virtually closed to Canadian borrowers. Fortunately, and unexpectedly, the Soviet Union started to buy Canada's wheat on a large scale. Without that windfall, the Canadian balance of payments would have been in deep trouble. Even so, the Bank of Canada pursued a cautious monetary policy, allowing chartered bank reserves to rise more slowly than output.

More shocks lay ahead. In December 1965 the American government published guidelines that were meant to reduce the flow of American direct foreign investment and speed the repatriation of profits by American-owned businesses. At first finance minister Mitchell Sharp did not object, believing that the new rules were consistent with Canada's own policy of discouraging further direct investment. To help the Americans, he had already reduced the target for Canadian reserves of foreign money. But in Montreal the financial world complained loudly, and Sharp soon explained that he disliked the guidelines.

In March 1966, therefore, Minister of Trade and Commerce Robert Winters published some Canadian guidelines. Foreign-owned businesses were asked to do many things, in particular to keep enough profits in Canada for the financing of Canadian expansion. And the Americans told Sharp and Winters that 'the United States government was not requesting United States companies to induce their Canadian subsidiaries to act in ways that differed from their normal business practices.'

There was another crisis late in 1967, when the British pound was devalued. The pound had been under pressure for some time, and more than once other nations had helped with emergency finance. In November 1967 London at last admitted that it would have to devalue the pound from $2.80 US to $2.40. Although the Canadian dollar had been strong, following the British devaluation it did experience some problems, and the more nervous international investors moved funds out of Canada in the expectation that it might follow Britain downward. There was no question of Canada's doing so, however, and Mitchell Sharp insisted that the dollar would stay at 92.5 American cents. Nevertheless, for no very good reason, speculators began to suspect that other relatively weak currencies, such as the Canadian dollar, would be devalued too. The Canadian currency was weak in the sense that every well-informed person knew that Canada needed regular borrowings to cover its regular deficits on current account. Hence funds began to flow out of Canada. The flow continued well into 1968.

By year's end the speculative pressures had spread to the American dollar itself. Everyone, especially the French, expected that the United States would have to raise the price of gold. There was, accordingly, a flight from American dollars into gold, and into such strong currencies as the mark. On January 1, 1968, the American government announced new and more stringent guidelines. Canada had been consulted about these guidelines and was not much worried, because Sharp thought that the curbs would not affect the behaviour of American-owned firms in Canada. However, it appears that, within days, there was an unexpectedly large transfer of funds from American-owned firms back to the United States. In addition, the Canadian dollar was still under some speculative pressure because of the nervousness about the international monetary situation. By January 21 the government had begun to make emollient pronouncements and to take defensive moves. But as the world financial system moved ever more deeply into speculation against gold, Canada's position became ever more uncomfortable.

The governor of the Bank of Canada later wrote, 'For most of the first half of 1968 the Bank gave top priority to the defence of the exchange value of the Canadian dollar.' What Canada wanted, and got, was another confidence trick. On March 7, 1968, the Americans gave Canada some new exemptions. They had been trying to discourage US multi-nationals from transferring funds abroad and to encourage them to bring profits back home. Now these rules would not apply to Canada. Canada arranged to borrow from the International Monetary Fund, the American Export-Import Bank, the Bank of International Settlements, and the central banks in West Germany and Italy. In effect the government was mobilizing its resources so as to defend the dollar, and by telling the public how strong its defences were it hoped to end the speculative pressure. The trick worked: the drain slowed at once, and stopped on March 17.

Nevertheless the world-wide speculation continued, reaching a crisis in mid-March, when it was necessary to close the gold markets both in London and in Canada. The speculation had got completely out of hand. After three days of frantic negotiation the countries of the Western world announced that there would be a new regime. Among themselves, the world's central banks would trade gold at the old price of $35.00; on the open market, gold could be bought and sold at any price; the central banks would neither buy new gold on the open market nor supply gold to it. In effect newly mined gold was now a commodity like wheat or copper. Canada welcomed this innovation and early in April allowed its own gold markets to reopen.

Canada liked the new arrangements, if only because they would end the speculation. Immediately the Bank of Canada returned to an expansionary course. Nevertheless, the monetary expansion did not keep interest rates low enough to prevent an accretion of foreign exchange, as capital funds flowed into Canada. By December 1968, for the first time, these holdings were above the 1963 ceiling.

As speculators moved from gold and foreign money back into Canadian dollars Canada's position quickly improved, and by the end of 1968 Sharp had wound up most of the emergency loans and lines of credit that he had negotiated in the first three months of the year in an atmosphere of political crisis. Underlying this improvement were two factors: the current account balance was improving, and Canada was still importing long-term capital funds, both to finance new foreign direct investments and to expand Canadian businesses and governments.

But now the US exemptions of July 1963 and March 1968, once so eagerly sought, had turned into a strait-jacket that placed the Bank in an impossible position. Whenever capital came flowing into Canada with especial speed, the Bank would have to make credit easy (thus creating inflationary pressure, about which the Bank and the government were increasingly worried) so as to discourage Canadians from borrowing abroad, lest holdings of foreign money rise. Once more Canada's monetary mandarins made a pilgrimage to Washington. At last, late in December 1968, the American authorities, who now understood the position, discarded the 1963 rule. Once more Canada could let its foreign exchange holdings rise if it wanted to. Thus after five years the Bank recovered a modicum of freedom with respect to domestic credit policy, which no longer had to be conducted with both eyes glued firmly on national holdings of foreign money.

Having shed the strait-jacket, Canadians did not always remember that in 1963 they had designed it themselves and willingly donned it. At that time inflation had not seemed much of a danger, and the balance of payments seemed much more precarious than in the late sixties, by which time everyone was much more worried about inflation. As circumstances and perceptions had changed, the warm and comforting security blanket of 1963 had become a too-restricting swaddling.

As monetary policy evolved, so did Canada's financial structure. During the 1960s the changes were numerous and striking. In 1967 the banks were allowed freely to lend on mortgage, and after a slow start they moved massively into mortgage lending, as the government had intended when Parliament changed the law. Throughout the period, the banks were also extending their consumer lending, a field they had once left to the specialized instalment-finance companies, household-finance companies, and loan sharks. By the seventies the media were full of advertisements from banks, urging households to rush in and borrow. The sedate and nervous bankers of the forties, perhaps remembering the Depression of the thirties, could not have imagined any such development, and certainly would not have tolerated it.

Until 1967, the banks could not charge more than 6 per cent interest, and they were allowed to agree among themselves on the interest they could charge borrowers and pay on deposits. These rules had originally been devised to protect borrowers and banks in equal measure. Then the law was changed: the banks could no longer collude, and they could charge or pay whatever rates of interest they thought right and proper. The result was a sudden outbreak of competition that quickly extended from charges to such important matters as opening hours and such unimportant ones as personalized scenic cheques. As for the ceiling on bank charges, there was much protest when its abolition was proposed, but by 1975 it had been long forgotten and the public was accustomed to a situation where banks, like supermarkets and car dealers, eagerly sought its business while charging and paying what the traffic would bear.

Until 1985 there would never be any doubt that Canada's banks were secure, safe, and solvent. None had failed since 1923; in case of need, any bank could borrow from the Bank of Canada. In 1965, however, the government decided to make assurance doubly sure. It was seriously worried not about banks but about 'near-banks' – trust companies, mortgage companies, and credit unions – which did bank-like business but were less closely regulated and could not borrow from the Bank of Canada. In the fifties and sixties near-banks mushroomed all over Canada. Some were ancient and well managed; some were new but well run; some were neither.

In 1965 a financial house, Atlantic Acceptance Corporation, collapsed noisily and messily. This collapse involved a large and long-established near-bank, British Mortgage and Trust of Stratford, Ontario, which had lent a lot to Atlantic. The Ontario government and the Ottawa authorities were afraid that the public would lose confidence in near-banks and try to withdraw deposits, quickly producing a wave of near-bank failures. The Bank of Canada provided emergency help and urged the chartered banks, some of which had close links with the near-banks, to do likewise. Another trust company absorbed British Mortgage, and to preserve public confidence in banks and near-banks the national government introduced deposit insurance.

The Canada Deposit Insurance Corporation (CDIC) was modelled on lines followed in the United States since 1933. All banks and all federally incorporated near-banks were obliged to insure their smaller deposits; provincially incorpo-rated companies could join so long as their provincial authorities approved. Nine provincial governments did so, while the tenth, Quebec, set up its own deposit insurance plan. Credit unions were not covered, but most enjoyed protection under other provincial statutes.

The CDIC made little difference to the banks, but it must have helped the near-banks to expand still more quickly. By the mid-seventies they were very much in evidence, competing energetically with the chartered banks. Most strik-ing in some regions were the credit unions. Long established in Quebec and in a few French-speaking areas elsewhere, by the seventies credit unions had come out of the closet almost everywhere and were making a major splash with hand-some new buildings and massive advertising campaigns. Relative to the char-tered banks the credit unions and the other near-banks were still rather small, but in the sixties and seventies they had a considerable impact. In Quebec there were interesting developments. The Banque Provinciale, one of the 'French banks' based in Montreal, made a serious effort to expand its business, especially in Ontario. In 1979 it merged with the Banque Canadienne Nationale to form the Banque Nationale du Canada, known in Quebec simply as la Banque Nationale. Whether this merger had turned the 'Big Five' into a 'Big Six' remained to be seen.

Meanwhile the banks built glass towers and decorated city centres with pla-zas and art works. Toronto acquired the Toronto-Dominion Centre and Com-merce Court, in addition to First Canadian Place. Social commentators thought the glass symbolic: banks were now open, welcoming, eager to see and be seen, no longer the costive, introverted institutions of the old days.

While the banks were sheathing themselves in glass, consumers were bedeck-ing themselves in plastic. At the end of the war it was still quite difficult for households to borrow money. Of course there were mortgage loans and instal-ment plans, but the latter were closely regulated with respect to downpayments and terms of repayment, lest consumers create inflationary pressure by trying to buy too much. Department stores ran charge accounts and some oil companies were beginning to issue credit cards, but both systems were small in scale and impact, and neither made much provision for extended credit. In the fifties things began to change. As wartime inflation receded, the government stopped controlling instalment credit. As stores and oil companies competed harder they spread their plastic manna more widely and paid less attention to the credit-worthiness of cardholders. By 1960 American Express, Diners' Club, and Carte Blanche had begun to distribute general-purpose credit cards; even so, their stan-dards were high, they insisted that accounts be paid when rendered, and there were still relatively few places that would accept the things. American Express said that you could go around the world on your card without spending a dollar in cash. True, but only if you wanted to travel first class. The breakthrough came in the sixties with Chargex (later called Visa), and Mastercharge (later Mastercard), the first really general-purpose cards that also allowed for extended payment. These were also the first credit cards to be distributed quite widely. Because the chartered banks and near-banks ran the new credit cards, plastic money slipped neatly not only into the Canadian way of life but also into the Canadian financial fabric. Later, in the 1980s, they would be used in another novelty, the cash-dispensing 'money machine.'

Other developments, less obvious to ordinary people, were digested with equal smoothness. As Canadians grew richer and Canadian business grew more sophisticated the financial scene became much more complex. There were new kinds of specialized financial business and new sorts of instruments for borrowing and lending. Canadian chartered banks expanded their external operations in some directions, such as western Europe, while cutting back in others, such as Cuba and the Caribbean, where the political climate had become increasingly uncomfortable.

Whatever the long-run impact of monetary developments, the Pearson era itself was a time of boom, based on a rising tide of exports and a wave of domestic investment, both domestically owned and foreign owned. And what a boom it was! The list of projects is almost endless. Quebec was building a steel mill and Montreal and Toronto were digging subways. In Nova Scotia the government was manufacturing heavy water, or trying to, and bribing Clairtone Radio to move from Ontario to Pictou. New Brunswick was building the Mactaquac hydro project, and Newfoundland began work at Churchill Falls. Manitoba, too, was building new hydroelectric capacity on the Nelson River, and British Columbia on the Columbia and on the Peace.

Saskatchewan battened on the new wheat sales, and its potash deposits, where production had begun in 1951, began to bulk large. In 1964 Great Canadian Oil Sands began to build its Alberta plant. In the Northwest Territories the Pine Point lead-zinc complex began to produce, and Canada Tungsten reopened its mine. In Quebec there was to be a government-owned plant that would assemble Renault and Peugeot cars; in Nova Scotia there was hope that a Japanese car firm would join Volvo. And alongside these dramatic and newsworthy schemes were developments less picturesque but equally important. Rapidly the country was building its new urban framework – factories, houses, commercial buildings, shopping centres, roads, sewers, and universities.

In the export trade many things were happening. The Communist states were buying Canada's wheat; Americans began to buy its cars. In 1963 the Soviet Union signed a massive wheat contract. Never before had Canada shipped more than 400 million bushels a year, but in 1963-4, thanks to this contract, it would have to ship 550 million. In 1965 the Soviet Union bought another 187 million bushels. It has been buying ever since. China, having contracted in 1963 to buy up to 187 million bushels by 1966, reached that figure in June 1965 and at once signed another contract to buy up to 187 million bushels by mid-1969. The United States was not happy about these deals, but Ottawa paid no attention to its complaints. Meanwhile, in November 1963, Canada introduced an export incentive scheme to encourage car exports. Studebaker promptly shut down its American plant and shifted to Canada; Washington as promptly complained. The Canadian government was worried because Canadians were importing more cars and parts than they exported; the Americans objected because the Canadian government was proposing to subsidize exports, thus diverting jobs from American auto cities to Canadian ones. In 1964, therefore, at Canada's initiative, the two governments began to discuss an alternative – a kind of free-trade arrangement for cars and parts – whereby North America would be a single market. In January 1965 an agreement was reached. The United States would eliminate tariffs on Canadian-made cars and parts; Canada would allow the car companies to import cars and parts duty-free from the United States so long as they satisfied certain conditions – a definite minimum level of work in Canadian plants, and a definite ratio between Canadian manufacture and Canadian sales. These qualifications to free trade would later be known as 'safeguards.' At once the car companies began to rearrange their production so as to get the benefits of continental specialization. In Canada production went up, and so did employment. By the early 1970s cars and parts were the largest single export. In Canada, thanks to government pressure, car prices fell a little relative to American cars, and car-buyers hoped for a larger pay-off in due course. The Autopact was not genuine free trade, because Canada continued to protect Canadian production and because Canadian citizens were still not allowed to import cars duty-free: only the car firms could do so. By the mid-1980s the Autopact had become sacrosanct, even to the NDP and the autoworkers' union, which had strongly opposed it in its early years.

On the trading horizon there were two kinds of clouds. The European Economic Community (EEC), established in 1958, was still shaping its common agricultural policy, but by 1963 it was already obvious that this policy would be highly protectionist. Along with the United States, Canada pressed for a more open market for foodstuffs in continental Europe; predictably it got nowhere. Meanwhile Oriental goods were providing awkward competition, especially for Canada's textile producers. In 1963, new and more stringent import quotas on Japanese and other textiles were imposed, thus providing more effective protection while reducing certain tariff rates.

In 1963 the Kennedy administration had proposed that all tariffs be cut by 50 per cent. It wanted multilateral negotiations through GATT – the General Agreement on Tariffs and Trade. In Ottawa, the cabinet was split. Should Canada accede to the American initiative? After all, since 1944 the government had supported much multilateral tariff bargaining, and in a general sort of way Canada wanted other people to reduce their tariffs so long as it did not have to concede very much. Walter Gordon was afraid that Canada could not bargain without making concessions; Mitchell Sharp believed the bargaining could be turned to its advantage. In 1964 Canada agreed to take part in the talks, which had quickly been labelled the Kennedy Round. Canada won an exemption from the across-the-board cuts. Its heavy exports of numerous primary products, on which other countries' duties were already low or non-existent, meant that if everyone were to reduce tariffs by 50 per cent Canada could not possibly hope to gain as much as it would have to give. Instead, a list of 'offers of concessions' was prepared. Canada also hoped, through the Kennedy Round discussions, to maintain its pressure on the EEC. Bargaining went on until September 1966, by which time the EEC had fixed its agricultural policies on basically protectionist lines; this fact was especially alarming to Canada in that Britain was once more seeking to join the Community. Canada supported British membership so long as its own export interests could be safeguarded, but it was already clear that in the future Britain would not be a large market for Canadian goods. Indeed, when the Kennedy Round negotiations ended in May 1967 it was with the Americans that Canada had done best. Gains in other directions, although valuable, were not nearly so large. Tariff cuts covered $3 billion worth of export trade, of which $1.9 billion went to the United States. Canada's own concessions covered $2.5 billion worth of imports, $2 billion of which came from the United States. The agreements were far from 'unrestricted reciprocity,' and all tariff cuts were extended symmetrically to all fifty GATT members. But so far as Canadian imports and exports were concerned, the new arrangements would integrate the Canadian economy more closely with the American.

Nowhere was this interpretation more apparent than in energy. On balance Canada was still importing oil. But during the Pearson years its hydrocarbon exports went steadily up, and the United States was the only market. In the American Midwest and far west, Canadian oil and gas had become quite important. Something similar had happened with electric power. In the early sixties the Diefenbaker government had hoped for a Canadian national electricity grid. By 1965, however, it was clear that the connections would run north and south, not east and west. Regional electricity systems were connected with their American opposite numbers so that loads could be shared and power could be imported or exported whenever the need arose. The results could be dramatic, as

Canadians learned in 1965, when a mechanical failure on the Niagara Frontier blacked out everything from Toronto to New York. In energy, at least, continental integration had come to stay. Or so it seemed in 1968.

Present-day governments normally use their taxing and spending programs to steer the economy. In Canada the practice began during the Second World War. We have seen that, in the Diefenbaker years, there was a good deal of budgetary tacking, and it was often suspected that the helmsman did not know where he was going. But when Lester Pearson took office he installed Walter Gordon as his finance minister. The Toronto accountant had written eloquently of the need for 'confidence.' He had helped to form the economic planks of the Liberal platform. The nation expected that he would devise a business-like budget, one that would help to revive the economy. When Gordon brought down his first budget on June 13, 1963, however, the country received a rude shock.

So as to stimulate investment and cut unemployment the finance minister imposed an 11 per cent sales tax on machinery, equipment, and building machinery and made various minor tax changes meant to reduce the budget deficit. Economists were agreed that these measures would tend to *increase* unemployment and *reduce* investment, other things being equal. Gordon did not care. He was much more interested in a series of tax tricks that were meant to discourage foreign takeovers and encourage foreign subsidiaries to place shares on the Canadian market. At once there was a horrendous outcry from the stock exchanges, and on July 8, Gordon, having retreated in disorder, produced a second budget. He cancelled the tax on takeovers and diluted the proposals to tax the remittance of interest and dividends to foreigners. As for the new sales tax, he exempted some buildings and decided to impose the tax in stages, rising to the full 11 per cent only in 1965.

Both Parliament and the public were most distressed by the fact that Gordon had relied on three financial advisers whom he had brought from Toronto; the financial community was worried by the foreign investment measures; only economists seemed to notice how foolish it was to *raise* taxes, especially on capital goods, when the economy needed more investment so as to absorb the unemployment and raise the growth rate. In later years Gordon still defended his budget. Admitting that it was inconsistent, he wrote that this did not matter; because he was trying to do two things at once, naturally his budget had contained contradictory measures, and observers were wrong to object. When the first budget appeared, Mel Watkins remarked that it was not merely pre-Keynesian but positively Precambrian. The description still seems to apply. If we take the Gordon budgets together, we can see that they provided the sort of medicine that Canada did not need. One budget discouraged new spending on plant, equipment, and structures; another encouraged households to consume more. Yet Gordon was eager to encourage Canadians to save and invest in Canada so as to drive out the foreigner.

Fortunately for the Pearson government the forces of economic expansion were strong enough to defeat these manoeuvres. And on December 17, 1965, following Gordon's resignation, Mitchell Sharp became Minister of Finance. In the St Laurent years Sharp had been Deputy Minister of Trade and Commerce. Soon after the Diefenbaker victory in 1957 he had left the civil service, first for the business world and then for politics. He distrusted Gordon's gimmickry, and, except in respect of banking, he did not worry much about foreign investment. He thought the Canada Development Corporation, which Gordon had promised but never produced, a waste of time and money.

With Sharp at the finance department Canada experienced another period of macroeconomic management along the standard lines that Keynesian economics prescribes. To the professional economist Sharp's budget speeches sounded like echoes from the last of the King years and from the St Laurent years, when Ilsley and Abbott and Harris had tried to explain the modern principles of Keynesian economic policy. To social reformers in the Liberal cabinet and outside, Sharp's policy was less attractive. Taking office when inflationary pressures were beginning to worry the nation, Sharp was often obliged to raise taxes and to oppose, defer, or reject new spending programs, especially on the social services. To socialists and economic nationalists, such as Walter Gordon, Sharp was, of course, anathema. Not only did Sharp force the cabinet to defer medicare for a year, but he opposed the publication of the Watkins Report on foreign ownership that Gordon had sponsored, and he did not establish the Canada Development Corporation.

In November 1968, Sharp introduced an orthodox anti-inflationary package of the sort that any academic economist would have applauded. Naturally it was unpopular; even in good times nobody likes to pay extra taxes and nobody wants government to spend less on the services one actually uses. It was easy to make fun of the fact that Sharp kept changing his mind and changing the taxes also. But Sharp could and did explain that he was doing the right thing. When the economic climate changes in unexpected ways the government *should* change its taxing and spending plans. However, it might be argued that Sharp was too eager to 'fine tune' the economy. When tax rates change, households and businesses may not change their ways at once. But governments and politicians want fast results.

To everyone's surprise, on February 19, 1968, the House rejected the budget measures on third reading. Sharp then had to design a new tax package that would do the same things. Now, however, he had new reasons for haste and for concern. In January 1968 the Canadian dollar had begun to fall. To hold it close to the peg fixed in 1962, the government was borrowing abroad and spending its reserves of foreign money. If the government could take a firm anti-inflationary line, speculators might be more willing to hold Canadian dollars. Indeed, money might flow back into the country. Hence, on March 6, Sharp proposed an 'austerity' package much like the Conservative measures of 1962. In addition, however, he now proposed to create a review board that could discourage wages and prices from rising too fast. Ever since 1966 some Canadian publicists had wanted an anti-inflationary 'incomes policy.' In 1966 Sharp had seen little hope for such a device. Now he was willing to try. But the thing would be voluntary; it might urge and complain, but it could not make anyone *do* anything.

By 1968 Canada's finance minister faced a much harder task than in 1962 or 1957. The civil service had acquired a vegetable life of its own: unless carefully watched it would grow by 4 per cent or more every year for no very obvious reason. But much more serious was the enormous range of new spending programs to which the Pearson government had committed itself. Many of these – medicare, Canada Assistance, aid for universities, decent old age pensions, and a whole range of shared-cost programs – were virtually uncontrollable. For this depressing fact there were two reasons. First, many were propelled by 'need' or by demography. Second, most were run by the provinces. Ottawa provided much of the money, but it did not control the standard of service or its cost, and neither the federal nor the provincial governments controlled the demand. In the Trudeau and Mulroney years, federal-provincial wrangling would revolve in large part around the problems of control. The roots of this trouble were to be found in the Pearson years, when the federal authorities set up new programs without any rational assessment of their costs or controllability. In 1966, it was said, federal-provincial medicare would cost $80 million. How wrong can a cabinet be?

What are we to make of the Pearson budgets? Were they expansionary or contractionary, inflationary or anti-inflationary? To answer the question we have to rearrange the budget data from the *Public Accounts* into the more logical categories of the *National Income and Expenditure Accounts*. When we do this, we find that from January 1963 until December 1968 the federal government took in $56,922 million, spent $18,908 million on current operations, and distributed $36,044 million in transfer payments to persons, businesses, and junior governments. Thus it 'saved' $1,970 million. However, it spent an additional $2,190 million on buildings and equipment. Setting this 'gross capital formation' against the savings, we find that the government's true deficit was only $220 million – 0.06 per cent of total gross national product in the years 1963-8. The Canada Pension Plan even ran a surplus. Obviously government spending can hardly have been inflationary.

Over the whole period GNP grew 69 per cent, federal revenue 75 per cent, current expenditure 44 per cent, capital outlays 85 per cent, and transfer payments 73 per cent. The budget was outgrowing the economy, but as yet the divergence was small, and some of the new federal outlays may have replaced outlays that would otherwise have been made in the private sector. Perhaps, if taxing and spending had both been less, the economy would have grown faster, and by 1968 or 1978 Canadians might have been even richer. Many observers think this would have been so, but others believe the idea is nonsense. There is really no way to settle the question. Still, it is reasonably clear that the economy grew because business investment and exports were growing, not because of government policy.

25

The Sixties: Nationalism and Culture

In another day, Walter Gordon's fumblings as finance minister, his unpopularity with the business community, with American investors, and with nearly all economists, would have doomed him to political obscurity and disgrace. This was not so in the sixties. This tweedy scion of the Canadian 'establishment' became a patron to an economic-nationalist movement, which was itself a part of a rambunctious ferment that disrupted what many Canadians thought of economics and society. In a period in which traditional standards and ideas stood condemned because they were traditional, Gordon's visionary quality and his rejection of the economics of the academy became an emblem that permitted him to pass where few others of his kind could go.

Gordon wanted to limit the amount of foreign investment in Canadian business and to control the activities of foreign-owned firms. The times seemed propitious as America's Vietnam adventures spread an ever-denser fog of suspicion and dislike that soon shrouded all things American. Tactless American interventions in Canadian affairs and a tendency to claim an 'extraterritorial' control over the foreign activities of US-based firms increased Canadian fury. Gordon had expressed his concern about foreign investment in the 1957 Royal Commission on Canada's Economic Prospects, which he had headed. Gordon's conclusions, some critics noted, did not rest on a strong foundation of commission research and, in some cases, conflicted directly with what researchers had found. The Diefenbaker goverment could easily ignore the report; a Liberal government would likely have done the same. But the Liberals in opposition were tempted by this modern Jeremiah's call to end our old ways and doings, especially since this prophet brought with him money and friends to rebuild a shattered party.

In 1963 Mike Pearson appointed Walter Gordon Minister of Finance, and Gordon's first budget and its failure became not proof of Gordon's political or economic naïveté but rather indication of the strength of the 'malevolent' forces working against him. Out of the cabinet after the 1965 election, Gordon became ever more the prophet, decrying his country's relationship with the new Babylon. The chorus accompanying him swelled, and in January 1967 he returned to the cabinet as a 'senior member without portfolio.' He immediately set up a 'task force' that would investigate the effects of American influence in the Canadian economy.

Because Gordon's task force was organized by M.H. Watkins, its output was known as the Watkins Report. After many delays, in February 1968 Watkins and his associates issued their findings. They argued that Canada should extract more information from the multinational corporations, while regulating their activities and forcing them to accept orders from Communist buyers. The nation should also make sure that such firms were paying a fair share of taxes, and it should devise new tax incentives that would encourage the multinationals to sell shares in Canada. The report proposed that Canada should prohibit Canadian compliance with foreign anti-trust decrees, orders, or judgments, and also, perhaps paradoxically, proposed that the nation should devise a more active antitrust policy of its own. Finally, the report urged the government to set up an enormous investment trust – a Canada Development Corporation, which Gordon had been demanding for years.

Partly because Gordon left the cabinet in March 1968, the government did not act on any part of the Watkins Report, which seemed at first to sink without trace. Nevertheless, in succeeding years the report was like a yeast, gradually leavening the lump of public opinion, especially in central Canada. In the next chapter we shall sniff at some of the gaseous bubbles that resulted during the Trudeau years.

Watkins and his associate, Abraham Rotstein, were economic historians who rejected what they termed the sterility of mainstream economic thought in favour of a romantic vision that asserted the importance of reasons of the heart. In this case, their hearts led them to a definition of American interests as fundamentally antagonistic to Canadian interests. This led Watkins, personally, to discard the muted business suit of an academic liberal economist with a bachelor of commerce degree and assume instead the open-shirted, leather-jacketed garb of a theorist of the New Left. Watkins and the publicist Jim Laxer became the leading figures in the Marxist-nationalist 'Waffle' movement that very nearly overwhelmed the forces of moderate democratic socialism in the New Democratic Party. The appeal was straightforward: Canada could never possess its own soul so long as it remained a bourgeois-capitalist nation on this bourgeois-capitalist continent. Government ownership of the economy could alone recapture for Canada its purity and its identity.

That the Canadian left shared so many qualities of the American left is hardly surprising; politically, both shared the same critique of bourgeois democracy and, above all, a profound distrust of 'technology,' a term that seemed often to mean all things that limited what they might want to do. The Canadian and American New Lefts shared another trait: they were both dominated by the young. So was society, and this gave the decade its predominant image, that of a boisterous uprising of the young that threatened and sometimes tumbled over the fundamental institutions of our society.

John Grierson, the noted film-maker, dubbed the movement 'The Children's Crusade,' and it was as confusing and sometimes as tragic as that remarkable medieval adventure. In the universities the crusade made its deepest mark. Throughout the sixties, the young had left their families for the classrooms as never before. In 1962-3 there were 196,700 post-secondary students, 11.1 per cent of the population aged eighteen to twenty-four; ten years later, there were 513,400, 18.4 per cent of the same age group. This meant more classrooms, and also, inevitably, that what went on in those classrooms would not be the same as before. The numbers of young people, their parents' and teachers' doubts, and the corrosive effects of rapid change all played their part in the explosion that shattered the traditional image of the university. The shock effects were widely felt. Writing in 1969, the novelist Hugh MacLennan despaired at finding his generation of liberal, humane academics 'assaulted and blackmailed by the Youth [sic] with unprecedented contempt as The Establishment.' His generation, MacLennan wrote, had 'embarked on a lifelong Odyssey that took us through more than one cave of the winds, under the legs of more than one man-eating Cyclops, but we never deviated in our unconscious aim, which was to recreate the old Victorian patriarchal world in the image of an indulgent mother wearing pants. Now we find ourselves cursed by the young for all the things we were proud of, for our voyage did not end in the Ithaca we had deserted, but in the land of the Lotus Eaters.'[1]

The new land at MacLennan's McGill was startlingly unlike the old. Even Frank Scott, a poet, lawyer, and civil libertarian, who had long defended socialist and liberal values, was a subject of abuse during 1967 demonstrations which demanded that McGill become 'French,' a part of the ferment about it. Perhaps for the first time in Canada, the universities became objects of public suspicion. The normal question was: why should the state subsidize these institutions so highly if they contribute to the disruption rather than the enrichment, economic and otherwise, of society? At first this complaint could be easily dismissed, but by the end of the decade the arguments against it were no longer so convincing. 'Standards' in educational institutions obviously were falling, especially in non-

---

1 Hugh MacLennan, 'Reflecting on Two Decades,' in George Woodcock, ed., *The Sixties* (Vancouver: University of British Columbia Press, 1969), p. 28.

professional programs, as student activists demanded – and often got – an end to such symbols of 'psychological oppression' as examinations and required courses. Issues abounded. At Simon Fraser University in British Columbia, politics became theatre in that striking mountaintop university's central mall. Margaret Trudeau, a student there at that time, recalled that 'all hell broke loose' with every local headline proclaiming 'Riots at Simon Fraser.' Summing up the experience over a decade later, she wrote: 'We fought, we protested, we had good times, and in the end we lost.' To outsiders, the reasons for protest were obscure; the good times, however, were all too obvious.

'Good times' meant experimentation – with sex, with drugs, with fashion, with political extremes. Social researchers in the United States in the 1920s (and, of course, F. Scott Fitzgerald) had noticed that college students behaved differently from the general population. In the sixties, too, they were in the vanguard, and, because there were so many young, that vanguard was extremely visible. The externals of tradition and convention were first assailed. Academic gowns were an early casualty, and the campuses became a showplace for the eclecticism that marked fashion in the 1960s. Blue jeans were everywhere, and, by 1967, the mini-skirt, created by Britain's Mary Quant, abounded on campuses, if not yet in offices. But in offices, at cocktail parties, and in shops, hemlines crept up inch by inch, and the plumage became thinner elsewhere as well. Even if Rudi Gernreich's topless bathing suits appeared rarely, if at all, on Canadian beaches, skimpy coverings were the rule. Midriffs often were uncovered or barely concealed by filmy gauze. It would be wrong to suggest that such styles were the fashion, for fashion itself ceased to have a clear direction. More than ever, clothes were 'statements' about the 'identity' and personality of the wearer, whether this meant a billowing skirt reminiscent of ages long past or army surplus jackets, reminder of wars we would not fight. Fashion was a reflection of the age, an age of change and chaos.

Measurement of change in and confusion about personal attitudes and behaviour is always difficult. In Canada we have no counterpart to the large-scale Kinsey report on sexual behaviour, or its updates by Masters and Johnson. What evidence we do have suggests that Canada followed the United States into a 'sexual revolution' during the 1960s. One study, carried out by C.W. Hobart and W.E. Mann, looked at university and trade school students in the late 1960s in three Canadian cities and showed an acceptance of increased permissiveness and fewer feelings of guilt about sexual activity. In Hobart's survey, two-thirds of the English-Canadian sample said that they were increasingly permissive in their dating habits, but only 39 per cent of the French-Canadian sample reported increasing permissiveness. A majority of both groups, however, accepted premarital sex where 'love' was present. A cross-national survey of 2,230 male and female students from the United States, Canada, England, Norway, and West Germany found Canadians more conservative, both in their attachment to a double standard for male and female behaviour, and in their coital experience, in which Canadian men ranked fourth and Canadian women fifth.

Even if Canadians were more conservative than the English, they were less so than their fathers and mothers. Moreover, they knew more and thought more about sex. This arose not only from the pervasiveness of sex in the magazines at the corner store, but also from the increased concern for sex education in Canadian society. In this case at least, there is good evidence that what was taught in schools, churches, popular magazines, and even newspapers was remembered. One long-term study of sexuality and family planning among married couples in low-income urban areas of Quebec revealed a distinction between the periods before and during 1969-70. In the earlier period two-thirds of pregnancies were unplanned, and one-fourth of the couples used contraceptives after marriage or after the first pregnancy. In the 1969-70 interviews, however, researchers found that 86 per cent of the couples were using contraceptives, with 49.5 per cent of the women taking oral contraceptives.

Birth rate statistics reflect the impact of the more widespread use of contraceptives, among other factors. The crude birth rate for Canada declined from 27.4 in 1959 to 21.3 in 1965 to 17.6 in 1969. Other evidence, too, showed that more families were being 'planned.' In 1961, the percentage of childless married women between twenty and twenty-four was 26.3; ten years later it was 42. This meant more time for education, for careers, and for double incomes, and for society this presaged major changes in what women would do and how they would live.

In 1967, these changes could not be predicted, but many sensed that women's future in Canada would not be like the past. The Pearson government, prodded by Judy LaMarsh and by groups such as the National Council of Women, appointed a Royal Commission on the Status of Women. Many newspapers ignored it editorially, others were condescending, a few were critical. The *Calgary Herald* blamed 'vocal militants who make a fetish of women's rights' for this unnecessary commission. 'Men and women are not equal,' the *Herald* declared. 'Nature has ascribed roles to women which makes it impractical for them to be regarded on the same basis [as men] in many instances.' Besides, most women would not trade 'exerting an immeasurable, if subtle, influence on society ... to compete outright in all things with men.' By the time the Royal Commission reported, such sentiments seemed anachronistic.

One area where women were already competing very well was in literature. Margaret Atwood won the Governor General's Award for poetry in 1966, and, after intermittent production for some years, P.K. Page and Miriam Waddington began to publish regularly a richer and more reflective poetry. In fiction, the *Literary History of Canada* noted the change from the 1950s, when the 'point of view of the time was male,' to the 1960s, 'the decade of Malcolm Lowry ... and of Margaret Laurence.' Laurence, W.H. New wrote, 'explored the essential differences between middle class expectations and other values, articulated a female perspective, and offered evidence to many younger writers that the simple act of being alive was a political act.' Not only for Laurence and other women had writing become a political act.

Canadian literature was not unique in the political spirit of its art in the later 1960s. Still, even though in Canada the stream flowed in a parallel direction to the American stream, its shadings were different. Both in French- and English-Canadian literature, politics in art meant nationalism. The title of Dave Godfrey's first short-story collection, published in 1967, *Death Goes Better with Coca Cola*, was the cultural counterpart of the Watkins Report. Vietnam, the charnel-house of the American dream, marked Godfrey's pages. He decried the Canadian colonial mentality that made Canadians accept the death cloud of Americanism on our culture. Godfrey, Atwood, Dennis Lee, Robert Kroetsch, and other young writers sought creative freedom through a search for other traditions and through shrill rejection of Americanism. In French-Canadian literature, such writers as Hubert Aquin and Marie-Claire Blais were equally strident and even more determined to break through conventional language and content. Theirs, admittedly, was a different kind of nationalism, one that directed its fury at all things Anglo-Saxon and seemed often to equate vulgarity and the English influence. There could be no common meeting ground for these two nationalisms, and Canadian literature remained divided at its linguistic core.

The nationalism of art in the later 1960s is easy to understand given the large numbers of new writers who appeared and the disillusionment with American values. Later, writers like Atwood, Lee, and Blais would treat the period as a 'necessary stage' whose importance lies in the foundations it created. In denying America, Canadians were forced to define themselves. They did so not only in novels and poetry, but even in movies and art. The Canadian film industry that had died so many times was given a strong restorative in the form of the Canadian Film Development Corporation. Artists, too, found a government caught up in the self-celebrating mood of Centennial year much more willing to be a patron. On occasion the patronage was repaid. Before her return to a Canada that was changing quickly, Joyce Wieland created a quilt for a politician who in 1968 symbolized that change and promised to hasten it. In our future, Wieland stitched on the quilt, we would have 'reason before passion.' The man, Pierre Trudeau, would not fully be his message.

PART SIX

Into the Seventies and Beyond

26

The Centennial and the
Early Trudeau Governments

Canada's centennial was more than anyone expected. Coming so soon after the scandals that soured Canadian politics and after the first clear threats to the future of Confederation, Centennial year seemed to promise little. In 1966 the preparations occasioned mostly derision. Expo '67, the first Canadian World's Fair, was still a muddy, incomplete site, and its projected deficit rose ever higher. Ottawa's plans appeared similarly troubled; cynics also thought them mawkish and redolent of small-town boosterism. Nor did Canadian leaders inspire excitement or confidence. Both the Liberal and Conservative parties were clearly waiting for a change, for the appearance of a new generation of politicians untainted by the bitter parliamentary battles of the minority Liberal governments. And yet, when the new year came, even the cynics changed their mood. In the *Canadian Forum,* one of the authors of this book confessed that he had looked forward to Centennial celebrations with a sense of impending nausea. He later admitted that the nausea had not come and that he shared the peculiar exuberance that was to capture Canadians for those twelve months. The sensation was perhaps like that of the middle-aged man who has saved up so long he does not know how much he is worth. Suddenly he stands back and recognizes that he has done far more than he knew or had a right to expect.

One can only speculate about what produced this mood of gentle nationalism. Certainly, a major factor was the turmoil in the United States caused by the Vietnam war. The Canadian sense of inferiority was replaced by a strong gust of moral righteousness which exalted many of those values that had embarrassed Canadians in 1960: their placidity, caution, and even innocence. One could find the more militant forms of nationalist sentiment in *Canadian Dimension* and even in *Maclean's,* but for most Canadians nationalism meant telling the pollsters that they were more concerned about the effects of American influence on Canadian life and waving our new flag.

The red maple leaf became ubiquitous in 1967. The centre of angry debate when first introduced to the House of Commons in June 1964, the flag now seemed an emblem for younger Canadians. They wore it on their backs in Europe to get rides that would be denied the 'uglier' Americans. Charms, icons, and even automobiles bore the imprint of the red maple leaf. The flag seemed to have become what Pearson had hoped it would be: an expression of the willingness of the young to break with their past. John Diefenbaker, of course, would not have agreed; neither would many other Canadians. Yet in 1967 Diefenbaker was to learn how much his land had changed and how much an anachronism he had become.

Diefenbaker's problems had really begun during the flag debate when his French-Canadian colleagues, notably Léon Balcer, broke finally and firmly with him. Balcer demanded a leadership convention in February 1965, and no doubt the movement would have gained impetus had not the 1965 election interfered. Despite Diefenbaker's surprisingly good performance in that election, many of his colleagues had had enough of him. His performance during the scandals debate was notable for its histrionics, but it embarrassed many of his colleagues. Moreover, the 1965 election results showed that the party had lost the youth and the cities. With Diefenbaker, it seemed that the Conservatives could be a party only of an ever more remote past.

By the end of 1965 leading members of the Conservative executive were discussing how best the Chief might go. Eventually they found a leader – the party president, Dalton Camp. On September 20, 1966, Camp publicly called for an assessment of the leadership of his party. But Camp had a problem. One of the few remnants of conservatism in the party was the absence of a procedure for leadership review. Camp thus disguised his attempt to overthrow Diefenbaker as a movement to reform the party. He staked his own presidency on the issue of reform. At the party's November 1966 convention those who voted for Camp as president were voting for leadership review; those who voted for Arthur Maloney were voting for John Diefenbaker. The byzantine manoeuvres involved in making this choice need not concern us. What is interesting is the support Camp received. It was from the young, the urban, the professionals, and the French Canadians. Their organizational skills brought them to Ottawa in greater numbers than the rural and traditional Tories who supported Diefenbaker.

Camp won the presidency, and Diefenbaker became from that moment a lame-duck leader. In Parliament, however, he seemed more a wounded bear lunging after whatever irritated him. Polls showed in early 1967 that the nation was as embarrassed as the party. Conservative strength fell below that of the New Democratic Party and far behind the Liberals. This news hastened the calling of the leadership convention, which was set for early September 1967 in

Toronto. The abundance of candidates revealed that leading Conservatives thought that their party's future was bright without Diefenbaker. It seemed that Dief would not run, but he remained characteristically silent. He kept his silence as the crowd pushed into Maple Leaf Gardens to hear what it thought – and, in the case of most, hoped – would be the Chief's farewell. But Diefenbaker would not go gently into the night. He raved at his detractors and summoned up his own version of Canadian history to deny the claims of the present. The next day he filed his nomination papers, the last of the ten leadership aspirants to do so. On the first ballot Diefenbaker finished a dismal fifth and by the third could muster only 114 votes, compared with the 717 of Nova Scotia premier Robert Stanfield, the front-runner. Diefenbaker withdrew and left the Gardens. He returned to honour Stanfield the winner. Ironically, he called for loyalty to the new leader. He would not heed his own call, but on that night no one knew the depths of Diefenbaker's bitterness.

As the Tories left for home, they had reason to be contented. Stanfield had been an effective provincial premier. His personality was dull, but it was such a welcome contrast to his predecessor's that scarcely anyone noticed. Within two months of the convention's end, the Conservatives had moved significantly (9 per cent) ahead of the Liberals in the Gallup Poll. Unlike Diefenbaker, Pearson recognized that his day had finally passed. His health was not particularly good; his wife wanted his time; and Centennial year had brought emotional rewards that previous years had denied. On December 14, 1967, he announced his resignation. There was no obvious successor as there had been in 1948 and 1958. The Liberal tradition of French-English alternation seemed more necessary than ever before, but Jean Marchand, the best-known French-Canadian prospect, was disinclined, and his personality was unsuited to the task of leadership. Pearson shared the belief in alternation and tried to persuade Marchand to run, but the former labour leader knew his limitations better than his leader did. Pearson then turned to Pierre Trudeau, who had in his brief tenure as justice minister attracted the attention of the liberal media with his divorce reform as well as his articulateness in both languages. On Valentine's Day 1968 he announced his decision to run. His remarks on that day revealed how, after the tenth decade, candour, novelty, and even inexperience had become political values of considerable weight.

Throughout the country, the meetings to choose delegates were filled with the faces of those new to Liberal gatherings. Most of them were young; many were at universities or taught there. Trudeau offered a chance that could not be missed. With the zeal and commitment of youth, the Trudeau forces were remarkably successful at the local level. Politicians like Paul Martin and Paul Hellyer who had so carefully tended the Liberal party found that the friends they

'Where the devil is that "one nation" speech!'
Opposition leader Robert Stanfield searches for inspiration (McNally, c1968).

had met at so many fund-raisers, at so many long political evenings, could not control their constituencies. By the opening of the convention on April 4, Trudeau was clearly in the lead. Mitchell Sharp had already withdrawn, throwing his support to Trudeau. On the first ballot Trudeau led, with 752 votes, followed by Paul Hellyer, 330; Robert Winters, 293; John Turner, 277; Paul Martin, 277; Joe Greene, 169; Allan MacEachen, 165; Eric Kierans, 103; and the Reverend Lloyd Henderson, 0. Still, it took four ballots; on the final one Trudeau bested Winters 1,203 to 954.

The new prime minister called a federal election for June 25, 1968. What had happened at Ottawa's civic centre in April now swept the country. Mackenzie King's Canada could not have imagined what occurred. While Diefenbaker in 1958 had stirred emotions, he did so in the style of Elmer Gantry. Trudeau was Bogart in the trenchcoat. The offhand kiss, the sideward glance, the flip insult, the smile, and the tears it brought, all seemed perfectly timed. He ran against his own party as well as the opposition. He did it with a style and a grace that even Liberals hardly noticed. He hectored his audiences, blaming them for a past that had 'hamstrung' them and daring them to change. The mood was propitious for the appeal. In the United States Bobby Kennedy and Eugene McCarthy were rousing the young by striking similar notes. The past was a dead hand that must be lifted; in the jargon of the day, it was irrelevant.

Stanfield never had a chance. The Liberals took 45.5 per cent of the vote and 155 seats, the Conservatives 27.3 per cent of the vote and 72 seats (lower than any Diefenbaker total), and the NDP 17 per cent of the vote and 22 seats.

The strongest vote for Trudeau, then and in the future, came from his native province. There can be little doubt that his support in the other provinces came partly because it seemed that this Quebecker could speak most easily, most effectively, and most harshly to that troubled province. Within Quebec, critics of Trudeau's anti-nationalist viewpoint cited this fact as evidence that Trudeau appealed to anti-French feelings in English Canada to obtain his majority. This is surely unfair. Trudeau during the campaign had spoken French from the Kootenays to Halifax; every speech was punctuated by sentences in French. The response was invariably cheers from the anglophone audiences, most of whom did not understand the language. The spontaneity of the gesture belies any interpretation of hypocrisy. Comparing it with what happened later makes one realize how fresh hopes were in that early summer of 1968 and how little Canadians realized what fears and hates still lingered.

Trudeau's major appeal in English Canada – and in Quebec – flowed from a broader and more salubrious stream. The crusty dowager of the Canadian press, the *Globe and Mail,* expressed it well in its editorial endorsing Trudeau: 'The argument most frequently made against [Trudeau] is that he is unknown, that we have no long-term record of Mr. Trudeau as an administrator, that we can't be certain how he will react in any given situation. But perhaps it is one of the facts of life in the sixties that Canada no longer needs the great certainties that are largely born of fear. Canada is willing to adventure. It may be that what Canadians see in Mr. Trudeau is this new side of themselves, a readiness to gamble on the unknown, to move into areas not explored before.'

Trudeau's election reinvigorated the Liberal party. In the fall of 1967, an outside observer might well have concluded that the party was likely to suffer the fate of so many of its counterparts elsewhere. When *Canadian Dimension* asked several Canadian academics, politicians, and journalists what party they thought would succeed in the decade ahead, almost half thought there would be a non-Liberal government of the left. Only Ed Schreyer expressed the belief (and perhaps the hope) that there might be an NDP-Liberal coalition governing Canada. The strong NDP standing in the polls before Trudeau and the leftward drift of public opinion in Canada, as in the Western world generally, seemed to threaten Liberalism. In a polarized society, there is little room for a party whose appeal is as a mediating force in that society. The victory of 1968 brought youth into the party; it made Liberal committee rooms respectable to youthful idealists as they had not been in 1965. Not surprisingly, the new Liberals were anxious to shrug off what they regarded as old barnacles, and they were not at all upset when Trudeau failed to observe the niceties of political leadership – as, for example, when he did not permit a day for speeches to honour his predecessor in the House. Nor did they dissent when Trudeau attacked the inefficiency and the conservatism of the bureaucracy, an institution so long identified with the Liberal party. In short, Trudeau accepted the Liberal party's traditional mediatory role, but he rejected its style. Liberalism could be tough and direct.

In this case, the style was definitely the man. Mackenzie King had dominated his cabinet through his experience, through his careful sifting of ministers' emotions, and through delicate intrigue. He judged his men shrewdly and knew those on whom he could rely and those whom he must simply court, or, in a few cases, endure. St Laurent shunned intrigue, shared responsibilities, and controlled his cabinet through the respect that his intelligence and integrity commanded. Pearson gave his ministers much freedom and relied on his ability to charm and to cajole to move his cabinet toward decision. With Trudeau, apparently, there were no favourites. The cabinet atmosphere was not unlike a high-quality academic seminar where one's weaknesses were continuously probed. A minister knew that neither political weight nor personal charm could excuse a weak brief. Thus Trudeau had from his ministers respect but not love, sometimes not even sympathy. One minister once remarked on the difference between Trudeau and Pearson in the House of Commons. When Pearson fumbled and the opposition scored, his ministers rallied behind him in common cause. When Trudeau was under fire, he stood alone. His ministers watched but stood beyond the fray.

Trudeau also changed the style and shape of Canada's administrative substructure. Since the Second World War Canadian governments had adopted various devices for coping with the increasing complexity of administration. Under Mackenzie King a Privy Council secretariat was created to keep minutes and guide committees and subcommittees of cabinet in their deliberations. The cabinet secretaries and assistant secretaries combined with the new expert generation of senior civil servants ('the mandarins') to keep Ottawa in working order. St Laurent exploited the system to enhance his direction of cabinet business, using his control of the agenda to guide cabinet discussions and conclusions. As a preliminary to cabinet discussions, issues were fought out in interdepartmental committees of senior bureaucrats so that by the time a problem reached the cabinet its solution had usually been determined.

Under Pearson, however, some slippage occurred. 'Pearson let everybody talk,' one of his ministers recollected. 'The trouble was, nobody knew what the conclusions were.' Confronted by the institutional rigidity of the regular civil service, Pearson sought refuge in special task forces and the creation of new departments to stir things up. But these measures were, at best, palliatives.

Trudeau, who became a member of the Pearson cabinet in the spring of 1967, observed the Pearsonian chaos closely. 'I was quite concerned about the machinery of government,' he told a reporter soon after becoming prime minister. 'One of the reasons why I wanted this job, when I was told it might be there, is because I felt it very important to have a strong central government, build up the executive, build up the Prime Minister's Office, strengthen Parliament.' Under Trudeau, cabinet committees were strengthened and reorganized. Ministers were expected to fight out their problems in committee, bringing only the most critical or the most insoluble to cabinet as a whole.

Cabinet committees proved, in the experience of the ministers and officials who attended them, to be a great equalizer and an immense bore. Obliged to stay in Ottawa and tend the store, the ministers as a group came more and more to resemble administrators and less and less practising politicians. But the ministers' bargaining power was limited: 'We're here because he's here,' they told themselves, looking down the table at the Prime Minister. By solving one problem, Trudeau created another.

The relationship with ministers in some ways mirrored the relationship with the party. Trudeau's people in 1968 had little experience in the party and, like him, tended to enter from the top. They were naturally resented and responded with distrust. As with the cabinet so too with the party; the Prime Minister's Office (PMO) became the barrier that shielded the political element from the leader. Trudeau would not go to party fund-raisers. He refused to soothe tender egos. Although a politician like Paul Martin continued to have much influence in southwestern Ontario, Trudeau would not hesitate to place him beyond politics (in the Senate) and to do it in a fashion that prevented Martin from attaining a record for political longevity. Trudeau sought to change the texture of Canadian politics, to remove it from the concerns of the local constituency and from the sway of traditional belief. No election revealed this better than that of 1972.

Disdaining traditional election machinery and appeals, Trudeau's campaign was managed by three former academics whose direct electoral experience was negligible. They and others around Trudeau in his PMO seemed to shield Trudeau from the emotions that the country felt. Indeed, Trudeau appeared determined to make the contest not an election at all. The slogan was 'The Land Is Strong,' and the technique, in the parlance of the day, was dialogue with Canadians. 'We're not fighting any party,' Trudeau said. 'The other parties can fight us if they want, but we're going to be talking to Canadians.' Theoretically, it seemed that the technique might work. But it did not. Party workers, ignored since 1968, shunned the campaign. The press seemed bored when it was not angry. Although the Conservatives also ran a dispirited campaign, it was the Liberals who revealed too much distance from the electorate. When the results came in on October 30, the Liberals had lost their majority and very nearly the government. They had won 109 seats; the Conservatives, 107; the NDP, 31; the Créditistes, 15; and independents, 2. Clearly the attempted dialogue had not occurred.

The day after the 1972 election most commentators spoke of a Liberal defeat and a Conservative victory. Although the Liberals had two more seats than the Tories, the pattern was clear, and Trudeau, it was thought, might recognize it with his resignation. The Liberal-supporting Ottawa *Citizen* did urge Trudeau to remain on as a lively leader of the opposition and congratulated Stanfield on his 'victory.' But the reports of Trudeau's death were much exaggerated. Disillusioned yet combatant, hurt yet prideful, Trudeau did stay on, and within a couple of months had the press writing about a new Trudeau – more human, more tender, more willing to listen to Canadian complaints. His office was reorganized and made more political, and the Liberal party was no longer the shabby mate one dragged along in the campaign, but a coy maiden for whom the Prime Minister had ample world and time. The popular Martin O'Connell, a defeated MP, replaced Marc Lalonde as Trudeau's principal secretary, and, in the spring of 1973, Keith Davey, Pearson's very political campaign chairman, was named chairman of the next Liberal campaign. These appointments were more important symbolically than practically. On Trudeau's part they indicated an understanding that he must reinvigorate English-Canadian Liberalism and that he could not remain an elusive, aloof political animal because the mood of English Canada would not accept such a leader. If anything, the election had made Trudeau more cynical about the democratic process, but he quickly realized he would have to change if the government were to survive. The government scrambled together a legislative program of wide range but of little coherence for the January session. The *Toronto Star* immediately hailed Trudeau as a 'willing learner' and the legislation as the kind that would have brought him victory a few months before. The *Star* called for the NDP, which held the balance of power in the Commons, to stand by Trudeau and the program. This decision wasn't hard for NDP leader David Lewis. The program was loaded with bait – especially in social policy and nationalist economics – that Lewis's party could easily swallow. Moreover, Lewis remembered what had happened in 1958, and he feared that another election could have the same result as that earlier Conservative triumph – the decimation of the third party. Thus Trudeau won time, but at some cost. At one point, he complained, 'If a government wants to do the popular things, it will ruin the economy – real quick.' And yet for two years his government had to do the popular thing. He was obviously uncomfortable, and as we suggest in our comments on the economy, his apprehensions about the result of doing 'popular things' had considerable substance.

The apparent transformation of Trudeau once more drew attention to this remarkable politician and away from his opponents. The fascination returned, if not the adulation. In Parliament Trudeau seemed to take from Stanfield the advantage that an opposition leader normally has. In his attacks on the Tories, he had the assistance of David Lewis's sharp-tongued eloquence, as Lewis sought to justify his party's support of Liberal programs. Trudeau did not always say the popular thing, however. After the election he told Parliament that the opposition had exploited anti-French-Canadian feelings, and he implied more than once that the opposition to his bilingualism program was sheer bigotry. He accused some Conservatives of trying to divide the country by using the language issue. English-Canadian editorial opinion denounced Trudeau, but on this matter he would not retreat. In his own words, he wanted 'to put people on notice that I will not be silent on this. I don't want to create hysteria about it, but I want people to know that wherever I find traces of bigotry, I will fight it whether it be in the province of Quebec or in any other province.'

These remarks were not popular, but they were largely ignored. After the trouncing the Parti Québécois received in the October 1973 provincial election, when Robert Bourassa's Liberals won 102 of 110 seats, Quebec as a 'problem' attracted much less attention. Moreover, the Trudeau government had, after the 1972 election, slowed down the bilingualism program. What captured attention instead was the flood of legislation that the government introduced: an election expenses act that fundamentally changed the rules of the political game, and not in a way that benefited the Liberals; a Foreign Investment Review Agency, which partially quelled the complaints of Liberal nationalists like Walter Gordon; increases in all kinds of pensions that Canadians received from the federal government; a tax cut that benefited most Canadians; and, after OPEC's 1973 success in raising oil prices, a pricing policy that sheltered Canadians from the impact of the world increase. Because of the tendency to identify social legislation with a broad concern for humanity, the press began to see Trudeau as 'someone who cared,' a man who understood human needs better than before. No matter that Trudeau himself was obviously embarrassed by the political inspiration for much of this legislation and probably believed that human needs in the longer term would have been better served by a less hectic pace of social welfare expansion; the public perception of the government had changed.

Both Tories and New Democrats were confused. In the spring of 1974

Trudeau was daring them to defeat his government. That year's budget was calculated both to please an electorate and to force the New Democrats to make a choice. Lewis, whose pre-budget demands had obviously been ignored, could not back down. On May 8, 1974, the Trudeau Liberals were defeated. They were delighted.

In the campaign that followed Trudeau kept his opponents on the defensive. For Lewis it was difficult to attack the government's legislative record when he was claiming that he was its intellectual inspiration. It was much easier to turn on Robert Stanfield, the apparent front-runner, whose party was committed to a badly thought out wage and price control scheme. Trudeau revelled in his fate; the insider as outsider, slashing away at his opponents with a freedom he had never had since those days when he tried to bring Duplessis down. He ignored the media, refused interviews, and staged encounters with the press. Harking back to the campaign style of old, he took a train through the small towns and into the hearts of the large cities, all the time promising a brighter future and revealing, it seemed, a new Liberalism with a human face.

Although many across the country remained unconvinced, and the newspapers strongly favoured the election of Stanfield's Conservatives, the proposed wage and price freeze hurt him badly in both Ontario and British Columbia. Later analyses of the election revealed that leadership was decisive in 1974 and that Stanfield was not perceived as a leader. On July 8, 1974, urban and industrial Ontario and British Columbia swung decisively behind the Liberals and gave Trudeau his majority once more. He won 141 seats (43.2 per cent of the vote), the Conservatives only 95 seats (36 per cent), and the NDP 16 seats (15.4 per cent). The *Globe and Mail,* which had supported Stanfield, was impressed.

Trudeau had won – but what? The party was now thoroughly his; even the reluctant now admitted that Trudeau had proved that his political skills were the equal of, if not better than, those of any Liberal leader since King. He thus gained more freedom to shape the party into the mould he required, and his perpetuation of a very political Prime Minister's Office showed that he intended to exercise his power in the party. He also had time. Unlike the minority period, when legislative flurry was calculated to keep the opposition off balance, there was now an opportunity for reflection.

His first gestures after the election revealed his intentions. Both the cabinet and Prime Minister's Office set about determining policy and setting objectives. The appointment of Michael Pitfield as Clerk of the Privy Council Office and Secretary of the Cabinet gave Trudeau a personal and political friend at the apex of the bureaucracy. His job was to integrate programs and to steer the bureaucracy in the direction that the cabinet and Trudeau had decided it must move. Pitfield's familiarity with and experience in the bureaucracy made him an ideal person to play such a part. And yet, by the autumn of 1975 it was clear that the exercise had failed. As a study of the policy and planning experiment discovered, the departments were expected to propose new policies that would help the government accomplish its declared aims.[1] They did not; instead, 'in bureaucratic fashion, department officials sent mainly self-serving responses' that normally said, 'This is how our existing programs and proposals fit your plan for the next four years.' By spring 1976 the attempt to plan had clearly failed.

Even without the bureaucratic response, the long-range plans of January 1975 would not have been realized. Inflation and rising unemployment bedevilled political planning in that year. The government's attempt to deal with the problems produced growing scepticism and irritation. In his June budget, Minister of Finance John Turner paraphrased Keynes: 'Economics is too important to be left to economists. The choices to be made are essentially political decisions.' But as a political decision-maker Turner was unconvincing even to some Liberal friends. His performance was ridiculed by the *Toronto Star* as one of much show and little substance.

A few months later Turner was gone. His department had become a strong advocate of the wage and price controls that he and Trudeau had so vociferously and effectively opposed during the 1974 campaign. In early September Turner, who seems to have been undecided about controls themselves, quit cabinet, causing the press to interpret the puzzling resignation as an indication of impending economic disaster. The plea for controls – never defined and most often misunderstood – became a clamour. Wage settlements were higher than anyone could ever remember; there seemed to be no end to the rate of increase and to the concomitant inflation. Columnists wrote regularly of the possibility that 'the British disease' was crossing the Atlantic and infecting us, but rarely did they note the dismal history of peacetime controls in Britain and in other countries. Trudeau was the last to be convinced; he reportedly capitulated when Robert Bourassa informed him that his government intended to grant some civil servants a yearly increase of over 30 per cent. The lack of will was startling enough to show even the most doubtful that controls might be the psychological shock treatment the country so clearly needed. On Thanksgiving Day 1975 Trudeau announced the controls, warning, however, that controls would not be some miraculous palliative for the nation's ills. They would only purchase time 'to understand and adopt the real cure, which is a basic change in our attitudes.'

The effectiveness of controls we assess elsewhere; it is chiefly their political effect that concerns us here. In this respect, they didn't work. Although the press had led the movement for controls, it was not prepared to give Trudeau credit

1   Colin Campbell and George Szablowski, *The Superbureaucrats: Structure and Behaviour in Central Agencies* (Toronto: Macmillan, 1979).

for introducing them. The press and, it seems, the public became more suspicious of the government's direction, if indeed it had one. Even the normally quiescent Liberals had their doubts. At the November 1975 biennial convention of the Liberal party, opposition to Trudeau was surprisingly open. Corridors were filled with whispers of doom and disgruntlement. In the vote on the question of whether there should be a leadership review, 19.2 per cent voted yes, almost twice as much as the figure after the disastrous 1972 election.

The reaction to Trudeau's year-end interview, usually an occasion for banalities of the season, compounded his difficulties. The remarks themselves are unexpectional; indeed, they are the commonplace of economic textbooks. In answering a question about the evil of 'bigness,' Trudeau said: 'We can't destroy the big unions and we can't destroy the multinationals, we can control them ... That means the Government is going to take a larger role in running institutions, as we're doing now with our anti-inflation controls.' Tom Cossitt, Conservative MP for Leeds, declared that Trudeau had revealed his true intentions, 'namely to take Canada right down the road to a dictatorial form of socialism or a similar form of plain old fascism.' For once, Cossitt found many who agreed, especially in the business community, which even the staid *Canadian Annual Review* described as 'paranoiac' in its reaction to Trudeau's remark. *Le Devoir* asked whether the Canadian Chamber of Commerce had gone mad and whether collective hysteria had seized business circles. The editorialist correctly saw the reaction to the speech as the culmination of a growing distrust of Trudeau and of the economic aims of the government.

For Trudeau the unexpected reaction surely brought further disillusionment with his government and with the electorate. The feeling was mutual. In early 1976 there were widespread rumours that Trudeau would not long remain leader. These rumours began partly because the Conservatives did change their leader in February 1976. As conventions so often do, the Tory convention focused attention upon and attracted support to the party and its new leader, a young Alberta MP named Joe Clark. Before the convention the Liberals had every right to be fairly optimistic about the outcome. The Conservatives were fighting each other with the skill and the vindictiveness characteristic of their internal wars. The frontrunners, Claude Wagner and Brian Mulroney, were subjected to intense scrutiny and criticism, and by the opening of the convention their positions had much deteriorated. Several other candidates could not be taken very seriously: Paul Hellyer, a Liberal retread; Sinclair Stevens, a financier whose record gave rise to some uneasiness; Jack Horner, taken seriously only by himself and John Diefenbaker; Patrick Nowlan; Heward Grafftey; and John Fraser. Although it was fashionable to wear Flora MacDonald's buttons, commitment to her was like the River Platte, a mile wide and an inch deep. This left Joe Clark, whose greatest advantage was that hardly anyone had noticed him. He was young, bi-lingual, and from the west, where Tory strength lay. As Mulroney and Wagner stumbled, Clark moved ahead to take the convention on the fourth ballot. Over-all the effect of the convention was better than the Tories had hoped and, for the Liberals, worse than they had feared. Apart from some individual cases of bitter-ness, the only regret many had was the loss of Bob Stanfield as leader. On the night he was honoured Stanfield gave the best speech at the convention – witty, intelligent, and probably effective in its call upon Tories to be more loyal to their new leader than many of them had been to him. A cacophonous period ended on a note of grace.

Still, few Liberals feared Clark until the Tories began to pull ahead of the Grits in the public opinion polls in the summer of 1976. By August the lead was eighteen points (47 per cent to 29 per cent), the worst Liberal performance since the Diefenbaker sweep of 1958. It seemed as if Trudeau could do nothing to halt the slide, except resign. The temptation must have been great. His attempt to explain his policies had been met with misunderstanding and misinterpretation, which he no doubt thought was deliberate in some cases. In 1976 he seemed to be afraid to say anything; perhaps he thought it not worth the trouble that any definite statement would surely cause. His family, too, brought pressures of an-other kind. His third child, Michel, was born in October 1975, and the desire to spend more time with his young sons was understandably strong. As well, he had begun to realize that something had gone seriously wrong in his relationship with his wife, Margaret. Anyone who has seen a marriage break up – as this one eventually did in the spring of 1977 – can understand the enormous strain Tru-deau must have endured. But this and the bad polls and the bad press he did en-dure.

He probably stayed because in November 1976 the battle he had long feared finally came when René Lévesque won power in Quebec. During the early sum-mer of 1976 the controversy about bilingual air traffic control had alerted Tru-deau to the dangerous divisions within the country. On June 25, as pilots refused to fly and controllers to guide unless bilingualism in the air was abandoned, Tru-deau told the Commons: 'This country is in danger of very seriously being di-vided ... as it has not been for 34 years.' While Quebec newspapers interpreted the illegal strike as an irrational anti-French outburst, the *Toronto Sun* blamed the strike on 'a bone-headed, bloody-minded federal government determined to shove French down throats.' Each reaction intensified the other. There is no doubt that René Lévesque's arguments gained much force among francophones as a result of the strike. In terms of English-French relations, this crisis was probably the most serious since 1944, yet when Trudeau suggested that this might be the case, the *Globe and Mail* accused him of the hyperbole that would create a real crisis. In the House of Commons, Trudeau found similar disbelief, and the attitudes of Clark and Broadbent troubled him very much. The former he thought opportunistic; the latter, ill-informed and emotionally distant from French Canada. Given Trudeau's perception of himself and his purpose in politics, these events surely steeled his determination to remain.

Stay he did, and, after Lévesque's election, English Canadians began to see him once more as the only leader to meet the challenge of separatism. Despite clear evidence in the public opinion polls, non-Québécois had refused to believe that the Parti Québécois could win. On election night, November 15, 1976, the surge of emotion that swept Paul Sauvé arena as Lévesque spoke jolted Canadians into recognition of the depth of the separatist commitment and the power of its appeal. Clark's response was clumsy, and the NDP's ambiguous, since the Parti Québécois espoused social democracy as well as separatism. Trudeau's eloquent and obviously sincere response won plaudits from all but separatists and obdurate opponents. His popularity and that of his party rose quickly; by mid-summer 1977 the Liberals had the support of over 50 per cent of Canadians, according to the Gallup Poll. In Conservative ranks there were bitter complaints about the party leadership; there were even questions about whether Clark would survive until the general election. The press and social critics were often savage. In autumn 1977 Mordecai Richler wrote: 'While Trudeau is easily the intellectual equal of René Lévesque, Clark, even if he sat on three telephone directories, would still have the fiery Quebec premier looking down on him.' Richler was especially disturbed because Clark had not disavowed Roger Delorme, a Conservative candidate in a May by-election, even though Delorme had claimed that 'only' one million Jews had died in the holocaust and had declared that 'I have dealt with Zionists and Nazis and it was the same thing.' And yet two years after his by-election defeat many Jewish voters marked Conservative ballots for the first time in their lives.

Had the people who remember most forgotten so quickly? The Tory votes in 1979 were surely not won by Clark's impossible election promise to move the Canadian embassy from Tel Aviv to Jerusalem. It seems more likely that this item is merely further evidence of the discontinuity of Canadian public life in the late seventies. As rapidly as Trudeau rose in the polls in the winter of 1977, he fell in the summer and autumn of 1978. A political study published in 1979 revealed how willing Canadians were to change their political preferences and how far they had come from those days when party affiliation was a badge one wore unto death. Old loyalties faded as did old perceptions, and they did so as rapidly as the changing seasons.

One thing most people expected in late 1977 or early 1978 was an election, but Trudeau held off. In the late summer of 1977, as the polls showed almost two-to-one support for the Liberals over the Conservatives, Trudeau ignored his leading advisers, but not his nervous caucus, saying: 'As far as I am concerned, just because one is convinced he is going to win an election is not a good enough reason to go to the people.' Mackenzie King would have been horrified. Then, a year later, in September 1978, with the Liberals still ten points ahead in the polls (forty-five to thirty-five), Trudeau once again refused to call an election, opting instead for a so-called mini-election of fifteen by-elections. Despite the large Gallup lead, there was more concern in autumn 1978 because private Liberal polls revealed growing animosity toward Trudeau himself. He was thought to be insensitive and unaware of Canadian needs. There was, moreover, what *Maclean's* termed 'a chilling anti-French bias in parts of English Canada which is aimed at Trudeau personally – although it is often thinly disguised in passionate advocacy of the monarchy.' These perceptions could not easily be changed; and they weren't.

The by-elections were a disaster for the Liberals. Support among the urban middle class dropped precipitously, and soon the polls were showing the Conservatives and the Liberals almost even in support. By this time, January 1979, Trudeau's queen in the political chess match – the freedom to choose the election date – was almost lost. In September 1978 the press had already begun to question whether Trudeau could long remain as leader. Serious political observers, whatever their political bias, knew that Trudeau would and must stay. To leave the Liberal leadership in response to anglophone pressure when separatists governed Quebec was impossible for Trudeau and, for that matter, for the Liberal party, which might never have recovered. In the late winter and spring of 1979, Trudeau thus played out his part.

He finally called the election for May 22, and, at the beginning of the campaign, many Liberals believed that they would win once more. The issue, they thought, would be leadership, and the polls clearly showed that Trudeau was perceived by Canadians as a more competent leader in nearly every respect. Joe Clark's January world trip, during which he almost impaled himself on a bayonet, walked into a door in an officers' mess, and invariably seemed to have left his luggage one country behind, seemed proof, in the words of one reporter, that Clark was 'dwarfed on the world stage.' But it really didn't matter. Change – not Clark – became the major issue, and the Conservative organization protected Clark well, as Trudeau and the Liberals assailed Clark's leadership capacity. Clark did make mistakes, especially in his contradictory statements about Quebec's ability to 'vote its way out of Canada,' but Trudeau did too. His moods varied, his style was inconsistent, and his staff showed exceptional qualities only in offending party workers in the constituencies. The Liberal campaign was a disaster.

By the final week of the campaign, the Liberals knew that the Tories had won. The NDP alliance with labour was not swinging votes in industrial Ontario. A television debate a week before the election also changed little. Most thought Clark had been bested (with the exception of the *Toronto Sun,* which, in a headline reminiscent of the partisan newspapers of the nineteenth century, declared Clark the winner), but the final opinion poll showed that his party had not lost support.

On May 22, 1979, more Canadians voted for the Liberals than the Conservatives (about 4 per cent more), but the Liberals had too much of their support in Quebec. The Conservatives used the system better than the Liberals, doing poorly in Quebec (two seats), but extremely well west of the Ottawa River, especially in southern Ontario, where cabinet ministers and Liberal strongholds fell with astonishing ease on election night. In the west, where Laurier and King Liberalism did so very well, Trudeau Liberalism garnered the support of one out of five voters and carried only one seat west of Manitoba. Only NDP strength in Saskatchewan and, to a lesser extent, in British Columbia kept Clark from a western sweep and a majority. Still, after appointing James Jerome, a Liberal, as speaker, he was just a few seats short, and the pattern of support outside Quebec offered Conservatives much consolation. They had recaptured the support among the urban middle class that Diefenbaker had lost in the sixties. More important was the remarkable rise in Conservative support among youth, a segment of the electorate that had tended to vote Liberal since Pierre Trudeau became leader. In 1979, unlike 1968, young people were conservative in their style and, apparently, their political tastes. Voting Conservative seemed to be the counterpart of taking the economics and business courses that the young now so eagerly sought out.

Commentators were quick to find signs of a conservative temper everywhere. Geoffrey Stevens saw 'the story of Canada in the 1970s' as the change from Trudeau's 1970 love beads to the yellow cardigan Joe Clark donned after work. When Diefenbaker died in mid-summer 1979, the Conservative government presided over an emotional farewell that emphasized the richness of the Diefenbaker personality while ignoring so many personal bad memories of Diefenbaker's political legacy. Indeed, in his cabinet choices, Clark had shown how little he owed to (and, perhaps, thought of) the party's oldtimers. Absent from his cabinet were such leftovers from the Diefenbaker era as Alvin Hamilton, George Hees, and Marcel Lambert. In their place were younger, feistier Tories, many of whom had cut their political teeth a decade earlier in the campaign to rid the party of John Diefenbaker.

To the Clark Conservatives, Canada and especially its federal government reeked of Liberalism and Trudeauism. Although many Conservatives wished quickly to erase the Liberal tinge in the bureaucracy, the government decided not to risk arousing the ire of its public servants any more than it absolutely had to. After all, there were other tasks that were more important in consolidating the new government.

The Conservative political dilemma since 1917 had been the party's weak presence in Quebec. In 1979, however, western Canada for the first time had more seats than Quebec, and the demographers told us that the western tilt of the political balance would grow in the future. This offered consolation; it was also reflected in the government's policy. Clark and his government seemed to shift the focus of federal politics away from the so-called problem of Quebec. 'Cool it,' was the typical jargon so often heard when Quebec came up in Clark press conferences during the summer of 1979. Unlike Trudeau, Clark said he would take little direct part in the debate that would occur before the referendum. Attacking the 'confrontation' politics of previous federal-provincial diplomacy, Clark promised 'co-operation' with the provinces and vaguely suggested that his 'flexibility' could embrace Quebec's demands as well as those of other provinces. What this flexibility meant remained elusive. During the campaign, Clark had spoken of Canada as a 'community of communities,' which presumably foretold a decentralization unparalleled in Canadian history. Clark did not have time to clarify what he meant, although some signs did appear during his period in office. Clarification came later from Clark's successor, Brian Mulroney.

Troubles came early for Clark, most of them arising from Tory carelessness in the courtship of the Canadian electorate before May 22. The first problem was the promise to move the Canadian embassy in Israel to Jerusalem. When Clark made the promise during the campaign the press scarcely noticed, although international relations specialists, had they been consulted, would quickly have pointed to the dangers. Once in office Clark faced the protests of business groups fearing the economic consequences of such a move. He reluctantly reversed his decision, but his credibility suffered. Even more serious were the problems with the economy. In the campaign, the Conservatives had promised to 'privatize' Petrocanada, to grant a generous mortgage interest deduction to homeowners, to maintain lower interest rates, and to cut income taxes while reducing the budget deficit in the longer run. None of these things occurred.

Aware that many thought him a weak leader, Clark tried to seem decisive. But decisiveness meant decision, and this brought problems. Petrocanada had become popular after the election. To many it became – quite wrongly – a symbol of lower oil prices. According to Peter Newman, if Clark 'privatized' Petrocan, he would 'deprive us of the least costly, most efficient method of achieving Canada's energy goals.' But to leave it intact would deprive Clark of much political credibility. Again he hesitated, and he barely survived a non-confidence vote on the issue.

This vote made Clark and his ministers breathe more easily. They thought they had time enough to build their new structure of government. The Liberals were listless, Trudeau strangely ineffective in debate. In the House the Tories had several fine performers who could easily match or surpass Liberal or NDP critics in intellectual debate or parliamentary repartee. Minister of Finance John Crosbie rumbled and roared in a Newfoundland accent that attracted laughter and diverted attention from the many sensible things he had to say. Other cabinet members, such as David MacDonald and Don Mazankowski, impressed in quieter ways. There were disappointments. Ron Atkey as Minister of Employment and Immigration fumbled badly, and Roch LaSalle, the Minister of Supply and Services, embarrassed the government with his candour about patronage. His performance was not unexpected. LaSalle, the sole Tory francophone MP from Quebec, was not cabinet material, but Clark had no choice.

Clark himself could be seen as an asset the next time in Quebec. He was the first anglophone leading a major party to speak French. In the Commons he replied in the language of the questioner, and those few who watched Question Period usually gave him good parliamentary grades. Whatever the policy problems the party kept a united front, perhaps feeling that after an election a couple of years hence the elusive majority might be theirs. They needed time, and, on November 21, they appeared to get it. Pierre Trudeau unexpectedly announced that 'it's time for a new leader to take up this work.' In the Commons, Clark thanked Trudeau for his past service and hoped that he would continue 'to contribute his formidable talents to Parliament and Canada.' Few had thought that he would remain after the upcoming Quebec referendum, and even there Claude Ryan was making it clear that Trudeau was not wanted. At the age of sixty, Trudeau's future meant Michel, Sacha, and Justin, perhaps a university chair, and surely a large mark on his nation's history. In a little-noticed comment that had major implications, Clark said that Trudeau's departure 'will allow us to move more quickly than we might have otherwise in getting some of the legislative initiatives that we have wanted to move on.' The statement betrayed the fears that had made Conservative policy tentative and contradictory. Without a leader, the Liberals could only watch as the minority Conservatives acted like a majority. According to several reports, it was only after Trudeau resigned that the Conservatives decided that they could go ahead with some harsh economic measures that were sure to offend the already troubled and politically volatile province of Ontario.

Trudeau's resignation was, for Tories, an opiate that stilled fears but blurred vision. There was much that should have disturbed the government. The Gallup Poll for November, which appeared just after Trudeau's resignation, showed a startling nineteen-point Liberal lead. The Liberals, moreover, were not the well-disciplined party Canadians had so long known. But Joe Clark as prime minister was unconvincing. In cartoons Clark's chin receded ever farther. Ethnic jokes became respectable as Clark jokes. 'Have you heard the latest Joe Clark joke?' became an all-too-familiar staple of bar-room and even family dinner conversation. Tories didn't help. Dalton Camp gave Clark a mixed review in his best-selling *Points of Departure*. 'If you were ever in a fight,' Camp wrote, 'the safest man around to hold your coat would be Clark.' Six months later Camp's introduction to another book no longer even granted that Joe Clark was safe.[2]

Into this setting came John Crosbie (in mukluks) on December 11 to deliver his budget address. 'Don't be defensive,' Crosbie reportedly told the Tory caucus. 'This is an offensive Bodjit.' It was, but it was not really the 'tough' medicine Crosbie and his detractors later claimed it to be. Its true significance was political. Ontario provincial Conservatives reacted as expected to the budget's provisions for an 18 cent per gallon excise tax and for regular increases of wellhead prices which would soon bring Canadian prices to 85 per cent of the rapidly increasing world price. Premier Lougheed, however, beamed on budget night, proclaiming the budget to be proof that Albertans finally had a government in Ottawa that they could call their own. Lougheed's glee and Ontario Premier Davis's grumblings were remembered as Liberal MPs began their boisterous annual Christmas party on Wednesday evening, December 12.

The members drank away their doubts and fears as the night passed into morning. There was an NDP non-confidence motion to be voted on on Thursday. On the last non-confidence motion, enough Liberals had had political 'flu to allow the government to endure and to taunt them afterward. This time the Tories would face the taunts – or else. The next morning, as the party's late stragglers awoke, they discovered that it might well be 'or else.' The Liberal whip, directed by the strong arm of Allan MacEachen, was coming hard. Even Liberal hospital patients felt its sting, and Trudeau did nothing to stop MacEachen's skilful directing of errant Liberals into the fold for the night's vote. What made the vote so portentous was Social Credit leader Fabien Roy's decision to demand changes in the excise tax proposal as a price for his five MPs' support. By noon on Thursday, December 13, the young government's survival seemed doubtful. Strangely, it seemed not to care. Clark later said that he had never expected the Liberals to defeat him, and for that reason he neither delayed the vote nor bargained with the Socreds. It was a game of bluff, and the Tories thought that the high cards were on their side. They weren't. The government fell, six months after the election, by 139 votes to 133.

2 For Camp's comments on Clark, see *Points of Departure* (Ottawa: Deneau and Greenberg, 1979).

The next morning Trudeau met his caucus, and Clark went to see the Governor General. The election would be on February 18. Trudeau told his caucus that he would head the party if it could find no other leader and then left for a weekend in Montreal to brood over his future. His caucus, once again guided by MacEachen, made his decision. Since the Pearson years, MacEachen had toiled with little personal celebrity in Liberal party vineyards. He had built up a substantial number of credits; more important, his judgment was trusted. That Friday morning he cashed in his credits. Many were wary, especially the Quebec members, who worried about Trudeau's impact on English Canada. Because of their overwhelming numbers and these worries, the Quebec members withdrew, leaving the decision to those from English Canada. The caucus continued into the evening. Some members spoke despairingly of Trudeau's unpopularity with their constituents, but by late evening these voices had stilled. The caucus 'unanimously' called on Trudeau to lead it into the next election.

The next morning some members of the Liberals' national executive fumed, and the meeting carried on to an embarrassing length. Yet it too called on Trudeau to accept the draft to remain as leader. Several days later the CBC began the delayed Trudeau press conference with a discussion of the forthcoming Liberal leadership convention. There would be none; Trudeau would stay, but not forever. The Liberal general took off his stripes, but he still stood above his enlisted men. The new 'Liberal team' prepared to face the enemy without a platform, but with a keen awareness of the fatal weaknesses of its Tory opponents.

The Conservatives' greatest weakness was their leader, who, polls soon revealed, was wanted as prime minister by fewer than one out of seven Canadians. As Clark stumbled, too many Tories failed to rush to pick him up. Premier Davis of Ontario, whose treasurer's anti-budget statements Liberals gleefully quoted, found southern climes politically salubrious. Premier Lougheed of Alberta announced that he would remain silent until February 19. He did so even though a Lougheed statement indicating refusal to accept Trudeau's vague energy proposals would probably have helped the Tories in Ontario. Perhaps nothing would have helped.

Ontario Conservatives hoped that the hostility toward Trudeau that they had found in May would endure, but this hope soon vanished. The early polls generally showed Conservatives twenty points behind in Ontario, the Liberals an astonishing fifty to sixty points ahead in Quebec. The ingredients for a Liberal majority were present even if western Canada would not beckon to the Liberal appeal. The Liberal strategy was to make no mistakes, to arouse none of the old fears of Trudeau's arrogance. The promised Liberal platform never appeared, nor did any definite statement on energy prices. Liberal strategy was simple. Clark was already fatally wounded. Trudeau became a sniper circling at a

Duncan Macpherson
Toronto Star

Joe Clark's brief government (Macpherson, 1980). Reproduced with the permission of
The Toronto Star Syndicate

Table 4
Results of 1980 General Election

Province	Seats			Liberal popular vote (rounded)	
	Lib.	Cons.	NDP	1979	1980
Yukon/NWT	0	2	1	33	37
BC	0	16	12	23	22
Alberta	0	21	0	21	21
Saskatchewan	0	7	7	20	24
Manitoba	2	5	7	23.5	28
Ontario	52	38	5	37	41.5
Quebec	73	1	0	62	68
NB	7	3	0	45	50
NS	5	6	0	35.5	40
PEI	2	2	0	40	47
Newfoundland	5	2	0	38	47
Total	146	103	32	39.8	43.9

distance, refusing contact, never committing himself lest he come too near to the range of return fire. Trudeau read his speeches from a prepared text in which banality and cliché abounded. He became what he had almost never been before – boring. As he walked into one rally, a woman said, 'Please be your old arrogant self.'

If Trudeau lacked arrogance before the crowds, he retained it for the press. At the news conference at which he announced his resignation he had told the reporters – in a wry echo of Richard Nixon – that he would not have them to kick around anymore. Immediately on his return he began kicking again, leaving in the middle of a reporter's question at the press conference at which he announced his decision to remain as leader. The press's response, not surprisingly, was generally hostile. Richard Gwyn spoke of two decent party leaders and one who lacked honour and decency. His bitterness did not diminish during the campaign, nor did that of Allan Fotheringham, who irritated Trudeau's aide Jim Coutts into a lawsuit. The Liberals did not do well in newspaper endorsements either. Of the major papers, only *La Presse* and the *Toronto Star* supported the Liberals.

What did matter was energy prices – especially in Ontario and eastern Canada – and the perception of Clark as an inadequate leader. Not even the famous episode late in the campaign when the Canadian ambassador to Iran, Kenneth

Taylor, cleverly managed the escape of six American diplomats from Tehran could establish Clark as an international figure of substance. Canadians gave credit to Taylor, not to Clark. Clark's strong support for a planned Olympic boycott in response to the Soviet invasion of Afghanistan had much public approval, and it caused Trudeau to stumble briefly into contradictory statements, but Clark reaped few political rewards.

On February 18, 1980, eastern Canadians had elected a Liberal majority before the Manitoba returns came in. With a relatively small shift in the popular vote, the Liberals garnered thirty-two more seats than they had in May 1979. Because the Tories in 1979 had won so many Ontario seats with narrow margins, the Grits were able to recoup many, again with small margins. The Conservatives had, in fact, done much better (by 5 per cent) than the pre-election Gallup Poll suggested they would, but they would face a Liberal majority. No consolation removed the grief. The NDP, too, could point to more seats and more voters (19.8 per cent), but it had remained too much a regional party, the opposition in the west perhaps only while Trudeau led the Liberals.

'Welcome to the 1980s,' the victor greeted his followers on election night. Eight months before, few had thought he would make it into the eighties; now, just as few could explain how he had. There remains much that is puzzling in Trudeau's survival. If Liberals had polled their party members on leadership in September 1979 Trudeau would surely have lost. As one who entered politics when the Conservatives were ridding themselves of Diefenbaker, he knew how few high cards an electoral loser holds. He thus threw in his cards because he could not bluff and probably was tired of the game. Certainly Trudeau seemed to relish the freedom his resignation brought. The Crosbie budget and the Clark government's political clumsiness meant a new deal with a high trump. He could not refuse; reason and passion joined to give his answer. He became the master of his fate. In December 1979, René Lévesque's referendum, the promise of 1976, was still to come, and for Trudeau, of course, it was still to be fought. There was, too, Trudeau's promise of 1968, the vision of a juster society, and this found its echo – sometimes a hollow one – in the leftish, nationalist tinge of the Liberal campaign of winter 1979-80. And, finally, there was the Trudeau record after the 1974 majority. His personal life in tatters, he had given too little to public life. In private life in 1979 he was starting over; in public life he wanted a second chance. He got it. He had already left his mark on Canada's history; he was now determined to give this mark a clearer shape.

27

Economic Developments, 1968-79

Trudeau carried Quebec in the 1980 election because Quebec's concerns were not only emotional but economic. In the seventies the economic fabric of the country was transformed and the part played by government in that transformation was great. Longer-term trends were naturally at work – rising employment, rising real income, rising living standards, increasing economic involvement with the United States. As we argued in Part I, such developments should not be credited to any particular government or blamed upon it. But the seventies saw profound changes in many directions that made the whole structure different. Ottawa might seem increasingly impotent, but it could still affect the economy greatly. Because these structural changes are so many and so important for shaping the Canada in which we now live, the first and longest section of this chapter is given over to them. The second section treats traditional economic management – taxing, spending, money, and the foreign exchanges. We shall see that in wielding these traditional macroeconomic weapons the Trudeau government was relatively unskilled and increasingly diffident, not to say inept. However, with respect to gimmickry and structural fiddling – the matter of the first section – it was more imaginative and active than any peacetime government in Canadian history.

The 1970s saw various shifts in the balance of economic power. In part because of government subsidy and encouragement, life in the Atlantic region improved relative to that in central Canada. By autumn 1979, indeed, thanks to off-shore discoveries, a wave of gaseous and oily enthusiasm was sweeping Nova Scotia and Newfoundland. But the manufacturing industries of Quebec, based so largely on textiles, clothing, footwear, and other rather uncompetitive consumer goods, faced increasingly vigorous competition from imports. Here political events had some effect, and new developments did not arrive with sufficient speed or vigour to help meet new conditions, although in the late seventies the Quebec economy was performing surprisingly well. In so far as the Québécois encouraged an exodus of anglophone firms and businessmen they made matters worse for themselves, at least in the short run. In Ontario, although the Committee for an Independent Canada spoke of 'de-industrialization,' the industrial and financial community continued its rapid development. Regrettably, however, neither in Ontario nor in Quebec did labour productivity rise fast enough to provide the extra consumer goods that people thought they needed and should have. Also, the public was probably confused by the ever-growing wave of protest against 'extortionate' corporation profits; one seldom heard that corporations pulled in less than 10 per cent of GNP and that, on the average, they paid at least 35 per cent tax on the profits they garnered. Hence, doubtless, some of the pressure for extra money wages – a pressure that many blamed for the inflationary trends of the decade. In western Canada, the Trudeau years began with agricultural impoverishment and with flaccid markets for Alberta oil. But in 1973, when OPEC initiative transformed world oil markets, western Canada found itself more wealthy than ever before. Wheat farmers, too, did well on world markets for several years in the mid-seventies. Paradoxically, as westerners became more prosperous, they seemed to resent eastern Canada more than ever. In the mid- and late seventies, 'western alienation' was a vogue phrase that was also a fact of life.

Another fact of life in the seventies was concern for 'ecology,' a word whose meaning was elusive but whose effect was clear. Influenced by American models, Canadians talked and chattered and regulated and protested and legislated and delayed in an effort to ensure that things would stay as natural as possible – whatever that might mean. Greenpeace tried to safeguard whales and caribou. Brigitte Bardot was not alone in worrying about the baby seals of the St Lawrence. Much was heard about the fragile Arctic environment. Determined to appear to protect that fragility, Ottawa delayed approval of pipelines and created Justice Thomas Berger's inquiry to help find reasons for doing so. Some provinces drew up more stringent regulations regarding pollution and tried to undo the ravages of earlier decades. By 1979 the Great Lakes were noticeably less polluted than in 1968, although at Montreal the St Lawrence was still an open sewer. The federal authorities passed new laws and negotiated with the United States. Ontario pressed ahead with the development of nuclear power, and Ottawa did its best to peddle Canada's very own CANDU reactor from China to Peru, but there was widespread nervousness about nuclear safety, the impact of nuclear installations on the environment, and, most of all, nuclear proliferation. Canada could not escape the informational backwash from Pennsylvania's Three Mile Island incident; in Ontario especially, politicians ignored advisers' insistence that nuclear energy was safe. In many relatively small respects there was a good deal of tidying up, although never enough to satisfy the real enthusiasts. And as usual there was some sign of overshooting. Good though it might be in the abstract to preserve some Ungavan brook against pollution, prevention may also cost society a good deal, and a cost in one direction implies some sacrifice in another. Is it better to have a pure stream in Ungava, or a great big swimming pool in a crowded Montreal suburb? This sort of question was, if anything, even harder to raise and more difficult to answer in 1979 than in 1968.

A government had to care about the environment; it also had to care about people. Hence, presumably, the imaginative and unwise experiments with the unemployment insurance system that had been designed in 1940 and extended somewhat during the 1950s. In 1968 the scheme covered those who earned less than $7,800 per year, on the sensible grounds that the more prosperous were unlikely to become unemployed and that, if they did, they could look after themselves. The St Laurent and Diefenbaker governments extended the system to cover fishermen and farm workers and added the 'seasonal benefit' for the winter months, when persons had not worked long enough to qualify for ordinary benefit. Benefits came out of a fund, which was theoretically self-sustaining and fed by contributions from employees, employers, and the exchequer. For the new world of the Just Society, where problems of poverty and deprivation were much discussed, the old arrangements seemed too restrictive. The government therefore devised a new scheme, which it announced in 1969. Presenting it to the House, the Minister of Labour spoke in terms that made the government's intention perfectly clear: the plan would not simply insure against unemployment but provide 'individual development coupled with adequate income support.' In other words, unemployment insurance would become part of the welfare system. Everyone would be covered. Benefits would be raised, and they would be easier to get. Employees would pay a smaller share of the cost, and the national exchequer would contribute more. In 1971 the necessary bill was introduced and passed.

Some of the results became part of the national folklore. In certain parts of eastern Canada whole communities lived for much of the year on unemployment insurance, just as they had once lived on seasonal benefit; but now they lived much more comfortably than before and had less incentive to seek new jobs in other places. Some of the results were bizarre and unexpected. In the great cities, musicians and artists found that their living standards had a new underpinning, and the system provided a new and hidden subsidy to the arts.

Although unemployment insurance proved to be an income support plan for Quebec and eastern Canada, the Trudeau government was anxious to devise a more organized and purposive plan to help the poorer regions. In so doing, it should be remembered, it was concerned partly to develop a new nation-wide constituency that would naturally look to Ottawa for help, as, for example, manufacturers had looked to Ottawa in the bad old days of protectionism. The ARDA and FRED schemes for rural redevelopment, and also an Area Development Incentives plan that was due to expire in 1970, had been inherited from the Diefenbaker and Pearson years. Before 1968 was out, Trudeau had appointed Jean Marchand to a new portfolio, Regional Economic Expansion, soon christened DREE. In 1969, Parliament transferred ARDA and FRED to DREE and, under the Regional Development Incentives Act, gave DREE quite remarkable powers. By 1979, DREE was spending half a billion dollars a year.

Many observers thought that DREE worked with unemployment insurance to make the Canadian economy less flexible and less productive than it would otherwise have been. Ironically, these new arrangements coexisted with initiatives in competition policy, tariffs, and taxation, all of which were meant at first to make us *more* flexible and productive. But nothing much came of these new initiatives; it was 'DREE-ism' that triumphed in the end. In agriculture the triumph was delayed a little, but by 1975 it was complete.

So far as prairie farmers were concerned, the Trudeau government could do nothing right. They blamed it for transport problems, boxcar shortages, and bad conditions on world markets. They never forgot that in a moment of irritation the Prime Minister had asked, philosophically, 'Why should I sell your wheat?' But, given the Canadian Wheat Board, wheat marketing *was* Ottawa's responsibility. And as a marketer the Wheat Board's performance was not at all bad. From 1968 to 1975, annual cash receipts from wheat farming rose from $605 million to $1.7 billion, comfortably outstripping inflation and bringing new prosperity to the prairie provinces. Regrettably, in the late seventies wheat prices fell back, and wheat farmers' incomes shared in the retreat. Also, there were ever-increasing difficulties in the transport of wheat, chiefly because grain-shipping rates were controlled at so low a level that the railways had no incentive to provide rolling stock or to maintain track and stations. In addition, there were troubles in grain handling at the ports.

In summer 1979 the situation verged on a national scandal. The Clark government appointed a commissioner to see what could be done. In the 1979-80 campaign, Trudeau astonished most railway experts and convinced few farmers with a pledge to doubletrack the railways to the Pacific. During all this time, Alberta was awash in oil revenues, and Saskatchewan was doing relatively well out of oil, potash, and forest products. The wheat situation came to matter much less in the late seventies than it had in the late sixties, although naturally the wheat farmers did not see things that way. The wheat problem was difficult because so much of the output was exported under conditions that the Wheat

Board might hope to influence but could not control. Further, as in the sixties, a great deal depended on crop results in the Communist world. Thus China and Russia became Canada's principal customers, but their purchases were erratic, and, in the longer run, they were trying to become self-sufficient in grain. As for the British market, its future was dim once Britain had joined the European Economic Community in 1973. Europe's agricultural protectionism would soon drive Canadian wheat off Britain's markets.

As with wheat, so with other foodstuffs: after some years of reluctance the Trudeau government responded to pressure from producers who wanted more security and higher incomes. Here, however, the medicine was already available – more protection, more subsidy, and more power for the marketing boards.

By 1975 there were 108 of these, providing 57 per cent of farm income. Ottawa did what it could to co-ordinate and strengthen the boards, and in 1972 it provided a federal umbrella which, on provincial and producer request, would shelter producers whenever the provincial umbrellas proved leaky. Soon there were federal arrangements for eggs, turkeys, various fruits and vegetables, chickens, corn, tobacco, and – yes – pregnant mares' urine. Eugene Whelan, the Minister of Agriculture, conducted a continuous campaign to convince consumers that they should be glad to pay whatever prices the marketing boards might choose to extort.

These price-raising policies were especially odd given that the government also claimed to be fighting inflation. Sometimes the results were painful and absurd. At one time there was a mountain of powdered milk that the government could not give away. At another time there was a chain of egg warehouses whose contents the egg agency absentmindedly allowed to rot. One journalist suggested that by combining the rotten eggs with the skim milk the government could bake an enormous custard and use it as a symbol of national unity – or a platform for Arctic oil drilling. Few laughed.

In competition policy the government evinced a characteristic pattern of advance and retreat. On taking office its members seem to have believed that there could be and should be fundamental reform, and they planned to model that reform on the best textbook principles, as transmitted to the cabinet by the economists on the Economic Council of Canada staff and the Watkins task force. But as time passed the political realities gradually became clearer. Reform would hurt too many vocal interests. Consumers, who would stand to gain, were badly organized and mute. As the government became unpopular it could less readily carry a series of measures that excited so much opposition, especially from the business classes. The government proceeded cautiously, deciding to legislate gently, and in stages. In 1974 it introduced a mild measure, one that said nothing about mergers but that gave new powers to the authorities to prohibit many new things, including the extension of foreign laws and directives into Canada. This measure died, was reintroduced, provoked fierce controversy, and was finally passed. Meanwhile, nothing had been heard of monopolization and inefficiency. In 1975 the government set up a royal commission to examine the concentration of economic power. At length the commission reported that Canadians had almost nothing to worry about under that heading.

From the Carter Royal Commission on Taxation, which Diefenbaker had appointed in 1962, the Trudeau government inherited a 2,600-page report in six volumes (not counting the many research studies that accompanied it). Among specialists in public finance the report excited world-wide admiration. But, because the commission wanted to tax capital gains as income and also to tax the oil and mining industries more heavily, the reception within Canada was rather less joyous. In November 1969 Edgar Benson, the finance minister, tabled a White Paper on tax reform that already represented partial retreat from the full logical rigour of the Carter plan. Once again there was an outcry. Thus when in 1971 the government actually moved to modify the income tax system there was little relation between its proposals and Carter, and not much resemblance to the 1969 White Paper. Capital gains were to be taxed, but at a concessionary rate, and principal residences would be exempt. Although mining companies were taxed more heavily for the time being, these arrangements were soon changed as the nation worried more about energy. Not much was done about corporation taxation, which retained many allowances, concessions, and special arrangements – devices that would expand later in the decade and would shortly provide the basis for the NDP cry, 'Corporate welfare bums!'

Benson described the whole process – the steps from Carter to the White Paper and then to the bill – as an exercise in participatory democracy. The historian is much more likely to call it an exercise in futility and a splendid case study of pressure-group activity.

In trade policy, as in tax policy, there were inheritances from earlier governments that at first seemed to place the government's feet firmly on the path of liberalization – fewer and lower tariff barriers, as well as fewer non-tariff obstructions to trade. But here the inheritance was mixed, and the retreat to interventionism and protectionism even more pronounced.

Having committed itself to help poor countries' exports, the government in 1970 promised to reduce tariffs on many of these items. But it exempted the 'sensitive' goods, those on which Canada had imposed quotas. Charity began at home, chiefly in Quebec and the Atlantic region. In 1969 the government introduced the tariff cuts that had been negotiated under the Kennedy Round at GATT during the 1960s, and in the 1970s it participated actively in GATT's Tokyo Round. In 1979, when these talks were brought to a satisfactory conclusion,

High meat prices for Easter
(Wicks, 1973). Reproduced with the permission of Canada Wide Feature Service Ltd

there was much congratulation in Ottawa. In 1971, when President Nixon decided to subsidize American exports and to raise American tariffs, Canada did not retaliate, perhaps in large part because so many Canadian goods were exempted. Instead, while complaining bitterly in Washington, it provided transitional assistance to domestic industries. Recognizing that Commonwealth preferential tariffs now made little difference to Canada's transatlantic trade, when the British entered the European Economic Community in 1973 Canada wished Britain well and did not complain. In February 1973, many food tariffs were reduced as an anti-inflation device. But by October, when there was a chance that American beef imports would really have an effect on Canadian prices, John Turner raised the beef duties, more than offsetting the February reductions. From then on, Canadian trade policy seemed to become steadily more protectionist. The process was more visible with respect to non-tariff barriers. The Pearson government had begun in the sixties to impose import quotas so as to control the flow of cheap textiles, clothing, and shoes from the efficient low-wage countries of Asia and Latin America. In the seventies the quotas were retained, extended, and made more restrictive. Canada did agree to the tariff reductions in the 1979 GATT revision, and the rhetoric of freer multilateral trade continued to ring out from Ottawa. But as the unemployment problem became more pressing, Ottawa was less inclined to protect consumers and more inclined to protect farmers, industrialists, and workers in the endangered industries, especially those located in Quebec.

With respect to foreign investment, the same sort of shift toward protection-ism took place. In the sixties most professional opinion argued that the country had gained by welcoming so much foreign capital and that where harm had been done the fault had been Canada's. The government's proper task, therefore, was to manage things so as to increase the gains relative to the costs, remembering that the former were already much larger than the latter. This line had been tak-en in the Watkins Report of 1968, by the economist A.E. Safarian, and by al-most all qualified observers. Certainly in the late sixties the business community did not want the government to move from the benign acquiescence of the late sixties to the systematic screening and interventionism of 1971 and thereafter. The credit – if that is the word – belongs to three groups: nationalist sectarians among the intelligentsia and their echoes in the media; like-minded people with-in the Liberal party and caucus; and eager officials, anxious to 'regulate' foreign-owned firms in the national interest. In 1973 and afterward, additional pressure came from the oil price crisis and from later developments on the ener-gy front. In the background was an ever-increasing but unacknowledged echoing of American populist opinion, which held that large business is Bad, multina-tional business is Worse, and oil companies are Worst of All. Without infuriat-ing its own business supporters in Canada, the government could do little or nothing about the Bad. But by acting to 'control' the Worse and the Worst of All it could pacify its populist supporters and give its bureaucrats more work and more power.

The Watkins task force reported in February 1968. It called for more compe-tition, lower tariffs, more information about the foreign-owned firms, more taxa-tion of such firms, and a Canada Development Corporation. Most of the sugges-tions eventually made their way into law or regulation, although not soon enough to satisfy Professor Watkins or Walter Gordon. In 1972, Ottawa officials produced the Gray Report on the costs and benefits of foreign investment. It was much more hostile and interventionist than the Watkins Report. At once the gov-ernment introduced a measure that would have set up a takeover tribunal. In 1974 the tribunal did appear in the form of the Foreign Investment Review Agency (FIRA). Thereafter, until 1985, almost all takeovers and transfers of own-ership to foreign interests, or among them, were subject to screening – with ulti-mate decisions at cabinet level – as were most direct foreign investments in new enterprises and any foreign expansion into any new and unrelated areas of busi-ness.

What FIRA actually meant was hard to say. Naturally its promoters thought it did not go far enough, while many Canadian economists and businessmen thought it went rather too far. Tories and Americans liked to mutter about its iniquities. Certainly FIRA was not as all-encompassing as the Gray Report had suggested. Certainly, too, its results could be odd. Most academic observers, Canadian and otherwise, believed that the FIRA procedures were more rigorous and arbitrary than those of any other developed industrial country, several of which have similar schemes. More than two-thirds of all applications were approved, but gradually it became clear that the screening agency and the cabinet were developing criteria that went beyond the explicit letter of the act (the act also gave the cabinet a complete discretion that it was certainly willing to use). For example, by 1979 it was unwilling to permit foreign takeovers and transfers in publishing, even when the firm in question was already foreign-owned. The act did not provide a special status for publishing; presumably the government had decided that national virility required a Canadian-owned book industry. In Edmonton, publisher Mel Hurtig doubtless rejoiced.

There was more artillery used in the battle against the foreign firm. There were special rules to extrude foreigners from Canadian broadcasting and cable networks. Although the Canada Development Corporation, established in 1971, was not meant to buy back Canada, by 1979 it had purchased control of one multinational firm from American interests, fought takeover battles in Alberta oil, and collected a pharmaceutical firm that in earlier days would probably have passed into foreign control. In 1974 the government bought De Havilland Aircraft of Toronto from Hawker Siddeley of Britain, and Canadair from General Dynamics of the United States, in the hope that it could sell the two firms to Canadians. By 1979 it had not managed to do so. More or less by accident, Canada had nationalized most of its aerospace industry. Even more striking and most pregnant with possibilities was the arrival of Petrocanada.

On December 6, 1973, Trudeau told the House that the government would set up a national petroleum company. This body was meant to arrange for oil imports, work oil sands in Alberta, and explore for conventional oil and gas – in short, to coexist with multinationals such as Imperial, Texaco, and Gulf. In 1975 an appropriate bill was introduced and passed. The Conservatives thought it was not needed; the NDP (which wanted to nationalize Imperial Oil) thought that it did not go far enough.

Did Petrocanada do more than the multinationals would have done? Had it cost Canada less? No one knew. The truth is that in the national energy picture Petrocanada made very little difference. In the quagmire of federal energy policy it was more like a piece of floating turf than an island of safety and security. Canada could not escape the world-wide disturbances that swept the oil markets in 1973 and thereafter. Many Canadians thought that Petrocanada would insulate them from the external cold blasts, but *that* it could never do, although Trudeau and Broadbent hinted that it could. It was hardly surprising that Canadians were confused.

Until 1973 Canada's main problem had been to find markets for its oil. Ottawa worried about restrictive American quotas and preserved intact Diefenbaker's National Oil Policy, by which Ontario and western Canada were sequestered, protected markets for high-cost Alberta crude: in the early seventies, Iranian oil landed in Montreal for about $2.50 per barrel, while in Ontario Alberta oil cost $3.00. To keep out cheap foreign oil and gasoline, Ottawa maintained a sort of documentary dyke just west of the Ottawa River and kept the transcontinental oil pipelines well short of Montreal: after all, pipelines can move oil in either direction. But by November 1973, imported oil cost $7.50 per barrel, and by the end of the year it was over $10.00. The government spliced together a policy. The Montreal and Mackenzie pipelines were to be expedited. The Alberta tar sands were to be developed. Petrocanada was to be invented. Eastern Canada would use more price-controlled Canadian crude and import less. The improvisations were desperate; the pressure from the left was consistent; the goal was 'self-sufficiency' – or perhaps 'self-reliance'; the result was a vagueness too common in Canadian public life after 1973.

Now there was a natural conflict between the eastern provinces, which used most of the oil, and the western provinces, which owned it. Alberta wanted to get the world prices while Quebec and the Atlantic region bitterly resented that price and hankered after Alberta's artificially cheap crude, or, if they could not have that, a subsidy. Canada's oil imports roughly equalled its exports, but there was no convenient way to replace the former with the latter, given the pipeline systems and the long-term commitments to export.

All the provinces agreed that to establish a single nation-wide price the federal government could subsidize oil imports for Quebec and the Atlantic provinces. It was agreed that to stimulate domestic exploration and development the Canadian price would have to drift upward, though not necessarily to world levels. Meanwhile, by taxing oil export Ottawa would have some extra funds to help subsidize oil imports. Of course the effect of this package was to ensure that Canada would consume more oil, import more, and export less, than if prices were not held below world levels. Thus by 1979 the country was again a large net importer. The subsidies were a new and heavy burden; the country was more exposed than in 1973 to the next turn of the OPEC screw, which came in 1979 as the OPEC price rose rapidly toward $35 per barrel. The subsidy now cost over two and a half billion dollars a year.

The Alberta authorities controlled most domestic conventional production, which came from shrinking reserves. Hence it was believed that Canada would have to depend ever more on the costly oil from the tar sands, on heavy oil, and on new discoveries in faraway places – the Arctic, the off-shore Atlantic shelf, maybe even the Gulf of St Lawrence. In light of these facts it might have seemed sensible to cut domestic consumption as fast as possible by letting prices rise to the world level at once. But there were obvious political reasons for not doing this. The oil-importing zones were the poorer parts of the country in the 1970s; Quebec was solidly Liberal; and the NDP would not stand for any such thing.

If Canada was to be more 'self-reliant,' it would have to produce more oil. In the acrimonious disputes of 1974 Premier Lougheed of Alberta clearly recognized the implications for development. Trudeau probably did not. By early 1975, however, he had come to understand that there would have to be a compromise. Oil prices would have to rise in Canada; the provinces would have to receive a larger take, and the oil companies would have to get enough to encourage new exploration and development. Thus from 1975 through 1979, although the domestic oil price was kept consistently below the world price it was adjusted upward from time to time, after discussion and agreement with the provinces. Ottawa and Edmonton agreed to share the loot.

By early 1979 the universe of oil was unfolding as it should. Domestic oil, which brought $12.75 a barrel, had risen near the OPEC world price of $14.75. Within Canada new oil-sands production had come on stream, and exploration and development were proceeding apace, even though there was still no pipeline to the Arctic. But in 1979, the Iranian revolution produced a constriction in world supply at a time when world demand was rising rapidly once more. The result was a new upsurge of oil prices by OPEC and its imitators, such as Mexico. Within Canada the phenomena of 1974 quickly reappeared.

In autumn 1979 the Clark government argued about energy policy and negotiated anxiously with Premier Lougheed. Clark wanted an energy self-sufficiency bank and a much heavier federal tax on gasoline. The goal, he said, was self-sufficiency by 1990. But no one could be sure if the increases, or the new share-out, would satisfy the Albertans.

John Crosbie, the finance minister, naturally had to work the energy package into his December 11 budget. The proposals attracted fascinated and horrified attention. The government proposed to raise the gasoline tax by 4 cents per litre, or nearly 18 cents per gallon. The domestic oil price would rise $4 per barrel in 1980 and $4.50 per barrel in each of 1981, 1982, and 1983. A new federal tax would skim off $1 per barrel in 1980 and still more in 1981-3. Much of the new revenue would go into a new energy bank. Predictably these plans infuriated the consuming provinces, which had hoped to give less, and the producing ones, which had hoped to get more. Unfortunately there was no way to be sure that the measures would produce Clark's goal – self-sufficiency by 1990.

Meanwhile, Canada had been working hard to develop unconventional fuels. After the adventures of 1973 there was renewed interest in coal, both in British Columbia and in Nova Scotia, where it was hoped that coal-fired generators would help reduce the province's dependence on OPEC oil. Fundy tidal power, that perennial will-o'-the-wisp, once more made headlines but not electricity. There was some renewed interest in atomic power and in Canada's very own CANDU reactor. There were more wood stoves, some bio-gas generators, the occasional windmill, and a few solar water heaters. More interesting and much more promising were developments in Alberta and Saskatchewan, where oil sands and heavy oil were being tapped at last. The costs admittedly were very high, but so was the cost of conventional oil, especially from OPEC.

It may seem an easy step from oil price control to general wage and price control. Indeed, nothing makes the lurch toward interventionism clearer than the imposition of general control in 1975. Nevertheless, all the evidence suggests that the government was reluctant to take this step. When the Trudeau team was formed in 1968 there was already much talk about incomes policies. Britain had experimented several times with wage freezes and wage controls. In many countries it was thought that wage increases were causing prices to rise. But the government then believed that in Canada controls could not work. Much of the inflationary pressure came from abroad via Canada's immense import and export trade. Worse still, there was no consensus about controls; that is to say, the unions would not stand for them. So compulsion was pointless.

In December 1968 the authorities invented the Prices and Incomes Commission, and Dr John Young travelled from British Columbia to head it. The Commission could issue reports and recommendations, although it could not actually make anybody do anything at all. Nevertheless, the unions would have nothing to do with it, so Young really achieved very little. In 1972 his Commission itself asked for general but temporary controls on prices and wages. Many newspapers agreed with Young, but the government abolished the Commission.

In 1973, because food prices were rising especially rapidly, the government restricted the export of meat and subsidized the domestic consumption of wheat; but it was still unwilling to control food prices directly. Instead it invented the Food Prices Review Board, chaired by Beryl Plumptre. This board had no power, but, in accordance with current fashion, it was to 'monitor' price movements. It quickly set up a research division, and 'Plumptre's posses' descended on supermarkets. From time to time Mrs Plumptre announced that the great food chains were *not* the villains, and now and then she crossed swords with Eugene Whelan, whose price-raising activities in the Department of Agriculture should already have been a public scandal. But the result was copy for the journalist, nothing more.

At the same time, house prices continued to rise in most of Canada, and mortgages cost more than ever. The government's response was twofold: it would finance a land assembly and development scheme; it would support research on cheaper ways to service land. In the short run, both plans would cost money, not save it, and neither could quickly affect the housing market. Meanwhile, to prevent mortgage rates from going sky-high, funds were pumped into CMHC. The extra money raised house prices even faster and increased inflationary pressure throughout the economy; but at least the government seemed to be 'doing something about the housing crisis.'

As inflationary pressure continued, in 1973-5 there was new militancy among organized labour, especially in Quebec and more especially in public employment. Teachers, postmen, air traffic controllers – all were asking for wage increases that ranged from 20 per cent to 80 per cent. Strictly speaking such demands were not inflationary. Since most of the services in question were not *sold* to anyone, the demands implied higher taxes but usually not higher prices. Still, private employers faced the same sorts of demands, and there it was obvious that the results would be some mixture of higher prices, a weaker dollar, and fewer jobs.

By December 1974 the finance minister was trying to orchestrate a new program of voluntary restraint. Early in 1975 he announced that the chief cause of inflation was now wage push. But by May 1975 it was clear that labour would not co-operate in a voluntary program, and it had long been clear that John Turner did not want a compulsory one. At budget time, in June, Turner told the Commons that he and the cabinet had discussed controls but had rejected the idea. Then Turner left the cabinet in September, and the way was clear. On October 13 the Prime Minister told the House that there would be controls after all. The plan was to last for three years at least. The CLC planned a national day of protest, but no one paid much attention because the controls were really very popular. The provinces swung quickly into line, some of them using the federal initiative as an excuse for comprehensive rent controls. Prices and wages still rose, but the rate of increase fell, and academic studies suggested that the controls program might actually be credited for some of this decrease. By 1978 prices were rising much less rapidly than in 1974-5, and the extraordinary wage demands seemed to be bad memories from the past. But there was still plenty of wage push, and the money supply was still growing very fast – by over 14 per cent in 1977, and over 10 per cent in 1978. The country was running a massive deficit on current account, and the government's financial position had changed from comfortable to disastrous.

Would controls actually end in 1978? The *coup de grâce* was administered after the Prime Minister had visited West Germany, whose record of stable prices and rapid growth was the envy of the world. In mid-summer 1978, after his return from Bonn, Trudeau announced that controls would end that autumn. He went on to say that the real problem was the government deficit: this time there would be genuine cuts in public spending!

As for labour relations, the West German success offered no solution for Canada. Experience since 1970 suggested to thoughtful scholars that no miracle cures existed for a labour relations system that observers on all sides admitted was close to breakdown. Labour union membership in Canada had grown continuously since the 1960s (unlike in the United States), primarily because of the rapid expansion of public service unions. In 1962 there were slightly over one and a half million organized workers, in 1973, well over two and a half. In the 1970s the man-days lost from strikes and lockouts soared to levels over four times that of the early 1960s. The Woods Commission which investigated why this happened found many explanations but no easy palliatives. In 1975, the CLC talked much about 'tripartism,' pointing to the successful labour-management-government co-operation in prosperous West Germany and Scandinavia. After a feeble attempt to initiate this by labour and government, many concluded that such a system could come to Canada only slowly. Most, in labour, government, and the press, concluded that it should not come at all.

Meanwhile, as the federal-provincial shared-cost programs had become ever more expensive and alarming, labour began to worry about losing some of its gains. By agreeing to split the cost of health, education, and welfare with the provinces, Ottawa had committed itself to make outlays that it could not control. From time to time the federal government would try to negotiate a rearrangement by which its own costs were controlled. In 1977 it was obliged to impose a solution: for the next five years its contributions would escalate automatically in step with the growth of GNP, not with actual spending on higher education and medicare. Understandably the provinces, no matter how much they valued their own financial autonomy, were reluctant to swallow Ottawa's medicine. Over and over again Ottawa had to impose a solution on the provinces. By 1975 the great federal initiatives had come, although their full long-run cost was yet to be digested. Unemployment insurance and welfare had been modernized; health and old age had been provided for; eastern Canada was running on subsidized oil. Now the bills were coming in. They were horrendous. But again the economic situation made solutions difficult to find.

Year after year the problem was inflation. Or so a succession of finance ministers and central bankers told the Canadian people. There was, in addition, an unemployment problem. Although employment and output went up year by year, unemployment figures also increased both because the labour force was

(Donato, c1978). Reproduced with the permission of Canada Wide Feature Service Ltd

growing quickly and because, as we saw in the last section, structural changes tended to raise them. Not only were the boom babies of the forties and fifties coming on to the job market; more women were entering the work-force. Further, in spite of the unemployment figures, immigrants flocked to Canada whenever the government would give them visas – and often when it would not.

For inflationary pressure the orthodox fiscal medicine is higher tax rates, lower government spending, or both. But these weapons create more unemployment, at least in the short run. Hence any government would be reluctant to use them when unemployment is already a political issue. Further, year by year federal spending was ever more clearly out of control. Too many uncontrollable items had been built into the budget, both in the federal outlay pattern and in the system of grants and subsidies to persons, junior governments, and businesses. Ottawa could reduce its own capital outlays, but these were small relative to everything else. It could restrict growth in the civil service, but officials could not readily be fired, and, in a relatively young service, attrition was bound to be slow – especially given the generous salaries and benefits that Pearson had introduced and that the Trudeau government greatly augmented. There was also genuine doubt among economists in the seventies about the efficacy of traditional fiscal policy. Suppose that the main inflationary pressure came from wage push? If income tax rates were raised, what would happen? Might not workers just demand higher money wages, offsetting the effect of the higher taxes?

At first there was an attempt to use traditional weapons in traditional ways. But after 1972 matters became more complicated, and the macroeconomic direction became very unclear indeed. Late in 1973 Prime Minister Trudeau announced that the government would battle inflation by raising various welfare payments and subsidies – exactly the wrong medicine. In May 1974 the budget was equally perverse. Finance minister John Turner proposed to reduce personal tax rates and to cut some sales taxes, while taxing corporations, vehicles, and alcohol more heavily. The budget, Turner explained, was meant to increase *supply*, thereby fighting inflation. But in the short run supply could not increase much, while inflation must be fought from month to month and week to week. In June 1975, price controls not yet having been introduced, Turner presented a 'neutral' budget. To increase supply and maintain investment there were various new gadgets. Some sales and excise taxes were raised and others were lowered, but now the main thrust was toward cost control. The unemployment scheme would be changed so as to save money, and so would medicare grants to the provinces. Government spending would be restrained in a sense; it would grow only 15 per cent instead of the 20 per cent that had originally been intended. The next year saw a new finance minister and another change of direction. In 1977 and 1978, although none of its critics thought that it was going far enough, the

Trudeau government responded by systematically cutting taxes and raising outlays in the face of its ever-widening budget deficit.

Although no one would have predicted such a development from the tenor of
the spring election campaign, by December 1979 it seemed that the Conservative cabinet had decided that austerity was the watchword. When John Crosbie
presented his budget on December 11, he told Canadians that the problem was
inflation; the government would have to manage its affairs with prudence so as
gradually to restore a balance between income and outgo; gone without trace
was the Clark plan for a sharp but temporary cut in the income tax. Corporations
would pay more tax at once, and so would consumers of beer, wine, cigarettes,
and gasoline. Unemployment insurance premiums would go up.

When inflation coexists with economic growth, as in Canada during the
1970s, government revenues will rise automatically unless tax rates are cut. If
old programs do not become more costly or if new programs are not invented,
the result will be a steady growth in the government surplus, and this surplus
will have an ever-larger anti-inflationary effect. But Canada's federal government had gradually adopted many programs whose costs could not easily be
controlled. Further, by indexing personal exemptions and by raising so many
pensions and other benefits to offset the effects of inflation, the government had
connived at an erosion of its own tax base and a further increase in its uncontrollable outlays. To make matters worse, from time to time the government transferred more of the shared-tax fields, especially the income tax, to the provinces.
Then there was lavish if temporary expansion of some old programs, such as
DREE, coupled with a tendency to invent new programs. One notable example
was the oil import subsidy. Meant originally to be self-balancing through the tax
on oil exports, the subsidy soon became a heavy charge on the exchequer. There
was also a noticeable and increasing tendency to cut business taxes rather than
personal income taxes so as to encourage business investment. Even though in
1975-8 federal revenues marched on upward, expenses grew faster. To finance
its operations the government had to borrow from the Bank of Canada and from
anyone else who would lend to it. Throughout the seventies it was an active borrower because it had to finance so many things – CMHC, extra holdings of US
dollars in certain years, and also the investment plans of the Canadian National
Railways and of so many other Crown corporations.

Lavish though the developments of the Trudeau years had been, as taxer and
spender the federal government had in fact long since lost primacy to the junior
governments. In 1974 the federal surplus was only 0.4 per cent of GNP. It
seemed that the government might be wise to ignore the macroeconomic impact
of its own taxing and spending, concentrating instead on the manipulation of
business investment. In the mid-seventies, indeed, some economists thought

themselves foolish to spend so much time analysing Ottawa's deficits and surpluses. But the period 1975-8 saw an explosion of federal spending. Deficits reappeared, and they yawned ever wider, so that in 1978 the federal deficit was 5 per cent of GNP – quite large enough to affect unemployment, inflation, and the value of the dollar.

After 1974 the federal fiscal position went from bad to worse. Every year there were deficits, and these grew steadily. It is no wonder that in the 1979 election the Tories could say that the budget was out of control, and the Liberals could not defend themselves very well. But the problem had complicated origins. Federal revenues grew quite steadily, from $29 billion in 1974 to $37 billion in 1978, a gain of 28 per cent. Federal spending on goods and services – that is, on salaries and commodities – rose $5 billion, of which $1.6 billion was extra defence outlays. The cost of the debt more than doubled, rising from $3 billion to $6.4 billion. But transfer payments to persons, such as unemployment insurance, rose from $8.7 billion to $14.6 billion, while payment to the provinces rose from $6 billion to $10.5 billion; subsidies to businesses, including the oil import subsidies, rose from $2.8 billion to $4 billion. In percentage terms, *every* kind of spending was outgrowing revenue. But there was plenty of extra revenue to cover the extra outlay on goods and services. Thus in a sense it is all the other things – subsidies to persons, businesses, and provinces, plus debt-service – that pushed the federal exchequer so very deeply into the red. Indeed, by 1978, to bring the budget back into balance *without* cutting these subsidies and grants would have forced Ottawa to reduce its basic outlays on goods and services from $12 billion to $0.6 billion. In 1979 the Clark government would talk of shrinking the public payroll by 60,000 persons. But it could not possibly shed enough public servants to dent the deficit very much.

Whatever the government may have been saying at the time, it would be absurd to maintain that Ottawa was really fighting inflation in 1975-9. If federal taxing and spending were aimed in any particular direction, that direction was anti-unemployment. But we should ask ourselves whether, given the origins of the deficits, Ottawa could really have done much better. To a quite remarkable extent deficits came from things that the government could change slowly or not at all. Indeed, in real terms federal spending on goods and services was almost constant, and it was certainly rising less rapidly than national output. In principle, of course, Ottawa could have raised tax rates. But in 1978, to balance the budget would have implied a 31 per cent increase in federal taxation. Need we wonder why no one tried or why federal finance ministers came and went?

Whatever the frustrations of macroeconomic management in a federal state where spending is out of control, Ottawa certainly could and did manage the exchange rate and the national holdings of foreign money, the foreign exchange reserves, all by itself. Occasionally a province would bleat that it should be allowed a voice. But although Ottawa politicians certainly listened to the voters all across the country, with respect to the exchange rate they did not listen to the provincial premiers. Nor, after December 1968, did they need to heed the Americans with respect to the foreign exchange reserves.

By that time Bank of Canada Governor Louis Rasminsky, seriously worried about inflation, wanted to control the money supply quite tightly. Thus in 1969 national output grew 5.3 per cent, while chartered bank reserves *fell* slightly, and in 1970 reserves and output grew in step with one another. These arrangements were part of an anti-inflation campaign that probably created more unemployment in 1969-70 than either Rasminsky or the government had intended. When unemployment rose still more in 1971-2, the monetary system expanded very rapidly indeed, and it is tempting to suspect that this expansion was an anti-unemployment policy.

The anti-inflation campaign of 1969-70 attracted funds from abroad. Also, in 1970, for the first time in nearly twenty years, we began to run a *surplus* in the current account of our balance of payments. Foreign purchases fell slightly. Receipts from abroad jumped sharply upward; the result was a current account surplus of nearly one billion dollars.

These developments produced enormous pressures on Canada's monetary system. The government could keep the exchange rate pegged at 92.5 American cents only by massive purchases of foreign money on the foreign exchange market. But, as we have noted several times in earlier chapters, to make such purchases the Bank basically creates Canadian money in the required amount, adding to the money supply and to inflationary pressure. Although the causes were not quite the same as in early 1950 (when the fixed exchange rate had last been abandoned), the manifestations were basically similar, and the authorities responded in the same way: on May 31, 1970, the Canadian dollar was allowed to float away from its 1962 peg.

For the rest of the 1970s the Canadian dollar floated. It floats still. But the float has been a very dirty one. Trying to moderate the movements of the floating rate, the government built up reserves of foreign money at some times, while at others it spent its reserves, or even, by the late 1970s, borrowed abroad. Sometimes, as in 1970-1, when Canada's exports exceeded its imports, the dollar was strong. At other times, and increasingly, it was weak. The strength of the dollar on foreign exchange markets depended critically on international movements of capital. When a lot of foreign money was flowing into Canada, the dollar tended to be strong; when foreign money and Canadian money was leaving, it was weak. A strong dollar tended to moderate inflationary pressures by making imports cheaper; a weak dollar had the opposite effect.

Although fiscal policy and exchange-rate policy were sensibly anti-inflationary at least some of the time in the early and mid-seventies, most of the time the Bank of Canada and the financial system were systematically stoking inflationary fires. Except in 1970, the money supply regularly outgrew the output of goods and services.

Until after 1974 the government's own deficit was not to blame, because in 1969-74 there was a cumulative federal-government surplus. But in 1975-8 the federal deficits were so large that the Bank of Canada had to create a great deal of extra money just to help finance the government of Canada. Also, some government projects – CMHC, the exchange reserves, the Crown corporations – often needed more finance than the budget could provide from current taxation. Further, the inflationary process itself created a need for more money and credit, just to keep the wheels of commerce turning. If the price level doubles, the typical household will need twice as many dollars, on average, just to bridge the distance between one payday and another. Credit cards, which proliferated in the seventies, provided a considerable cushion offset, but not a complete one.

In principle the Bank of Canada could have followed the same sort of tight-money policy that James Coyne had followed in the late fifties. Since the dollar was floating in both decades, the effect would have been much the same – a more valuable dollar, more imports, fewer exports, a much larger inflow of foreign capital, more unemployment. Prices would therefore have risen more slowly; but these unpleasant side-effects would have been unpopular, to say the least. However, the Bank and the government might have argued that they were simply following the same sort of expansionary path that other countries, especially Britain and the United States, were taking. Indeed, in 1973-5 it was usual for Ottawa to say that because inflation was a world-wide phenomenon Canada could not really avoid it. This was a half-truth at best. West Germany is as tied to the world economy as Canada is. So is Switzerland. Yet the German mark and the Swiss franc rose ever higher, and in both countries there was little inflation. Perhaps this was one of the many things that the Prime Minister learned on that fateful visit to Bonn in summer 1978.

The Bank knew perfectly well that its policies were adding to inflation. By the late seventies it had begun to announce its targets for monetary expansion, and it said that it would lower these targets year by year so as to convince people that there would not be enough money to fuel further inflation. Regrettably, just when the Bank was announcing this new line of policy, the federal budget deficit was moving out of control. It would remain to be seen who would give way – the Bank's governor or the finance minister. By late 1979 some observers were expecting to see a revival of the Diefenbaker confrontations, with a different cast but with the same basic plot.

During the 1970s Canadians all learned new lessons. The Canadian economy became a major topic for debate at dinner parties and for concern in corporate boardrooms. The decade disappointed most Canadians, perhaps because their expectations had been so high in 1970. That was not so in 1979.

28

Quebec and the Constitution: Phase One

The constitution, Pierre Trudeau told the House of Commons in January 1968, was 'not very high on the list of priorities as things that this country must do.' Yet under Trudeau the Canadian constitution changed as much as it had in the previous century; to many of his supporters, it was his principal monument.

The paradox was present from the beginning. Trudeau had given considerable thought to constitutional questions before he became prime minister. His interest was not restricted to any special area: questions of the division and balance of powers, of individual political rights, and of language had all received his attention and comment before he arrived in Ottawa. Once there, he quickly put together a team consisting of Carl Goldenberg, a distinguished Montreal lawyer and frequent royal commissioner, and Ivan Head, a law professor from the University of Alberta. Soon, Prime Minister Pearson announced, he would ask the provinces to consider a bill of rights, to be embedded in the Canadian constitution. Change, apparently, was in the wind.

Trudeau rejected any idea that the British North America Act, as it then was, needed fundamental revision. His view was much the same as St Laurent's: the provinces already had all the power they needed to shape their own destinies. Demands for more power and more money were, by the same token, unreasonable, reflecting not so much real needs as the appetite for power of their sponsors – the provincial politicians and provincial bureaucracies. Such demands took little account of either the national interest or its guardian, the federal government. It was up to the Trudeau government to stand firm and preserve Ottawa's freedom to act as an arbiter in Confederation and as a leader for the country in international affairs.

Trudeau represented a legitimate strand of Quebec thought or opinion, one often overlooked both inside that province and in the rest of Canada. Most articulately represented by Henri Bourassa at the turn of the twentieth century, it urged French-speaking Quebeckers to seek their future in a larger Canada rather than a narrower Quebec; it stressed safeguards for individual rights rather than the collective responsibilities of a beleaguered French-Canadian people. It denied that the Quebec government was the sole or even the predominant repository of the French-Canadian nation in North America. As St Laurent once put it, Quebec was a province like the others. St Laurent had compromised on the matter, but Trudeau had a different personality, and different experience.

Trudeau's views notwithstanding, there was substantial demand for change in the country, especially in Quebec where it was most forcibly expressed by the Union Nationale premier, Daniel Johnson. Johnson, too, had written a book, *Egalité ou Indépendance* (Equality or Independence), which preached a new, provincially centred destiny for the French Canadians in their real homeland – Quebec. Johnson's own feelings were ambivalent and, perhaps, vacillating. At times he seemed to be veering toward indépendance; at others he seemed prepared to let events take their natural course toward an unknown destination. But Johnson's position was highly significant, not just for its influence on Quebec government policy, but also for the appeal it had for an increasing number of Québécois – whether Union Nationale supporters or not – who demanded that Ottawa's power over their province be diminished and that Quebec be accorded a larger influence over whatever federal powers remained. At its crudest, 'equality' meant giving Quebec an equal say in the running of the central government. And that directly challenged the basis of representation – as well as the foundations of political power – across the country.

It is not surprising that this proposition was not taken seriously. In 1968, Quebec had roughly 28 per cent of the population. In wealth and population, it was outdistanced by Ontario alone. English Canadians outside Quebec could see little justice in the demand for equality; as far as most English-language commentators could judge, Québécois enjoyed the same opportunities as other Canadians, as individuals, and it was for them to make the most of things. Any other solution would give the inhabitants of Quebec extra privileges at the expense of other Canadians and their national government.

But Johnson's preaching could not be ignored altogether. The Premier of Ontario, John Robarts, had admitted as much when he summoned the representatives of the provinces to a public think-tank, the Confederation of Tomorrow conference. Ensconced on the fifty-fourth floor of the Toronto-Dominion Centre, overlooking the distant smokestacks of Buffalo, the premiers encouraged one another with centennial goodwill. Changes might possibly be made, and, Johnson was told, they might be enough to justify Quebec's continued presence in Canada. But it would have to be a modernized sixties version of Canada, a much reformed country.

The Pearson government succumbed to the pressure of Robarts's example. It summoned a constitutional conference to meet in Ottawa in February 1968 to consider what needed to be done about the hoary old BNA Act. The mere fact that the conference had been summoned indicated that something new was needed; by tossing the constitution in the pot, the federal government brought it into question: a subtle, but tangible, delegitimization of the federal position.

The federal government's prescription for constitutional reform faithfully represented Trudeau's commitment to individual rights over those of groups. Guarantees of language rights, entrenchment of a bill of rights in the constitution, binding commitments from all the provinces, and the transfer of the power to amend the BNA Act from Westminster to Canada were the federal government's proposals. In May 1970, the Minister of Justice, John Turner, announced that 'substantial agreement had been reached.' Language rights, access to taxation, regional disparities, and shared-cost programs were among the areas of 'substantial agreement.'

The way seemed to have been smoothed by the election of a Liberal government in Quebec in April 1970. The new Bourassa government was committed to demonstrating that federalism was 'profitable' for Quebec; at the same time, Bourassa and his advisers, including Claude Morin, stood out for a larger role for the province in social policy and, later, communications. Morin's view was encapsulated in some remarks he made to Jean Chrétien: 'We'll separate from Canada the same way that Canada separated from England: we'll cut the links one at a time, a concession here and a concession there, and eventually there'll be nothing left.'[1] Some of these concessions were to be debated in a constitutional conference scheduled for Victoria in June 1971.

That conference at first seemed successful. After a lengthy negotiating session, a 'Canadian Constitutional Charter, 1971' was proclaimed. The charter was much more modest than Trudeau's original intentions. It entrenched a limited number of personal freedoms, but only 'subject to such limitations ... as are reasonably justifiable in a democratic society in the interests of public safety, order, health or morals, of national security, or of the rights and freedoms of others.' Such a compromise would have guaranteed the courts a busy time in the years ahead as lawyers and judges struggled to penetrate the murky language of the Charter.

Language rights, too, represented a compromise. The right to use French in Parliament and the legislatures was guaranteed, except in Saskatchewan, Alberta, and British Columbia. French could be used in federal courts, and in other courts in New Brunswick, Newfoundland, and Quebec – but not in Ontario, with

1   Quoted in Ron Graham, *The One-eyed Kings: Promise and Illusion in Canadian Politics* (Toronto: Collins, 1986), p. 66.

its 482,000 French-speakers. The constitution of the Supreme Court was to be altered to permit provincial participation in the nomination of judges and to ensure that any case involving Quebec's civil law would always be heard by a panel with a majority of Quebec justices. There was to be a domestic amending formula, involving varying numbers of the provinces, but giving Ontario and Quebec a veto over any change. And there was to be a compromise on social policy, with Ottawa conceding provincial primacy in the important areas of pensions and social benefits.

It is remarkable that so much could be agreed, even if the agreement was 'tentative.' It was decided that all provinces and the federal government must state their concurrence within ten days. Bourassa, who had not achieved as much as he wanted, returned home with deep forebodings. These proved justified. Within days a storm of protest swept through Quebec. The federal government still had too much power; Quebec had been faced with an ultimatum; equal status, special status, or anything remotely resembling them, was not conceded. The Victoria Charter would not do. And so Bourassa said, on June 23.

'If there isn't agreement, then that is the end of the matter, for now, or for a while, I hope,' Trudeau had said. Although some expressed the hope that all was not lost, it was evident that no new initiatives were likely. To some, Bourassa's refusal meant that no accommodation was possible with Quebec inside the federal system. To some Quebeckers, it meant that no accommodation was possible with English Canada; that in turn implied that French Canada would never be able to speak to English Canada 'd'égal à égal.' And, if equality meant a province with vastly increased powers inside and outside the federal government, that impression was correct. To English Canadians, Victoria was not a stage on the route to either total decentralization or 'two nations,' but a means to make the existing constitution more workable, and, it was hoped, more palatable to Quebec as well as to themselves. If neither aim could be achieved, then the present arrangements would have to do.

Although federal-provincial discussions over the constitution were suspended for the moment, ordinary federal-provincial diplomacy continued. Fiscal agreements for 1972-7 had to be negotiated; as usual they resulted in further redistribution of federal tax revenue to the provinces, so that the provincial share of the income tax 'take' reached 30.5 per cent. Because Quebec had long since 'opted out' of most federal shared-cost programs, the level of federal income taxation remained much lower there than elsewhere, and the provincial share, collected directly by the province, much higher.

Shared-cost programs remained a large proportion of the federal budget. Some of them were costly – too much so in the minds of the Trudeau cabinet and its officials. The temptation to apply a 'Quebec solution' to the other provinces was therefore financially tempting and philosophically congenial; once again Quebec would be a province just 'like the others.' Medicare was the first target. The federal government announced that it intended to place a ceiling on its contributions to a scheme which it had itself fathered; the provinces could pay the balance, if they wished, or make cutbacks. As might have been expected, the federal démarche produced a storm of indignation among the provinces. Indignation spawned unity: all the provinces agreed that they wanted more money – much more – from Ottawa if the national government intended to leave them footing the bill. At the end of 1976, when the fiscal agreements for 1977-82 were complete, they had largely obtained what they wanted.

In one aspect of economic management, as we shall see, the federal government compounded its own weakness through concessions to the provinces to manage the marketing of agricultural products. That, added to the provinces' pronounced tendency to conduct their own economies as far as possible in the narrowest interests of their own work-forces or industries, helped to intensify economic divisions within the country. Although still largely intact, the Canadian common market was flawed. The provinces, one economist commented, 'have not failed to infringe on the spirit, and sometimes on the letter, of the Constitution. They have thus impaired the Canadian common market.' This was exaggerated, but it would not seem unreasonable to predict that, left to their own devices, the provinces will most often act to impair the spirit and the letter of the constitution and where caught out – as the Maritime provinces were over offshore mineral rights, or Quebec over cable TV jurisdiction – will rely on political pressure to give them what the courts do not. The Trudeau government's overall record in federal-provincial relations was sometimes mixed: bold in approach, but often enfeebled and infirm in withstanding the provinces' political demands. No matter: the provinces refused to be satisfied, and Trudeau, surveying the record, drew his own conclusions. The brief Clark government was less bold even than Trudeau partly because of idological preconceptions, expressed in the phrase 'a community of communities.'

Before 1979, for most English Canadians the constitution meant Quebec. Here hopes were brightest in 1968. Canadians outside Quebec expected that Trudeau, a Québécois with a distinguished command of both languages and a reputation for saying the same thing in both, would restore Quebec to a state of harmony inside the Canadian federal family. Some commentators (not to mention the Lévesque government) have interpreted this to be a desire 'to put Quebec in its place,' presumably beside the national coal scuttle, ready to fetch and carry for its bloated anglophone brethren. This was, and is, a misconception. Trudeau hoped to give the Québécois, as individuals, a stronger place in the Canadian federal system; as for their government, that was in Ottawa as well as Quebec City. The same links of patriotism and self-interest that bound the citizen to the one should apply to his or her relations with the other. Most Canadians agreed.

This perception of the proper relations between the province and the central government did not attract large sections of the Quebec intelligentsia, who were for the most part committed to a conception of 'deux nations' in a single state, with the province of Quebec equalling in the balance of power the 70 per cent of Canadians who lived outside it. And only one step beyond 'deux nations' was its intellectual twin, the 'souveraineté-association' preached by René Lévesque. It might be said that in the final analysis 'souveraineté-association' was the same as 'deux nations'; it was simply that the first required a more drastic rupture of the constitutional balance in order to convince English Canadians that Quebec would in the future occupy a place that was separate but equal inside a confederal state of very limited powers.

It was obvious that Trudeau's ideas were seriously at variance with the conception that Quebec (and all the French-speaking Quebeckers inside it) formed a 'collectivité' animated by collective cravings for separate institutions, jurisdictions, and destinies, focusing on what was local and controllable, and denying that on important matters the Québécois could or should share their experiences or interests with their neighbours. In this conception the contrary also obtained: non-Québécois influence on Quebec society should be reduced to a minimum. And that applied particularly on the touchy issue of language.

Officially, English and French enjoyed equal status in the Quebec legislature (renamed in a grand gesture the 'National Assembly' in 1968) and Quebec courts, as well as in the federal Parliament and courts. The Protestant minority in Quebec and the Catholic minority in Ontario had a right to their own separate schools, thanks to compromises at the time of Confederation. But it was not along Protestant and Catholic lines that conflict developed, but along those of language. There were, in 1971, 888,000 persons using the English language at home in Quebec, and 4,870,000 who used French. The English-speakers were and are overwhelmingly concentrated in or around the Island of Montreal; English-speaking pockets elsewhere in the province were and are relatively insignificant – except, of course, to their inhabitants.

The English minority in Quebec has a peculiar composition. As of the 1971 census, 36 per cent of those identifying themselves as English-speaking Quebeckers had been born outside the province; in addition, outside the province, there were some 713,000 persons of English mother tongue who had been born in Quebec (more than the native-born Quebec remnant of anglophones inside the province). Thus, while the English-language group in Quebec has continued to grow, slowly, in absolute numbers, it has suffered a steady hemorrhage of its

'Of course it's difficult for outsiders to grasp the subtle complexities of the situation here in Québec.'
(Aislin, c1977). Reproduced with the permission of Aislin: *The Montreal Gazette*

members, who have departed to what are presumably more congenial climes elsewhere in Canada. This process has been going on for some considerable time and is neither a phenomenon simply of the past decade nor a direct consequence of the emergence of the Parti Québécois as a political force. The list of towns outside Montreal that were once English and are now French provides mute but eloquent testimony to decades of out-migration by Quebec's English residents: Sherbrooke, Magog, Waterloo, Huntingdon, and Ormstown are useful examples.

These facts might have been comforting to Quebec's nationalists if they had not had their eyes firmly fixed elsewhere. The percentage of Quebec residents of French mother tongue dipped slightly between the censuses of 1951 and 1961, from 82.5 per cent to 81.2 per cent, and it dipped again, to 80.7 per cent in 1971 (although it had been 79.6 per cent in 1931). It did not take long for some demographers to draw a picture of a tidal wave of English-speakers, with their immigrant allies, swamping the French institutions of Quebec, first in Montreal and then in the rest of the province.

It was in Montreal that the first trouble came. In the autumn of 1969, a dispute over educational facilities offered to the children of Italian immigrants in the Montreal suburb of St Léonard – fanned by extremist elements – turned into a riot. The Union Nationale government of Jean-Jacques Bertrand (who had succeeded Daniel Johnson on the latter's death in 1968) responded in three ways: it unsuccessfully prosecuted those prominently involved in the riots; it appointed a royal commission to study the whole problem of language in Quebec; and it introduced Bill 63, affirming that parents in Quebec had freedom of choice in their children's language of education. The bill stipulated that every child attending school in Quebec should, as a matter of course, learn French, but that proviso was lost to view in the brouhaha that followed. Freedom of choice, for the nationalists, was the worst solution of all: a heavy dose of legislative coercion was what they demanded. The outcry was loudest, as was to be expected, from the French-language teachers and among students in French-language universities. The latter staged a one-day strike in protest, but the bill was passed all the same.

It is not surprising that the agitation over Bill 63 stirred deep feelings on both sides. There was hostility on the part of those nationalists who believed that Quebec's French future and identity were threatened and who drew sustenance from a study for the Royal Commission on Bilingualism and Biculturalism that showed French-speaking Quebeckers clinging to the bottom of the economic ladder and English-speaking Quebeckers clustering near the top. The English-speaking Quebeckers reacted with alarm at the threat to rights and institutions they had always enjoyed and for which, as private citizens and as taxpayers, they had paid.

A provincial election was due in 1970. In January, the Liberal party found itself a new leader. The principal candidates were Claude Wagner, Attorney General under the old Lesage government, Pierre Laporte, the former Minister of Municipal Affairs, and Robert Bourassa, a young economist elected for the first time to the assembly in 1966. There might have been a fourth candidate, Jean Marchand, the Minister of Regional Economic Expansion in Ottawa, but Trudeau dissuaded his Quebec lieutenant from running. He did not prevent him from intervening in the Liberal convention, however, and it was with Marchand's strong support that Bourassa became Liberal leader.

Bourassa immediately led his party in the Quebec general election, called for April 29. The Liberals stressed two themes in their campaign. In French-language ridings, they stressed economic development and the economic dangers of separatism; in English-language ridings they had no difficulty using the threat of separatism pure and simple. Immigrant groups, remembering the separatist Parti Québécois's fervent opposition to Bill 63, had no difficulty in voting against separatism. In the election, the Liberals received 45 per cent of the vote and seventy-two seats. The Parti Québécois got 24 per cent of the vote and seven seats; the Union Nationale, with fewer votes, got more seats, and the title of official opposition.

The Bourassa government was markedly different from its predecessors in style and, some might argue, in content as well. The new premier fervently believed in keeping in close touch with the grass roots of his party; the telephone was his talisman, carrying out appeals for help and information at all hours and bringing in return advice and warnings. Through the grass roots, and the Liberals' fund-raisers, Bourassa kept close contact with the Ottawa Liberals – this despite the official and public distance maintained between the two parties.

Relations between the federal and provincial Liberals were never simple or easy. It was generally true that Liberals federally were Liberals provincially, and the two parties had a common anti-separatist ideology that drew them closer together. But Bourassa, gawky, young, and inexperienced, cut an unimpressive figure beside the dashing Trudeau; it was easy for opposition propagandists to claim that Ottawa was dominating Quebec through its novice premier.

This became painfully apparent during and after the October Crisis in the autumn of 1970. To all intents and purposes, the federal and Quebec governments stood shoulder to shoulder against terrorism and against extra-constitutional attempts to exploit the crisis in the interests of a Quebec united against Ottawa. But it was suspected that during the crisis Trudeau had operated at long range, imposing his will on a confused and terrified Bourassa through his personal emissary in Quebec City, Marc Lalonde. This image is doubtless exaggerated, but the October Crisis blurred so many images, and this is merely one.

There had been little political violence in Canada in the twentieth century. Moreover, Canada was also at peace externally, a happy contrast to its belligerent southern neighbour, then bogged down in the Vietnam War. With a philosopher-prime minister known to disapprove of the military (which had just been drastically reduced in size), this state of affairs seemed likely to continue.

The military, certainly, was discontented, but its opinions counted for little. It found new roles to play: in the autumn of 1969, when the police of Montreal went out on strike, the army was called in by the civil authorities to restore order after a night of rioting. In the fall of 1969, however, the Montreal authorities had something else on their minds: terrorism. The cause of an independent Quebec had not yet flourished at the polls, and some of its sympathizers, especially those on the extreme left, thought it was time to hurry things along with a few well-placed bombs. In their view the illegitimate capitalist state was by its very existence in an attitude of war with its subjects. Capitalism could be purged only by violence, and, in Montreal, with its highly visible and generally prosperous

English-speaking minority, anti-capitalism could easily blend with anti-colonialism. National liberation struggles overseas, especially in Algeria, Bolivia, and Cuba, furnished ready-made models of heroic struggle, and the rest was easy: thefts from armouries, construction sites, or gun stores provided the arsenal of the revolution.

Omelettes are not made without breaking eggs, according to the jargon of the period, and revolutions are not won without at least some incidental deaths: such violence could be justified afterward in press releases, or more often shrugged off. The press was eager to publicize it, and horror was always good copy, so that the terrorists of the Front de libération de Québec (or FLQ) could always be assured of an instant audience. The Front was a self-perpetuating entity. Current evidence suggests that it never had much of a formal organization; rather, small groups of individuals appropriated the title from time to time, thereby preserving the illusion of a continuing, hydra-headed conspiracy.

It was such a conspiracy that the municipal authorities of Montreal depicted in testimony in Ottawa. But their testimony had little effect. Ordinary police procedures turned up terrorists from time to time, and these men were periodically brought before the courts and sent off to the penitentiary. Their crimes, though serious, did not demand more than the ordinary powers of justice for their suppression. It was true that terrorism was growing more frequent: in November and December 1969 there were five separate bombing incidents in Montreal. In June 1970, a plot to kidnap the Israeli consul in Montreal was uncovered. The well-publicized arrests of two revolutionary theorists, Pierre Vallières and Charles Gagnon, contributed to the general excitement. And in August 1970 there was a new twist: FLQ terrorists, training with the Palestinian terrorists, announced that they would soon renew their struggle, using selective assassination as a weapon.

When, on October 5, 1970, the British trade commissioner in Montreal, James Cross, was abducted from his home, terrorism was very much in the air. Before long a press release arrived from the FLQ announcing its terms for the release, unharmed, of Cross. They included a ransom ('voluntary tax') of $500,000 in gold ingots, the release of a list of 'political prisoners' then serving time for their crimes, re-employment of some former post office drivers in Montreal, no police pursuit, free transport out of the country, and the reading of the FLQ manifesto and all subsequent communiqués on radio and television.

The manifesto, a hysterical and abusive potpourri of grievances combined with a distorted view of history, attempted to justify FLQ actions in terms of the rhetoric of colonial revolution and national struggle. In tone and substance it was not greatly different from thousands of bygone leaflets that had passed unhindered from the printing press into the wastebasket. But this time it was different: the FLQ had a hostage, and the price for his life was national attention.

The ultimate responsibility for a diplomat's safety rests squarely in the hands of the federal government. But police power is, for the most part, a local matter, and in this case responsibility lay with the city of Montreal and the Quebec provincial police. There were anxious consultations among the various levels of government as to the proper policy to be adopted, but it is impossible, even now, to say just what proposals were made during these discussions. What is certain is the result: a decision to bargain with the FLQ by agreeing to comply with some of its less dangerous demands. As the terrorists had demanded, the FLQ manifesto was published and broadcast, safe passage was guaranteed for the kidnappers, and the Attorney General of Quebec promised that he would support parole for some of the 'political prisoners.'

The partial surrender by the constituted authorities in Ottawa and in Quebec was well intentioned: if Cross's life could be saved, then some concessions, even in the face of terror, were worthwhile. But concessions enforced at the barrel of a gun may tend to give the impression that more can be extracted if the price is raised; and so, while the first kidnapping cell of the FLQ continued to hold on to Cross, another self-constituted group, describing itself as the 'Chenier financial cell,' swept up Quebec's Minister of Labour, Pierre Laporte, as he played ball with his children outside his suburban house on October 10.

Although the Cross kidnapping was taken seriously, the authorities remained calm; but the abduction of Laporte threw many in the Quebec government into a state of panic. Ministers flew their families out of the province: the less timid to Ottawa; others as far as New York. Pierre Laporte was the second minister in the Quebec government; he had been a strong contender for the Liberal leadership only nine months before. Laporte's disappearance affected the innermost circles of Quebec politics.

Events moved quickly to a crisis. As the police, quarrelling among themselves, pursued the search for Cross and Laporte, the provincial government dithered over what to do. It was speculated that a coalition government might be formed comprising all the parties in a kind of national union in order to find a way out of the crisis. Bourassa himself did not engender sufficient confidence, and it was darkly suspected that he would cave in to hardline pressure from Trudeau. A hard line, in the eyes of many influential Québécois, would mean refusal to comply with some, at least, of the terrorists' demands, such as the release of 'political prisoners.' The lives of two men were concrete: the legitimacy and authority of the state were abstract. Many intellectuals and journalists and some politicians plumped for the concrete, but the situation is by no means as clear-cut as these individuals then seem to have believed it to be. Terrorism poses both a theoretical and a practical problem to those who confront it (naturally it poses no problem at all to those who sympathize with or support it). As one recent student of the phenomenon of terrorism has argued, 'It is an important, sometimes over-riding, terrorist aim to undermine the political will, confidence and morale of liberal governments and citizens so that they are made more vulnerable to political and social collapse.'[2] More practically, one terrorist act, if one is to judge by experience abroad, will most likely lead to another. Events in Brazil in the same year, 1970, furnish an illustration: in September 1969 terrorists seized the American ambassador. The price for his release was fifteen prisoners. The West German ambassador's turn came in June 1970: his ransom was forty prisoners. The Swiss ambassador followed in December 1970: his release was extorted at the cost of seventy prisoners. And, once undertaken, the tactic of conceding terrorist demands takes on a crazed logic of its own: what was given for one must be given for the next.

As we know, some of these considerations were in the minds of Canada's federal and provincial governments as they contemplated the difficult question of what to do. Evidence of confusion and demoralization was painfully apparent in the days after the Laporte kidnapping, when it was argued that only a new government (even though the democratically elected government of Quebec was only six months old) could have the authority and legitimacy to deal with the real crisis.

What could that crisis be? In the eyes of many observers, it was the rigid and inflexible attitude that Ottawa was said to be taking in refusing to contemplate any further concession to the terrorists' demands: for any further concession, as Trudeau and his ministers knew, meant the release, before their sentences were served, of many or all of the 'political prisoners' then held in federal penitentiaries. Bourassa was said to be inclined to a softer line (although some evidence that has appeared since contradicts this). In order to 'strengthen' Bourassa's hand, therefore, sixteen prominent Quebec personalities, including various labour and business leaders, Claude Ryan, and René Lévesque, urged the Premier to persevere 'despite and against all obstruction from outside Quebec' in order to negotiate the 'exchange of the two hostages for the political prisoners.' The use of the term *political prisoners* without quotation marks surprised some, even when Ryan justified it as a 'question of fact and not law,' in itself a curious phrase. The implication that it was up to Quebec to solve its own problems, and that interference from 'outside' (meaning the rest of Canada) was illegitimate, was familiar enough in the separatist camp, but alarming when it came from those not already committed to Quebec's independence.

That same day, October 14, less respectable elements in Quebec society were

---

2 Paul Wilkinson, *Terrorism and the Liberal State* (London: Macmillan, 1977), p. 80.

taking action designed to support the FLQ. The lawyer negotiating on behalf of the terrorists urged a meeting of Université de Montréal students to boycott classes; the boycott began the next day. At another Montreal college, students occupied their rector's office, proclaiming that they would stay there 'until the victory of the FLQ.' That evening, a rally was held in Montreal's Paul Sauvé arena, with an audience of three thousand chanting 'FLQ ... FLQ ... FLQ.' Michel Chartrand, a Montreal labour leader, told the audience that the FLQ was going from strength to strength. 'There is no doubt,' he said, 'that there are infinitely more people now in accord with them, who understand and sympathize with the objectives of the FLQ than there were in 1963 and 1966.' Chartrand was doubtless right. Some of those who, in 1963, condemned the first bombings now remained uneasily silent, either convinced that it was not their fight, or frightened to speak out. One Montrealer who did speak out while in Toronto was reproached by his fearful family when he came home: it was dangerous, they explained, to draw attention to oneself.

By Thursday, October 15, a climax was approaching. That evening, a curious conversation took place between the premier of Quebec and a PQ member of the assembly. 'What do you want me to do?' Bourassa asked. 'You must immediately form a coalition government,' the Péquiste replied. He urged Bourassa to get rid of the more hesitant members of his cabinet and replace them with members of the opposition and other public bodies, including the trade unions. 'That coalition government will oppose Ottawa and negotiate with the FLQ. We haven't a minute to lose. It's your last chance.' Bourassa, however, refused. It was, he said, already too late.

As the two men spoke, the Canadian army was taking up positions around Montreal, Quebec City, and Ottawa. At the invitation of the government of Quebec, the troops had come to reinforce the hard-pressed police. It was the first intimation that the general public had had of the gravity of the crisis, and of the two governments' determination to resist further concessions to terrorist pressures. More was to come. At three o'clock on the morning of Friday, October 16, the federal government invoked the War Measures Act, declaring that an 'apprehended insurrection' existed in Quebec and giving the police extraordinary powers of arrest and detention against anyone suspected of belonging to, or sympathizing with, the FLQ.

That morning the police began a series of raids across Quebec, rounding up anyone suspected of belonging to the FLQ. We know now that police intelligence was seriously flawed, and that ministers found police work most unsatisfactory. But it was all they had. The size of the round-up seems to have surprised its authors, the federal cabinet, who had seen a list of only some seventy suspects. In sum, some 436 persons were arrested and detained under the authority of the

War Measures Act during the whole time of the crisis. The selection of whom to arrest was left in the hands of the police, and the police did not always proceed with due regard for reasonable evidence. In one notorious case, they entered the home of the federal Secretary of State, Gérard Pelletier, in search of a different Gérard Pelletier. Their source of information in this case seems to have been the telephone book.

The immediate effect of the imposition of the War Measures Act was the silencing of the vocal support for the FLQ which had been so much in evidence in the previous weeks. Of those arrested, sixty-two were eventually brought to trial, and twenty were convicted. The War Measures Act could not rescue Laporte or Cross, although it did allow the police to divert more resources to the pursuit of their kidnappers. The FLQ group holding Laporte murdered its helpless victim on Saturday, October 17 ('executed' is the revolutionary cant it employed) and left his body in the trunk of a car to be picked up.

Cross was eventually found and released, early in December. His captors traded the British diplomat's life for their own safe passage out of the country, to Cuba, where they lived, more or less discontentedly, for several years. They later moved to France, which admitted them as 'political refugees.' Eventually some returned to Canada, where they were tried, convicted, and, in view of their stated repentance for past misdeeds, given light sentences. The murderers of Laporte were uncovered in the corner of a country basement later the same month. They too were tried and convicted; because of the gravity of their offence, they received heavier sentences.

Most of the terrorists' demands were not achieved. No 'political prisoners' won their freedom. Despite the raucous rhetoric that surrounded the first stages of the kidnapping crisis, the seizure of the two victims did not touch off revolutionary festivities in the streets of Montreal. Nor was the October Crisis the first of many, as those who believed in the existence of revolutionary conditions in 'oppressed Quebec' had predicted. Instead, there was a decline and then a cessation of terrorist activity. That may have been coincidence, or it may have derived from the vigorous employment of the power of the state to confront and crush terrorism. Once the stakes were raised in the game of revolutionary theatre, once the governments made plain that those who played at parlour revolution faced real and immediate sanctions, the enthusiasm for a day of the barricades, FLQ style, noticeably diminished.

The bases of the government's reasoning were explained in a speech by Prime Minister Trudeau on the night of Friday, October 16. 'Should governments give in to this crude blackmail,' Trudeau informed his television audience, 'we would be facing the breakdown of the legal system, and its replacement by the law of the jungle ... Freedom and personal security are safeguarded by laws; those laws must be respected in order to be effective.' But under the threat of terrorism, extraordinary dangers required extraordinary measures: 'The criminal law as it stands is simply not adequate to deal with systematic terrorism' – a discovery that other countries besides Canada have made. Finally, Trudeau emphasized, 'This government is not acting out of fear. It is acting to prevent fear from spreading ... It is acting to make clear to kidnappers and revolutionaries and assassins that in this country laws are made and changed by the elected representatives of all Canadians – not by a handful of self-selected dictators.'

Trudeau's actions provoked much discussion at the time, and much condemnation since. Some alleged that the government had acted on the basis of inadequate information; it had panicked and used a sledgehammer to squash a gnat. Others suggested that the government knew well what it was doing: and that was to crush separatism, legal and democratic, under the guise of suppressing an illegal revolutionary conspiracy. Still others decried the use of troops to protect public figures and public buildings during the crisis and complained loudly when Trudeau replied that he would do anything that was necessary to protect constituted authority in Canada. Trudeau was short with the last variety of questioner. 'Yes,' he said, 'well there are a lot of bleeding hearts around who just don't like to see people with helmets and guns. All I can say is, go on and bleed, but it is more important to keep law and order in the society than to be worried about weak-kneed people.'

The first two objections merit serious consideration. In answer to the first complaint, that the government acted hastily and panicked, it is possible to observe that governments are neither omniscient nor omnipotent. The concrete information that the government had to hand indicated that the arms and dynamite thefts of the previous couple of years were largely unaccounted for and that the wild threats of the revolutionaries themselves now had to be taken more seriously than before. The politicians concluded that the will to resist revolutionary violence in Quebec was demonstrably weakening. There was a reasonable basis for all this conclusion, and it is not surprising that the federal government acted as it did to shore up and restore the political will to resist violence in Quebec.

As for the objection that Trudeau was acting to squash separatism and its most prominent proponents, the Parti Québécois, we have the statements of both the Prime Minister and one of his supporters, Bryce Mackasey, during the crisis. On October 17, Mackasey stressed to the House of Commons that the Parti Québécois was 'a legitimate, political party. It wants to bring an end to this country through democratic means, but that is the privilege of that party.' Trudeau himself made the same point in November to an interviewer. Those who claim that Trudeau was acting to discredit the PQ must fly in the face of explicit public statments by Trudeau and his ministers.

The War Measures Act crisis produced one of the highest favourable ratings in public opinion that any Canadian government has ever achieved. Eighty-seven per cent of Canadians, with no significant variation between English and French, signified their approval of the government's course. Even so, the government's reputation has suffered because of its actions. The benefits have been hard to seize upon, the defects and injustices (and there were many in the way the police applied their powers) easy to criticize. In retrospect it is difficult to understand what else, legally and politically, could have been done. The government was bound to uphold the law and its application. It would have been ultimately foolish to concede much of the terrorist program, and it may have been unwise to concede any. Politically, it is the government's duty to try to manage conditions, including public opinion, so that danger to the fabric of the Canadian state is avoided or repaired. That it also seems to have done, averting the possibility of a coalition government in Quebec City, and uniting with, rather than opposing, the government of Quebec to put down manifestations of support for revolution and terror. In this it acted wisely and properly.

Nevertheless, the crisis caused Trudeau to lose respect for Bourassa. Other factors later exaggerated the differences between Ottawa and Quebec: Bourassa's inability to impose an agreement on his cabinet and party over the Victoria Charter; the excursions of some Quebec ministers into federal jurisdiction; and the Bourassa government's attempts to compromise with the nationalists over language policy. Trudeau responded publicly and intemperately, which must have further diminished the esteem in which Bourassa was held inside Quebec.

The most apparent divergence between the federal Liberals and Quebec Liberals took place over the Bourassa government's Bill 22, introduced into the legislature in May 1974. Bill 22 was designed to affect both the economic life and the language of education of the province: it enacted incentives for firms to expand the use of French in their daily operations ('francization') and in their dealings with customers; but it also abolished the freedom of parental choice that Bill 63 had guaranteed. In future, admission to English-language schools was conditional on whether one's maternal language was English or on a language test administered to determine if a toddler really had sufficient knowledge of English to slip through the loopholes of the bill. In a final fillip, French was made the sole official language of Quebec.

The enactment of Bill 22 was probably unnecessary to protect the French character of Quebec or of Montreal, given the steady emigration of English-speakers from the province and the probability that there would be fewer immigrants in the seventies and eighties than in the fifties and sixties. It was, moreover, not only the English who were leaving. Of those immigrants who came to Quebec and assimilated to the English community only a minority chose to remain indefinitely. The rest packed their bags and, like their native-born fellow citizens, departed. Worse, from Bourassa's point of view, Bill 22 failed to appease the hysteria expressed in Quebec nationalist circles, as the following editorial on the subject from *Le Jour,* Montreal's separatist daily, made plain: 'A whole people is in the process of being dispossessed of its collective rights by an immigration that is massively anglophone. It has the right to know what is happening.'[3] Moreover, the bill made explicit what many English Quebeckers had long feared: their government intended to rework the context of their lives, from the language spoken in the workplace down to the signs on shops (these were, after a certain delay, to become bilingual, at least in English-speaking areas). They were unhappy about it, and they let the Premier and the Prime Minister know about it. Across the country there were demands that Bill 22 be disallowed, or at least reviewed by the Supreme Court to determine its constitutionality.

Trudeau steered a careful path among the linguistic minefields. He did not like Bill 22 but explained that his government could not disallow a law simply because it was foolish or unjust. That would have depopulated the provincial statute books. Perhaps he sensed that Bill 22, for all its fallacies, was indeed better than any alternative that the separatists could dream up; and, as time would show, he was right.

If Bourassa's language policy embarrassed the federal government, events in the federal sphere helped to undermine the position of the provincial Liberals. The occasion was the attempt by the federal government to expand the use of French in air traffic control – to put, as the saying went, 'français dans l'air,' by making several airports in Quebec bilingual. The proponents of French pointed out that 90 per cent of controllers in Quebec had French as their mother tongue and that most Quebec pilots were French. The Canadian Airline Pilots Association (CALPA) was distressed at the possibility that incoming aircraft, using and understanding only English, might be endangered by French communications between air traffic control and local air traffic. There was no reconciling the two points of view; the pilots went on strike in June 1976 over the issue of 'air safety.' Opinion in English Canada overwhelmingly backed them, and, although there was no particular danger in airports outside Quebec, pilots of foreign airlines professed to believe that any intrusion into Canadian airspace endangered the safety of their passengers. 'This debate,' Richard Gwyn wrote in the *Toronto Star,* 'as everyone knows full well, isn't over safety but over bilingualism,'

3   Un peuple entier est en voie d'être dépossédé de ses droits collectifs par une immigration massivement anglophone. Il a le droit de le savoir.

which most English Canadians disliked, as the massive English-Canadian support for the pilots demonstrated. French Canadians took notice.

Although the air traffic control dispute was terminated by an agreement by the federal government to study the whole matter at greater length, its repercussions undoubtedly lasted far beyond the immediate inconvenience to passengers and public that the strike had caused. Bourassa later singled out the air traffic control dispute as an important factor in his party's defeat in the provincial election of November 15, 1976.

The other reasons were common enough: economic unrest, inflation, Bill 22, and 'pseudo-scandals' promoted by the opposition Parti Québécois. It is difficult not to sympathize with Mr Bourassa, on this last count at least. 'Name one case,' he challenged Lévesque in a televised debate. Lévesque, evidently surprised by the question, referred only to 'generalized cancer' in his reply. But more Quebeckers by then preferred Lévesque's version of recent history to Bourassa's.

Lévesque had learned some valuable lessons in his years in opposition. Independence, immediate separation from Canada, perturbed the electorate. As long as independence remained the party's principal stock-in-trade, the PQ's chances of electoral success were doubtful. But if independence were defused, put, so to speak, in cold storage, the Bourassa government was sufficiently unpopular to be defeated.

The solution was proposed by Claude Morin, who had resigned from the civil service in 1971 and publicly proclaimed his adherence to the separatist cause. Morin's experience in federal-provincial relations had persuaded him of the efficacy of gradualism: if the electorate were pushed, a little at a time, to accept that the PQ could govern, it might then be prepared to swallow the PQ's independence option. Morin's reasoning was accepted by the party. Henceforth, independence would be on the instalment plan: first a PQ government, and then, somewhere down the road, a referendum on its special nostrum, souveraineté-association.

The Quebec electorate approved. On November 15 an emotional Lévesque saw his party swept to victory after victory as Liberal bastions fell one after another. Even Bourassa was defeated. The English-language voters did not, it is true, choose the PQ, but they split their votes between the Liberals and a revived Union Nationale. 'The divided anglophone vote,' Bourassa later admitted, 'allowed dozens of PQ candidates to capture their respective ridings.' Without accepting that 'dozens' of seats changed hands according to the whim of the anglophones, it is probably true that the Liberal vote (33.8 per cent and twenty-six seats) would have been more impressive in an election focused more clearly on separatism. Lévesque's 41.4 per cent garnered a majority government of seventy-one seats.

English Canadians were startled. Trudeau had recently assured the country

The Parti Québécois is elected in Quebec (Aislin, 1976). Reproduced with the permission of Aislin: *The Montreal Gazette*

that separatism was dead; now it was alive and well and governing Canada's second-largest province. Observers, including the Prime Minister, drew comfort from the fact that the real battle was just beginning. This would be the battle of the referendum, now inevitable. In a partial response, Trudeau dredged up the constitution and appointed a national unity task force. His constitutional propo-

...NOT A CREATURE WAS STIRRING, NOT EVEN A MOUSE...

Prime Minister Trudeau reads a story to his children (Christmas, 1978), as René Lévesque approaches from the rear (Mallette, 1978). Reproduced with the permission of the *Globe and Mail*, Toronto

sals, revealed with great fanfare in the summer of 1978, were a badly written and worse-conceived potpourri of Senate reform and Supreme Court fiddlings. They fell with a dull thud before an astonished and somewhat bemused populace. The national unity task force perambulated the country after the fashion of its bilingualism and biculturalism predecessor. After much labour and droning, it emitted a report that repeated most of the myths about Canadian history dearly beloved of Quebec nationalists; in token of apology for past injustice (112 years of it) it tendered a decentralized constitution.

The Canadian academic community also rushed to the barricades, but whether to build them up or tear them down no one could be certain. Universities vied with one another in holding national unity rituals: York held a conference, so Toronto, Queen's, even Harvard must hold theirs too; one after another their products marched from the printing presses to accumulate unread on groaning academic shelves. The *Canadian Forum*, the addled matriarch of left-wing ferment, surprised its readers by publishing the manifesto of a Committee for a New Constitution. This new proposal looked to decentralization and two nations for Canada's (or Canada-Quebec's) salvation. It stopped just short of promoting separatism as a good, desirable in and for itself.

While the rest of Canada talked and bickered, Quebec acted. The Lévesque government sponsored labour and electoral reforms and encouraged Crown cor-

porations. It also, naturally, passed a law concerning referenda. But its most notorious enactment, in the eyes of the rest of Canada, was its language legislation.
The PQ had promised to revise, reform, and improve Bourassa's Bill 22. So it
did – in nationalist eyes. In the new version, children of English-speaking parents were automatically guaranteed a place in English schools for themselves so
long as the parents had been educated in Quebec. Given the rate of emigration of
English-speaking natives of Quebec, this would not be a difficult promise to fulfil. (Those with English as mother tongue declined from 14 per cent of the population in 1941 to 10 per cent in 1986.) The younger sisters and brothers of children already enrolled in English-language schools were also guaranteed an English education. But there the concessions ended. The children of all immigrants
to Quebec, including immigrants from other Canadian provinces, were to attend
French-language schools. A partial exemption, for three years or less, was accorded the children of temporary residents in Quebec.

The language of instruction in the schools was, however, only a part (although an important one) of the Lévesque government's linguistic policy. That
policy was explained in a white paper issued in March 1977, and stated in legal
terms by the PQ's Bill 1 (later, because of a procedural problem, renamed Bill
101). The bill started off unequivocally by defining Quebec and Quebeckers as
French. French members of Quebec society enjoyed rights – rights that now had
the force of law behind them; others, including the long-established English
community, were treated as 'exceptions.' They would, nevertheless, have to
conform to the PQ's legislation, institute programs of 'francization' in their businesses, rewrite their signs, and make their municipalities (in some of which the
English are still a majority) conform to the dictates of a law that proclaimed
French to be the only legal medium of public affairs.

The Office de la Langue française was set up to enforce the new law and to
devise detailed regulations to speed the task on its way. The White Paper described the widespread appearance of English in Montreal as 'difficult and embarrassing.' English signs that might offend the public were to be expunged, although signs that had already been changed to conform with the previous language law were given a brief stay of execution. Thus, signs on private businesses in English-language areas were henceforth to be in French only; internal
signs, for example in English-language bookstores, were also to be in French.
One zealous bureaucrat at one point decided that English-language churches
should conform as well and translate their liturgy and hymnals into French, but a
last-minute reprieve was permitted in this case. The language police were ever
vigilant, however. When a contraband shipment of Dunkin' Donuts bags was
uncovered it was immediately subjected to the full rigour of the law – and
burned.

Snap, Crackle and Pap

Bill Vander Zalm, Pierre Trudeau, and René Lévesque deal with Canadian culture (Peterson, 1976). Reproduced with the permission of Roy Peterson, *Vancouver Sun*

After the federal election of 1988, the Supreme Court of Canada upheld lower court decisions which declared that certain sections of Bill 101 contravened the Quebec and Canadian Charters of Rights. Bourassa had pledged in his election campaign that he would restore bilingual signs. Once in power, he hesitated to act, claiming that he wanted the courts to decide. When the Supreme Court decided, Bourassa disagreed. He banned English language outside signs and required interior English signs to be smaller than French signs. He invoked the 'notwithstanding' clause of the constitution. In doing so, he threatened the future of the Meech Lake accord which its proponents had claimed would protect minority language rights. It would do nothing of the sort; Meech Lake's critics were proven correct.

It would be comforting to be able to dismiss Bill 101 and its excesses as an exercise in comic opera bureaucracy straight out of the *Inspector General*, but both its principle and practice disturbed many. As Claude Ryan pointed out in *Le Devoir* at the time of Bill 101's first appearance, it is 'rigid, dogmatic and authoritarian,' in keeping with the 'narrow and chauvinistic brand of nationalism' of the bill's authors. In protecting the language of the majority against imagined terrors, the Parti Québécois saw fit to negate the rights of a minority of close to one million persons, to treat them almost as non-citizens, and their language as a non-entity. In so doing it violated basic individual rights and appealed for the first time to the power of the state to coerce private citizens with respect to the language they speak in their private, business lives. That anglophone provinces had also behaved badly is certainly true, but this is, of course, no excuse. Some of them, New Brunswick and Ontario in particular, had repented and were expanding French-language rights in the 1970s and 1980s, with New Brunswick becoming officially bilingual. In any case, the English-language provinces stopped short of prohibitions on signs and shops.

Many English-speaking citizens of Quebec voted with their feet. In the last half of 1977 some 50,000 people left Quebec, compared to the 33,000 who left in the corresponding part of 1976 and the 28,000 during the last six months of 1975, 'the bus people,' according to a contemporary quip. Many companies also left, with the Sun Life Insurance Company as the flagship of the departing fleet.

The effect has certainly been to enhance the official French character of Quebec, although at the expense of some hundreds of thousands of the province's well-educated and productive citizens. The large French-speaking population will, for the most part, be spared the strain of bilingualism (although an economic analysis might tell us that knowledge of two languages is a definite economic advantage), and the leaders of Quebec will no longer be embarrassed by anglophone signs as they contemplate the uniquely French character of their diminished province.

Graduates of Quebec universities and technical colleges have taken some of the places of the departed English; as more of these become available (either through migration or through economic growth) the French character of workforce and workplace will be reinforced. There may well be an inflow of skilled and educated francophones from other provinces. These processes will proceed at a somewhat faster pace and with greater disruption than the simple effluxion of time would have brought about. But if the language measures do prove to be the last gasp of nationalist fervour in Quebec, the provincial economy will probably evolve, in the long run, much as if nothing had been done, and its élite, whether francophone or anglophone, will continue to find English a useful tool of business.

There have been economic and social elements of the emerging Quebec nationalism whose impact on economic growth might prove very unattractive. The nationalization of the asbestos industry by the PQ as an act of linguistic and cultural revenge may prove to be one of these, as may the determination to bring Crédit Foncier Franco-canadien, long controlled by Paris interests, under Québécois control. On the labour front, construction work was reserved for those actually living in the province of Quebec, provoking a dispute with the neighbouring province of Ontario. Although it was pointed out that Quebec workers probably derived more benefit from working in Ontario than Ontario workers did from working in Quebec, this was a minor consideration for the government of Quebec, which was, from an ideological standpoint, uninterested in the mobility of labour. Increasingly, such things appeared to be straws in the wind.

The political fortunes of the Lévesque government had remarkably little effect on the strictly political destinies of the Trudeau regime. Trudeau's support in Quebec remained relatively constant throughout the 1972 and 1974 elections, and an attempt to persuade Quebeckers to vote Social Credit in the 1979 election as a protest against federalism fizzled. In the 1980 election the federal Liberals even improved on past performance, taking every seat but one in Quebec and swamping the opposition in the popular vote.

As federal politics eddied back and forth the provincial Liberals took the time to reconstruct their party under a new leader, Claude Ryan. Ryan's selection provoked misgivings among many. He was anything but a doctrinaire Liberal and had on many occasions in the past opposed the party's federal and provincial policies. His often dry oratorical style provoked misgivings among the electorally minded. But Ryan was not without his supporters, as by-elections proved. Nor was he without a program of his own.

What Ryan and Lévesque stood for became clearer as the Parti Québécois's promised referendum approached. At the beginning of November 1979 the Quebec government published a White Paper on the referendum in which it outlined its proposed scheme of 'sovereignty-association.' Grandiloquent, tendentious, and emotional, the White Paper chronicled past wrongs to make current points. The history sometimes seemed to be that of another country. Omitting those parts of Quebec history that might have demonstrated co-operation, agreement, or mutual advantage between French and English, the White Paper selected events that illustrated opposition and discord. In 1914, the White Paper inaccurately declared, 'despite firm and virtually unanimous opposition [from Quebec], Canada entered the war.' The National Policy of 1879, which enshrined protection of industry, appeared to the authors of the White Paper to have benefited Ontario alone. As Senator Maurice Lamontagne, a Liberal critic, noted, the tariff arrangements of the central government had probably favoured Quebec more than Ontario – and continued to do so. The Quebec government also detected a 'formidable centralizing attack' on the provinces by Ottawa since the war, one that had intensified in recent years. These misreadings of history were, of course, mere transparent flourishes that underlined the paper's central appeal, in which Quebec was asked 'to choose the only road that can open up the horizon and guarantee us a free, proud and adult national existence'; in other words, sovereignty.

Once sovereignty was achieved, there would be association. The White Paper proposed four Quebec-Canada agencies: a community council, a commission of experts, a court of justice, and a monetary authority. The first would be chaired alternately by Quebec and Canadian representatives, and Quebec and Canada would possess 'fundamental legal equality.' In some cases these agencies could be 'modifications' of existing institutions such as the Bank of Canada. In all cases the 'adjustments' were made to seem the essence of sweet reasonableness. 'Monetary union' and 'free circulation' of people and goods (already impaired under existing federal arrangements) would remain. For Quebec, sovereignty 'will have a legal impact on the power to make laws and to levy taxes, on territorial integrity, on citizenship and minorities, on the courts and various other institutions, and on the relations of Quebec with other countries.' An adult national existence perhaps, but one might suggest that in this plan the adolescent was leaving home with the keys to father's house and mother's Mastercard.

That, of course, was the impression that the White Paper sought to convey to a worried and divided Quebec electorate. Knowing that the electorate, even after four years of PQ rule, would not support independence pure and simple, the Lévesque cabinet sought to reassure its potential voters. There would be no sovereignty without association. Regardless of the frequently voiced warnings of the other nine premiers, Lévesque told an audience, the other provinces would come round – 'on their knees' – in the face of a popular mandate for sovereignty-association. PQ supporters elsewhere in Canada, accepting the inevitability and the righteousness of Lévesque's position, urged their fellow Canadians to 'respect Quebec's right to self-determination' by accepting sovereignty-association.

English Canadians, however, looked to Claude Ryan for an alternate vision of the constitutional future. On January 9, 1980, Ryan presented his proposals for 'A New Canadian Federation.' The document was clearly the product of Ryan's logical, intense mind. More wooden and less tendentious than the Lévesque White Paper, the Ryan proposals, unfortunately dubbed the 'beige paper,' hailed the achievements of Canadian federation while demanding fundamental changes in its structure. Central to the constitutional reform was a Federal Council that would serve as a provincially based watchdog over a new, decentralized constitutional structure and numerous government appointments. The importance of preserving and expanding language rights across Canada and of correcting regional disparities was recognized. Nationalist yet Canadian, the 'beige paper' affirmed the Liberals' belief that they were 'a part of the wave of cultural, economic, social and political affirmation which is presently sweeping over Quebec.' Liberals refused, the paper continued, 'to choose between Quebec and Canada, as if one should necessarily exclude the other. On the contrary we choose Quebec AND Canada because each needs the other to fulfill itself.'

To anglophones the rhetoric of this paper was more appealing than its substance. The response to it was tepid. Ontario's premier, William Davis, hesitated to reply and was vague when he finally did. Press comment often ignored the details while lauding Ryan's undeniable commitment to Canada. Péquiste strategist Claude Morin called Ryan's plans a 'mixed up federalism that could lead us to another 40 years of continuing discussion with the rest of Canada.' More disturbing was the political scientist Léon Dion's extended series in *Le Devoir* which echoed Morin's doubts that English Canada would accept much while arguing that the paper would not appeal to francophones. Better no statement, Dion argued, than the over-complex paper of January. For the referendum the 'beige paper' was a clumsy weapon, too heavy to tote into battle, and too scattered in its aim. Ryan's party, reinvigorated through an intensive membership campaign, nevertheless endorsed it unanimously at a convention in late February. As the referendum neared, the debate about Quebec's and Canada's future began. The two papers were but the first step; later the route would become more treacherous for both parties.

At first, however, the Lévesque government seemed to have events running its way. The referendum question was announced and debated in the Quebec National Assembly in March. The question was relatively lengthy:

The Government of Québec has made public its proposal to negotiate a new agreement with the rest of Canada, based on the equality of nations;

this agreement would enable Québec to acquire the exclusive power to make its laws, levy its taxes and establish relations abroad – in other words, sovereignty – and at the same time, to maintain with Canada an economic association including a common currency;

no change in political status resulting from these negotiations will be effected without approval from the people through another referendum;

on these terms, do you give the Government of Québec the mandate to negotiate the proposed agreement between Québec and Canada?

The strategy behind the referendum question was the same that had led to the Parti Québécois's victory in the 1976 election. The electorate was not asked to approve immediate independence or effective change of any sort; but its approval would be a tangible step on the way. Party orators in the National Assembly left their television audience in little doubt of the true symbolism of the referendum. A 'oui' answer to the government's question would be positive, prideful, nationalistic, and assertive. Reading, for the most part, texts prepared for them by others, Lévesque's troops scored a brilliant theatrical success. By contrast, Ryan's deputies, reading speeches they had written for themselves (at their leader's insistence), seemed hesitant, negative, and parochial.

Relying on the momentum of the legislative debate, Lévesque chose an early date for the referendum: May 20. 'Oui' and 'non' committees were established, as required by the referendum law, under Lévesque's and Ryan's respective direction. Lévesque set off on a quasi-papal progress through the province, dispensing certificates identifying their proud holders as original supporters of Quebec nationhood. Ryan's campaign meanwhile failed to catch fire in the eyes of the media. The result, until the first public opinion poll, seemed a foregone conclusion.

Yet Lévesque's campaign showed from the beginning some curious features. Although the referendum question itself was clearly based on negotiations for 'sovereignty,' the premier himself tended to avoid the term. 'It is a question of honour,' Lévesque said, 'to demand equality and the first *déblocage* ... at least, dammit, to say that this is the direction we want to go in.' Unfortunately for the would-be voter, these nuances were not present in the referendum question itself. While denaturing the question, the 'oui' supporters also suggested that only by going to the extreme of supporting the option of sovereignty-association could Quebeckers show English Canadians that they were serious in their complaints about the country. Thus, to vote 'non' was also in some fashion to ratify continuing subordination of French to English in Canada.

Gradually, as April turned into May, it became apparent that Lévesque's message had convinced only a minority of the voters. The premier had failed, in particular, to convince the 18.5 per cent of Quebec's population who spoke a language other than French that they should entrust their destinies to a separate and independent Quebec governed by the Parti Québécois. The negative anglophone reaction was explained away as the result of brain-washing by media slavishly responding to the dictates of their 'foreign' (non-Quebec) owners. More probably the English-language and ethnic voters were simply interpreting the evidence that the last three years had placed before them. Bill 101, with its limitations on the use of the English and other languages, was hardly encouraging. Some of the expressions of the Parti Québécois's cultural supporters, who voiced their nationalism in vociferously anti-English ways (as in the play *Medium Saignant* or the poem *Speak White*), were particularly disturbing. Those anglophones who proclaimed a new-found allegiance to the cause of a sovereign Quebec had to work with unpromising material in their efforts to persuade the English community that there was positive benefit in abandoning Canada for a future as a minority in an independent Quebec. More negative benefits were stressed by other Parti Québécois orators, who warned the obdurate English of the danger of alienating the francophone majority, or of cheating it of its rightful prize.

Lévesque and his followers also protested against the periodic interventions from outside Quebec of other provincial premiers and of federal politicians. The latter should confine themselves to minding the store in Ottawa, keeping their noses strictly out of a 'provincial' matter (that this provincial matter involved the very existence of the federal government was held to be of small account). The federal politicians not surprisingly ignored Lévesque's strictures. Marshalled by the Minister of Justice, Jean Chrétien, a parade of federal Liberals and Conservatives descended on Quebec to support the 'non' side. (The New Democrats, citing obscure reasons of their own, abstained.) Joe Clark made a particularly effective excursion, but the *pièce de résistance* was the Prime Minister himself. Trudeau made three speeches in Quebec in the course of the campaign, orations rated among the best he had ever given. Placing Quebec's leaders side by side, even 'oui' supporters leaned massively toward Trudeau; 53 per cent of Quebeckers (and 46 per cent of francophones) placed Trudeau squarely ahead of Lévesque (22 per cent and 27 per cent, respectively) in preference.

Contrary to initial expectations, pride in Trudeau and attachment to Canada both played a significant role in the campaign. The bread-and-butter issues that the federalists had emphasized in the provincial elections of 1970, 1973, and 1976 no longer worked quite the same magic: polls showed that 57 per cent of francophone voters expected that economic conditions would either improve or remain the same if Quebec won its sovereignty-association. At the same time, 72 per cent of francophone voters (and 96 per cent of anglophones) confessed to a deep attachment to Canada.

Up to the last moment the result appeared uncertain. But within minutes of the polls closing on the evening of May 20 the results became clear. The 'non' side seized a decisive margin and maintained it. At the 'oui' headquarters defeat was finally conceded at 9:30 p.m., two and a half hours after the polls closed, and an emotional Lévesque informed his followers that the ball was once again in the federal court. He naturally added that the 'non' campaign had been unfair and reprehensible. Watching Lévesque's ungracious concession from a suburban hockey rink, justice minister Chrétien was overheard to mutter, 'Hypocrite.'

Across Canada there was an audible sigh of relief, tempered by a rush of wind as commentators and provincial politicians proclaimed the result to be a mandate for 'renewed federalism' and not for the 'status quo.' Opinion polls from within Quebec tended to confirm this, though what 'renewed federalism' might mean varied greatly from person to person, and place to place. That French Canadians expected to become more 'equal' in the result seems indisputable, but whether this could be satisfied by constitutional or more orthodox political means remained unclear. For the moment only one thing was evident. A solid 59.5 per cent of Quebec's voters had rejected 'sovereignty-association.' The 'non' vote was widespread within Quebec, where only one major geographic region voted in the majority for 'oui' (the north shore and Saguenay region), and a majority of French Canadians (52 per cent) had voted 'non.'

In Alberta, Premier Lougheed opined that the people of Quebec had really been concerned about economic issues within Confederation, all evidence from public opinion polls notwithstanding. More constructively, Saskatchewan called for immediate federal-provincial negotiations on the renewal of national institutions and the redistribution of federal and provincial powers. In Ontario the Simcoe County Council contributed its mite by condemning the provincial government's efforts to 'push bilingualism on Canada,' by opening a French high school for the francophone minority in the area.

There were still, obviously, great difficulties to be overcome. In the stampede of provincial politicians for more power there remained the danger that Quebec's real expectations of Canada might well be forgotten, and equally the danger that the remnant of federal power that might be left behind by provincial rightists would not be enough to organize a real country around. As the historian Terry Copp reflected, shortly before the referendum, 'How can we in the rest of the country have the nerve to ask [Quebeckers] to make an emotional or political identification with Canada when we ourselves are in the process of building a consensus on decentralization and emasculation of the powers of the national Government?'[4]

4 *Globe and Mail,* May 10, 1980.

29

Quebec and the Constitution:
The Canadian Constitutional Revolution

The origins of what came to be Canada's 'renewed federalism' dated back to the constitutional imbroglio of the late 1970s. At that time the several provinces had confronted Ottawa with a series of demands for 'reform,' a reform that invariably pointed to a devolution of powers from the central government toward the provinces.

At the end of 1978 the Trudeau government appeared to incline toward the provincial position. 'Positions' would probably be a more accurate description, for each province had its own shopping list: British Columbia wanted control of off-shore resources, as did Newfoundland, but also wanted a radically reformed Senate to be appointed by the provinces and with no federal representation; Saskatchewan and Alberta wanted more control over natural resources, including aspects of international trade, and indirect taxation; fisheries were a maritime desideratum. A committee of federal and provincial ministers examined these and other issues over the winter of 1978-9, in the hope of reaching an agreement that would also include patriation of the constitution, an amending formula, and a charter of rights.

A draft did emerge from these meetings; had it been accepted, it would have had the effect, as some Saskatchewan commentators later put it, of 'a major redirection of Canadian federalism ... augmenting provincial powers at the expense of federal authority.'[1] But the draft was not accepted. For one thing, Quebec did not want any progress to be made until after it had held its referendum. For another, the assembled provincial premiers fully expected the Trudeau government shortly to be defeated; they were unwilling to do anything that might have enhanced the federal Liberals' credibility at the polls.

Trudeau, as might be expected, drew an unfavourable conclusion from the

1 Roy Romanow, John Whyte, Howard Leeson, *Canada ... Notwithstanding* (Toronto: Carwell-Methuen, 1984), p. 53.

exercise. To the premiers, the Prime Minister lamented at the time that 'we've almost given up the shop to you' and still failed to satisfy provincial demands. Privately, he indicated that his withdrawal from politics at the end of 1979 was stimulated by a belief that he could never get the provincial governments to agree on constitutional reform.

Events overtook Trudeau; even more they overtook the premiers. Trudeau's mandate was on the point of expiring in February 1979; a year later he was heading a newly elected majority government, and three months after that his forces demolished the separatists in the Quebec referendum. Whatever Lévesque spoke for after May 1980, he could not pretend that it was majority opinion in Quebec. With separatism a dead issue, at least for the moment, the PQ leader became a secondary player. 'Lévesque was a political eunuch,' one western premier explained. 'It was up to the rest of us to take on Trudeau.'[2]

And they did, first by proxy when Jean Chrétien toured the provincial capitals in May after the referendum, and then in person, in first ministers' conferences in June and September 1980. In between there was a last attempt to find common ground between Ottawa and the provincial governments, centring around a charter of rights, the entrenchment of English and French as official languages, minority language rights in education, equalization, some kind of amending formula, and patriation. To this list, familiar from the 1970s, Trudeau added the 'economic union' of Canada, arguing that national power over the economy ought to be strengthened in return for concessions to provincial demands in other areas. Cleverly, Trudeau differentiated among the items up for negotiation. Some were 'people's issues,' such as equalization or an entrenched charter of rights; others were really of concern only to governments – a rejection, if the premiers needed to be reminded, of their contention that only they spoke on constitutional matters for their 'peoples.'

It was, of course, inherently unlikely that the provincial governments would concede that Ottawa was better at managing the economy than they were. In any case, they proclaimed as an article of faith that Ottawa's economic policies were designed to favour central Canada and that equity demanded that they protect their own economies from the iniquitous depredations of the federal power. This point of view had deep roots in the Maritimes and western Canada, and we have seen it emerge during the Quebec referendum campaign, with some apparent effect. The use of local manufacturing requirements, of province-first purchasing policies, and of the provincial licensing power responded to the perception that Canadians needed ten little economies rather than one bigger one – even if

---

2   Quoted in Robert Sheppard and Michael Valpy, *The National Deal: The Fight for a Canadian Constitution* (Toronto: Fleet, 1982), p. 41.

the bigger one were smaller and poorer than, say, California's.[3]

But management of the economy was hardly the only issue. To Newfoundland's Brian Peckford, a basic principle was at stake, namely that the national government was properly 'the agent of the provinces ... and not the other way round.'[4] In September, at the second first ministers' conference, he told Trudeau to his face that he had come to prefer René Lévesque's vision of Canada to the Prime Minister's. Presumably Peckford knew how offensive his remark would be to those who had just fought the referendum on the Canadian side; in any case it prompted Jean Chrétien to lean forward and whisper in Trudeau's ear, 'Have you got a bag? I want to vomit.'[5]

Peckford was admittedly extreme, but there was no lack of extreme positions. Some premiers espoused parliamentary supremacy and contrasted it with an entrenched charter of rights. Others held out to the end for an amending formula they knew to be unacceptable to the national government. Most of them held out for further devolution of powers as a necessary preliminary consideration before they would agree to any amending formula or to bring final jurisdiction over the constitution home from London. To show Trudeau where they thought he stood, and what they thought of federal paramountcy, they insisted that he accept a premier as co-chairman of the conference. They even combined all their demands in the so-called Chateau consensus (named after the Chateau Laurier hotel in Ottawa): the ultimate exercise in mutual back-scratching which would have devolved federal authority to a far greater extent even than the failed proposals of 1979.

Under the rules of the constitutional game as developed in the 1960s and 1970s, this should have been enough to send the premiers and the Prime Minister back to their respective corners while academic observers wrung their hands and deplored the lack of goodwill, compromise, and diplomacy. But Trudeau had already come to accept that goodwill was lacking, compromise impossible, and diplomacy irrelevant. As a British wit observed, 'When I hear the word devolution, I reach for my devolver.' As it happened, Trudeau had a devolver to hand.

A memorandum signed by one of his advisers, Michael Kirby, had delineated the possible outcomes of the conference, ranging from total success through various forms of partial failure to complete breakdown. Barring genuine agreement, Kirby advised on August 30, 1980, Trudeau should search for a spectacular fail-

3 See Romanow, Whyte, and Leeson, *Canada ... Notwithstanding,* pp. 70-1, for a restatement of provincialist axioms on this subject. See also David Milne, *Tug of War: Ottawa and the Provinces under Trudeau and Mulroney* (Toronto: Lorimer, 1986), p. 86, for a similar point of view.
4 Quoted in Sheppard and Valpy, *National Deal,* p. 39.
5 Ibid., p. 64.

ure, putting the blame on the provinces. The preference was, obviously, for genuine agreement, contrary to the dark suspicions of the provincial delegations to Ottawa; that was nothing new. What was new was the existence of an alternative strategy.[6]

The strategy was defined in the weeks following the break-up of the September conference. When it was presented to the national Liberal caucus on September 17, there was enthusiasm: 'Allons-y Cadillac,' one member said. 'To go Cadillac,' Trudeau responded. 'I will use it. I understand that this caucus wants us to go with the full package. To be Liberal ... all the way down the line. Not temper our convictions with political expediency. If that is your will, I'm delighted to follow it.'[7]

The federal government would act unilaterally to patriate the constitution. It would do more. It would incorporate an amending formula and embody a charter of rights, including language and mobility of labour so that Canadians from one province could not be discriminated against in another. It would entrench equalization and guarantee a national standard of public services to all Canadians. The government would present a resolution to that effect to the House of Commons. Once passed by Parliament, it would be sent on to London to be enacted as a British statute, the last amendment that the British Parliament would be called on to make to the hoary British North America Act, 1867.

Trudeau presented his solution to the country in a televised speech on October 2. 'In this complex and turbulent world,' he said, 'Canadians can no longer afford to have fundamental aspects concerning the nature of our country left unresolved and uncertain, to feed confrontation, division and disunity. We are summoned to a great act of national will: we must take unto ourselves and for our children, the ultimate responsibility for the preservation of our country.' On October 6 the constitutional resolution was moved in the House of Commons: it provided among other things for a national constitutional referendum on a type of double majority principle to determine a proper amending procedure. Lévesque's referendum was still bearing fruit: federal fruit, as it happened, growing in democratic soil.

The constitutional resolution was not the only business that confronted the federal government in October 1980. At the end of the month the finance minister, Allan MacEachen, presented his budget to Parliament; embodied in it was the National Energy Program, or NEP. It guaranteed that Ottawa and Edmonton would find themselves in a state of war over the parcelling out of energy rev-

---

6 *Canadian Annual Review of Politics and Public Affairs, 1980* (Toronto: University of Toronto Press, 1982), p. 65; provincial suspicions are voiced in Romanow, Whyte, and Leeson, *Canada ... Notwithstanding*, pp. 94-5.

7 Quoted in Sheppard and Valpy, *National Deal*, p. 65.

enues for the first part of 1981, and it inflamed western regionalists who interpreted the energy policy an eastern raid on western resources. The constitution served as just another dreadful example of centralist exploitation; reactions varied from discontent to outright separatism.

Trudeau hoped that his constitutional package would be complete and ready for proclamation on July 1, 1981, Canada Day. That did not happen. The federal Progressive Conservative party, under Joe Clark, determined to fight the proposals. The New Democrats under Ed Broadbent supported the government; eventually, however, their party split on the issue, with four MPs from Saskatchewan following their provincial premier rather than their national leader. It is interesting to discern a divergence between the liberal and socialist strands of NDP thought on this issue; while Premier Allan Blakeney of Saskatchewan followed a conservative-socialist road, stressing legislative supremacy, Broadbent took a different path, toward individual rights. Although the government successfully guided the constitutional package to a special joint committee, it did not succeed in getting it passed by the end of the year. It escaped from committee only on February 13, 1981.

It then returned to the House of Commons where it sat, mired in debate and procedural wrangling, until the end of April. Two NDP amendments were accepted, one explicitly clarifying the equality of the sexes under the constitution, while another referred any changes to the rights of native people to a future federal-provincial amending conference.

To sustain its position the Trudeau government had been negotiating with Nova Scotia and Saskatchewan (it already had Ontario and New Brunswick in the bag), but in neither case could the necessary compromises be made. Meanwhile, the remaining six provinces referred the propriety and legality of federal unilateral action on the constitution to their courts of appeal. Three were chosen: Quebec's, as reflecting the civil law tradition and a francophone atmosphere, and Manitoba's and Newfoundland's, as being the most likely to favour the provincial case. From that point (October 23, 1980) forward, the rhythm of constitutional action was determined by the courts; it was a foregone conclusion that once the appeals judges had rendered their opinions, the Supreme Court of Canada would be called on by one side or the other to pronounce. Meanwhile, anticipating that the constitutional package would eventually reach London, the provincial governments began to lobby British politicians.

They were not without success. Led by Quebec's agent general in London, the provincial governments stimulated the British House of Commons Foreign Affairs Committee, chaired by Sir Anthony Kershaw, to investigate conventions that governed the amendment of the Canadian constitution. The committee's proceedings and its conclusions, which argued that the federal government had never before unilaterally altered the distribution of powers in the Canadian constitution, stimulated sharp debate. When the committee proffered its own criteria for the constitutionality of the federal amendments, involving a substantial measure of provincial consent, the federal government was moved to issue a rebuttal. Critics pointed out that the Kershaw committee's three expert witnesses were not expert in Canadian constitutional law and that two out of three had been retained by the Quebec government as consultants. But others have responded that Kershaw and company had the better of the argument and that the balance of past practice sustained the provincial arguments.[8]

The provincial governments were not disappointed in Newfoundland, but their views were vigorously rejected in Manitoba and Quebec, though by divided tribunals. At the end of April 1981 the Supreme Court of Canada began to hear the constitutional reference; its decision was rendered five months later, on September 28.

The Supreme Court decision was lengthy and somewhat confusing. It separated the issues of law and convention. The federal government's manner of proceeding was, in the Court's view, legal but unconventional. It could be done, for the law allowed it; but it had not been done before.

Both sides promptly proclaimed victory. The federal government rejoiced that the courts had sustained its legal right to act; the provincial governments argued that what the courts had done was to rule the federal government's procedure legal but illegitimate. (Why, then, was it still legally possible?) The federal government could go ahead and send its constitution to Westminster, where the provinces had every reason to expect that it would receive a scorching reception and very doubtful passage. Both sides were right; what the court had done was to clear the ground for compromise. After all, the governments of Alberta and Canada had recently reached agreement on energy, removing a notorious irritant to federal-provincial relations; the understanding was a contribution to, and a precedent for, agreement on other matters.

To demonstrate that compromise was at least possible, Trudeau called a meeting with the provincial premiers in Ottawa at the beginning of November. The eight dissenting premiers ('the Gang of Eight') understood that another failed meeting would be a prelude to a submission to the British Parliament, with incalculable consequences if British MPs obstructed it. They had in the mean time altered their position from the intransigence of September 1980; in April 1981 they agreed to a 'Provincial Patriation Plan,' which allowed for patri-

---

8 E. McWhinney, *Canada and the Constitution, 1979-1982* (Toronto: University of Toronto Press, 1982), pp. 70-1; Peter Russell, 'Bold Statescraft, Questionable Jurisprudence,' in Keith Banting and Richard Simeon, eds., *And No One Cheered: Federalism, Democracy and the Constitution Act* (Toronto: Methuen, 1983), pp. 222-3.

ation and an amending formula that involved compensation for provinces that opted out of future amendments; but most important, it involved the abandonment of Quebec's claim to a veto over constitutional change. Although their plan was immediately rejected by the federal government, it remained alive as a negotiating position; and it was this position that the Gang of Eight brought to the negotiating table in November.

The negotiations that followed were complex, but from Trudeau's point of view fruitful. Trudeau managed to win Quebec's consent to a referendum on the constitution, with the possibility of the federal government appealing to the people over the heads of the provincial premiers; this disrupted the provincial common front. Then Chrétien detached the remaining seven of the Gang of Eight from Quebec, working out a compromise that was announced, with due fanfare, on November 5, 1981.

There would be patriation. The federal government accepted the provincial amending formula (from April) without any compensation for provinces that 'opted out' of any amendment. Minority language rights and mobility rights – up to a point – were guaranteed. There would be a Charter of Rights and Freedoms, although its pledges were subjected to a legislative override, the 'notwithstanding' clause. The federal government gambled that no government would wish to take advantage of the clause to admit that its legislation was not in conformity with accepted definitions of fundamental rights. Natural resources, equalization, forestry, and electrical energy were made the subject of a special compromise. Manitoba's Progressive Conservative government reserved consent on minority language rights, but within two weeks it was gone, blown away by its electors. Its NDP successor accepted the measure.

The Quebec government took these developments badly. It had misjudged the balance of federal-provincial diplomacy, acting, in the opinion of some provincial observers, with 'wilful blindness' in overestimating its partners' readiness to stand fast by the April provincial position. In any case, Lévesque shattered the psychological unity of the Gang of Eight when he jumped at Trudeau's offer of a solution by referendum.[9] Subsequent complaints from the Quebec government were taken to be sour grapes; the referendum had rendered them irrelevant. Lévesque took what satisfaction he could from using the 'notwithstanding' clause on every single piece of legislation passed by his legislature.

The result of the constitutional conference was transmitted to Britain, whose Parliament passed the Canada Act on March 8, 1982. It was duly signed and proclaimed by Queen Elizabeth II, with a very pleased Pierre Trudeau and Jean Chrétien in attendance, on a rainy day in Ottawa, April 17.

9   Romanow, Whyte, Leeson, *Canada ... Notwithstanding,* pp. 264-5.

Not everyone was pleased, but it is not quite true to say, as a group of academic critics has done, that 'No One Cheered.'[10] Certainly no one in that group cheered, a point not without its relevance in the future. Even among critics there was hope that the lesser good of the Charter of Rights and Freedoms would somehow outweigh the great harm done to process by Trudeau and his Liberals; they refused to contemplate the possibility that Trudeau might have been right and that the process was an obstacle to rational government rather than a totem for political scientists to worship. Many in various parts of Canada were pleased that the great constitutional conundrum that had bedevilled every Canadian government since 1967 had been resolved, and that its interpretation now belonged to the courts rather than the politicians.

The 1984 federal election was not, on the face of it, fought on the constitution. Trudeau was gone, and so, shortly, were the Liberals, too long in office, with too many enemies and too little to offer in response. Renovation and freshness, time for a change, were what the electorate sought, and the massive majority bestowed on Brian Mulroney and the Progressive Conservatives bore witness to the high expectations of Canadians.

Mulroney promised change, and to a very large extent – more than many realized at the time – he brought change. The National Energy Policy was dismantled. Newfoundland, which had unwisely taken its claim to off-shore jurisdiction to court, and lost, got most of what it wanted, including royalties, anyway. Nova Scotia, which had settled earlier with Ottawa, had its settlement topped up to match. The Trudeau government had fought for Ottawa's right to tax energy, in order to make up the central government's large deficit; by 1986 its Petroleum and Gas Revenue Tax was only a memory.

In one respect Mulroney carried on Trudeau's legacy. He was the first Quebec-centred leader of the Conservative party, and as such he was prepared to promote bilingualism, especially when it ran into a series of roadblocks in Manitoba. 'French power' in Ottawa was not reversed; francophones continued to receive encouragement to occupy high positions in the national civil service even though they still did not occupy places proportionate to their numbers in the country as a whole.

There was, it appeared, a more favourable climate for federal-provincial accord. In 1985 the provincial Liberals swept out the discredited and divided Parti Québécois government and returned to power under Robert Bourassa. Bourassa had not been noted for his ability to get on with Pierre Trudeau, and his cabinet included a number of Liberals who were anything but devotees of Trudeau's line

10 See above, note 8.

on constitutional balance. His Minister of Intergovernmental Affairs, Gil Rémillard, a constitutional scholar, had characterized Trudeau's constitutional revolution as 'legal but illegitimate,' reminiscent of the nineteenth-century ultramontanes in its willingness to impose correct values on a public that it had failed to consult. This would not prevent Rémillard from co-operating in a similar exercise, but with results he liked better, some years later.[11]

Mulroney carried forward Trudeau's campaign for 'la francophonie,' rather against the inclinations of the French government. But Mulroney prevailed, with the result that Quebec sat beside Ottawa in francophone summits in Paris in 1986 and in Quebec in 1987. Early signs were mixed, since the Quebec delegation to Paris immediately searched for, and found, ways of differentiating itself from its federal colleagues. And, as Mulroney discovered, hosting *la francophonie* in 1987 meant standing by blandly while the French premier Jacques Chirac, an acolyte of the late Charles de Gaulle, praised the latter's perception and genius in shouting 'Vive le Québec libre' back in 1967. But as Chirac observed, things were different now.

They were different because in the spring of 1987 Mulroney had 'brought Quebec back into the constitution,' by securing the unanimous consent of Canada's first ministers to a package of constitutional reforms. The federalist Liberal government of Quebec had enunciated a set of demands: the explicit guarantee of Quebec as a distinct society; increased provincial powers in immigration; the restriction of the federal spending power; the recognition of Quebec's right to a veto, traded away by Lévesque back in 1981; and a place for Quebec in nominating Supreme Court judges. With these demands before them, Mulroney assembled the premiers without their respective entourages or advisers in his chalet at Meech Lake north of Ottawa. When they emerged, Mulroney had their signatures on what came to be called the Meech Lake accord.

The Meech Lake accord conceded everything that Quebec wanted. It did more. It restored the constitutional veto to all provinces. By placing an explicit guarantee of a 'distinct society' in the preamble, it may have created an opportunity for Quebec to override the pledges contained in the Charter of Rights and Freedoms; but on this opinions differed. It handed over nominations to the Supreme Court and the Senate to provincial governments. The Prime Minister retained the power to appoint, it is true, but only from a list of provincial nominees. And the provinces got the right to opt out of federal programs, subject only to a vague warranty of similarity, with compensation. And Mulroney had resuscitated a particularly badly thought out Conservative constitutional proposal from the early eighties: there would be an annual conference on the constitution,

11 See Rémillard's interesting essay, 'Legality, Legitimacy and the Supreme Court,' in Banting and Simeon, *And No One Cheered*, pp. 189-209.

apparently ad infinitum. This feature certainly promised to make Canada's constitution unique. It is not surprising that Mulroney got unanimous consent.

The strongest argument for Meech Lake was precisely that it 'brought Quebec back into the constitution,' that it belatedly secured the consent of the government of Quebec to amendments to the constitution that had affected that government's powers. The agreement had been made with the federalist government of Quebec, worthy of trust, with no ulterior agenda. A high price for this consent was justified, the argument continued, since the Quebec government's consent legitimized the authority of the Canadian constitution in that province.

Acting on the principle of 'all for one and one for all,' the eleven Canadian governments announced that they would pass Meech Lake through their legislatures without changes. They would, it is true, hold hearings on the package, to allow their opponents to blow off steam, but the hearings themselves would not be taken seriously by the governments concerned. Critics of the agreement argued that Meech Lake would make the Canadian constitution, already inclined to provincial power, dangerously unbalanced. The critics included Trudeau, who emerged from retirement to write a scathing denunciation of the weakness and folly that had undermined his constitutional achievement. But if there was one thing that leaders of all three political parties in Ottawa agreed on, it was that they wanted no more of Trudeau and his bothersome habit of confronting contradictions. Lorne Nystrom, an NDP MP from Saskatchewan, put a blunt question to Trudeau when the latter appeared before the joint parliamentary committee 'studying' the accord. Referring to the premiers who had crafted Meech Lake, Nystrom demanded to know, 'Are all those people just weaklings and snivellers? ... Are all those people wrong? ... Are you right? ... Or has the country changed in the last few years?'

Trudeau was uncharacteristically mild in his response. 'Maybe I'm passé,' the former prime minister conceded. 'Maybe there's a new Canada now.'

On his television news commentary that evening, journalist Peter Trueman decided to improve on Trudeau's answers. To Nystrom's question, whether the Meech Lake negotiators were weaklings and snivellers, 'The answer is no, although none of them is very strong ... Two or three of them are barely bright enough to tie their own shoes; at least one of them is the invention of a marketing agency; in the midnight feeding frenzy that developed, only two of them fought to defend federal rights, and the Prime Minister was not one of them; the best of them appear merely ordinary; ... and some of them we wouldn't allow in our own living rooms.' As for Nystrom's final question, 'Has the country changed in the last few years?' Trueman responded: 'It certainly has, and not for the better ... It now appears that the joint committee will swallow the Meech Lake accord whole, and if the country does the same thing it will deserve what it

Trudeau testifies against Meech Lake – 1987 (Donato, c1987). Reproduced with the permission of the *Toronto Sun*

gets.'

Not surprisingly, Quebec swiftly ratified the Meech Lake agreement, and most of the other provinces followed along. At the time of writing, the ratification of the accord by all the provinces is probable; what the country will get as a result of course remains to be seen.

With respect to constitution-remaking, there was a certain symmetry in the Mulroney government's actions. Not content to rebuild Canada's main constitution through the Meech Lake accord, in April 1988 it also abolished our supplementary constitution – the War Measures Act of 1914. This pithy, ten-clause, four-page statute allowed the Governor in Council to 'do or authorise such acts and things, and make such orders and regulations, as he may by reason of the existence of real or apprehended war, invasion, or insurrection, deem necessary and advisable.' The provinces were not mentioned; under the act their powers and prerogatives could be, and regularly were, overruled, not only in 1914-18 but in 1939-45. Individuals, too, could find their civil liberties less than secure once the act had been proclaimed. Indeed, in the 1960s Parliament had amended the act so as free it from the trammels of the Diefenbaker Bill of Rights. Hence the rage with which civil libertarians greeted the proclamation of the act during the 1970 October Crisis. Although Parliament could always require the government to put the act back on the shelf, there was no provision for parliamentary surveillance, nor did a proclamation expire through the effluxion of time.

To replace the old statute Parliament passed a very different measure – the Emergencies Act. Now there were four sorts of emergency – public welfare, public order, international, and war. The Governor in Council could still act, but any proclamation would expire in no more than 120 days unless it was explicitly renewed. In a war emergency the government's powers would still seem to be effectively unlimited, but in all other sorts of emergency its special powers were carefully listed. Furthermore, even in a war emergency, there was to be prior consultation with the provinces, except where time did not permit, and there were careful clauses designed to ensure that Ottawa would not trench upon provincial powers and sensibilities.

Here the historian sees a sign of the times – and not an attractive one. The Emergencies Act hopes to handle crises by aligning provincial activities and regulations, without superseding these. The new act will therefore tend to hobble and castrate Canada's national government. In World War Two, it was thanks to the War Measures Act that Ottawa could act with decision and energy in every corner of the nation, and in all spheres of the national life. If the Emergencies Act had then existed, Canada's wartime economy would certainly have been managed very differently, and we find it hard to believe that either mobilization or management would have been very effective. We hope that the Emergencies Act will never have to face this sort of test.

30

Living after 1970:
Culture, Education, and Social Trends

In 1974 Pierre Trudeau reportedly decided not to make a speech on his government's cultural policy because the topic was deemed politically too sensitive. Twenty-five years before it would have been simply ludicrous. In the quarter-century since the Massey Commission, the state had become the major supporter of cultural activity in Canada, and an articulate pressure group had appeared to assure that the source that had brought life continued to nurture what it had created. Through content quotas, direct subsidies, and tax relief, the state recognized that culture was a legitimage area for large-scale operations. Sometimes the contrasts with the past were astonishing. In the mid-seventies British Columbia's Minister of Public Works (a portfolio usually associated with bridges and roads) referred to art as 'the sensitizing object' and 'an essential ingredient in our society.' The head of the Cultural Development Division in Alberta's Ministry of Government Services dreamed of Alberta as 'the cultural capital of the North American continent.' Money builds capitals, and here Alberta's commitment in 1976 to spend $400 million on cultural facilities suggests that there was more than rhetoric in Canada's most prosperous province. Quebec, of course, had less money, but its nationalism and the close ties between the Liberal and Péquiste politicians and the university community meant that the government inevitably took responsibility for promotion of culture.

Throughout Canada the munificence was remarkable. In 1964, government support for Canadian museums, art galleries, and related institutions was $6,060,067; six years later it was $22,478,511. The Federal Cultural Policy Review claimed that the federal government alone spent $1.2 billion on cultural matters in 1981-2, a figure that it claimed was too low. Canada's per capita support of the arts throughout the 1970s and 1980s was estimated to be almost ten times that of the United States. Canada was no longer a nation whose art collectors embarrassed art's finest critics and whose professional artists were as scarce as palm trees and, like palms in Canada, something to be kept inside in sheltered corners. In 1952, Canadian artists exported 52 works; in 1962, 1,116; and in 1974, 9,131. Similarly, Canadian buyers imported 1,329 works of art in 1952, 5,222 in 1962, and 32,680 in 1974. State support for artists thus paralleled, and was the corollary of, public sympathy for the arts that had not been present earlier.

It is hoped that the reader will not necessarily regard as special pleading (although admittedly university professors are given to such activity) the suggestion that the major factor in this creation of new tastes among Canadians is the expansion of educational opportunity in Canada. Leisure and affluence are, of course, important factors; yet when one considers the creation of culture, the part played by education is clear. A survey of artists by *Arts Canada* in 1976 indicated that 10 per cent of artists' incomes came from sales, 10 per cent from direct grants, and 40 per cent from teaching and related occupations (10 per cent also came from unemployment insurance and welfare). The discontent in the artistic community in the late 1970s and early 1980s can, therefore, be seen as directly related to the ailments that afflicted Canadian education; having endured severe growing pains in the 1950s and 1960s the educational system now faces, in the vernacular, a severe mid-life crisis.

Urged by Quebec and the other provinces, the Trudeau government gradually disengaged itself from the educational system that federal money had done so much to build up in the 1950s and 1960s. Ottawa continued to finance much of the training and retraining of adults. Through the Canada Council and the other research councils it still financed a great deal of research in the universities. It still operated the military colleges at Kingston, Victoria, and St Jean. Through DREE, it helped finance schools in the backward regions. But it did not renew the provisions for financing secondary vocational and technical education that it had devised in the early sixties. And in university finance it made a gradual exit. The universities were not happy about this. In province after province, the fiscal net was gradually tightened around them. Provincial authorities now controlled fee scales. Sometimes they treated endowment income as an offset that reduced provincial grants. Generally they failed to raise grants in step with inflation, although the pattern differed from province to province. By 1985 the 'underfinancing' of Ontario universities had become an election issue. It was obvious that Ontario, a rich province, had not funded higher education as well as it might. In the early fifties, faced with a similar squeeze, the universities had won federal subsidies to supplement provincial grants. It was apparent that in the eighties Ottawa would not listen, and a conference that tried to resolve the financing problem in 1987 ended without agreement.

For the universities the Trudeau years were difficult; and the troubles were not all financial. Full-time enrolments continued to rise, but much less rapidly than in the sixties. Indeed, by the mid-seventies some locales saw enrolments falling, and, especially where enrolments determined grants, there were already some signs of a scramble for students. Part-time studies expanded greatly, and much better arrangements came to be made for the part-time student, but the numbers did not explode as the futurologists had forecast in the late sixties. In any case, part-time students did not fit neatly into curricula that had been designed for full-time study, and in general it was the curriculum that gave way, as one university after another, in response to economic and student pressure, adopted some form of the American 'credit system.' This system had already firmly rooted itself in many provincial secondary systems. The credit system was a neat way to meet the demands for 'flexibility' and 'freedom of choice' that were so often heard in the late sixties, when a great deal of time and effort had had to go into redesigning curricula.

At the same time (the late sixties), on many campuses there were disorders that reflected or imitated developments in Europe and the United States. Journalists began to write 'think pieces' about student revolutionaries. Student politicians brooded on an American tract, *The Student as Nigger*, and began to suffer from delusions of grandeur in which terrified administrators often encouraged them to indulge. At Toronto and elsewhere students repeatedly sat in; at Sir George Williams in Montreal they occupied part of a building and destroyed the computer. There was pressure to insert students into administration at all levels, from appointments committees to boards of governors. There were demands for black studies, native studies, women's studies, urban and environmental studies, and, of course, Canadian studies. In addition, because some student leaders – and some faculty members – wanted changes that would make university study more flexible and, probably, easier than before, the old curricular arrangements came under attack.

By the late seventies many of these stresses had passed. The revolutionary student had largely vanished, at least partly because it was now clear that a university degree did not guarantee a good job. Students were working harder and choosing the more structured and vocationally oriented courses (such as commerce) where job prospects were thought to be good and where rewards were quicker and more certain. There were demands for return to a more vertebrate program of study, although there were endless arguments about the shape that structure should take.

Controversy developed when three historians, one of them an author of this book, entitled a work on Canadian universities *The Great Brain Robbery*. Their allegation that the decline of Canadian universities – the decline seemed to be admitted on all sides – stemmed from laxity on the part of faculty and administration as well as from governments neglect was met with howls of outrage from many quarters, especially the Canadian Association of University Teachers. Nevertheless, most observers within and outside the university did accept that the quality of education could be improved at all levels. Governments were reluctant to act because entrenched interests were strong and easy solutions were not present. Public expenditure on education remained relatively high, at 8 per cent of GNP in 1987, as compared to 5.1 per cent in France, 5.7 per cent in Japan, and 6.8 per cent in the United States. Over one-third of the population over twenty-five had some post-secondary education, and a roughly equal percentage had completed secondary education, although what that meant did vary from province to province. The population had a high degree of literacy, but statistics indicated that Canada compared poorly with other Western nations in some key indicators of how that literacy was used. The average Canadian in 1981 spent only 3.5 hours reading per week and watched 13.3 hours of television. Canada had 1.7 persons per television receiver compared to 2.4 in West Germany and 3.0 in the United Kingdom. The Canadians tied the Americans for the lowest figure, but even the Americans read more. There were, in 1986, 217 newspapers circulated per 1,000 Canadians; the United States stood at 267, the United Kingdom at 421, and Japan at 565. Maybe Marshall McLuhan, and his *Understanding Media,* influenced his fellow Canadians more than we realize.

In 1977-8 enrolments finally began their predicted fall. Everyone had said that a decline was on the way, but the change came more quickly than most people expected. Some universities responded by lowering their entry standards. Others were more imaginative. For instance, in autumn 1979 Karma Buddhist College enrolled its first students. Affiliated with Brock University, Karma had been founded to perpetuate the Kargyu strain of Tibetan Buddhism. Although its courses were not to count for academic credit, Karma claimed (or at least hoped) to bring students 'to a greater, higher level of self-realisation.' To the optimists, it represented a last flutter from the flower people of the sixties. To the pessimists, it looked like a desperate step, meant to bring more students to Brock. Few other universities would adopt equally unusual expedients. And in the eighties, enrolments were rising again.

The early seventies saw a boom in Canadian studies and 'Canadianization.' From Carleton University, Professors Robin Mathews and James Steele were issuing anti-American manifestos. In Ontario a legislative committee called for measures to bring about a Canadianization of faculties. Gradually the immigration authorities responded, not only to such demands but also to protect the job prospects of Canadian graduate students. As so few universities were hiring by the mid-seventies little Canadianization or feminization was possible, but where jobs were available there was natural pressure to favour the Canadian candidate, the female one, or both. And no doubt in some places there was a great deal that could properly be done. Without substantial drafts of foreigners the university expansion of the sixties and early seventies could not have happened. But the recruitment arrangements of the sixties had not always been quite fair to Canadian candidates. A widespread feeling developed that the universities should be more Canadian, both in staff and in program. Hence the efflorescence of courses in all aspects of Canadian life, literature, and society. The wave of Canadian content even spread abroad. Responding to sarcastic comment and anxious to strengthen Canada's links with Europe and the Far East, Ottawa began to subsidize Canadian studies programs in Japan, Britain, and continental Europe, as well as in the United States. The results were sometimes funny, and often ineffective, but at least the government was trying to dispel that ignorance about Canada of which travelling Canadians had so often complained. In the United States, for example, undergraduate courses on Canada multiplied; and serious academic studies of Canada reappeared.

The universities and the community colleges had 789,690 students in 1986-7. Approximately 42 per cent of the eighteen-to-twenty-one age group were in some kind of higher education. The percentage was one of the highest in the world, though it was still higher in the United States. But in the seventies an ever-growing amount of university-type work was being done in the community colleges, which also offered a vast range of career programs. In 1966, 14.2 per cent of all Canadians aged eighteen to twenty-four were enrolled in some sort of full-time schooling, almost entirely in the universities. By 1976 the percentage had risen to 19.4 per cent, partly because the community colleges offered so many new and attractive alternatives to university study. Enrolments rose in the 1980s largely because of a higher female participation rate. More Canadian students seemed to want easier entrance requirements, shorter courses clearly focused on jobs, and a somewhat less pressured academic environment. All these things the community colleges could offer. Indeed, most of them had been designed to do just that.

Although there had been a few junior colleges in Canada, the sixties were a time of new foundations – institutes of technology, community colleges of various kinds in the anglophone provinces, and in Quebec the CEGEPs. By 1968 Ontario already had some twenty Colleges of Applied Arts and Technology (CAATs), and Quebec soon came to possess some thirty-seven CEGEPs, of which four operated in English. Some twenty-eight classical colleges had survived in Quebec, but they were now of much less significance than before. In the early seventies, Alberta and British Columbia saw a flowering of junior colleges, while in Saskatchewan, Manitoba, and the Atlantic provinces, governments showed some inclination to adopt or adapt the Ontario CAAT. The expansion halted in the 1970s; the expansionary mistakes of the 1970s were frozen in place.

What did all this expansion mean in terms of learning? It was hard to say. Many of the institutions, such as Ryerson in Toronto and the BC Institute of Technology in Vancouver, successfully developed rigorous training schemes whose graduates were welcomed in the work world. But Quebec's Collèges d'enseignement générale et professionel (CEGEPs) were a very mixed bag, especially in their university transfer streams. In British Columbia, some university people thought that transfer students from the junior colleges were not really ready for senior work in the universities, and some observers regretted the passing of the old senior matriculation system, by which some high schools offered what was in effect first-year university.

Whatever the junior colleges and other community colleges were trying to do, like the universities they were working with students who often seemed to have learned less than expected in secondary school. No one quite knew what had gone wrong, but by 1979 most observers agreed that something had. In Ontario, it was usual to blame the erasure of the old high-school curriculum with its limited freedom of choice, the introduction of a credit system with free options, and the abolition of external examinations for high-school exit or university entrance. In the mid-1980s, David Peterson's Liberal government won support by calling for fewer options, more rigour, and more compulsion. In other provinces the same general pattern could be detected during the seventies and eighties, and if these criticisms were proper in one province, presumably they applied in others. In Quebec it was often believed that the state secondary schools had grown too fast, staffing themselves with ill-prepared young enthusiasts whose main interests were political. The late 1970s and early 1980s saw many signs of a reaction, partly because parents, discovering what was actually happening in the schools, began to protest. But both teachers and educational establishments had grown attached to the new system; it remained to be seen how much change they would allow.

In the 1980s complaints about laxity in the arts curriculum were echoed by scientists who complained bitterly about the lack of governmental support for their work. The so-called technological revolution of the 1980s found Canada scrambling to keep up; in few fields was Canada's record in the 1970s and 1980s impressive. Politicians made silly remarks about the need to improve science education in order that Canada 'keep up' with many supposed threats. These tended to be ignored, but when the University of Toronto chemist John Polanyi, who won the Nobel Prize in 1986 for his work on infrared chemiluminescence, said that he was telling his best students to go to the United States if they wanted a career in science, Canadians took notice. There was some irony in the remarks of Polanyi, a leading peace activist as well as a great scientist. American support for science derived in considerable part from the large military budget. In Canada, defence spending was one-third of the American rate. Needless to say, the difference was not devoted to Canadian universities or Canadian science.

The slippage in standards was doubly surprising because for the first time in a quarter of a century the schools did not have to cope with an ever-rising wave of pupils. Enrolments in elementary and secondary schools peaked in 1970, and thereafter they dropped nearly 10 per cent in the course of the decade, reflecting the falling birth rates of the 1960s. The result was panic in the teachers' unions, and joy in ministries of education. Teachers' colleges closed or reduced their intakes. Ministries raised the standards for certification, especially in elementary teaching. In universities, fewer students concentrated on the humanities subjects that would have led in the fifties and sixties to a secure if demanding career in schoolteaching. In the schools themselves, pupils were allowed to shift away from the more academic or difficult subjects. Thus the free-choice curriculum made things worse so far as many teachers were concerned. These trends were especially noticeable and alarming with respect to the study of French in the anglophone provinces. Although many schools were extending and improving their French instruction, and although many school districts were mounting impressive immersion schemes, fewer anglophone pupils were actually studying the other national language in university. Trudeauvian bilingualism was unpopular, and French was supposed to be difficult. In francophone Canada, it seems that more pupils were studying English, but chiefly because more teenagers were staying in school. Some observers thought that the average Quebec pupil was actually mastering less English than before.

As parents came to believe that in the public schools their children would learn little, not enough, or nothing, private schools flourished. Their enrolments rose from 140,000 in 1971 to 182,000 in 1975, even though total enrolment was falling from 5.8 million to 5.6 million. They then levelled off as costs rose. Many new schools were founded, and some old ones managed to raise not only the calibre of their intakes but also the quality of their efforts. Of course some of the private schools specialized in trendy trivia; but others offered remarkably rigorous academic programs. One new foundation, the Lester Pearson College on Vancouver Island, was planned with a view to build international friendship by mixing pupils from different countries.

It was often thought that the separate and parochial schools did a better job than the public schools, even though they had less money, because both pupils and teachers took discipline more seriously. Whether or not this was so, in many cities separate school enrolment went on rising long after public school enrolments had begun to fall. This was largely because so many immigrant families were Roman Catholic. More pupils meant better morale, but the results could sometimes look grotesque, as separate school boards put up new schools while public school boards worried about empty classrooms.

There were still some disputes about the financing of denominational schools. In British Columbia, Roman Catholics campaigned from time to time to acquire tax dollars. In Ontario, where tax support for separate schools ended with Grade 10, there were efforts to extend support through Grade 13 and to make it more generous. In 1985 these efforts succeeded. In Ontario, too, there was some agonizing about government financing of church-related colleges and theological faculties, but they too were funded in the 1980s. But by the mid-seventies this kind of worry had come to seem increasingly anachronistic. In disputes about schools and schooling, it was now language that mattered; not religion.

Of the many social changes of the seventies and eighties, we cannot yet be sure what future generations will deem significant. Our comments are admittedly eclectic, some might say eccentric, but they represent our impression of some of those trends that might endure and some of those events that will stay in Canadians' memories.

The seventies neither roared nor soared nor were dirty. Adjectives shun the decade, but for Canadians, change came quickly yet not in a regular pattern. This was the decade in which the sexual revolution really hit the dominion of the north. Birth rates, having fallen for almost a decade, stabilized at or slightly below the net reproduction rate. For the first time since the thirties, one-child families were chic. In the great cities there were more varieties of family structure, and these families were far less stable than ever before. Premarital intercourse was now reported to be so common as to be commonplace. Divorce was also more common as a result of the 1968 changes in the divorce law. Between 1971 and 1974 divorces rose from 20,685 to 45,019; the latter number was almost seven times the figure for 1961. In 1985 there were 60,928. The stigma attached to illegitimacy all but disappeared. For the first time, the one-parent family became a noticeable fact in Canadian urban life. However, the unwanted baby was a vanishing species, as the adoption agencies discovered. In spite of a vocal right-to-life movement, legal abortion was now frequent, simple, often easy, and getting steadily easier. In 1987, it appeared to become easier still when the Supreme Court struck down the existing law in a dramatic and much debated assertion of its power. The Pill was readily available, although its effects worried many women who chose interuterine devices instead – until these too occasioned alarms. Condoms could be bought almost everywhere, now that it was no longer illegal to display or sell them. As for pornography, although the really hard and nasty material was still not widely sold, there was far more soft porn in the late seventies than ever before. By then there were signs of a change of heart with respect to these materials. From the late 1970s the government that had taken the policeman out of the bedroom was actively considering bringing him back to the magazine rack, the video store, and the art gallery. Indeed, its proposals would have let any local authority ban almost any printed material, from *Pericles* to *Penthouse*, if local sensibilities found it offensive. But whatever might happen to the porn industry, there was no reason to expect any general sexual counter-revolution – until AIDS.

AIDS was unheard of in the late seventies; by the mid-1980s it was known everywhere and was greatly influencing private behaviour and public debate. Although Canadian AIDS cases were not large in number by 1988, the impact of the epidemic on public health and sexual behaviour was profound. Toronto's bath houses, which gay rights activists fought to keep open despite continuous police raids, were closed by the gays themselves as the contagion of AIDS spread. At first it appeared that AIDS could be spread only through sexual contact, but it soon became clear that AIDS was transmitted through the bloodstream: cuts, lesions, needle punctures – anything that allowed contaminated blood or bodily fluids to enter the system. It was well known that some AIDS cases had developed from blood transfusions, but rumours about saliva-spread AIDS were generally unfounded. What was not in doubt was its seriousness: the virus meant death, and there was no known cure and none on the horizon. For the gay community at least sexual liberation came to an abrupt end.

As with sex, so with drugs. During the seventies the drug culture peaked, and parts of it became respectable. In 1969 LSD and STP became 'restricted drugs,' and thereafter fewer Canadians went tripping on hallucinogens. But the LeDain Commission recommended that marijuana should be 'decriminalized,' and although nothing was formally done, the drift of police and judicial action was clearly to de-emphasize the cannabis problem. More and more people came to believe that reefers were no more harmful than rye. There seemed to be less social smoking – the ritual passing-around of a joint. But as the adolescents of the sixties became the young executives and professionals of the seventies and eighties, perhaps there was more scope for extended and private enjoyment. As for heroin and the other drugs that everyone admitted were really dangerous, the addiction problem certainly did not diminish, and the crime it generated did not grow less. But by the mid-seventies the teenager was a dying breed, killed off by the Pill. Both absolutely and relatively there were fewer adolescents than there had been ten years before. Also, there were plenty of signs that the young were turning back to the traditional solace of earlier generations – booze. Now most provinces let the young drink at eighteen or nineteen, and sales statistics showed that the young would be even more tempted by John Barleycorn and his friends than their parents had been. Total alcoholic-drink consumption increased from 394,532,000 gallons in 1970 to 520,068,000 in 1978, as the drinking age fell. Though the drinking age rose slightly in the years that followed, consumption rose too, to roughly 636,086,000 gallons in 1985-6.

Nearly all the social indicators that Canadians had traditionally used to measure the stability of their society seemed to reflect instability in the 1970s. The abortion rate rose from 8.3 per 100 live births in 1971 to 17.4 in 1978 but fell to 16.5 in 1985. Suicides increased from 2,559 in 1971 to 3,317 in 1977 to 5,850 in 1987; especially troubling were the rises in rape conviction from 1,019 in 1969 to 1,886 in 1977 to 2,550 in 1983 and in murder convictions from 342 to 624. The latter, however, declined in the 1980s. What these indicators mean is no longer so certain as it seemed when Sir Wilfrid Laurier proudly compared our divorce and crime rates to those of the decadent Americans. Many commentators followed Christopher Lasch in suggesting that the pattern of changes in social behaviour reflects the narcissism of modern culture. This idea generated the phrase 'the me decade,' a common label for the seventies. Perhaps the label fits and will stick, but it would be unfortunate if these trends, which reflect the decline of restraints on individuals and diminished concern for the welfare of the community as a whole, were seen through the narrow focus of a decade and a single nation. Even in Canada itself, regional variation was striking: the divorce rates in British Columbia and Newfoundland were, in 1978, 326.7 per 100,000 and 75 per 100,000 respectively. In all these things Canada followed the Western world generally, and the changes reflected patterns already apparent in earlier decades. Moreover, if so many social critics lamented the way we lived now, there were many positive changes which the critics of an earlier generation had demanded but never really expected. We had artistic and educational opportunities beyond our fondest hopes in 1945, and a much greater proportion of the population took advantage of them.

The sixties were the great decade of building to house the arts. Alberta built two identical concert halls, one for Edmonton and one for Calgary. Vancouver built the Queen Elizabeth Theatre and the smaller Playhouse. Thanks to the Centennial celebrations of 1967, Charlottetown got a theatrical showpiece, Toronto eventually got the St Lawrence Centre for the Performing Arts and Roy Thomson Hall, and, most important and most valuable, Ottawa got the National Arts Centre. More theatres and halls opened in 1970. Thereafter, little occurred: although in 1988 there was talk of a new opera house for Toronto and a new concert hall for Montreal, the last major project had been the Shaw Festival Theatre in Niagara-on-the-Lake. But the good work had been done. Provided at last with suitable venues, Canada's performing arts blossomed. By 1970 there were repertory companies in Halifax, Fredericton, Montreal, Ottawa, Toronto, Edmonton, Vancouver, Victoria, and more. Some summer festivals, such as Vancouver's, sank without trace. Others, such as Stratford's, tended to wither steadily in artistic merit while triumphing at the box office and at the subsidy trough. Still others, such as the Shaw Festival, went from strength to strength.

And off the great and very expensive stages there was a flowering of less expensive and less lavish theatre. This kind of thing was most noticeable in Toronto, Vancouver, and Montreal, but other cities were affected too. Subsidies helped, of course. So did unemployment insurance. Quality varied, partly because so few companies really had to depend on pleasing the public, and partly because acting had become a form of self-expression, not a form of discipline. There were troubles with directors, too. Some were criticized, especially Stratford's Robin Phillips, who was accused of mingling disrespect for the classic texts with an interest in gimmickry. Others, such as George Luscombe in Toronto, did well in spite of Marxist and populist obsessions. Not that such obsessions were peculiar to directors. Playwrights shared them, and as subsidies spread and theatres sprang up there were opportunities for the 'genuinely Canadian play' – everything from Merrill Denison's *March Hay* to Robertson Davies's *Pontiac and the Green Man* and Michel Tremblay's *Belles soeurs* and *St Carmen of the Main,* surely one of the most boring pieces of theatre ever thrust upon the public. But at least for Tremblay's play there *was* a public, both in English and in French. For the outpourings of many other Canadian playwrights this could not be said. Subsidized companies *performed* the plays, yes. But often the audience stayed away in droves. And the Toronto Truck Theatre, which did well at the box office on things like *The Mousetrap,* was vilified by the 'arts community' because it was both popular *and* unsubsidized.

In parallel with all this there was some genuinely commercial theatre activity. In 1970, *Hair* ran for a year at the Royal Alexandra Theatre in Toronto and for twelve weeks in Montreal. Ed Mirvish, having grown rich as a retail merchant, bought Toronto's Royal Alex, ran it as a commercial proposition, and appeared to grow still richer. Summer stock companies performed popular plays without subsidy. In some cities, touring companies still came from Britain and from New York. Affluent Canadians were increasingly inclined to use theatre as a decoration to their lives, and the theatres, both subsidized and unsubsidized, mounted massive campaigns to get the public away from the TV screens and into the stalls.

As for theatre, so for opera, ballet, modern dance, and music. Although the subsidies never seemed large enough, the trend was certainly upward, and provinces and cities joined corporations and the Canada Council in underwriting the massive budgets, while, from time to time, the banks presumably carried the massive deficits. Sometimes patience failed, of course. In 1979 the Festival Singers of Canada went messily bankrupt. In 1987 the Vancouver Symphony Orchestra did the same. The Canadian Opera Company stuck largely to things that it knew the public wanted to hear. Admittedly, in 1967 and thereafter it had performed Somers's *Louis Riel*. But this was a Centennial project, with special foundation subsidies. Anyway, Riel was on his way to secular beatification, and no one could deny that he was genuinely Canadian. The three major ballet companies toured and polished and trained, daring to face critical audiences in New York, London, and even the Soviet Union (the same could not be said of the subsidized theatre companies). Ottawa's National Arts Centre, opened in 1969, quickly earned a distinguished reputation as home of a summer opera festival and as year-round base for Mario Bernardi and the National Arts Centre Orchestra. There were more symphony orchestras, too, and more of these were approaching international standing. Vancouver brought Richard Bonynge to run its new opera, and, from a base in Halifax, Symphony Nova Scotia toured ceaselessly, except when its members were on strike.

Every so often there were nervous twinges about all this. Was the whole thing *too* dependent on subsidy? What would happen if the money ran out? In the 1980s the Vancouver and Windsor symphonies ran into serious trouble. The federal and provincial governments appointed numerous bodies to look at problems in the arts. The most notable was the so-called Applebaum-Hebert commission (Federal Cultural Policy Review) which generally applauded what had been done but called on government to respect the arm's-length relationship concept which it found had fallen into disrepute among politicians and senior bureaucrats. There was some emphasis on better use of the private sector as a provider and subsidizer. By 1988 little had come of these recommendations. The arts community complained about cutbacks by the federal government, and there were indications that in another recession the arts would have a most difficult time.

In cinema, too, subsidy combined with tax gimmickry was working a miracle, both in quantity and in artistic quality. The latter, of course, was mixed: at one extreme, *Mon Oncle Antoine*; in the middle, *Goin' down the Road*; at the other, *Meatballs*. The distributing industry was largely Canadianized. Although the number of movie houses was falling, small new houses were still opening, and they usually belonged to local interests. American multinationals still owned Famous Players and Twentieth Century theatres, but in 1978 a Canadian entrepreneur brought Odeon from Britain's Rank interests. By the mid-1980s Cineplex, which was controlled by the fashionable Toronto entrepreneur Garth Drubinsky, was Canada's largest chain and was very active in the United States. Ironically the Americans now complained about the Canadian invasion. One might suspect that the Canadian film production industry was doing its best to follow the appropriate line. The Film Development Corporation would lend government money for 'Canadian' films, no matter whether the stars came from Napanee, Beverly Hills, or Lower Slobbovia. But Canadian movie-goers now had the chance to see bits of Vancouver Harbour and slices of Trinity College and gobs of King township on film – although only as background. In Quebec things were much better. And, strangely, hovering on the fringe but making money were such companies as Canukr Films, which made movies in Ukrainian. At first it had trouble because all its casts spoke Ukrainian with Canadian accents. Also, the specially constructed Ukrainian village near Oshawa did not look sufficiently weatherbeaten and decayed to be believably Ukrainian. But a little practice and experience cured the first problem, and a couple of Ontario winters cured the second.

There was some pressure for a quota system, like that in Britain, by which a certain percentage of all showings would have to be Canadian. This was not provided for the movies, but the Canadian Radio and Television Commission (CRTC) did persevere with quotas, not merely for television but also for radio. The government had already acted, in 1968, to ensure that in any broadcasting company 80 per cent of the voting shares had to be Canadian and that all such companies had to have Canadians as directors and chairmen. With the boardrooms purified, Canada's electronic media could presumably do their nationalist best, while the CRTC would do what it could to make sure that the public would watch and listen. At first it said that it would stress quality, not quantity, although, perhaps not surprisingly, that did not last long. It quickly moved to tighten the content rules it had inherited.

The result was quite complicated. In 1970, following the Commission's ruling, the record companies and the Canadian Association of Broadcasters got together and examined the situation. To their surprise they found that there were already 7,000 discs that could be called Canadian. At that time, Helmut Kallmann wrote, 'The whole effort seemed to be designed as much to promote the employment and marketing aspects of the music industry as to make the listener familiar with the home-grown product.' Indeed, the listener can seldom have known whether any particular singer or disc was 'Canadian.' Yet after the quota was invented there certainly was a flowering of Canadian pop records and pop performers – all sorts, from folk through rock to country and western. Indeed, the popular arts came together in Tremblay's *St. Carmen*, about a Québécoise cowgirl singer who goes to Kentucky to improve her yodelling but whose political consciousness is somehow raised during the process. Meanwhile, the gurus of international pop had their huge Canadian followings, and the tides of musical fashion did not stop at the Atlantic seaboard or the forty-ninth parallel. Some

Canadians such as Bryan Adams did very well internationally. Nevertheless, there were fewer teenagers, so that the youth culture, which was so largely musical, subtly changed its texture. Side by side with the music of the young ran a trend in instant nostalgia, as young and not-so-young adults relived the music of their own youths, all the way back through the Beatles and Elvis to the big band sound of the forties.

As for the music that was not pop, there was at last some chance for Canadians to buy their own performers on disc. To find Canadian compositions was admittedly more difficult, but not impossible. In 1967 the CBC had begun to produce some records for distribution through ordinary business channels. In the Trudeau years this arrangement continued at first, only to be superseded by a much larger project of CBC recordings. Regrettably, for some years these records were not sold in stores; to get them one had to write to Toronto, thus encountering what had become the worst postal-sorting office in the capitalist world. Besides the CBC's labours, the commercial companies themselves began to seek out Canadian performers and orchestras, especially those whose conductors were known abroad. The Toronto Symphony made several discs; so did the Festival Singers. By 1988 there was concern lest the Canadian record-pressing companies might not survive under free trade.

One might think that because so many Canadians lived next to the United States the CRTC's labours would be in vain. As the cable systems expanded they could and did carry ever more American TV, and even FM radio. Further, the quality of the American product was rapidly improving thanks to the new and relatively generous funding of American public broadcasting, whose ad-free programming competed directly with the CBC's. But the CRTC had an answer, or thought it did. It would regulate cable as well. Some provinces (Quebec, for one) sought to annex this right but were not allowed to do so, although both Quebec and Ontario were at length permitted to set up their own broadcasting stations. As for cable, it would have to give priority to Canadian advertisers and sources of programming, and it would have to provide 'community' channels no matter how few people might watch these feeble dribblings of local self-expression. Further, the cable systems could carry American channels only when *all* relevant Canadian channels were already on line, even where the Canadian signals duplicated or triplicated one another. In the event, the cable technology was too much even for the CRTC. For a time the Commission made it illegal to import American signals by microwave; but nothing could stop the cable converter, which could increase the number of channels from ten to forty or even more, thereby providing room for American signals in plenty. Although the Commission might strain every nerve to make sure that every anglophone family would be watching *The King of Kensington,* all it achieved was a rupture for itself − and, increasingly, a belly laugh from the public. In the 1980s the CRTC struggled to Canadianize pay television, but again Canada's small market and the popularity of American programming bedevilled the efforts.

By 1980 many Canadians were questioning whether CBC television could survive the defection of viewers and the effects of new technology. Few had doubts about the survival of Canadian literature. At the beginning of the decade Margaret Atwood had published a primer on Canadian literature, *Survival,* which argued for the persistence of certain themes (most notably 'survival') in Canadian literature and which, in evangelical fervour, called on Canadians to recognize a unique literary heritage. As Malcolm Ross pointed out, Atwood's intellectual structure left out a great deal of Canada's heritage – in particular those parts that were not defensive and obsessed with survival. But few read Ross; and many read *Survival.* Indeed, after *Survival* it seemed that Atwood had given a formula to which Canadian authors must conform. Certainly her novel *Surfacing* was an elaboration of what she thought had been and, in the future, must be. Fortunately, by the end of the decade, the stridently defensive tone of *Survival* was no longer necessary, as Canadian writers got increasing and favourable notice at home and elsewhere.

Atwood herself became a critical and popular success, and a missionary for Canadian studies, although her novels received more praise in the United States than in Canada. About Marian Engel's and Alice Munro's work there seemed to be more consensus, and the latter author's extraordinary sense of time and place put her short stories and novels on both history and literature reading lists. Certain western Canadian authors had similar fortunate fates. Rudy Wiebe and Robert Kroetsch had vastly different styles, but as representatives and interpreters of a distinct Canadian literary tradition they attracted much attention. So did Robertson Davies, whose voice was unique yet Canadian and whose novels sold well in Canada and elsewhere. French-Canadian literature became less nationalist and political as the decade passed. Most writers remained separatist, but, as Marie-Claire Blais admitted, that commitment meant far less in their art. The most acclaimed work in French during the 1970s was a novel by Antonine Maillet that won the Prix Goncourt, and its subject was the Acadians, not modern or even old Québec. Few would read Maillet, and in Canada far more Canadians read the sports pages than the book reviews. The gap between popular and high culture widened in the 1970s, although governments worried about the former as well as the latter, so that in sports, too, nationalism became central to public debate.

When, for example, Canadian football clubs enforced blackouts locally on televised games, they presumably diverted a few bodies into the bleachers but switched many more eyeballs to the telecasts of the (US) National Football

League games of the week. There was little that the government or the CRTC could do about this. By the mid-1980s the Canadian Football League was near collapse. The CRTC did impose tax penalties for Canadian firms that advertised on American TV. But if enough Canadian sets were tuned to the border stations Canadian business would find that it paid to advertise there, tax penalty or no. Fortunately for the nationalists, the seventies saw all sorts of new initiatives on the sports front. Canada hosted the 1976 Summer Olympics and the 1988 Winter Olympics; Canadian football was saved from complete Americanization. But Canada did other things too.

In 1970, Mayor Jean Drapeau announced that Montreal had won out over Moscow. In 1976 his city would host the Olympics. There would be a splendid stadium for 80,000 people. Just in case the Québécois got interested in cycling, there would be a velodrome. For athletes and journalists there would have to be an Olympic village, for which Ottawa would help pay because it would turn into public housing afterward. As for the rest, the Mayor assured his electors, it would not cost Montreal a penny.

Where would the money come from? Gradually the picture unrolled. There would be a national Olympic lottery – which fathered Loto Canada. There would be Olympic coins, stamps, and so on – promoted by the dominion, but aimed at financing Drapeau's dream. On ticket sales, one supposes, Drapeau hoped to raise some advance money.

Meanwhile, the country would have to get ready. Canada had already allowed the National Hockey League to add many US teams, but the effect on the calibre of hockey was disastrous, and anyway Canadians were already losing on international rinks to the Russians and the Swedes. Ironically, the nation that had given birth to hockey had no Olympic team between 1968 and 1980. In 1984 and 1988 the teams were quickly eliminated. To ready the athletes for competition there would be Canada Games from time to time and Ottawa would contribute funds to help athletes, coaches, and so on. Canada's national self-respect seemed to demand some sort of sporting life, especially after the ignominy of the 1968 Olympics in which Canada ranked fourteenth in the winter events and nineteenth in the summer. There was some consolation: Gordie Howe had scored his 700th goal and continued to score more; Nancy Greene was great on skis; Karen Magnussen was superb on skates; Nijinsky, son of Northern Dancer, was a magnificent horse. But none of this was enough.

In the end, the Montreal Olympics came near to being a national and municipal disaster. Buildings were overambitious; workers were rapacious but not diligent; money was not forthcoming; and everything cost more than expected. Almost up to the moment the Olympics commenced, people wondered whether they would happen at all. Almost certainly the International Olympic Committee had arranged for some sort of fall-back position. Some structures, including the great stadium, were not finished on opening day; a few could never be completed as designed. Still, some things went better than expected. In 1970 the superannuated runner Bruce Kidd had predicted that the Olympics would bring violence to Montreal. Quebec's poor, he said, would not stand for such a lavish extravaganza when their own needs were so great. Kidd was no prophet. For many Montreal workers the construction binge meant good jobs and big money. For everyone, the events themselves meant good spectacle and big excitement. Canada's showing, admittedly, was not brilliant, but no one had really expected it to be. As for the financial mess that the Olympics left behind, the less said the better.

From the Olympic adventure two things followed. One was the lottery. The other was sporting subsidy. In 1988, both were still very much alive. And if Ottawa could have a lottery, there was no reason why the provinces could not. Thus the Olympic Lottery begat not only Loto Canada but also Lottario, Wintario, the Western, the Provincial, Loto Quebec, and so on. Little or none of the net receipts went into general revenue; most was pumped out as subsidies to sports and culture. In 1979, when the Clark government said it might abolish Loto Canada, the sporting community rose as one and yelped with pain. It then tried to make common cause with the arts community, which was also yelping. (As a political alliance or lobby, the result is certainly a most implausible coupling.) As for the lotteries, people seemed to like them. Revenues far exceeded expectation. The TV spectaculars at which winners were announced attracted large audiences. As a form of tax, a lottery is inefficient because the costs of collection are so high; but at least it is a voluntary tax. It is no wonder that in 1979 the Clark government wondered about a lottery for the hospitals. Shades of the Irish Sweepstakes!

Western Canada did much better than Montreal with extravaganzas in the seventies and eighties. In 1986 Vancouver held Expo '86, which had as its themes the appropriately Canadian subjects of transportation and communication. World Fairs were no longer so elaborate as Montreal, but Vancouver was a success by any standards. There was some grumbling about its architectural value, but by 1986 there was a great deal more grumbling about what modern architecture had done to the urban landscape since the advent of the international style. Calgary's landscape seemed rather inhospitable to winter Olympics, but the mountains were nearby and the city was rich. After their successful bid for the 1988 Winter Olympics, Calgarians saw huge expenditures for new ski runs, skating rinks, and all kinds of public facilities. Canada spent four times as much as Yugoslavia in 1984 and ten times as much as the Americans had for the Lake Placid Olympics in 1980. Nevertheless, most critics regarded the games as a huge success, an effective advertising device for a city little known internationally. The performance of the Canadian athletes, unfortunately, was not so successful. Complaints abounded on the sports pages, and Bruce Kidd called for closer relations with East Germany which had swept so many events.

In earlier times Canadians might well have resisted the lottery temptation. But the seventies were a decade of moral change. It seemed that everything was acceptable – women's liberation, gay liberation, abortion on demand – you name it, some Canadian offspring of an American organization was lobbying for it. The old certainties were going fast. In Quebec, the Catholic school and welfare systems were quickly secularized as the religious fled from classroom and bedside. In Ontario, the Mackay Committee wanted to abolish religious instruction. The Anglican Church said that it could see no reason not to ordain women and homosexuals. The pope was still opposed to birth control, but many Canadian papists were manifestly not. Even the United Church, bastion of conservative radicalism, stopped fighting the good fight against beverage alcohol and in 1988 decided that it would 'consider' the ordination of lesbians and gays. In the process it narrowly escaped becoming the 'Disunited Church.'

In the old mainline churches there was a collapse of morale. In Quebec it was not the government's secularizing onslaught that killed the triumphalist church. If the hierarchy and the parishes had not lost their self-confidence, life would have been much harder for Quebec's politicians and officials. Deploring Methodist doctrine with respect to priests and bishops, the Anglicans nevertheless appropriated Methodist practice with respect to female ordination and abortion, and their leaders accepted not only the social gospel but, occasionally, the theology of revolution. In 1978, the Primate of All Canada was explaining on national television why he was quite willing to give money to some African movements that were terrorist as well as revolutionary. Anglicans were scarcely the Conservative party at prayer. Indeed the church hierarchy joined others in opposing free trade and many other policies of the Mulroney Tories. Admittedly, in one respect Anglican tradition was intact: there was still one religion for the clergy and another (or more than one) for the people. The difference was that the clergy were trying to redirect and trendify the popular religion.

To some extent the same thing was happening in the Roman Catholic Church, where vernacular liturgies, theological modernism, and revolutionary theology quickly filtered down from bishops' conclave to catechism class. But there was a difference. The Roman reforms were genuinely about religion; the Anglican reforms were not. Indeed, many Anglican priests were so anxious to be modern that they were quite prepared to abolish the denomination's most cherished and only unique possession – its liturgy. The United Church, having little to lose by way of liturgy or doctrine, had much self-confidence to lose. No longer could it see itself as the Church of Canada; one heard this claim rarely in the eighties. Membership was falling; Sunday school classes were emptying; more and more innercity churches were redundant; immigrants rarely joined the United Church. Now and then, moderators opined that the government was admitting too many Catholics. But there was not much heat in such complaints, and the 'death of the WASP' was commonly proclaimed by 1988.

Equally painful was the collapse of the church-union discussions. In the seventies the United Church digested two small Protestant sects, but the Anglican Church, the one big fish it had hoped to catch, eluded it, and the union talks, begun decades before on Anglican initiative, lapsed. Soon afterward the Anglicans themselves were facing a minor schism. Following the decision to ordain women, a few Anglican priests and some lay people seceded, affiliating themselves with the new Anglican Church of North America, an American schismatic body. The apparent cause seemed too slight to provoke such a response, and of course the real cause lay far deeper. The schismatics were protesting not just against female ordination but against the whole tendency of 'reform' in Canadian Anglicanism. One schismatic thus remarked: 'Christianity is not about Zimbabwe and the guaranteed annual income. It is about Jesus Christ who died for our sins and who is present in the Blessed Sacrament.' By 1988, many main-line clergy would not have agreed.

For some, the changing times were summed up in Ontario's debate about government money for separate schools. In 1985 the Tory government decided to extend government funding to the end of high school. As the Liberals and NDP had long favoured this step, the electorate really had no chance to express an opinion, although it is thought that some folk voted Liberal just to punish the Tories. After a year's discussion and investigation the money began to flow. Among the most vocal opponents was the Anglican Archbishop of Toronto, who rode out to battle like King Billy on a white horse. But what did the archbishop object to? The lack of public discussion! Nor did his intervention focus the opposition, which was led by the teachers of the public schools: these folk had no objection that earlier generations would have thought principled, but they certainly feared for their jobs. And there was great dismay when it was realized that, at least in the more distant future, the separate schools might hire only Catholics; the literati and the media folk could not cope with the idea that a school system might actually expect its teachers to believe anything in particular.

The real competition was not among the big old denominations – Protestant, Anglican, Roman – all of which were stumbling erratically, and most of which had become far too polite to proselytize. It was between the old denominations and the new – the fundamentalists, the Pentecostals, the Mormons, and a vast array of deviant young people's groups, some Christian and some not. The media people, so often agnostic and liberal, did not know what to make of all this. Clearly it was good that the old denominations were shedding 'obsolete dogma' and devoting themselves to good works. They were even purging the sacred texts of 'sexist, non-inclusive' language, so that 'God the Father' was becoming 'God the Parent,' and 'God the Child' was replacing 'God the Son.' What a pity that the main-line churches were shrinking, while the unreconstructed, roughneck, ill-educated, unpolished fundamentalist sects were growing in numbers and in wealth.

As Christian fundamentalism flourished at one extreme, so did a whole series of movements that seemed to be secular religion substitutes – jogging, consumerism, anti-pollutionism, gay liberation, women's liberation, and pro- and anti-abortion enthusiasm. Under all these headings there were certainly injustices to be remedied and wrongs to be put right. But it was regrettable that the new votaries so often lacked either sense of humour or sense of proportion. There was rapid evolution in the law, especially during the late Pearson and early Trudeau years. The criminal code was changed to allow abortion in certain circumstances and to permit homosexual relations among consenting adults. As Trudeau explained, Parliament had taken the policeman out of the bedroom. Province after province passed human rights measures, meant in part to improve the status of women and to outlaw sexual, religious, or racial discrimination. By 1979 it was common to ask whether such measures could, should, or did outlaw discrimination on the basis of 'sexual orientation.' To the annoyance of the fundamentalists but to the applause of many of the media people, all over Canada the gays were coming out of their closets.

Women were coming out of the kitchen too. There were many signs of changed attitudes. Many women kept their own names at marriage, or hyphenated them. Women were more prominent not only in the labour force but in many professions and occupations once dominated by men. Law, medical, and theological schools saw female enrolment rise, in some cases to over 50 per cent. It was said that increasingly women were paid as well as men, but this statement was incorrect. Equal pay legislation was the answer, it was thought, but its effectiveness remains unknown. To help working mothers there were far more nurseries and crèches – in the jargon of the period, 'day-care centres.'

To help the Inuit and other native peoples, there were new subsidies and new kinds of consultation. In 1969, the government had proposed to abolish the 'Indian Problem' by repealing the Indian Act, integrating the native people into the larger society, and giving the provinces control over their welfare. But the native people did not like the idea, and the government withdrew hastily. In the middle and late seventies there was much concern about native land claims, not merely in the far north but elsewhere, and about Inuit hunting rights. When the James Bay native residents objected to the hydro-power developments in that region, the Quebec authorities felt constrained to offer a large sum as compensation. By the mid-1980s it could be argued that Canada had made some progress in removing all sorts of old injustice and that the secular religionists had provided much of the push, but that a good deal remained to be done. The effect of the Charter promised to be greater than was originally expected, especially in the area of abortion rights.

Replacing the old exportable religion of the medical missionary was the new religion of foreign aid, complete with ministry, consistory, and pope – the director of the Canadian International Development Agency (CIDA). Canada set up a Canadian International Development Institute, whose purpose was cloudy and whose activities were invisible. CUSO volunteers went overseas, both to anglophonie and to francophonie, with special attention to Africa. Canada brought in people for specialist training and sent experts abroad. It gave more aid – not much, relative to our rising national wealth, but enough to require a large CIDA staff. In 1987 government responded to numerous complaints and urged CIDA to send more of its staff to the field. Canada, studies indicated, had administered grass-roots projects from Hull's bureaucratic bunkers. Much Canadian aid was unpopular with the clerisy of foreign aid, but it was very attractive to the suppliers and recipients. On the whole, this aid seems to have been welcome, and most of it was probably well applied, although there were some well-publicized disasters. Repeatedly Canadians were told that they were not giving or doing enough. Sometimes they were urged to pay higher prices for imports from poor countries. Often they were urged to 'untie' their aid. Always they were urged to give more. Since nothing Canada could do was likely to make a large impact on world poverty, it could always be argued that Canadians were not doing enough (the devout will readily spot the parallel with traditional religion). The foreign aid lobby was large, and vocal, while the foreign aid interest that battened on Canada's aid program had every reason to be pleased. As an American economist had said twenty-five years before, 'There's money in poverty.'

By the early eighties, thoughtful Canadians knew that the stability their parents had had a generation ago was gone, and, for their children, it would not return. Few regretted the vanishing of the conservative social behaviour of the 1950s. Most Canadians had shed their greatcoats, buttoned-up vests, and tight corsets, although without the protection of tradition some feared the ever-colder blasts outside. But like the Americans and the people of western Europe, Canadians would have to shape their individual lives in a world where all standards were mutable, and all conduct debatable.

31

Canada and the World Beyond

No previous Canadian prime minister attracted so much international attention as Pierre Elliott Trudeau: none seemed so well prepared by academic training and breadth of interests to play a large part in international affairs, and certainly none was so cosmopolitan in style. Yet Pierre Trudeau's time in office was marked by alternating spasms of domestic concentration and international flourishes; and the internationalism that Trudeau displayed was markedly different from that of his predecessors. It was true that, like Pearson, Trudeau had spent time in the United States and in England; unlike Pearson he had gone beyond, to the Sorbonne, as might be expected, but then on through the Middle East as far as China and Vietnam. Both those countries were then in the midst of civil war; and to China he would return some years later to investigate how it was getting on under its Communist masters. As a junior civil servant in the Privy Council Office, Trudeau witnessed Canadian foreign policy at its most active, during the Korean War. As a journalist, Trudeau was not reluctant to tackle foreign policy issues in his magazine, *Cité libre*. What he had to say there might have given the mandarins in External Affairs some cause for uneasiness.

Trudeau's views on nuclear arms, on Vietnam, and even on the United States were unorthodox by the standards of Pearson's generation. Some believed that they might logically have led him into the NDP rather than the Liberals, but since for Trudeau the problem of Quebec was foremost, he chose the Liberals as the party best able to deal with that province and its discontents. In any case Trudeau was not alone, either in the cabinet or in the Liberal party, in questioning the nostrums of Canadian foreign policy. Walter Gordon, under Pearson, was a notable sceptic where the United States and Vietnam were concerned; some at least of the younger and newer generation of Liberal ministers in 1968 felt closer to Gordon's opinions than they did to Mike Pearson's or Paul Martin's.

Many Canadians interpreted Trudeau as the bringer of a freer spirit; in an age when freedom was thought to mean impulsiveness if not actual licence, they looked to the prime minister to feed them change for change's sake. That was not Trudeau's style at all. In conjunction with Michael Pitfield, an assistant cabinet secretary and after 1975 the Clerk of the Privy Council, he was determined to improve the methods by which the federal government formulated its policies and transacted its business. Cabinet committees were strengthened; central control was reinforced; and departmental autonomy was in some (but not all) cases diminished. It was a time of systems, models, and formulae, planned program budgeting, and computers. 'Cybernetics,' implying the replacement of fallible humanity by reliable mechanisms, became a watchword. The age of social science had arrived.

During 1968-70 the cabinet, and the civil servants, conducted two major policy reviews: defence and foreign policy. Defence was completed first, in March 1969. Though it was the Department of National Defence that was principally affected, the Department of External Affairs was vitally concerned, for on the defence review turned the size and even the existence of Canada's NATO commitment. The defence department and its diplomatic allies would have preferred the commitment to stand, just as it was. This would cost money, more money than was currently being spent, but it would maintain alliance solidarity in the face of a continuing Soviet threat.

Not everyone felt the same way. Some senior civil servants, including some in the Privy Council Office, regarded NATO as an object frozen in time, an obsolete response to a non-existent threat. Peace was preserved, not by NATO and certainly not by Canada's brigade group or air division in Europe, but by the American nuclear umbrella. Others believed that the military had just become too costly. The government needed, or would soon need, money for its social programs. A reduction in military spending would be very timely.

Trudeau was determined to review all possible options, from neutrality to the existing alliance status quo. When he discovered that the military and the diplomats refused to play the game by his rules, he simply moved around them, using his own staff to generate alternative policy proposals. While the alternatives did not survive cabinet scrutiny, neither did the status quo. It was decided, on March 29, 1969, to reduce Canada's NATO contingent, which Trudeau duly announced to the House of Commons on April 3. Protests from allies before and after were received with studied indifference; the only ally whose views counted, the United States, disapproved but did not retaliate. National defence minister Léo Cadieux, who had fought the changes in cabinet, had the unpleasant task of announcing Canada's unilateral action at a ministerial meeting in Brussels in May: 5,000 troops only would be staying in Europe. The British, at least, were very rude: 'Canada [is] passing the buck to the rest of us,' their defence minister stated. (He did not, however, mention that Canada was paying for its own troops out of its own resources; the British drew on the West Germans for the subsistence of Britain's Army of the Rhine.)

Back home, the Canadian armed forces were reduced. Their numbers had already been falling, from 126,000 in 1962 to 100,000 in 1968; by 1975 they were down to 80,000. In current dollars they cost the same as they once had, but when inflation is considered, the military budget was steadily shrinking. To match their shrinking numbers, the military's role was redefined: the protection of Canadian sovereignty was henceforth their principal task: a 1971 White Paper said as much. Collective defence came a long way after.

With the defence review out of the way, the Trudeau government proceeded to a re-examination of the rest of Canada's foreign policy. The 'foreign policy review' took the best part of a year to complete, and consumed a fair proportion of External Affairs's resources of time, labour, and money. The labour may have been educational, possibly even beneficial, for those involved. The result was not, however, free from absurdity or irony.

To explain Canada's foreign policy its reviewers had recourse to a colour-coded hexagon which they proudly displayed to an incredulous cabinet committee. The hexagon symbolized the various facets of Canada's policy and demonstrated that no one side had primacy over any other. The astonished ministers rejected the concept and the symbol; it looked too much like a stop sign, one snorted. The colours, however, remained, and the review was embodied in six brief booklets (Latin America, the Pacific, Europe, the United Nations, international development, and a general overview), each with its appropriate shade.

Foreign Policy for Canadians paid homage to strange gods. The principal object of Canadian policy, the booklets implied, was economic growth, followed by social justice and the quality of life. One observer was struck by 'the government's evident willingness to abandon the past. Canada's "national interest" was defined as the touchstone of policy.' Another critic, Peyton Lyon, charged that the new foreign policy was a retreat into irresponsibility, if not fatuity: 'We are retreating from Europe,' he wrote, '... and taking a giant step in the direction of continental isolationism. If not quite a free ride in world affairs, we are taking one that will be much cheaper, and more sharply focused on national interests.'[1]

Lester Pearson, in retirement, wrote a savage critique of the new foreign policy. Canada's security, he argued, was dependent on the solidity of its collective relationships and not on a selfish and mistaken definition of the national interest. Since the government was not inclined to pay for armed neutrality on the scale of Sweden or Switzerland (that would have required a reversal of the money-

1 J.L. Granatstein, 'External Affairs and Defence,' in the *Canadian Annual Review for 1970* (Toronto: University of Toronto Press, 1971), p. 314.

saving conclusions of the defence policy review) Canada was bound to depend on the strength of others for its sovereignty and independence. The unique feature of Canada's foreign and defence policies in the early 1970s was that they simultaneously acknowledged and ignored this uncomfortable fact.

Indeed in the early 1970s Canada expanded rather than contracted its jurisdiction. The result was not visible on conventional maps, but it was doubtless felt by the fish and seagoing mammals who dwelt within two hundred nautical miles of Canada's coasts. Canada was not alone in seeking to extend its jurisdiction into what had previously been King Neptune's watery realm. Technology created the opportunity to mine the seabed for fuels and metals, and after 1958 (when a convention on the law of the sea concluded that the continental shelf was fair game) all coastal states leapt at the opportunity. They at least fell within the realm of the technically and legally possible; and Canada hoped for its 'slope' and 'rise' as well.

There was some difficulty in reconciling control over the resources of the sea with traditional rights of free navigation. The United States, as a major naval power, objected to zones of national control choking off straits and proved or at least asserted a point when it sent the tanker *Manhattan* sailing across the north in 1969. In an age of tanker spills and environmental concerns, this suggested that the Arctic ecosystem (like cybernetics, a word to conjure with in Ottawa in 1969) was endangered. So Ottawa passed the Arctic Waters Pollution Prevention Act of 1970, designed to assert Canada's right to prevent pollution, or the possibility of pollution, within a hundred miles of its northern coasts. The North-West Passage forthwith became a bone of contention between Canada and the United States, and remains so at the time of writing.[2]

The sea was not the only new focus for Canadian policy. There was a review of Latin American policy designed to match limited resources (and even more limited public interest) with the political and economic needs of Latin America. Unfortunately Canadian interests and those of some Latin American countries were often opposed; the most tangible connection with the southern continent in the 1970s was the billions of dollars in loans by Canadian banks to debtor nations. The fate of these loans by 1988 was absolutely certain: few, or none, would ever be paid in full, or at all.

Foreign Policy for Canadians was notable for its omission of the United States from its survey of areas or topics inherently important to Canada. The omission was forcibly drawn to Canadians' attention in 1971 when the US government of Richard Nixon implemented a series of protectionist measures de-

2   The events of the 1969-76 period are chronicled and explained more fully in Barbara Johnson and Mark Zacher, *Canadian Foreign Policy and the Law of the Sea* (Vancouver: University of British Columbia Press, 1977).

signed to shore up the weakening American balance of payments and to protect US gold reserves. The package was announced on television one August evening; a few hours before, the Autopact with Canada had been removed from the list of obligations that the United States proposed, unilaterally, to scrap. (The removal was at the insistence of the US State Department, not the Canadian government, which remained blissfully unaware of the Autopact's narrow escape.)

The Canadian government's response to the 'Nixon shokku,' as the Japanese called it, was one of the most curious foreign policy statements in Canadian history: External Affairs minister Mitchell Sharp's *Canada-US Relations: Options for the Future,* published during the election campaign in October 1972. This became known as the Third Option paper. Option 1 was maintaining Canada's existing relationship with the United States; option 2 was closer integration with the Americans; and option 3, reduction of 'Canadian vulnerability' to American actions. As in all papers of this kind, the 'right choice' was obvious. Option 3, however, presented some problems. If we wanted to reduce our dependence on the Americans the obvious connection to make was with the Europeans, who had recently been ignored when the Canadian government consulted its own narrowly defined interests in reducing Canada's NATO commitment. Some did suggest the Third World as an appropriate venue for Canadian action, but as one of the authors has suggested elsewhere, 'It was inherently improbable that public opinion could swallow a facile identification between Canada and the Third World.' So Europe it was.

In April 1974 Canada handed an aide-mémoire to the Commission of the European Economic Community and its nine member governments. What Canada wanted was recognition of its distinctiveness from the United States, and also some European trade connections. In October 1974 Trudeau travelled to European capitals in search of substance for his vague policy. The results were not happy. Some Europeans were still unhappy about the NATO reduction; in any case why sign a trade agreement with Canada when new GATT negotiations were under way? Even Trudeau admitted that Canada's proposals were 'banal.' He persisted nevertheless, and in June 1975 his efforts were crowned by the signature of a 'contractual link' between the EEC and Canada. Because the Arab oil embargo and the dramatic increase in oil prices were a major economic blow to industrialized Western nations, the value of such a link soon depreciated. But it had never been great. By 1979 the contractual link was seldom heard of, and Europeans were blunt in their refusal to give special treatment to anything but Canadian exports of natural resource materials. What they wanted was the one thing Canadians did not want. We were back to options 1 and 2.

It did not help that one of Canada's proposed European partners, France, was engaged in some incidental mischief-making at Canadian expense. After de

Gaulle's unfortunate visit to Canada in 1967 the French government (or, more properly, some elements in that government) gave publicity and symbolic encouragement to the government of Quebec in its efforts to enhance its international status as a prelude to its eventual complete independence. There was little that Canada could do. Canadian ill-will was not held to be of much account in Paris, and it was tacitly conceded that opinion in Quebec would be excessively disturbed if Canada actually broke relations with France. For France, it was a 'costless' even if pointless foreign policy, which gratified small but vocal sections of its intellectual and political community. For Quebec, where the deputy minister of intergovernmental affairs, Claude Morin, called the diplomatic shots, it afforded a considerable opportunity, but only a step at a time. (Morin, of course, eventually became a politician and a minister in René Lévesque's separatist government.)

Part of the battle between Ottawa, Paris, and Quebec was fought in the savannahs and deserts of Africa, where France's ex-colonies formed the world's largest collection of francophone states. Starting under Pearson, a procession of Canadian ambassadors, ministers, and aid-givers headed for French-speaking Africa. Somewhat bemused African politicians found themselves receiving long explanations of the state of the Canadian constitution along with libraries and scholarships, truly the most bizarre example of 'tied aid' in Canadian history. (An indirect reflection of Ottawa's differences with Quebec is to be found in Canada's support for the Nigerian federal government in the Biafran civil war of 1969.)

In its dealings with 'la francophonie' Canada's ultimate object was to create an association similar to the English-speaking Commonwealth. France, which preferred to keep its relations with its ex-subjects cosy and bilateral, based on a preponderance of French wealth, technology, and, occasionally, arms, was notably less enthusiastic. But Canada kept at it, in good times (as between 1971, when Morin quit the Quebec service, and 1976, until Lévesque won his first provincial victory) and bad (1976 to 1980, or until Trudeau demolished Lévesque and his cause in the Quebec referendum). French enthusiasm, and the opportunity for French action, waxed and waned according to the political health of separatism in Quebec; but ultimately the impasse in Ottawa's relations with France was solved with the victory in 1981 of François Mitterand and the Socialist party. Brian Mulroney reaped the reward, with a francophone summit that included the federalist premier of Quebec, and as a culmination, the 1987 visit of a French president to Canada (even to Saskatchewan) – the first since de Gaulle.

The victory of the Parti Québécois in the 1976 Quebec election coincided with the victory of Jimmy Carter and the Democrats in the US presidential election. Carter was, needless to say, concerned by the evidence of political change to the north. He responded by committing his administration, unofficial-ly and behind the scenes, to support the federal government in Ottawa and to give no encouragement to the separatist government in Quebec City. In February 1977 Trudeau visited Washington, where he addressed Congress in a speech whose real audience was clustered around televisions and radios back in snow-bound Canada. (In Washington the Canadian embassy put on a special effort to secure enough visible bodies in congressional chairs to serve as a backdrop for the Prime Minister.)

Carter evidently hoped that he, a genuine American liberal, would achieve fellow-feeling and common policy with his Liberal counterpart in Ottawa. When, in October 1980, the Liberals brought in the National Energy Policy, which discriminated against US investment in Canada, Carter was disappointed, to use no stronger term; but by then his writ had only a few more months to run.

The Americans, both under Carter and his Republican predecessor, Gerald Ford, had supported Canada's attempts to gain admission to the World Econom-ic Summit, known after the accession of Canada and Italy as the Group of Seven or G-7. Trudeau actually hosted a G-7 meeting near Ottawa in 1981, greatly to the delight of the capital's hotelkeepers. It was certainly a lesson in stage man-agement, proving that the entourage of the new American president, Ronald Reagan, had mastered the art of masking illusion as substance. In 1988 the sum-miteers came to Toronto, and seemed to enjoy themselves. But what these sum-mits, or any other summits, really produced is debatable. Communiques are hard enough to draft; concerted international action has proved harder still.

Trudeau did not much like the stiff formality required and expected at the gatherings of the political leaders of the world's seven most prosperous democ-racies. He preferred the more ramshackle arrangements of the Commonwealth conferences, where he made it possible for heads of government to exchange views in informal, because closed, meetings. He tried, and largely failed, to work the same magic at NATO conferences; there eyes tended to glaze as Canadi-an delegates got up to make their contributions to the alliance's deliberations, a legacy, some said, of 1969. As for the economic summit, Canada's interest was expressed in its presence – a matter of sufferance, not substance. Perhaps little more was required.

This is not, however, to say that under Trudeau or his two Conservative suc-cessors, Joe Clark and Brian Mulroney, Canada had no views on issues that were not strictly domestic. Trudeau especially worried over the East-West split. There is no evidence that he tried or seriously contemplated getting Canada out of the Western alliance. But he took a less worried attitude than his predecessor toward the Soviet Union. In an age of 'détente,' when the Western powers gen-erally hoped for reconciliation with the Soviet Union based on a perception of a shared interest in world order, Trudeau was not unusual. For Canada, as for other Western nations, 'détente' was not a straight line; the process was subject to interruptions when the Soviet Union invaded its neighbours (Czechoslovakia in 1968, Afghanistan in 1979) or backed up the actions of its satellite governments (Poland in 1980-1). Worsening relations between East and West prompted Trudeau to go on an international peace mission in the fall and winter of 1983-4. We doubt that it greatly altered the view that East took of West, or vice-versa.

One thing that was certain was that the US government, Ronald Reagan's, had little regard for Trudeau or his views. It was prepared to be polite, and it was prepared, in the interest of harmonious Canadian-American relations, to refrain from hostile or retaliatory acts for what it perceived to be grievances, such as the National Energy Program. But it was not prepared to listen intently when Trudeau came bearing messages of international comity. Nor, if the truth be told, would Trudeau have been much more attentive if Reagan had chosen to expound *his* view of the world and its problems.

Matters were different when Mulroney (at one slight remove) succeeded Trudeau. Mulroney was strongly pro-American, and he showed it. He promised to do better than Trudeau had done in defence. He castrated FIRA and terminated the National Energy Program. He promised to satisfy American concerns over pharmaceutical patents (a promise that took time, and a bizarre legislative history, to fulfil). He would have free trade with the United States. He held a singing summit in Quebec City to symbolize the new harmony (since it was March 17, 1985, the tune chosen was 'When Irish Eyes Are Smiling').

Only time will tell whether Mulroney's agenda was well chosen. The United States had problems. A booming domestic economy cohabited with severe difficulties of adjustment in some industries, especially in the midwestern 'rust bowl.' The US balance of payments had gone into deficit on current account, although by mid-1988 that deficit was falling. The US federal budget was also in deficit, and there was little sign that it would quickly return to balance. All these cirumstances diminished US willingness and political capacity to deal with Canada in a forthcoming way. The 1980s were thus different from the 1940s or 1950s. Canadian demands for special treatment puzzled American politicians, who preferred to put Canada on an equality with other countries. The idea that Canadian-American relations are somehow exceptional does not sit well with the descendants of Franklin D. Roosevelt, while the legatees of Mackenzie King have trouble visualizing any other way of proceeding.

32

Encounters of the Strangest Kind:
Politics in the 1980s

In the eighties Canadians came to prefer brief affairs to long-term political relationships. Old attachments to party which had weakened during the 1970s eroded almost completely as the Liberal and the Conservative parties changed leaders with little regard to past attitudes and actions. What occurred at the leadership conventions of the Conservative and Liberal parties in 1983 and 1984 respectively would have horrified partisans of an earlier day. The Tories in 1983 chose as leader a young Quebec businessman who had never run for elective office and who had embraced many policies, notably bilingualism and biculturalism, which many Tories believed were a Liberal hex upon the nation. The Liberals turned to John Turner, who had served the party admirably in the 1960s and early 1970s but who had come to represent the natural opponent to Pierre Trudeau, the Liberals' leader for just less than a generation.

The Trudeau years were already passing by the early 1980s, and their monuments were finally in place: the Charter of Rights and Freedoms; official bilingualism; a wealth of programs to support symphonies, ballet, publishers, and broadcasters; the Foreign Investment Review Agency; and the National Energy Program. Many of these items were testimony to the influence of nationalist youth in Quebec and the rest of Canada in the late 1960s and early 1970s. Others, notably the Charter, were testimony to the longevity and the persistence of Pierre Trudeau. With the Charter in place, many Canadians and many Liberals saw that Trudeau's time had passed. Moreover, some of the monuments to interventionist Liberalism were suffering from a new and harsh environment. The nationalist icons, the National Energy Program and FIRA, faced a cyclone of criticism from various quarters as Canada endured its worst recession since the war and the public became increasingly sceptical of government interventionism.

Canadians, it seemed, were becoming conservative. Polls in spring 1982 suggested that more Canadians considered themselves 'Conservative' than 'Liberal,' something which had not been true in 1979 when the Tories won the election. Moreover, the influence of the United States on Canada was conservative in the 1980s. Neo-conservatism in the United States had many articulate backers: intellectuals like George Will and Norman Podhoretz and businessmen like Donald Regan and David Packard. Canadians were often sceptical about the depth of Ronald Reagan's intellect and personal commitments, but by 1983 Reagan's bold attempt to have 'America stand tall' attracted much admiration among certain Canadians, especially those in business circles. *Western Report,* the most broadly circulated conservative journal in Canada, contrasted the thin ideological gruel of the Canadian Conservatives with the hearty broth of Reaganism. Canada, it argued, needed a stronger serving of conservatism than the feckless federal Tories could provide.

These westerners found more agreement on Bay Street than in earlier times. The National Energy Program (NEP) annoyed central Canadian business leaders almost as much as those in Calgary and Edmonton. The *Globe and Mail,* which had become more the voice of business interests, railed against the NEP and made common cause with western complaints against the arrogant and interventionist federal government. The foundations for a new conservative coalition were thus emerging. This coalition was gradually taking form as social conservatives opposed to abortion and supporting capital punishment merged with economic conservatives who opposed government intervention and pointed to the deregulatory actions of the Reagan administration as a model for Canadian governments. The trouble was that Joe Clark, the leader of the Progressive Conservative Party, fitted the form very badly. He was more progressive than conservative, and in those days Ronald Reagan's telegenic charms overwhelmed the quiet sincerity and decency of Clark. Lacking both communication style and conservative substance, Clark never acquired the confidence of his party's natural constituency. His days were numbered.

Brian Mulroney was doing the counting. Defeated by Clark in the Conservative leadership convention of 1976, Mulroney had stood aside from active politics, partly because the defeat shattered him emotionally but partly because he entered upon a career as the president of the Iron Ore Company of Canada. Some have sneered at Mulroney's presidency as little more than a public relations flak for the parent American company which wanted to shut down its Quebec operation at Schefferville. The task, however, was difficult, and Mulroney's legendary charm and skills as a labour negotiator served him well. After all, branch plant presidencies are often little more than public relations roles; so too are politics. By 1983 Brian Mulroney managed to look attractive to the motley crowd that made up Canada's Conservative party. Most important, it looked as if he could win. Joe Clark had been and would be a loser.

In the sixties Clark had been part of the effort to make the Conservative leader accountable. Now the rules he helped to establish became his nemesis. The party's general meeting in 1981 had voted two to one not to hold a leadership convention. The issue failed to die as western Tories offended by Clark's Red Tory outlook, Quebec Tories eager for a victory, Ontario Tories fearful of a Liberal leadership change, and various others who were overlooked when appointments were made in 1979 continuously stoked the flames which they hoped would consume Clark. Another meeting was scheduled for Winnipeg in January 1983, and during 1982 the battle lines were drawn. Clark's friends told him that he had to do better than he had done in 1981; that is, he had to receive more than two-thirds of the ballots in the crucial vote on whether to hold a leadership convention. Memories of the 1980 defeat should have faded by 1983; the Tories had moved well ahead in the polls; and Clark had made a strong effort to win support in Quebec where his strongest opposition was found in 1981. Clark's chances looked especially good when Brian Mulroney with Clark beside him endorsed the leader and called for no review on December 6, 1982. But did he perform in private as he promised in public?

Whereas Dalton Camp became a pariah to most Tories because of his challenge to the increasingly erratic Diefenbaker, and, in 1986 Keith Davey, who had toiled so long in Liberal vineyards, faced vituperative denunciation from his former colleagues when he suggested that John Turner's leadership should be reviewed, Brian Mulroney escaped the arrows deftly. When the Tories assembled in Winnipeg in late January, all knew that the Quebec delegates opposed to Clark had been organized by Mulroney's friends. Nevertheless, the blood of many bitter constituency battles was not upon his hands. Looking leaner and more handsome than ever, Mulroney was poised to challenge his leader if Clark had to face a leadership convention. The vote came in after too many tense moments on the night of January 31. A stunned Clark read the figures: 66.9 per cent favoured no review. A short time later, Clark emerged to tell the waiting delegates that the result was not good enough. He wanted a leadership convention to 'clear the air,' and he would be a candidate. His advisers were almost unanimous in recommending that course; it was probably the worst political advice in Canadian history.

The leadership convention took place in Ottawa in June 1983. Clark took the lead on the first ballot and held it for two more. It was down to Mulroney and Clark on the last ballot, and Mulroney won. Clark did win more support in Quebec than did Mulroney, but Mulroney won more in Clark's home province, Alberta, than did Clark. Both seemed to do best where they were known least.[1]

1 See the delegates' poll in Patrick Martin, Allan Gregg, and George Perlin, *Contenders: The Tory Quest for Power* (Scarborough: Prentice Hall, 1983), Appendix B.

Mulroney, the thoroughly bicultural Québécois, carried the right-wing Tories who had so strongly opposed the Official Languages Act. Clark did well among francophone Québécois. The Tories did send a message that June evening: more than anything else they wanted to win, and, for once, it seemed they had a winner.

The polls did nothing to dispute these claims. Ed Broadbent and the New Democratic Party were going through their most difficult period since the party's foundation. Broadbent's principled stand in favour of the Charter of Rights and Freedoms had deeply offended some western New Democrats. Others were troubled when Broadbent hired the former Waffle member James Laxer, whose nationalism remained intense but whose zeal to nationalize had waned considerably. Laxer urged on a sympathetic Broadbent policies that would bring the party closer to the mainstream of European social democratic parties which had abandoned nationalization and had supported collective security through NATO. At a time when the Canadian peace movement was vehemently denouncing NATO as a warmongering alliance, these notions fell on deaf ears in Canada. The NDP's troubles were too well known, and the New Democrats began to tumble in the polls, reaching the lowest levels in their history in 1983 and 1984. Their future seemed in doubt; there were solid rumours that Laxer and others might defect to the Liberals. A few Liberals and New Democrats talked about a coalition to turn back the surging Tories, who by late 1983 not only stood high in national opinion polls but also governed every Canadian province except Quebec and British Columbia. In the case of British Columbia, the Social Credit government of Bill Bennett was the farthest right in Canada. These were gloomy days for Canadian socialists and liberals. In Quebec, the Parti Québécois had fallen from grace, and rumours abounded about intrigues within the party.

The Parti Québécois's ailments reflected its defeats in the referendum and in the constitutional negotiations, but Trudeau's victories did not bring him political gains. His caucus contained many malcontents who recalled Trudeau's 1980 comments about that election being his last and who believed that John Turner, so long the crown prince, now deserved his coronation. The pressures grew as the government entered its fourth year, and Trudeau finally took a 'walk in the snow' on a February evening and decided to leave politics. A few around him wanted him to stay; most hinted that he should leave. He seemed a sad figure that day he announced that he would resign. Unlike King, St Laurent, and even Pearson, Trudeau knew that he could do little to influence the choice of his successor or, for that matter, the policies that his successor might follow. Nevertheless, the traces of his governments touched nearly all aspects of Canadian life. He had not left his land as it was when it found him a generation earlier. For his successors, his shadow constantly hovered about them and made them seem lesser leaders than he. In the spring of 1984, however, Brian Mulroney and the leading candidate for the Liberal leadership, John Turner, tried to distance themselves from Trudeau's presence as much as they could.

Turner had been in Jamaica when Trudeau resigned the last day of February. He had stunned everyone in 1979 when he announced that he would not stand for the leadership after Trudeau said that he was resigning. That decision, which meant nothing because Trudeau returned, probably helped Turner's cause in 1984, for the Liberals, like the Tories, were inclined to look beyond the House of Commons for their next leader. Very quickly Liberal notables rushed to join the Turner team, a team that had especially strong representation from Quebec. Jean Chrétien, who had fought so many of the Trudeau government's battles in the Commons and the country, found his support much less than he had expected. After momentary hesitation, Chrétien announced that he would run against Turner, and until the mid-June convention Chrétien never stopped running. His was a brilliant campaign, which subtly played upon the theme of party loyalty. Other candidates – Don Johnston, John Roberts, Eugene Whelan, Mark MacGuigan, and John Munro – confused matters but never threatened the front runners. Turner's appeal was straightforward: he was a winner. The polls proved this point conclusively. Canadians wanted a new approach, and if the Liberals who had governed for more than twenty years wanted to appear 'new' they had to choose a leader who was untainted by the bitter debates of the past decade. Turner had experience yet he was fresh; the combination was most seductive on those early summer days at Ottawa's civic centre. Turner led on the first ballot and won on the third. The Liberals soared in the polls, and the gnomes of political sociology seemed secure in their thrones.

More thoughtful students of polling, who were usually those who did not reap rich consultancy fees, warned that public opinion polling was being done too casually and that major assumptions about political behaviour were being derived from shaky evidence. In the summer of 1984, these reservations were scarcely noticed. Conventional wisdom had it that Turner call an election as soon as possible to take advantage of the publicity generated by the leadership convention and of his high standings in the polls. Although both the Queen and the Pope were coming in the fall, Turner could not afford to wait. After a quick flight to Britain to ask Her Majesty's forbearance, Turner called a press conference for July 9, 1984. At the press conference he spoke clearly, answered questions well, and looked thoroughly prime ministerial. Then he stunned the crowd by announcing seventeen patronage appointments, some his own, others done at the insistence of Trudeau. The latter clearly made him uncomfortable, and he did not hide his feelings. Michel Gratton, who was working for Mulroney at the time, felt uneasy at first, but he and the others watching the press conference

The Tory government takes a new attitude to patronage – 1984 (Aislin, 1984).
Reproduced with permission of The Toronto Star Syndicate

immediately realized that Turner had given them an issue the Tories 'had hardly
dared to hope for.' Not only had Turner appointed a long list of people whose
primary qualifications for their new position was Liberal political activity, but
also on that list 'was a name that leapt off the page like a squirt of grapefruit
juice in the eyeball': Bryce Mackasey was named Ambassador to Portugal.[2]

After that day Turner looked more shopworn; Mulroney was visibly fresher.

2 Michel Gratton, *'So, What Are the Boys Saying?' An Inside Look at Brian Mulroney in Power*
(Toronto: McGraw-Hill Ryerson, 1987), p. 14.

Broadbent, the most seasoned campaigner, quickly demonstrated his skills. His shrill style (radio journalists had privately dubbed him 'rent a rant') gave way to a folksy bonhomie. The NDP began to regain its strength, especially in the west, where Turner's western background had led many Liberals to expect big gains now that the party was freed from the yoke of Trudeau. Turner's campaign manager was Bill Lee, also a veteran of political wars of the 1960s who had had a successful private career in the 1970s and 1980s. The organization never coalesced, as Trudeau Liberals, resentful of the Turner supporters' refusal to court them, and the traditional Liberals whom Turner attracted back to the party eyed each other suspiciously. The short time had healed no wounds.

The July Gallup Poll had shown the Liberals at 49 per cent, the Tories at 38 per cent, but the gap quickly began to close. Turner agreed to face his opponents in a debate both in French and in English. Although Mulroney's French was colloquial and excellent, Turner's was remarkably good for one who grew up on the Pacific. Broadbent's was poor. No one expected much, for Canadian political debates in the past had changed little and were notable for their dulness. These debates were a historic exception. Turner was nervous in the first English debate; Mulroney was sharp and forceful. The patronage question came up quickly, and Turner looked down, away from the camera, and said, 'I had no option.' Mulroney exploded in righteous indignation: 'You had an option, sir. You could have said, "I am not going to do it. This is wrong for Canada, and I am not going to ask Canadians to pay the price." ' The words haunted Turner for the remainder of the campaign; they would haunt Mulroney afterward.

By early August, the Tories had moved clearly into the lead; the NDP was sopping up left-leaning Liberal support in English Canada. The Liberals panicked; Bill Lee left, and Keith Davey became Turner's campaign manager. The press hovered over the crumbling Liberals. It focused principally in late September on party president Iona Campagnolo's buttocks, which party leader Turner had patted in public. Symbolically, the incident represented the dated nature of Turner's response to women's issues. In the last week of the campaign, leading Liberals hastened their return to their own constituency and tried to salvage what was left of a lost campaign. The returns on September 1984 astonished even the most optimistic Tories. They won 211 seats, the Liberals only 40, the rejuvenated NDP 30. Only Robert Borden's Unionists in 1917 and Diefenbaker's Tories in 1958 had achieved a higher popular vote. The results were testimony to Mulroney's effective campaign and to the incredible disintegration of the Liberal efforts. Underlying this change were profound shifts in the relationship between Canada's regions and its central government and between citizens and their governors.

Beginning at the constituency level, one finds that the member of Parliament had become an ombudsman and that Burkean theories of representation had been supplanted by more populist notions. The member was to serve his constituents and would do so with the help of a full-time staff paid for by the state. These notions derived in part from the ruminations about participatory democracy in the 1960s and also from the sense that parliamentarians must stay close to the grass roots in an age of increasing complexity and distance. This change tended to weaken the party system; certainly the capacity of the leader to influence party members was less than it had been in the age of King and St Laurent. The isolation of the leader and his distrust of the party are a frequent result. In his study of the Liberal party, Joseph Wearing criticizes Trudeau for failing to build up an informal network of Liberals throughout the country with whom he checked his policies and from whom he sought advice. The result was that John Turner's supporters 'became a kind of opposition from within the party' and that Trudeau retreated into the Prime Minister's Office and 'came to regard his staff there as the only group whose loyalty was unquestioned.' This description of Trudeau's actions is correct, but it fails to note how frequently one finds the Trudeau response among contemporary political leaders at the provincial and federal levels.[3]

The way in which politicians present their message has also altered because of fundamental changes in the nature of the mass media. The impact of the television debate in the 1984 campaign underlines the extraordinary effect that medium can have. American studies have argued that the presidency has become 'rhetorical' since the spread of television, and the evidence of recent Canadian history suggests that such an interpretation fits in Canada too. Presidents talk directly to the voters without intermediaries who, by their very nature, are distrusted. When Trudeau gave his brilliant farewell speech at the 1984 convention, he got the loudest applause when he boasted about how he had 'gone over' the heads of the press and the bureaucracy and had spoken directly to the people. John Turner found quickly that the easy camaraderie that marked press relations with politicians in the 1960s, when the press gallery was small and reporters were susceptible to the flattery of politicians, had vanished by the 1980s, when suspicion marked the relationship. Studies carried out on the political sympathies of the press gallery by the University of Western Ontario School of Journalism confirmed what Trudeau, Turner, and (very soon) Mulroney believed. Journalists saw themselves as forces of opposition, and most of them were sceptical of political leaders and the two major parties. The NDP was the favoured party by a considerable margin. Even in 1979, when the Tories formed a government, they won less support than either the Liberals or the New Democrats

3   Joseph Wearing, *The L-Shaped Party: The Liberal Party of Canada 1958-1980* (Scarborough: Prentice Hall, 1981), p. 236.

among members of the press gallery. Tory claims of ingrained leftist bias on the part of the journalists would seem to have some merit.

In fact, the attitude of the reporters probably has to do with their relationship to politicians less than to the newspaper owners. By the 1980s most newspapers were owned by conglomerates, notably the Southam and Thomson chains. Reporters gained greater freedom, although, paradoxically, they probably had less status in their communities and were less significant figures nationally. The *Toronto Star* was a curiosity, since its editorial page and its reporters also clearly reflected its Liberal-nationalist bias. The *Toronto Sun* and its tabloid affiliates and imitators also harked back to earlier partisanship. Even in the case of the Tory *Sun*, however, some reporters strove to maintain their independence. The most strident critiques of Brian Mulroney and William Davis were written by Claire Hoy, a *Sun* columnist. It should be added that Hoy was moved to Ottawa after his exposé of Davis and lost his job after his attack on Mulroney. Other newspapers in the great chains reflected a variety of viewpoints in their pages. The *Globe and Mail* became ever more a business newspaper, and its publisher claimed that its major role was to reflect the business community's interest. For a newspaper which proclaimed itself Canada's national newspaper, the *Globe* had a curious view of that nation.

Other roles had changed. The bureaucracy under Trudeau was discussed in an earlier chapter (see chapter 26). Although Joe Clark's brief reign did not lead Conservatives, apart from Flora MacDonald, to allege that the bureaucracy was against them, suspicion lingered when Mulroney took office that many of the senior bureaucrats were Liberal partisans. They further believed that the structure of the bureaucracy under Trudeau, where the Privy Council Office (PCO) controlled the co-ordination of decision-making, had undermined the position of ministers and enhanced the power of bureaucrats. The latter, in this view, were creatures of the PCO and the PMO and not committed to departments and to ministers. The changes, however, were the product not so much of Trudeau autocracy as of government complexity. In an excellent study of government influence, John Sawatsky described how the Mulroney government and its supporters came to recognize that the fault lay more in the stars than in the men and women who held office: 'With the Trudeau government finally gone, some businessmen had hoped that a friendly administration would remove much of the need for consultants and lobbyists. But just the opposite proved to be true. Mulroney arrived in government with a forty member cabinet which rarely met as a group, and contained junior and senior ministers with a variety of ambitions, capabilities, interests and levels of influence.'

Business found that this sympathetic government still required careful attention to assure that the right contracts were issued, the right decisions made.

Mulroney centralized power in the PMO after his initial flirtation with decentralization, and the trend that had begun much earlier continued without a break. As Sawatsky concluded: 'Clearly, politicians and the new generation of Tory backroom boys would be making the major decisions, not the bureaucrats. This centralization of power meant that Ottawa was increasingly following Washington towards the hired-gun approach to government relations.' Hired-gun Bill Lee had run Turner's campaign; his former partner Bill Neville had been one of Mulroney's closest advisers. 'Public affairs' was one of the greatest growth industries, and the governance of Canada would never be the same.[4] If the cosy relationship between reporters and politicians had broken down, so too had the familiarity between bureaucrats and politicians that had marked the King and St Laurent eras. The style had changed, but so had the substance.

The trends we have identified had effect over a long term. The Mulroney government's impact is obviously still short term and difficult to assess. What stands out at this point is the lost trust. The Conservative campaign in 1984 was deliberately vague, since, as an opposition party, the best tactic is to avoid offending any significant group while letting the government defeat itself, which we have seen it did. The promises were inherent in the style rather than the substance. Two major emphases were present under the label 'national reconciliation,' which meant both a more conciliatory attitude toward provincial government demands and a more pro-business attitude. In both cases, the Mulroney government's policies reflected these emphases in its initiatives. Why, then, was trust lost? The answer here again seems to relate more to style than substance. Bill Neville, one of Mulroney's closest advisers in the early months, argues that the shallowness of the government's commitments and of Mulroney's personal beliefs has hurt the government most. 'The most important thing,' Neville has said, 'is for people to think, "Here's a guy you can rely on to act in a certain way because he really believes in that." Successful leaders have that quality. Mulroney and the government let that slip away.'[5]

There is, then, this strong contradiction. Mulroney is seen as one who lacks strong principles and who cannot give strong leadership. And yet his government has taken some strong initiatives which have reflected what he promised in the election campaign. Whatever happens to the Mulroney government when it faces the polls, several programs and policies will be seen as significant. The

4   John Sawatsky, *The Insiders: Government, Business, and the Lobbyists* (Toronto: McClelland & Stewart, 1987), p. 349. See also the important study by David Bercuson, J.L. Granatstein, and William Young, *Sacred Trust: Brian Mulroney and the Conservative Party in Power* (Toronto: Doubleday, 1986).

5   Quoted in Claire Hoy, *Friends in High Places: Politics and Patronage in the Mulroney Government* (Toronto: Key Porter Books, 1987), p. 132

most prominent are the dismantling of the nationalist structures of the Pearson-Trudeau era in the economic field, notably the Federal Investment Review Agency, the National Energy Program, and the restrictions on foreign involvement in the financial services sector; the shift of powers from the federal to the provincial governments embodied in the energy agreements and the Meech Lake accord; and the free trade treaty with the United States.

As we argue in the next chapter, FIRA and the NEP had begun to disintegrate in the late Trudeau years, and they found few friends among the Turner Liberals. They retain a symbolic importance to their creators and to important segments of the media. Many Mulroney initiatives revealed an anti-interventionist and pro-market philosophy on the part of the government. In part, the tone derived from the rapid internationalization of markets which occurred in the 1980s. There could be no doubt, however, that the Liberals and New Democrats would have handled matters differently.

In the case of Mulroney's most remarkable initiative, the Meech Lake accord, both opposition parties supported the government. Indeed, John Turner and Ed Broadbent hastened to shake the Prime Minister's hand when he returned from the ten-hour negotiation at Meech Lake on April 30, 1987. Provincial premiers lavished their praises on Mulroney, with Ontario Liberal premier David Peterson boasting that 'he felt good about his country.' Few expected much of the gathering of the premiers and the Prime Minister at Meech Lake. Since the election, the Tories had not done well in provincial elections. In Ontario, the resignation of William Davis led the Tories toward the right and the amiable Frank Miller. Miller faced a reinvigorated Liberal party led by Peterson, which during the election campaign in the spring of 1985 quickly took over the middle of the electoral spectrum. The final results showed the Liberals with more votes but the Tories with more seats. In an unusual move, the New Democrats agreed to support the Liberals subject to their agreement to several policy demands from the New Democrats. There was no request for a coalition government, but there was a promise of two years of support for the government so long as the general agreement between the two parties was honoured. Thus the most enduring political regime in Canadian history fell ignominiously and without much grace.

Quebec also turned toward the Liberals, now led by a recycled Robert Bourassa. The Parti Québécois was a victim, first, of the harsh medicine it administered to some of its bureaucratic and academic supporters during the economic gloom of the 1980s, second, of the physical and emotional deterioration of its leader, René Lévesque, who resigned in early 1985, and, third, of its own success in advancing the cause of the French language and culture within the province. The loss of the referendum also had a soporific effect on some separatist supporters. The party lost its balance and its élan; its new leader, Pierre Marc

Johnson, could not keep the fires burning with so few embers. Bourassa won a sweeping victory. During the campaign he promised that he would not relent in Quebec's demands on the federal government. Specifically, he would insist on fundamental constitutional change if Quebec were to approve the accord which the other provinces had accepted in 1982. His close personal relationship with Mulroney, established when both seemed to be tragic political has-beens, was an advantage that Bourassa recalled.

Mulroney had given vague promises during the campaign that he would bring Quebec into the constitution, but what that meant specifically was quite unclear. Bourassa responded to his friend's vagueness with some specific proposals, the most important being his demand that Quebec's 'distinctiveness' be constitutionally recognized and protected. For a generation Canadian politicians had squabbled over this Quebec demand; opposition to it had been part of Trudeau's appeal in 1968 and a continuing theme of Trudeau's prime ministerial period – but not always. In the troubled period before his defeat in 1979, Trudeau's government had flirted with proposals first presented by the Pépin-Robarts commission which pointed in the direction of special status and decentralization. Gordon Robertson, the long-time constitutional adviser, had been most active in promoting these ideas. When, however, the constitutional reform took place in the early 1980s, Trudeau's original vision of a Canada where no province or people had a special status prevailed, and Robertson was excluded from the constitutional deliberations. The group around Robertson, the advisers of Pépin-Robarts, and numerous other 'advisers' who favoured greater accommodation of Quebec's constitutional demands than had Trudeau re-emerged with the election of the Mulroney government.

Mulroney, then, had considerable bipartisan and non-partisan support for a leap beyond what had gone before. Urged on by the provincial premiers, who played on his labour arbitrator's disposition toward good times and compromise, Mulroney took a breathtaking leap. The details of the accord are discussed elsewhere; their political impact concerns us here. The opposition parties stood behind Mulroney, fearful as both now were of alienating Quebec. The Liberals, however, split badly, with ethnic members and Trudeau Liberals profoundly disturbed by the accord. Don Johnston left the Liberal party to sit as an independent Liberal; Pierre Trudeau emerged from silence to denounce Mulroney as a weakling and the accord as a defeat for Canada. In the case of the New Democrats, there was much private grumbling, but their high standing in the polls in Quebec allowed Ed Broadbent to maintain party unity: only BC MP Ian Waddell consistently opposed the accord. Ironically, the provincial branch of the NDP, which constitutionally was not separate from the federal, did oppose the accord because it did not go far enough. Outside the Commons many traditional New

Democrats lamented the fact that the party which had long called for national social programs had so enthusiastically supported an arrangement that might well make new programs and national standards impossible. The provinces stood fast behind the agreement until New Brunswick elected Frank McKenna's Liberals, who were mildly opposed, and Manitobans elected a hung legislature, where one party, the Liberals, vehemently opposed Meech Lake. At the end of 1988, Meech Lake, nevertheless appeared likely to become part of Canada's constitution and, to its opponents, an enduring testimony to rampant provincialism and Mulroney weakness.

Free trade had briefly entered the Conservative leadership campaign in 1983 when John Crosbie endorsed the concept. Mulroney borrowed a Trudeau metaphor and compared it to sleeping next to an elephant, which was fine until it twitches but then it rolls over and 'you're a dead man.' These views persisted through the 1984 election campaign, but a shift began soon after. When Mulroney crooned 'When Irish Eyes Are Smiling' to a beaming Reagan on St Patrick's Day 1985, there were already hints that the American president was telling his fellow Irishman and conservative that he would make sure that Canada would not suffer from the protectionist sentiment in the United States. Indeed, Reagan had talked about a North American free trade area in the 1980 presidential campaign, and, for ideological reasons, free trade bore special meaning to him. Mulroney had based much of his appeal on his ability to repair Canada's wounded relationship with the United States. A shift in direction became easier when the four western provinces, including New Democratic Manitoba, endorsed a vague proposal for freer trade. Certainly the public opinion polls suggested that the issue might swing many voters toward the increasingly unpopular government. In the fall of 1986, polls showed that three times as many Canadians thought the idea of free trade was good as thought it was bad. There were dangers among the nettles of negotiations, but the flower of safety might well be plucked.

Negotiations began formally on May 21, 1986, in Ottawa, with Simon Reisman, who had been closely tied to John Turner in the past, as chief Canadian negotiator. Pat Carney, like Reisman an outspoken advocate of the concept of free trade, was the minister responsible. For over a year the negotiations dragged on and the popularity of free trade diminished somewhat. By the summer of 1987 Canadians seemed bored with the issue, and the government's apparent mishandling of the negotiations was regarded as one of the reasons for its low standing in the public opinion polls. Then, just as it seemed that all the negotiation was for naught, a deal was salvaged at the last possible moment, given the congressional timetable. On October 4th, after frantic last-minute phone calls, and presidential intervention, Reisman and his American counterpart announced that they had a deal. Mulroney crowed in the Commons; Broadbent ranted; Turner proclaimed that he would 'tear it up' when the Liberals took power.

The end of 1987, the Mulroney government began to creep up in the polls, but only slightly. The Conservatives stood in third place as they had for most of the past year. Mulroney's personal popularity was remarkably low; indeed, one comparative poll indicated that it was the lowest of any major Western leader. Fewer than one in six Canadians thought that he was doing a 'good job.' Here we return to the paradox mentioned earlier. Mulroney's major policies attracted some strong support. Meech Lake was very popular in Quebec, but after its announcement Tory support fell. Free trade was strongly supported by many westerners, yet the strongly anti-free trade New Democrats continued to lead the Gallup Poll in western Canada. The early charges that Mulroney was incapable of making decisions could surely not be sustained after Meech Lake and free trade. The problem was different. Very simply, he was not trusted. His government could not shun the atmosphere of slick deals and sleaze that it acquired in its early days. By February 1988, eight ministers had resigned from the Mulroney government as a result of various sins. A couple were venial. Some were very serious, as in the case of Sinclair Stevens, a senior minister, and André Bissonette, who faced criminal charges. (He was later cleared.) Mulroney's righteous denunciation of Liberal patronage in 1984 now rang so hollow, and his depiction of himself as the poor boy from Baie Comeau seemed outrageous deception as Canadians learned about his sixty pairs of Guccis and expensive tastes.

Writing in 1986, three historians argued that 'If Mulroney goes the way of Diefenbaker, his four years or so in power will have served only one enduring national purpose – it will have given the Liberals the rest and rejuvenation they so badly needed.'[6] They judged too quickly. As the summer of 1988 advanced, Liberal and NDP fortunes ebbed. The Conservatives rose steadily in the polls. John Turner faced grumbling and menaces from his caucus, and, in September, a damaging (and best-selling) book on his record as Liberal leader. When, on October 1, Prime Minister Mulroney announced that a general election would be held on November 21, the Liberals appeared to go into free fall in the polls, standing behind both the Conservatives and the NDP. NDP leader Ed Broadbent prophesied the demise of the Liberals and the emergence of a two-party system, on the model of the confrontational politics of Great Britain and British Columbia. (That such a system would heavily favour the right wing did not seem to worry Broadbent.)

The Liberals, like Robert Borden in 1911 and Sir John Macdonald in 1891,

6   Bercuson, Granatstein, and Young, *Sacred Trust,* p. 296.

chose to play the patriotism card. Free trade imperilled Canada's future, Turner told his sparse audiences; and Broadbent said much the same thing. The Conservatives confined themselves to lofty assurances that all would be well once free trade was in: investment, jobs, and prosperity would abound in the land.

The major parties agreed to two three-hour television debates in mid-October, first in French and then, the next night, in English. In 1984, Mulroney had demolished Turner in such a debate, and Liberal partisans in 1988 glumly expected the worst. The worst, however, did not occur. Turner gave the show of his life, telling a spluttering Mulroney that 'you sold us out' in the free trade deal. The Liberal campaign took fire, and the party soared in the polls to challenge the Conservatives.

The prospect that free trade might actually be defeated astounded and apparently terrified the Canadian business community. Premier Bourassa of Quebec, a free trade partisan, tried to get his legislature to pass a supportive motion. Because Liberal support, and fears about free trade, were strongest in Ontario, Conservative orators like Secretary of State Lucien Bouchard denounced free trade opponents as Ontario plotters attempting, once again, to do Quebec down, a theme that was highly congenial to pro-Conservative organs like *The Globe and Mail*, which commended Bouchard for his vision and perception. Expensive pro-free trade advertising appeared in newspapers across the country, and on television Conservative workers appeared in simulations of person-on-the-street interviews to denounce Turner as an opportunistic, incompetent liar.

The tide turned. Pollsters estimated that perhaps 15 per cent of the electorate was 'issue-driven' by free trade; and the 15 per cent began to switch back to the Tories. The Liberals had meanwhile run out of the borrowed funds that were sustaining their campaign and could do little to counter the advertising blitz.

On election night, Canadians returned a majority Conservative government with 169 seats, including 63 out of 75 in Quebec. The Liberals took 83; they had done well, but not well enough, in the Maritimes, Ontario, and Manitoba. The NDP declined in those regions, but improved its standing from Saskatchewan to British Columbia; it won 43 seats. Opponents pointed out that the Conservatives had got only 43 per cent of the popular vote but with the opposition divided between the Liberals (32 per cent), the NDP (20 per cent), and a bunch of largely right-wing fringe parties, 43 per cent was definitely enough.

The 1988 election confirmed that a political revolution, and not a fluke, had occurred in 1984. The Conservatives replaced the Liberals as the party of choice in Quebec; they were supported by an astonishing cross-section of Quebec opinion, from previously separatist journalists and politicians to more moderate nationalists who had plumped, like Mulroney, for the federalist side in the 1980 referendum. The Liberals emerged as the standard-bearers of Canadian nationalism; this was signified by the passage of NDP nationalists like Jim Laxer, a former national secretary of that party, and one-time leader of its radical waffle wing, to the Liberal camp. The Liberal loss of key ridings in Toronto and Vancouver was attributed to the abstention of free-trade Liberals from the party's cause, or to the disaffection of those whom Turner had alienated.

The NDP had improved its seat total, but had not won the breakthrough it had, once again, sought. What the future would hold for it in the Age of Mulroney no-one could say.

33

The Economy in the 1980s:
Disenchantment, Deregulation, and Deficits

In the eighties Canada experienced some painful economic shocks. Both inflation and interest rates rose to unprecedented heights, and then fell away. In
1981-2 the economy experienced its first genuine recession since the 1930s. The
slump was mild by comparison with that earlier disaster, and especially in central Canada recovery was swift, but the shock to confidence was profound. Unemployment rates, moreover, remained high, especially in the west and in Atlantic Canada, while for many people living standards declined, stagnated, or rose
only slowly – the natural result of stagnating labour productivity, unemployment, and weakening world markets for the nation's primary products. The resource boom of the seventies and early eighties ended gloomily, with depression
in those western centres that depended so heavily on development spending. The
main growth industries were still the services, and white-collar employment rose
along with this expansion, even though governments, frightened by rising deficits, worked hard to control and even to reduce their bureaucracies. The result
was disappointment and shock for those many professionals who had been carefully brought up to work for government and for no one else. Worse shocks
were to come from the financial troubles of various great enterprises. Chrysler
Canada, like its American parent, required government bail-outs. So did
Massey-Ferguson, renamed Varity in 1986. Inco, the victim of world-wide recession, lost money. Dome Petroleum, swollen by acquisitions and burdened by
debts, went bankrupt. So did some trust companies and two small banks – Canada's first bank failures since 1923. The larger banks worried about their loans to
Massey, to Dome, and to the Third World – wasting and uncertain assets by
1983. Farmers, too, were in trouble.

But all was not gloom and doom. After 1982 employment began to rise again,
so that by 1988 there was little slack in the labour markets of central Canada,
where more than 60 per cent of Canadians lived. Chrysler recovered, Varity re-

turned to profit, and government subsidy attracted new Japanese auto-makers to Ontario. Oil took a tumble, especially in 1986 and again in 1988. In mid-1987 the oil patch came alive again, and The *Globe and Mail* could write, 'If energy deregulation remains the vogue in Ottawa, and if OPEC holds together, Alberta is looking good.'[1] OPEC, however, was coming apart fast. The social welfare system, though somewhat damaged by federal and provincial cutbacks, survived. Even unemployment insurance, excoriated by the Forget commission of inquiry in 1987, was little changed. Like other social programs, such as medicare, it had become an 'entitlement,' or to the Conservative government a 'sacred trust,' though others might see it as a sacred cow.

New social programs, admittedly, were not introduced, except for an expensive proposal for national day-care. This federal plan appeared in 1988. There was some pressure for a guaranteed minimum income and for special measures that would help the aged. Some of these ideas ought to have been politically attractive. Working wives were ever more numerous, and so were the old. But Canada's governments were too financially embarrassed to tackle anything really expensive. In so far as new spending schemes could be contemplated at all, they were targeted at the unemployed, at day-care, and at industrial renewal. Nevertheless there was some tidying-up, especially with respect to medicare.

In 1984 the Trudeau government passed the Canada Health Act, a measure that would discourage the provinces from collecting user-fees and from allowing physicians to 'extra-bill.' Initially supported by the Tories, the new act was not repealed under the Conservatives, and although some provincial governments disliked it, others welcomed the Ottawa initiative. Long after the federal measure had passed, Ontario doctors objected to a provincial act that would bring it into effect. Some doctors went on strike. But in Queen's Park the minority Liberal government took courage, counted its bank balances, and braved the wrath of organized medicine, which, in turn, proved to be a paper tiger. Yet the feline received its pound of flesh. In the final bargain there would be no more extra-billing, but a great deal more government money would flow to the doctors.

The financial dramas were more absorbing than the medical ones. In 1985, after strenuous governmental rescue efforts, the Canadian Commercial Bank of Edmonton collapsed, shortly followed by the Northland Bank. Both banks, it seemed, had been scandalously mismanaged but had also suffered from the slump in western property values. Some other small banks were saved only by purchase and merger. Foreign banks acquired both the Mercantile and the Bank of British Columbia. No doubt Walter Gordon, who died in 1987, spun in his sepulchre. But takeovers and rescues were not the only instances of foreign pen-

1   The *Globe and Mail* lead editorial, July 29, 1987.

etration. Foreign banks were now allowed to set up wholly owned subsidiaries – 'Schedule B banks' – in Canada. By 1987 there were several dozen of these. And starting in June 1987, foreign financial interests were allowed to enter that most carefully guarded precinct of Canadianism, the securities industry. At the same time, Ottawa allowed banks and federally regulated insurance and trust companies to enter the securities businesses. The 'universal financier,' or 'financial department store,' seemed to be on the way.

Because it was legal for small groups of investors to control them, the trust companies became honey-pots for financial speculation. The general public, after all, could hardly tell one from another, and the pace of mergers and buyings-out increased the confusion. Anyway, why should the public have cared? Most trust-company liabilities were insured, by a government agency. Regulation, nevertheless, was lax, and overtrading and bad lending were all too easy, while the recession and the property-slump spelt trouble for some trust companies, especially in western Canada. But the dramatic collapse of Seaway Trust, Greymac Trust, and Crown Trust could not be explained by reference to the 'conjuncture.'

These three firms were controlled by a small group of speculators, whose practice it was to trade properties, raising prices steeply at each transaction, and to finance each sale by a mortgage advance from one of the trust companies that they controlled. The responsible financiers were said to have made off with $329 million, and the Canada Deposit Insurance Corporation had to pay out $680 million in addition. The culmination to the speculative pyramid occurred in 1982; in a matter of days the financiers bought 10,921 Toronto apartments for $312 million and sold them for $500 million. The province seized the trust companies; in 1986 the three principal speculators were charged with fraud and conspiracy. One, William Player, pleaded guilty on thirty-five charges.

Equally dramatic was the bankruptcy in August 1987 of Alberta's Principal Group, soon dubbed the 'unprincipled group.' It contained at least twenty-nine subsidiary companies, including a Cayman Islands bank and an Edmonton trust company, as well as mutual funds and a brewery. After the bankruptcy the prospects for depositors and other claimants were dim. Hundreds of millions of dollars had vanished without trace. As many as twenty-five Alberta Hutterite communities, for instance, appeared to have lent $30 million to Principal. These loans, like most of Principal's liabilities, were not insured.

Many credit unions, also, were in dire trouble. Quebec's *caisses populaires* were not in distress, and their provincial central agency had become a purchaser of industrial and financial assets not only within the province but outside it. Elsewhere in Canada, credit unions enjoyed less happy fates, largely because of bad judgment and terrible luck. At least two landed in hot water because their managers were dishonest.

All these financial troubles sparked waves of outrage, spates of scrutiny, and multiform cries for better and tighter regulation – certainly not for deregulation. The police investigated. So did the Parliament of Canada. Jurisdictions, of course, were divided. Ottawa regulated the banks and some trust companies and insured deposits (except in Quebec trust companies); the provinces supervised the rest of the deposit-takers. The situation was ironic in that these financial distresses erupted just when the rest of the Western world was moving toward *de*regulation. Meanwhile, in Canada, people wondered who would regulate the new 'financial department stores.' Ottawa looked after the banks, but the provinces dealt with securities; what about the new securities businesses of the banks? In February 1987 Ontario was poised to extend its net of control, and the federal Minister of State for Finance said that there would have to be a 'harmonious resolution' – but not what that might be.

Transport, also, was thought to be ripe for deregulation, partly because the Americans had already moved in that direction. Under federal legislation of 1987, it would be much easier for new trucking lines to establish themselves and for railways to quote confidential rates. Because the provinces have some say with respect to highways, they would have to enact concurrent legislation, and it remained to be seen what each province would do. Ottawa and Ontario expected that the new arrangements would start in 1988, although they would be only gradually phased in.

There was also talk of new freedom for the airlines. In preparation, Air Canada assembled a grouping of tributary regional feeder airlines, while Pacific Western first bought Canadian Pacific and then acquired its own tributaries. The new carrier was tentatively named Canadian International Airlines, but the initials were unfortunate; in 1987 the new firm settled on Canadian Airlines International Limited, or CAIL. To the annoyance of the logo-designers and name-tailors, people still called it 'CP AIR.'

Outside transport and finance, deregulation made little headway. Indeed, in some respects things were moving in the opposite direction. For non-financial businesses there was a new Competition Act – a major achievement of the Mulroney government, and something that the Trudeau government had never been able to consummate. The new measure came into effect in June 1986, replacing the ancient, creaking, and ineffective Combines Investigation Act. Unlike the old law, the new one treated many questions as civil rather than criminal offences. It had long been thought that, because property and civil rights belong to the provinces, Ottawa could not regulate competition and monopoly without using the criminal law. But everyone had tacitly agreed to ignore the problem, presumably because the provinces saw the logic of leaving competition policy – an obscure topic that annoyed businessmen – to Ottawa. Now there was a tribunal, with wide powers to maintain competition by restraining mergers, and a new Bureau of Competition Policy, which could scrutinize any acquisition, give prior approval, or bring matters to the tribunal. The Bureau and the tribunal were supposed to consider not just market share or industrial concentration, but also any potential for improving efficiency through mergers.

By 1988 few observers thought that the new act would make any difference, and those who believed in competition were pinning their hopes, instead, on the prospect of freer international trade. Indeed, the eighties saw a remarkable spate of corporate takeovers and reshufflings, all lovingly chronicled by the media. Long gone were the days when Canadian capitalists could do their deals in dignified obscurity. Some of the transactions were immense. The Reichmann brothers bought control of Gulf Canada from Gulf USA, kept most of the assets, and resold some to Petrocanada and to the British firm Ultramar. In a complicated series of manoeuvres to avoid a takeover, Simpson's department store sold its part of Simpson's-Sears to Sears USA. But the Hudson's Bay Company bought Simpson's just the same. The Bay then sold its northern operations to a new concern, appropriately named the North-West Company and based in Montreal. Carling-O'Keefe Breweries, long controlled by the Rothman tobacco interests, was sold to the Australian brewers Elders IXL. Merchandisers, such as Coles Books and Canadian Tire, acquired US operations, lost money on them, and then disposed of the residue. In western Canada Woodward's department store chain sold its money-losing supermarkets to Canada Safeway. Dominion Stores, part of the Argus conglomerate, was partly dismembered and in large part sold to the German-controlled firm of A&P (its rival, Loblaws, went from strength to strength). And W.H. Smith bought Classic Books.

Canadian agriculture stayed as regulated as before. The marketing boards and price supports continued, as did the Canadian Wheat Board, whose markets were now overwhelmingly in China and the Soviet Union. How would the marketing-board apparatus survive under continental free trade? It seemed that most of their traditional practices would have to be outlawed, or harmonized with American arrangements. But the negotiators from Washington proved unusually accommodating. Nevertheless, there were other disquieting tendencies on farmers' horizons. The world wheat market was depressed. The public was increasingly concerned about pesticides, additives, antibiotics, and chemical fertilizers, and there were efforts to mobilize public opposition to food irradiation – a technique that the federal Crown corporation AECL was busily promoting. Some of these high-tech agricultural devices might upset the ecology; others might upset human biology. 'Organic farming' was a refuge, but only for a few. And in 1988 came a serious drought.

Especially among Conservatives, deregulation was tangled with privatization. But there was not really much connection. Britain's Thatcher government was eager to sell off state assets but restricted its deregulation to transport and finance; the Reagan administration, having few assets to sell, thought that deregulation was 'good for the economy.' These ideological currents from the south and east had their backwashes in Canada, where, in addition, many of Mulroney's western supporters were critical of the Trudeau experiments with nationalization and control. But the provincial governments, regardless of party, were not uniformly interested. They had no intention of selling off their natural resources. Indeed, the east-coast provinces argued energetically and successfully not for the privatization of off-shore oil and gas but for a share in the control and the revenue. Quebec sold some money-losers; Ontario sold its Urban Transport Development Corporation; Alberta disposed of Pacific Western Airlines; in Saskatchewan the Devine government sold some Crown corporations and hoped to sell others; Premier Vander Zalm of British Columbia, hoping to raise $3 billion, embarked on a fire sale of provincial assets, including the highway-maintenance service. But for some provincial agencies it would have been hard to find a buyer. Nova Scotia's Sydney steel works, for instance, was out-of-date and bankrupt, operating only because federal agencies fed it with orders. The Mulroney government, with fifty-four Crown corporations to survey, took a different line: some had outlived their usefulness, while others might be more efficient and vital if they were privately owned. By mid-1988, therefore, Ottawa had sold DeHavilland Aircraft, Canadair, Teleglobe, Canadian Arsenals, the Canada Development Corporation, the CN Hotel chain, and four smaller enterprises. It decided to sell Eldorado Nuclear and at least three minor firms, as well as many shares in Air Canada. And it badly wanted to sell Petrocanada too. By August 1988, it was estimated, privatization had raised $4.6 billion – $2.1 billion for Ottawa, $1.1 billion for Victoria, $0.8 billion for Quebec, and $0.4 billion for Regina.[2]

Federal sales, naturally enough, produced angry comment. Had the government charged enough? Had it protected the workers' jobs? Was it selling the nation's high-tech heritage? This last question came most often from the numerous worshippers of the Avro Arrow, that high-tech, high-cost aircraft of the 1950s. But others asked it too. Since Canadair and DeHavilland were losing hundreds of millions a year, the government was doing well to get anything more than zero dollars for them. But the high-tech lobby and the unions naturally did not see things that way.

The row about Petrocanada, involved as it was with the Trudeau govern-

2   The *Globe and Mail*, August 13, 1988, p. B1.

ment's energy missteps and with the National Energy Program of 1980-4, proved more complicated. The Clark minority government intended to dismantle Petrocanada, privatize it, or, as was suggested in the 1980 campaign, give half the shares to Canadian citizens and sell 20 per cent, keeping 30 per cent, and effective control, in government hands. The new Trudeau government took no such action. Instead, it encouraged Petrocanada to go on a buying spree that led to absorption first of Belgian Petrofina and then of British BP. In Allan Mac-Eachen's budget of October 28, the Liberal National Energy Program – the NEP – was unveiled.

The program would annoy almost everyone, except some nationalist ideologues. Gas and oil were to be taxed much more heavily. The oil price would rise. Canadians would pay a 'blended average' of world and domestic oil prices, and this average would be less than the world price. There would soon be no more depletion allowances, but instead a Petroleum Incentives Program – the PIP – which would encourage exploration not in the provinces but in the 'Canada lands' – off-shore and up north – where Ottawa had full control. Months of negotiation with Alberta having failed, Ottawa would now set prices for crude oil and natural gas. The domestic crude-oil price would rise from $16.75 per barrel in autumn 1980 to $66.75 per barrel on July 1, 1990, at which time the world price was expected to be a great deal higher than that. Domestic oil from non-conventional sources, such as the Alberta tar sands, would receive a specially high domestic price and would even be allowed to earn depletion allowances. The PIP grants would be much lower if the firms were operating inside a province, if they were not Canadian-owned and controlled, or both.[3] Further, only Canadian companies – those at least 50 per cent Canadian-owned – would be allowed to produce on the Canada lands, where the Crown would reserve the right to take an interest of 25 per cent – the 'back-in' affecting old leases as well as new. To finance Petrocanada's campaign of acquisitions there would be a new tax. New and more energetic 'off oil' schemes, well-subsidized from Ottawa, were planned.

Albertans were furious. So were the oil companies. And so was Washington's new Reagan administration, which objected to the differential PIP and the 'back-in.' Capitalists do not like surprises, and neither does the American government. Alberta maintained that, so far as provincial lands were concerned, the NEP would bring exploration to an end; it was also outraged because Ottawa now fixed energy prices and because the new taxes meant a smaller provincial share

3 If a company were less than 50 per cent Canadian-owned, and if it were exploring on provincial lands, by 1984 it would have no depletion allowances and no PIP. But if it were exploring on 'Canada lands' and were at least 75 per cent Canadian-owned, PIP would cover 80 per cent of its exploration costs.

in the growing bonanza of oil revenues. When Alberta did its sums and discovered that, in spite of the new federal taxes, because the price of crude was to rise so sharply, Alberta's revenues would in fact increase 50 per cent in three years, Edmonton's politicians were somewhat mollified. Nevertheless, when they learned that the NEP had been designed by a senior civil servant who had a doctorate in economics, they wondered about his doctoral dissertation. Finding it treated socialism in Tanzania, one of Africa's many basket cases, they were dismayed but not surprised: the Liberals, they thought, had pointed Canada – or at least Alberta – in a Tanzanian direction. And certainly the signs did point that way. Imperial Oil quickly suspended its heavy-oil plan for Cold Lake, and the Alsands oil-sands scheme was put on hold. The drilling rigs, meanwhile, would soon be leaving Alberta – heading for the sunny south or for the Canada lands on the Beaufort Sea.

The PIP grants were discriminatory, and the back-in was provided because Ottawa wanted 50 per cent Canadian ownership of the oil industry by 1990. Petrocanada's buying program served the same end. This was nationalism, but it also looked like common sense. From 1980 through 1983, the NEP forecast, the oil industry would garner $27.5 billion in ordinary revenues, and another $2.5 billion in PIP. The more of the industry Canadians owned, the more of that money would stay in Canada.

It looked as if Ottawa wanted Canadians to buy out the foreigners. Aided by bank loans, they almost at once began to do so. Nova, Sulpetra, Turbo, and the Canada Development Corporation all made large acquisitions, and Dome bought the American-owned Hudson's Bay Oil and Gas. Even the Conservative government of Ontario got into the act, buying 25 per cent of Suncor. Ontario had got things wrong. Twenty-five per cent did not give control, nor did it make Suncor 'Canadian' for purposes of PIP.

If the NEP forecasters had been right about world oil prices, or if the newly bloated firms had quickly found marketable oil on the Canada lands, all would have been well. But by 1987, billions of dollars having been spent, there was still no new production[4] in the north or off-shore. As for the world price, Ottawa's planners had overestimated the long-run power of OPEC and underestimated the joint impact of non-OPEC production and world-wide conservation. The ink had hardly dried on the NEP when, in 1982, the world price began to slip downward. Thereafter, year by year, it went on down. Dome was already in trouble: in summer 1981 it realized that it could not pay the interest on its $5.3 billion of borrowed money. In a more remorselessly capitalistic world the firm would simply have gone broke. But Ottawa and the banks, anxious to save this

4 The long-known field at Norman Wells was further developed and a little more oil was produced there. But this was a drip in the oil-can.

new flagship of Canadianization, arranged a bail-out. Things got no better: in 1986 Dome ceased to pay any interest at all, and the Canadian banks, having carried the firm for six years, were not pleased when Dome proposed to sell out to Amoco, an American company. The Amoco deal of 1987, the banks said, gave the shareholders too much, the creditors – especially the banks – too little. But they were eventually mollified, and the deal proceeded.

Meanwhile, the NEP was providing plentiful scope for federal-provincial diplomacy. In 1981, following an angry series of Albertan ripostes in which the province deliberately reduced its oil production, Edmonton and Ottawa reached a new agreement on oil pricing. Prices would rise more steeply than under the original NEP. 'New oil' – that discovered after December 31, 1980, extracted from oil sands, or garnered by means of enhanced recovery – would receive very nearly the world price. The price of 'old oil' would also rise until it received 75 per cent of the world price. Ottawa relented with respect to its gas-export tax. And there would be more money for everybody – Ottawa, Edmonton, and the oil companies. But this pact, and the parallel agreements with Saskatchewan and British Columbia, had to be renegotiated almost at once, because the world price was sliding downward. Ottawa and Edmonton made new concessions in favour of oil companies and for the unconventional-oil projects. These schemes, which expensively extracted hydrocarbons from unpromising raw materials, were thought to be the great hope: without them Canada could not hope for self-sufficiency by 1990, the Liberal target date. The first such plant, Great Canadian Oil Sands, dated from 1967. The second, Syncrude, began production in 1978.[5] New projects, among them Alsands, or expansions of the old ones, were desired. There was also to be 'enhanced recovery' from conventional wells, and the refractory 'heavy oil' would somehow be sucked up and made usable.

Cold Lake, a heavy-oil site, would be a 'megaproject.' So would Alsands. The Trudeau government put great faith in megaprojects, not only for energy self-sufficiency but for general macroeconomic stimulation. Such projects could create interesting work and helpful orders for high-tech Canadian industry. But it was hard to keep the megaprojects trundling along, given the evolution in world energy prices. In 1983, indeed, Ottawa pressed for a rollback in domestic oil prices, observing that, under the 1982 agreements, the domestic oil price could not be more than 75 per cent of the world price. Alberta resisted, claiming that there was no provision for a rollback. In March 1983 it was decided, in view of the declining world price, to forgo the domestic-price increase scheduled for the summer. At the end of June, Ottawa and Edmonton agreed to freeze the domestic price until December 1984. The domestic price for 'old oil' was now

5 For details about the Syncrude saga see our first edition.

83 per cent of the world level. But this was still falling, and it would drop a good deal further – from almost $30 US in mid-1983 to under $10 US at the end of 1986. Admittedly, over the same period the Canadian dollar also fell somewhat – but not enough to dispel the pain.

During the short-lived Turner government things began to change. On July 14, 1984, Turner announced that the NEP, including its PIP grants and its federal tax on oil and gas, would be re-examined and that domestic prices would rise to world levels – though not at once. Under Mulroney the changes would come more quickly still.

Pat Carney, the new energy minister, said the same sorts of thing as Turner; on November 15, Michael Wilson, the finance minister, announced that oil prices would at once rise to world levels. Since oil prices were tending to fall, this was less painful than it might have been. For the time being Wilson retained the NEP energy taxes, and indeed raised them. These levies, however, did not all survive the declining oil price, the resulting plight of the oil companies and the exploration industry, and the importunities of the provinces. Within two years came a new federal-provincial Western Accord, which eliminated several of the taxes, almost completing the ruin of the NEP. Under the original plan, in 1980-3 Ottawa would collect 24 per cent of the revenue from oil and natural gas, leaving the provinces with 42.5 per cent and the industry with 33.5 per cent.[6] In 1986, however, the federal government collected only 4.5 per cent of upstream revenues, and the provinces only 24.8 per cent, while the industry retained 69.6 per cent of the much-reduced total.[7] Meanwhile, in the course of 1985-6 the rest of the NEP – PIP, 'back-in,' and the preferential treatment of Canada lands – all vanished. The NEP was dead. But in the United States, and in western Canada, it was not forgotten.

The designers of NEP had expected that oil would produce a torrent of money for government and for Canadian-owned business. But by 1983 there was little prospect of oil-begotten loot for Canadian governments, investors, or shareholders. The government of Alberta was hard-hit. It was forced to reduce its spending and to float its first bond-issues in many years, even though its Heritage Fund was producing $3 billion per year. For the governments of Newfoundland and Nova Scotia, where off-shore oil had yet to flow, the disappointment was greater still. Although the courts had ruled that they had no claim on off-shore oil or gas, the Mulroney government was willing to let them share in the management, and in the revenue. In 1988 Mulroney's government contrived a mixture of grant and guarantee which, it hoped, would bring Newfoundland's Hiber-

6   Federal receipts are net of PIP payments, which in turn are included with industry receipts.

7   These figures do not include Ottawa's receipts from the federal sales and excise taxes. Even so, between 1985 and 1986 Ottawa's total receipts fell from $6.3 billion to $3.6 billion.

nia field into production. With oil hovering around $20 per barrel, in real terms a lower price than in 1973, businesses were reluctant to pump from the expensive off-shore sites. Meanwhile, for the newly bloated Canadian energy conglomerates the problem was one of survival. In 1986, for instance, oil-company revenue was $8.3 billion; a year before it had been $13.1 billion. The debts, and the debtors, sat and waited, while early in 1988 the price of oil fell yet again.

Petrocanada, a Crown corporation created not by the NEP but by the minority government of 1973, could not go bankrupt. Indeed, it burgeoned: when the Reichmann family bought control of Gulf Canada, Petrocanada, with the Mulroney government's permission, bought part of the company from the Reichmanns. By 1987 the logo, the service stations, and the advertising of the Crown corporation were facts of life almost everywhere. Privatization might come, and management might welcome it; meanwhile, as the Israelis say, Petrocanada was 'making facts.'

Another inheritance from the Liberal 1970s, and another thorn in Tory and American flesh, was the Foreign Investment Review Agency – FIRA. Canadians also criticized FIRA because they thought that, in the recession of the early 1980s, it had discouraged external investment, thus, like NEP, making the recession worse. No doubt it did. But its effect was probably small, not because it approved most applications but because it affected mainly foreign takeovers, not new capital formation. The latter creates new output and employment; the former just helps some people to sell their assets at a good price. It was quite wrong, therefore, to say that FIRA was in any serious way the cause of the recession – which indeed came as much from an export decline as from an investment slump. But the general public and the politicians could not have cared less about such fine-spun arguments. In any event, by 1984 FIRA had become another symbol of bureaucratic interference, and the logic of deregulation was bound to clip its wings. After all, its proceedings cost time and money, nor was there any appeal from its mixture of bureaucratic and political decision. Further, after the NEP mess many people were sceptical about such decisions: why would anyone believe that the denizens of Ottawa could outguess the market with respect to national benefits and costs? The economic mishaps of the Trudeau years had discredited that idea for at least a generation. Hence the Mulroney forces quickly laid FIRA to rest. From its grave rose a new agency, Investment Canada, which retained some regulatory powers but was intended chiefly to *attract* new investment. As the ads proclaimed in the *Economist* and the *Wall Street Journal*, 'Canada is open for business.'

In Ronald Reagan's United States, the ideology of deregulation cohabited with the idea of fiscal reform. Many Republicans wanted to cut income-tax rates and to hack a path through the thickets of exemptions and special deductions that generations had planted and fertilized. If Congress would lower tax rates, it was suggested, Americans would respond creatively. The result would be a 'supply-side' explosion that would raise output and productivity; in the end there would be more government tax revenue than ever. Early in the 1980s Congress did what Reagan wanted, and during his second term it also simplified the exemptions. At the same time, while cutting its social outlays, the administration spent a great deal more on defence. The result was not a supply-side recovery from the recession. Rather, the simple Keynesian prescription – cut tax rates and raise spending in a slump – produced a classic Keynesian recovery – rapidly growing output and employment, dramatic worsening of the balance of payments on current account, a flood of imports, and eventually a weaker US dollar. Because the Federal Reserve System kept credit tight, the deficit also tended to raise interest rates – although the inflationary expectations and realities of the early 1980s were pushing the same way. Throughout the world, local interest rates followed suit. In 1981 the Canadian long-term rate on corporate bonds averaged 16.3 per cent; in 1982 it was 15.9 per cent, and in 1983, 12.7 per cent.

If Canada suffered from American interest rates, it benefited from Washington's unconscious Keynesianism. Having fallen painfully in the early 1980s, our export sales recovered smartly. Canadian governments, however, were not anxious to swallow a domestic dose of Reagan's Keynesian medicine. Unemployment rose, passing 12 per cent during the worst of the slump. Even in 1988, after five years of recovery, the national rate was 8 per cent, although in central Canada it was a great deal lower. Keynesianism had fallen into disfavour during the 1970s, and few Canadians recognized just how Keynesian American policy actually was. Ottawa, in any event, had other problems. During the late 1970s the federal budgetary position had dramatically deteriorated, partly because of rising transfer payments to persons and provinces, partly because Ottawa gave away much of the income tax to the provinces – several of which, in turn, had worrisome deficits. Budgetary policy in the 1980s, therefore, revolved partly around unemployment but chiefly around the federal deficit – and the fight to contain or reduce it. Tax reform, also, was on the federal agenda.

Returning to office in 1980, the Liberals experienced some pressure for new spending. Allan MacEachen resisted these, worrying much more about inflation than about unemployment. In his first budget, in 1981, he made a few structural changes with respect to pension and retirement incomes, but his second, in 1982, contained a much stronger push for equity in taxation. There was to be a complicated set of adjustments in personal, corporate, and sales tax arrangements. The 1982 budget set off a storm of criticism – vehement and vituperative, but hardly devastating, and often amounting to no more than the proposition that prosperous taxpayers and their lawyers did not want to lose some of their customary tax shelters, gimmicks, and dodges. 'Entitlements' had surfaced once again. Certainly a budget that reduced many tax rates while leaving government revenue essentially unchanged could hardly be a budget of gloom and doom. Nevertheless the outcry continued, and after six months the Department of Finance began a retreat that the government would later complete. MacEachen, meanwhile, continued to believe that it was important to fight inflation so as to provide more jobs and to reduce unemployment in the longer run – views that enjoyed professional support among many economists, not only in Canada but abroad. Keynesian pump-priming, MacEachen believed, was unhelpful medicine. Besides the tax reforms, therefore, the main innovation of the 1982 budget was the scheme of 'six and five': there would be pay-restraint in the public sector, holding wage increases to 6 per cent for the first year and to 5 per cent for the second. None the less, MacEachen's 1982 budget did contain some pump-priming, directed chiefly toward new housing. The annual deficit was now pushing the $20-billion mark.

In September 1982 Marc Lalonde succeeded MacEachen at Finance. In an October mini-budget the new minister provided a little new stimulation, a little new taxation, and an announcement that in the current fiscal year the deficit would reach $23.6 billion. In April 1983, bringing down his first complete budget, he offered about $2 billion in extra pump-priming. But this was less than 2 per cent of total federal outlays, and it was offset by an increase in the federal sales tax. Federal expenditure was still outgrowing revenue, and the expected deficit was now over $30 billion, or 6.7 per cent of GNP in the fiscal year 1982-3.

The deficit might or might not have been a problem. Few economists thought it was; few businessmen, even when government spending provided their sales and their profits, would admit that it was not. But the media and the public had little interest in technical debates, or in the undoubted fact that the recession itself had made the deficit worse: government revenue was less than expected, while some sorts of outlay, especially on unemployment insurance and welfare, were higher. High interest rates, further, increased the cost of servicing the debt. At least the government was not dramatically raising tax rates, nor was it cutting outlays, in an effort to reduce the deficit or to get rid of it. To that extent, at least, its policy was Keynesian. The medicine may not have been sufficient. On the left, where simplified or crude Keynesianism was popular, few thought it was. Yet the public suspected that the deficit was somehow a Bad Thing – some kind of failure inside the Trudeau government.[8]

8 We cannot review all the technical debates about the virtues and vices of deficits. But two points ought to be made. It is hard to believe that any businessman would refuse to build a new plant, or buy a new piece of equipment, or refrain from profitable production, merely because he was

By 1984 the Liberal government seemed to agree with the public. Lalonde's February budget provided only a gentle stimulus, and it phased out the unpopular 'six and five.' When John Turner became Prime Minister in June 1984, he put the February budget on hold, in preparation for an election.

The Tories campaigned on a platform that included tax cuts, reform of the personal income tax, some new spending, and some paring of existing programs. Early in November 1984 the new finance minister, Michael Wilson, began to work out the logic of this platform. The process would continue for the next three years and was not complete by summer 1987, when Wilson produced a 'White Paper' – in reality another budget – on tax reform.

In 1984 Wilson cut expenditures, raised tax rates, wondered whether social programs had to be universal, and talked seriously about limiting and reducing the deficit. This he expected to rise from $32 billion in 1983-4 to $35 billion in 1987-8 – if the Conservatives could control spending, and if the auguries for revenues had been correctly read. But the deficit would fall in relation to GNP.

In fact, unless he was willing to abolish some major, much-loved spending program or to impose a really swinging rise in tax rates, Wilson could not quickly conjure deficit away. In 1982 government revenue was $64.9 billion, while transfer payments, subsidies, and interest on the public debt amounted to $65.8 billion. Ottawa was spending $20.1 billion on goods and services. If *all* such outlays had been abolished, the national exchequer would still have been running a small deficit. And the transfer payments were almost all of two sorts – contractual obligations, such as interest on the public debt, and 'sacred trusts,' like federal-provincial equalization payments, old age pensions, medicare, and unemployment insurance. In these circumstances, which the Tories inherited from the Liberals, petty economies would really make little difference. This fact did not deter the Mulroney government from imposing them.

The challenge to 'universality' proved not to be serious: faced with a cry of rage from the public, the Conservatives quickly backed down. Nevertheless, the government was serious about controlling expenditure, and one may suppose that its eagerness increased when Ottawa's oil revenues collapsed. Soon there were the task forces of Erik Neilsen, the Deputy Prime Minister, busily scrutinizing government spending. There were talks with the provinces about shared-cost programs, such as medicare and university education. And wherever possible there were cuts, freezes, or some mixture of the two. Only defence was

worried about the deficit, which, therefore, cannot have made the recession worse. Nor can it have squeezed out business investment by raising the cost of credit. In the early eighties interest rates were high throughout the Western world, but that was not Canada's fault, and Canadian businessmen could borrow abroad, thereby escaping any 'crowding-out' that Ottawa's deficit might produce on Canada's own capital market.

spared: on Reaganesque lines, Mulroney launched a new and badly needed plan to re-equip the Canadian armed forces. Meanwhile, among the sufferers were the CBC, the Canada Council, with its $69-million grant budget,[9] the federal research councils, and other federal laboratories. Arts groups were naturally loud in their protest. So were scientists. The government paid little attention. Perhaps it had not realized that for every three farmers there was, by 1981, a worker in 'cultural, artistic, and recreational pursuits.' Or perhaps it thought that such people would never vote Tory, no matter what the government might do.

The Conservatives inherited an economy in which employment, after falling 3.3 per cent in 1982, had begun to rise. In 1983 employment and unemployment rose together, because the labour force was growing, so that the unemployment rate rose from 11 per cent in 1982 to 11.9 per cent in 1983. In 1984 things got better: employment rose 2.5 per cent while the labour force grew only 1.8 per cent, and the unemployment rate therefore began to fall. For the year as a whole it averaged 11.3 per cent, but at year-end it was down to 10.9 per cent. The pattern continued in 1984-8: employment rose, while the unemployment rate drifted downward. This recovery was concentrated in central Canada: in Alberta and British Columbia, the resource industries were deeply troubled, and so were the construction trades that depended so heavily on them. Albertans blamed the NEP. Its abolition, however, did not produce a local recovery – much less a 1970s-style boom.

The rate of inflation was falling dramatically. During the 1970s the consumer price index rose 8 per cent per year. In 1981 it shot up 12.5 per cent, and in 1982, 10.2 per cent; in 1983 the year-end figure was 4.5 per cent and in 1984, 3.8 per cent. The 1984 pattern continued in later years. In 1987, for example, at mid-year the consumer price index was rising at an annual rate of 4.8 per cent – still a comparatively high figure by the standards of the 1950s or 1960s, but a blessed relief after the experience of the 1970s and of 1981-2. The Canadian experience precisely paralleled that of the United States and was reflected in much though not all of western Europe. Growing deficits, it seemed, could coexist with falling inflation. The Conservatives did not deserve any particular praise for 'de-inflating' the Canadian economy, and to their credit they did not claim any.

By summer 1987 the Americans had completed a major simplification of their income-tax system, and the Canadian government, committed to an 'open' discussion of tax proposals, made no secret of its intentions: it would do its best to follow the US example. Meanwhile, Michael Wilson had introduced a lifetime exemption for capital gains: each taxpayer, he announced, would be able eventu-

9   Less than 0.01 per cent of total federal spending.

ally to receive up to $500,000 in such tax-free gains. But the new concession would be phased in gradually. Pension deductions, also, were gradually to be liberalized. And the government also wanted to change its sales taxation. The federal manufacturers' sales tax, collected on certain manufactured goods and on comparable imports, would be replaced by some version of the European 'value-added tax,' or VAT.

The government seemed to like VAT because it could be applied to services, which by 1987 accounted for more than 50 cents out of every dollar the consuming public spent. It could also be applied to food. But these ends could have been attained in different and simpler ways. The public was afraid of VAT, partly because it could become a new money-cow, partly because it might well be applied to food and other 'necessities,' and partly because it would be an administrative nightmare for small business. Horror stories about European VAT began to circulate. In 1987, a government poll revealed that 68 per cent of Canadians feared a 'broadly-based sales tax' of the VAT type, especially if it were applied to food.

On June 18, 1987, Wilson presented his White Paper on tax reform; in summer 1988 Parliament passed the necessary legislation. The White Paper embodied the most drastic and sweeping tax changes that Canada had seen since the First World War. Personal income tax rates would fall, and there would be three rates instead of ten. Corporation income tax would also be reduced. But many personal and corporate exemptions would be abolished, and some others would be converted into tax credits. The capital-gains exemption would be capped at $100,000, except for farmers. About 850,000 Canadians would vanish altogether from the income-tax rolls. There would be some kind of new VAT-like tax, the precise form to be determined through federal-provincial consultation. Wilson hoped for an integrated federal-provincial tax, the rate presumably varying as between one province and another; if the provinces would not agree Ottawa would go it alone. In the end, Wilson explained, 1.5 million households would pay heavier income taxes, 9 million would pay less – and the government would get less revenue from the modified personal income tax, making up the difference from corporations and from the new sales tax. Low-income families would avoid the pain of the higher sales taxation, because they would get sales-tax credits. This scheme naturally did not satisfy the anti-poverty lobby, which at once pointed out that there was a problem: the poor folk would pay the extra sales tax now and get the credit only later.

The government and the media suggested that the reform was a 'supply-side' plan, one that would liberate and stimulate individual initiative. In fact it might work the other way. Lower tax rates may make people work harder because they keep more of the loot, but people may also work *less* hard, because less work now produces the same after-tax income. Much more interesting, in the longer run, would be the shift from personal income to sales taxation. To tax sales is to tax consumption; savings escape entirely. Therefore, a sales tax ought to encourage thrift, saving, and investment – just what Canada would need if its productivity performance, dismal during the period 1975-83, was to improve. Again, however, the anti-poverty lobby pointed to the flip side: the better-off do not spend all of their incomes, while the poor spend every penny – and then some.

Free trade is another way to raise productivity.[10] The Trudeau government continued its support for the approach embodied in GATT – a multilateral approach to the control and reduction of trade barriers, whether tariff or non-tariff. Both Ottawa and Washington frequently invoked GATT in their endless bickering over trade-related issues in 1980-4. Ottawa was, nevertheless, eager to explore new bilateral trade relations, especially with the newly prosperous lands of OPEC and the Pacific Rim. Indeed, when the government's departmental structure was reshuffled in 1982, one aim was to ensure that, in trade promotion, External Affairs and Industry, Trade and Commerce would never work at cross-purposes: trade promotion moved from IT&C to DEA, whose building thereupon bulged at the seams.

The Trudeau government also, in 1983, began a 'sectoral free trade initiative' with the United States as its target. A new government statement, *Trade Policy for the 1980s*, defined the direction. The days of the 'third option,' when Trudeau had wanted to encourage Canada to do more of its trade off-shore, seemed long past. That was not really so: Ottawa was still anxious to push overseas sales as hard as it could. But now there was hope that in certain industries, such as steel, agricultural and urban transportation equipment, petrochemicals, and 'informatics,' Canadian factories could win large sales in the United States.[11]

Negotiations began in 1983 and continued in 1984 but did not get anywhere. The times were not propitious. Both the United States and Canada had suffered recession in 1981-2, but for Canada, unlike the United States, the current account of the balance of payments moved into surplus in 1982 and stayed in sur-

10 Because it displaces labour and machinery from low-productivity uses into higher-productivity uses. It may also encourage investment, in so far as it encourages business to build capacity that it would not otherwise have built. The former effect is quite certain, unless workers are unwilling or unable to move from one job to another; the latter is entirely uncertain, partly because free trade *saves* resources and partly because it lets businessmen build their plants abroad. Finally, some people believe that free trade forces everyone to work harder and more efficiently. This is the 'cold shower effect,' and it is very uncertain indeed.

11 In fact, every study by professional economists, since the pioneering work of the Wonnacotts in the 1960s, concluded that there were plenty of industries where this would happen. The attention of government and public was concentrated on a few 'leading sectors'; the actual opportunity was almost certainly a great deal broader.

plus during 1983 and 1984. Further, Canada was doing very nicely out of the 1965 Autopact, which meant free trade on the American side but, because of Ottawa's 'safeguards,' something less than free trade on the Canadian. Not only among the American auto workers but in Congress, there was strong criticism of the results, which looked very much like unfair trade. To such foreign critics, new schemes for sectoral free trade were bound to look self-serving and partial.

In 1984 there were pressures for a more comprehensive initiative. The Americans were increasingly inclined to impose various unexpected burdens, both tariff and non-tariff, on Canadian exports, and as the American balance of payments continued to run a deficit on current account, such inclinations were naturally strengthened. Canadians began to worry about American 'contingent protectionism.' This was the risk that if Canadian competition became awkward the Americans would take new restrictive action, GATT commitments or no. Indeed, during 1985 and 1986 there were instances of this. The Americans imposed new levies on Canada's tiny shake and shingle industry, and they claimed that the Canadian provinces subsidized their lumber industries by collecting unduly low fees for the cutting of trees on Crown lands. This was a silly assertion,[12] but the Canadians handled their case ineptly, and the Americans would not listen to reason. Finally, to obviate the penal 32 per cent tax that the Americans proposed, in January 1987 Ottawa imposed its own 15 per cent export levy, pending an increase in provincial logging fees.[13]

More free-trade pressure came from the federal Royal Commission on the Economic Union and Development Prospects for Canada, better known as the Macdonald Commission. Originally appointed in November 1982, it produced a short interim report in April 1984 and an enormous final report in 1985. The full substance of the Commission's labours, and of recommendations, need not concern us here. In most respects its work was as stillborn as the labours of past royal commissions. But with respect to trade this was not so. After pointing to the appearance of wasteful interprovincial barriers within Canada, the commission called for a comprehensive free-trade agreement with the United States. It noted that free trade would produce efficiency-gains, possibly enough to raise Canadian incomes by 10 per cent, while controlling American protectionism and

12 The value of the standing timber has to be deduced backward, so to speak, from the selling price in the relevant market, where the American loggers never supplied less than two-thirds of the demand, ensuring that in that market the Canadians were 'price-takers' not 'price-makers.' If the provinces do not collect enough for the standing timber, and/or if logging-industry wages do not rise enough to offset provincial 'restraint,' the Canadian suppliers will have a *cost* advantage that translates into a larger market share. But this is not a subsidy.
13 The federal government certainly had the constitutional power to do this, but to abbreviate new yelling and screaming in the provincial capitals the Mulroney cabinet distributed the yield to the provincial governments.

attracting investment from businessmen now oscillating between the enormous American market and the small Canadian one but frightened by American 'contingent protectionism.'

Even though they came from a body that the Tories believed to be dominated by Liberal hacks, the Macdonald recommendations were highly convenient for Mulroney, who had become eager to negotiate freer trade. President Reagan, it seemed, shared the Prime Minister's eagerness. As Canada's senior negotiator Ottawa chose Simon Reisman, once a senior mandarin and now a consultant. At one time it would have seemed more natural to appoint a bureaucrat or to let a cabinet committee conduct the negotiations. But by using Reisman the cabinet could actually distance itself from the proceedings and from the results. If the talks succeeded, Mulroney could take the credit; if they failed, perhaps Reisman would bear the blame.

There followed a characteristic Canadian wrangle. What was 'on the table'? Culture? The Autopact? Foreign investment? Under FIRA Ottawa often tried to make foreign-owned firms buy in Canada. This was clearly an unfair practice, and one that the United States had often challenged. The Americans showed signs of larger ambitions: they wanted to restrict Canada's right to regulate foreign investment as such. The Autopact mattered because of the safeguards – also obviously unfair in principle, even though for almost twenty years the Canadian auto industry had been building more cars than the rules required. Regional incentives mattered because they could give some Canadian firms an unfair advantage in a continental market. And culture mattered because Canada's tax and subsidy rules discriminated in favour of Canadian-owned magazines, book-publishers, and printers, and against American border-television stations.

Canada's culture lobby naturally claimed that the entire apparatus of culture-subsidy was imperilled. Some actors, actresses, producers, and publicists may even have believed this. By cutting the CBC and Canada Council budgets, Mulroney had made them more fearful still. In fact, it would have been quite easy for Ottawa to defend the subsidies that really benefit culture and national identity – those that go to the people who actually produce cultural and national services, such as plays, concerts, books, broadcasts, and movies. There was no evidence that the Americans wanted Ottawa to discontinue these. Indeed, as one American negotiator wryly remarked, 'Why should we worry about *that*? After all, Canadian culture isn't an export good.' But no one could defend the arrangements by which Canadian-owned businesses, such as cable companies and TV stations, get special treatment in the vain hope that they will hire more Canadian performers and producers. Indeed, some observers hoped that the free-trade deal might force Ottawa to abandon various schemes that were not only silly but ineffective.

ACTRA, the actors' union, did not see things this way. In summer 1987 it joined with the Canadian Auto Workers, the United Church of Canada, and various interest groups in the 'Coalition to Oppose Free Trade.' The group promptly sponsored a 'Free Trade's No Picnic' picnic. The Roman Catholic bishops, while at first not willing to oppose free trade, were clearly nervous about the idea. In the vain hope that their parishes would 'study the topic,' they provided a guide which, to say the least, accentuated the negative. And in due course GATT-FLY, a lobby financed by the large churches, announced that free trade was immoral.

Ottawa could conduct and ratify a trade pact without consulting the provinces, which certainly had no constitutional power of veto. But in the GATT Tokyo Round of the 1970s the provinces had been regularly consulted, and in a Canadian-American pact there would be many matters that worried the Americans and clearly fell within provincial jurisdiction. In the United States, a trade agreement or treaty would bind the junior governments; in Canada it would not. Sad to say, because the provinces managed the Crown lands, bought wine and liquor, controlled beer, issued contracts of all kinds, and distributed subsidies, they would have to accept some limitations of their powers.

On October 3, 1987, after various tribulations, including a carefully orchestrated walk-out by Canada's chief negotiator, an agreement of sorts was reached. To sign an agreement is not to bring one into force: in summer 1988 the US Congress approved, but Mulroney would face an election on the free-trade issue. Naturally the various interest groups complained; the public interest in cheapness and economic efficiency quickly began to vanish from sight.

It was predicted that, even though some industries would shrink, the pact would create many additional Canadian jobs – perhaps as many as 350,000. Canadian consumer prices would drop by 3 to 6 per cent, the equivalent of one to two years' inflation. Yet, as always, the free-trade pact delivered less than either government had desired. Also, because many non-tariff barriers were allowed to continue, Canada's efficiency-gains would be less than economists might have hoped. On the one hand, Canada was allowed to continue its farm marketing boards, its cultural subsidies, and its content quotas for radio and television (the Canadian agricultural and culture lobbies had nothing to complain of, but none the less they wailed). Nor was Canada obliged to rationalize its brewing industry. Thus 'jobs were saved' in brewing, while Canadians would continue to pay unnecessarily high prices for beer because the regulatory framework wasted resources. On the other hand, Canada committed itself to end all discriminatory mark-up and pricing arrangements for wine within seven years. The nation's 3,500 grape growers were dismayed; the nation's wine-bibbers had cause to rejoice. So did the purchasers of records, films, and tapes, on which duties were to be phased out. Canada promised to give up the 'duty-remission scheme' under which overseas auto-makers could earn credits toward their tariff bills by buying and exporting Canadian-made parts – a form of export subsidy that is expensive to Canada, and that international tribunals have often denounced. In other respects the Autopact survived in a form that was *more* protectionist with respect to overseas producers. The 'safeguards' for Canadian production were intact, and it was agreed that no additional car companies could work under the pact. Similarly, the Defence Production Sharing Agreement was untouched. The two governments' 'buy-at-home' procurement policies were somewhat liberalized, but not abolished.

By January 1, 1988, all Canadian-US tariffs would be gone, and so would some non-tariff barriers. Canada's meat, potato, oilseed, and grain producers could expect more ready access to the US market. The uranium trade was to be liberalized, and in energy there could be no discrimination in pricing and supply arrangements of the sort that Ottawa had imposed on US oil- and gas-buyers in the 1970s. Thus, although Americans could buy only as much energy as Canadians were willing to sell, Canada could not return to practices that, in the 1970s, had been economically wasteful and politically stressful, both at home and abroad. Also, there were important provisions that would ensure more transborder competition in services.

Canada did not get the 'binding mechanism for dispute resolution' that the Mulroney government wanted. Each country could go on applying, and modifying, its own anti-dumping and anti-subsidy measures. Each country could take disputes to a new binational tribunal, which could consider whether any particular measure was in accordance with the law of the nation that had imposed it. If the tribunal found in the negative it could issue a binding cease-and-desist order. There was to be a working party that would try to develop, within seven years, an agreed 'substitute system of rules in both countries for anti-dumping and countervailing duties' (articles 1906, 1907). Few observers believed that this effort would or could succeed. More useful, perhaps, were the agreed limitations on punitive 'emergency action.' After 1998 neither party could unilaterally restrict a damaging flow of imports from the other; until that time, any such action would have to last no more than three years and could not be imposed without compensation.

Strictly speaking, international investment need not form part of a free-trade agreement, which by definition is about movement of outputs, not movement of inputs. But Canada's investment regulations were on Washington's 'must list,' and it is doubtful if the Mulroney government, anxious to shed the memory of FIRA, argued much. Thus, with respect to new legislation, there was to be 'national treatment' for all new businesses. Also, to the rage of the self-styled

'Canadian nationalists,' Canada agreed to raise the threshold for reviews of take-overs of existing businesses and to phase out the review of 'indirect takeovers' – where an already-foreign-owned firm experiences a change in ownership because its foreign parent has been taken over. None of the new arrangements would apply to oil, gas, unbottled water, or uranium.[14]

Neither the Trudeau nor the Mulroney government wanted to put all its eggs in the American basket. Admittedly, by 1984 the United States was taking 80 per cent of Canada's exports, and under free trade it would take still more. Some traditional markets, such as the British, had shrunk to insignificance, and western Europe as a whole, once a major market for our wheat, aluminum, and forest products, was now exporting the first commodity and buying little of the second or the third. Indeed, by the mid-1980s almost all Canada's wheat exports went to the socialist countries of the 'second world,' especially to the Soviet Union and China. Japan had long since emerged as a very important market – a larger one than Britain. But to Ottawa's rage, the Japanese bought chiefly raw materials and semi-fabricates – forest products, iron ore, and coal. Indeed, by 1987 the trans-Pacific coal trade had become a major national scandal. Canada's national government had joined with British Columbia and with various private interests to develop the massive new Quintette coal enterprise in northern British Columbia and to link it with the sea at Prince Rupert, but the project was barely working before the Japanese began to cut back on their purchases and to lower their buying prices. Another mega-project, it seemed, would bite the dust.

Canada's export-credit system and its aid program, meanwhile, made new overseas markets for Canada's manufactures. The practice of 'tying aid,' begun long before by the Liberals, was continued with new energy by the Tories. The aid lobby exaggerated the extent of the practice, and its dangers: after all, some aid is better than no aid, and because so much Canadian aid was multilateral while much bilateral aid was untied, less than half of all our aid was in fact tied. Nevertheless, by 1987 there were whole Canadian sectors, such as the locomotive industry, which were heavily dependent on CIDA, and others, such as the aircraft and atomic reactor industries, for which export credit was crucial.

In these industries were to be found some of the typical firms of the eighties – indeed, both successes and failures. The Canadian-owned firm of Bombardier, for instance, supplied 'CIDA locomotives,' and thanks to export credits it even sold subway cars to New York. After acquiring Canadair, which had lost $1.4 billion in its last year of Crown ownership, Bombardier no doubt hoped that

14 The long and complicated agreement contains many details that are not mentioned here. For the full text, plus Canadian official comment, see Department of External Affairs, *The Canada-US Free Trade Agreement* (Ottawa: Department of External Affairs, 1988). This document runs to 315 pages.

more credits would help it export the Canadair line of executive jets. The atomic industry, specializing in Canada's very own CANDU reactor and impeded by world-wide suspicion of atomic power, soldiered on. But its sales were few, and its successes, as in Argentina, Romania, and South Korea, always involved concessions and suspected bribes as well.

The American relationship and the subsidy system were two pillars of Canada's trade regime; the third was GATT. The international body was somewhat battered by the world-wide advance of non-tariff barriers (NTBs) and 'voluntary' arrangements for trade limitation, such as those with which Canada controlled its imports of textiles and Japanese cars. But it was still alive and still useful. Disputes could still be taken to GATT, and a favourable verdict, though not self-enforcing, had a valuable effect. Further, there were things that the multilateral GATT could do – or might be able to do – but that Canada could not possibly do on its own. And of these the most important for Canada, by the mid-1980s, related to grain.

By 1986 the United States had again built up large grain holdings, as in the 1960s, because it possessed a domestic price-support system that encouraged domestic production while restricting domestic consumption. The European Community, a large grain importer as late as the mid-1960s, was in the same position as the United States, and for the same reasons. These two great trading blocs, therefore, became involved in a trading war – the competitive subsidization of their wheat exports, not only to the Third World and OPEC (where Saudi Arabia also, incredibly, had a surplus of exportable grain), but to the Soviet Union. The world price of wheat therefore fell sharply, so that in summer 1987 it was lower than it had been for fifteen years or more. Ottawa did not subsidize the nation's wheat export, but it did subsidize the wheat farmers, to the tune of nearly $3 billion in 1986. Ottawa must have been hoping to keep the vote solid and the industry alive until better times should come. Those times, however, could not arrive unless and until the United States and the Community changed their policies. Canada, therefore, took an active part in the 'Cairns Group,' a collection of the smaller wheat-exporting countries, all suffering in the same way as Canada. The Group voiced its concerns at GATT. When, in summer 1987, President Reagan called for the world-wide phasing-out of agricultural subsidies, the Canadian government voiced its support. What the European Community would concede remained to be seen. Few observers hoped for much.

Interacting with these trade developments was the saga of the exchange rate. During the 1980s the rate, expressed as US cents per Canadian dollar, moved sharply downward, first to the 82-cent mark and then to 70 cents, touching levels, as the press loved to announce, not seen since the Great Depression. In 1987 there was some recovery: from February to July our dollar was trading around the 75-cent mark. Relative to other world currencies the movements were very different. The Canadian dollar first rose with the American, then, in 1986-7, fell with it.

The Canadian dollar remained a 'managed currency.' The Bank of Canada continued to buy and sell Canadian dollars and foreign monies in the foreign exchange market; from time to time the government borrowed foreign monies and spent them to support the rate; domestic interest rates were managed with an eye to the exchange rate, so that credit became looser and interest rates lower when the Bank wanted a lower exchange rate, and vice versa. Such fiddling became easier after November 1982, when the Bank abandoned its seven-year-old practice of setting explicit monetary targets.

Central banks, such as the Bank of Canada, manage interest rates and credit so as to 'induce' international flows of capital funds. In the world of the 1980s the entire capitalist world was awash with funds. Individuals and corporate treasurers watched interest rates and exchange rates, moving money promptly when they detected, or expected, a profit. In most respects the capitalist world had become a single financial community, so that a truly autonomous monetary system could no longer exist. If a smallish country like Canada kept money particularly tight, foreign money would flow in, pushing up the exchange rate; if such a country tried for specially easy credit and 'cheap money,' as many thought Canada should do in the early 1980s when inflation and recession were both serious, its exchange rate would tend to fall, other things being equal. In the 1980s Canada could have had an exchange-rate target. Or it could have had a money-growth target. it could not have both. And after 1982, the government seems to have opted for managing the exchange rate.

For things like inflation and interest rates, money still mattered. But it was the money supply of the capitalist world, not of a small country like Canada, that mattered. Canada's financiers and analysts were slow to understand this fact. They watched the figures on the nation's money supply, like Roman augurers studying chicken-entrails. What they learned was hard to say. 'Tight money' was widely blamed for the recession of 1981-2. Of course no one liked to pay the high nominal interest rates of 1981-2. Mortgages were written at more than 20 per cent. Even the Government of Canada paid over 17 per cent on one issue of Canada Savings Bonds. But the public had grown more sophisticated about interest rates. It had learned to distinguish the 'nominal' from the 'real,' the latter being adjusted for inflation and sometimes even for taxation.[15] Certainly real interest rates stood well below nominal. One estimate suggests that the real

15 Sad to say, there is no right way to calculate 'the' real interest rate. The calculation is different for households and businesses, for borrowers and lenders, for the future and for the past. It is also sensitive to the particular tax status of the person, or the business, for whom it is attempted.

long-term rate of interest was only 2.8 per cent in 1981 and 3.4 per cent in 1982 – hardly high enough to deter new investment. In fact, real interest rates seem to have *risen* along with the recovery of 1983 and thereafter, presumably because many folk expected that inflation rates would not stay low. But the comparatively high real interest rates did not prevent recovery. To anyone who closely studies the arithmetic of interest, taxation, and investment, this fact will not be surprising.[16]

Recovery, however, was uneven. In the Atlantic provinces, as usual, nothing much was happening, while in the four western provinces the recession lingered. Given the depressed condition of wheat, oil, timber, and the construction and development activities that battened on these primary industries, it could do little else. Various nostrums were suggested. In 1987, indeed, a conference of westerners resolved that Ottawa should encourage people to move westward. There would then be a larger local market. What would the migrants *do*? This was less clear. Naturally the depressed provinces, and their politicians, looked to Ottawa for help. They always have, and they always will. But it was far from clear that Ottawa could do much. The federal deficit was one problem. So was the shortage of ideas. Equalization payments, begun in 1957, naturally continued. Without them the several Atlantic provinces would have been bankrupt.

Administrative reshuffling, certainly, did not do much. In 1982 the Trudeau government combined the old Department of Regional Economic Expansion (DREE) with parts of the old Department of Industry, Trade and Commerce, erecting a new Department of Regional Industrial Expansion (DRIE) which continued to spend money. In 1984-5, for instance, DRIE spent over $600 million on its two largest programs,[17] of which 35 per cent went to the Atlantic provinces and 22 per cent to the prairies and British Columbia. It follows that over 40 per cent of the money went to Ontario and Quebec – prosperous provinces that could hardly be said to be disadvantaged. Why did such things happen? Of course both Ontario and Quebec *did* contain 'stagnant pockets' where the local economy was anything but healthy. In addition there were politics, 'entitlements,' and bureaucratic inertia. When a journalist asked a senior DRIE official

16 Suppose a new machine will produce an income of $1,000 per year. If the materials cost $300 and labour costs $500, while other charges cost $100, there is $100 left over. Suppose the firm borrows at 10 per cent to buy the machine. Its profit is zero, and unless it expects a rise in the price of the output that exceeds the rise in the costs of materials, labour, and other charges, it won't buy the machine. But at *any* rate of interest below 10 per cent the machine is profitable, so long as profits are taxed at less than 100 per cent. A fall in the nominal interest rate or a rise in the expected price level, therefore, will affect only projects that had previously been unprofitable or balanced precisely on the 'margin of indifference.'

17 Federal-provincial Economic and Regional Development Agreements (ERDA) and the Industrial and Regional Development Program (IRDP).

in summer 1987 to provide a policy outline, he said that he could not do so, because he did not have one.

Regional dissatisfaction prodded the Mulroney government into a new wave of agency-creation. In June 1987 came the Atlantic Canada Opportunities agency, which took over DRIE's responsibilities in that part of Canada. In July came the Western Diversification Initiative, which was to spend $1.2 billion over five years – 'all new money.' Westerners were sceptical. Said the president of Calgary's Canada West Foundation, 'We've heard all this before.'

The provincial governments, meanwhile, pursued their own recovery and development programs, displaying the mixture of interventionism, *étatisme*, gimmickry, and folly that historians would expect. Only a few examples will be offered here. Nova Scotia did its best to keep Sydney Steel alive, even though the steel industry has global excess capacity. In Quebec the return of Bourassa's Liberals in 1985 produced some retreat from the extreme interventionist policies of the *Péquistes*. In Ontario under the Peterson government there was special interest in high-tech and in higher education, mixed with extreme unease about the future of the booming auto industry. In British Columbia both the Bennett government and its Vander Zalm successor believed that provincial salvation was to be found through union-bashing, cost-trimming, high-tech tourism, and an industrial park at the University of British Columbia – into which Vander Zalm proposed to parachute five Professors of Film. After all, was Vancouver not 'Hollywood North'? In all provinces and all regions, without exception, the politicians welcomed foreign investment. Neither origin nor direction seemed to matter very much. Everything was welcome – yen, marks, francs, and especially dollars, both American and Hongkongolese.

By 1988 it seemed that few Canadians worried about 'the problem of foreign investment.' Most Canadians seemed to have accepted the situation: Canadian business was a fact of foreign life, and foreign business was a fact of life in Canada. And although foreign businesses still faced criticism whenever they closed Canadian plants, most thoughtful folk recognized that the multinationals had not caused the slump of the early eighties, nor were they responsible for the uneven pattern of recovery. Indeed, by 1988 Canadians and their political leaders were, if anything, too optimistic about the good that new foreign investment would do.[18]

18 Professional economists now treated the whole topic with caution. Foreign firms, like domestic firms, *might* misbehave. Foreign enterprises could and often did bring new products, new technology, new methods. Foreign projects might or might not involve new capital formation, new jobs, and a wider tax base. It all depended. But the effects, whatever they might be, would be dampened: by 1988 new foreign investment was simply too small, relative to the whole Canadian economy, to make very much difference to anything.

The conservative eighties (Raeside, 1988). Reproduced with the permission of Adrian Raeside, Victoria *Times Colonist*

Thanks to the media and to the controversy over foreign ownership that raged from the mid-fifties to the early eighties, Canadians became accustomed to one item in the nation's balance of international indebtedness[19] – the value of foreign claims on the Canadian economy. They also heard plenty about the value of foreign direct investment. Both numbers were only part of the story, because Canadians have assets abroad, as well as liabilities. To measure 'burden' one really ought to subtract external assets from liabilities. From 1946 to 1969 both assets and liabilities grew, but so did Canada's GNP, so that in 1969 net liabilities were still only 35 per cent of GNP – not much more than the 32 per cent they had been in 1946. By 1984 they were 36 per cent of GNP – not much more than in 1946. Recent developments reflected massive Canadian foreign investments

19 A sort of inventory of all external claims and obligations, all assets and liabilities, struck for the whole Canadian economy, generally on December 31, and including businesses and persons as well as governments.

during the 1970s and 1980s, as well as the several surpluses[20] on the current account of the balance of payments. It was in those years that the great Canadian property companies went to work in US cities, and in the United Kingdom; in the early eighties Canadian oil companies bought many foreign firms. In 1986 the international payments of interest and dividends still consumed only 3.4 per cent of Canada's GNP and 13.1 per cent of export receipts, compared with 2.4 per cent and 8.6 per cent, respectively, in 1946. In 1985-8 the economy, and its external assets, again outgrew external liabilities. Canada certainly did not resemble a Third World debtor.

The years after 1945 saw some dramatic developments: the diminishing importance of the British market, new opportunities for wheat sales in the Soviet Union and China, new demands from the United States for forest products, iron ore, oil and natural gas, uranium, aluminum, and other non-ferrous metals, and, after 1965, motor cars and parts. Without these new export markets Canada would not have been able to pay for its imports. It is unlikely that it could have borrowed all the foreign money needed to fill the gap. Growth would have been throttled had the nation not been able to pay for the imports the country wanted. As it was, Canada filled the remaining gap by importing capital funds and by welcoming a large amount of direct foreign investment.

In this whole process Canada's trade became ever more closely bound up with the American market, in spite of the new opportunities in Japan and the socialist world. In 1946 Britain took 26 per cent of our exports and the United States 38 per cent; in 1986 the percentages were 2.2 and 78, while continental western Europe's total share had risen to 5 and Japan's from less than 1 per cent to 5. On the import side the changes were less dramatic, but equally significant. In 1946 the United States provided 75 per cent of our imports, and in 1986, 76 per cent; Britain's shares were 7.5 per cent in 1946 and 3.6 per cent in 1978, while Japan's share had risen from almost nothing to 7.5 per cent, and continental Europe's to more than 9 per cent.

These changing percentages reflected many things. The British economy, although growing, found itself outgrown by all the other western European economies, and Japan grew faster still; in terms of design, quality, and price many British goods lost the competitive edge that they had had in the late forties and the fifties; American multinational firms often preferred to draw supplies from their parents and to send their exports to the United States; continental Europe and Japan emerged as producers of machines, equipment, and consumer goods that were highly competitive in design, quality, and price – not merely with

20 In 1970, 1971, 1973, and 1982-4 inclusive. The current account of the balance of payments records all receipts and payments arising from current production and spending and from the servicing of past obligations, plus a few small miscellaneous items.

British goods but also with American; as Britain gradually withdrew into the protective agricultural arrangements of the European Community after 1973, the British market became less open to Canadian grain and other foodstuffs; once the stresses and strains of war and reconstruction had been surmounted, Britain naturally drew more of its foodstuffs from continental Europe and more primary products from Scandinavia and even from the Soviet Union, because these supplies were close by.

As the years passed Canadians were vaguely aware that Britain mattered less and Japan mattered more. They certainly noticed when the Soviet Union and China began to buy Canada's wheat. Nor could they ignore the extent to which American goods and American opportunities had become pre-eminent in the nation's external trade. Without doubt they would have noticed that American firms were very much present in the Canadian market-place even if publicists and politicians had not regularly reminded them of the fact.

By 1968 foreign-owned corporations held 62.8 per cent of the assets in Canada's mining corporations and 58 per cent of the assets in manufacturing. In other sectors foreign ownership, chiefly American, was less striking; it ranged from 7.8 per cent of assets in transport, communication, and public utilities (where most installations are government-owned) to 12.6 per cent in financial corporations, 13 per cent in construction, 20 per cent in services, and 31 per cent in wholesale trade. The foreign-owned sector had grown partly by new investment and partly by purchase; it had financed its growth partly by importing capital funds, partly by borrowing within Canada, and partly by accumulating earnings from its Canadian operations. In the seventies the percentages fell, especially in the resource industries, as some large foreign-owned firms shifted to Canadian private control while others were taken over, directly or indirectly, by governments. These trends continued during the eighties. Thus by 1986, the last year for which data are available, Canada was the locus of control for 53 per cent of the capital in manufacturing, 69 per cent in petroleum and natural gas, 67 per cent in mining and smelting, 100 per cent in railways, and 97 per cent in other utilities. For these industries, plus merchandising and construction, in 1984 Canadians controlled 78 per cent of total assets. Among manufacturing, petroleum, natural gas, mining, and smelting firms, Canadian control had been increasing steadily and substantially since the mid-1970s.[21]

By 1987 the 'foreign-controlled economy' so much beloved of pamphleteers was beginning to look like a myth. Canadian capitalism, it seemed, had grown up: it frolicked not only at home, but throughout the Americas and in western Europe as well. Admittedly foreign-owned firms still seemed to dominate some

21 Statistics Canada, *Canada's International Investment Position 1981-1984* (catalogue number 67-202, table 32).

parts of the resource industries and some manufacturing lines, though certainly not all. In the resource industries they still used resources, such as oil and timber, that Canadian governments owned. In the industries and in manufacturing, as C.D. Howe had pointed out more than thirty years before, Canadian law and policy conditioned their actions. In managing manufacturing, exports, and energy policy, Ottawa had learned by the mid-sixties that foreign-owned firms could be bent to the national will – indeed, that they could be instruments of Canada's national purpose. In FIRA and the NEP, Ottawa applied this lesson anew. Washington raged, but without effect, until a more tractable government had taken power in Ottawa.

So far as jobs were concerned, foreign firms mattered little. Very few people worked in the relevant resource industries. In manufacturing, employment was shrinking in comparison with the growing labour force, and the new jobs were chiefly in the service sectors, where foreign ownership was insignificant or altogether absent. The vast majority of Canadians did *not* work for a foreign-controlled firm. No doubt Canadians were increasingly steeped in American ideas and increasingly inclined to adopt American styles and attitudes, both in life and in politics. But the blame, if that is the appropriate word, belongs with prosperity, travel, family contacts, the media, and the absence of any persuasive alternative models for life and conduct – not with foreign investment. Similarly, if tranquil Toronto has become a clone of demented Detroit by 2000, the cause will not be foreign investment – and it certainly will not be free trade.

Many years have now passed since George Grant sang his *Lament for a Nation*. Perhaps Grant is right to regret that Canadians are now so very like their neighbours to the south. It is open to anyone to imitate Grant in imagining hypothetical histories of Canada, historical trajectories different from the one on which the Dominion of the North launched itself so long ago. And anyone can deplore some of the things that some foreign-owned firms have done or left undone. But it is equally important to criticize the native product. Most of what went wrong with post-war Canada was inevitable, unavoidable, or Canada's own damn fault.[22]

---

22 This chapter uses those statistical materials that were available up to September 1988.

PART SEVEN

Conclusion

34

Conclusion

In 1944 the Canadian Chamber of Commerce undertook to look into the future. It polled Canadians in Kitchener and Vancouver to discover what they hoped for and expected at war's end. The responses indicated a desire for a richer material life: refrigerators, cars, and a house in the suburbs. Possibly because they were not asked, they did not express a desire for a new constitution, world government, or international workers' solidarity. They did not get any of these latter things, but they did get a patriated constitution, as well as refrigerators, cars, and a house in the suburbs, not to mention television sets, snowmobiles, and microwave ovens. They also got family allowances, unemployment insurance beyond their wildest dreams, health insurance, and contributory old age pensions. Economic progress made all these things possible. The period from 1945 to 1980 was one of almost uninterrupted economic growth, the benefits of which were shared widely among all levels of Canadian society and in all regions. In the eighties growth has been uneven and its benefit not so widely shared.

Even the unemployed, the native people, and other groups considered disadvantaged have gained from Canada's economic growth. We are now more critical of deprivation, poverty, and oppression than we could have afforded to be in the 1940s. Those who hoped for more fundamental social and economic change are of course disappointed. Whether or not one shares their disappointment, one must recognize that in fact society has undergone a massive transformation since 1945, and with that transformation has come an unprecedented abundance of material prosperity.

Canadians in 1945 could not have anticipated all the consequences of their desire for a better material life. More of them had to live in larger cities to which were also attracted very large numbers of immigrants. Their lives have consequently become more complicated; in the process they have been forced to become more tolerant of diversity, and many of them have actually come to enjoy the variety and freedom that the great cities have made possible. What their parents believed has often been discarded. They live differently, behave differently, and presumably believe different things.

The rise in living standards was accompanied by increased organization, larger corporations, larger cities and their attendant problems, and larger government. Most Canadians had more comfort and security than ever before, but they were dependent for these things on distant and impersonal institutions both private and public. The wish for new and expensive services created certain tensions and unhappinesses which may or may not be regarded as inevitable. People distrusted bureaucracy, feared large corporations, and resented the power of larger labour unions and other special interest groups. Some parts of Canadian public life often seemed to visibly malfunction, such as the schools, the post office, and the Canadian system of labour relations. By the late 1980s these problems seemed to matter less.

Rising prosperity has nevertheless created new demands and an ability to pay for these demands on a scale inconceivable in 1945. It became relatively easy for governments to imagine that they could solve problems by throwing money at them. Pressure groups also came to believe that government could finance any and all of their obsessions; indeed, even in 1988 government itself often seemed to believe this. This tendency increased in the 1960s and 1970s when the public came to think that budgets need not be balanced and that the supply of money need not be rigidly controlled. For obvious reasons, one found little dissent from this new orthodoxy in the governments or in the media. The results could be seen in the financial disarray of the 1970s and the 1980s.

The services that were demanded – such as education, roads, health care, social assistance – belonged constitutionally to the provinces and had largely been supplied traditionally by the municipalities. Thus only a major constitutional overhaul would have prevented steady expansion of provincial activities relative to those of the federal government. Decentralization was therefore inevitable, given the existing constitutional structure of Canada and the economic and social developments of the period. In addition there was a noticeable tendency for the provinces to offer services that the national government had initiated and was still willing and able to offer. Because of the rivalry between the two levels of government, federal-provincial conferences became a regular feature of Canadian life – all too regular in the opinion of some. The culmination was the Meech Lake potlatch, and the constitutional cookery it attempted.

The planners of 1945 tried to avoid this problem by proposing a restructured constitution in which decisive powers would belong to the national government. This was politically impossible, as the 1945 dominion-provincial conference proved; thereafter the King and St Laurent governments largely avoided the problem by abandoning most of the social welfare schemes so popular during the Second World War. But in the heady prosperity of the sixties, it seemed possible to use the federal spending power to resolve constitutional difficulties by throwing money at the provinces in order to produce a welfare state.

Federal incursions into the sphere of social welfare were encouraged by reductions in spending in areas that were unquestionably national in scope, such as defence. If it had been necessary throughout this period to maintain a defence effort comparable to that of the early 1950s, there would have been less room for much of this. The unexpected and unsought result of social welfare planning and accomplishment was that the national government was weaker in terms of its undoubted responsibilities at the end of the period than at the beginning.

In the case of one provincial government, that of Quebec, an activist outlook exacerbated the tensions that would in any event have been present. The federal government feared, with much justification, that it might soon have little or no direct contact with Canadians in Quebec. Moreover, the Quebec government moved into areas of shared jurisdiction with its own deposit insurance, pension plan, and cultural policy. Other provinces were less adventurous and their motivations less ideological, but their actions contributed to the conflict in the same fashion.

One sees this in the field of natural resources, where the interest of the national government in the 1940s and 1950s was directed to the solution of national problems such as unemployment, growth, and imbalances of payment. As constitutional conflict intensified, debate over the exploitation of natural resources, which had previously been considered to require co-operation, became more bitter. Because provincial governments own these resources, they were naturally interested in using them and especially their revenue for provincial ends. But the national government remained interested in resources, and its underlying reasons for such an interest have not changed, although new concerns have emerged in Ottawa also. Of course all conflict is not federal-provincial; provinces differ among themselves with respect to resource exploitation. Ontario and Alberta would have feuded over oil prices if Ottawa had not existed. Indeed, without a strong national government, rational arbitration of their differences would likely have proved impossible. Similarly, Ontario, Manitoba, and Quebec would have warred over egg marketing and chicken sales.

The courts theoretically might have solved these difficulties; practically they have not. The perplexities of divided jurisdiction have remained unclarified by the courts, and special interest groups have taken advantage of this ambiguity and of the division itself. Business, for example, has often used one level of government to obtain a privilege the other level had refused. But business was sometimes a victim as well. In the cases of cable television permits and mining regulations, both levels of government demanded that companies comply with the regulations of each. What was involved in these disputes was the question of government patronage in its largest and most legitimate sense. It could be argued that some of the federal government's more surprising activities in the late sixties and the seventies might be interpreted as an attempt to maintain a clientage. Thus a splendid, empty airport was built at Mirabel; national historic sites appeared everywhere; a Department of Regional Economic Expansion tried to look after those perennial federal clients, the less advantaged provinces; and ethnic groups, recent beneficiaries of Ottawa's immigration policies, benefited again from large grants to maintain the visibility of their various national heritages. Provinces naturally responded with their own historic plaques and their own multicultural grants. Such bidding and counter-bidding continue still.

The character of the change in public life is relatively easy to describe. The change in the texture of private life occurred mainly behind curtains, and its implications are much more difficult to discern. We cannot psychoanalyse the Canadian people, but we can suggest that Canadians now live different lives than their parents did. Many paths lead to different ends, and many old trails are now overgrown. What this means remains uncertain. Some observers have concluded that since 1945 Canadians have become more Americanized. We think that this interpretation is misleading because it is too easy. We were not, in fact, much different from the Americans in 1945. Since that time both societies have developed in similar ways, responding to many of the same ideological and economic developments. We do not mean to understate the very real difference between Canada and the United States. After all, the United States is eleven times larger than Canada, and proportionately richer. Its place in the world reflects this difference. The two nations have different political cultures and systems. Canada still enjoys some of the comforts of a small and closely linked society. Nevertheless, like Americans, we have become less local and parochial in the last quarter-century. Like the citizens of Denver, Birmingham, and Munich, our lives have become more varied and broader.

Survey data have shown that Canadian attitudes and values were less diverse in the late 1970s than they were in the early 1960s. This means that anglophones and francophones are more alike today than before. Yet there is an apparent paradox: the people have become more homogeneous as the polity has become less integrated and less organized. People can be pardoned for being confused. According to the best liberal theory, greater similarities and prosperity should lead to understanding and happiness. Few would agree that it has. In 1945 Canadians had relatively little, hoped for much, but did not really expect it. Surely they never expected exactly what they got.

Select Bibliography

Writings about Canada since the Second World War can (and do) fill the shelves of many libraries in Canada and even some abroad. Yet the material is of such variety and complexity that researchers or students are tempted to give up before they get properly started. Certainly there are few short-cuts, but some handy guides do exist through the thicket of information. The purpose of this bibliographical essay is to introduce the reader to some of the books and other materials that are likely to be helpful.

First among the guides is the grandmother of governmental handbooks, *The Canada Year Book,* crammed full of useful information from the statistical to the statutory, in annual editions in English and French. For the period down to 1960 the *Year Book,* literal and tedious though it often is, remains the only consistent guide to legislation and regulations in force throughout Canada, as well as to a host of statistics otherwise difficult of access for the ordinary reader using the ordinary library. In 1960 the *Year Book* was supplemented by the revival of a long-defunct Canadian institution, the *Canadian Annual Review,* published in annual volumes by the University of Toronto Press. Orginally conceived on a grand scale to cover everything from provincial politics to mass media and sports, the *Review* has since 1971 focused more narrowly on political and economic happenings. Without these two series our task would have been infinitely more difficult, if not downright impossible. J.L. Granatstein, *Canada 1957-1967: The Years of Uncertainty and Innovation* (Toronto: McClelland & Stewart 1986) is a splendid culmination to the Canadian Centenary Series. Morris Zaslow's *The North 1914-1967* (Toronto: McClelland & Stewart 1988), the last volume in the series to appear, is less incisive and critical; it was also rather dated by the time it was published.

There is no general account of economic development in Canada since 1945. *The Canadian Encyclopedia* (Edmonton: Hurtig, 1985) has a wealth of useful information. Some material may be found in William L. Marr and Donald G. Paterson, *Canada: An Economic History* (Toronto: Macmillan 1979), especially Chapters 2, 7, 8, 9, 12, and 13. The older *Canadian Economic History* by W.T. Easterbrook and Hugh G.J. Aitken (Toronto: Macmillan 1956) has only a few pages on the post-war years. Quantitative studies covering part of our period have been published by, among others, Harvey Lithwick (*Economic Growth in Canada: A Quantitative Analysis* [Toronto: University of Toronto Press 1967]) and W.C. Hood and A.D. Scott (*Output, Capital, and Labour*, [Royal Commission on Canada's Economic Prospects, Ottawa: Queen's Printer 1957]). The most convenient and important source of primary quantitative data remains Statistics Canada (formerly the Dominion Bureau of Statistics). In the notes to Chapter 1 we have mentioned the most significant publications. There is also an annual *Catalogue,* through which the reader can track down a wealth of specialized statistical publications both periodical and regular. Ottawa produces a monthly indexed *Canadian Government Publications Catalogue,* and the National Library issues a monthly and annual compendium (*Canadiana*) listing all new Canadian Books. Every year the University of Toronto Press issues its *Subject Guide to Canadian Books in Print.* Scholarly papers relating to economic affairs are published by the Fraser Institute, the C.D. Howe Research Institute, the Economic Council of Canada, the *Canadian Journal of Economics,* and *Canadian Public Policy.* Both of these periodicals review new books relating to the Canadian economy; before 1967 such reviews appeared in the *Canadian Journal of Economics and Political Science,* which for many years also contained a 'Bibliography of Canadian Economics.' From time to time useful papers appear in the *Journal of Canadian Studies,* and the scholarly literature can be searched thoroughly with the aid of the quarterly *Journal of Economic Literature* and its occasional summary in the *Index of Economics Journals* (Homewood, IL: Richard D. Irwin). Much can be gleaned from the various introductory economics textbooks that have been prepared for the Canadian market. Of the current textbook crop the best is perhaps by Richard G. Lipsey, Douglas D. Purvis, and Peter O. Steiner, *Economics,* sixth edition (Cambridge etc.: Harper and Row 1988). Not only are its two principal authors Canadians; they are also distinguished scholars. For a vast range of particular topics in economics, politics, and constitutionalism, guidance both substantive and bibliographical can be found in the scores of research studies that were commissioned by the Royal Commission on the Economic Union and Development Prospects for Canada – the Macdonald Commission. These *Collected Research Studies* (Toronto: University of Toronto Press 1986) fill seventy-two volumes.

Passing from general treatments and bibliographical aids, we must first note the distinction between semi-popular treatments of controversial topics and scholarly treatments of topics that may or may not be in the public eye. Second, we should observe that in economic affairs both controversial writing and public discussion have concentrated disproportionately on two topics – the foreign investment question and, in the seventies, the energy problem. On each topic an ocean of ink has been spilled, leaving the public not much wiser than it was thirty years before. The controversy over foreign investment is embalmed in: Royal Commission on Canada's Economic Prospects, *Report* (Ottawa: Queen's Printer 1957), M.H. Watkins and others, *Foreign Ownership and the Structure of Canadian Industry* (Ottawa: Queen's Printer 1967), Harry Johnson, *The Canadian Quandary* (Toronto: McGraw-Hill 1963), M.H. Watkins, 'A New National Policy,' in T. Lloyd and J. McLeod, eds., *Agenda 1970* (Toronto: University of Toronto Press 1970), Task Force on Foreign Investment, *Report* (better known as the *'Gray Report'*) (Ottawa: Information Canada 1972), and A.E. Safarian, *Foreign Ownership of Canadian Industry* (Toronto: McGraw-Hill 1966 and later editions). H.C. Eastman and S. Stykolt, *The Tariff and Competition in Canada* (Toronto: Macmillan 1968) is also relevant. Kari Levitt's account (*Silent Surrender* [Toronto: Macmillan 1970]) can mislead. With respect to energy policy the same could be said of James Laxer, *The Energy Crisis* (Toronto: Lorimer 1975). It would be better to begin with Leonard Waverman, ed., *The Energy Question: An International Failure of Policy* (Toronto: University of Toronto Press 1974), and with the annual reports of the National Energy Board. Something can also be learned from Larry Pratt, *The Tar Sands* (Edmonton: Hurtig 1976). The view from Ottawa can be glimpsed neatly in National Energy Board, *Canadian Natural Gas: Supply and Requirements* (Ottawa: National Energy Board 1979). The National Energy Policy still awaits its historian.

Passing to fiscal, monetary, and trading matters, much of the scholarly literature consists of papers that only professional economists can make much of. With respect to trade and international finance there is a good deal of information in the series *Canada in World Affairs* (Toronto: Canadian Institute of International Affairs, roughly annually), which now extends to 1965. The general reader can learn something from textbooks, such as R. Craig McIvor, *Canadian Monetary, Banking, and Fiscal Development* (Toronto: Macmillan 1958) or D.E. Bond and R.A. Shearer, *The Economics of the Canadian Financial System* (Scarborough: Prentice-Hall 1972), from Scott Gordon, *The Economists versus the Bank of Canada* (Toronto: Ryerson 1962), and, after 1960, from the summaries in the *Canadian Annual Review,* especially the excellent treatments by D.F. Forster. For a 'monetarist' view of the Bank of Canada's more recent behaviour, see Thomas J. Courchene, *Money, Inflation, and the Bank of Canada* and *The Strategy of Gradualism* (Montreal: C.D. Howe Research Institute, 1976 and 1977). The Bank's earlier record is treated by E.P. Neufeld, *Bank of Canada*

Operations and Policy (Toronto: University of Toronto Press 1955 and later editions). An invaluable treatment of monetary and exchange rate policy is Paul Wonnacott, *The Canadian Dollar 1948-1962* (Toronto: University of Toronto Press 1965).

In matters of economic organization, business, agriculture, and labour, it is hard for the general reader to get much beyond the textbook, and in some areas, such as agricultural organization and policy, there are very large gaps in the literature. Don Mitchell, *The Politics of Food* (Toronto: Lorimer 1975) has some useful material but the tone is polemical and the analysis incomplete. On labour one may consult Gordon Bertram, *The Contribution of Education to Economic Growth* (Economic Council of Canada Staff Study no. 12, Ottawa: Queen's Printer 1966), John Crispo, *International Unionism* (Toronto: McGraw-Hill, 1967), J. Hamelin and F. Harvey, *Les Travailleurs Québécois 1941-1971* (Cahiers de l'Institut Supérieur des Sciences Humaines, Québec: Université Laval 1976), R.O. Miller and F. Isbister, eds., *Canadian Labour in Transition* (Scarborough: Prentice-Hall 1971), S. Ostry and M.A. Zaidi, *Labour Economics in Canada* (Toronto: Macmillan 1972), and Task Force on Industrial Relations, *Report* (Ottawa: Privy Council Office 1968). On industry see D.H. Fullerton and H.A. Hampson, *Canadian Secondary Manufacturing Industry* (Royal Commission on Canada's Economic Prospects, Ottawa: Queen's Printer 1957), Economic Council of Canada, *Interim Report on Competition Policy* (Ottawa 1969), the books by Safarian and Eastman and Stykolt mentioned above, G.L. Reuber and F. Roseman, *The Takeover of Canadian Firms 1945-1961* (Economic Council of Canada Special Study no. 10, Ottawa 1969), N.C. Stewart, *Concentration in Canadian Manufacturing and Mining Industries* (Economic Council of Canada Background Paper, Ottawa 1970), and Royal Commission on Corporate Concentration, *Report* (Ottawa: Ministry of Supply and Services 1978), along with the staff studies relating thereto. In the literature there is little systematic treatment of the growth and development of particular industries. To find out about such things one must turn to the Statistics Canada materials, beginning with the *Canada Year Book*.

External affairs and defence have inspired a plentiful but variable literature. First, there are the official, scholarly compilations by the Department of External Affairs itself, the *Documents on Canadian External Relations* (Ottawa: Queen's Printer and successors 1967-). For many years the Department also published the useful *External Affairs Bulletin,* later transformed into an opinionated house organ as *International Perspectives. International Perspectives* was eventually privatized. Another feature of the post-war years was the appearance of a scholarly journal on international relations, the *International Journal,* sponsored by the Canadian Institute of International Affairs (CIIA). Its

French-language counterpart, *Etudes Internationales,* also repays careful perusal. An indispensable source of information is the CIIA's monograph series, *Canada in World Affairs* (Toronto: Oxford University Press and successors 1941 to date), which has been recently revived to cover the post-1963 period. Other documents on external relations have been published by the Carleton Library: R.A. MacKay, ed., *Canadian Foreign Policy, 1945-1955* (Toronto: McClelland & Stewart 1971) and Arthur Blanchette, ed., *Canadian Foreign Policy, 1955-1965* (Toronto: McClelland & Stewart 1977) and Blanchette's sequel, *Canadian Foreign Policy, Selected Speeches and Documents, 1966-1976* (Carleton Library 1980). On defence policy, a handy collection is Larry Stewart, ed., *Canadian Defence Policy: Selected Documents, 1964-1981* (Kingston: Centre for International Relations, Queen's University 1982). An often ignored source of information about Canadian external activities is the documentary collection of the American Department of State, *Foreign Relations of the United States,* in its many volumes. Since 1984 the Norman Paterson School of International Affairs at Carleton University has been publishing a new series of annual volumes, *Canada among Nations* (Toronto: Lorimer 1985-). It effectively replaces the CIIA's formerly current series, *Canada in World Affairs.*

The continuing and important work of James Eayrs, *In Defence of Canada* (Toronto: University of Toronto Press 1964-), contains much useful information. Three prominent figures from the Department of External Affairs have written reminiscences of their careers: John Holmes, *The Shaping of Peace* (Toronto: University of Toronto Press 1979), Escott Reid, *Time of Fear and Hope* (Toronto: McClelland & Stewart 1977), and A.F.W. Plumptre, *Three Decades of Decision* (Toronto: McClelland & Stewart 1977). For Canada's Commonwealth connection, see Joe Garner, *The Commonwealth Office* (London: Heinemann 1978), Nicholas Mansergh, *Survey of British Commonwealth Affairs: Problems of Wartime Cooperation and Post-War Change, 1939-1952* (Oxford: Oxford University Press 1958) and J.D.B. Miller's excellent volume, *Survey of Commonwealth Affairs: Problems of Expansion and Attrition, 1953-1969* (London: Oxford University Press 1974). Extremely useful for Canadian-American relations are two works by J.L. Granatstein and Robert Cuff, *Canadian-American Relations in Wartime* (Toronto: Samuel Stevens Hakkert 1975) and *American Dollars, Canadian Prosperity* (Toronto: Samuel Stevens 1978). Denis Stairs's unique study of Canada in the Korean War, *The Diplomacy of Constraint* (Toronto: University of Toronto Press 1974), is also useful. Douglas Ross, *In the Interests of Peace: Canada and Vietnam, 1954-73* (Toronto: University of Toronto Press 1984) is a distinguished addition to Canada's diplomatic history despite some necessary bows in the direction of political science totems. Some interesting essays on Canadian foreign policy, reflecting changing styles in the interpretation of international affairs, may be found in Stephen Clarkson, ed., *An Independent Foreign Policy for Canada?* (Toronto: McClelland & Stewart 1968) and Norman Hillmer and Garth Stevenson, eds., *A Foremost Nation* (Toronto: McClelland & Stewart 1977). Two collections of essays by John Holmes, *The Better Part of Valour* (Toronto: McClelland & Stewart 1970) and *Canada: A Middle-Aged Power* (Toronto: McClelland & Stewart 1976), offer wise observations on Canadian foreign policy since the war. A great deal about Canada's foreign policy under Pierre Trudeau can be learned from Paul Martin's ably edited *The London Diaries, 1975-1979* (Ottawa: University of Ottawa Press 1988).

The finest source for Canadian political history until 1950 is the Mackenzie King Diary, now available on microfiche (University of Toronto Press 1980), or in the useful and authoritative *Mackenzie King Record,* edited by J.W. Pickersgill and Donald Forster in four volumes (Toronto: University of Toronto Press 1961-70). For King's wartime career, J.L. Granatstein's *Canada's War* (Toronto: Oxford University Press 1975) functions almost as a biography of Canada's wartime prime minister. Louis St Laurent presents a greater challenge for a biographer. Nevertheless, two of his advisers, Dale Thomson (*Louis St Laurent: Canadian* [Toronto: Macmillan 1967]) and J.W. Pickersgill (*My Years with Louis St Laurent* [Toronto: University of Toronto Press 1975]), have written useful accounts, unlikely to be speedily superseded. Robert Bothwell and William Kilbourn have also written *C.D. Howe: A Biography* (Toronto: McClelland & Stewart 1979) on St Laurent's principal colleague.

John Diefenbaker's memoirs, *One Canada,* 3 volumes (Toronto: Macmillan 1975-7) are fascinating, but also exceedingly badly organized and often misleading. Peter Stursberg's first two-volume collection of interviews, *Diefenbaker: Leadership Gained* and *Diefenbaker: Leadership Lost* (Toronto: University of Toronto Press 1975-6) are greatly to be preferred. Lester Pearson's memoirs, *Mike* (Toronto: University of Toronto Press 1972-5), are better written than Diefenbaker's, and better on foreign policy than on domestic political affairs. Stursberg also compiled two volumes on Pearson, *Lester Pearson and the Dream of Unity* and *Lester Pearson and the American Dilemma* (Toronto: Doubleday 1978, 1980). Three of Pearson's colleagues have written their memoirs. Judy LaMarsh's *Bird in a Gilded Cage* (Toronto: McClelland & Stewart 1968) presents a frequently jaundiced view of her former leader; Walter Gordon's *A Political Memoir* (Toronto: McClelland & Stewart 1977) explains and justifies its author's political career. Paul Martin published a frequently engrossing two-volume memoir, *A Very Public Life* (Ottawa and Toronto: Deneau 1983, 1985), while Pearson's principal policy adviser, Tom Kent, published his extremely readable memoir and analysis of the 1960s, *A Public Purpose* (Montreal and Kingston: McGill-Queen's University Press, 1988). The best book to date on Pierre Trudeau is George Radwanski's *Trudeau* (Toronto: Macmillan 1978). Christina McCall-Newman's long-awaited *Grits: An Intimate Portrait of the Liberal Party* (Toronto: Macmillan 1982) furnishes some fascinating sketches of the prominenti of the 1970s. The authors confess to a fondness for Ron Graham's well-written and penetrating *One-eyed Kings: Promise & Illusion in Canadian Politics* (Toronto: Collins 1986) and for Jeffrey Simpson's *The Discipline of Power: The Conservative Interlude & Liberal Restoration* (Toronto: Personal Library 1980). Both books show that fine political journalism is not a lost art in Canada. On the academic side, there is much to be learned from Joseph Wearing, *The L-Shaped Party: The Liberal Party of Canada 1958-1980* (Toronto: McGraw-Hill Ryerson 1981).

Some of Canada's provincial figures have also produced or stimulated memoirs or biographies. Joey Smallwood of Newfoundland is best served in Richard Gwyn's *Smallwood* (Toronto: McClelland & Stewart 1968); his own memoirs are best forgotten. Maurice Duplessis has received authoritative treatment in Conrad Black's well-researched book, *Duplessis* (Toronto: McClelland & Stewart 1976). The most useful book on René Lévesque is Peter Desbarats' *René: A Canadian in Search of a Country* (Toronto: McClelland & Stewart 1976). Tommy Douglas of Saskatchewan has received worshipful treatment in a relentlessly favourable biography by Doris Shackleton (Toronto: McClelland & Stewart 1975). Richard Hatfield, New Brunswick's controversial premier, has been the subject of a book timed to coincide with his electoral defeat: Richard Starr, *Richard Hatfield: The Seventeen Year Saga* (Halifax: Formac 1987). John Robarts, Hatfield's Ontario counterpart, is the subject of a dreary biography by A.K. McDougall, *Robarts* (Toronto: University of Toronto Press 1986).

Provincial politics receive comprehensive treatment in Martin Robin, ed., *Canadian Provincial Politics* (Scarborough: Prentice-Hall 1971). Richard Simeon, *Federal-Provincial Diplomacy* (Toronto: University of Toronto Press 1972) is indispensable for federal-provincial relations in the sixties. Extremely useful for the debate on separatism are the Accent Québec series of the C.D. Howe Research Institute, particularly Judith Maxwell and Caroline Pestieau, *Economic Realities of Contemporary Confederation* (Montreal: C.D. Howe Research Institute 1980). Papers relating to federal and provincial politics may also be gleaned from the *Canadian Journal of Economics and Political Science* until 1967 and since that time in the *Canadian Journal of Political Science*. Books relating to the topic are reviewed in the two aforementioned journals, and in the *Canadian Historical Review,* which publishes a comprehensive bibliography on the subject.

Material relating to Canada's cultural, educational, and literary life can be found in Julian Park, eds., *The Culture of Contemporary Canada* (Toronto:

Ryerson 1957). The revised edition of Carl Klinck, ed., *Literary History of Canada: Canadian Literature in English,* 3 vols. (Toronto: University of Toronto Press 1976) offers excellent surveys of the various types of English-Canadian writing. Norah Story's *Oxford Companion to Canadian History and Literature* (Toronto: Oxford University Press 1967) and William Toye's *Supplement to the Oxford Companion* ... (Toronto: Oxford University Press 1973) also furnish many interesting details. The most recent edition of George Woodcock's *The Canadians* (Toronto: Douglas & McIntyre 1979) is an important social and cultural commentary. Lastly, there are some books on Canadian political culture which cannot be omitted. Donald Creighton's book, *The Forked Road* (Toronto: McClelland & Stewart 1976) is tendentious but readable. George Grant's *Lament for a Nation* (Toronto: McClelland & Stewart 1965) presents much the same point of view, though at much shorter length. Peter Newman's two popular histories, *Renegade in Power* (Toronto: McClelland & Stewart 1963) and *Distemper of Our Times* (Toronto: McClelland & Stewart 1968) contain a wealth of colourful detail, though they have now been superseded on many issues. Within the last decade several first-class studies of Canadian political parties have been written. Foremost among them is Reg Whitaker's *The Government Party* (Toronto: University of Toronto Press 1977), based on exceptional access to the papers of the Liberal party; also noteworthy is George Perlin, *The Tory Syndrome* (Montreal: McGill-Queen's University Press 1980). More speculative and less reliable is Walter Young's account of the CCF, *Anatomy of a Party* (Toronto: University of Toronto Press 1969). All three books prove that political scientists can on occasion still write English.

Quebec and Quebec politics have been the subject of some interesting recent work. Dale Thomson's best book, *Vive le Québec Libre* (Toronto: Deneau 1988) makes amends for his rather disappointing biography of Jean Lesage. Graham Fraser's *PQ: René Lévesque and the Parti Québécois in Power* (Toronto: Macmillan 1984) is lucid and comprehensive for the PQ's political rise; it should be supplemented by L. Ian Macdonald's *From Bourassa to Bourassa: A Pivotal Decade in Canadian History* (Montreal: Harvest House 1984). Claude Morin's *L'Art de l'impossible: la diplomatie québécoise depuis 1960* (Montreal: Boréal 1987) is as interesting for what it omits as for what it includes. Last but not least, Morin's great rival Pierre Trudeau demonstrated, in a collection of articles and speeches edited by Donald Johnston, why he so dominated Canadian politics for almost two decades: *With A Bang, Not a Whimper* (Toronto: Stoddart 1988).

Index

Abbott, Douglas 59, 70-2, 116-18, 176
Abortion 407, 417, 419-20, 430
Acheson, Dean 121
Acquired Immune Deficiency (AIDS) 10, 408
Adams, Bryan 413
Aerospace industry 346
Afghanistan, Soviet invasion of 337, 428
Agricultural Rehabilitation and Development Act (ARDA) (1961) 215-16, 290, 341
Agriculture 23-5, 66-8, 198, 214-18, 314, 446, 449; demography and 139 141, 266, 289; 'Food for Peace' and 195; marketing and 165, 195, 214, 342, 363, 449; policy re 53, 290, 301-2; price support for 67, 126, 165, 175, 215, 341-2; problems in 23-5, 141, 195; protectionism and 175, 191, 195, 301, 342, 344
Air Canada 448
Air Force (RCAF). See defence
Air traffic control dispute (1976) 356, 375-6
Alberta 11, 75, 105, 196, 218, 333-4, 361, 387, 393, 404, 409; economy of 31, 144, 166-7, 187, 199, 220, 300, 339, 341, 347-8, 388, 447, 450-4, 459; Her-
itage Fund 454; politics in 117, 157, 179, 237, 288, 400
Alcohol. See liquor
Allan, Andrew 95
American Federation of Labor (AFL). See unions
American Import-Export Bank 71
Anglo-Canadian wheat agreement (1946) 67-8
Anka, Paul 161
Aquin, Hubert 312
Architecture 28, 83, 243, 299
Argue, Hazen 241
Armed forces, Canada. See defence
Art 98, 242, 340, 400-1, 459
Arts, the 242-3, 400-1, 409-14. See also culture
Atkey, Ron 332
Atlantic Acceptance Corporation 298
Atlantic alliance (1948) 90, 119-21, 262. See also North Atlantic Treaty Organization (NATO)
Atlantic Canada Opportunities Agency 470
Atlantic provinces. See Maritime provinces
Atomic bomb, development of 40-1, 143-4, 231, 241, 259
Atomic Energy of Canada Limited (AECL)